2.9<u>5</u>

W9-ARX-893

LANGENSCHEIDT'S
UNIVERSAL DICTIONARY

LATIN-ENGLISH
ENGLISH-LATIN

Edited by
C. D. N. Costa, M. A., B. phil.
and
Mary Herberg, M. A.

LANGENSCHEIDT
NEW YORK · BERLIN · MUNICH
VIENNA · ZURICH

Introduction

This Latin-English dictionary is essentially an abridgment of the Pocket Latin Dictionary prepared for Langenscheidt by Mr. S. A. Handford, and it retains in its smaller compass the principles of presentation and, usually, the word-definitions of that work. Vocabulary of the same literary period, from Plautus to the early second century A.D., is covered, and it is hoped that a wide range of words is still preserved in spite of the reduction in size. This reduction has been achieved by abbreviating, where possible, the definitions, and by omitting most of the words which occur only once, and many words of infrequent occurrence, especially those which seem to be confined to the less commonly read authors.

The English-Latin section of the dictionary offers a Classical prose vocabulary. Equivalents have been drawn wherever possible from Cicero and Caesar, and where notes on a word's construction are given they are likewise based on the best prose usage.

In a dictionary of this size it is not possible to distinguish fully between the different meanings of one English word. Often the notes on construction will help to show which sense is being translated, but if there is any doubt the word must be checked in the Latin-English section, and this rule holds good wherever the Latin word is unfamiliar.

The Latin Alphabet and Pronunciation

In the time of Cicero the Latin alphabet contained the following twenty-one letters:

A B C D E F G H I K L M N O P Q R S T V X,

and shortly afterwards Y and Z were added, to represent respectively *v* and *ζ* in Greek loan-words. The letter i represented both a vowel sound (igitur, ignis) and a semi-vowel or 'consonantal' sound (iubeo, ieiunus), pronounced like English y and sometimes written j in older editions of Latin texts. Similarly, the letter u (V) represented a vowel sound (unda, usus), and a semi-vowel or 'consonantal' sound (ualeo or valeo, uiuo or vivo), pronounced like English w. Following the prevailing contemporary practice this dictionary groups vowel and consonantal i together, but vowel and consonantal u separately under u and v.

Vowels in Latin are by nature either long (as in crās, rūpēs) or short (as in ăvĭdŭs). This is known as their 'quantity', and approximate English equivalents of the vowels are as follows:

Latin	English	Latin	English
ā	f*a*ther	ŏ	n*o*t
ă	s*a*t	ū	tr*u*ce
ē	f*a*te	ŭ	p*u*t
ĕ	p*e*t	y	(no near parallel in
ī	mach*i*ne		English, but similar
ĭ	s*i*t		to French *u* or
ō	d*o*se		German *ü*)

The chief Latin diphthongs are ae (as English time), au (as English foul), and oe (as English boil).

The consonants were pronounced approximately as in English, but note:

(a) c and g were always 'hard', as in English cat and go (not as in centre and gender); ch (pulcher) was like kh (as English pack-horse);

(b) consonantal i (iaceo, iubeo) was pronounced like English y in yet;

(c) consonantal u (valeo [ualeo], vulnus [uulnus]) was pronounced like English w in win. Thus qu, as in English, was pronounced kw.

In Latin, as in other languages, words were pronounced with an 'accent' on one or other syllable. This accent must not be confused with the 'quantity' (i.e. length) of the vowel in the syllable accented, and it is uncertain whether the Latin accent was one of pitch or stress, or both. However, it is certain that the rules for the position of the accent are as follows:

(a) in words of two syllables it falls on the first syllable (ámo, tándem);

(b) in words of more than two syllables it falls

(i) on the penultimate syllable, if it is long (amabátur, legátus);

(ii) on the antepenultimate syllable, if the penultimate is short (aúfěro, monúěrit).

Notes on Using the Dictionary

The following features of the Pocket Latin Dictionary are retained:

(a) where assimilation takes place in compound words formed with a preposition, the assimilated form is given (e.g. ac-curro for ad-curro, col-loquor for con-loquor), and the unassimilated form is included by cross-reference;

(b) both forms of common variant spellings appear by cross-reference (e.g. vulnus or volnus, verto or vorto);

(c) regularly formed adverbs are not given unless their meanings differ from the corresponding adjectives;

d) vowels known to be long are so marked (ā, ē, ī), while short ones are left unmarked;

(e) the figures 1, 2, 3, 4, after verbs indicate the conjugation; the figures 2, 3, after adjectives, participles, and pronouns indicate the number of terminations of the nominative singular.

Abbreviations

abbr. abbreviation	*mus.* musical term
abl. ablative	*n* neuter
acc. accusative	*naut.* nautical term
adj. adjective	*nom.* nominative
adv. adverb	*P.* passive
cj. conjunction	*part.* participle
comp. comparative	*perf.* perfect
dat. dative	*pers.* personal
dim. diminutive	*pl.* plural
esp. especially	*pol.* political term
f feminine	*poss.* possessive
fig. figuratively	*prep.* preposition
gen. genitive	*pron.* pronoun
impers. impersonal	*relat.* relative
indecl. indeclinable	*rhet.* rhetorical term
indef. indefinite	*sc.* scilicet (that is to say)
indic. indicative	*sg.* singular
inf. infinitive	*subj.* subjunctive
int. interjection	*subst.* substantive (noun
intens. intensive	or pronoun)
interrog. interrogative	*superl.* superlative
intr. intransitive	*thea.* theatrical term
jur. juridical term	*trans.* transitive
lit. literally	*usu.* usually
liter. literary term	*vb.* verb
loc. locative	*v/i.* verb intransitive
m masculine	*v/t.* verb transitive
med. medical term	*voc.* vocative
mil. military term	*vulg.* vulgar

A

A *abbr.* **1.** = Aulus; **2.** = absolvo; **3. a. d.** = ante diem; **4. a. u. c.** = anno urbis conditae

ā, āh *int.* alas!, ah!

ā, ab *prep.* with *abl.* (*of space*) from, away from, out of; distant from; at, on, in; (*of time*) after, since; (*of relation*) by, from, of, on the part of, on account of, against

abacus, ī *m* table; counting board

ab-aliēnō 1 to alienate; to sell; to deprive; to estrange

ab-dicō 1 to renounce; to disown, reject; to resign, abdicate

ab-ditus 3 hidden, secret

ab-dō, didī, ditum 3 to remove, put aside; to hide, conceal; **se abdere** to hide oneself, escape [paunch]

ab-dōmen, inis *n* belly,

ab-dūcō 3 to lead away from, take away, rob; to separate, seduce, draw away; to reduce, degrade

ab-eō, iī, itum, īre to go away *or* off; to resign; turn out, end; to pass away, disappear; to deviate from; to be transformed

ab-errō 1 to wander, lose one's way; to wander in thought

ab-hinc *adv.* from this time, ago

ab-horreō, uī, — 2 to shrink back from, abhor; to be averse to; to differ from, be inconsistent with

āb-iciō (*and* **āb-**), **iēcī, iectum** 3 to throw away *or* down; to squander; to give up, abandon; to degrade, humble; **se ābicere** to prostrate oneself

ab-iectus 3 cast away *or* down; dispirited; mean, contemptible; cowardly

abiēs, etis *f* fir(-tree); ship; spear

ab-igō, ēgī, āctum 3 to drive away *or* off; to procure abortion; to banish

ab-itus, ūs *m* a going away, departure; outlet

ab-iungō, iūnxī, iūnctum 3 to unyoke, detach

ab-iūrō 1 to deny on oath

ab-lēgō 1 to send away; to banish

ab-luō, luī, lūtum 3 to wash (away), cleanse

ab-negō 1 to deny, refuse; to disown

ab-nuō, nuī, nuitūrus 3 to

deny, refuse, decline (by a sign); to reject; to disclaim

ab-oleō, ēvī, itum 2 to destroy, do away with; to take away

ab-olēscō, lēvī, — 3 to disappear, vanish

ab-olītiō, ōnis f abolition; amnesty

ab-ōminor 1 to deprecate as an evil omen; to detest, execrate

ab-rādō, rāsī, rāsum 3 to scrape or shave off

ab-ripiō, ripuī, reptum 3 to snatch away, drag off

ab-rogō 1 to repeal, annul; to take away

ab-rumpō, rūpī, ruptum 3 to break off or away; to tear, burst; to sever; to violate

abs-cēdō, cessī, cessum 3 to go away, withdraw; to desist from, give up; to disappear, be lost

abs-cessus, ūs m departure, absence

abs-cīdō, cīdī, cīsum 3 to cut off; to separate

ab-scindō 3 to break off; to rip open; to divide, separate

abs-cīsus 3 cut off; precipitous; short

abs-condō, con(di)dī, conditum 3 to conceal

ab-sēns, tis absent, remote

ab-sentia, ae f absence; want

absinthium, iī n wormwood

ab-sistō, stitī, — 3 to go away, withdraw; to desist from

ab-solūtiō, ōnis f acquittal; perfection [perfect]

ab-solūtus 3 complete,

ab-solvō 3 to loosen; to set free; to acquit, absolve; to complete, finish; to relate

ab-sonus 3 discordant; incompatible

ab-sorbeō, uī, — 2 to swallow down, devour

absque prep. with abl. apart from, without

abs-tergeō 2 to wipe off, dry by wiping; to remove

abs-terreō 2 to frighten away, drive away; to deter

abs-tinēns, tis abstinent, continent; chaste

abs-tinentia, ae f abstinence; self-denial

abs-tineō, tinuī, (tentum) 2 to keep off or back; to abstain, refrain

abs-trahō 3 to draw or drag away or off; to remove, detach; to estrange

abs-trūdō 3 to thrust away, conceal

ab-sum, ā-fuī (ā-futūrus) ab-esse to be away from, be absent; to stand off, take no part, be missing; to abandon, not to help; to be inconsistent with, be different; to be free from

ab-sūmō 3 to take away, consume; to waste; to destroy; to spend (*time*). P. to perish

ab-surdus 3 out of tune, harsh; foolish, silly; incongruous

ab-undantia, ae *f* abundance, plenty; an overcharging

ab-unde *adv.* plentifully, more than enough

ab-undō 1 to overflow, stream over; to be rich in; to enjoy

ab-ūtor 3 to use up, consume; to abuse, use wrongly

ac = atque

acanthus, ī *m* (and *f*) bear's-breech (*a plant*); gum arabic

ac-cēdō 3 to go or come to, approach; to approach as an enemy; to enter upon some work; to agree; to be like; to be added

ac-celerō 1 to accelerate; *intr.* to hasten

ac-cendō, cendī, cēnsum 3 to set on fire; to lighten up; to excite, arouse

ac-cēnsus, ī *m* attendant of a magistrate

ac-ceptus 3 welcome, pleasing

ac-cersō 3 = arcesso

ac-cessiō, ōnis *f* a coming to, approach; addition, appendage

ac-cessus, ūs *m* 1. = accessio; 2. entrance

ac-cidō[1], **cidī, —** 3 to fall down; to fall at the feet of; to reach, strike (*the senses*); to come to pass, happen; accidit ut it happens that

ac-cidō[2], **cidī, cīsum** 3 to cut or hew at; to consume; to weaken, ruin

ac-cingō 3 to gird to or on; to equip with, arm

ac-ciō 4 to call to, summon

ac-cipiō, cēpī, ceptum 3 to take, receive; to suffer, bear; to approve of; to receive as a guest; to hear, perceive; to learn, understand; to interpret; to suffer

accipiter, tris *m* a hawk, bird of prey

ac-citus, ūs *m* summons, call [shout]

ac-clāmātiō, ōnis *f* cry,/

ac-clāmō 1 to call, cry, shout at; to name by acclamation

ac-clīnis, e leaning on, inclined to

ac-clīnō 1 to lean on, incline to

ac-clīvis, e 3 inclined upwards, sloping

ac-cola, ae *m* one who dwells near, neighbour

ac-colō 3 to dwell near

ac-commodātiō, ōnis *f* an adjusting; complaisance

ac-commodō 1 to put on, apply; to adjust, adapt; to attribute; to make use of ac-commodus 3 fit for, suitable

ac-crēscō 3 to grow, increase; to come as an addition [at table]

ac-cubitiō, ōnis f a lying

ac-cubō 1 to lie or recline at table

ac-cumbō, cubuī, cubitum 3 to lie at table

ac-cumulō 1 to heap up, amass, give in abundance; to overwhelm

ac-cūrō 1 to do carefully

ac-currō, (cu)currī, cursum 3 to run to or up, hasten to

ac-cursus, ūs m a running to

accūsātiō, ōnis f accusation, complaint; indictment

accūsātor, ōris m accuser, prosecutor

accūsātōrius 3 like an accuser

ac-cūsō 1 to accuse, prosecute; to complain of, blame

ācer, ācris, ācre sharp, piercing; pungent, shrill; acute, sagacious; violent, active, spirited; passionate, fierce

acerbitās, ātis f bitterness, sourness; harshness; painfulness; misery

acerbus 3 bitter, sour; raw, unripe; harsh, rough, morose; grievous

acernus 3 of maple (wood)

acerra, ae f casket for incense

acervātim adv. in heaps; to sum up, briefly

acervus, ī m heap, pile; multitude (vinegar; wit)

acētum, ī n sour wine,

acidus 3 sour, sharp; disagreeable

aciēs, ēī f sharp edge, point; keenness (of sight); eye; insight, acuteness; line of battle; army; battle

acipēnser, eris m a sea-fish, sturgeon

aconītum, ī n a poisonous plant, aconite

ac-quiēscō 3 to come to rest, to repose; to die; to have peace; to be content with

ac-quīrō, quīsīvī, quīsītum 3 to acquire in addition; to obtain, win

ācrimōnia, ae f sharpness; energy

ācriter adv. of acer

acroāma, atis n musician, reader, actor

acta[1], ae f sea-shore

acta[2], ōrum n/pl. actions, deeds; public or legal acts, ordinances; register, records; gazette

āctiō, ōnis f a doing; enterprise, business; public action; a performing (of an orator or actor); action in a court of justice

āctitō 1 to do or perform often

āctor, ōris m agent, performer; manager; accuser; actor, player

āctuārius 3 easily driven, swift

āctum, ī *n*, see acta[2], orum

āctus, ūs *m* a driving, impulse; gesture, presentation of a play; division of a play, act

actūtum *adv.* immediately

aculeus, ī *m* sting, point; sarcasm

acūmen, inis *n* point; spear-point; cunning; acuteness

acuō, uī, ūtum 3 to point, sharpen; to exercise, practise; to stimulate; to raise, enhance

acus, ūs *f* needle

acūtus 3 pointed, sharp; pungent, piercing; cunning, sagacious; crafty

ad *prep.* with *acc.* (*of space*) to, towards, against, before; at, near; (*of time*) about, toward; till, up to; at, on; (*of relation*) (*with numbers*) about, almost; for the purpose of; with respect to; compared with; besides, in addition to

ad-aequē *adv.* in like manner

ad-aequō 1 to make equal; to compare to; to come near to

adamantēus 3, **-tinus** 3 of steel; hard as steel

adamās, antis *m* steel; adamant; hardness, inflexibility

ad-amō 1 to fall in love with

ad-aperiō 4 to throw open

ad-augeō 2 to increase

ad-bibō, bibī, — 3 to drink (in); *fig.* to listen eagerly to

adc..., *see* acc...

ad-dīcō 3 to assent, be propitious; to award, adjudge; to knock down to (*in auctions*); to sell; to dedicate; se addicere to give oneself up to; **addictus**, ī *m* 3 debtor, bondsman [dition]

ad-discō 3 to learn in ad-]

ad-dō, didī, ditum 3 to give *or* put to; to add to, increase; to bestow; to add (*in reckoning*); to say *or* write in addition

ad-dubitō 1 to incline to doubt, to hesitate; *trans.* to doubt

ad-dūcō 3 to draw (tight) to oneself, draw together; to lead to; to bring to a certain condition *or* state of mind; to prevail upon

ad-ductus 3 drawn together, wrinkled; stern

ad-edō, ēdī, ēsum 3 to gnaw at; to consume

ad-ēmptiō, ōnis *f* a taking away

ad-eō[1], iī, itum, īre to go *or* come to *or* up, approach; to accost, apply to; to visit; to attack; to enter on, take in hand; to undergo, incur

ad-eō[2] *adv.* to that point, thus far; so long; so much; indeed, truly, precisely

adeptiō, ōnis *f* an obtaining

ad-equitō 1 to ride up to

adf..., see aff...

adg..., see agg...

ad-haereō 2 to cleave, stick or hang to, to adhere; to border on, be near

ad-haerēscō, haesī, haesum 3 to stick to, adhere; to cling to; to stick fast, stop

ad-hibeō, uī, itum 2 to bring to, hold to, lay on; to apply to, use, show; to summon; to consult; to treat, handle [long for]

ad-hinniō 4 to neigh to; to

ad-hortātiō, ōnis f exhortation, encouragement

ad-hortātor, ōris m one who exhorts

ad-hortor 1 to exhort, encourage, rouse

ad-hūc adv. thus far, hitherto; up to the present time; still; besides, in addition

ad-iaceō 2 to lie at or by the side of; to adjoin

ăd-iciō (and ăd-), iēcī, iectum 3 to throw to, to direct to; to apply to, to add

ad-iectiō, ōnis f addition

ad-igō, ēgī, āctum 3 to drive to; to compel, urge

ad-imō, ēmī, ēmptum 3 to take away; to take from

adipātus 3 fatty, greasy; turgid, bombastic

ad-ipīscor, adeptus sum 3 to reach, come up to; to obtain, get

ad-itus, ūs m a going to, approach; entrance; audience; admittance; beginning; opportunity

ad-iūdicō 1 to award, adjudge; to assign

ad-iūmentum, ī n help, support

ad-iūnctiō, ōnis f a joining to, union; addition

ad-iūnctus 3 closely joined, united; belonging to; subst. adiūnctum, ī n characteristic or essential attribute; accessory circumstance

ad-iungō 3 to yoke or bind to; to join, attach; to add, associate; to win as a friend; to give, attribute

ad-iūrō 1 to swear in addition; to swear to; to confirm by oath

ad-iūtō 1 to help, assist

adiūtor, ōris m helper; aid, adjutant; deputy; secondary player (in the theatre)

adiūtrīx, īcis f female helper

ad-iuvō, iūvī, iūtum 1 to help, assist; to encourage; to be useful

adl..., see all... [out to]

ad-mētior 4 to measure]

adminic(u)lum, ī n prop, support, stake; aid, help

ad-minister, trī m assistant, servant; fig. tool

ad-ministra, ae f female helper

ad-ministrātiō, ōnis f help, aid; management; administration, government

ad-ministrō 1 to direct, administer, manage, execute

ad-mīrābilis, e admirable, wonderful; strange, astonishing

ad-mīrābilitās, ātis *f* admirableness

ad-mīrandus 3 = admirabilis

ad-mīrātiō, ōnis *f* admiration; wonder, astonishment

ad-mīror 1 to admire; to wonder at, be astonished at

ad-misceō 2 to mix with; to join, mingle; to implicate

ad-missārius, ī *m* stallion

ad-missum, ī *n* trespass, crime

ad-mittō 3 to let go, set in motion; to admit, give audience; to allow; to commit (*a crime*)

ad-mixtiō, ōnis *f* admixture

ad-modum *adv.* (*with numbers*) to full measure, at least; (*of degree*) wholly, quite, altogether; (*in answers*) certainly

ad-moneō 2 to remind; to put in mind of a debt; to warn; to advise; to urge

ad-monitiō, ōnis *f* a reminding; suggestion, exhortation

ad-monitor, ōris *m* admonisher

ad-monitus, ūs *m* = admonitio

ad-mordeō, momordī, morsum 2 to gnaw at

ad-moveō 2 to move to *or* near; to bring up, lead on; *fig.* to apply *or* direct to   [murmuring]

ad-murmurātiō, ōnis *f* a]

ad-murmurō 1 to murmur

adn..., *see* ann...

ad-oleō, uī, — 2 to burn

ad-olēscentia, ae *f* = adulescentia

ad-olēscō, olēvī, (ultum) 3 to grow up, grow

ad-operiō 4 to cover; to close

ad-optātiō, ōnis *f* = adoptio

ad-optiō, ōnis *f* adoption

ad-optīvus 3 adopted

ad-optō 1 to choose in addition, to select; to adopt

ador, ōris (*and* ŏris) *n* spelt

adōrea (*or* -la), **ae** *f* praise, glory, reward of valour

adōreus 3 of spelt

ad-orior 4 to rise against; to attack; to address; to undertake, attempt

ad-ōrnō 1 to fit out, equip, provide; to adorn

ad-ōrō 1 to speak to; to implore; to worship; to ask for

adp..., *see* app...; **adqu...,** *see* acqu...; **adr...,** *see* arr...

ad-rādō 3 to scrape at; to cut

ads..., **adsc...,** **adsp...,** **adst...,** **adt-...,** *see* ass..., **asc...,** **asp...,** **ast...,** **att...,**

ad-sum, *see* as-sum

adūlātiō, ōnis *f* a fawning; flattery

adulēscēns, entis *m* young man; *f* young woman

adulēscentia, ae *f* youth; young people

adulēscentulus, ī *m*, ula, ae *f* a young man, woman

ad-ūlor 1 to fawn on; to flatter

adulter, erī *m* adulterous; adulterer; paramour

adultera, ae *f* adulteress

adulterīnus 3 counterfeit, false

adulterium, ī *n* adultery

adulterō 1 to commit adultery; to falsify, corrupt

adultus 3 grown up, mature

ad-umbrō 1 to sketch, shade; to represent vaguely; ad-umbrātus 3 unreal, feigned

ad-uncus 3 bent inwards, hooked

ad-ūrō, ussī, ustum 3 to set on fire; to scorch; to nip, freeze

ad-usque *prep.* with *acc.* = usque ad; *adv.* all the way

ad-vehō, vexī, vectum 3 to carry *or* bring to a place; P. to be brought *or* conveyed to; to arrive

ad-vēlō 1 to veil; to crown

ad-vena, ae *m* stranger, foreigner; novice

ad-veniō 4 to come to, arrive at; to approach, appear   [eign)

adventicius 3 strange, for-

adventō 1 to approach, advance

ad-ventor, ōris *m* visitor, guest

adventus, ūs *m* approach, arrival

adversārius 3 opposed, hostile, noxious; *subst.* ∼, ī *m* opponent, enemy; adversāria, ōrum *n/pl.* memoranda; notebook

ad-versor 1 to resist, oppose

ad-versus[1] 3 turned towards, opposite, in front; opposed, hostile; odious; unfavourable; *subst.* adversa, ōrum *n/pl.* misfortune, disaster

ad-versus[2] *or* -sum 1. *adv.* in the opposite direction, to meet; 2. *prep.* with *acc.* opposite, towards; contrary to; compared with

ad-vertō 3 to turn to *or* towards; to steer, land; to perceive; to punish; animum advertere to direct one's attention to, to heed

ad-vesperāscit, āvit, — 3 evening approaches

ad-vigilō 1 to watch, guard

ad-vocātiō, ōnis *f* a summoning to advise; legal advice; the bar, body of advocates; delay for consultation

ad-vocātus, ī *m* one who is called to aid in a trial; advocate, witness ad-vocō 1 to call, summon; to call as an adviser *or* witness

ad-volō 1 to fly to; to hasten towards

ad-volvō 3 to roll to; P. to throw oneself at the feet of

ad-vors-, -vort-, *see* advers-, -vert-

adytum, ī *n* the holiest part of a temple, inmost recess (*generally in pl.*)

aedēs (*or* aedis), is *f* 1. temple, apartment; temple; 2. *pl.* a dwelling, house

aedicula, ae *f* small building, temple, *or* room

aedificātiō, ōnis *f* act of building; building

aedificātor, ōris *m* builder

aedificium, ī *n* building, structure

aedi-ficō 1 to build, erect, establish

aedilicius 3 of an aedile; *subst.* ~, ī *m* ex-aedile

aedīlis, is *m* aedile, superintendent of public works

aedīlitās, ātis *f* office of an aedile

aedituus, ī *m* guardian of a temple

aeger, gra, grum sick, suffering; feeble; troubled; painful, sad

aegis, idis *f* shield of Jupiter, aegis

aegrē *adv.* painfully, distressingly; with difficulty; unwillingly

aegrēscō, —, — 3 to fall sick; to become worse

aegrimōnia, ae *f* sorrow, distress

aegritūdō, inis *f* sickness; grief

aegrōtātiō, ōnis *f* sickness

aegrōtō 1 to be sick *or* ill; to suffer

aegrōtus 3 sick, ill, suffering

aemulātiō, ōnis *f* rivalry; jealousy

aemulātor, ōris *m* rival; imitator

aemulor 1 to vie with, rival; to envy

aemulus 3 vying with; jealous

aēneus 3 of copper, bronze

aenigma, atis *n* riddle, mystery

aēnus 3 = aeneus; *subst.* aēnum, ī *n* bronze vessel

aequābilis, e uniform, similar, equal; equable; impartial, just

aequābilitās, ātis *f* equality, uniformity; impartiality

aequaevus 3 of equal age

aequālis, e like, equal; even; uniform, steady; equal in size *or* age

aequālitās, ātis *f* equality

aequanimitās, ātis *f* fairness, impartiality; calmness, kindness

aequē *adv.* equally, in like manner; fairly, justly

aequi-noctium, ī *n* equinox

aequi-perō 1 to compare; to equal, rival

aequitās ātis *f* uniformity, evenness; calmness; fairness, justice

aequŏ 1 to make level, smooth, straight *or* equal; to compare

aequor, oris *n* even surface; plain; (surface of the) sea

aequoreus 3 belonging to the sea

aequus 3 equal; even, level; favourable; friendly; equal in size; even-tempered, calm; impartial, fair

āēr, āeris *m* air, atmosphere; mist, cloud

aerārius 3 of copper *or* bronze; belonging to money, pecuniary; *subst.* aerārius, ī *m* citizen of the lowest class; aerāria, ae *f* copper-mine; aerārium, ī *n* public treasury

aerātus 3 fitted with brass

aereus 3 = aeneus; = aeratus

aeri-pēs, pedis brazen-footed

āerius 3 belonging to the air, aerial; lofty, high

aerūgŏ, inis *f* verdigris; envy; avarice

aerumna, ae *f* toil, hardship, suffering

aerumnōsus 3 full of hardship, miserable

aes, aeris *n* copper, bronze; copper vessel, statue, tablet; money, coin, the as; aes alienum debt

aesculētum, ī *n* oak-forest

aesculeus 3 of the oak

aesculus, ī *f* the winter oak

aestās, ātis *f* summer

aesti-fer 3 heat-bringing

aestimābilis, e valuable

aestimātiō, ōnis *f* an appraising, valuation, esteem

aestimātor, ōris *m* appraiser

aestimō 1 to appraise, estimate; to value, esteem, judge

aestīvus 3 of summer; *subst.* aestīva, ōrum *n/pl.* summer camp; campaign; summer pastures

aestuārium, ī *n* lagoon; creek, bay

aestumō = aestimo

aestuŏ 1 to blaze; to burn, boil, seethe; to swell; to be agitated; to hesitate

aestuōsus 3 glowing, hot; surging, agitated

aestus, ūs *m* fire, heat; fever; a raging, seething; surge, swell; fervour; unrest, hesitation

aetās, ātis *f* age, lifetime; time of life, generation

aeternitās, ātis *f* eternity, immortality   [tal]

aeternus 3 eternal, immor-f

aether, eris *m* the upper air, sky, heaven

aetherius 3 relating to the upper air; celestial, heavenly

aethra, ae *f* the clear sky

aevum, ī *n* 1. eternity; 2. = aetas

af-fābilis, e affable, approachable

af-fatim *adv.* sufficiently, abundantly

af-fātus, ūs *m* a speaking to, address

affectātiō, ōnis *f* a striving

affectiō, ōnis *f* disposition, state of mind

affectō 1 to grasp; to pursue, strive after; to try, win over

affectus[1], ūs *m* condition, state, disposition; passion, feeling; affection

affectus[2] 3 furnished, provided; disposed, inclined; impaired, weakened

af-ferō, attulī, allātum 3 to carry, bring to; to report, announce; to produce; to cause; to help, be of use

af-ficiō, fēcī, fectum 3 to treat in a certain way, influence, affect; to weaken, impair, oppress

af-fīgō 3 to fasten to, attach

af-fingō 3 to form in addition; to add falsely

af-finis, e adjoining, neighbouring; connected with, accessory to; related by marriage

af-finitās, ātis *f* relationship by marriage

af-firmātiō, ōnis *f* affirmation, solemn assurance

af-firmō 1 to strengthen; to confirm, assert; to assure

af-flātus, ūs *m* a blowing or breathing on; blast, breath; inspiration

af-flīctātiō, ōnis *f* pain, torture

af-flīctō 1 to beat or strike repeatedly; to trouble, torment; to grieve

af-flīctus 3 beaten, damaged; miserable, wretched; spiritless; vile

af-flīgō, xī, ctum 3 to strike or dash against; to throw down; to injure, distress; to weaken, humiliate; to dash to pieces [on]

af-flō 1 to blow or breathe)

af-fluēns, tis abundant, plentiful, rich, full of

af-fluentia, ae *f* abundance, plenty

af-fluō 3 to flow to; to glide on; to flow with, abound

af-for 1 to accost, address, implore

af-fulgeō 2 to shine upon

af-fundō 3 to pour into; affūsus prostrate

agāsō, ōnis *m* groom, hostler; churl

agellus, ī *m* little field or estate

ager, grī *m* field, estate; open country; territory, district

agger, eris *m* heap, mound, soil; rampart, dam; fortification, wall

aggerō 1 to heap up; to increase

ag-glomerō 1 to attach

ag-glūtinō 1 to glue to, stick on

ag-gravēscō, —, — 3 to become worse

ag-gravō 1 to make heavier or worse; to oppress

ag-gredior, gressus sum 3 to step *or* go to, approach; to apply to, address; to attack, fall upon; to begin, undertake, attempt

ag-gregō 1 to add to, join to

ag-gressiō, ōnis *f* introduction (*to a speech*)

agilis, e easily moved; quick, nimble; lively

agilitās, ātis *f* quickness, agility

agitātiō, ōnis *f* motion; agitation; pursuit, management

agitātor, ōris *m* driver; charioteer

agitō 1 to set in violent motion, drive about *or* onward, chase, hunt, shake; to incite, pursue; to trouble, rouse, disturb; to practise, exercise; to discuss, debate; to consider, deliberate

agmen, inis *n* band, crowd, troop; army on the march, column, army in line of battle

agna, ae *f* ewe-lamb

a-gnāscor, agnātus sum 3 to be born in addition

a-gnātiō, ōnis *f* blood-relationship on the father's side

a-gnātus 3 born after; related on the father's side

a-gnōscō, agnōvī, agnitum 3 to perceive, observe; to recognize, identify

agnus, ī *m* lamb

agō, ēgī, āctum 3 to drive, lead, chase, urge; to set in motion; to drive away, rob; to accuse, impeach; to excite, prompt; to direct, steer, push; to construct; to pass, spend, live; to pursue, practise, perform; to keep (*a festival*); to act (*a play or part*); to consider, discuss; to plead, conduct a lawsuit; **se agere** to behave, bear oneself

agrārius 3 relating to land *or* fields

agrestis, e living in the fields *or* country; wild, savage; rustic, uncultivated, clownish; agricultural; *subst.* ~, is *m* countryman, peasant

agri-cola, ae *m* farmer

agri-cultiō, -cultor, -cultūra, *see* **ager** *and* **cultiō** etc.

āh, ā *int.* ah! alas!

ahēneus, ahēnus = **aeneus, aenus** [assert, say]

āiō to say yes, assent; to

āla, ae *f* wing (*of a bird or army*); armpit, shoulder; troop (*of cavalry*)

alacer, cris, cre lively, quick, eager, active, cheerful

alacritās, ātis *f* liveliness, quickness, eagerness

alapa, ae *f* box on the ear

ālārius 3, belonging to the wing of an army; *subst.* **ālāriī, ōrum** *m/pl.* auxiliary troops ālātus 3 winged

albātus 3 clothed in white

albeō, uī, — 2 to be white

albēscō, buī, — 3 to become
white

albus 3 white; pale; fortunate,
propitious; *subst.* album, I
n white colour; white
tablet; register, list

alcyōn, ōnis *f* kingfisher

ālea, ae *f* game with dice,
die; hazard, risk

āleātor, ōris *m* dicer,
gambler

āles, itis winged; swift;
subst. (*f* and *m*) bird; prophetic bird; omen, augury

alga, ae *f* sea-weed

algeō, alsī, — 2 to be or feel
cold

algor, ōris *m* cold

aliās *adv.* at another time;
elsewhere; in another
way; aliās ... aliās at one
time ... at another time

alibī *adv.* elsewhere; in
other respects; alibī ... alibī
here ... there

alicunde *adv.* from somewhere, from any place

aliēnātiō, ōnis *f* alienation
(*of property*), transfer;
separation, desertion

aliēni-gena, ae *m* alien,
foreign; foreigner

aliēnō 1 to make a thing
another's, transfer; to
cast off, disown; to sell; to
drive mad; to estrange,
alienate

aliēnus 3 belonging or

relating to another; not
acquainted with, strange
to; averse, hostile; unsuitable, disadvantageous;
subst. aliēnus, ī *m* stranger,
foreigner; aliēnum, ī *n*
another man's property
or affair

āliger, gera, gerum bearing
wings

alimentum, ī *n* food, provisions; return due to
parents for the bringing
up of children

aliō *adv.* to another place,
person or thing

aliō-quī(n) *adv.* in other
respects, otherwise; be-
sides, moreover, in any
case [swift-footed]

āli-pēs, pedis wing-footed,

aliquā *adv.* (sc. viā) by any
way; somehow

aliquam-diū *adv.* for a
pretty long time

aliquandō *adv* at any time,
at some time, once, ever;
finally, sometimes

aliquantisper for a while

aliquantulus 3 very little *or*
small

aliquantus 3 some, con-
siderable; *subst.* aliquantum, ī *n* a considerable
amount

ali-quī, a, od some, any

ali-quis, a, id some one,
something, anyone, any-
thing; aliquid (*adv.*) in
some degree

ali-quō *adv.* to some place,
somewhere

ali-quot some, a few, several

ali-quotiē(n)s *adv.* several times

aliter *adv.* otherwise, in another way; in the contrary manner, in other respects

ālium, ī *n* = allium

ali-unde *adv.* from another direction, from elsewhere

alius, a, ud another, other; different, of another kind

al-lābor 3 to glide *or* flow to

al-labōrō 1 to add to by toil

al-lēgō¹ 1 to send on business, as a negotiator *or* deputy

al-legō² 3 to choose in addition

al-levātiō, ōnis *f* alleviation

al-levō 1 to lift up, raise; to lighten, alleviate

al-liciō, lexī, lectum 3 to allure, entice

al-līdō, sī, sum 3 to strike against

al-ligō 1 to bind *or* tie to; to make fast; to fetter; to bind by kindness

al-linō, lēvī, litum 3 to smear on, bedaub

allium, ī *n* garlic

al-loquium, ī *n* a speaking to, address; encouragement, consolation

al-loquor 3 to speak to, address; to exhort, comfort

al-lūdō 3 to play *or* sport with

al-luō, luī, — 3 to wash (*against*)

almus 3 nourishing, giving food; kind, bountiful

alnus, ī *f* alder; ship, boat

alō, aluī, altum *or* alitum 3 to nourish, feed, rear; to support; to strengthen, increase

altāria, ium *n/pl.* (high) altar

alter, era, erum one of two, the one, the other; neighbour, fellow-man

altercātiō, ōnis *f* debate, quarrel

altercor 1 to dispute, quarrel

alternō 1 to do by turns *or* alternately; to change; to hesitate

alternus 3 one after the other, alternate; alternīs (*adv.*) by turns

alter-uter, utra, utrum one of two, one *or* the other

altilis, e fat; *subst.* fattened fowl

altitūdō, inis *f* height; grandeur; depth; reserve, secrecy

altor, ōris *m* nourisher, sustainer

altrix, īcis *f* foster-mother, nurse

altus 3 1. a) high; b) lofty, great; *subst.* altum, ī *n* height; heaven; 2. deep; secret, profound; ancient; *subst.* altum, ī *n* depth, far distance

alucinor 1 to wander in mind, to ramble in speech

alumna, ae *f* foster-daugh-
ter; pupil

alumnus, ī *m* foster-son;
pupil

alūta, ae *f* soft leather;
shoe; purse

alv(e)ārium, ī *n* beehive

alveolus, ī *m* small trough;
gaming board

alveus, ī *m* hollow, cavity;
trough, basin; boat; bed
of a river

alvus, ī *f* belly; womb;
stomach; beehive

amābilis, e lovely, lovable

ā-mandō 1 to send away,
remove

amāns, tis loving, friendly;
lover

amāracus, ī *m* marjoram

amarantus, ī *m* amaranth

amārus 3 bitter; morose

amātor, ōris *m* lover

amātōrius 3 loving, amo-
rous

ambactus, ī *m* vassal

amb-āgēs, um *f/pl.* (*abl.
sg* āge) digression, dif-
fuseness; evasion, am-
biguity

amb-igō, —, — 3 to doubt,
hesitate; to dispute, argue

ambiguitās, ātis *f* ambiguity

ambiguus 3 inclined to both
sides; wavering, uncer-
tain; obscure

ambiō, īvī *and* iī, ītum 4 to
go round; to avoid; to
surround; to go round
canvassing for votes; to
entreat

amb-itiō, ōnis *f* a going

about; pomp; canvassing
for an office; a striving
after honours, flattery;
ambition

ambitiōsus 3 twining
around; striving after
honours; vain, preten-
tious

amb-itus, ūs *m* circuit,
revolution, circle; illegal
canvassing for an office

ambō, ae, ō both, the two

ambrosius 3 divine; *subst.*
ambrosia, ae *f* ambrosia,
food of the gods

ambulātiō, ōnis *f* a walking
about; promenade

ambulō 1 to walk about;
to travel; to traverse

amb-ūrō 3 to scorch, burn
up; to benumb

ā-mēns, tis senseless, mad;
foolish

ā-mentia, ae *f* madness,
folly

āmentum, ī *n* strap, thong

amīca, ae *f* female friend;
mistress

amiciō —, ictum 4 to
clothe, wrap round

amīcitia, ae *f* friendship;
alliance

amictus, ūs. *m* garment,
covering

amiculum, ī *n* cloak, mantle

amīculus, ī *m* (dear) friend

amīcus 3 friendly, loving,
kindly; pleasing; *subst.*
amīcus, ī *m* friend

ā-missiō, ōnis *f* loss

amita, ae *f* aunt (*father's
sister*)

ā-mīttŏ 3 to send away, let go; to loose; to lose

amnis, is *m* river, stream; current

amō 1 to love; to be wont, be fond of

amoenĭtās, ātis *f* pleasantness, loveliness, charm

amoenus 3 pleasant, lovely, charming

ā-mōlior 4 to move (away) with effort, remove

amōmum, ī *n* an aromatic shrub

amor, ōris *m* love, affection; love-affair; object of love; longing

ā-moveō 2 to move away, remove; to steal; to banish

amphi-theātrum, ī *n* amphitheatre

amphora, ae *f* two-handled vessel (*for wine*), pitcher; a measure for liquids

am-plector, plexus sum 3 to encircle, surround, embrace; tc love, welcome; to consider, understand; to discuss

amplexor 1 = amplector

amplexus, ūs *m* a surrounding, encircling; embrace

ampli-fĭcātĭō, ōnis *f* an enlarging, increasing

ampli-ficō 1 to enlarge, extend; to glorify

amplĭō 1 a) = amplifico; b) to adjourn, delay a judgment

ampliter *adv.* amply, fully; splendidly

amplitūdō, ĭnis *f* wide extent, size; greatness

amplius *adv.* (*of time*) more, longer; in a higher degree; (*with numbers*) more than; besides, in addition

amplus 3 large, spacious; full, abundant; strong; splendid, glorious; distinguished, noble

ampulla, ae *f* a flask for unguents; bombast

amputō 1 to cut off; to prune; to curtail

an *cj.* 1. *in disjunctive* (*direct or indirect double*) *questions*: or; utrum — an whether — or; annon or not; 2. *in indirect simple questions* = num whether; 3. *in simple direct questions*: or then, or rather

anas, atis *f* duck

an-ceps, cĭpĭtis two-headed; twofold; from *or* on both sides, doubtful, undecided; dangerous

ancīle, is *n* the shield said to have fallen from heaven in the time of Numa; shield

ancilla, ae *f* maidservant

ancillula, ae *f* a young maidservant

ancora, ae *f* anchor

ancorāle, is *n* (anchor-) cable

andro-gynus, ī *m* manwoman, hermaphrodite

ān-frāctus, ūs *m* a turning, bending round; diffuseness; intricacies

angi-portus, ūs *m or* -um, ī *n* narrow lane; by-street

angō, (anxī), — 3 to squeeze; to choke, strangle; to vex, torment

angor, ōris *m* strangling, suffocation; anguish, trouble

anguis, is *m and f* serpent, snake

angulus, ī *m* corner; angle; nook, recess

angustiae, ārum *f/pl.* narrowness, narrow place; defile; difficulty, poverty, distress, trouble; meanness

angustus 3 narrow, short; confined, limited; difficult; base, mean

an-hēlitus, ūs *m* a panting, short breath; vapour

an-hēlō 1 to pant, gasp; to breathe out; to pant for

an-hēlus 3 panting; causing to pant   [woman]

anicula, ae *f* little old/

anīlis, e of an old woman

anima, ae *f* current of air, wind; breath; soul, life; departed spirit; living being; mind

anim-adversiō, ōnis *f* observation, inquiry; censure; punishment

anim-advertō 3 to attend to, notice, observe; to blame; to punish

animal, ālis *n* living being, creature; beast

animālis, e of air; animate, living

animāns, tis living; *subst.* ~, tis *m and f* = animal

animātus 3 disposed, minded; courageous

animō 1 to animate, give life; to dispose; to encourage

animōsus 3 courageous, audacious, passionate

animus, ī *m* 1. *poet.* = anima; 2. soul, mind; intellect, reason; thought, judgment, opinion; feeling, affection; disposition, nature; courage, spirit; arrogance, pride; passion, wrath; desire, purpose, intention

annālis, e relating to a year, annual; *subst.* annālēs, ium *m/pl.* yearly records, annals

an-ne = an

an-nectō 3 to tie *or* fasten to; to connect

an-nītor 3 to lean upon; to exert oneself, take pains

anni-versārius 3 yearly

an-nō 1 to swim up to

annōna, ae *f* yearly produce, crop, corn; price of grain and other provisions

annōsus 3 full of years, aged

an-notō 1 to remark, observe

an-numerō 1 to count among, reckon; to count out, pay

an-nuō, nuī, — 3 to nod to, make a sign; to agree, grant

annus, I *m* a year; season; harvest

annuus 3 lasting a year; yearly

an-quīrō, sīvī, sītum 3 to seek carefully; to inquire into; to conduct judicial inquiry; to accuse, impeach

ānsa, ae *f* handle; opportunity

ānser, eris *m* (*and* *f*) goose

ante 1. *adv.* in front, before, forwards; previously; 2. *prep.* with *acc.* (*of space*) before, in front of; (*of time*) before; (*of relation*) before, more than

anteā *adv.* before, formerly

ante-capiō 3 to take beforehand, preoccupy; to anticipate

ante-cēdēns, tis foregoing, preceding

ante-cēdō 3 to go before, precede; to excel, surpass

ante-cellō, —, — 3 to be prominent; to surpass

ante-cessiō, ōnis *f* a preceding; antecedent cause

ante-cursor, ōris *m* fore-runner; advanced guard

ante-eō iī, īre to go before, precede; to surpass

ante-ferō, tulī, lātum, ferre to bear *or* carry before; to place before, prefer

ante-hāc *adv.* before this time, hitherto

ante-lūcānus 3 before daybreak

ante-merīdiānus 3 before midday

ante-mittō 3 to send before

antenna (-mna), ae *f* (sail-)yard

ante-pīlānus, I *m* soldier who fought before the triariī

ante-pōnō 3 to place before; to prefer

ante-quam *cj.* before

ante-signānus, I *m* soldier who fought before the standards; leader

an-testor 1 to call as a witness

ante-veniō 4 to come *or* arrive before; to anticipate

ante-vertō 3 to precede; to anticipate; to prefer to

anticipō 1 to take before; to anticipate

antīquitās, ātis *f* ancient time, antiquity; the ancients

antīquitus *adv.* from antiquity; in former times

antīquō 1 to reject (*a law*)

antīquus 3 (anticus) old, ancient, former; venerable, oldfashioned; *subst.* antīquī, ōrum *m/pl.* the ancients, ancient writers

anti-stes, itis *m and f* overseer of a temple, chief priest(ess)

antrum, I *n* cave, cavern

ānulus, I *m* finger-ring, seal-ring

anus¹, ūs *f* old woman

ānus², I *m* fundament

anxietās, ātis *f* anxiety, trouble

anxius 3 anxious, troubled; tormenting, troublesome

aper, prī *m* wild boar

aperiō, ruī, rtum 4 to uncover, open; to display, make known; to explain

apertus 3 uncovered, exposed; open; accessible, free; clear, evident; frank, candid

apex, icis *m* point, extremity, summit; helmet; cap of a priest; crown

apis, is *f* bee

apium, ī *n* celery

aplustre, is *n* stern

apo-thēca, ae *f* store-room, warehouse

ap-parātus[1], ūs *m* a preparing; tool, instrument; splendour, pomp

ap-parātus[2] 3 well prepared, ready; splendid, sumptuous

ap-pāreō 2 to appear, become visible; to be clear, evident; to attend, serve

ap-pāritor, ōris *m* public servant, lictor

ap-parō 1 to prepare, make ready, equip

appellātiō, ōnis *f* an addressing, speaking to; appeal; name, title

ap-pellō[1] 1. to address, speak to, greet, to entreat, request; to appeal to; to summon; to call by name, name

ap-pellō[2], pull, pulsum 3 to drive, move, bring to; P. (*and intr. active*) to reach land

ap-pendix, icis *f* supplement, addition

ap-pendō, ndī, nsum 3 to weigh out

ap-petēns, tis striving after, eager for; grasping, avaricious

ap-petitiō, ōnis *f* a grasping at; longing for [petitiō]

ap-petītus, ūs *m* = ap-

ap-petō 3 to strive after, desire, seek; to approach, draw near; to attack

ap-plicātiō, ōnis *f* attachment, inclination

ap-plicō, cāvī, cātum (*or* cuī, citum) 1 to apply, attach, join to; P. to land; to turn to, direct towards

ap-pōnō 3 to put *or* place at, by, beside; to serve, set before; to add to

ap-portō 1 to carry, bring to

ap-positus 3 placed *or* situated near, contiguous; appropriate, proper

ap-prehendō 3 to seize, take hold of

ap-prīmē *adv.* chiefly, exceedingly

ap-probātiō, ōnis *f* approval; assent; proof

ap-probō 1 to approve, assent to, favour; to make acceptable; to prove

ap-properō 1 to hasten, accelerate; to make haste

ap-propinquō 1 to approach, draw near

ap-pulsus, ūs *m* approach, landing; influence

aprīcus 3 open to the sun, sunny

Aprīlis, e belonging to April; *subst.* Aprīlis, is *m* April

aps..., *see* abs...

aptō 1 to fit *or* adapt to, to adjust, accommodate; to prepare, make ready

aptus 3 fastened, joined; prepared, equipped; suitable, fit, proper

apud *prep.* with *acc.* at, near, by, with; in the presence of, among; at the house of; in the opinion of; in the writings of

aqua, ae *f* water; sea, lake, river, rain

aquātiō, -ōnis *f* a fetching of water

aquila, ae *f* eagle; the standard of a Roman legion

aquili-fer, ferī *m* eagle-bearer

aquilō, ōnis *m* the north-wind; north

aquor 1 to fetch water

aquōsus 3 watery, rainy

āra, ae *f* altar, hearth; refuge, shelter

arānea, ae *f* spider; spider's web

arātiō, ōnis *f* a ploughing; agriculture; arable land

arātor, ōris *m* ploughman, farmer; cultivator of public lands

arātrum, ī *n* plough

arbiter, trī *m* spectator, eyewitness; arbiter, umpire; judge; master, ruler

arbitrātus, ūs *m* free-will, choice, pleasure

arbitrium, ī *n* decision of an arbiter, judgment; dominion, mastery

arbitror 1 (*and* arbitrō 1) to give judgment; to consider, think, believe

arbor (*and* ōs), oris *f* tree (*coll.* trees); mast, oar, ship

arboreus 3 of a tree; tree-like

arbustum, ī *n* plantation, orchard, vineyard; trees, shrubs

arbuteus 3 of the strawberry-tree

arbutum, ī *n* fruit of the strawberry-tree

arbutus, ī *f* strawberry-tree

arca, ae *f* chest, box for money; coffin; cell

arcānus 3 secret, hidden

arceō, uī, — 2 to shut in *or* up, confine; to restrain, hinder, keep at a distance

accessō, īvī, ītum 3 to call, summon; to summon before a court of justice, accuse

archi-pīrāta, ae *m* pirate chief

architectus, ī *m* architect; inventor; plotter

Arctos, ī *f* the Great Bear; the two Bears

Arctūrus, ī *m* the brightest star of Boötes

arcus, ūs *m* a bow; rainbow; arch, vault; curve

ārdēns, tis burning, glowing, hot; glittering; fiery, impassioned

ārdeō, ārsī, ārsum 2 to burn, be on fire; to sparkle, flash; to be inflamed *or* excited, desire ardently

ārdēscō, ārsī, — 3 to become inflamed; to glitter; to become furious

ārdor, ōris *m* flame, fire, heat; brightness; eagerness; love

arduus 3 steep, lofty; difficult, hard

ārea, ae *f* open space; building ground; threshing-floor; playground

arēna, ae *f* sand; desert; sea-shore; arena in an amphitheatre

arēnōsus 3 sandy

ārēns, tis dry, arid; thirsty

āreō, uī, — 2 to be dry *or* arid

argentārius 3 of silver; of money; *subst.* argentāria, ae *f* banker's shop; argentārius, ī *m* money-changer, banker

argenteus 3 made of silver; ornamented with silver; of a silver colour; *subst.* ⁓, ī *m* silver coin

argentum, ī *n* silver; silver plate; money

argilla, ae *f* white clay, potter's clay

argūmentātiō, ōnis *f* a proving, argumentation

argūmentor 1 to adduce proof

argūmentum, ī *n* subject, story; theme; plot, tale; proof, conclusion; token

arguō, uī, ūtum 3 to make clear *or* known, show, prove; to accuse, censure

argūtiae, ārum *f/pl.* quick movement; cleverness, wit; cunning

argūtus 3 piercing, noisy, melodious; clear; acute, witty; sly, cunning

āridus 3 dry, parched; thirsty; meagre, scanty

ariēs, etis *m* ram; battering-ram

arietō 1 to butt like a ram, strike violently

arista, ae *f* ear of corn

arma, ōrum *n/pl.* tools, implements, tackle; weapons, armour; war; armed men

armāmenta, ōrum *n/pl.* tackling, equipment of a ship

armāmentārium, ī *n* arsenal, armoury

armārium, ī *n* chest, cupboard

armātūra, ae *f* armour; armed soldiers

armātus[1], ūs *m* = armatura

armātus[2] 3 armed, equipped; *subst.* armātī, ōrum *m/pl.* armed men, soldiers

armentārius, ī *m* herdsman

armentum, ī *n* herd, cattle (for ploughing)

armi-fer 3 bearing arms, warlike

armi-ger 3 shield-bearing; *subst.* ~, ī *m* shield-bearer

armilla, ae *f* bracelet, arm-ring   [arms]

armi-potēns, tis mighty in]

armō 1 to equip, fit out; to arm; to strengthen, help

armus, ī *m* shoulder: flank

arō 1 to plough, till; to farm

ar-rēpō 3 to creep to, approach gently

ar-rīdeō 2 to laugh *or* smile at, laugh with; to be favourable; to please

ar-rigō, rēxī, rēctum 3 to erect, lift up; to excite, rouse

ar-ripiō, ripuī, reptum 3 to snatch, seize; to drag into a court; to accuse

arrogāns, tis arrogant, haughty

arrogantia, ae *f* arrogance, pride

ar-rogō 1 to appropriate, claim; to confer upon

ars, artis *f* skill; profession, trade; fine *or* liberal art, letters; science, knowledge; principles of art; manual of any art *or* science; practice, method, work of art; character, habit; cunning, trick

artē *adv.* of artus[2]

articulus, ī *m* a joint; finger; part, division; moment, crisis

arti-fex, icis *m* and *f* 1. *adj.* clever, skilled; 2. artist; maker, contriver

artificiōsus 3 skilful; artistic

artificium, ī *n* skill, ingenuity, art; trick, craft; trade, handicraft

artus[1], ūs *m* joint, limb (*mostly pl.*)

artus[2] 3 tight, narrow, close; dense; scanty, needy

arundō, *see* harundo

aruspex, *see* haruspex

arvum, ī *n* ploughed land, arable field; field, plain

arx, arcis *f* citadel, fortress; height, eminence; protection, refuge

as, assis *m* a copper coin, the as

a-scendō, ndī, ēnsum 3 to mount, ascend; to rise, reach

a-scēnsus, ūs *m* a going up, ascent; place of ascending, approach

a-sciō 4 to take to oneself, adopt

a-scīscō 3 to take to oneself, receive, adopt

ā-scrībō 3 to write in addition; to enter in a list; to appoint; to reckon among

asellus, ī *m* little ass

asinus, ī *m* ass; blockhead

a-spectō 1 to look at attentively; to lie towards

a-spectus, ūs *m* a looking at, glance; appearance

asper, era, erum rough,

stormy; cold, harsh, hard; bitter, abusive; cruel, severe; troublesome, dangerous

a-spergō[1], rsī, rsum 3 to sprinkle; to taint

a-spergō[2], inis f a sprinkling; drops, spray

asperitās, ātis f roughness; sharpness, harshness; rudeness; calamity, adversity [reject]

a-spernor 1 to despise, f

asperō 1 to make rough; to excite, exasperate

a-spiciō, spexī, spectum 3 to look at, observe; to face; to consider, ponder

a-spīrō 1 to breathe at or upon; to be favourable, assist; to strive for, aspire to; trans. to infuse, instil

as-portō 1 to carry or bring away

asprētum, I n rough or stony place

assecla, ae m = assectator

as-sectātiō, ōnis f attendance

as-sectātor, ōris m attendant, follower; disciple

as-sector 1 to follow, accompany

assecula, ae m = assectator

as-sēnsiō, ōnis f an assenting, applause

as-sēnsus, ūs m = assensio; echo

assentātiō, ōnis f an assenting; flattery

assentātor, ōris m flatterer

as-sentior, sēnsus sum (and as-sentiō) 4 to assent, agree

as-sentor 1 to assent; to flatter

as-sequor 3 to overtake, reach; to obtain; to understand

asser, eris m stake, pole, post

as-serō, seruī, sertum 3 to join to; to claim; to set free

as-servō 1 to keep carefully, preserve; to watch

as-sevērātiō, ōnis f earnestness, perseverance; earnest assertion

as-sevērō 1 to assert earnestly

as-sideō, sēdī, sessum 2 to sit near; to attend, wait upon; to besiege

as-sīdō, sēdī, sessum 3 to sit down

assiduitās, ātis f constant attendance; constant repetition; perseverance

assiduus 3 untiring, incessant; perpetual

assignātiō, ōnis f an assigning, allotment

as-signō 1 to assign, allot; to ascribe, attribute

as-siliō, siluī, (sultum) 4 to leap at

as-similis, e like, similar

as-simulō 1 to make like, copy; to compare; to feign, pretend

as-sistō, stitī, — 3 to stand

at, by, near: to help, defend

as-soleō, —, — 2 to be wont, accustomed

as-suēfaciō 3 to accustom to

as-suēscō 3 to become accustomed; to accustom; assuētus 3 usual, customary

assuētūdō, inis *f* custom, habit

as-sum, affuī, adesse to be at, by, near; to be present; to arrive; to appear before a tribunal; to be present to support, defend; animo adesse to give attention

as-sūmō 3 to take to oneself, receive; to claim

as-surgō 3 to rise up; to mount

assus 3 roasted

ast = at

a-stipulātor, ōris *m* supporter

a-stō, stitī, — 1 to stand at, by, near; to stand upright

a-strictus 3 drawn together, tight; concise, brief

a-stringō 3 to draw together, contract, bind together; to bind, oblige, to circumscribe, condense

astro-logia, ae *f* astronomy

astro-logus, ī *m* astronomer; astrologer

astrum, ī *n* star, constellation; (*pl.*) heaven, immortality

a-struō 3 to build in addition; to add

astus, ūs *m* cunning, craft

astūtia, ae *f* skill; cunning

astūtus 3 shrewd; cunning

asȳlum, ī *n* place of refuge, sanctuary

at *cj.* but, yet, moreover

at-avus, ī *m* great-great-great-grandfather; ancestor

āter, ātra, ātrum black, dark; gloomy, sad, dismal, unlucky

āthlēta, ae *m* wrestler, athlete

a-tomus, ī *f* indivisible body, atom

atque *cj.* (*before consonants* ac) and, and also, and even, and especially; *after words of comparison* (*aequus, similis, alius, etc.*): as, than; and so, and thus

at-quī *cj.* yet, however, nevertheless, rather

ātrāmentum, ī *n* black liquid, a blacking, ink

ātriēnsis, is *m* house-steward

ātrium, ī *n* forecourt, hall; principal room of a house

atrōcitās, ātis *f* fierceness, harshness, barbarity

atrōx, ōcis horrid, terrible; savage, cruel, severe; perilous

at-tāctus, ūs *m* a touching, touch

at-tamen *cj.* but yet, but nevertheless

at-temptō 1 to try to corrupt; to attack

at-tendō, dī, tum 3 to

stretch to, direct to; **animum attendere** to give attention to

at-tentō = attempto

at-tentus 3 attentive, engaged; intent on, striving after

at-tenuō 1 to make thin; to lessen; to weaken, impair

at-terō 3 to rub against; to wear away; to destroy, injure

at-tineō, tinuī, (tentum) 2 to hold fast, detain; to delay; *intr.* to pertain to; to concern

at-tingō, tigī, tāctum 3 to touch against; to arrive at; to border on; to strike, attack; to come in contact with, be related to; to engage in, undertake; to mention, refer to

at-tollō, —, — 3 to raise up, lift up; to exalt, distinguish

at-tondeō, ndī, nsum 2 to shear, shave; to lessen

at-tonitus 3 thunder-struck; terrified, senseless; inspired, frantic

at-trahō 3 to draw to, attract; to drag; to allure

at-trectō 1 to touch, handle; to appropriate

at-tribuō 3 to allot, assign to; to confer, bestow; to pay out, to attribute, impute

at-trītus 3 worn; shameless

au-ceps, cupis *m* bird-catcher, fowler

auctiō, ōnis *f* auction

auctiōnārius 3 pertaining to an auction

auctiōnor 1 to hold an auction

auctor, ōris *m* (*and f*) writer, author; example, teacher, voucher, security; promoter, producer; counsellor; originator, founder, inventor

auctōritās, ātis *f* warrant, security; right of possession; full power, authorisation; example, precedent; weight, dignity, influence, power; will, pleasure, decision; decree (*of the Senate*)

auctumnus, ī *m* = autumnus

auctus[1], **ūs** *m* increase, growth

auctus[2] 3 increased, enlarged

aucupium, ī *n* bird-catching, fowling; the hunting after a thing

aucupor 1 to strive for, hunt after

audācia, ae *f* courage, daring, boldness; temerity, insolence; bold action

audāx, ācis (*adv.* audācter) courageous, bold; foolhardy, rash

audēns, tis daring, bold

audeō, ausus sum 2 to dare, venture, risk

audiēns, tis _m_ hearer, listener

audientia, ae _f_ a hearing, listening

audiō 4 to hear; to perceive, learn; to listen to; to hear a case; to give credence to; to obey, follow; to be called, named, reported

audītiō, ōnis _f_ a hearing, listening; hearsay, report

audītor, ōris _m_ hearer, listener; pupil, scholar

au-ferō, abstulī, ablātum, auferre to carry away, bring away; to rob, steal; to destroy, kill; to gain, obtain

au-fugiō 3 to flee away

augeō, xī, ctum 2 to increase, enlarge; to extol; to furnish abundantly, enrich; to honour

augēscō, —, — 3 to become greater

augur, uris _m_ augur, diviner

augurālis, e pertaining to an augur

augurātus, ūs _m_ office of an augur

augurium, ī _n_ divination, augury; prophecy; omen, sign

augurō 1 _and_ **auguror 1** to act as an augur, interpret omens; to predict, prophesy; to conjecture, forebode

augustus 3 sacred, vener-able, majestic; **Augustus, ī** _m_ August

aula, ae _f_ yard, forecourt; palace

aulaeum, ī _n_ canopy, curtain (_esp. in a theatre_)

aura, ae _f_ breath of air, breeze, air (_pl._ the upper air, heaven); odour, exhalation; breath of favour

aurātus 3 gilded; golden

aureolus 3 = **aureus**

aureus 3 of gold, golden; (_nummus_) gold coin; gilt; glittering like gold; beautiful, magnificent

auricula, ae _f_ lobe of the ear; ear

auri-fex, ficis _m_ goldsmith

aurīga, ae _m_ charioteer, driver

auris, is _f_ the ear; (_pl._) sense of hearing, critical judgment

aurītus 3 long-eared; listening

aurōra, ae _f_ dawn, daybreak; the east

aurum, ī _n_ gold; vessel _or_ ornament of gold; money; golden lustre, brightness

auscultō 1 to listen to; to obey

au-spex, icis _m_ bird-seer; interpreter of omens; leader, protector; witness at a marriage

auspicium, ī _n_ divination by means of birds, auspices; command, authority; will; sign, omen

auspicor 1 to take the auspices; to begin under
good auspices; auspicātus
3 inaugurated, conse-
crated; fortunate, lucky

auster, strī *m* the south
wind; the south

austērus 3 harsh; severe,
morose

austrālis, e southern

ausum, ī *n* venture, bold
undertaking

aut *cj.* or, or else; aut ...
aut either — or

autem *cj.* but, however, on
the other hand, moreover;
besides, further

autumnālis, e autumnal

autumnus, ī *m* autumn

autumō 1 to assert,
affirm

auxiliāris, e, -ārius 3 help-
ing, assisting; *subst* auxili-
liārēs, ium *m/pl.* auxiliary
troops

auxilior 1 to help, assist

auxilium, ī *n* help, assistance, aid; *pl.* auxiliary
troops

avāritia, ae *f* avarice,
greediness

avārus 3 greedy, avari-
cious; eagerly desirous;
adv. avārē

ā-vehō 3 to carry off *or*
away; P. to ride, sail,
drive away

ā-vellō, vellī *or* vulsī, vulsum 3 to tear, rend, pull
off, snatch away

avēna, ae *f* oats, wild oats;
straw

aveō[1], —, — 2 to long for,
crave

aveō[2] 2 to fare well; avē,
avēte hail!, farewell!

ā-verruncō 1 to avert
(*evil*)

ā-versor 1 to shrink from;
to repulse

ā-versus 3 turned away *or*
backward; back; un-
favourable, hostile

ā-vertō 3 to turn away *or*
off, to avert, divert;
intr. to turn away; to
carry off, steal; to alienate

aviditās, ātis *f* eagerness,
longing; covetousness

avidus 3 eager, desirous,
longing; greedy; avari-
cious, covetous

avis, is *f* bird; omen,
portent

avītus 3 of a grandfather,
ancestral

āvius 3 out of the way,
remote, unfrequented;
wandering

ā-vocō 1 to call away; to
remove; to divert, dis-
tract

ā-volō 1 to fly away; to
vanish

ā-vors-, -vort-, *see* ā-vers-,
-vert-

avunculus, ī *m* maternal
uncle

avus, ī *m* grandfather;
ancestor

axis, is *m* axle-tree; wagon,
chariot; the North Pole;
the heaven

2*

B

bāca (bacca), ae *f* berry; round fruit, olive; pearl

Bacchānālia, ium *n/pl.* feast of Bacchus

bacchor 1 to celebrate the festival of Bacchus; to revel, rage

baculum, ī *n* stick, staff

bālātus, ūs *m* a bleating

balbus 3 stammering

balbūtiō 4 to stammer, stutter

balineum, ī *n* = balneum

ballaena, ae *f* whale

ballista, ae *f* military engine for hurling stones

balneāria, ōrum *n/pl.* bathing-rooms [keeper]

balneātor, ōris *m* bath-

balneum, ī *n* bathroom, bath; balnea, ōrum *n/pl.* or balneae, ārum *f/pl.* public baths

bālō 1 to bleat

balsamum, ī *n* balsam(-tree)

balteus, ī *m* (and -um, ī *n*) sword-belt, baldric

barathrum, ī *n* abyss, chasm

barba, ae *f* beard

barbaria, ae (and barbariēs, ēī) *f* foreign country; rudeness, savageness

barbaricus 3 barbarian, foreign

barbarus 3 foreign, strange; rude, uncivilized, cruel; *subst.* ~, ī *m* foreigner, barbarian

barbātus 3 bearded; *subst.* ~, ī *m* an old Roman

barbitos, ī *m* lyre, lute

bārō, ōnis *m* simpleton

basilicus 3 royal, princely; *subst.* basilica, ae *f* basilica, public building (*law-court*, *exchange*)

basis, is *f* base; pedestal

bāsium, ī *n* kiss

beātus 3 happy; prosperous, rich; fertile; blessed, fortunate

bellātor, ōris *m* warrior; warlike

bellātrix, īcis *f* warlike

bellē *adv.* of bellus

bellicōsus 3 warlike, martial

bellicus 3 belonging to war; warlike; *subst.* bellicum, ī *n* war-signal

belli-ger 3 warlike

belli-gerō 1 to wage war, fight

bellō 1 (*and* bellor 1) to wage war, fight

bellum, ī *n* war; fight, contest

bellus 3 pretty, charming

bēlua, ae *f* wild beast, monster, brute

bene *adv.* (melius, optimē) well (better, best), properly, rightly, prosperously; thoroughly, fully, very much

bene-ficentia, ae *f* kindness, liberality

bene-ficiārius, I *m* privileged soldier (*exempt from menial work*)

bene-ficium, I *n* kindness, favour, service; distinction, honour

bene-ficus 3 kind, generous, liberal

bene-volēns, tis = bene-volus

bene-volentia, ae *f* goodwill, benevolence, favour

bene-volus 3 well wishing, benevolent, kind

benignitās, ātis *f* friendliness, courtesy; liberality

benignus 3 kind; good-natured, friendly, pleasing; liberal, obliging; fruitful, rich

beō 1 to make happy, bless, gladden

bēstia, ae *f* beast, animal

bēstiārius *m* one who fights with wild beasts

biblio-thēca, ae *f* library

bibō, bibī, — 3 to drink; to absorb, drink in

bibulus 3 fond of drinking; absorbent

bi-color, ōris two-coloured

bi-cornis, e two-horned; two-pronged

bi-dēns, tis with two teeth; *subst. m* hoe, fork; *f* sheep

bīduum, I *n* space of two days

bi-ennium, I *n* space of two years

bi-fāriam *adv.* in two ways *or* parts

bi-foris, e having two doors *or* openings

bi-fōrmis, e two-formed; two-shaped

bīgae, ārum *f/pl.* pair of horses; two-horsed chariot

bīgātus 3 bearing the figure of a pair of horses; *subst.* ~, I *m* silver coin so stamped

bi-iugis, e *and* bi-iugus 3 yoked two together; *subst.* biiugī, ōrum *m/pl.* = bīgae

bi-linguis, e speaking two languages; false, double-tongued

bīlis, is *f* bile; anger, wrath

bi-maris, e lying on two seas

bi-membris, e with double members; *subst.* ~, is *m* centaur

bīmus 3 two years old

bīnī, ae, a two each; a pair, two

bi-partītus, bi-pertītus 3 (*adv.* -ō) in two parts, in two ways

bi-pedālis, e two feet long

bi-pennis, e double-edged; *subst.* ~, is *f* double-edged axe

bi-pēs, edis two-footed, biped

bi-rēmis, e two-oared; *subst.* ~, is *f* ship with two sets of oars

bis *adv.* twice; in two ways

bitūmen, inis *n* mineral pitch, bitumen

bi-vius 3 having two ways; *subst.* **bivium, ī** *n* place where two roads meet

blaesus 3 lisping, stammering [ditia]

blandīmentum, ī *n* = **blan-**

blandior 4 to flatter, caress, coax; to please, gratify

blanditia, ae *f* flattery, caress; allurements

blandus 3 flattering, caressing; charming, enticing

blatta, ae *f* moth, cockroach

boārius (*and* **bovārius**) 3 relating to cattle

bōlētus, ī *m* mushroom

bonitās, ātis *f* goodness; virtue, integrity, kindness

bonus 3 (*comp.* **melior, us,** *superl.* **optimus** 3, *adv.* **bene**) good; excellent, proper, suitable, clever; brave; noble, distinguished, aristocratic; wealthy; large; favourable, kind; honest, virtuous, faithful; patriotic, loyal

boreās, ae *m* the north-wind; the north

bōs, bovis *m* and *f* ox, bull, cow

brācae ārum *f/pl.* breeches, trousers

brācātus 3 wearing breeches; foreign; Transalpine

bracchium, ī *n* the whole arm; fore-arm; branch of trees

brevis, e short; small, narrow, shallow; brief, concise; **brevī** *adv.* in short, shortly; short in time; **brevī** (*tempore*) in a short time

brevitās, ātis *f* shortness; conciseness

breviter *adv. of* brevis

brūma, ae *f* the winter solstice; winter time, wintry cold

brūmālis, e wintry

būbō, ōnis *m* (f) owl

bubulcus, ī *m* ox-driver, ploughman

bucca, ae *f* cheek, mouth

būcina, ae *f* horn, trumpet

būcula, ae *f* young cow, heifer

bulla. ae *f* boss, stud; amulet

bustum, ī *n* place for burning the dead; pyre, tomb

buxus, ī *f and* **buxum, ī** *n* box(tree); boxwood; object made of boxwood

C

C. *abbr.* 1. = Gaius; 2. = condemno; 3. = centum

caballus, ī *m* pack-horse, nag

cachinnus, ī *m* loud laugh

cacūmen, inis *n* point, extremity, height

cadāver, eris *n* dead body, corpse

cadō, cecidī, cāsum 3 to fall; to descend; to slip, drop;

to be thrown; to go down, set; to be killed; to be conquered *or* destroyed; to decline, decay, cease; to get into, fall under, be subject to; to agree, be suitable, fit; to happen; to come to pass

cādūceātor, ōris *m* herald, officer bearing the flag of truce [staff]

cādūceus, ī *m* a herald's

cādūcus 3 falling, fallen; hurled; frail, perishable, transitory; *in law:* rendered void, having no heir *or* owner

cadus, ī *m* wine-jar

caecitās, ātis *f* blindness

caecō 1 to make blind

caecus 3 blind; mentally *or* morally blind; dark, obscure; invisible, hidden; unknown; doubtful, uncertain

caedes, is *f* a killing, slaughter, massacre

caedō, cecidī, caesum 3 to cut, hew; to strike, beat; to slay, kill

caelātor, ōris *m* engraver, carver

caelebs, libis unmarried, single

caeles, itis heavenly; *m/pl.* the gods

caelestis, e heavenly, celestial; divine, superhuman, glorious; *subst.* … is *m* god, deity

caeli-cola, ae *m* dweller in heaven, god

caelō 1 to engrave in relief, chase, carve; to adorn

caelum, ī *n* the sky, the heaven; clime, zone, region; air, atmosphere, weather; highest joy, immortality

caementum, ī *n* unhewn stone

caenum, ī *n* dirt, mud

caepa, ae *f and* caepe, is *n* onion

caerimōnia, caeremōnia, ae *f* holy dread, reverence; religious usage, ceremony

caeruleus *and* caerulus 3 dark-blue, blue-black; (blue-)green; dark

caesariēs, ēī *f* the hair of the head

caesim *adv.* by cutting

caesius 3 (with) bright blue (eyes)

caespes, itis *m* turf, grass; altar of turf

caestus, ūs *m* boxing-glove made of thongs

caetra, ae *f* short Spanish shield

caetrātus 3 armed with a short shield

calamister, trī *m* curling-iron; artificial ornament in speech

calamistrātus 3 curled with the curling-iron

calamitās, ātis *f* loss, disaster, ruin; defeat in war

calamitōsus 3 disastrous, destructive; suffering damage, unhappy

calamus, ī *m* reed, cane;

reed-pen, reed-pipe, arrow

calathus, ī *m* wicker-basket; bowl, cup

calcar, āris *n* spur; incitement

calceus, ī *m* shoe, half-boot

calcō 1 to tread on, to trample upon; to despise

calculus, ī *m* small stone, pebble; stone used in reckoning *or* for voting

caldus 3 = calidus

cale-faciō 3 to make warm *or* hot; to heat, excite

Calendae, ārum *f/pl.* the calends, first day of each month

caleō, uī, calitūrus 2 to be warm *or* hot; to be inflamed *or* enamoured; to be urged on zealously

calēscō, luī — 3 to grow warm *or* hot, glow

cal-faciō = calefacio

calidus 3 warm, hot; fiery, rash, eager

cālīginōsus 3 dark, obscure, gloomy

cālīgō[1], inis *f* darkness, night; mist, vapour; calamity, affliction

cālīgō[2] 1 to cover with darkness, obscure; to be dark *or* gloomy

calix, icis *m* cup, goblet

calleō, uī, — 2 to be clever *or* skilful; to know by experience

calliditās, ātis *f* shrewdness; cunning, slyness

callidus 3 skilful; practised,

shrewd; well-wrought, ingenious; crafty, cunning

callis, is *f (and m)* foot-path, mountain-path; alpine meadow

callum, ī *n* thick skin; insensibility

cālō, ōnis *m* groom, soldier's servant

calor, ōris *m* warmth, heat; heat of passion, zeal

calumnia, ae *f* artifice, deceitful pretence; malicious prosecution; penalty for false accusation

calumniātor, ōris *m* intriguer, false accuser

calumnior 1 to intrigue; to prosecute maliciously; to calumniate

calvus 3 bald, without hair

calx[1], cis *f (m)* limestone, lime; goal in a race-course

caix[2], cis *f (m)* heel, hoof

camēlus, ī *m (f)* camel

camera, ae *f* vault, arch

camīnus, ī *m* fire-place; furnace, forge

campester, stris, stre pertaining to a field *or* plain, flat, level; of the Campus Martius, used in sport

campus, ī *m* field, plain, open country; the Campus Martius

canālis, is *m (f)* water-pipe, channel, canal

cancellī, ōrum *m/pl.* lattice, enclosure, railings

cancer, crī *m* crab (*also* C∼

sign of the zodiac); south, summer heat

candēla, ae *f* wax-light, candle

candēlābrum, ī *n* candlestick, lamp-stand

candeō, uī, — 2 to be shining white, glow

candidātus, ī *m* candidate

candidus 3 shining white, glittering; bright, fair, beautiful; honest, upright

candor, ōris *m* whiteness, lustre, brightness; beauty; sincerity, frankness

cāneō, uī, — 2 to be grey, white, hoary

cānēscō, —, — 3 to become grey, white, old

Canīcula, ae *f* the Dog-star, Sirius

canis, is *m* and *f* dog; insolent, shameless person; the Dog-star

canistra, ōrum *n/pl.* plaited basket

cānitiēs, ēī *f* grey colour; grey hair

canna, ae *f* reed, cane

canō, cecinī, (cantum) 3 to sing; to crow; to play on a musical instrument; *trans.* to sing, compose (*poems*); to celebrate, praise; to prophesy

canor, ōris *m* song, sound

canōrus 3 melodious, harmonious

cantharus, ī *m* tankard

canticum, ī *n* musical monologue; song

cantilēna, ae *f* silly prattle, gossip

cantō 1 a) = cano; b) to recite incantations, enchant

cantor, ōris *m* singer; poet; player

cantus, ūs *m* song, a crowing; music, sound; incantation

cānus 3 white; old

capāx, ācis wide, large, spacious; capable, apt, fit for

capella, ae *f* (little) she-goat

caper, prī *m* he-goat

capessō, sīvī, sītum 3 to seize eagerly, lay hold of; to take in hand, engage in; to strive to reach, resort to

capillus, ī *m* hair of the head

capiō, cēpī, captum 3 to take, seize, grasp; to capture, hold; to arrive at, reach; to win, gain; to undertake, engage in; to win, charm, deceive; to injure, attack; to choose, select; to receive, obtain; to enjoy, reap; to contain, hold; to comprehend mentally

capistrum, ī *n* halter, muzzle

capital, ālis *n* capital crime

capitālis, e relating to life; capital, deadly; distinguished

capra, ae *f* she-goat

caprea, ae *f* wild goat, roe

capri-fīcus, ī *f* wild fig-tree

caprīnus 3 of goats

capsa, ae *f* chest, box, case

captātor, ōris *m* one who seizes eagerly; legacy-hunter

captiō, ōnis *f* deceit, fraud; fallacy, sophism

captiōsus 3 deceitful; sophistical, captious

captīvus 3 taken in war, captured; *subst.* captīvus, ī *m* prisoner, captive

captō 1 to strive to seize, snatch at; to try to obtain; desire, seek

captus, ūs *m* power of comprehension, capacity

capulus, ī *m* handle; hilt of a sword

caput, itis *n* the head; man, individual; summit, point; origin, source, mouth (*of a river*); life; civil rights, citizenship; the chief point; chief, leader, author; principal place, capital; principal sum, stock

carbaseus 3 of linen

carbasus, ī *f*, carbasa, ōrum *n/pl.* linen garment, sail

carbō, ōnis *m* coal, charcoal

carcer, eris *m* barrier, starting-place; prison, jail

carchēsium, ī *n* drinkingcup

cardiacus 3 suffering in the stomach

cardō, inis *m* door-hinges; crisis

carduus, ī *m* thistle

careō, uī, — 2 to be without, be free from, be destitute of; to abstain from; to want, miss

carīna, ae *f* keel of a ship; vessel, ship

cāritās, ātis *f* dearness, high price; high esteem, respect, love, affection

carmen, inis *n* song; poem, lyric poetry; formula (*religious* or *legal*); incantation, oracle

carni-fex, icis *m* executioner, hangman; murderer; villain

carnificīna, ae *f* rack, torture, torment

carnu-, *see* carni-

carō, carnis *f* flesh

carpentum, ī *n* two-wheeled carriage, coach

carpō, psī, ptum 3 to pluck; to graze on, eat; to gather; to enjoy, make use of; to divide into parts; to take one's way, pass over; to tear to pieces; to weaken; to blame, slander, revile; to harass, alarm

carptim *adv.* by pieces; by degrees

carrus, ī *m* cart, wagon

cārus 3 dear, valued, loved

casa, ae *f* hut, cottage, cabin

cāseus, ī *m* cheese

casia, ae *f* cinnamon; spurge-laurel

cassis[1], idis *f* helmet of metal

cassis[2], is *m* (*mostly* cassēs, ium *m/pl.*) hunting-net; snare

cassus 3 empty, hollow devoid of; vain, fruitless

castanea, ae *f* chestnut (tree)

castellānus 3 pertaining to a castle *or* fortress

castellum, ī *n* castle, fort, stronghold; refuge

castigātiō, ōnis *f* a correcting, censure, reproof

castigō 1 to correct, reprove; to punish; to amend

castimōnia, ae *f* purity, chastity

castrēnsis, e of a camp

castrum, ī *n* 1. = castellum; 2. *pl.* military camp; military service; a day's march

castus 3 pure, innocent; chaste; pious, religious; continent, disinterested

cāsus, ūs *m* a falling; destruction; end; event, occurrence; disaster, calamity, death

cata-phractus 3 mailed

cata-pulta, ae *f* engine of war for throwing arrows

catellus, ī *m* (*and* catella, ae *f*) little dog

catēna, ae *f* chain, fetter; barrier, restraint

catēnātus 3 chained, fettered

caterva, ae *f* crowd, troop, throng

catervātim *adv.* in companies, in troops

cathedra, ae *f* arm-chair, sedan-chair

catīnus, ī *m* bowl, dish

catulus, ī *m* young animal, whelp; young dog

catus 3 intelligent, sagacious, wise

cauda, ae *f* tail

caudex, icis *m* trunk of a tree; wooden tablet for writing, book, account-book

caulae, ārum *f/pl.* spaces, opening

caulis, is *m* stalk of a plant; cabbage

caupō, ōnis *m* innkeeper

caupōna, ae *f* inn, tavern

caurus, ī *m* the north-west wind

causa, ae *f* cause, reason, motive; good reason; pretext, feigned cause; affair, business; lawsuit; question, matter for discussion; party, faction; relation of friendship; causā *with gen.* on account of, for the sake of

causi-dicus, ī *m* advocate

causor 1 to give as a reason, pretend

caussa, ae *f* = causa

cautēs, is *f* sharp rock, crag

cautiō, ōnis *f* precaution, circumspection; security; bail

cautus 3 wary, careful; secured, safe

cavea, ae *f* den, cave, stall; auditorium in a theatre, the spectators

caveō, cāvī, cautum 2 to be on one's guard, take care, take heed; to have a care for; to lend aid to; to give security or bail for; to make oneself secure; to order, decree

caverna, ae f hollow, cave

cavillor 1 to jest, jeer, mock

cavō 1 to make hollow; to pierce through

cavus 3 hollow, excavated, concave; *subst.* ... ī *m* (*and* cavum, ī *n*) a hollow, hole

cedo[1] (*pl.* cette) here with it! give here!; out with it! let us hear!; only look!

cēdō[2], cessī, cessum 3 to go, move; to fall to the lot of; to turn out, result; to give place, go away, withdraw, to yield, cede; to pass away, vanish; to submit to; to obey

cedrus, ī f cedar, juniper

celeber, bris, bre frequented, populous; renowned, distinguished, celebrated; solemn, festive

celebrātiō, ōnis f numerous assembly; festival

celebrātus 3 = celeber

celebritās, ātis f festivity, celebration; multitude, large assembly; fame, renown

celebrō 1 to visit frequently *or* in great numbers, crowd round; to celebrate, keep a festival; to do frequently, practise; to make known, proclaim; to praise, honour; to fill with

celer, eris, ere swift, quick;

quick in mind, lively; hasty; *adv.* celeriter

celeritās, ātis f swiftness, quickness; adroitness

celerō 1 to quicken, accelerate; to make haste

cella, ae f chamber, room; granary, store-room; cell of a beehive; sanctuary

cēlō 1 to conceal, hide from

celsus 3 high, lofty, elevated; noble, high-spirited; haughty

cēna, ae f principal meal, dinner

cēnāculum, ī *n* dining-room; tenement, attic

cēnō 1 to dine, eat; *trans.* to eat up, dine upon

cēnseō, suī, sum 2 to tax, value, assess; to take the census; to value, appreciate, weigh; to be of opinion, think, judge; to vote, propose; to decree, resolve

cēnsor, ōris *m* a Roman magistrate, censor; censurer, critic

cēnsōrius 3 relating to a censor; rigid, severe

cēnsūra, ae f censorship

cēnsus, ūs *m* a registering of citizens and property, census, amount of property

Centaurus, ī *m* centaur (*half man, half horse*)

centēnī 3 one hundred each

centēsimus 3 the hundredth

centiē(n)s *adv.* a hundred times

centi-manus 3 having a hundred hands

centō, ōnis *m* a covering of rags, patch-work

centum a hundred; many

centum-virī, ōrum *m*/*pl.* the centumviri (*a college of judges*)

centuria, ae *f* a division of one hundred; company of soldiers

centuriātim *adv.* by centuries

centuriātus, ūs *m* office of a centurion; division into centuries

centuriō[1], ōnis *m* centurion, commander of one hundred soldiers

centuriō[2] 1 to divide into centuries

cēpa, ae *f* = caepa

cēra, ae *f* wax; writing-tablet covered with wax

cerasus, ī *f* cherry(-tree)

cērātus 3 covered with wax

cerdō, ōnis *m* workman

Cereālis, e belonging to Ceres

cerebrum, ī *n* brain; understanding

cēreus 3 waxen, pliant

cernō, crēvī, crētum 3 to separate; to distinguish, discern, perceive; to understand, comprehend; to decide, determine

certāmen, inis *n* contest, struggle; rivalry; fight, battle

certātim *adv.* in rivalry, emulously

certātiō, ōnis *f* contest, competition

certē *adv.* surely, certainly, really; at least

certō[1] *adv.* with certainty, surely

certō[2] 1 to fight, struggle, contend; to emulate, vie with

certus 3 decided, resolved; settled, established, fixed, definite; sure, true, to be depended on; informed, assured

cerva, ae *f* hind deer

cervīnus 3 of a stag *or* deer

cervīx, īcis *f* (*mostly pl.*) the nape, neck

cervus, ī *m* stag; forked stakes (*in a fortification*)

cessātor, ōris *m* loiterer, idler

cessō 1 to delay, loiter; to be remiss, idle; to cease, stop; to be unemployed

cēterō-quī(n) in other respects, otherwise

cēterus 3 the other, the rest, remainder; *adv.* a) cēterum *and* cētera for the rest, in other respects; b) cēterum however, but

cētus, ī *m* (*pl.* cētē *n*) sea-monster, whale

ceu *adv.* as, just as; as if

chalybs, ybis *m* steel

chaos *n* boundless, empty space; the shapeless mass out of which the universe was made

charta, ae *f* Egyptian papyrus, paper; writing, letter, poem

chelys f tortoise-shell lyre

cheragra, ae f gout in the hand

chīro-graphum, ī n hand-writing, autograph

chlamys, ydis f (*military*) cloak

chorda, ae f string

chorēa (*and* chorēa), ae f dance in a ring

chorus, ī m choral dance; dancing troop, chorus; band, crowd

cibāria, ōrum n/pl. food, provisions

cibus, ī m food, fodder; nourishment, sustenance

cicāda, ae f cicada, tree-cricket

cicātrīx, īcis f scar

cicer, eris n the chick-pea

cicōnia, ae f stork

cicūta, ae f hemlock; flute of hemlock-stalks

cieō, cīvī, citum 2 to move, stir, set in motion; to summon; to call by name; to cause, excite

cinaedus, ī m sodomite, unchaste person

cincinnātus 3 with curled hair

cinctus, ūs m a girding

cingō, cīnxī, cīnctum 3 to gird; to gird up, make ready; to surround, invest; to escort

cingulum, ī n girdle, belt

cinis, eris m (f) ashes; ashes of a corpse; destruction

cinnamum (and -on), ī n cinnanon

cippus, ī m tomb-stone; sharpened stake

circā adv. around, round about, near; prep. with acc. (of space) around, round, near to; (of time or number) about

circēnsis, e belonging to the circus; subst. (ludi) circēnsēs m/pl. the circus-games

circiter adv. about, near; prep. with acc. = circa

circu-eō = circumeo

circu-itiō, ōnis f a patrolling; circumlocution

circu-itus, ūs m a going round; circuit, compass

circulor 1 to form a circle of persons

circ(u)lus, ī m circle; orbit; ring; company, social gathering

circum adv. and prep. with acc. around, near

circum-agō 3 to drive, turn round; to pass away, be spent

circum-cīdō, cīdī, cīsum 3 to cut around, clip; to diminish

circum-cīsus 3 steep, precipitous

circum-clūdō, sī, sum 3 to shut in, enclose

circum-dō, dedī, datum 1 to put or place around; to surround with, invest, besiege

circum-dūcō 3 to lead or draw around

circum-eō iī, itum, ire to go round, travel *or* march around; to surround, encircle

circum-ferō, tūlī, lātum, ferre to bear *or* carry round; to spread around

circum-fluō 3 to flow round; to abound in, be rich

circum-fluus 3 flowing around, flowed around

circum-fundō 3 to pour around, P. to flow round; to enclose, overwhelm with; to surround, encompass

circum-iciō, iēcī, iectum 3 to throw *or* cast round, enclose with

circum-itiō, -itus = circuitio, -itus

circum-ligō 1 to bind with, encompass

circum-linō, —, — 3 to smear around; to cover

circum-mittō 3 to send round

circum-mūniō 4 to fortify, enclose by a wall

circum-plector, plexus sum 3 to embrace, enclose

circum-saepiō 4 to hedge *or* fence around

circum-scrībō 3 to enclose in a circle; to define, limit; to restrain, confine; to cheat, defraud; to cancel, annul

circum-scriptiō, ōnis *f* circumference; boundary, limit; a deceiving, cheating

circum-sedeō 2 to sit around; to besiege, blockade

circum-sīdō, sēdī, — 3 to besiege

circum-sistō, stetī, — 3 to stand round, surround

circum-sonō 1 *intr.* to resound on all sides; *trans.* to make echo, surround with noise

circum-spectō 1 (*intens.*) = circumspicio

circum-spectus, ūs *m* consideration; prospect, view

circum-spiciō, spexī, spectum 3 to look round; to observe; to survey; to look for, seek for; to consider, weigh

circum-stō, stetī, — 1 *intr.* to stand round; *trans.* to surround, encircle; to threaten, beset

circum-vādō, sī, — 3 to attack, assail on every side

circum-vallō 1 to surround with a wall, blockade

circum-vehor 3 *trans.* to ride *or* sail round

circum-veniō 4 to surround, enclose; to invest, beset, oppress, distress; to cheat, deceive

circum-volitō 1 to fly round

circum-volō 1 to fly round

circum-volvor 3 to roll round; to revolve through

circus, ī *m* circle; racecourse, circus

cis *prep.* with *acc.* on this side of

cis-alpīnus 3 lying on the Roman side of the Alps, Cisalpine

cista, ae f chest, box

citerior, ius on this (the Roman) side; nearer, closer

cithara, ae f cithara, lyre

citharista, ae m and citharistria, ae f player on the cithara

cithar-oedus, ī m one who sings to the cithara

citō[1] adv. of citus

citō[2] 1 to put in quick motion; to excite, rouse; to call, summon; to call a defendant or a witness; to name, recite

citrā adv. nearer, on this side; prep. with acc. on this side; except

citreus 3 of citrus-wood

citrō adv. to this side; ultrō et citrō hither and thither, to and fro

citus 3 swift, quick, rapid; non citō not easily

cīvicus 3 = civilis

cīvīlis, e pertaining to citizens; civil, civic, public; courteous, polite

cīvis, is m and f citizen; fellow-citizen

cīvitās, ātis f citizenship; rights of a citizen; the citizens; state, commonwealth

clādēs, is f injury, disaster, defeat, slaughter

clam adv. secretly, privately; prep. with abl. and acc. without the knowledge of, unknown to

clāmitō 1 intens. of clamo

clāmō 1 to cry aloud, shout; to proclaim, declare; to call upon, invoke

clāmor, ōris m loud shout, cry; acclamation, applause; outcry, complaint; noise, echo

clāmōsus 3 noisy

clanculum = clam

clandestīnus 3 secret, hidden

clangor, ōris m sound, clang, noise

clārēscō, ruī, — 3 to become bright or clear; to become brilliant or illustrious

clāritās, ātis f clearness; renown, fame

clāritūdō, inis f = claritas

clārus 3 bright, clear; distinct, loud; plain, evident; illustrious, renowned; notorious

classiārius 3 belonging to the navy; subst. ~ ī m soldier on a ship, marine

classicum, ī n trumpet-call for battle, war-trumpet

classicus 3 belonging to the fleet

classis, is f class or division of citizens; fleet, navy

claudeō 2 = claudico

claudicō 1 to limp, be lame; to waver, halt

claudō, ō, sī, sum 3 to shut, close, shut up; to end, conclude; to shut in, imprison; to intercept; to surround

claudus 3 limping, lame; crippled, defective

claustra, ōrum *n/pl.* lock, bolt, barrier; gate, barricade; bulwark, entrenchment

clausula, ae *f* close, conclusion [staff]

clāva, ae *f* cudgel, club;

clāvi-ger 3 club-bearing; *subst.* ―, ī *m* club-bearer

clāvis, is *f* key

clāvus, ī *m* nail; rudder, helm; purple stripe on the tunic

clēmēns, tis mild, calm, kind, merciful

clēmentia, ae *f* mildness, kindness, moderation

cleps-ȳdra, ae *f* water-clock

cliēns, tis *m* dependant, client; retainer, follower

clientēla, ae *f* clientship, patronage; clients, dependants

clipeātus 3 bearing a shield

clipeus, ī *m* (and **clipeum**, ī *n*) round brazen shield; oval medallion

clītellae, ārum *f/pl.* pack-saddle

clīvōsus 3 hilly, steep

clīvus, ī *m* gentle ascent, slope, hill

cloāca ae *f* sewer, drain

clūdō, *see* claudo

clueō 2 to be spoken of, be reputed

clūnis, is *f* or *m* buttock

clupeus = clipeus

Cn. (*abbr.*) = Gnaeus

co-acervō 1 to heap together, accumulate

co-āctor, ōris *m* collector of money

co-āctus, ūs *m* compulsion

co-aedificō 1 to build on

co-aequō 1 to make equal

co-āgmentō 1 to join, connect

co-alēscō, aluī, alitum 3 to grow together, unite; to become strong

co-arguō 3 to prove fully; to demonstrate; to prove guilty; to refute

co-artō 1 to pack, confine; to shorten

coccum, ī *n* scarlet dye

cochlea, coclea, ae *f* snail, snail-shell

cocus, ī *m* = coquus

cōda, ae *f vulg.* = cauda

cōdex, icis *m* = caudex

cōdicillī, ōrum *m/pl.* writing tablet; note, billet

co-emō 3 to buy up

co-ēmptiō, ōnis *f* marriage by fictitious sale

co-eō, iī, (itum), īre to go or come together, assemble; to meet in battle; to be united, combine; to agree

(coepiō), coepī, coeptum 3 to begin

coeptō 1 (*intens.*) = incipio

coeptum, ī *n* an undertaking, work begun

co-erceō, cuī, citum 2 to enclose, encompass; to restrain, control, curb

co-ercitiō, ōnis *f* a restraining; (right of) punishing

coetus, ūs *m* assembly, company

cōgitātiō, ōnis *f* a considering, deliberating; power of thinking, reflection; thought; plan, design

cōgitō 1 to think, reflect upon, ponder; to intend, purpose; *subst.* **cōgitātum, ī** *n* thought, idea; purpose

cognātiō, ōnis *f* blood-relationship; kindred, relations; resemblance, affinity

co-gnātus 3 related by blood; connected, similar; *subst.* ~, **ī** *m* kinsman

cognitiō, ōnis *f* a knowing, knowledge, acquaintance; legal inquiry, trial

cognitor, ōris *m* advocate, attorney; witness

cognōmen, inis *n* family name; name

co-gnōscō, gnōvī, gnitum 3 to become acquainted with, learn, perceive, understand; *perf.* to know; to inquire into, investigate; to recognize, identify

cōgō, coēgī, coāctum 3 to drive together, bring together; to assemble, summon; to collect (*money*); to urge, force, compel

co-haereō, haesī, — 2 to be united, cohere, adhere; to hold together, subsist

co-hērēs, ēdis *m* and *f* coheir

co-hibeō, buī, bitum 2 to hold together, contain, comprise; to restrain, hinder, control

co-honestō 1 to honour, celebrate

co-hors, tis *f* division of soldiers, cohort; retinue *or* suite of a governor; crowd, multitude

co-hortātiō, ōnis *f* exhortation, encouragement

co-hortor 1 to exhort, encourage

cō-iciō = coniciō

co-itiō, ōnis *f* a coming together; conspiracy, plot

co-itus, ūs *m* meeting

colaphus, ī *m* box on the ear

col-lābor 3 to fall to pieces, collapse

col-lacrimō 1 to bewail

col-lātiō, ōnis *f* a bringing together, contribution of money; comparison

col-laudō 1 to praise very much

col-lēctiō, ōnis *f* a gathering

collēga, ae *m* partner in office, colleague

collēgium, ī *n* colleagueship; association, guild, fraternity

col-libet 2 it pleases, it is agreeable

col-līdō, sī, sum 3 to strike *or* dash together

col-ligō¹ 1 to bind together; to combine; to restrain

col-ligō², lēgī, lēctum 3 to bring together, collect,

assemble; to gain, acquire; to consider, conclude

collis, is *m* hill, elevation

col-locātiō, ōnis *f* a placing; a giving in marriage

col-locō 1 to place, lay, set; to station, settle; to invest (*money*); to settle (*a woman*) in marriage; to employ, occupy

col-locūtiō, ōnis *f* conversation

colloquium, ī *n* conversation, talk

col-loquor 3 to speak, converse with; to negotiate with

col-lubet = collibet

col-lūceō, —, — 2 to shine, be clear *or* bright

collum, ī *n* the neck

col-lūsor, ōris *m* playmate

col-lūstrō 1 to illuminate; to survey

col-luviēs, ēī *f* = colluvio

col-luviō, ōnis *f* dregs, offscourings

colō, coluī, cultum 3 to care for; to till, cultivate; to dwell in a place; to protect, honour, cherish, love

colōnia, ae *f* colony, settlement

colōnus, ī *m* peasant, farmer; colonist, settler

color (*and* colōs), ōris *m* colour, complexion; outward show, external appearance; style, character

colōrō 1 to colour, dye

coluber, brī *m* serpent, snake

colubra, ae *f* female serpent

columba, ae *f* pigeon, dove

columen, inis *n* column, pillar; prop, support

columna, ae *f* column, pillar

colus, ūs *and* ī *f* (*m*) distaff

coma, ae *f* the hair of the head; foliage, leaves

comāns, tis hairy; having leaves

comātus 3 long-haired

com-bibō, bibī, — 3 to drink up, imbibe; to swallow

comb-ūrō 3 to burn up, consume

com-edō 3 to eat up, consume; to waste, squander

comes, itis *m and f* companion, comrade; attendant; *pl.* retinue

comētēs, ae *m* comet

cōmicus 3 of comedy, comic

cōmis, e affable, courteous, amiable

cōmissātiō, ōnis *f* a revelling, riotous banquet

cōmissātor, ōris *m* reveller, rioter

cōmissor 1 to revel, carouse

cōmitās, ātis *f* affability, kindness, friendliness

comitātus, ūs *m* train, escort, retinue; travelling company

comitiālis, e pertaining to an election

com-itium, ī *n* place of assembly; comitia, iōrum

n/pl. assembly of the people for electing magistrates, etc.

com-itor (com-itō) 1 to accompany, attend, follow

com-meātus, ūs *m* a going to and fro; leave of absence. provisions, food

com-meminī, isse to remember

com-memorātiō, ōnis *f* a mentioning, reminding

com-memorō 1 to remember; to remind of; to mention, recount

commendātiō, ōnis *f* recommendation; excellence

com-mendō 1 to intrust to; to recommend; to make agreeable

commentārius, ī *m* (*and* um, ī *n*) notebook, diary, memorandum; *pl.* memoirs, records

commentātiō, ōnis *f* careful consideration, deep reflection

commentīcius 3 invented, feigned, false

commentor 1 to meditate, think over; to study, practise speaking

commentum, ī *n* invention, fiction, falsehood

com-meō 1 to go to and fro, go about; to visit frequently

com-mercium, ī *n* commercial intercourse, trade; the right of trade; communication, communion

com-mereō 2 to deserve fully; to be guilty of

com-migrō 1 to migrate; to remove to

com-mīlitō, ōnis *m* fellowsoldier, comrade

com-miniscor. mentus sum 3 to devise, invent; to feign

com-minor 1 to threaten

com-minuō 3 to break into small pieces, to crush; to weaken, reduce

com-minus *adv.* at close quarters; near

com-misceō 2 to mix together; to unite, join

com-missum, ī *n* transgression, crime, fault; secret, trust

com-mittō 3 to bring together, join, combine; to commence or fight (*proelium*); to commit, be guilty of; to give cause, allow it to happen; to intrust, commit to; to expose, abandon

commoditās, ātis *f* fitness, convenience, advantage; courtesy, indulgence

commodō 1 to please, oblige; to furnish, give

commodum[1] *adv* just, just now

commodum[2], ī *n* convenience, opportunity; advantage, profit

com-modus 3 fit, convenient, suitable; agreeable, useful; obliging, friendly com-monefaciō 3 = com-moneo

com-moneō 2 to remind

com-mōnstrō 1 to show distinctly

com-moror 1 to tarry, linger, sojourn

com-mōtiō, ōnis f excitement, agitation

com-moveō 2 to remove, drive away, displace; to excite, agitate, disturb; to rouse, produce

commūnicātiō, ōnis f imparting, communication

commūnicō 1 to share with, have in common with, impart; to take counsel with

com-mūniō[1] 4 to fortify on all sides, strengthen

commūniō[2], ōnis f communion, mutual participation

com-mūnis, e common, general, usual, public; affable, courteous; subst. commūne, is n common property; commonwealth, state

commūnitās, ātis f community, fellowship

com-mūtābilis, e (ex-) changeable

com-mūtātiō, ōnis f a changing, alteration

com-mūtō 1 to change, alter; to exchange

cōmō, cōmpsī, cōmptum 3 to adorn, arrange; to dress

cōmoedia, ae f comedy

cōmoedus, ī m comic actor

compāgēs, is f connection, joint, structure

com-pār, aris like, similar, equal

comparātiō, ōnis f preparation; a procuring, acquiring; a comparing, comparison

com-pāreō, ruī, — 2 to appear, be visible, exist

com-parō[1] 1 to pair, match; to compare

com-parō[2] 1 to prepare, make ready; to equip; to ordain, establish; to procure, provide, obtain

com-pellō[1] 1 to accost, address; to rebuke, reproach; to accuse

com-pellō[2] pulī, pulsum 3 to drive together; to incite, urge, compel

compendium, ī n a short way; a saving, profit

com-pēnsō 1 to balance; to compensate

com-perendinō 1 to adjourn a trial to the third day

com-periō, perī, pertum 4 to find out, learn, discover

com-pēs, edis f fetter or shackle (for the feet)

compescō, uī, — 3 to restrain, check, suppress

com-petitor, ōris m rival, competitor

com-pīlō 1 to plunder, rob

com-pingō, pēgī, pāctum 3 to join together, construct; to fasten up

compitum, ī n cross-roads

com-plector, plexus sum 3

to clasp, embrace; to surround, enclose; to comprehend, comprise; to understand; to esteem, care for

com-pleō, ēvī, ētum 2 to fill up, make full; to complete; to accomplish, finish; to live through

complexiō, ōnis f combination; sentence, period

complexus, ūs m embrace, affection

com-plōrātiō, ōnis f (and -us, ūs m) wailing, lamentation

com-plūrēs, a several, very many

com-pōnō 3 to place, put together, collect; to bury; to compare; to construct, fashion; to compose, write; to agree upon, settle, to invent; to arrange, set in order; to allay, appease, quiet

com-portō 1 to carry or bring together

com-pos, otis partaking of, possessing, master of

com-positiō, ōnis f a putting together, arrangement, settlement, reconciliation

com-positus 3 well arranged; suitable, prepared; calm

com-prehendō 3 to express, describe; to seize, grasp, capture; to perceive, comprehend

com-prehēnsiō, ōnis f a seizing, perception

com-prēndō = comprehendo

com-prīmō, pressī, pressum 3 to press together; to embrace; to restrain, check, hinder; to conceal

com-probō 1 to approve of, assent to; to prove, confirm

com-putō 1 to sum up, reckon

cōnāmen, inis n effort, attempt

cōnātum, ī n attempt, undertaking; effort

cōnātus, ūs m = conatum

con-cavus 3 hollow, curved

con-cēdō 3 intr. to go away, retire; to yield, submit; trans. to concede, grant, allow; to pardon; to resign

con-celebrō 1 to celebrate a festival; to proclaim; to honour

con-centus, ūs m harmony, music; unanimity, concord

con-certō 1 to contend eagerly, dispute

con-cessus, ūs m only in abl. -u by permission of

concha, ae f mussel, mussel shell

conchȳlium, ī n oyster; purple dye, purple clothing

con-cīdō[1], cīdī, — 3 to fall down; to be slain, overthrown, defeated

con-cīdō[2], cīdī, cīsum 3 to cut up; to destroy, kill;

to beat severely; to prostrate, strike down

con-cieŏ, cīvī, citum 2 = concio

conciliábulum, ī n place of assembly, market-place

conciliátiō, ōnis f a making friendly, winning over

conciliō 1 to reconcile, win over; to cause, bring about; to acquire, gain

concilium, ī n assembly, meeting; council

con-cinnus 3 elegant, pretty, polished; courteous

con-cinō, cinuī, (centum) 3 to sing or sound together; to celebrate, praise; to agree

con-ciō, cīvī, cītum 4 to assemble, summon; to stir up, rouse, excite; to cause

con-cipiō, cēpī, ceptum 3 to take in, draw in; to conceive, become pregnant; to perceive, understand; to imagine, think; to adopt, harbour; to express in words

con-citātiō, ōnis f sedition, tumult; violent passion

con-citō 1 to stir up, excite, rouse up; to cause, produce

con-clāmō (and -mitō) 1 to shout together; to bewail

conclāve, is n room, chamber

con-clūdō, sī, sum 3 to shut up, confine; to compress, include; to end;. to infer

con-clūsiō, ōnis f a blockade; conclusion

con-color, ōris of the same colour

con-coquō 3 to digest; to consider

concordia, ae f concord, harmony

concordō 1 to agree

con-cors, dis of one mind, agreeing [commit]

con-crēdō 3 to intrust,]

con-cremō 1 to burn up

con-crepō uī, — 1 to resound, clash, creak

con-crēscō 3 to grow together, harden, stiffen, congeal; to grow, be formed

con-cubīna, ae f concubine

con-cubitus, ūs m a lying together, copulation

con-culcō 1 to trample upon, despise

con-cumbō, cubuī, cubitum 3 to lie with

con-cupīscō, pīvī and piī, pītum 3 to long for, covet

con-currō, (cu)currī, cursum 3 to run together, meet; to meet in conflict; to happen at the same time

con-cursātiō, ōnis f a running together, concourse; a running about

con-cursō 1 intr. to run to and fro; to skirmish; trans. to visit

con-cursus, ūs m a concourse, throng; a collision; an attack, assault con-cutiō, cussī, cussum 3 to shake violently, agitate; to disturb, alarm, impair, weaken

con-demnō 1 to sentence, condemn; to blame, disapprove

con-dēnsus 3 dense, close, thick

con-diciō ōnis f agreement, condition, terms; marriage-contract; position, situation, rank, nature, manner

condīmentum, ī n spice, seasoning

condiō 4 to make savoury; to soften, temper

con-discō 3 to learn thoroughly

conditor, ōris m founder, maker, author

con-dō, didī, ditum 3 to found, establish, build; to compose, write; to store up, hide, bury; to pass (time)

con-dolēscō, luī, — 3 to feel pain, suffer

con-dōnō 1 to give, present, surrender, deliver up; to forgive, pardon

con-dūcō 3 to assemble, gather; to hire, employ, contract for, farm; condūcit it is useful or profitable

cō-nectō, nexuī, nexum 3 to bind together, join, link

cōn-fectiō, ōnis f a composing, completing

cōn-ferciō, rsī, rtum 4 to cram together; cōnfertus 3 dense, crowded, filled full

cōn-ferō, tulī, collātum, cōnferre to bring together, unite, join; to discuss; to bring into hostile contact, set together; to pay in, contribute; to compare, contrast; to remove, transfer; to put off, defer; to change, transform; to ascribe, impute

cōn-fessiō ōnis f confession, acknowledgment

cōn-festim adv. without delay, immediately

cōn-ficiō 3 to make ready, prepare, accomplish; to pass over, complete (of time or space); to produce, provide; to weaken, diminish, kill, destroy

cōn-fīdēns, tis bold; audacious, impudent

cōn-fīdentia, ae f boldness, arrogance, impudence

cōn-fīdō, fīsus sum 3 to trust, rely on; to be assured, believe firmly

cōn-fīgō 3 to pierce through

cōn-fingō 3 to invent, devise

cōn-fīnis, e bordering, adjoining

cōn-fīnium, ī n common boundary, confine, border

cōn-fīō, —, fierī to be brought together; to be accomplished

cōn-firmātiō, ōnis f encouragement; a confirming

cōn-firmō 1 to make firm, strengthen; to confirm, prove; to encourage, console; to assert, affirm

cōn-fiteor, fessus sum 2 to confess, acknowledge

cōn-flagrō 1 to be in flames

cōn-flīctō 1 to strike together; P. to struggle, fight; to be tormented *or* afflicted

cōn-flīgō, xī, ctum 3 to be in conflict, struggle, fight

cōn-flō 1 to blow up, kindle; to bring together, make up; to cause, produce

cōn-fluō, fluxī, — 3 to flow together; *subst.* cōnfluēns, tis *m* confluence

cōn-fodiō 3 to pierce through, stab

cōn-fōrmātiō, ōnis *f* form, shape; notion, conception

cōn-fōrmō 1 to form, fashion, educate

cōn-frag(ōs)us 3 uneven, rough

cōn-fringō, frēgī, frāctum 3 to break in pieces, destroy

cōn-fugiō 3 to flee, take refuge

cōn-fundō 3 to pour together, mingle, unite; to confuse, throw into disorder, disturb

cōn-fūsiō, ōnis *f* confusion, disorder

cōn-fūtō 1 to silence, check, refute

con-gelō 1 to freeze, harden

con-geminō 1 to (re)double

congeriēs, ēī *f* heap, pile, mass

con-gerō 3 to bring together, collect; to heap up; to build; to load

congiārium, I *n* distribution, largess

con-globō 1 to gather into a ball; to press together in a mass

con-glūtinō 1 to glue together, unite

con-gredior, gressus sum 3 to come together, meet; to fight

con-gregō 1 to collect, gather together, associate

con-gressiō, ōnis *f* = congressus

con-gressus, ūs *m* a meeting; conversation, conference; encounter, fight

congruēns, tis agreeing, appropriate, consistent, harmonious

con-gruō, uī, — 3 to coincide; to agree, harmonize, suit

cōn-iciō (*and* cōn-), iēcī, iectum 3 to conjecture, guess, infer; to throw, cast, drive; to direct, urge, force

con-iectō 1 to conjecture, guess, infer

coniectūra, ae *f* conjecture, inference; soothsaying

con-iectus, ūs *m* a throwing, hurling; a directing

cō-nītor 3 to strive, struggle, exert oneself

coniug(i)ālis e conjugal

con-iugium, ī *n* marriage; wife

con-iūnctiō, ōnis *f* union, connection; friendship; relationship

con-iūnctus 3 adjoining, bordering on; associated, allied, kindred; agreeing with

con-iungō 3 to connect, join; to contract (*a union*)

con-iūnx, iugis *f* wife (*more rarely m* husband)

con-iūrātiō, ōnis *f* conspiracy, plot

con-iūrō 1 to swear together; to conspire, plot

coniunx, *see* coniunx

cō-nīveō, (nīvī *or* nīxī), — 2 to wink, shut the eyes; to overlook, connive

conl..., *see* coll...

cōnor 1 to attempt, try, venture, endeavour

con-queror 3 to bewail, lament, complain

con-quiēscō 3 to rest, repose

con-quīrō, sīvī, sītum 3 to seek for, bring together

con-quīsītiō, ōnis *f* a seeking out, collecting; a levying, conscription

con-quīsītor, ōris *m* recruiting officer

conr..., *see* corr...

cōn-saepiō 4 to fence in, hedge in

cōn-salūtō 1 to greet, salute

cōn-sanguineus 3 related by blood, kindred

cōn-sanguinitās, ātis *f* blood-relationship

cōn-scelerātus 3 wicked, villainous

cōn-scendō, dī, sum 3 to ascend, mount; to go on board

cōn-scientia, ae *f* joint knowledge, a being privy to; consciousness, feeling; good *or* bad conscience; remorse

cōn-scīscō 3 to resolve publicly; to bring *or* inflict upon

cōn-scius 3 knowing with another, conscious

cōn-scrībō 3 to enrol, levy, enlist, to write, compose

cōn-secrō 1 to dedicate, consecrate; to execrate; to deify

cōn-sector 1 to pursue, overtake; to strive after, emulate

cōn-secūtiō, ōnis *f* effect, consequence

cōn-senēscō, senuī, — 3 to become old *or* grey; to become weak, decay, fade

cōn-sēnsiō, ōnis *f* = cōnsensus

cōn-sēnsus, ūs *m* agreement, unanimity; conspiracy

cōnsentāneus 3 agreeing, suitable; reasonable, consistent

cōn-sentiō 4 to agree, accord, harmonize; to conspire, plot

cōn-sequor 3 to follow,

pursue; to imitate, obey; to result; to overtake, attain to; to understand, perceive

cōn-serō[1], sēvī, situm 3 to sow, plant

cōn-serō[2], seruī, sertum 3 to connect, join, bind; to engage (*in battle*)

cōn-servātor, ōris *m* preserver, defender

cōn-servō 1 to preserve, maintain, keep safe

cōn-servus, ī *m* fellow-slave

cōn-sessus, ūs *m* assembly, audience

cōnsīderātus 3 well considered; prudent, cautious

cōn-sīderō 1 to look at, contemplate; to consider, weigh

cōn-sīdō 3 to sit down, settle; to be in session; to encamp, station oneself; to sink down, subside

cōn-signō 1 to seal, sign; to attest; to write down, note

cōnsiliārius, ī *m* counsellor, adviser

cōnsilior 1 to take *or* give counsel

cōnsilium, ī *n* deliberation, consultation; council, senate; understanding, judgment; wisdom; resolution, plan, device; advice, suggestion

cōn-similis, e similar, like

cōn-sistō, stitī, — 3 to take one's stand; to exist, take place; to be based upon,

consist of; to stand still, stop, halt; to continue, endure; to dwell, abide

cōn-sociō 1 to unite, make common, share with

cōn-sōlātiō, ōnis *f* a consoling, comfort

cōn-sōlor 1 to console, comfort, encourage; to alleviate, relieve

cōn-sonō 1 to resound, echo

cōn-sors, tis having an equal share; *subst.* ~, tis *m* partner, associate, comrade

cōn-spectus, ūs *m* look, sight, view

cōn-spergō, sī, sum 3 to sprinkle, moisten

cōn-spiciō, spexī, spectum 3 to look at, perceive, observe; P. to attract notice, be distinguished

cōn-spicor 1 to see, behold

cōn-spicuus 3 visible; striking, remarkable, conspicuous

cōn-spīrātiō, ōnis *f* union, harmony; conspiracy

cōn-spīrō 1 to agree, harmonize; to conspire, plot

cōn-stāns, tis firm, steady, constant; steadfast, faithful

cōnstantia, ae *f* firmness, steadiness, perseverance; agreement, harmony; steadfastness

cōnsternātiō, ōnis *f* dismay, alarm, fright, tumult

cōn-sternō[1] 1 to cause confusion, terrify, alarm

cōn-sternō² 3 to strew over, cover, thatch, pave

cōn-stituō, uī, ūtum 3 to place, put; to station; to appoint, settle; to erect, set up; to establish, build, organize, manage; to designate, assign; to determine, resolve

cōnstitūtiō, ōnis f constitution, arrangement

cōnstitūtum, ī n agreement, appointment

cōn-stō, stitī, stātūrus 3 to stand firm, to remain; to agree, be consistent; to be certain or known; to exist; to consist of, be composed of; to cost

cōn-stringō 3 to bind, fetter; to restrain, limit

cōnstructiō, ōnis f a construction, building

cōn-struō 3 to heap up; to construct, build

cōn-suēfaciō 3 to accustom

cōn-suēscō 3 to accustom oneself to; perf. to be accustomed, be wont

cōnsuētūdō, inis f custom, habit, practice; social intercourse, intimacy

cōnsul, ulis m consul

cōnsulāris, e relating to a consul, consular; subst. ~ is m ex-consul

cōnsulātus, ūs m consulship

cōnsulō, luī, ltum 3 to deliberate, consider; to take care for, be mindful; to resolve, take measures;

to ask the advice of, consult

cōnsultātiō, ōnis f deliberation, consultation

cōnsultō 1 to consider, weigh

cōnsultor, ōris m adviser; one who asks advice

cōnsultum, ī n deliberation; resolution, decree

cōnsultus 3 well considered; knowing, experienced, learned; adv. cōnsultō (and -tē) deliberately, purposely

cōn-summō 1 to finish, accomplish, complete

cōn-sūmō 3 to use up, consume; to spend, waste, exhaust

cōn-surgō 3 to rise, stand up

cōn-tabulō 1 to cover with boards; to build in stories

con-tāctus, ūs m = contagio

con-tāgiō, ōnis f (also -gium, ī n) a touching, contact; contagion, infection

con-tāminō 1 to pollute, contaminate

con-tegō 3 to cover; to protect; to bury

con-temnō, psī, ptum 3 to despise, slight

contemplātiō, ōnis f a viewing, contemplation

contemplor (and -ō) 1 to look at, survey, consider

contemptim adv. contemptuously, scornfully

contemptiō, ōnis f / contempt, disdain

contemptor, ōris m despiser

contemptus, ūs m = contemptio

con-tendō, tendī, tentum 3 to stretch, draw tight; to compare, contrast; to strive with, contend, dispute; to hurl; to exert oneself; to strive, hasten, try to reach; to demand, ask; to assert, maintain

con-tentē energetically

contentiō, ōnis f comparison, contrast; contest, combat, dispute; exertion, zealous pursuit

contentus[1] 3 [contendo] stretched, tense; eager, zealous

contentus[2] 3 [contineo] contented, satisfied

con-terminus 3 bordering on, neighbouring

con-terō 3 to grind, bruise; to wear away, waste, consume, destroy

con-terreō 2 to terrify, frighten

con-testor 1 to call to witness

con-texō 3 to weave, entwine, connect, build

con-ticēscō, ticuī, — 3 to become silent or still

con-tignātiō, ōnis f floor, story

contiguus 3 bordering, near

con-tinēns, tis moderate, temperate; bordering,

neighbouring; following, continuous; subst. continēns, tis f mainland, continent

continentia, ae f temperance, self-restraint

con-tineō, tinuī, (tentum) 2 to hold together, connect, join; to retain, preserve; to shut in, enclose, limit; to contain, comprise; to hold back, restrain, curb

con-tingō, tigī, tāctum 3 to touch, take hold of, seize; to arrive at; to border on, be near; to concern, affect; to defile, pollute; intr. to happen, come to pass

continuātiō, ōnis f succession, series

continuō[1] adv. immediately, at once

continuō[2] 1 to connect, unite; to extend, carry on, continue

continuus 3 uninterrupted, continuous, successive; incessant

contiō, ōnis f assembly, public meeting; speech

contiōnālis, e of a public assembly; vulgar

contiōnor 1 to speak in public

con-torqueō 2 to twist, whirl, hurl

contrā adv. opposite; on the contrary; against; prep. with acc. opposite to; against, contrary to con-tractiō, ōnis *f* a drawing together; abbreviation

contrā-dīcō 3 to gainsay, speak against

con-trahō 3 to draw together, shorten, reduce, confine; to check, restrain; to collect, assemble; to bring about, accomplish, cause; to transact, bargain

contrārius 3 opposite; opposed, hostile, conflicting

con-trectō 1 to touch, handle

con-tremīscō, muī, — 3 to tremble, shake

con-tribuō 3 to unite, incorporate

con-trīstō 1 to make sad *or* gloomy

contrōversia, ae *f* quarrel, dispute, debate

contubernālis, is *m* (*and f*) tent-companion; comrade; attendant

con-tubernium, ī *n* common tent; tent-companionship; attendance

con-tueor, (tuitus sum) 2 to look on, regard

contumācia, ae *f* obstinacy, stubbornness

con-tumāx, ācis stubborn, obstinate

con-tumēlia, ae *f* insult, affront, abuse

contumēliōsus 3 insulting, abusive

con-tundō, tudī, tū(n)sum 3 to crush, bruise, break to pieces; to subdue, destroy

con-turbō 1 to disturb, confuse, disquiet; to be bankrupt

contus, ī *m* pole, pike

cō-nūbium (*and* -nūb-), ī *n* marriage, wedlock

cōnus, ī *m* cone; apex of a helmet

con valēscō, luī, — 3 to become strong, regain health

con-vallis, is *f* a valley

con-vehō 3 to carry together, collect

con-vellō 3 to tear away, pluck up; to shake, destroy

con-venientia, ae *f* agreement, harmony

con-veniō 4 to come together, assemble; to visit, meet, accost; to come to a decision, be agreed upon; to be fit *or* suitable *or* appropriate

con-ventiō, ōnis *f* (*and* conventum, ī *n*) agreement, contract

con-ventus, ūs *m* assembly; judicial session, court of justice; provincial corporation

con-versiō, ōnis *f* a turning round, revolution, change

con-vertō 3 to turn round, reverse; to throw back; to change, alter; to direct, turn; *intr.* to turn, return, change

convexus 3 vaulted, arched; sloping, steep

convīcium, ī *n* noise, clamour; altercation, contention; reviling, abuse

convictor, ōris *m* familiar friend

con-victus, ūs *m* social intercourse; banquet, feast

con-vincō 3 to convict, refute, prove guilty; to prove clearly

conviva, ae *m* table-companion, guest

convivium, ī *n* feast, banquet

con-vocō 1 to call together, assemble

con-volvō 3 to roll together, roll up

co-operiō, ruī, rtum 4 to cover over, overwhelm

co-optātiō, ōnis *f* election

co-optō 1 to choose, elect

co-orior 4 to arise, break forth, appear

cōpia, ae *f* plenty, abundance; wealth, riches; provisions. supplies; multitude, throng; power, opportunity, means; *pl.* troops, forces

cōpiōsus 3 well supplied, wealthy; abounding, plentiful; eloquent

cōpula, ae *f* band, tie

cōpulō 1 to bind together, unite

coquō, xī, ctum 3 to cook, bake; to burn, parch; to ripen; to meditate

coquus, ī *m* cook

cor, cordis *n* the heart; soul, feeling; judgment, mind; stomach

cōram *adv.* openly, publicly, face to face; in person; *prep.* with *abl.* in the presence of

corbis, is *f (m)* basket

corium, ī *n* hide, skin; leather

corneus 3 of horn; of cornelwood

corni-cen, inis *m* hornblower

corni-ger 3 horned

corni-pēs, pedis horn-footed

cornix, icis *f* crow

cornu, ūs *n* horn, antler; wing of an army; trumpet

cornum, ī *n* cornel-berry

cornus, ī *f* cornel(-tree)

corōllārium, ī *n* gift, present

corōna, ae *f* wreath, garland; crown; assembly, audience; surrounding army, besiegers

corōnō 1 to wreathe, surround

corporeus 3 bodily, of flesh

corpus, oris *n* body; corpse; person, individual; substance; mass, frame, structure

corpusculum, ī *n* little body

cor-rādō 3 to scrape together

cor-rēctor, ōris *m* corrector, censor

cor-rigō, rēxī, rēctum 3 to make straight; to correct, improve, reform

cor-ripiō, ripuī, reptum 3 to snatch up, seize; to attack; to blame, rebuke; to hasten cor-rŏborŏ 1 to strengthen, invigorate

cor-rogŏ 1 to collect by begging

cor-rumpŏ 3 to break, destroy, ruin; to injure, mar; to falsify; to pervert, seduce, mislead; to bribe

cor-ruŏ 3 to fall down; to be ruined

cor-ruptēla, ae f a corrupting, seducing, bribing

cor-ruptor, ōris m corrupter, seducer, briber

cortex, icis m (and f) bark, shell; bark of the cork-tree

cortīna, ae f kettle, caldron

corulus, ī f hazel(-tree)

cŏrus, ī m = caurus

coruscŏ 1 trans. to move quickly, vibrate; intr. to flash, glitter

coruscus 3 shaking; waving; flashing, glittering

corvus, ī m raven

corylus, ī f = corulus

corymbus, ī m cluster (of ivy-berries)

cŏrytus, ī m quiver

cŏs, cŏtis f flint-stone; whet-stone

costa, ae f rib; side

costum, ī n balsam-shrub; unguent

cothurnus, ī m high shoe of tragic actors; hunting-boot; tragic style, tragedy

cot(t)īdiānus 3 daily

cot(t)īdiē adv. daily, every day

crābrŏ, ōnis m hornet

crāpula, ae f intoxication

crās adv. to-morrow

crassitūdŏ, inis f thickness

crassus 3 thick, dense, solid

crāstinus 3 of to-morrow

crātēr, ēris m (and crātēra, ae f) mixing-vessel, wine-bowl

crātis, is f (mostly pl.) wickerwork, hurdle; fascines; joint, rib

creātrix, icis f mother

crēber, bra, brum thick, crowded together, close, numerous, repeated; adv. crēbrŏ frequently, repeatedly

crēb(r)ēscŏ, b(r)uī, — 3 to become frequent, increase; to spread abroad

crēdibilis, e worthy of belief, credible

crēditor, ōris m creditor

crēdŏ, didī, ditum 3 to commit, intrust; to lend; to trust, confide in; to believe, think, suppose

crēdulitās, ātis f credulity

crēdulus 3 easy of belief, confiding, unsuspecting

cremŏ 1 trans. to burn

creŏ 1 to produce, make, beget, bring forth, to cause; to choose, elect

crepida, ae f sandal

crepidŏ, inis f edge, border, dam

crepitŏ 1 to rattle, creak, rustle

crepitus, ūs m a clattering, creaking, rustling

crepō, uī, itum 1 *intr.* to rattle, creak, rustle, crack; *trans.* to cause to sound, talk much of

crepundia, ōrum *n/pl.* a child's rattle

crepusculum, ī *n* twilight

crēscō, crēvī, (crētum) 3 to grow, spring up; to increase, thrive, prosper

crēta, ae *f* chalk, clay

crīmen, inis *n* accusation, charge; offence, crime

crīminātiō, ōnis *f* accusation

crīminor 1 to accuse; to complain of, denounce

crīminōsus 3 slanderous, reproachful

crīnālis, e of the hair

crīnis, is *m* the hair

crīnītus 3 having hair, hairy

crispō 1 to swing, brandish

crispus 3 curly; quivering

crista, ae *f* crest, comb

cristātus 3 crested, plumed

croceus 3 of saffron; yellow

crocus, ī *m* saffron

cruciātus, ūs *m* torture, execution

cruciō 1 to torture; to afflict, grieve

crūdēlis, e cruel; hard, severe, fierce

crūdēlitās, ātis *f* cruelty, severity

crūdēscō, —, — 3 to become violent, grow worse

crūditās ātis *f* indigestion

crūdus 3 raw; unripe; fresh, vigorous; with full stomach; unfeeling, cruel

cruentō 1 to make bloody

cruentus 3 bloody; bloodthirsty

crumēna (and -mina), ae purse; money

cruor, ōris *m* blood, gore; bloodshed, murder

crūs, ūris *n* leg, shin

crusta, ae *f* crust, shell; inlaid *or* embossed work

crust(ul)um, ī *n* cake, confectionery

crux, crucis *f* cross, gallows; trouble, misery

cubiculārius, ī *m* valet

cubiculum, ī *n* bedroom

cubīle, is *n* den, bed, seat

cubitum, ī *n* elbow; cubit (1½ feet)

cubō, buī, bitum 1 to lie down, rest; to sleep; to recline at table; to lie sick

cucullus, ī *m* hood

cucūl(l)us, ī *m* cuckoo

cucumis, (er)is *m* cucumber

cūiās, ātis of what country?, whence?

cūius 3 (*interrog.*) of whom?, whose?; (*relat.*) whose

cūius-modī of what kind?

culcita, ae *f* mattress, pillow

culex, icis *m* gnat, midge

culīna, ae *f* kitchen; food

culleus, ī *m* bag, sack

culmen, inis *n* top, summit, roof

culmus, ī *m* stalk, straw

culpa, ae *f* guilt, error, fault; unchastity

culpō 1 to reproach, accuse, blame

culter, trī *m* knife; razor

cultiō, ōnis *f* cultivation

cultor, ōris *m* cultivator, farmer; inhabitant; supporter; worshipper

cultrīx, īcis, *fem. of* cultor

cultūra, ae *f* = cultus

cultus, ūs *m* cultivation, labour; training, education; culture, refinement; worship; luxury; dress, adornment

culullus, ī *m* drinking-vessel

cum¹ *prep.* with *abl.* with, in the company of, in connection with

cum² *cj.* when; whenever; as, since; although, whereas

cumba, ae *f* small boat

cumera, ae *f* box, corn-chest

cumulō 1 to heap up, fill, load; to augment, increase; to crown, complete, bring to perfection

cumulus, ī *m* heap, pile, mass; increase, surplus, summit

cūnābula, ōrum *n/pl.* cradle; dwelling

cūnae, ārum *f/pl.* cradle; nest

cūnctātiō, ōnis *f* a lingering, delaying

cūnctātor, ōris *m* delayer, loiterer

cūnctor 1 to linger, delay; to hesitate, doubt

cūnctus 3 all, all together, the whole

cuneātus 3 pointed like a wedge

cuneus, ī *m* wedge; troops drawn up in form of a wedge

cunīculus, ī *m* rabbit; underground passage, mine

cunnus, ī *m* unchaste woman

cūpa, ae *f* tub, cask

cupiditās, ātis *f* a longing, desire, passion; avarice; party-spirit

cupīdō, inis *f* (*m*) = cupiditas

cupidus 3 longing, desiring, eager, passionate; covetous; amorous; partial

cupiō, īvī *and* iī, ītum 3 to long for, desire, wish; to be favourable; be devoted

cupressus, ī (*and* ūs) *f* the cypress

cūr *adv.* why?

cūra, ae *f* care, attention, diligence; administration, management; anxiety, trouble, grief; object of love, mistress

cūrātiō ōnis *f* a taking care (of), management; treatment

cūrātor, ōris *m* manager, overseer

cūria, ae *f* senate-house; senate; division of the Roman people

cūriātus 3 relating to the curiae

cūriōsus 3 careful, attentive; inquisitive, prying

cūrō 1 to care for, attend

to; to administer, manage, command; to cure, heal

curriculum, ī *n* a running, race; chariot; career, course

currō, cucurrī, cursum 3 to run, hasten, fly

currus, ūs *m* chariot, team

cursim *adv.* hastily, quickly

cursitō *and* **cursō** 1 to run to and fro

cursor, ōris *m* runner

cursus, ūs *m* a running, course, march, voyage; direction, way

curtus 3 shortened, mutilated

curūlis, e belonging to a chariot; curule

curvāmen, inis *n* a bending, arching

curvō 1 to bend, curve

curvus 3 bent, crooked, curved

cuspis, idis *f* point; lance, javelin

custōdia, ae *f* watch, guard,

protection; watch-station; sentinel; confinement, imprisonment, prison

custōdiō 4 to watch, guard, keep; to preserve; to hold in custody

custōs, ōdis *m and f* watchman, -woman; keeper, protector; spy; jailer

cutis, is *f* skin

cyathus, ī *m* ladle for filling drinking-cups; a liquid measure

cybaea, ae *f* transport-vessel

cycnēus (*and* **cyg-**) 3 of a swan

cycnus (*and* **cyg-**) ī *m* swan

cylindrus, ī *m* cylinder, roller

cymba, ae *f* = **cumba**

cymbalum, ī *n* cymbal

cymbium, ī *n* drinking-vessel

cynicus 3 doglike, Cynic

cyparissus = cupressus

cytisus, ī *f* clover

D

daedalus 3 skilful, artfully constructed

damma, ae *f* deer

damnātiō, ōnis *f* condemnation

damnō 1 to condemn; to sentence; to disapprove, blame; to consecrate

damnōsus 3 injurious, destructive

damnum, ī *n* loss, damage, injury; fine, penalty

daps, dapis *f* (*mostly pl.*) feast; food, victuals

datiō, ōnis *f* a giving; the right to give away

dator, ōris *m* giver

dē *prep.* with *abl.* (*of space*) from, down from, out of; (*of time*) from, after, during; (*of relation*) from, out of a number; on account of; according to; with relation to; concerning

3*

dea, ae f goddess

dē-bacchor 1 to rave

dē-bellō 1 to finish a war; to subdue, vanquish

dēbeō, uī, itum 2 to owe, be in debt; to be bound, one ought, must, should; to be destined *or* fated; *subst.* **dēbitum, ī** n debt

dēbilis, e infirm, frail, weak, helpless

dēbilitās, ātis f lameness, weakness

dēbilitō 1 to lame; to weaken, unnerve, disable

dēbitor, ōris m debtor

dē-cantō 1 to sing; to repeat often, harp on

dē-cēdō 3 to go away, depart, retire; to give place, yield; to cease, disappear, subside

decem ten

december, bris, bre of December; *subst.* **December, bris** m December

decem-vir, ī m one of a commission of ten men

decem-virālis, e relating to the decemvirs

decemvirātus, ūs m office of a decemvir

decēns, tis becoming, seemly; handsome, beautiful

deceō, uī, — 2 to be seemly, become, be suitable *or* proper

dē-cernō, crēvī, crētum 3 to decide, determine, decree; to judge, resolve, settle; to decide by combat

dē-cerpō, psī, ptum 3 to pluck off, take away; to enjoy

dē-certō 1 to fight out

dē-cessiō, ōnis f departure; decrease

dēcessus, ūs m retirement; [death]

dē-cidō¹, cidī, — 3 to fall down; to sink down, die; to fail

dē-cīdō², cīdī, cīsum 3 to cut off; to decide, terminate, settle; to agree, compromise

deciē(n)s *adv.* ten times

decimānus 3 belonging to tithes; belonging to the tenth cohort; *subst.* ~, **ī** m tithefarmer

decimus 3 the tenth; *subst.* **decima, ae** f a tithe

dē-cipiō, cēpī, ceptum 3 to deceive, elude, beguile

dēcīsiō, ōnis f agreement, settlement

dē-clāmātiō, ōnis f practice in public speaking; loud talking

dē-clāmātor, ōris m rhetorician

dē-clāmitō 1, *intens. of* declamo

dē-clāmō 1 to practise public speaking, speak loudly, declaim

dē-clārō 1 to declare, explain, proclaim

dēclīnātiō, ōnis f a turning away, avoiding

dē-clīnō 1 to turn away, avoid; to deviate, digress

dē-clīvis, e sloping downwards

dē-coctor, ōris *m* spendthrift, bankrupt

dē-color, ōris discoloured; dark; degenerate

dē-coquō 3 to boil down

decor, ōris *m* charm, beauty, grace

decorō 1 to adorn, embellish; to honour, distinguish

decōrus 3 fitting, seemly, becoming; beautiful, graceful, adorned

dē-crepitus 3 very old, decrepit

dē-crēscō 3 to decrease, lessen, disappear

dēcrētum, ī *n* decree, resolution

decuma, decumānus = decima, decimanus

dē-cumbō, cubuī, cubitum 3 to lie down; to fall down

decuria, ae *f* a division of ten; division, class

decuriō[1] 1 to divide (into *decuriae*)

decuriō[2], ōnis *m* commander of ten horse-soldiers; member of a municipal senate

dē-currō, (cu)currī, cursum 3 to run down, fly or sail down; to hasten, travel; to march, manœuvre; to have recourse to; to pass through

dē-cursus, ūs *m* a running down; manœuvre, attack; course, career

decus, oris *n* ornament, beauty, glory, honour;

virtue; deed of honour, exploit

dē-cutiō, cussī, cussum 3 to shake off, throw down

dē-deceō 2 to be unbecoming *or* unseemly

dē-decorō 1 to disgrace, dishonour

dē-decus, oris *n* disgrace, dishonour, shame; crime

dē-dicātiō, ōnis *f* consecration, dedication

dē-dicō 1 to dedicate, consecrate

dē-dignor 1 to disdain, reject, scorn

dē-discō 3 to unlearn, forget

dēditīcius 3 one who has surrendered; prisoner

dēditiō, ōnis *f* surrender, capitulation

dēditus 3 surrendered; given to, addicted

dē-dō, didī, ditum 3 to give up, surrender

dē-doceō 2 to cause to unlearn

dē-dūcō 3 to lead down; to draw away, remove; to conduct, escort; to dispossess; to mislead; to compose; to divert, reduce

dē-ductiō, ōnis *f* a leading down *or* away; a colonizing; diminution

dē-errō 1 to go astray

dē-fatīgātiō, ōnis *f* weariness, exhaustion

dē-fatīgō 1 to weary out, fatigue, tire

dēfectiō, ōnis *f* desertion,

rebellion; disappearance; weakness

dēfectus, ūs *m* = defectio

dē-fendō, dī, sum 3 to ward off, drive away; to defend, protect; to maintain, assert

dēfēnsiō, ōnis *f* a warding off; defence

dēfēnsor, ōris *m* defender, protector

dē-ferō, tulī, lātum, ferre to bring, carry, throw down; to remove, drive off; to deliver, grant; to report, announce; to inform against, accuse; to register

dē-fervēscō, fervī (**ferbuī**), — 3 to cease boiling or raging

dēfetīgō 1 = defatigo

dē-fetīscor, fessus sum 3 to become tired, grow weary

dē-ficiō 3 to revolt, desert; to be wanting, fail, cease; to sink, faint, lose courage

dē-fīgō 3 to fix or fasten into; to turn intently, direct; to stupefy, astonish

dē-fīniō 4 to bound, limit; to define, explain; to restrict

dē-fīnītiō, ōnis *f* a limiting; definition

dē-flagrō 1 to burn down, be consumed

dē-flectō, flexī, flexum 3 to bend or turn aside; to lead astray

dē-fleō 2 to weep for, bewail

dē-flōrēscō, ruī, — 3 to fade, wither

dē-fluō 3 to flow or fall down; to vanish

dē-fodiō 3 to dig up; to bury, hide

dē-fōrmis, e deformed, hideous, ugly

dē-fōrmitās, ātis *f* deformity, ugliness

dē-fōrmō 1 to deform, disfigure; to disgrace

dē-fraudō 1 to deceive, cheat

dē-fringō, frēgī, frāctum 3 to break off

dē-frūdō 1 = defraudo

dē-fugiō 3 to flee away; to avoid, shun

dē-fundō 3 to pour down or out

dē-fungor 3 to finish, complete, discharge; to die

dē-gener, eris degenerate, unworthy, base

dē-generō 1 to become degenerate

dēgō, —, — 3 to pass (*time*); to live

dē-gravō 1 to weigh down; to burden, distress

dē-gredior, gressus sum 3 to march or walk down

dē-gustō 1 to taste; to try, test

dehinc *adv.* from this time, henceforth; thereupon, for the future; next

dē-hīscō, —, — to gape, split open

de-honestō 1 to dishonour

de-hortor 1 to dissuade

dē-iciō, iēci, iectum 3 to throw *or* hurl down; to destroy, kill; to avert, turn away; to drive out, expel; to deprive

dē-iectus, ūs *m* a throwing down, fall; declivity, depression

dein *adv.* = deinde

deinceps *adv.* successively, in order; immediately

deinde *adv.* from there, then, next; thereafter, afterwards

dē-lābor 3 to glide *or* fall down, sink

dē-lātor, ōris *m* informer

dēlectāmentum, ī *n* delight, amusement [pleasure]

dēlectātiō, ōnis *f* delight,)

dēlectō 1 to delight, please, charm

dē-lēctus, ūs *m* a) selection, choice; b) = dīlectus

dē-lēgō 1 to send away; to refer to, entrust, assign, attribute

dē-lēnīmentum, ī *n* blandishment, charm

dē-lēniō 4 to soothe, charm, caress

dēleō, ēvī, ētum 2 to blot out, destroy, finish

dēlīberātiō, ōnis *f* deliberation, consideration

dē-līberō 1 to weigh carefully, consider; to resolve, decide

dē-lībō 1 to take, enjoy; to detract

dē-libūtus 3 besmeared, anointed

dēlicātus 3 delightful, charming; voluptuous, effeminate

dēliciae, ārum *f/pl.* delight, pleasure, luxury; darling, sweetheart

delictum, ī *n* fault, crime

dē-ligō[1], lēgī, lēctum 3 to choose, pick out, select

dē-ligō[2] 1 to bind together, fasten

dē-linquō, līquī, lictum 3 to fail, commit a crime, transgress

dē-līrō 1 to be silly, mad, insane

dēlīrus 3 silly, mad, crazy

dē-litēscō, litui, — 3 to conceal oneself, lie hid

(delphīn, īnis *and*) delphī-nus, ī *m* dolphin

dēlūbrum, ī *n* shrine, temple

dē-lūdō, sī, sum 3 to mock, deceive

dē-mandō 1 to intrust

dē-mēns, tis mad, insane, foolish

dēmentia, ae *f* folly, madness

dē-mergō, rsī, rsum 3 to submerge, plunge; to cast down, overwhelm

dē-metō, (messuī), messum 3 to mow, reap

dē-migrō 1 to migrate, depart from

dē-minuō 3 to diminish, take away

dē-minūtiō, ōnis *f* a lessening, decrease

dē-mīror 1 to wonder, be amazed

dē-mittō 3 to let down, lower, drop; to drive or plunge into; dēmissus 3 low; humble; downcast, dispirited

dēmō, dēmpsī, dēmptum 3 to take away, remove

dē-mōlior 4 to throw down, destroy

dē-mōnstrātiō, ōnis f a pointing out, description

dē-mōnstrō 1 to show, indicate, describe; to prove

dē-morior 3 to die

dē-moror 1 to hinder, delay

dē-moveō 2 to remove, drive out; to divert

dēmum adv. at length, not till then; only; certainly

dēnārius, ī m a Roman silver coin

dē-negō 1 to deny, refuse

dēnī, ae, a ten each, by tens

dēnique adv. at last, finally; in short; then indeed; certainly, at least

dē-notō 1 to indicate, point out [prong]

dēns, tis m tooth; spike,

dēnseō, —, — 2 and dēnsō 1 to thicken, press together

dēnsus 3 thick, close, crowded together; frequent

dē-nūdō 1 to lay bare, uncover

dē-nūntiātiō, ōnis f announcement, declaration; threat

dē-nūntiō 1 to announce, declare; to menace, threaten; to order, command

dēnuō adv. anew, again

de-orsum (and -us) adv. downwards, down

dē-pacīscor 3 = depeciscor

dē-pāscō (and -scor) 3 to feed on, consume

dē-peciscor, pectus sum 3 to make an agreement; to bargain for

dē-pectō —, pexum 3 to comb

dē-peculātor, ōris m plunderer, embezzler

dē-peculor 1 to plunder, rob

dē-pellō, pulī, pulsum 3 to drive away, remove; to wean; to avert

dē-pendeō, —, — 2 to hang down, hang from

dē-pendō, ndī, nsum 3 to pay

dē-perdō, didī, ditum 3 to lose

dē-pereō 4 to perish, be lost; to be desperately in love (with)

dē-pingō 3 to portray, describe

dē-plōrō 1 to weep violently, bewail; to give up as lost

dē-pōnō 3 to place or lay down; to commit to, intrust; to give up, renounce

dē-populātiō, ōnis f a laying waste, pillaging

dē-populor 1 to lay waste, pillage

dē-portō 1 to carry down, take away; to bring home

dē-poscō, poposcī, — 3 to demand *or* request earnestly

dē-prāvātiō, ōnis *f* a distorting; perversion

dē-prāvō 1 to pervert, corrupt [intercession]

dē-precātiō, ōnis *f* appeal,)

dē-precātor, ōris *m* intercessor, averter

de-precor 1 to avert by entreaty, beg to escape; to pray for, intercede in behalf of

dē-prehendō 3 to seize, catch; to surprise, detect; to perceive, understand

dē-prēndō 3 = deprehendo

dē-primō, pressī, pressum 3 to press *or* weigh down, sink; to depress, oppress

dē-prōmō 3 to draw forth, bring out; to derive, obtain

dē-pugnō 1 to fight out

dēpulsiō, ōnis *f* a driving off; defence

dē-putō 1 to reckon, estimate

dērēctus 3 = directus

dē-relinquō 3 to forsake wholly, abandon

dē-rīdeō 2 to laugh at, mock

dē-rīgēscō, riguī, — 3 to become stiff

dē-rigō = dirigo

dē-ripiō, ripuī, reptum 3 to tear off, snatch away

dē-risor, ōris *m* derider, mocker

dē-rīvō 1 to lead off, divert; to derive

dē-rogō 1 to take away, detract

dē-ruptus 3 precipitous, steep

dē-saeviō 4 to rage furiously

dē-scendō, ndī, nsum 3 to go down, descend, sink; to stoop, agree to

dēscēnsus, ūs *m* descent, way down

dē-scīscō, scīvī *and* sciī, scītum 3 to revolt from, desert

dē-scrībō 3 to copy; to sketch, draw, describe; to define, assign, allot

dē-scrīptiō, ōnis *f* copy; disposition, arrangement; description

dē-secō, cuī, ctum 1 to cut off

dē-serō, seruī, sertum 3 to forsake, abandon, neglect; dēsertus 3 deserted, lonely, waste [runaway]

dēsertor, ōris *m* deserter,)

dē-serviō 4 to serve diligently

dēses, idis idle, indolent

dēsīderium, ī *n* a longing, desire, wish

dē-sīderō 1 to long for, desire, ask; to miss, lack, lose

dēsidia, ae *f* inactivity, idleness

dēsidiōsus 3 idle; causing idleness

dē-sīdō, sēdī *and* sīdī, — 3 to sink down, fall

dē-signō 1 to mark out; to designate, represent; to appoint to a magistracy

dē-siliō, siluī, (sultum) 4 to leap down

dē-sinō, siī, situm 3 to leave off, cease, end

dē-sipiō, —, — 3 to be silly, act foolishly

dē-sistō, stitī, — 3 to leave off, cease   [alone]

dē-sōlō 1 to forsake, leave

dē-spectō 1 = despicio

dēspectus, ūs m view, prospect

dē-spērātiō, ōnis f hopelessness, despair

dē-spērō 1 to be hopeless, despair

dēspicātus 3 despised, contemptible

dē-spiciō, spexī, spectum 3 to look down upon; to despise, disdain

dē-spoliō 1 to plunder, despoil

dē-spondeō, spondī, spōnsum 2 to promise, pledge; to betroth

dēstinō 1 to make firm; to fix, determine; to intend, choose

dē-stituō, tuī, tūtum 3 to set down, place; to leave, abandon, betray

dē-stringō 3 to strip off, draw (the sword); to touch lightly, graze

dē-struō 3 to pull down, demolish

dēsuētūdō, inis f disuse, want of practice

dē-suētus 3 out of use; unaccustomed

dē-sum, fuī, esse to be absent, be wanting, fail, abandon, neglect

dē-sūmō 3 to choose, select

dē-super adv. from above

dē-tegō 3 to uncover, reveal, disclose

dē-tergeō 2 to wipe off, cleanse; to break off

dēterior, ius comp. worse, lower, poorer, meaner; superl. dēterrimus 3 worst, lowest

dē-terō 3 to rub off, wear away; to lessen, weaken

dē-terreō 2 to frighten off, deter, prevent

dētestābilis, e detestable, abominable

dē-testātiō, ōnis f a cursing

dē-testor 1 to curse, execrate; to avert, ward off

dē-tineō, tinuī, tentum 2 to keep back, check

dē-tondeō, tondī, tōnsum 2 to shear off

dē-tonō, uī, — 1 to thunder; to cease to thunder

dē-torqueō 2 to turn away, avert; to twist, distort

dē-tractiō, ōnis f a taking away, removal

dē-tractō = detrecto

dē-trahō 3 to draw or pull down, take away, remove, drag; to disparage, slander

dē-trectō 1 to decline, refuse; to disparage

dētrīmentum, ī n damage, loss; defeat

dē-trūdō 3 to thrust down, drive away; to compel; to postpone

dē-truncō 1 to cut off

dē-turbō 1 to thrust down, drive away

de-ūrō 3 to burn, destroy

deus, ī m a god, deity

dē-vāstō 1 to lay waste, devastate

dē-vehō 3 to carry down or away [arrive]

dē-veniō 4 to come to,

dē-versor 1 to lodge as a guest

dēversōrium, ī n inn

dēverticulum, ī n by-road; digression; refuge; inn

dē-vertō 3 to turn aside; to go to lodge; to digress

dēvexus 3 sloping, steep

dē-vinciō 4 to bind, tie fast; to lay under obligation

dē-vincō 3 to conquer completely, subdue

dē-vītō 1 to avoid

dē-vius 3 out of the way, secluded; inconstant, foolish

dē-vocō 1 to call away or off; to allure

dē-volō 1 to fly down, hasten away

dē-volvō 3 to roll down

dē-vorō 3 to swallow, devour; to consume, waste; to endure

dē-vors-, -vort-, see devers-, -vert-

dē-vōtiō, ōnis f a consecrating; incantation

dē-voveō 2 to vow, offer, consecrate; to curse; to destine

dexter, t(e)ra, t(e)rum right, on the right hand; propitious; suitable; skilful; subst. dext(e)ra, ae f right hand, right side; adv. dext(e)rā on the right

dext(e)rē adroitly

dextrōrsum (or -sus) adv. to the right

dia-dēma, atis n royal headdress, diadem

dia-lecticus 3 dialectical

diālis, e of Juppiter

diārium, ī n daily ration

dica, ae f lawsuit, action

dicāx, ācis satirical, witty

diciō, ōnis f authority, power, control

dicō¹ 1 to dedicate, consecrate, give up to

dicō², dīxī, dictum 3 to fix, appoint, name; to say, speak, tell, declare

dictamnus, ī f dittany (a plant)

dictātor, ōris m dictator

dictātōrius 3 of a dictator

dictātūra, ae f dictatorship

dictiō, ōnis f a saying, uttering; diction, style

dictitō 1 to say often, maintain

dictō 1 to dictate

dictum, ī n a saying, word, maxim; order, command

dī-dō, dīdidī, dīditum 3 to distribute, spread

dī-dūcō 3 to separate, divide; to disperse, scatter

diēs, ēī *m* (*and f*) day; daylight; fixed day, appointed time; space of time, period

differentia, ae *f* difference

dif-ferō, distulī, dīlātum, differre to spread abroad, disperse, scatter; to delay, postpone; *intr.* to be different, vary

dif-fertus 3 stuffed full

dif-ficilis, e difficult, troublesome; dangerous; morose, surly; *adv.* difficulter

difficultās, ātis *f* difficulty, poverty, distress

dif-fīdentia, ae *f* distrust

dif-fīdō, fīsus sum 3 to distrust

dif-findō 3 to cleave asunder, split

dif-fluō 3 to flow away; to be dissolved, disappear

dif-fugiō 3 to flee, disperse, be scattered

dif-fundō 3 to pour forth, spread, scatter, extend; to gladden, cheer up

dī-gerō 3 to separate, divide, distribute; to arrange

digitus, ī *m* finger; a finger's breadth, inch

dī-gladior 1 to fight fiercely

dignātiō, ōnis *f* honour, rank

dignitās, ātis *f* merit; dignity, splendour, distinction, honour, rank, high office

dignor 1 to deem worthy, deign, condescend

dīgnus 3 worthy, deserving; fitting, suitable

dī-gredior, gressus sum 3 to go apart, depart; to digress

digressiō, ūs *f* a separating, parting, departure

dī-iūdicō 1 to decide, determine; to distinguish

dī-iungō, dī-iūnctiō, = disiungo, disiunctio

dī-lābor 3 to fall to pieces, dissolve, disappear; to flee, disperse

dī-lacerō 1 to tear to pieces, ruin

dī-laniō 1 to tear to pieces

dī-lātiō, ōnis *f* a delaying

dī-lātō 1 to spread out, enlarge

dī-lēctus, ūs *m* a picking out; levy, recruiting

dīligēns, tis careful, attentive, diligent, scrupulous

dīligentia, ae *f* carefulness, attentiveness, diligence

dī-ligō, lēxī, lēctum 3 to prize, value, love

dī-lūcēscō, lūxī, — 3 to grow light, become day

dī-luō 3 to wash away, dissolve; to weaken, impair

dīluviēs, ēī *f and* -vium, ī *n* flood, deluge

dī-mētior, mēnsus sum 4 to measure out, lay out; to be measured

dīmicātiō, ōnis *f* fight, struggle

dī-micō 1 to fight, contend, struggle

dīmidiātus 3 halved, half

dīmidius 3 half; *subst.* dīmidium, ī n a half

dī-mittō 3 to send about, send forth; to dismiss, dissolve; to discharge, release; to renounce, abandon

dī-moveō 2 to part, separate; to remove, take away

dī-nōscō, —, — 3 to distinguish, discern

dī-numerō 1 to count up, reckon

dī-rēctus straight, direct; upright; plain, simple

dīreptiō, ōnis f a plundering, sack

dīreptor, ōris m plunderer

dī-rigō, rēxī, rēctum 3 to set straight; to send, aim, steer; to dispose, order

dir-imō, ēmī, ēmptum 3 to separate, divide; to interrupt, end, break up

dī-ripiō, ripuī, reptum 3 to plunder, pillage, rob

dīritās, ātis f cruelty

dī-rumpō 3 to break, shatter

dī-ruō 3 to pull down, destroy

dīrus 3 ill-omened, awful, dreadful; dīrae, ārum f/pl. the Furies

dīs, dītis = dives

dis-cēdō 3 to separate, disperse, to go away, depart; to desert, forsake; to get away, come off

disceptātiō, ōnis f discussion, debate, dispute

disceptātor, ōris m arbitrator, judge

dis-ceptō 1 to discuss, debate; to decide, arbitrate

dis-cernō, crēvī, crētum 3 to separate, divide; to distinguish, discern

dis-cerpō, psī, ptum 3 to pluck to pieces, tear asunder

dis-cessiō, ōnis f *and* -sus, ūs m separation; a going away, departure

discidium, ī n separation; disagreement

dī-scindō 3 to tear asunder, rend

dis-cingō 3 to ungird

disciplīna, ae f instruction, teaching; learning, knowledge; training, education; custom, habit [scholar]

discipulus, ī m pupil,

dis-clūdō, sī, sum 3 to shut up apart, separate

discō, didicī, — 3 to learn, find out; to study

dis-color, ōris of a different colour; different

dis-cordia, ae f disagreement, discord

dis-cordō 1 to disagree, quarrel

dis-cors, dis disagreeing, discordant, at variance

dis-crepō, uī, — 1 to disagree, be different

dī-scrībō 3 to divide, distribute, assign

dis-crīmen, inis n interval, distance; difference, distinction; crisis, danger dis-crīminō 1 to separate, divide

dī-scrīptiō, ōnis f distribution, assignment

dis-crucio 1 to torture, torment

dis-cumbō, cubuī, cubitum 3 to recline at table; to go to bed

dis-currō, (cu)currī, cursum 3 to run different ways, run about

dis-cursus, ūs m a running about

discus, ī m quoit

dis-cutiō, cussī, cussum 3 to dash to pieces, shatter; to disperse; to destroy

disertus 3 eloquent, clever, fluent

dīs-iciō, iēcī, iectum 3 to drive asunder, disperse; to destroy, frustrate

dis-iūnctiō (or dī-iūnctiō), ōnis f separation; logical dilemma

dis-iungō (or dī-iungō) 3 to unyoke; to separate, remove; to estrange

dis-pār, aris unlike, different

dis-parō 1 to separate, divide

dis-pellō, pulī, pulsum 3 to drive asunder, disperse

dis-pendium, ī n expense; loss

dis-pēnsātiō, ōnis f management, administration

dispēnsātor, ōris m steward, treasurer

dis-pēnsō 1 to distribute,

pay out; to manage, arrange

dis-perdō 3 to ruin, destroy

dis-pereō to be lost, undone, ruined

dī-spergō, sī, sum 3 to disperse, scatter

dis-pertiō (and -ior) 4 to divide, distribute

di-spiciō, spexī, spectum 3 to discern, discover

dis-pliceō, uī, (itum) 2 to displease

dis-pōnō 3 to arrange, draw up, assign

disputātiō, ōnis f a reasoning; discussion

dis-putō 1 to discuss, argue, examine

dis-quīsītiō, ōnis f inquiry, investigation

dis-rumpō 3 = dirumpo

dis-sēminō 1 to sow, spread

dis-sēnsiō, ōnis f (and -sus, ūs m) disagreement, discord

dis-sentiō 4 to disagree; to be different

dis-serō, ruī, rtum 3 to discuss, argue

dissiciō = disicio

dis-sideō, sēdī, sessum 2 to disagree, be at variance

dis-signō 1 to arrange, dispose

dis-siliō, luī, — 4 to leap or burst asunder

dis-similis, e dissimilar, unlike

dis-similitūdō, inis f unlikeness, difference

dis-simulanter adv. secretly

dis-simulātiō, ōnis *f* a dissembling, concealing

dis-simulātor, ōris *m* dissembler, concealer

dis-simulō 1 to disguise, conceal

dissipātiō, ōnis *f* a scattering, dispersion

dis-sipō 1 to scatter, spread abroad; to put to flight; to destroy, squander

dis-sociābilis, e dividing; incompatible

dis-sociō 1 to separate; to estrange

dis-solūtiō, ōnis *f* a dissolving, destruction; dissoluteness

dis-solūtus 3 loose, lax, negligent; dissolute

dis-solvō 3 to separate, dissolve; to abolish; to refute; to pay

dis-sonus 3 discordant, confused; different

dis-suādeō 2 to advise against, resist

dis-sultō 1 to leap *or* burst asunder

dis-tendō, tendī, tentum 3 to stretch asunder, extend; to fill full; to divide

distinctiō, ōnis *f* distinction, difference

distinctus 3 separated, distinguished; decorated, adorned

dis-tineō, tinuī, tentum 2 to keep asunder, separate; to occupy, engage; to hinder

di-stinguō, īnxī, īnctum 3 to

decorate, adorn; to distinguish, discriminate

di-stō, —, — 1 to be distant *or* remote; to be different

dis-torqueō 2 to twist, distort

dis-trahō 3 to pull asunder, tear to pieces; to distract, perplex; to estrange

dis-tribuō 3 to divide, distribute

dis-tribūtiō, ōnis *f* division, distribution

di-stringō 3 to occupy, engage

dis-turbō 1 to demolish, destroy; to disturb, confuse

dītēscō, —, — 3 to grow rich

dīthyrambus, ī *m* dithyramb

dītō 1 to enrich

diū *adv.* a long time, long while

diurnus 3 by day, daily

dīus 3 = dīvus

diūtinus 3 lasting, of long duration

diuturnitās, ātis *f* long duration, length of time

diuturnus 3 lasting, long

dī-vellō, vellī (vulsī), vulsum 3 to tear apart, remove, separate

dī-vendō 3 to sell in separate lots

dī-verberō 1 to cut, divide

dīversitās, ātis *f* diversity, contradiction

dī-versus 3 opposite, contrary; apart, separate; different, discordant

dīves, itis rich; fertile, copious; precious, costly

dī-vidō, vīsī, vīsum 3 to separate, divide; to distribute, allot

dīviduus 3 divided, separated

dīvīnātiō, ōnis f divination, prophecy

dīvīnitās, ātis f godhead, divinity

dīvīnitus adv. by divine influence; excellently

dīvīnō 1 to prophesy, forebode

dīvīnus 3 of a god, divine; inspired, prophetic; admirable, godlike

dīvīsiō, ōnis f division; distribution

dīvīsor, ōris m divider, distributor of bribes

dīvitiae, ārum f/pl. riches, wealth

dī-vors-, see **dī-vers-**

dī-vortium, ī n separation; divorce

dī-vulgō 1 to make public, spread abroad

dīvus 3 divine; deified; subst. **dīvus**, ī m god

dō, dedī, datum, dare to give, offer; to give up, hand over; to grant, yield, permit; tell, utter, announce; to attribute, impute; to cause, produce

doceō, cuī, ctum 2 to teach, inform, tell; to prove, explain

docilis, e easily taught, docile

doctor, ōris m teacher, instructor

doctrīna, ae f instruction, teaching; learning, knowledge

doctus 3 learned, skilled, experienced

documentum, ī n lesson, example, proof; warning

dōdrāns, tis three fourths

dolābra, ae f pickaxe

dolenter adv. painfully

doleō, luī, litūrus 2 to suffer pain, grieve, be afflicted; to cause pain

dōlium, ī n cask; wine-jar

dolō[1] 1 to hew

dolō[2], ōnis m pike, swordstick; fore-topsail

dolor, ōris m pain, sorrow, affliction; indignation, resentment [ning]

dolōsus 3 deceitful, cun-/

dolus, ī m fraud, deceit, trickery, malice

domesticus 3 domestic; private, native

domicilium, ī n dwelling, abode, home

domina, ae f lady, mistress

dominātiō, ōnis f rule, dominion; tyranny

dominātus, ūs m = dominatio

dominor 1 to be lord or master, rule

dominus, ī m master, lord; owner; ruler, despot

domitor, ōris m tamer, subduer

domō, uī, itum 1 to tame, subdue, conquer

domus, ūs *f* house, home, household, family

dōnātiō, ōnis *f* a giving, gift

dōnec *cj.* as long as, while; until

dōnō 1 to give, grant; to pardon

dōnum, ī *n* present, gift; offering, sacrifice

dormiō 4 to sleep; to be idle

dormītō 1 to be drowsy; to fall asleep

dorsum, ī *n* (*and* -us, ī *m*) the back; ridge of a mountain

dōs, dōtis *f* dowry; gift, quality, talent

dōtālis, e belonging to a dowry

dōtō 1 to endow

drach(u)ma, ae *f* drachma

dracō, ōnis *m* serpent, dragon

dubitātiō, ōnis *f* doubt, uncertainty; hesitation

dubitō 1 to doubt; to deliberate; to hesitate, waver

dubius 3 uncertain, doubtful, undecided; dangerous, critical

ducēnī 3 two hundred each

du-centī 3 two hundred

dūcō, dūxī, ductum 3 to draw, drag, pull; to receive, admit; to drink, inhale; to incite, allure; to form, compose, build; to prolong; to lead, conduct, command; to marry; to consider, think, regard

ductō 1, *intens. of* duco

ductor, ōris *m* leader, commander

ductus, ūs *m* a leading, conducting; command

dūdum *adv.* a short time ago; formerly, of old; iam dūdum now for a long time

duellum = bellum

dulcēdō, inis *f* sweetness, charm

dulcis, e sweet; pleasant, charming, dear

dum *cj.* while, as long as; until; provided that; *adv.* (*joined to other words*) now

dūmētum, ī *n* thicket, thorn-hedge

dum-modo *cj.* = dum provided that, if only

dūmōsus 3 bushy

dum-taxat *adv.* exactly, only, merely; at least

dūmus, ī *m* thorn-bush; thicket

duo, ae, o two; both

duo-decim twelve

duo-dēnī 3 twelve each

duo-virī = duumviri

du-plex, icis twofold, double

duplicō 1 to double; to bend; to enlarge

duplus 3 double

dūrēscō, ruī, — 3 to grow hard

dūritia, ae *f* hardness, austerity, harshness

dūrō 1 *trans.* to make hard *or* hardy; to endure; *intr.* to become hard; to continue, last

dūrus 3 hard; rough; strong, enduring; unfeeling, stern, severe; difficult, painful, distressing; *adv.* **dūriter** *and* **dūre**

duum-virī, **ōrum** *m/pl.* a commission of two men

dux, **ducis** *m* (*and* *f*) leader; commander, general; ruler

dynastēs, **ae** *m* ruler, prince

E

ē, **ex** *prep.* with *abl.* (*of space*) out of, from; (*of time*) since, from, immediately upon; (*of relation*) from, of; on account of, through; according to

eā (*sc. viā*) *adv.* there, that way

eādem *adv.* by the same way

ē-bibō 3 to drink up

ē-blandior 4 to obtain by flattery

ēbrietās, **ātis** *f* drunkenness

ēbriōsus 3 given to drink; drunkard

ēbrius 3 drunk, intoxicated

ebur, **oris** *n* ivory; work of ivory

eburneus (**-nus**) 3 (made of) ivory

ē-castor *int.* by Castor!

ec-ce *adv.* lo!, behold!

ecf..., *see* **eff...**

echidna, **ae** *f* adder, viper

echīnus, **ī** *m* sea-urchin

ec-quandō *adv.* ever?

ecquis, **quī**, **ecqua**(**e**), **ec-quid**, **quod** (*is there* any) (**-one**)?, whether any(one) (**-one**)?; *adv.* **ecquid** *interrog. particle* (whether) at all?

eculeus, **ī** *m* young horse; rack

edāx, **ācis** greedy; consuming

ede-pol *int.* by Pollux!

ē-dīcō 3 to publish, proclaim; to decree, ordain

ē-dictum, **ī** *n* decree, proclamation, edict

ē-discō, **didicī**, — 3 to learn thoroughly

ē-disserō, **ruī**, **rtum** 3 to relate fully, explain

ēditīcius 3 announced, proposed

ēditus 3 elevated, high

edō[1], **ēdī**, **ēsum** 3 to eat, consume

ē-dō[2], **didī**, **ditum** 3 to give out, put forth; to give birth to; to publish, proclaim, ordain; to display, perform, cause

ē-doceō 2 to teach thoroughly; to inform, relate

ē-domō 1 to tame, subdue

ē-dormiō 4 to sleep out *or* off [up, education]

ēducātiō, **ōnis** *f* a bringing)

ē-dūcō[1] 1 to bring up, rear, educate

ē-dūcō[2] 3 to draw out, take away; to lead out; to bring before a court; to raise, build; to bring up, rear

effectus, ūs *m* execution, performance; result, consequence

ef-fēminō 1 to make effeminate

ef-ferō[1] 1 to make wild; to enrage

ef-ferō[2], extulī, ēlātum, efferre to bear, take out; to carry to the grave, bury; to produce, bear; to utter, spread abroad, make known; to excite; to raise, lift up; to make haughty; to praise

ef-ferus 3 very wild, savage

ef-fervēscō, ferbuī (*or* fervī), — 3 to boil up; to burst forth

ef-fervō, —, — 3 = effervesco

ef-fētus 3 exhausted, worn out

efficāx, ācis efficient, effective

ef-ficiō, fēcī, fectum 3 to bring about, produce, make, cause, finish, complete; to prove

effigiēs, ēī *f* image, likeness, portrait; ideal; phantom

ef-fingō 3 to form, fashion; to represent, express

ef-flāgitō 1 to demand urgently, entreat

ed-flō 1 to breathe *or* blow out

ef-flōrēscō, ruī, — 3 to bloom, flourish

ef-fluō, uxī, — 3 to flow out, escape; to disappear, be forgotten

ef-fodiō 3 to dig up, tear out

ef-for, fātus sum 1 to speak out, utter; to consecrate

ef-frēnātus 3 unbridled, unrestrained

effrēnus 3 = effrenatus

ef-fringō, frēgī, frāctum 3 to break open

ef-fugiō, fūgī, (fugitum) 3 to flee away, escape, avoid

effugium, ī *n* a fleeing away, escape

ef-fulgeō, lsī, — 2 to shine forth

ef-fultus 3 supported by, resting upon

ef-fundō 3 to pour out, shed; to waste, squander; to utter; to loose, let go

ef-fūsiō, ōnis *f* a pouring forth; extravagance, profusion

ef-fūsus 3 widespread, extensive; let loose, disorderly; unrestrained

ef-fūtiō 4 to chatter, babble

egēns, tis needy, poor

egēnus 3 needy, poor

egeō, uī, — 2 to be in need, want [charge)

ē-gerō 3 to bring out, dis-

egestās, ātis *f* need, poverty, want

egō *pers. pron.* I

ē-gredior, gressus sum 3 to go out, come forth; to land; to ascend; to go beyond, pass

ē-gregius 3 distinguished, excellent, admirable

ē-gressus, ūs *m* a going out, departure; a landing

ehem *int.* = hem

ēheu *int.* ah!, alas!

eho *int.* ho!, indeed!

ei *int.* = hei

ēia *int.* ha!, well then!, quick!

ē-iciō, iēcī, iectum 3 to throw *or* drive out, expel, banish; to run aground; to hoot, disapprove

ēiectō 1 to throw out

ē-ierō 1 = eiuro

ē-iūrō 1 to refuse on oath, abjure

ē-lābor 3 to glide out, slip away, escape

ē-labōrō 1 to work out, elaborate; to work hard, strive

ē-languēscō, guī, — 3 to become languid

ē-lātiō, ōnis *f* exaltation

ē-lātus 3 exalted

ēlectrum, ī *n* amber; alloy of gold and silver

ēlegāns, tis choice, elegant, refined

ēlegantia, ae *f* taste, refinement, elegance

elegī, ōrum *m/pl.* elegiac verses

elementum, ī *n* first principle, element; *pl.* rudiments, beginnings

elephantus, ī (*and* elephās, antis) *m* elephant; ivory

e-levō 1 to lessen, impair

ē-liciō, cuī, citum 3 to entice out, lure forth; to elicit, invite, produce

ē-līdō, sī, sum 3 to strike *or* drive out; to shatter, crush

ē-ligō, lēgī, lēctum 3 to pick out, choose

ē-linguis, e speechless

ē-lixus 3 boiled, soaked

elleborum *and* -us = hell...

ēlogium, ī *n* epitaph

ē-loquēns, tis eloquent

ēloquentia, ae *f* eloquence

ēloquium, ī *n* = eloquentia

ē-loquor 3 to speak out, utter, pronounce

ē-lūceō, xī, — 2 to shine forth; to be conspicuous

ē-luctor 1 to struggle out, overcome

ē-lūdō 3 to elude, avoid; to mock, ridicule; to frustrate

ē-luō, uī, lūtum 3 to wash away, efface

ēluviēs, ēī *and* -viō, ōnis *f* inundation, flood

em *int.* there!, see!

ē-mancipō 1 to release from the paternal authority; to transfer, make over

ē-mānō 1 to arise, spring; to spread abroad, become known

ēmendātor, ōris *m* corrector

ē-mendō 1 to correct, amend

ē-mentior 4 to lie, feign, pretend

ē-mereō *and* -eor 2 to deserve; to serve out

ē-mergō 3 *trans.* to raise up; *intr.* to come forth, e-merge, extricate oneself

ē-mētior, mēnsus sum 4 to

pass over, traverse; to impart

ē-micō, uī, ātum 1 to spring forth, break out

ē-migrō 1 to wander forth, emigrate

ēminēns, tis projecting, lofty; illustrious

ē-mineō, uī, — 2 to project; to be conspicuous; to be eminent

ē-minus *adv.* at a distance, from afar

ēmissārius, ī *m* emissary, spy

ē-mittō 3 to send out; to hurl; to utter; to set free

emō, ēmī, ēmptum 3 to buy, purchase

ē-mollō 4 to soften

ēmolumentum, ī *n* advantage, profit

ē-morior 3 to die off, perish

ē-moveō 2 to remove, expel

emporium, ī *n* place of trade

ēmptiō, ōnis *f* a buying, purchase

ēmptor, ōris *m* buyer, purchaser

ē-mungō, mūnxī, mūnctum 3 to blow the nose; to cheat

ē-mūniō 4 to wall off, fortify

ēn *int.* lo!, behold!, see!, there!, come!

ē-nārrō 1 to explain fully

ē-nāscor 3 to grow out of, arise

ē-necō, cuī, ctum 1 to kill; to exhaust

ē-nervō 1 to weaken, make effeminate

ē-nicō 1 = eneco

enim *cj.* for; for instance, namely; truly, certainly, in fact

enim-vērō *adv.* truly, certainly; but indeed

ē-niteō, tuī, — 2 to shine forth

ē-nitēscō, tuī, — 3 to shine forth

ē-nītor, nīxus *or* nīsus sum 3 to struggle up, ascend; to strive; to bring forth

ē-nīxus 3 earnest, zealous

ē-nō 1 to swim away

ē-nōdis, e without knots, smooth

ē-normis, e exceedingly big

ēnsis, is *m* sword

ē-nūbō 3 to marry out of her station *or* town

ē-numerātiō, ōnis *f* a counting up, enumeration

ē-numerō 1 to reckon, count up

ē-nūntiō 1 to declare, announce; to disclose, betray

eō¹ *adv.* thither, to that place; so far, so much; on that account; therefore

eō², iī (*and* īvī), itum, īre to go [place]

eōdem *adv.* to the same

Eōus 3 of the morning, of the East

ephēbus, ī *m* a youth

ephēmeris, idis *f* day-book, diary

ephippium, ī *n* horse-cloth, saddle

epi-gramma, atis *n* inscription; epigram

epi-logus i *m* peroration, epilogue

epi-stula, ae *f* letter, epistle

epos *n* epic poem

ē-pōtō 1 to drink up, absorb

epulae, ārum *f/pl.* food, dishes; feast, banquet

epulāris, e belonging to a feast

epulō, ōnis *m* arranger of a feast

epulor 1 to feast, dine

epulum, ī *n* feast, banquet

equa, ae *f* mare

eques, itis *m* and *f* horseman, -woman, cavalry; knight, equestrian order

equester, tris, tre of cavalry, equestrian; of knights

e-quidem *adv.* truly, indeed; for my part

equīnus 3 of horses

equitātus, ūs *m* cavalry; knights, the equestrian order

equitō 1 to ride

equuleus, ī *m* = eculeus

equus, ī *m* horse, steed

era, ae *f* mistress

e-rādō 1 to erase, eradicate

ē-rēctus 3 upright, lofty, noble; haughty; attentive, eager; resolute

ēreptor, ōris *m* robber

ergā *prep.* with *acc.* towards, in relation to

ergastulum, ī *n* house of correction, prison

ergō *adv.* therefore, accordingly

ē-rigō, rēxī, rectum 3 to raise up, erect; to arouse, excite; to encourage, cheer

erīlis, e of a master *or* mistress

Erīnȳs, yos *f* goddess of revenge, Fury

ē-ripiō, ripuī, reptum 3 to tear out, snatch away, rob; to rescue, free

ē-rogō 1 to pay out, expend

errābundus 3 wandering about

errātiō, ōnis *f* a wandering

errātum, ī *n* error, fault

errō[1] 1 to wander, stray; to err, be mistaken

errō[2], ōnis *m* vagabond

error, ōris *m* a wandering, straying; uncertainty, doubt; error, mistake

ē-rubēscō, buī, — 3 to grow red, blush, be ashamed of

ē-rūctō 1 to belch forth, vomit

ē-rudiō 4 to instruct, teach; *adj.* ērudītus 3 instructed, learned

ē-rumpō 3 *trans.* to cause to break forth, emit; *intr* to break out, rush forth

ē-ruō 3 to dig up, throw out; to search out; to destroy utterly

ē-ruptiō, ōnis *f* a bursting forth, sally

erus, ī *m* master; owner

ervum, ī *n* vetch

ēsca, ae *f* food; bait

ē-scendō, ndī, ēnsum 3 to climb up, ascend

ē-scēnsiō, ōnis *f* a landing; climbing

essedārius, ī *m* fighter in a war-chariot

essedum, ī *n* war-chariot

ēs(s)uriō 4 to be hungry

et *cj.* and; et ... et both ... and

et-enim *cj.* for, and indeed

etēsiae, ārum *m/pl.* Etesian (summer) winds

etiam *cj.* as yet, still, even now; again; also, even, furthermore, certainly

etiam-sī *cj.* even if, although

et-sī *cj.* although; and yet

eu *int.* well!, well done!

euge *int.* well done!,}

euhoe, *see* euoe   [bravo!]}

eunūchus, ī *m* eunuch

euoe, euhoe *int.* the shout of the Bacchantes

eurus, ī *m* south-east wind

ē-vādō 3 to go *or* come out; to traverse; to climb, ascend; to escape; to turn out, result

ē-vagor 1 to wander, make evolutions

ē-valēscō, luī, — 3 to prevail, be able

ē-vānēscō, nuī, — 3 to disappear, vanish

ē-vāstō 1 to devastate

ē-vehō 3 to carry out; to lift up, raise; **P.** to proceed, advance

ē-vellō 3 to tear out, root out, erase

ē-veniō 4 to happen, occur; to turn out, result

ēventum, ī *n* = ēventus

ēventus ūs *m* consequence, result; occurrence, event

ē-verrō, —, rsum 3 to clean out, plunder

ē-versiō, ōnis *f* an overthrowing, destruction

ēversor, ōris *m* destroyer

ē-vertō 3 to overturn; to demolish, destroy; to drive out

ē-vidēns, tis clear, plain

ē-vinciō 4 to bind round

ē-vincō 3 to conquer, subdue utterly; to prevail over

ē-vītō 1 to avoid, shun

ē-vocō 1 to call forth, summon

ē-volō 1 to fly away, rush forth, escape

ē-volvō 3 to roll out, unfold; to strip; to read; to disclose

ē-vomō 3 to vomit forth, cast out

ē-vort- = ē-vert-

ex *prep., see* e

ex-acerbō 1 to exasperate

ex-āctiō, ōnis *f* a collecting of debts, tax

ex-āctor, ōris *m* collector, exactor

ex-āctus 3 accurate, precise

ex-acuō 3 to sharpen; to excite, stimulate

ex-adversum (*or*-adversus) *and* -sus *adv.* and *prep.* with *acc.* opposite

ex-aedificō 1 to finish building

ex-aequō 1 to make equal

ex-aestuō 1 to boil up, glow

ex-aggerō 1 to heap up; to magnify, heighten

ex-agitō 1 to chase, disturb, harass; to blame, reproach; to excite, stir up

ex-āmen, inis *n* swarm, multitude

exāminō 1 to weigh, consider

exanguis, e = exsanguis

ex-animis, e *and* **-mus** 3 lifeless; frightened

ex-animō 1 to deprive of breath; to kill; to exhaust, dismay

ex-ārdēscō, ārsī, — 3 to be kindled, inflamed

ex-ārēscō, āruī, — 3 to dry up

ex-arō 1 to plough up; to obtain by ploughing

ex-asperō 1 to make rough; to exasperate

ex-auctōrō 1 to dismiss from service

ex-audiō 4 to hear; to give heed to

ex-cēdō 3 to go out, depart, disappear; to exceed, surpass

ex-cellēns, tis excellent, distinguished, superior

excellentia, ae *f* superiority, excellence

ex-cellō 3 to be distinguished *or* eminent

ex-celsus 3 elevated, lofty, high

ex-ceptiō, ōnis *f* exception, limitation

ex-cernō 3 to sift, sort

ex-cerpō, psī, ptum 3 to pick out; to leave out, except

ex-cessus, ūs *m* departure, death

excidium, ī *n* destruction, annihilation

ex-cidō¹, cidī, — 3 to fall out *or* down; to slip out, escape; to perish, be lost

ex-cīdō², cīdī, cīsum 3 to cut out *or* down; to destroy, banish

ex-cieō, cīvī, citum 2 *and* **exciō** 4 to rouse, excite, frighten; to summon, call forth

ex-cipiō, cēpī, ceptum 3 to withdraw; to make an exception; to catch, capture; to listen to; to meet, be exposed to, sustain; to receive, welcome; to follow, succeed

ex-citō 1 to stir up, excite; to call forth, summon; to cause, produce; to erect, construct; to encourage, comfort

ex-clāmō 1 to cry aloud, call out

ex-clūdō, sī, sum 3 to shut out, remove, separate; to prevent, hinder

ex-cōgitō 1 to devise, contrive

ex-colō 3 to cultivate, improve, perfect

ex-coquō 3 to boil out, dry up

ex-cors, dis silly, stupid

ex-cruciō 1 to torture, plague, afflict

ex-cubiae ārum f/pl. a lying out on guard; sentries

ex-cubō 1 to keep watch

ex-cūdō, dī, sum 3 to hammer out, forge

ex-currō, (cu)currī, cursum 3 to run out, sally forth; to spread, project

ex-cursiō, ōnis f sally, attack, invasion

ex-cursus, ūs m = excursio

excūsātiō, ōnis f excuse, plea

ex-cūsō 1 to plead as an excuse, apologize for, excuse

ex-cutiō, cussī, cussum 3 to shake off, cast out, expel; to examine; to wrest, extort

exec..., see exsec...

ex-edō, ēdī, ēsum 3 to eat up, consume, destroy

exemplar āris n copy, image; model, example

exemplum, ī n copy; purport, contents; pattern, model; warning, punishment

ex-eō, iī, itum, īre to go out or away, withdraw; to result; to pass away, expire; to evade

exequiae, exequor, see exs...

ex-erceō, uī, itum 2 to keep busy, occupy; to trouble, harass; to exercise, practise, train; to pursue, administer

exercitātiō, ōnis f exercise, training

exercitātus 3 practised, trained

exercitus, ūs m army; multitude

ex-hālō 1 to breathe out, exhale

ex-hauriō 4 to draw out, empty; to take away; to exhaust, bring to an end; to endure

ex-hērēdō 1 to disinherit

ex-hibeō, uī, itum 2 to hold forth, present, furnish, display; to cause

ex-horrēscō, ruī, — 3 to tremble, shudder

ex-hortor 1 to exhort, encourage

ex-igō, ēgī, āctum 3 to drive out, expel; to demand, require; to inquire; to consider; to complete, live through

exiguitās, ātis f scantiness, shortness

exiguus 3 scanty, small, mean

ex-īlis, e thin, meagre; poor, wretched; cheerless

exiliō, exilium see exs...

exim adv. = exinde

eximius 3 excepted; distinguished, excellent

ex-imō, ēmī, ēmptum 3 to take out, remove; to free, release; to spend (time)

exin adv. = exinde

ex-ināniō 4 to empty out

ex-inde adv. then, next

exīstimātiō, ōnis f judg-

ment, opinion; good name,
reputation, honour
ex-īstimō 1 to consider,
suppose, reckon
existō = exsisto
exitiā(bi)lis, e destructive,
fatal
exitiōsus 3 destructive,
deadly
ex-itium, ī n destruction,
ruin, hurt
ex-itus, ūs m a going out,
departure; outlet, pas-
sage; end, conclusion;
death; result, event
ex-lēx, lēgis lawless
ex-olēscō, lēvī, (lētum) to
become obsolete, pass
away
ex-onerō 1 to unload; to
discharge, release
ex-optō 1 to wish greatly,
long for
ex-ōrābilis, e easily en-
treated
ex-ōrdior 4 to begin, commence
exōrdium, ī n a beginning;
introduction
ex-orior 4 to come out,
spring up, appear; to
originate, begin
ex-ōrnō 1 to equip, furnish;
to adorn, embellish
ex-ōrō 1 to prevail upon,
induce
ex-ōrsum, ī n = exordium
ex-ortus, ūs m a rising
ex-ōsus 3 hating, detesting
ex-pavēscō, pāvī 3 to be
terrified (of)
expectō 1 = exspecto

ex-pediō 4 to let loose, set
free; to arrange, set right;
to relate; to prepare, procure; to be profitable
or advantageous
expedītiō, ōnis f expedition
expedītus 3 unimpeded,
free; ready, at hand
ex-pellō, pulī, pulsum 3 to
drive out, expel, banish
ex-pendō, ndī, ēnsum 3 to
ponder, consider; to pay,
expend
expergīscor, perrēctus sum
3 to be awakened, wake
experientia, ae f trial,
proof; experience, practice
experīmentum, ī n proof,
test
experior, pertus sum 4 to
try, prove; to undertake,
attempt; to contend with;
to know by experience
ex-pers, tis devoid of, free
from
ex-petō 3 to long for, seek
after, desire
ex-pīlātiō, ōnis f a pillaging
ex-pīlō 1 to pillage, plunder
ex-piō 1 to atone for,
expiate [explain]
ex-plānō 1 to make plain,
ex-pleō, plēvī, plētum 2 to
fill up; to complete, finish;
to satisfy; to perform
explicātiō, ōnis f explanation
ex-plicō, cāvī or cuī, cātum
or citum 1 to unfold, spread
out, loosen; to arrange,
regulate; to explain, ex-
press

ex-plōdō, sī, sum 3 to hiss off (the stage); to disapprove

explōrātor, ōris m scout, spy

ex-plōrō 1 to examine, explore; to reconnoitre; explōrātus 3 ascertained, certain

ex-poliō 4 to smooth, embellish

ex-pōnō 3 to put out, expose; to disembark; to publish; to relate, explain [send away]

ex-portō 1 to carry out.}

ex-poscō, poposcī, — 3 to ask earnestly, entreat, demand

ex-postulō 1 to demand; to complain of

ex-primō, pressī, pressum 3 to press or force out; to extort, elicit; to represent, express, imitate;

expressus 3 distinct, clear

ex-probrō 1 to reproach with, blame for

ex-prōmō 3 to show forth, display; to utter, declare

expugnātiō, ōnis f a taking, storming

ex-pugnō 1 to take by assault, storm; to subdue, overcome

ex-pūrgō 1 to exculpate, excuse

ex-quīrō, sīvī, sītum 3 to search out, seek, inquire, ask; exquīsītus 3 choice, refined

ex-sanguis, e bloodless, lifeless; pale, weak

ex-satiō = exsaturō

ex-saturō 1 to satiate, satisfy

exscendō and exscēnsiō, ōnis f = escendo and escensio

ex-scindō 3 to destroy

ex-secō 1 to cut out

exsecrātiō, ōnis f curse; oath

ex-secor 1 to curse, execrate

exsequiae, ārum f/pl. funeral rites

ex-sequor 3 to follow, pursue; to investigate; to carry out, perform; to punish, avenge; to describe, relate

ex-serō, ruī, rtum 3 to stretch out, put forth; to bare

ex-siliō, luī, — 4 to leap out, spring forth

exsilium, ī n exile; place of exile

ex-sistō, stitī, — 3 to come forth, appear; to spring, arise; to exist, be

ex-solvō 3 to loose, release, set free; to discharge, pay (debts)

ex-somnis, e sleepless

ex-sorbeō, uī, — 2 to suck up, drink

ex-sors, tis free from; deprived of; chosen, choice

ex-spatior 1 to wander from the course, spread

exspectātiō, ōnis f an awaiting, expectation

ex-spectō 1 to await, expect; to hope, desire; to fear

ex-spīrō 1 to breathe out; to die

ex-spoliō 1 to pillage, plunder

ex-spuō 3 to spit out, expel

ex-stimulō 1 to goad, excite

ex-(s)tinctor, ōris m destroyer

ex-(s)tinguō, inxī, īnctum 3 to put out, quench; to destroy, abolish

ex-stirpō 1 to root out, eradicate

ex-stō, —, — 1 to stand out, project; to be extant, exist

ex-struō 3 to pile up; to raise, build up

ex-sūdō 1 to perform with sweating

ex-sul, ulis m and f exile

ex-sulō 1 to be banished, live in exile

ex-sultō 1 to spring, leap up; to exult, rejoice

ex-superō 1 to surpass, surmount, excel, overcome

ex-surgō 3 to rise up, stand up

ex-suscitō 1 to awaken, rouse

exta, ōrum n/pl. the internal organs

ex-templō adv. immediately, straightway

ex-tendō, tendī, tentum or tēnsum 3 to extend, stretch out; to increase, enlarge; to spend, pass

ex-tenuō 1 to make thin or small, diminish, weaken

exter, a, um outward, foreign; comp. exterior, ius outer, exterior; superl. extrēmus 3 outermost, utmost, extreme, last; highest, greatest, lowest, worst

ex-terminō 1 to drive out, expel; to remove

externus 3 outward, external; foreign, strange

ex-terreō 2 to frighten, terrify

exterus 3 = exter

ex-timēscō, muī, — 3 to be greatly afraid (of)

ex-tinguō 3 = ex(s)tinguō

extō, —, — 1 = exstō

ex-tollō, —, — 3 to lift up, raise, extol, praise

ex-torqueō 2 to twist out, wrest away, extort

ex-torris, e exiled, banished

extrā adv. and prep. with acc. on the outside, without, beyond; except, besides

ex-trahō 3 to draw or drag out; to release; to prolong

extrāneus 3 external, stranger

extrā-ōrdinārius 3 extraordinary, uncommon

extrēmus 3, superl. of exter

ex-trīcō 1 to disentangle

extrīn-secus adv. from without

ex-trūdō 3 to thrust out, drive away

extrūdō 3 = exstruo
ex-tundō, tudī, (tūsum) 3 to beat out, forge, fashion
ex-turbō 1 to drive out, thrust away
ex-ūberō 1 to grow luxuriantly, abound
exul, ulis = exsul
ex-ulcerō 1 to make worse, embitter

ex-undō 1 to flow out, overflow
ex-uō, uī, ūtum 3 to take off, pull off, divest; to despoil
ex-ūrō 3 to burn up, consume
exuviae, ārum *f/pl.* skin of an animal; equipment, arms; booty

F

faba, ae *f* bean
fābella, ae *f* short story, tale
faber, brī *m* workman, smith, carpenter
fabrica, ae *f* work-shop; trade; architecture; trick
fabricātor, ōris *m* artificer, contriver
fabricor (*and* -cō) 1 to construct, build
fabrīlis, e of a workman
fābula, ae *f* account, tale, story; play
fābulor 1 to talk, chat, speak
fābulōsus 3 fabulous
facessō, īvī *and* **iī, ītum** 3 to perform, execute; to cause; to go away, depart
facētiae, ārum *f/pl.* wit, humour
facētus 3 merry, witty, humorous
faciēs, ēī *f* outward appearance, shape, aspect; face, countenance
facilis, e easy; good-natured, willing, courte-

ous; *adv.* **facile** easily; certainly; willingly
facilitās, ātis *f* ease; willingness, courteousness
facinorōsus 3 criminal
facinus, oris *n* deed, action, crime, misdeed
faciō, fēcī, factum 3 to make, produce, perform; to write; to cause, occasion; to give, procure; to feign, assert; to value, consider; to suppose; to take part; to be of use
factiō, ōnis *f* class, party, faction   [tisan]
factiōsus 3 seditious; par-]
factitō 1 to do frequently, practise
factum, ī *n* deed, action
facultās, ātis *f* possibility, opportunity, means; skill; plenty, abundance
fācundia, ae *f* eloquence
fācundus 3 eloquent
faenerātiō, ōnis *f* usury
faenerātor, ōris *m* usurer
faeneror (*and* -rō) 1 to lend on interest

faenum, ī n hay

faenus, oris n gain, profit; interest, usury

faex, cis f sediment, dregs, refuse [beech

fāgineus and fāginus 3 of beech-tree

fāgus, ī f beech-tree

falārica, ae f fire-dart

falcātus 3 sickle-shaped

fallācia, ae f deceit, trick

fallāx, ācis deceitful, deceptive

fallō, fefellī, falsum 3 to deceive, cheat; to violate; to escape notice, be concealed

falsus 3 false, pretended; deceitful; subst. falsum, ī n falsehood, deceit; adv. falsō

falx, cis f sickle, scythe

fāma, ae f report, rumour; public opinion; reputation, renown, infamy

famēs, is f hunger; greed

familia, ae f household; slaves, servants; family

familiāris, e of a household or family; intimate, friendly: subst. familiāris, is m servant; friend

familiāritās, ātis f intimacy, friendship

fāmōsus 3 famous; infamous

famula, ae f female slave

famulātus, ūs m servitude

famulus, ī m servant, slave

fānāticus 3 inspired; frantic, furious

fānum, ī n temple, sanctuary

fār, farris n corn, grain; bread

farciō, sī, tum 4 to stuff, cram

farrāgō, inis f mixed fodder; medley

fās n (indecl.) divine law; what is right or lawful

fascia, ae f band, bandage

fasciculus, ī m small bundle

fascinō 1 to enchant, bewitch

fascis, is m burden, load; pl. bundle of rods with an axe; high office

fāstī, ōrum m/pl. register of judicial days; calendar, annals

fastīdiō 4 to loathe, dislike, despise

fastīdiōsus 3 full of disgust, disdainful

fastīdium, ī n a loathing; haughtiness; fastidiousness

fastīgātus 3 sloping; pointed

fastīgium, ī n slope, descent; top of a building; high rank or dignity

fastus, ūs m pride, disdain

fātālis, e ordained by fate, decreed; fatal, deadly

fateor, fassus sum 2 to confess, acknowledge

fāti-dicus 3 prophetic

fāti-fer 3 deadly

fatīgō 1 to weary, tire; to vex, harass

fatīscō, —, — 3 to gape or crack open

fātum, ī n oracle; destiny;

fate; ill fate; destruction, death

fatuus 3 silly, foolish

fauces, ium f/pl. throat, gullet; defile, strait

Faunus, ī m Faun

faustus 3 favourable, auspicious

fautor, ōris m favourer, promoter, protector

fautrix, īcis f patroness, protectress

faveō, fāvī, fautum 2 to favour, promote, befriend; to be silent

favilla, ae f (glowing) ashes

favōnius, ī m the west-wind

favor, ōris m favour, goodwill; applause

favus, ī m honeycomb

fax, facis f torch, firebrand; shooting-star; incitement, cause of ruin

febris, is f fever

Februārius 3 of February; subst. ~, ī m February

fēcunditās, ātis f fertility

fēcundus 3 fruitful, fertile; rich, abundant

fel, fellis n gall, bile

fēlēs, is f cat

fēlīcitās, ātis f happiness, good fortune

fēlīx, īcis fertile; happy, fortunate; favourable, propitious

fēmina, ae f woman, female

fēmineus 3 womanly, feminine

femur, oris or inis n thigh

fēnerātiō, fēneror, see faen...

fenestra, ae f opening, window

fēnum, fēnus, see faen...

fera, ae f, see ferus

fērālis, e of the dead, funereal

ferāx, ācis fruitful, fertile

ferculum, ī n litter, bier; dish, course

ferē adv. almost, about: in general, quite, entirely

feretrum, ī n litter, bier

fēriae, ārum f/pl. festival days, holidays

fēriātus 3 keeping holiday, idle

ferīnus 3 of wild beasts

feriō, —, — 4 to strike, beat; to kill

feritās, ātis f wildness, savageness

fermē adv. = ferē

ferō, tulī, lātum, ferre to bear, carry, bring; to suffer, endure; to report, tell; to plunder, spoil; to receive, win; to require, allow; to bring forth, produce, cause; to move, drive

ferōcia, ae f defiant or headstrong spirit, fierceness

ferōcitās, ātis f = ferocia

ferōx, ōcis bold, courageous; headstrong, overbearing

ferrāmenta, ōrum n/pl. iron tools

ferrātus 3 covered with iron

ferreus 3 of iron; hardhearted, cruel; firm, unyielding

ferrūgineus 3 rust-coloured, dusky

ferrūgō, inis *f* iron-rust; dark colour

ferrum, ī *n* iron; iron tool; sword

fertilis, e fruitful, fertile

fertilitās, ātis *f* fertility

ferula, ae *f* rod

ferus 3 wild, untamed, savage, uncivil; *subst.* **fera,** ae *f* wild animal

ferveō, ferbuī, — 2 (*and* **fervō,** —, — 3) to boil; to swarm, be busy; to glow, burn

fervidus 3 burning, glowing, vehement, impetuous

fervō, —, — 3, *see* **ferveo**

fervor, ōris *m* violent heat; ardour, passion

fessus 3 tired, exhausted

festīnātiō, ōnis *f* haste, hurry

festīnō 1 to hasten, be quick

festīnus 3 hasty, quick

festīvitās, ātis *f* gaiety, humour

festīvus 3 agreeable, pleasant; humorous, witty

festus 3 solemn, festive; *subst.* **fēstum,** ī *n* festival, feast

fētiālis, e belonging to the college of the **fētiālēs,** ium *m/pl.,* diplomatic negotiators

fētūra, ae *f* a breeding; offspring

fētus[1] 3 pregnant; fertile; newly delivered

fētus[2], ūs *m* offspring; fruit, produce

fibra, ae *f* fibre, filament; *pl.* entrails

fībula, ae *f* clasp, brooch

fictilis, e made of clay, earthen

fictor, ōris *m,* maker

fictus 3 feigned, false

fīcus, ī *and* ūs *f* fig-tree; fig

fīdēlis, e faithful, trusty; sure, safe, strong

fīdēlitās, ātis *f* faithfulness, trustiness

fīdēns, tis confident, bold

fidēs[1], eī *f* trust, faith, confidence, belief; sincerity, faithfulness; promise, pledge; protection, safeconduct

fidēs[2], is *f* (*mostly pl.*) stringed instrument

fidi-cen, inis *m* lute-player

fidi-cina, ae *f* female lute-player

fīdō, fīsus sum 3 to confide, trust

fīdūcia, ae *f* trust, confidence self-reliance; pledge

fīdus 3 = **fīdēlis**

fīgō, xī, xum 3 to fix, fasten, attach; to transfix, pierce

figūra, ae *f* form, shape, figure; kind, quality

figūrō 1 to form, fashion

fīlia, ae *f* daughter

fīliola, ae *f* little daughter

fīliolus, ī *m* little son

fīlius, ī *m* son, child

filix, icis *f* fern, bracken

filum, ī *n* thread, string, cord; texture

fimus, ī *m* dung; dirt

findō, fidī, fissum 3 to cleave, split, divide

fingō, finxī, fictum 3 to form, fashion, make, mould; to teach, train; to imagine, think; to invent, feign, pretend

fīniō 4 to limit, bound; to determine, prescribe; to put an end to, finish

fīnis, is *m* (*and* f) boundary, limit, border; highest point *or* degree; end, close; *pl.* territory, country

fīnitimus (*and* -umus) 3 bordering upon, neighbouring; connected, related

fīō, factus sum, fierī to be born *or* created; to be made *or* appointed; to happen, come to pass

firmāmentum, ī *n* support, prop

firmitās, ātis *and* -tūdō, inis f firmness, strength, endurance

firmō 1 to make firm, strengthen; to encourage; to confirm, prove

firmus 3 firm, strong, constant, faithful; *adv.* firmē (*and* firmiter)

fiscina, ae f basket

fiscus, ī *m* money-bag; treasury, public chest

fissilis, e (that may be) cleft

fistula, ae f shepherd's pipe

fīxus 3 fixed, immovable

flābellum, ī *n* fan

flābra, ōrum *n/pl.* breezes, winds

flagellum, ī *n* whip, scourge

flāgitiōsus 3 shameful, disgraceful

flāgitium, ī *n* shameful act, outrage; shame, disgrace

flāgitō 1 to ask urgently, entreat, demand

flagrāns, tis burning, blazing; passionate, eager

flagrō 1 to burn, blaze; to be inflamed *or* excited

flagrum, ī *n* whip, scourge

flāmen[1], inis *n* a blowing, breeze, wind

flāmen[2], inis *m* priest

flamma, ae f flame, blaze, fire; passion, fire of love; ruin

flammeum, ī *n* bride's veil

flammeus 3 flaming, fiery (-red)

flammō 1 to burn, inflame

flātus, ūs *m* a blowing, breathing; breeze

flāvēns, tis = flavus

flāvēscō 3 to become yellow

flāvus 3 (golden-)yellow

flēbilis, e lamentable, pitiable; weeping, tearful

flectō, xī, xum 3 to bend, curve; to persuade, prevail upon; to turn, change; to go, march

fleō, ēvī, ētum 2 to weep, bewail

flētus, ūs *m* a weeping, wailing

flexibilis, e flexible, pliant; fickle

flexilis, e pliant, pliable

flexus, ūs *m* a bending, curve; change

fiō 1 to blow

floccus, ī *m* flock of wool; trifle

flōrēns, tis blooming, flourishing

flōreō, uī, — 2 to bloom, blossom; to flourish, be prosperous

flōrēscō 3 to begin to blossom

flōreus 3 of flowers, flowery

flōridus 3 blooming; flowery

flōs, ōris *m* flower, blossom; prime, crown, splendour

flōsculus, ī *m* pride, ornament

fluctuō (*and* -**uor**) 1 to wave, undulate; to waver, hesitate

fluctus, ūs *m* flood, billow, surge; commotion

fluentum, ī *n* flow, stream

fluidus 3 flowing, fluid; languid

fluitō 1 to flow, float

fiūmen, inis *n* stream, river

fiūmineus 3 of a river

fiuō, uxī, (uxum) 3 to flow, stream; to flow away, vanish

fluviā(ti)lis, e of a river

fluvius, ī *m* river

fluxus 3 flowing, loose; frail, transient

foculus, ī *m* fire-pan; fire

focus, ī *m* fire-place, hearth; home, family

fodiō, fōdī, fossum 3 to dig, dig up; to prick, pierce

foederātus 3 allied

foeditās, ātis *f* foulness, hideousness

foedō 1 to defile, pollute

foedus[1] 3 foul, ugly, repulsive, horrible

foedus[2], eris *n* treaty, alliance; agreement

folium, ī *n* leaf; foliage

follis, is *m* bellows

fōmentum, ī *n* poultice; alleviation, mitigation

fōns, tis *m* spring, fountain, source; origin, cause

for, fātus sum 1 to say, speak

forāmen, inis *n* hole, opening

forās *adv.* out of doors, forth, out

for-ceps, ipis *f* pair of tongs, pincers

forēnsis, e belonging to the forum, public, forensic

foris[1], is *f* (leaf of a) door, gate; *pl.* folding-doors, entrance

foris[2] *adv.* out of doors, in public

fōrma, ae *f* form, shape, figure; beauty

formīca, ae *f* ant

formīdābilis, e terrible, formidable

formīdō[1] 1 to fear

formīdō[2], inis *f* fear, terror, dread

formīdolōsus 3 fearful, dreadful

fōrmō 1 to form, shape, make; to regulate, direct

fōrmōsus 3 finely formed, beautiful

fōrmula, ae *f* rule, prescription; contract, agreement; principle

fornāx, ācis *f* furnace, oven

fornix, icis *m* arch, vault; brothel

fors *f* (only nom. and abl. sg.
forte chance, luck, hazard;
adv. **fors** perhaps; **forte** by chance

fors-an, forsitan *adv.* perhaps

fortasse (*and* **fortassis**) *adv.*
perhaps, probably, possibly

fortis, e strong, enduring, brave, manly

fortitūdō, inis *f* manliness, fortitude, bravery, courage

fortuītus 3 (*adv.* -ō) casual, accidental

fortūna, ae *f* fate, fortune, luck; prosperity; adversity; circumstances, lot, position; (*mostly pl.*) property, possessions

fortūnō 1 to make prosperous *or* happy; **fortūnātus 3** prosperous, happy, fortunate

forum, ī *n* market-place; the forum; public affairs

forus, ī *m* gangway; row of seats

fossa, ae *f* ditch, trench

fossor, ōris *m* digger, navvy

fovea, ae *f* pitfall, pit

foveō, fōvī, fōtum 2 to warm; to cherish, foster, caress

fragilis, e brittle; weak, frail

fragmen, inis *n* = **fragmentum**

fragmentum, ī *n* broken piece, fragment

fragor, ōris *m* crash, noise

fragōsus 3 rough; roaring

fragrō 1 to smell (sweet)

frāgum, ī *n* wild strawberry

frangō, frēgī, frāctum 3 to break, shatter; to grind, crush; to break down, subdue, weaken, violate

frāter, tris *m* brother

frāterculus, ī *m* little brother

frāternus 3 brotherly, fraternal; friendly, allied

fraudō 1 to deceive, cheat, defraud

fraudulentus 3 deceitful

fraus, dis *f* a cheating, deceit, fraud; error, mistake; injury, damage; offence, crime

fraxineus 3 of ashwood

fraxinus, ī *f* ash-tree

fremitus, ūs *m* a roaring, noise, murmuring

fremō, uī, (itum) 3 to growl, resound, roar, grumble

frendō, —, frēsum 3 to gnash the teeth

frēnō 1 to bridle, curb, restrain

frēnum, ī *n* (*pl. usually* -ī, **ōrum** *m*) bridle, curb, bit

frequēns, tis numerous, full, crowded; frequent, repeated, common

frequentia, ae *f* concourse, throng

frequentō 1 to visit often, frequent; to assemble in numbers; to do often, repeat

fretum, ī *n* strait, channel; sea

fretus[1] **, ūs** *m* = fretum

frētus[2] 3 leaning on, supported; relying on, trusting

fricō, cuī, c(ā)tum 1 to rub

frīgeō, (xī), — 2 to be cold; to be inactive or languid; to be coldly received; be disregarded

frīgidus 3 cold, cool; inactive, feeble; dull, insipid

frīgus, oris *n* cold, frost

frondātor, ōris *m* pruner

frondeō, —, — 2 to be in leaf, become green

frondēscō, —, — 3 to put forth leaves

frondeus 3 covered with leaves

frondōsus 3 full of leaves

frōns[1] **, dis** *f* leaves, foliage; garland of leaves

frōns[2] **, tis** *f* forehead, brow, countenance; front, face

frūctuōsus 3 fruitful, productive; profitable

frūctus, ūs *m* enjoyment, satisfaction; fruit, produce; profit, income

frūgālitās, ātis *f* thrift (-iness), temperance

frūgī thrifty, temperate, honest, worthy

frūgi-fer 3 fruitful

frūmentārius 3 of or producing corn, of provisions

frūmentātiō, ōnis *f* a providing of corn, foraging

frūmentātor, ōris *m* purchaser of corn; forager

frūmentor 1 to fetch corn, forage

frūmentum, ī *n* corn, grain, wheat

fruor, frūctus sum 3 to enjoy, delight in

frūstrā *adv.* in vain; without reason

frūstrātiō, ōnis *f* deception, disappointment

frūstror 1 to deceive, disappoint, elude, frustrate

frūstum, ī *n* piece, bit

frutex, icis *m* shrub, bush

frūx, ūgis *f* (*usually pl.*) fruit, produce; result, value

fūcō 1 to dye, paint; to falsify

fūcōsus 3 counterfeit, spurious

fūcus[1] **,** ī *m* red colour; disguise, deceit

fūcus[2] **,** ī *m* drone

fuga, ae *f* flight, running away; banishment; an avoiding, shunning; speed

fugāx, ācis fleeing, swift; timid, shy; shunning

fugiō, fūgī, fugitum 3 to flee, run away; escape; to become an exile; to disappear, perish; to avoid, shun; to escape the notice of

fugitīvus 3 fleeing away,

fugitive; *subst.* ~, ī *m* runaway slave

fugitō 1 to flee, avoid, shun

fugō 1 to put to flight, drive away

fulciō, lsī, ltum 4 to prop up, support; to sustain, uphold

fulcrum, ī *n* bedpost; couch

fulgeō, lsī, — 2 (*and* **fulgō** 3) to flash, lighten; to shine, gleam

fulgor, ōris *m* lightning; brightness, splendour

fulgur, uris *n* lightning

fūlīgō, inis *f* soot

fulmen, inis *n* flash of lightning; thunderbolt; crushing blow

fulmineus 3 of lightning; destructive

fulminō 1 to lighten

fulvus 3 reddish yellow, tawny

fūmeus 3, **fūmidus** 3, **fūmifer** 3 smoking, smoky

fūmō 1 to smoke, steam

fūmōsus 3 smoky, smoked

fūmus, ī *m* smoke, steam

fūnāle, is *n* wax-torch

funda, ae *f* sling

(**fundāmen**, inis *n and*) **fundāmentum**, ī *n* foundation, base

funditor, ōris *m* slinger

funditus *adv.* from the bottom, completely, entirely

fundō[1] 1 to found, establish, confirm

fundō[2], fūdī, fūsum 3 to pour out, shed; to scatter, hurl, spread; to utter; to produce, bear; to overcome, rout

fundus, ī *m* bottom; farm

fūnebris, e of a funeral, funereal; deadly

fūnereus 3 = funebris

fūnestō 1 to pollute (by death)

fūnestus 3 in mourning; deadly, fatal

fungor, fūnctus sum 3 to perform, execute, administer, discharge

fungus, ī *m* mushroom

fūnis, is *m* rope, cord

fūnus, eris *n* funeral, burial; corpse; death, murder; destruction

fūr, fūris *m and f* thief; rogue

furca, ae *f* fork; forked prop

furci-fer, erī *m* rascal

furia, ae *f* rage, fury, madness; Goddess of Revenge, Fury

furiālis, e furious, raging

furibundus 3 furious, raging

furiō 1 to madden, infuriate

furiōsus 3 mad, furious

furnus, ī *m* oven, fireplace

furō, —, — 3 to rage, be mad *or* furious

furor[1], ōris *m* rage, madness, passion; frenzy, inspiration

fūror[2] 1 to steal, pilfer

fūrtim *adv.* by stealth, secretly

fūrtīvus 3 stolen; secret, furtive

fūrtum, ī *n* theft; a stolen thing; trick, stratagem; love intrigue

furvus 3 dark, gloomy

fuscō 1 to blacken

fuscus 3 dark, black

fūstis, is *m* cudgel, club

fūsus¹, ī *m* spindle

fūsus² 3 stretched out, extended; flowing

fūt(t)ilis, e vain, worthless, futile

G

gaesum, ī *n* long javelin

galea, ae *f* helmet

galērum, ī *n and* **galērus, ī** *m* skin cap

gallīna, ae *f* hen

gallus¹, ī *m* cock

gallus², ī *m* castrated priest of Cybele

gānea, ae *f and* **-eum, ī** *n* cookshop; brothel

gāneō, ōnis *m* glutton, debauchee

ganniō 4 to growl, snarl

garriō 4 to talk, chatter

garrulus 3 chattering, talkative

gaudeō, gāvīsus sum 2 to rejoice, be glad, delight in

gaudium, ī *n* joy, gladness, delight

gaza, ae *f* treasure, wealth

gelidus 3 icy cold

gelō 1 to freeze

gelū, ūs *n* (also **gelum, ī** *n*) frost, cold, ice

gemellus 3 = geminus

geminō 1 to double, repeat; to unite

geminus 3 double, twin; similar

gemitus, ūs *m* a groaning, sighing; roar

gemma, ae *f* bud; jewel

gemmātus 3 set with jewels

gemmeus 3 set with jewels; sparkling

gemō, uī, (itum) 3 to groan, sigh, lament

gena, ae *f* cheek

gener, erī *m* son-in-law

generātim *adv.* by kinds, by classes; in general

generō 1 to beget, produce

generōsus 3 of noble birth; superior, excellent

genetrīx, īcis *f* mother

geniālis, e nuptial; pleasant, joyous

genitālis, e fruitful, generative

genitor, ōris *m* begetter, father

genius, ī *m* tutelar deity, guardian spirit; inclination, taste

gēns, tis *f* race, family, clan; tribe, people

gentīlis, e of the same clan *or* family

genū, ūs *n* knee

genus, eris *n* birth, descent, family; noble birth; race, line; kind, sort, species; manner, style

germānitās, ātis *f* brotherhood

germānus 3 full *or* own (*brother or sister*); genuine, real

germen, inis *n* shoot, bud

gerō, gessī, gestum 3 to bear, carry, bring; to produce; to administer, manage, accomplish, perform

gestāmen, inis *n* thing carried *or* worn

gestiō 4 to exult, be joyful; to desire eagerly

gestō 1 to carry, bear, wear

gestus, ūs *m* bearing, carriage; gesture

gignō, genuī, genitum 3 to beget, produce; to occasion, cause

gingīva, ae *f* gum (in the mouth)

glaciālis, e icy, frozen

glaciēs, ēī *f* ice, frost

gladiātor, ōris *m* swordsman, gladiator

gladiātōrius 3 of gladiators

gladius, ī *m* sword

glaeba, ae *f* clod; earth

glāns, dis *f* acorn, nut; acorn-shaped ball

glārea, ae *f* gravel

glaucus 3 grey-green

glēba, ae *f* = glaeba

glīscō, —, — 3 to swell, grow

globōsus 3 spherical

globus, ī *m* ball, sphere; crowd, mass

glomerō 1 to form into a ball; to collect, assemble

glōria, ae *f* glory, fame; ambition, boasting

glōrior 1 to boast, vaunt

glōriōsus 3 glorious, famous; boasting

glūten, inis *n* glue

gnārus 3 knowing, skilled

gnāvus, *see* navus

gōrȳtus, *see* corytus

gracilis, e thin, slender, lean

gradātim *adv.* step by step

gradior, gressus sum 3 to step, walk, go

gradus, ūs *m* step, pace; advance; station, position; stage, degree, rank

grāmen, inis *n* grass; plant, herb

grāmineus 3 grassy

grammaticus 3 of grammar; *subst.* ~, ī *m* grammarian

grānārium, ī *n* granary

grand-aevus 3 old, aged

grandi-loquus 3 boastful

grandis, e aged, old; great, tall, full, strong

grandō, inis *f* hail

grānum, ī *n* grain, seed, corn

grassātor, ōris *m* rioter, footpad

grassor 1 to prowl about; to act, proceed; to attack

grātēs *f/pl.* thanks, thanksgiving

grātia, ae *f* favour, regard, friendship; kindness, courtesy; thanks, gratitude, requital; *abl.* grātiā for the sake of; grāt(i)īs for nothing, gratuitously

grātificor 1 to do a favour to, oblige; to give up, sacrifice grātiōsus 3 in favour, popular, beloved

grātor 1 = gratulor

grātuītus 3 without pay *or* reward, free, gratuitous

grātulātiō, ōnis *f* a wishing joy, congratulation; thanksgiving, festival

grātulor 1 to congratulate, rejoice

grātus 3 pleasing, agreeable, charming; thankful, grateful   [willingly]

gravātē reluctantly, unwillingly]

gravēscō, —, —, 3 to become burdened; to grow worse   [ed, full]

gravidus 3 pregnant, load-]

gravis, e heavy; burdensome, oppressive; severe, harsh; unwholesome, noxious; important, weighty; venerable; loaded, burdened

gravitās, ātis *f* heaviness, weight; importance, dignity, gravity, seriousness; oppressiveness, severity, harshness

gravō 1 to load, burden, oppress

gravor 1 to be annoyed, do unwillingly, shrink from

gregālis, e of a common soldier; *subst.* gregāles, ium *m/pl.* companions

gregārius 3 (of soldiers) common, private

gremium, ī *n* lap, bosom

gressus, ūs *m* step, course

grex, gregis *m* flock, herd; band, troop, crowd

grūs, uis *f* (*and m*) crane

gubernāc(u)lum, ī *n* helm, rudder; guidance, direction   [government]

gubernātiō, ōnis *f* direction,]

gubernātor, ōris *m* steersman, pilot; ruler

gubernō 1 to steer, pilot; to direct, govern

gula, ae *f* gullet, throat; appetite, gluttony

gurges, itis *m* whirlpool, gulf; stream, sea   [taste]

gustātus, ūs *m* (sense of)]

gustō 1 to taste; to enjoy

gutta, ae *f* drop; spot

guttur, uris *n* gullet, throat

gūtus, ī *m* narrow-necked jug

gymnasium, ī *n* physical training school; lecture-room

gynaecēum *and* -īum, ī *n* the women's apartments

gȳrus, ī *m* circle, ring circuit

H

habēna, ae *f* thong; rein, bridle; management, government

habeō, uī, itum 2 to have, hold; to keep, detain; to deliver (*orationem*); to treat, use; to think, regard; to know; to show, exhibit; to cause

habilis, e manageable,

handy; suitable, apt; nimble

habitābilis, e habitable

habitātiō, ōnis f dwelling, habitation

habitātor, ōris m inhabitant, tenant

habitō 1 to inhabit, dwell; to stay, remain

habitus, ūs m appearance; dress; condition, quality, nature [this way]

hāc adv. on this side, by

hāc-tenus adv. thus far; hitherto; to this extent

haedus, ī m young goat, kid

haereō, haesī, sum 2 to stick to, cling to, keep firm; to stand still, be perplexed or at a loss

haesitō 1 to stick fast; to hesitate

hālitus, ūs m breath, vapour

hālō 1 to breathe, be fragrant

hama-dryas, adis f wood-nymph

hāmātus 3 furnished with a hook; crooked

hāmus, ī m hook

harēna, ae f = arena

hariolor 1 to prophesy; to talk foolishly

harpagō, ōnis m hook, grappling-iron

harundineus 3 of reed

harundō, inis f reed, cane

haru-spex, icis m soothsayer, diviner

hasta, ae f staff, pole; spear, javelin; auction

hastātus 3 armed with a spear; subst. ~, ī m soldier of the first line

hastīle, is n spear-shaft, spear, stick

haud adv. not, not at all

haud-quāquam adv. not at all

hauriō, hausī, haustum 4 to draw up or out; to spill; to derive, gather; to drink in, exhaust, consume

haustus, ūs m a drawing; drinking, drink

haut = haud

hebeō, —, — 2 to be blunt or dull

hebes, etis blunt, dull; sluggish, stupid

hebēscō, —, — 3 to become blunt or dull

hebetō 1 to make blunt, dull, weak

hedera, ae f ivy

hei int. ah! woe!

hēia int. = eia

helleborus, ī m hellebore

helluō, ōnis m glutton, squanderer

helluor 1 to gormandize, devour

hem int. oh!, well!, indeed!

herba, ae f grass, herb, plant; weeds

herbidus 3 grassy

herbi-fer 3 producing grass

herbōsus 3 grassy

hercle int. by Hercules!

here adv. = heri

hērēditārius 3 hereditary, inherited

hērēditās, ātis f inheritance

hērēs, ēdis *m and f* heir, heiress

herī *adv.* yesterday

hērōicus 3 heroic, epic

hērōis, idis *f* demigoddess

hērōs, ōis *m* demigod, hero

hērōus 3 = heroicus

hesternus 3 of yesterday

heu *int.* oh!, ah!, alas!

heus *int.* ho!, there!, hark!

hiātus, ūs *m* an opening, aperture

hībernāculum, ī *n* tent for winter-quarters

hībernō 1 to pass the winter

hībernus 3 wintry, winter-...; *subst.* hīberna, ōrum *n/pl.* winter-quarters

hibiscum, ī *n* the marsh-mallow

hīc[1], (*and* hĭc), haec, hōc this; present, actual

hīc[2] *adv.* here; in this affair, on this occasion

hiemālis, e wintry

hiemō 1 to pass the winter; to be stormy

hiem(p)s, emis *f* winter, cold; storm

hilaris, e = hilarus

hilaritās, ātis *f* cheerfulness, gaiety

hilarō 1 to cheer, gladden

hilarus 3 cheerful, glad, joyful

hinc *adv.* from this place, hence; on this side, here; from this time; from this cause

hinnītus, ūs *m* a neighing

hiō 1 to gape, yawn; to be amazed; to long for

hircus, ī *m* he-goat; smell of a goat

hirsūtus 3 shaggy, bristly, rough

hirtus 3 = hirsutus

hirundō, inis *f* swallow

hīscō, —, — 3 to gape; to utter, speak

hispidus 3 shaggy, rough

historia, ae *f* inquiry, history; narrative, tale

historicus 3 historical

histriō, ōnis *m* actor, player

hiulcus 3 gaping

ho-diē *adv.* to-day, now

hodiernus 3 of this day, today's

holus(culum), holitor, *see* ol...

homi-cīda, ae *m and f* manslayer

homō, inis *m* a man; *pl.* mankind

homunciō, ōnis *m* little man

honestās, ātis *f* honour, reputation; honesty, integrity, virtue

honestō 1 to honour, dignify, adorn

honestus 3 honoured, distinguished, noble; worthy, virtuous, decent; beautiful

honor *and* -ōs, ōris *m* honour, respect, praise; public honour, office; reward, recompense; glory, ornament, grace

honōrārius 3 for the sake of honour, honorary

honōri-ficus 3 honourable

honōrō 1 to honour, respect

honōs, ōris *m* = honor

hōra, ae f hour; time, season
hordeum, ī n barley
hōrnus 3 of this year
horrendus 3 terrible, dreadful; wonderful
horreō, uī, — 2 to stand on end, bristle; to shudder (at), be afraid
horrēscō, ruī, — 3 to bristle up; to begin to shudder, be terrified (at)
horreum, ī n storehouse, barn, granary
horribilis, e terrible, dreadful, horrible
horridus 3 rough, shaggy; rude, wild, uncouth; terrible, frightful
horri-fer 3 dreadful, horrible [or terrible]
horri-ficō 1 to make rough
horri-ficus 3 dreadful, frightful
horri-sonus 3 sounding dreadfully
horror, ōris m a trembling, shuddering, dread
hortāmen, inis and hortāmentum, ī n incitement, encouragement
hortātiō, ōnis f encouragement, exhortation
hortātor, ōris m encourager, exhorter
hortātus, ūs m encouragement, exhortation
hortor 1 to incite, encourage, exhort
hortulus, ī m little garden
hortus, ī m garden
hospes, itis m guest; host; stranger

hospita, ae f hostess; guest
hospitālis, e hospitable, of a guest, of a host
hospitium, ī n hospitality, entertainment; lodging, quarters
hospitus 3 hospitable; strange, foreign
hostia, ae f victim, sacrifice
hosticus 3 hostile
hostīlis, e hostile, inimical
hostis, is m (and f) enemy, foe [hither; so far]
hūc adv. to this place,
huī int. ha!, ho!, oh!
hūmānitās, ātis f human nature, humanity; philanthropy kindness; education, refinement, good manners
hūmānus 3 human; humane, kind, gentle; well educated, refined; adv. hūmānē and hūmāniter
humilis, e low, small, slight; mean, humble, poor; base, abject
humilitās, ātis f lowness; meanness, insignificance; baseness, abjectness
humō 1 to bury, inter
humus, ī f earth, ground; loc. humī on the ground
hyacinthus, ī m kinds of red or purple flower
hydra, ae f water-serpent
hydrus, ī m water-serpent
Hymēn, enis m the god of marriage
hymenaeus, ī m marriage-song; wedding, nuptials; the god of marriage

I

iaceō, uī, (iacitūrus) 2 to lie, lie down; to lie dead; to be flat; to be despised

iaciō, iēcī, iactum 3 to throw, hurl; to establish, build

iactātiō, ōnis f a tossing, shaking, agitation; ostentation

iactō 1 to throw, hurl; to emit, spread; to utter, speak; to boast; to toss about, shake

iactūra, ae f loss, damage, sacrifice; expense

iactus, ūs m a throwing, hurling, cast

iaculātor, ōris m thrower, javelin-thrower

iaculor 1 to throw, hurl; to strike, hit

iaculum, ī n dart, javelin

iam adv. already; now; immediately; moreover

iambus, ī m iambus; iambic poem

iānitor, ōris m door-keeper

iānua, ae f door, entrance

Iānuārius 3 of January; subst. ., ī m January

iānus, ī m arched passage

iaspis, idis f jasper

ibī (and ibi) adv. in that place, there; then; in that matter

ibī-dem adv. in the same place; at that very moment

ībis, is and idis f the ibis

īcō, īcī, ictum 3 to strike, hit

ictus, ūs m blow, stroke, stab

id-circō adv. on that account, therefore

ī-dem, eadem, idem the same; likewise, also

identidem adv. repeatedly, several times

id-eō adv. on that account, therefore

idiōta, ae m ignorant person, outsider [ficient]

idōneus 3 fit, suitable, suf-f

īdūs, uum f/pl. the ides, middle of the month

iecur, oris n the liver

iēiūnium, ī n a fasting, hunger

iēiūnus 3 fasting, hungry; barren; poor, insignificant

igitur cj. then, therefore, accordingly

ī-gnārus 3 ignorant, inexperienced, unacquainted with; unknown

īgnāvia, ae f laziness, cowardice

ī-gnāvus 3 lazy, idle; cowardly

īgnēscō, —, — 3 to take fire, kindle

īgneus 3 fiery, burning hot

īgniculus, ī m little flame, spark

īgni-fer 3 fire-bearing

īgni-potēns, tis mighty in fire

ignis, is *m* fire; brightness, splendour; rage, fury; love, beloved object; destruction

ī-gnōbilis, e unknown, obscure; of low birth

ignōbilitās, ātis *f* obscurity; low birth

ī-gnōminia, ae *f* disgrace, dishonour

ignōminiōsus 3 disgraceful, degraded

ignōrantia, ae *f* ignorance

ignōrātiō, ōnis *f* = ignorantia

ī-gnōrō 1 not to know, be unacquainted with

ī-gnōscō, gnōvī, gnōtum 3 to pardon, forgive, indulge

ī-gnōtus 3 unknown, strange; low-born

īlex, icis *f* holm-oak, ilex

īlia, ium *n/pl.* groin, flanks

ī-licet *adv.* all is lost!; immediately, at once

ī-licō *adv.* on the spot, instantly, directly

īlignus 3 of the holm-oak, oaken

il-lābor 3 to fall, slip, flow into

illāc *adv.* on that side, there

il-lacrimābilis, e unwept; inexorable

il-lacrimō *and* -mor 1 to weep over, lament

il-laesus 3 unhurt, uninjured

il-laetābilis, e cheerless, sad

ille, a, ud that; he, she, it; the well-known; *adv.* illō to that place, thither

illecebra, ae *f* enticement, inducement, bait

illī *adv.* = illic

il-lībātus 3 undiminished, unimpaired

il-līberālis, e ignoble, ungenerous, mean

illic[1], aec, uc that, yonder; he, she, it

illic(c)[2] *adv.* in that place, there

il-liciō, lexī, lectum 3 to allure, entice, seduce

il-līdō, sī, sum 3 to strike against

il-ligō 1 to tie *or* fasten on, attach; to fetter, entangle

illim *adv.* = illinc

illinc *adv.* from that place, thence

il-linō 3 to smear over, anoint

il-litterātus 3 unlearned, unlettered

illō(c) *adv.* = illuc

il-lōtus 3 unwashed, dirty

illūc *adv.* to that place *or* point

il-lūcēscō, lūxī, — 3 to grow light, dawn

il-lūdō 3 to play at *or* with; to mock at, ridicule; to abuse, ruin

il-lūminō 1 to light up, adorn

il-lūstris, e lighted, bright; clear, distinct; distinguished, famous

il-lūstrō 1 to light up; to explain; to adorn

il-luviēs, ēī *f* dirt, filth

imāgō, inis *f* portrait, bust; ghost, apparition; echo; pretence, appearance; idea, conception

imbēcillitās, ātis *f* weakness, feebleness

im-bēcillus 3 weak, feeble

im-bellis, e unwarlike, peaceful

imber, bris *m* rain, storm; water, waves

im-berbis, e *and* -bus 3 beardless

im-bibō, bibī, — 3 to drink in; to conceive

imbrex, icis *f* hollow tile

imbri-fer 3 rain-bringing

im-buō, uī, ūtum 3 to wet, moisten; to steep, infect; to train, instruct

imitābilis, e imitable

imitāmen, inis *n* imitation

imitātiō, ōnis *f* a copying, imitation

imitātor, ōris *m* imitator

imitor 1 to imitate, copy; to resemble

im-mānis, e enormous, monstrous; frightful, horrible

immānitās, ātis *f* savageness, barbarity, frightfulness

im-mānsuētus 3 untamed, savage

im-mātūrus 3 unripe; premature, untimely

im-medicābilis, e incurable

im-memor, oris unmindful, forgetful, heedless

im-mēnsus 3 immense, boundless

im-merēns, tis not deserving, innocent

im-mergō 3 to dip *or* plunge into

im-meritus 3 not deserving, innocent; undeserved

im-migrō 1 to migrate *or* remove into

im-mineō, —, — 2 to project over, overhang; to threaten; to be near to; to be intent upon

im-minuō 3 to diminish, lessen; to weaken, destroy

im-misceō 2 to mix in, mingle with; to associate

im-mītis, e harsh, sour; rough, cruel, stern

im-mittō 3 to send in, dispatch, let loose; to discharge, shoot, to let grow

immō *adv.* no indeed, nay rather, by no means; indeed, assuredly

im-mōbilis, e immovable

im-moderātus immoderate, unrestrained

im-modestus 3 excessive, unrestrained

im-modicus 3 immoderate, excessive

im-molō 1 to sacrifice

im-morior 3 to die in *or* upon

im-mortālis, e undying, immortal

im-mortālitās, ātis *f* immortality

im-mōtus 3 motionless, unshaken, steadfast

im-mūgiō 4 to resound inwardly

im-mundus 3 unclean, impure

im-mūnis, e free from obligation, inactive; exempt from taxes; not sharing in, devoid of

immūnitās, ātis f exemption from burdens, immunity, privilege

im-mūnītus 3 unfortified

im-murmurō 1 to murmur at or against

im-mūtābilis, e unchangeable

im-mūtātiō, ōnis f change

im-mūtō 1 to change, alter

im-pācātus 3 warlike

im-pār, aris unequal, uneven; inferior

im-parātus 3 unprepared

im-pāstus 3 unfed, hungry

im-patiēns, tis unable to bear, impatient

im-pavidus 3 fearless, intrepid

impedīmentum, ī n hindrance, impediment; pl. baggage

im-pediō 4 to entangle, hold fast; to hinder, obstruct, check

impedītus 3 hindered, encumbered; impassable, inaccessible; difficult, intricate

im-pellō, pulī, pulsum 3 to strike, push, drive on; to rout; to incite, urge, persuade

im-pendeō, —, — 2 to overhang; to threaten, be at hand

impendium, ī n expense; interest

im-pendō, ndī, ēnsum 3 to expend, lay out; to employ, apply; impēnsus 3 expensive; earnest, great

impēnsa, ae f expense, cost

imperātor, ōris m ruler, commander

imperātōrius 3 of a general

im-perditus 3 not killed

im-perfectus 3 unfinished, incomplete

imperiōsus 3 far-ruling, powerful; imperious

im-perītia, ae f inexperience

imperītō 1 to rule, command

imperītus 3 inexperienced, ignorant

imperium, ī n command, order; power, control, authority; dominion, empire

imperō 1 to command, order; to levy, demand; to rule, govern

im-pertiō 4 to share with, bestow

im-pervius 3 impassable

impetrābilis, e attainable

im-petrō 1 to accomplish, obtain, procure

impetus, ūs m impulse, vehemence, rush; attack, assault; ardour, passion

im-pexus 3 uncombed

im-pietās, ātis f irreverence

im-piger 3 diligent, active, quick

im-pingō, pēgī, pāctum 3 to

drive at *or* into, strike, dash against

im-pius 3 ungodly, wicked

im-plācābilis, e implacable

im-plācātus 3 unappeased

im-placidus 3 ungentle, savage

im-pleō, ēvī, ētum 2 to fill up; to complete, finish, accomplish

im-plexus 3 entwined

implicātiō, ōnis *f* an entanglement

im-plicō, uī (*and* āvī), ātum *and* itum 1 to enfold, entangle; to unite, join; to perplex, embarrass

im-plōrātiō, ōnis *f* an imploring

im-plōrō 1 to implore, beseech

im-plūmis, e unfledged

im-pluvium, ī *n* small court open to the sky

im-polītus 3 unpolished

im-pōnō 3 to place upon *or* in; to embark; to impose, lay upon; to deceive; to apply, give

im-portō 1 to bring into, import; to cause

importūnitās, ātis *f* importunity, rudeness

im-portūnus 3 rude, cruel, savage

im-portuōsus 3 without a harbour

im-potēns, tis powerless, weak; without self-control, unbridled, violent

im-potentia, ae *f* ungovern-

ableness, passionateness, fury

im-prānsus 3 without breakfast, fasting

im-precor 1 to call down upon, imprecate

im-pressiō, ōnis *f* onset, attack

im-prīmīs *adv.* chiefly, especially

im-prīmō, pressī, pressum 3 to press upon, imprint, stamp

im-probitās, ātis *f* wickedness, dishonesty

im-probō 1 to disapprove, reject

im-probus 3 bad, dishonest, wicked; relentless, shameless

im-prōvidus 3 not foreseeing, heedless

im-prōvīsus 3 unforeseen, unexpected

im-prūdēns, tis not foreseeing, unaware, rash

im-prūdentia, ae *f* imprudence, ignorance

im-pūbēs, eris (*and* impūbis, e) under age, youthful

im-pudēns, tis shameless, impudent

im-pudentia, ae *f* shamelessness, impudence

im-pudīcitia, ae *f* unchasity, lewdness

im-pudīcus 3 unchaste, lewd

im-pugnō 1 to fight against, attack

impulsor, ōris *m* inciter, instigator

im-pulsus, ūs *m* push, pressure, incitement

impūne *adv.* with impunity, unpunished; safely

impūnitās, ātis *f* impunity, safety

im-pūnītus 3 unpunished; unrestrained

impūrātus 3 vile, infamous

impūritās, ātis *f* impurity, pollution

im-pūrus 3 unclean, defiled, infamous

im-putō 1 to reckon, attribute

īmus 3, *see* inferus

in *prep.* 1. with *abl.* in, on, among; during; 2. with *acc.* into, towards; till, for; in relation to, against, with a view to

in-accessus 3 inaccessible

in-aedificō 1 to build upon; to build up, barricade

in-aequālis, e unequal, unlike, changeable

in-aestimābilis, e priceless, inestimable

in-amābilis, e repulsive, odious

in-ambulō 1 to walk up and down

in-animus 3 lifeless, inanimate

in-ānis, e empty, void; deserted, abandoned; useless, vain; conceited; *subst.* ināne, is *n* empty space

in-arātus 3 unploughed

in-ārdēscō, ārsī, — 3 to kindle, glow

in-assuētus 3 unaccustomed

in-audiō 4 to hear tell

in-audītus 3 unheard of, unusual

in-augurō 1 to practise augury; to inaugurate, consecrate [gold]

in-aurō 1 to overlay with⟩

in-ausus 3 not ventured, not attempted

inb..., *see* imb...

in-caeduus 3 uncut, unfelled

in-calēscō, luī, — 3 to grow warm, glow

in-callidus 3 unskilful, unintelligent

in-candēscō, duī, — 3 to grow hot, glow

in-cānēscō, nuī, — 3 to become white *or* grey

in-cānus 3 quite white

in-cassum *adv.* in vain

in-cautus 3 incautious, heedless; unexpected; unsafe

in-cēdō, ssī, ssum 3 to go, advance, march; to happen, approach, appear

incendium, ī *n* fire, conflagration; vehemence, passion

in-cendō, ndī, ēnsum 3 to set on fire, light up; to inflame, excite

in-cēnsiō, ōnis *f* a setting on fire

in-cēnsus 3 not assessed, unregistered

in-ceptō 1 to begin, undertake

inceptum, ī *n and* -tus, ūs *m* a beginning, attempt

in-certus 3 uncertain, doubtful

in-cessō, (īvī)ī, — 3 to assault, attack

in-cessus, ūs *m* a walking, pace, gait

incestō 1 to pollute, defile

in-cestus[1] 3 impure, defiled, unchaste

in-cestus[2], ūs *m* unchastity, incest

in-cidō[1], cidī, cāsum 3 to fall into *or* upon; to attack; to incur, come upon; to happen, occur

in-cidō[2], cidī, cīsum 3 to cut into *or* through; to engrave; to break off, stop

in-cingō 3 to gird, surround

in-cipiō, *perf.* coepī, coeptum *and* inceptum 3 to begin, undertake

incitāmentum, ī *n* inducement, incentive

incitātiō, ōnis *f* an inciting; ardour, favour, energy

in-citō 1 to urge, rouse, excite

in-citus 3 rapid, swift

in-clāmō 1 to cry out to, call upon; to scold

in-clēmēns, tis unmerciful, harsh

in-clēmentia, ae *f* harshness, unkindness

in-clīnātiō, ōnis *f* inclination, favour; alteration

in-clīnō 1 to lean, bend, incline; to drive back; to sink; to change; to yield

inclitus 3 = inclutus

in-clūdō, sī, sum 3 to shut up, confine; to insert, include; to obstruct, hinder

in-clutus 3 famous, renowned

in-cōgitāns, tis inconsiderate

in-cognitus 3 unknown; unexamined

in-cohō 1 to begin, commence

incola, ae *m* (*and f*) inhabitant, resident

in-colō 3 to dwell, inhabit

in-columis, e uninjured, unharmed

incolumitās, ātis *f* safety

in-comitātus 3 unaccompanied

in-commoditās, ātis *f* inconvenience

in-commodō 1 to be troublesome, annoy

in-commodus 3 inconvenient, unsuitable; troublesome; *subst.* in-commodum, ī *n* inconvenience, trouble, injury, misfortune

in-compertus 3 unascertained, unknown

in-compositus 3 disordered, irregular

in-cōmptus 3 unkempt, unadorned; artless, rude

in-concessus 3 not allowed, forbidden

in-concinnus 3 awkward, inelegant

in-conditus 3 confused, disorderly; artless

in-cōnsīderātus 3 thoughtless, inconsiderate

in-cōnstāns, tis changeable, fickle

in-cōnstantia, ae *f* inconsistency, fickleness

in-cōnsultus 3 inconsiderate, indiscreet

in-cōnsūmptus 3 unconsumed

in-continēns, tis incontinent, intemperate

in-continentia, ae *f* incontinence

in-coquō 3 to boil in; to dye

in-corruptus 3 unspoiled, unadulterated, pure, upright

in-crēb(r)ēscō, b(r)uī, — 3 to grow, increase

in-crēdibilis, e incredible, extraordinary

in-crēmentum, ī *n* growth, increase; seed, progeny

in-crepitō 1 to call to; to reproach, rebuke

in-crepō, uī, itum 1 *intr.* to rustle, roar; to be noised abroad; *trans.* to cause to sound; to upbraid, rebuke

in-crēscō, crēvī, — 3 to grow, increase

in-cruentus 3 without bloodshed

in-cubō, uī, itum 1 to lie upon; to brood over

in-culcō 1 to impress, force upon

in-cultus¹ 3 uncultivated; disordered; unpolished, unrefined

in-cultus², ūs *m* neglect

in-cumbō, cubuī, cubitum 1 to lie upon, recline; to rush towards, fall upon; to devote oneself to; to incline towards

in-cūnābula, ōrum *n/pl.* cradle; origin

in-cūria, ae *f* carelessness, negligence

in-cūriōsus 3 careless, negligent

in-currō, (cu)currī, cursum 3 to run to; to rush at, assail; to meet, fall into

in-cursiō, ōnis *f* onset, attack; incursion

in-cursō 1 to run against, attack

in-cursus, ūs *m* = incursio

in-curvō 1 to bend, curve

in-curvus 3 bent, curved

in-cūs, ūdis *f* anvil

in-cūsō 1 to accuse, find fault with

in-custōdītus 3 unwatched, unguarded

in-cutiō, cussī, cussum 3 to strike *or* beat against; to inspire with, inflict

ind-āgō¹ 1 to reach, explore

indāgō², inis *f* an encircling, enclosing

in-de *adv.* from there, thence; from that time; from that cause

in-dēbitus 3 not owed, not due

in-decoris, e without honour, shameful

in-decōrus 3 unseemly, disgraceful

in-dēfēnsus 3 unprotected

in-dēfessus 3 unwearied; indefatigable

in-demnātus 3 uncondemned

in-dēprēnsus undetected

in-dex, icis *m* (*and f*) informer, betrayer; sign, indication; forefinger; title, inscription

indicium, ī *n* discovery, disclosure, evidence; mark, proof

in-dicō[1] 1 to point out, show, declare

in-dīcō[2] 3 to announce, proclaim; to impose, enjoin

in-dictus 3 unsaid

ind-idem *adv.* from the same place

indi-gena, ae *m and f* native, indigenous

indigentia, ae *f* need, want, insatiableness

ind-igeō, uī, — 2 to need, want; to long for

indiges, etis *m* native god, deified hero

in-dignāns, tis impatient, indignant

in-dignātiō, ōnis *f* indignation, displeasure

in-dignitās, ātis *f* shamefulness, indignity; indignation

in-dignor 1 to consider unworthy, be offended *or* indignant at

in-dignus 3 unworthy,

not deserving; innocent; shameful, undeserved

indigus 3 needy, in want of

in-dīligēns, tis careless

in-dīligentia, ae *f* carelessness, negligence

ind-ipīscor, deptus sum 3 to attain, obtain

in-discrētus 3 indistinguishable

in-dō, didī, ditum 3 to put into, give, apply

in-docilis, e unteachable; ignorant

in-doctus 3 untaught; unskilful

ind-olēs, is *f* inborn quality, nature; disposition, talents

in-dolēscō, luī, — 3 to feel pain, be grieved

in-domitus 3 untamed, wild

in-dormiō 4 to sleep upon *or* over

in-dōtātus 3 without a dowry, without gifts

in-dūcō 3 to draw over *or* on; to bring in, lead up; to move, persuade, seduce

in-ductiō, ōnis *f* a bringing in; intention, inclination

indulgēns, tis kind, indulgent

indulgentia, ae *f* kindness, forbearance; tenderness, affection

in-dulgeō, lsī, (ltum) 2 to be forbearing, yield, allow; to give oneself up to

in-uō, uī, ūtum 3 to put on, dress in; to cover, clothe; to entangle in-dūrēscō, ruī, — 3 to become hard

in-dūrō 1 to make hard, harden

industria, ae *f* diligence, activity, industry; (de) industriā intentionally

industrius 3 diligent, active

indūtiae, ārum *f/pl.* truce, armistice

in-edia, ae *f* abstinence from food, fasting

in-ēluctābilis, e inevitable

in-ēmptus 3 unbought

in-eō, iī, itum, īre to go in, enter; to begin, undertake

ineptia, ae *f* (*mostly pl.*) silliness, absurdity

ineptiō 4 to play the fool

in-eptus 3 unsuitable, unfit; silly, awkward

in-ermis, e *and* -mus 3 unarmed, defenceless

in-ers, tis without skill; lazy, idle

inertia, ae *f* inactivity, laziness

in-ēscō 1 to allure with a bait

in-ēvītābilis, e inevitable

in-exercitātus 3 untrained

in-exhaustus 3 unexhausted, inexhaustible

in-exōrābilis, e inexorable

in-expertus 3 inexperienced; untried, untested

in-expiābilis, e inexpiable; implacable

in-explēbilis, e insatiable

in-explētus 3 insatiable

in-explicābilis, e impassable; inexplicable

in-explōrātus 3 unexplored

in-expugnābilis, e impregnable, unconquerable

in-exstīnctus 3 unextinguished

in-exsuperābilis, e insurmountable

in-extrīcābilis, e inextricable

īn-fabrē *adv.* unskilfully

īn-facētus 3 dull, stupid

īn-fācundus 3 not eloquent

īnfāmia, ae *f* ill fame, shame, disgrace

īn-fāmis, e infamous, disgraceful

īn-fāmō 1 to disgrace; to accuse

īn-fandus 3 unspeakable, abominable

īn-fāns, tis speechless; young, little; *subst.* īnfāns, tis *m and f* (little) child

īnfantia, ae *f* lack of eloquence; infancy

īn-fatuō 1 to befool, infatuate

īn-faustus 3 unlucky, unpropitious

īn-fectus 3 not done, not made, unaccomplished

īn-fēcundus 3 unfruitful

īn-fēlīcitās, ātis *f* ill luck, unhappiness

īn-fēlīx, īcis unfruitful; unhappy, unlucky; ill-boding

īn-fēnsus 3 hostile

īnferiae, ārum *f/pl.* sacrifices in honour of the dead

īnferior, ius, *see* īnferus

īnfernus 3 lower; of the underworld

in-ferō, intulī, illātum, inferre to bring, carry in or to; to offer; to bring forward, produce, cause

īnferus 3 below, beneath; subst. īnferī, ōrum m/pl. the dead, the lower world; comp. īnferior, ius lower, inferior; superl. īnfimus 3 and īmus 3 lowest, last

īn-fēstus 3 unsafe; hostile, dangerous

īn-fīcētus 3 = īnfacetus

īn-ficiō, fēcī, fectum 3 to dye, colour; to taint, infect, corrupt

īn-fīdēlis, e unfaithful

īn-fīdēlitās, ātis f faithlessness [erous)

īn-fīdus 3 faithless, treach-]

īn-fīgō 3 to fasten in, affix; to impress

īnfimus 3, see īnferus

īn-findō 3 to cut into

īn-fīnītus 3 boundless, endless, countless

īn-firmitās, ātis f weakness, feebleness

īn-firmō 1 to weaken, refute, annul

īn-firmus 3 weak, feeble; timorous, inconstant; trivial

īn-fit he (she) begins

īnfitiae, ārum f/pl. a denying

īnfitiātor, ōris m denier

īnfitior 1 to deny, disown

īn-flammō 1 to set on fire; to inflame, excite

īn-flātus 3 swollen; pompous, haughty

īn-flectō 3 to bend, curve; to change, affect

īn-flētus 3 unwept

īn-filgō, xī, ctum 3 to strike against; to inflict

īn-flō 1 to blow into, swell; to inspire, encourage

īn-fluō, ūxī, — 3 to flow in

īn-fodiō 3 to bury

īn-fōrmis, e shapeless, hideous

īn-fōrmō 1 to form, shape; to conceive; to describe; to instruct

īn-fortūnātus 3 unfortunate, unhappy

īnfortūnium, ī n misfortune, calamity

īnfrā 1. adv. below, beneath; 2. prep. with acc. below, beneath; inferior to

īn-frāctus 3 exhausted, dejected

īn-fremō 3 to growl, bellow

īn-frendō 3 to gnash

īn-frēnis, e (and -us 3) unbridled

īn-frēnō 1 to bridle, harness

īn-frequēns, tis infrequent, in small numbers, not filled with

īn-frequentia, ae f small number, scantiness

īn-fringō, frēgī, frāctum 3 to break off; to weaken, subdue

īnfula, ae f (sacred) fillet

īnfumus = īnfimus

īn-fundō 3 to pour in or out; to spread over

īn-fuscō 1 to make dark; to stain, corrupt

in-geminō 1 to (re)double, repeat

in-gemīscō, muī, — 3 to groan over, lament

in-gemō 3 = ingemisco

in-generō 1 to implant; to produce

in-geniōsus 3 naturally gifted, talented; suited

in-genium, ī *n* natural quality, disposition, character; talents, abilities; man of genius

in-gēns, tis vast, huge, immense

ingenuitās, ātis *f* free birth; uprightness, frankness

in-genuus 3 native; free-born; noble, upright, frank

in-gerō 3 to throw *or* heap on; to inflict, force upon

in-glōrius 3 inglorious

in-gluviēs, ēī *f* gullet, maw

in-grāt(i)īs *adv.* unwillingly

in-grātus 3 unpleasant; ungrateful; unprofitable

in-gravēscō, —, — 3 to become heavier; to grow worse

in-gravō 1 to make heavy, make worse

in-gredior, gressus sum 3 to go into, enter; to walk, proceed; to begin, undertake

in-gressiō, ōnis *f* = ingressus

in-gressus, ūs *m* an entering; a walking, gait; a beginning

in-gruō, uī, — 3 to fall upon, assail

inguen, inis *n* the groin

in-gurgitō 1 (with *se*) to plunge in; to gormandize

in-habilis, e unmanageable, unwieldy

in-haereō, sī, (sum) 2 to stick fast, cling

in-haerēscō, haesī, haesum 3 = inhaereo

in-hibeō, uī, itum 2 to hold back, restrain; to row backwards; to practise, use

in-hiō 1 to gape (at); to regard longingly

in-honestus 3 dishonourable, shameful

in-honōrātus 3 not honoured, disregarded; unrewarded

in-horreō, —, — 2 to stand erect, bristle

in-horrēscō, ruī, — 3 to rise erect, bristle up; to shake, tremble

in-hospitālis, e inhospitable

inhospitus 3 inhospitable

in-hūmānitās, ātis *f* cruelty; rudeness, incivility, unkindness

in-hūmānus 3 rude, savage, cruel; uncultivated, uncivil

in-humātus 3 unburied

in-iciō, iēcī, iectum 3 to throw *or* put in *or* on to; to inspire, cause; to mention

inimīcitiae, ārum *f/pl.* (*rarely sg.*) enmity, hostility

inimīcō 1 to make hostile

in-imīcus 3 hostile, injurious; *subst.* ~, ī *m* enemy, foe

inīquitās, ātis *f* unevenness; unfavourableness, difficulty; unfairness, injustice

in-īquus 3 uneven, steep; unfavourable; excessive; unjust; hostile; unwilling

in-itiō 1 to initiate, admit

initium, ī *n* a going in; beginning; elements; secret mysteries

in-itus, ūs *m* arrival; beginning

in-iūcundus 3 unpleasant, harsh

in-iungō 3 to join *or* fasten to; to inflict, impose

in-iūrātus 3 unsworn

iniūria, ae *f* injury, injustice, wrong

iniūriōsus 3 unjust, hurtful

in-iūrius 3 wrongful, unjust

in-iussū without orders

in-iussus 3 unbidden

in-iūstitia, ae *f* injustice

in-iūstus 3 unjust; harsh, severe

inl..., inm..., *see* ill..., imm...

in-nāscor 3 to be born, grow in *or* upon

in-natō 1 to swim into *or* upon

in-nectō 3 to tie, fasten together

in-nītor 3 to lean upon

in-nō 1 to swim upon

in-nocēns, tis guiltless, innocent; harmless

innocentia, ae *f* innocence; uprightness

in-nocuus 3 = innoxius

in-nōtēscō, tuī, — 3 to become known

in-noxius 3 harmless; innocent; unhurt

in-nūbō 3 to marry into

in-nubus 3 = innuptus

in-numerābilis, e innumerable

in-numerus 3 numberless

in-nuō, uī, — 3 to nod to

in-nuptus 3 unmarried, virgin

in-observātus 3 unobserved

in-offēnsus 3 unobstructed, undisturbed

in-olēscō, lēvī, litum 3 to grow upon

inopia, ae *f* want, need, scarcity, helplessness

in-opīnāns, tis not expecting, unaware

in-opīnātus (*and* in-opīnus) 3 unexpected

in-ops, opis helpless, poor, needy, weak

in-ōrdinātus 3 not arranged

in-ōrnātus 3 unadorned

inp..., *see* imp...

inquam (*defective vb.*) to say

in-quiētus 3 restless, unquiet

in-quīnō 1 to stain, pollute, defile

in-quīrō, sīvī, sītum 3 to search for, examine

in-quīsītiō, ōnis *f* investigation, inquiry

in-quīsitor, ōris *m* investigator

inr..., *see* irr...

īn-sānābilis, e incurable

insānia, ae f madness; frenzy

īn-sāniō 4 to be mad, rage, rave

īn-sānus 3 mad, raving; monstrous, excessive

īn-satiābilis, e insatiable

īn-sciēns, tis not knowing, unaware

īn-scientia, ae f ignorance, inexperience

īnscītia, ae f unskilfulness, ignorance

īn-scītus 3 unskilful, blundering [ignorant]

īn-scius 3 not knowing,

īn-scrībō 3 to write upon, inscribe; to ascribe

īn-scrīptiō, ōnis f inscription, title

īn-sculpō 3 to engrave

īn-sectātiō, ōnis f pursuit; a railing at

īn-sector 1 to pursue, attack

īn-senēscō, nuī, — 3 to grow old in

īn-sepultus 3 unburied

īn-sequor 3 to follow after, pursue; to censure, reproach

īn-serō[1], **sēvī, situm** 3 to ingraft, implant; insitus 3 innate, natural

īn-serō[2], **ruī, rtum** 3 to put in, insert, introduce

īn-sertō 1 to put into

īn-serviō 4 to serve; to be devoted to

īn-sīdō, sēdī, sessum 2 to sit upon, be settled, occupy

īnsidiae, ārum f/pl. ambush, plot, trap, treachery

īnsidiātor, ōris m waylayer, lurker

īnsidior 1 to lie in ambush; to plot against

īnsidiōsus 3 deceitful, cunning, dangerous

īn-sīdō, sēdī, sessum 3 to sit down upon; to become fixed; to occupy

īnsigne, is n token, mark; badge, decoration; standard

īn-signiō 4 to make conspicuous, distinguish

īn-signis, e remarkable, distinguished, excellent

īnsignītus 3 distinguished, conspicuous

īn-siliō, luī, — 4 to leap or spring in or on

īn-simulātiō, ōnis f accusation, charge

īn-simulō 1 to charge, accuse

īn-sinuō 1 to push forward, penetrate [ish]

īn-sipiēns, tis unwise, foolīn-sistō, stitī, — 3 to stand upon; to enter on; to pursue; to persist, apply oneself; to pause, stop

īnsitiō, ōnis f a grafting

īnsitīvus 3 grafted; pretended

īn-sociābilis, e with whom no alliance is possible

īn-solēns, tis unusual; excessive; haughty, arrogant

īn-solentia, ae f strangeness; pride, arrogance

in-solitus 3 unaccustomed; unusual

in-somnia, ae f sleeplessness

in-somnis, e sleepless

in-somnium, ī n dream

in-sonō, uī, — 1 to resound, make a noise

in-sōns, tis innocent

in-spectō 1 to look at, view

in-spērāns, tis not hoping, not expecting

in-spērātus 3 unhoped for, unexpected

in-spergō, rsī, rsum 3 to sprinkle on

in-spiciō, spexī, spectum 3 to look upon, examine, inspect; to investigate

in-spīrō 1 to blow upon; to inspire, rouse; to instil

in-stabilis, e unstable, unsteady, inconstant

īnstar n (indecl.) likeness, resemblance; with gen. in the form of, like, as large as

īnstaurātiō, ōnis f renewal

īn-staurō 1 to establish; to renew, repeat

in-sternō 3 to cover over, spread upon

īn-stīgō 1 to incite, stimulate

īn-stillō 1 to drop in, instil

īn-stimulō 1 to arouse, incite

īn-stīnctus, ūs m incitement

īn-stinguō, īnxī, īnctum 3 to incite, impel

īnstita, ae f border of a lady's robe

īnstitor, ōris m hawker, pedlar

īn-stituō, uī, ūtum 3 to put into, fix, set; to build, construct; to draw up (troops); to designate; to undertake, begin; to determine, resolve; to introduce, institute; to teach, educate

īnstitūtiō, ōnis f arrangement; instruction

īnstitūtum, ī n custom, usage; purpose; decree

īnstō, stitī, (stātūrus) 1 to stand on; to press upon, urge, pursue; to be at hand, approach; to be intent upon, strive after

īn-strūctiō, ōnis f array

īnstrūctus 3 drawn up; provided with, furnished; instructed

īnstrūmentum, ī n tool, instrument, material; ornament; means

īn-struō 3 to build in; to draw up, set in order; to prepare, provide, equip; to teach

īn-suāvis, e unpleasant, disagreeable

īn-suēscō 3 to accustom oneself; to accustom

īn-suētus 3 unaccustomed; unusual

īnsula, ae f island; tenement house

īnsulsitās, ātis f absurdity, bad taste

īn-sulsus 3 without taste, insipid, absurd

in-sultō 1 to leap upon, jump; to taunt, insult

in-sum, infuī, inesse to be in *or* on, be contained in, belong to

in-sūmō 3 to take for, apply, expend

in-suō 3 to sew in

in-super *adv.* above, on the top; moreover

in-superābilis, e insurmountable; unconquerable [self]

in-surgō 3 to rise, lift one-

in-susurrō 1 to whisper to

in-tābēscō, buī, — 3 to melt; to pine away

in-tāctus 3 untouched, uninjured; unattempted; chaste

in-tēctus 3 uncovered

in-teger, gra, grum untouched, whole, unhurt; fresh, vigorous; undecided, open; healthy, sane, unbiassed; spotless, pure, honest

in-tegō 3 to cover, protect

integritās, ātis *f* soundness; purity, honesty, innocence

integrō 1 to renew, repeat

in-tegumentum, ī *n* covering, disguise

intellēctus, ūs *m* perception, understanding

intellegēns, tis intelligent, discerning

intellegentia, ae *f* intelligence, understanding, taste

intel-legō, ēxī, ēctum 3 to perceive, understand

in-temerātus 3 inviolate, pure

in-temperāns, tis immoderate, unrestrained

in-temperantia, ae *f* intemperance

in-temperiēs, ēī *f* excess, inclemency

in-tempestīvus 3 untimely, unseasonable

in-tempestus 3 timeless; unhealthy; nox intempesta the dead of night

in-temptātus 3 untried

in-tendō, ndī, ntum 3 to stretch, extend; to lay, fasten; to direct, aim; to intend, purpose

in-tentiō, ōnis *f* a straining, attention

in-tentō 1 to stretch *or* hold out threateningly

in-tentus 3 intent, eager

in-tepēscō, puī, — 3 to become warm

inter *prep.* with *acc.* (*space or relation*) between, among; (*time*) between, during

inter-calāris, e *and* -ius 3 inserted, intercalary

inter-calō 1 to intercalate; to defer

inter-cēdō 3 to go between; to intervene, happen; to protest against, oppose

interceptor, ōris *m* interceptor, embezzler

inter-cessiō, ōnis *f* intervention

inter-cessor, ōris *m* preventer; mediator

inter-cīdō[1], cīdī, cīsum 3 to
cut through *or* down
inter-cīdō[2], cīdī, — 3 to fall
between; to perish, be
forgotten
inter-cipiō, cēpī, ceptum 3
to intercept; to interrupt,
hinder; to snatch away
inter-clūdō, sī, sum 3 to
shut off, hinder; to separate
inter-currō, (cu)currī, cursum 3 to intercede; to
mingle   [tween]
inter-cursō 1 to run be-
inter-cursus, ūs *m* intervention
inter-dīcō 3 to forbid, prohibit; *subst.* interdictum,
ī *n* prohibition; praetor's
decree
inter-dictiō, ōnis *f* a pro-
hibiting
inter-diū *adv.* by day
inter-dum *adv.* sometimes
inter-eā *adv.* meanwhile;
however
inter-eō, iī, itum, īre to
perish, go to ruin
inter-equitō 1 to ride between
inter-fector, ōris *m* murderer
inter-ficiō, fēcī, fectum 3 to
destroy, kill
inter-for 1 to interrupt
inter-fūsus 3 flowing be-
tween
inter-iaceō, —, — 2 to lie
between
inter-iciō, iēcī, iectum 3 to
throw, place between *or*
among

interim *adv.* meanwhile
inter-imō, ēmī, ēmptum 3
to destroy, kill
interior, ius inner, interior;
more intimate
inter-itus, ūs *m* destruction,
ruin
inter-linō 3 to smear be-
tween; to falsify by era-
sure
inter-lūceō, xī, — 2 to shine
forth
inter-luō, —, — 3 to flow
between
inter-minor 1 to threaten,
forbid
inter-misceō 2 to mingle
inter-missiō, ōnis *f* a leaving
off, interval
inter-mittō 3 to separate; to
leave off, interrupt; to let
pass
inter-morior 3 to die off; to
faint away
inter-necīnus (-necīvus) 3
murderous, destructive
inter-neciō, ōnis *f* massacre,
destruction
inter-nōscō, nōvī, — 3 to
distinguish between
inter-nūntius, ī *m* and -tia,
ae *f* negotiator, go-be-
tween
internus 3 inward, internal
interpellātiō, ōnis *f* inter-
ruption
inter-pellō 1 to interrupt;
to prevent, hinder
interpolō 1 to furbish; to
falsify
inter-pōnō 3 to place be-
tween, insert, introduce;

to let pass; to allege as a reason

inter-pres, etis *m* and *f* negotiator, mediator; explainer, interpreter

interpretātiō, ōnis *f* explanation

interpretor 1 to explain, interpret, understand

inter-rēgnum, ī *n* interval between two reigns

inter-rēx, rēgis *m* regent

in-territus 3 undaunted

inter-rogātiō, ōnis *f* question, examination

inter-rogō 1 to ask, question; to examine judicially, accuse

inter-rumpō 3 to interrupt; to break asunder

inter-saepiō 4 to hedge in, shut off, separate

inter-scindō 3 to tear asunder, separate

inter-sum, fuī, esse to be between; to intervene; to be different; to put a stop to   [tion]

interventus, ūs *m* interven-

inter-texō 3 to interweave

inter-trīmentum, ī *n* loss, damage

inter-vallum, ī *n* distance, interval; pause

inter-veniō 4 to intervene, break in upon; to put a stop to

interventus, ūs *m* interven-

inter-vertō 3 to embezzle, intercept

inter-vīsō, sī, sum 3 to take a look

in-testābilis, e infamous

in-testātus 3 intestate

intestīnus 3 inward, internal; *subst.* **intestina, ōrum** *n/pl.* (*rarely sg.*) intestines

in-texō 3 to interweave, surround

intibum, ī *n* endive

intimus 3 inmost, deepest; intimate

in-tolerābilis, e unbearable

in-tolerandus 3 unbearable

in-tolerāns, tis impatient of, intolerant

in-tolerantia, ae *f* insolence

in-tonō, uī, — 1 to thunder; to resound

in-tōnsus 3 unshorn; uncouth

in-torqueō 2 to twist round; to hurl, launch

intrā *prep.* with *acc.* within, into; during; less than

in-tractābilis, e unmanageable, fierce

in-tractātus 3 not handled; unattempted

in-tremō, uī, — 3 to tremble

in-trepidus 3 undaunted, undisturbed

intrō¹ *adv.* inside, within

intrō² 1 to enter, penetrate

intrō-dūcō 3 to lead *or* bring into, introduce

intro-eō, iī, itum, īre to go into, enter

intrō-ferō, tulī, lātum, ferre to carry in

intrō-gredior, gressus sum 3 to enter

intro-itus, ūs *m* entrance; beginning

intrō-mĭttō 3 to send in, let in

intrōrsum *and* -sus *adv.* inwards; inside, within

intrō-rumpō 3 to break into

intrō-spĭciō, spexī, spectum 3 to look into, inspect, examine

in-tueor 2 to look at, gaze at; to consider, contemplate

in-tŭmēscō, muī, — 3 to swell up

intŭmus 3 = intĭmus

intus *adv.* within, inside

in-tūtus 3 unguarded, unsafe

in-ultus 3 unavenged, unpunished

in-umbrō 1 to overshadow, darken

in-undō 1 to overflow, inundate

in-ung(u)ō 3 to anoint

in-urbānus 3 rustic, unpolished

in-ūrō 3 to burn in; to brand, imprint

in-ūsĭtātus 3 unusual

in-ūtĭlis, e useless; hurtful

in-vādō 3 to go into; to undertake; to rush upon, attack; to seize

in-vălĭdus 3 weak, feeble

in-vehō 3 to carry in; me inveho, *or* P. to attack; to ride *or* drive into

in-vĕniō 4 to come upon, meet with; to find out, discover; to devise

inventor, ōris *m and* -trīx, īcis *f* inventor, discoverer

inventum, ī *n* invention, discovery

in-vĕnustus 3 without charm, ungraceful

in-vergō, —, — 3 to pour upon

in-vertō 3 to turn upside down, turn about; to pervert

investīgātor, ōris *m* inquirer, investigator

in-vestīgō 1 to trace out, search into

in-vĕterāscō, āvī, — 3 to grow old, become fixed

in-vĕterātus 3 long-established

in-vĭcem *adv.* by turns; mutually, on both sides

in-victus 3 unconquered; unconquerable

in-vĭdeō 2 to envy, grudge

invĭdia, ae *f* envy, jealousy, ill will, unpopularity

invĭdiōsus 3 envious; enviable; hateful

invĭdus 3 envious, jealous

in-vĭgĭlō 1 to watch over

in-viŏlābĭlis, e inviolable

in-viŏlātus 3 unhurt; inviolable

in-vīsĭtātus 3 unseen; new, strange

in-vīsō, sī, (sum) 3 to visit

in-vīsus 3 hated, hateful

invītāmentum, ī *n* allurement, incitement

invītātiŏ, ōnis *f* invitation; challenge

in-vīto 1 to invite, entertain; to allure, entice

in-vītus 3 unwilling, reluctant

in-vius 3 impassable

in-vocātus 3 uncalled, uninvited

in-vocō 1 to call upon

in-volō 1 to fly at, attack

involūcrum, ī n veil, covering

in-volvō 3 to roll upon; to wrap up, envelop

iō int. ho!, hurrah!

iocor 1 to jest, joke

iocōsus 3 humorous, facetious

ioculāris, e = iocosus

iocus, ī m jest, joke

ipse, a, um himself, herself, itself; just, very, exactly

īra, ae f anger, wrath, rage

īrācundia, ae f wrath, anger

īrācundus 3 irascible, angry

īrāscor, — 3 to grow angry

īrātus 3 angry, enraged

ir-remeābilis, e from which there is no return

ir-reparābilis, e irrecoverable

ir-rēpō 3 to creep into

ir-requiētus 3 restless

ir-rētiō 4 to entangle

ir-revocābilis, e irrevocable

ir-rīdeō 2 to laugh at

ir-rīgātiō, ōnis f a watering

ir-rigō 1 to water, irrigate, flood

irriguus 3 supplying water; well-watered

ir-rīsiō, ōnis f = irrisus

ir-rīsus, ūs m mockery, derision

ir-rītābilis, e irritable, excitable

irrītāmen, inis n and irrītāmentum, ī n incitement, incentive

irrītātiō, ōnis f incitement, irritation

irrītō 1 to excite, incite, provoke

ir-ritus 3 invalid, void; vain, useless

ir-rogō 1 to propose against; to impose, inflict

ir-rōrō 1 to bedew, moisten

ir-rumpō 3 to break or rush into; to intrude

ir-ruō, uī, — 3 to rush in, invade

irruptiō, ōnis f invasion, incursion

is, ea, id he, she, it; this or that; such

iste, a, ud that (of yours)

istic[1], aec, oc or uc = iste

istic[2] adv. there, here

istinc adv. from there, thence

istō(c) adv. thither, there

istūc adv. thither [way]

ita adv. thus, so; and so, consequently; yes, just so

ita-que cj. and so, therefore, for that reason

item adv. likewise, also

iter, itineris n journey, march, passage; road, path; method, means

iterō 1 to repeat

iterum adv. a second time, again

itidem *adv.* in like manner

itiō, ōnis *f* a going, travelling

iuba, ae *f* mane; crest

iubar, aris *n* radiance; sunshine

iubeō, iussī, iussum 2 to order, command; to ratify; to designate

iūcunditās, ātis *f* pleasantness, delight, cheerfulness

iūcundus 3 pleasant, agreeable, delightful

iūdex, icis *m (f)* judge; juryman; critic

iūdicātiō, ōnis *f* judgment

iūdiciālis, e *and* iūdiciārius 3 judicial, judiciary

iūdicium, ī *n* judicial investigation, trial; decision, opinion, judgment; discernment, discretion

iūdicō 1 to judge, decide, condemn; to resolve, determine; to consider, think; to declare

iugālis, e yoked together; nuptial

iūgerum, ī *n* a land measure (*about 2/3 of an acre*)

iūgis, e perpetual, never failing

iungō 1 to bind, marry

iugulō 1 to cut the throat, murder; to ruin, destroy

iugulum, ī *n (and* -us, ī *m)* throat

iugum, ī *n* yoke; pair, team; ridge, mountain heights [July]

Iūlius 3 of July; *subst.* ~, ī *f*

iūmentum, ī *n* beast of burden

iūnctūra, ae *f* a joining, connection

iuncus, ī *m* (bul)rush

iungō, iūnxī, iūnctum 3 to yoke, join, unite

iūnior, ōris comparatively young; younger

iūniperus, ī *f* juniper-tree

Iūnius 3 of June; *subst.* ~, ī *f* June

iūrgium, ī *n* quarrel, altercation

iūrgō 1 to quarrel, brawl, scold

iūris-dictiō, ōnis *f* administration of justice, jurisdiction

iūrō 1 to swear, affirm on oath; iūrātus 3 on oath

iūs[1], iūris *n* broth, soup

iūs[2], iūris *n* right, law, justice; privilege, authority; court of justice; iūre rightfully, justly

iūs iūrandum, iūris iūrandī *n* oath

iussū by order

iussum, ī *n* order, command, ordinance

iūstitia, ae *f* justice, equity

iūstitium, ī *n* judicial vacation, holiday

iūstus 3 just, fair, lawful, proper; *subst.* iūsta, ōrum *n/pl.* due forms and observances

iuvenālis, e youthful

iuvenca, ae *f* heifer; young woman

iuvencus, ī *m* young bullock

iuvenīlis, e youthful

iuvenis, is young; *subst.*

iuvenis, is *m* young man, youth

iuventa, ae (*and* iuventās, ātis) *f* age of youth

iuventūs, ūtis *f* time of youth; young people

iuvō, iūvī, iūtum 1 to delight, please; to help, aid

iuxtā 1. *adv.* near, close; in like manner, equally; 2. *prep.* with *acc.* near to, close to

K

Kal. = Kalendae, *see* Calendae

L

labāscō, —, — 3 to waver, yield

labe-faciō 3 = labefacto

labe-factō 1 to shake, weaken, ruin

labellum, ī *n* little lip

lābēs, is *f* a falling; ruin, destruction; stain, disgrace

labō 1 to totter, waver; to be undecided

lābor[1], lāpsus sum 3 to glide, slip, fall down; to vanish, pass away; to be mistaken, commit a fault

labor[2], ōris *m* work, toil; hardship, trouble, distress

labōri-fer 3 toil-enduring

labōriōsus 3 full of toil; industrious

labōrō 1 to work, toil, strive; to suffer, be troubled, be in distress; to work out, produce

labōs, ōris *m* = labor[2]

labrum[1], ī *n* lip, edge

lābrum[2], ī *n* bathing-tub, basin

labyrinthus, ī *m* labyrinth

lac, lactis *n* milk

lacer, era, erum mangled, torn

lacerātiō, ōnis *f* a mangling

lacerna, ae *f* cloak

lacerō 1 to mangle, tear to pieces; to censure, wound; to waste, ruin

lacerta, ae *f* lizard

lacertōsus 3 muscular

lacertus[1], ī *m* lizard

lacertus[2], ī *m* upper arm; strength, vigour

lacessō, īvī *and* iī, ītum 3 to excite, irritate, arouse

lacrima, ae *f* tear

lacrimābilis, e lamentable

lacrimō 1 to weep

lacrimōsus 3 lamentable; plaintive

lacrimula, ae *f* little tear

lacruma, -mō = lacrima, mo

lactēns, tis sucking (milk); young; sappy, juicy

lacteus 3 milky; milk-white

lactō 1 to contain milk

lacūna, ae *f* hole, pit, pool

lacūnar, āris *n* panelled ceiling

lacus, ūs *m* basin, tank, vat; lake, pool

laedō, sī, sum 3 to hurt, wound; to insult, annoy

laena, ae *f* cloak, mantle

laetābilis, e joyful, glad

laetitia, ae *f* joy, gladness

laetor 1 to be glad, rejoice

laetus 3 glad, joyful; pleasing, prosperous

laevus 3 left, on the left side; awkward, foolish; unfavourable, unfortunate; *subst.* laeva, ae *f* left hand

lagoena, ae *f* flagon

lagōna, ae *f* = lagoena

lambō 3 to lick, lap, wash

lāmenta, ōrum *n/pl.* lamentation

lāmentābilis, e lamentable, mournful

lāmentātiō, ōnis *f* a lamenting

lāmentor 1 to wail, moan; to bewail

lām(i)na *and* lammina, ae *f* thin plate, leaf, layer; money, coin

lampas, adis *f* torch, light, lamp

lāna, ae *f* wool; working in wool

lancea, ae *f* lance, spear

lāneus 3 woollen

langueō, guī, — 2 to be faint, languid, weary

languēscō, guī, — 3 to become faint, weak, languid

languidus 3 faint, weak, languid, dull

languor, ōris *m* weariness, feebleness, dullness

lāni-ficus 3 working in wool

lāni-ger 3 wool-bearing

laniō 1 to tear to pieces, mangle

lanista, ae *m* trainer of gladiators; instigator

lanius, ī *m* butcher

lanterna, ae *f* lantern, lamp

lānūgō, inis *f* down

lanx, cis *f* plate, dish; scale of a balance

lapidātiō, ōnis *f* a stoning

lapideus 3 of stone

lapidō 1 to rain stones

lapidōsus 3 stony

lapillus, ī *m* pebble; precious stone

lapis, idis *m* stone; milestone; jewel

lāpsō 1 to stumble

lāpsus, ūs *m* a gliding, flowing, falling

laqueāre, āris *n* = lacunar

laqueātus 3 panelled

laqueus, ī *m* noose, snare, trap

Lār, Laris *m* tutelary god of a house *or* city; home, hearth

lārdum, ī *n* bacon

largior 4 to give abundantly, bestow, grant; to bribe

largitās, ātis *f* liberality

largītiō, ōnis *f* a giving freely, bestowing; bribery

largītor, ōris *m* bestower, granter; briber

largus 3 liberal, bountiful;

abundant, plentiful; *adv.*
largē *and* largiter
lascīvia, ae *f* playfulness,
wantonness
lascīviō 4 to be wanton,
sport
lascīvus 3 playful, wanton
lassitūdō, inis *f* weariness
lassō 1 to make weary, tire
lassus 3 wearied, tired, faint
latebra, ae *f* hiding-place,
retreat; pretext
latebrōsus 3 full of hiding-
places, hidden
lateō, uī, — 2 to lie hid *or*
concealed; to be sheltered;
to remain unknown
later, eris *m* brick, tile
laterīcius 3 made of bricks
latex, icis *m* a liquid, water
latibulum, ī *n* hiding-place,
refuge
lātiō, ōnis *f* a bringing
lātitō 1 to be hidden
lātitūdō, inis *f* breadth,
width
lātor, ōris *m* mover, pro-
poser
lātrātor, ōris *m* barker, dog
lātrātus, ūs *m* a barking
lātrō¹ 1 to bark (at); to
growl, roar
lātrō², ōnis *m* highwayman,
robber
latrōcinium, ī *n* robbery,
piracy; villany
latrōcinor 1 to practise robbery
lātus¹ 3 broad, wide,
spacious
lātus², eris *n* side, flank;
the lungs; the body

laudābilis, e praiseworthy
laudātiō, ōnis *f* praise,
eulogy
laudātor, ōris *m* praiser,
eulogizer
laudō 1 to praise, commend
laurea, ae *f* = laurus
laureātus 3 crowned with
bay
laureus 3 of bay
laurus, ī (*and* -ūs) *f* bay-
tree; laurel (bay) wreath
laus, dis *f* praise, glory;
praiseworthy action, merit
lautia, ōrum *n/pl.* public
entertainment of am-
bassadors
lautumiae, ārum *f/pl.* stone-
quarry; prison
lautus 3 neat, elegant,
splendid
lavō, lāvī, lautum, lōtum *or*
lavātum 1 (*and* 3) to wash,
bathe; to wet
laxāmentum, ī *n* mitigation,
alleviation
laxō 1 to unloose, slacken;
to extend; to relax, relieve
laxus 3 loose, relaxed; wide,
open
lea *and* leaena, ae *f* lioness
lebēs, ētis *m* basin, cauldron
lectīca, ae *f* litter
lēctiō, ōnis *f* a selecting;
a reading
lectī-sternium, ī *n* feast
offered to the gods
lēctitō 1 to read often
lēctor, ōris *m* reader
lectulus, ī *m dim. of* lectus¹
lectus¹, ī *m* bed, couch

5*

lēctus[2] 3 chosen, picked

lēgātiō, ōnis f embassy

lēgātum, ī n legacy, bequest

lēgātus, ī m ambassador; deputy, lieutenant

lēgi-fer 3 law-giving

legiō, ōnis f a Roman legion; army

legiōnārius 3 of a legion

lēgitimus 3 lawful, legal; right, proper

lēgō[1] 1 to depute, send as an ambassador, commission; to bequeath

legō[2], lēgi, lēctum 3 to collect, gather; to pass along or over; to choose, select; to read, recite

legūmen, inis n pulse, bean

lembus, ī m cutter, boat

lemurēs, um m/pl. ghosts, spectres

lēna, ae f procuress, bawd

lēnīmen, inis n alleviation, solace [soothe]

lēniō 4 to alleviate, soften,

lēnis, e soft, smooth, mild, gentle, kind

lēnitās, ātis f mildness, softness, gentleness

lēnō, ōnis m pander, procurer

lēnōcinium, ī n a pandering; enticement

lentēscō 3 to become sticky or pliant

lentitūdō, inis f slowness; dullness

lentō 1 to bend

lentus 3 tenacious, tough, pliant; slow, sluggish

leō, ōnis m lion

lepidus 3 pleasant, charming, elegant

lepōs, ōris m pleasantness, charm; wit

lepus, oris m hare

lētālis, e deadly, fatal

lēti-fer 3 = letalis

lētō 1 to kill

lētum, ī n death

levāmen, inis and -mentum, ī n alleviation

levātiō, ōnis f alleviation

lēvis[1], e smooth; beardless, youthful

levis[2], e light; gentle, mild; quick, swift; trifling, unimportant; fickle, inconstant

levitās, ātis f lightness; mobility; inconstancy

lēvō[1] 1 to smooth, polish

levō[2] 1 to lighten, diminish; to relieve, console; to raise, lift up

lēx, lēgis f stipulation, terms; law, legal enactment; precept, rule

lībāmen, inis n libation, offering

lībella, ae f small coin ($^{1}/_{10}$ denarius)

libellus, ī m little book; petition; programme, announcement

libēns, tis willing, with pleasure; adv. libenter

liber[1], brī m bark of a tree; book, writing

liber[2], era, erum free, unrestricted

līberālis, e of freedom;

gentlemanly, noble, kind, generous

liberālitās, ātis *f* noble character; liberality, generosity

liberātiō, ōnis *f* a releasing, acquittal

liberātor, ōris *m* deliverer, liberator

liberī, ōrum *or* **um** *m/pl.* children

liberō 1 to set free, release; to acquit

liberta, ae *f* freedwoman

libertās, ātis *f* freedom, liberty, independence

libertīnus 3 of the class of freedmen; *subst. m, f* freedman, -woman

libertus, ī *m* freedman

libet, libuit *and* **libitum est 2** it pleases, is agreeable

libīdinōsus licentious, wanton

libīdō, inis *f* desire, pleasure, caprice; lust

libō 1 to touch, taste; to diminish; to offer, make a libation

lībra, ae *f* balance, scales; the Roman pound

lībrāmentum, ī *n* weight

lībrārius 3 of books; *subst.* ~, **ī** *m* copyist, scribe

lībrō 1 to poise, balance; to swing, hurl

lībum, ī *n* cake

liburna, ae *f* light warship

licentia, ae *f* freedom, licence; licentiousness, lawlessness

liceō, uī, — 2 to be valued

liceor, itus sum 2 to bid, offer a price for

licet, licuit *and* **licitum est 2** it is allowed, permitted; *cf.* even if, although

licium, ī *n* (*usu. pl.*) thread

lictor, ōris *m* lictor, official attendant of a magistrate

lignātor, ōris *m* wood-cutter

ligneus 3 wooden

lignor 1 to procure wood

lignum, ī *n* wood, firewood; tree

ligō[1], ōnis *m* mattock, hoe

ligō[2] 1 to tie, bind

ligūr(r)iō 4 to lick up, feed daintily; to lust after

ligustrum, ī *n* privet

līlium, ī *n* lily

līma, ae *f* file; a polishing

limbus, ī *m* hem, edge

līmen, inis *n* threshold; door, entrance; dwelling

līmes, itis *m* boundary; path, way, road

līmō 1 to file, polish; to file off, diminish

līmōsus 3 muddy

līmus[1], ī *m* mud, mire, dirt

līmus[2] 3 aslant, sideways

līnea, ae *f* linen thread, plumbline; bound, limit; line

līneāmentum, ī *n* (*usu. pl.*) outline, features

līneus 3 flaxen, linen

lingua, ae *f* tongue; speech, language

līniāmentum, ī *n* = **līneāmentum**

līni-ger 3 linen-wearing

linō, lēvī, litum 3 to be-smear, anoint

linquō, līquī, — 3 to leave, forsake, abandon

linter, tris f boat, skiff; trough

linteus 3 of linen; subst. linteum, ī n linen cloth, sail

līnum, ī n flax, linen; thread, fishing-line; net

lippus 3 with sore eyes; blind

lique-faciō 3 to melt, dissolve

liquēns (and lī-), tis liquid

liqueō, liquī or licuī, — 2 to be clear, evident

liquēscō, —, — 3 to melt (away)

liquidus 3 flowing, liquid; clear, bright, pure; adv. liquidō clearly, certainly

liquor¹, ōris m a fluid

līquor², — 3 to flow, melt away

līs, lītis f quarrel, dispute; lawsuit

lītātiō, ōnis f auspicious sacrifice

lītigiōsus 3 quarrelsome

lītigō 1 to dispute, quarrel

lītō 1 to sacrifice under favourable auspices; to propitiate

lītoreus 3 of the shore

littera, ae f letter of the alphabet; pl. letter, epistle; document, record; literature; learning, culture

litterātus 3 learned, liberally educated

litterula, ae f small letter (of the alphabet); pl. (knowledge of) literature

litūra, ae f erasure; blot

lītus, oris n sea-shore, beach; bank

lituus, ī m curved staff of an augur; trumpet

līveō, —, — 2 to be bluish, dark, livid

līvidus 3 bluish, blue-grey, livid; envious

līvor, ōris m bluish colour, livid spot; envy, malice

lixa, ae m sutler, camp-follower [leasing]

locātiō, ōnis f a letting out,]

locō 1 to place, put; to lease, farm out; to give out on contract

loculī, ōrum m/pl. receptacle, coffer, satchel

locuplēs, ētis rich, wealthy; trustworthy

locuplētō 1 to enrich

locus, ī m place, spot; station, post; district, region; topic, subject; position, rank; opportunity, occasion; condition, situation

lolium, ī n darnel

long-aevus 3 aged, old

longē adv. (of space) far off, at a distance; by far, very much; (of time) long, for a long time

longinquitās, ātis f length, extent, long duration

longinquus 3 distant, far, remote; long in duration, tedious longitūdō, inis *f* length

longus 3 long; vast; far off, remote; of long duration, tedious

loquācitās, ātis *f* talkativeness

loquāx, ācis talkative, garrulous

loquēla, ae *f* speech, language

loquor, cūtus sum 3 to speak, say

lōrīca, ae *f* leather cuirass; breast-work

lōrīcātus 3 armed with a cuirass

lōrum, ī *n* thong; rein; whip

lōtos and -us, ī *f* lotus

lubēns, lubet, lubīdō = libens, libet, libido

lūbricus 3 slippery; quickly moving, fleeting; uncertain, hazardous

lucellum, ī *n* small gain, little profit

lūceō, xī, — 2 to be bright, shine; to be conspicuous *or* clear

lucerna, ae *f* lamp

lūcēscō, lūxī, — 3 to grow light, become day

lūcidus 3 clear, bright

lūci-fer 3 light-bringing; *subst.* ~, ī *m* the morning-star; day

lūcīscō 3 = lucesco

lucror 1 to gain, win, acquire

lucrum, ī *n* gain, profit, advantage

luctātiō, ōnis *f* a wrestling, contest

lūcti-ficus 3 mournful, doleful

luctor 1 to wrestle, struggle

lūctuōsus 3 mournful, sorrowful

lūctus, ūs *m* sorrow, mourning

lūcubrātiō, ōnis *f* a working by lamp-light

lūcubrō 1 to work by night

lūculentus 3 bright; distinguished, splendid

lūcus, ī *m* grove, wood

lūdibrium, ī *n* derision, mockery; laughing-stock

lūdibundus 3 playful; without effort

(lūdicer), cra, crum sportive; belonging to public shows; *subst.* lūdicrum, ī *n* plaything; public games, scenic show

lūdificātiō, ōnis *f* a deriding, mockery

(lūdi-ficō *and*) lūdi-ficor 1 to ridicule, mock; to thwart [stage-player]

lūdiō, ōnis *and* lūdius, ī *m*]

lūdō, sī, sum 3 to play, sport; to ridicule, deceive

lūdus, ī *m* play, game; *pl.* public games, shows; jest, joke; school

luēs, is *f* plague, pestilence

lūgeō, xī, — 2 to mourn, lament

lūgubris, e of mourning, mournful; disastrous

lumbus, ī *m* the loin

lūmen, inis *n* light; lamp, torch; eye; glory, ornament

lūna, ae *f* the moon

lūnāris, e lunar, moonlike

lūnō 1 to bend into a crescent

luō, luī, — 3 to expiate, atone for; to suffer punishment

lupa, ae *f* she-wolf; harlot

lupātus 3 with wolf's teeth

Lupercālia, i(or)um *n/pl.* festival of Lupercus

lupīnus 3 of a wolf; *subst.* **lupīnus, ī** *m and* **lupīnum, ī** *n* lupin

lupus, ī *m* wolf

lūridus 3 sickly yellow, ghastly, lurid

luscus 3 one-eyed

lūsiō, ōnis *f* playing, game

lūsor, ōris *m* player; humourist

lūstrālis, e of expiation

lūstrātiō, ōnis *f* purification; a wandering about

lūstrō[1] 1 to light up, illuminate

lūstrō[2] 1 to purify by expiation; to review, survey; to go over, traverse

lūstrum[1], ī *n* den, lair; forest; brothel; debauchery

lūstrum[2], ī *n* expiatory

sacrifice; period of (five) years   [dalliance]

lūsus, ūs *m* play, game,|

lūteus[1] 3 of mud *or* clay; worthless

lūteus[2] 3 orange, yellow

lutulentus 3 muddy, dirty

lutum[1], ī *n* mud, dirt; clay

lūtum[2], ī *n* dyer's weed, yellow colour

lūx, lūcis *f* light, brightness; daylight, day; life; publicity; help, encouragement

luxuria, ae *f and* **-iēs, ēī** *f* luxuriant growth; riotous living, extravagance

luxuriō *and* **-or 1** to be rank of luxuriant, abound in; to be playful; to revel, run riot

luxuriōsus 3 luxuriant; dissolute, voluptuous, excessive

luxus, ūs *m* luxury, debauchery; splendour

lychnus, ī *m* light, lamp

lympha, ae *f* clear water

lymphātus 3 insane, frantic

lynx, cis *m* and *f* lynx

lyra, ae *f* lyre, lute; lyric poetry, song

lyricus 3 lyric

M

macellum, ī *n* food-market

macer, cra, crum lean, meagre

māceria, ae *f* wall

mācerō 1 to weaken, enervate; to tease, torment

māchina, ae *f* machine, engine; device, artifice

māchināmentum, ī *n* machine

māchinātiō, ōnis *f* machine, engine

māchinātor, ōris *m* engineer; contriver, inventor

māchinor 1 to contrive, scheme, plot

maciēs, ēī *f* leanness, thinness

macte (*voc. of* **mactus**) glorified; **macte virtute** hail to thee!, good luck!, well done!

mactō 1 to honour; to afflict, punish; to sacrifice, kill

macula, ae *f* spot, stain, blemish, fault

maculō 1 to stain, pollute, disgrace

maculōsus 3 spotted; stained, polluted

made-faciō 3 to wet, moisten

madeō 2 to be wet, be soaked

madēscō, duī, — 3 to become wet

madidus 3 wet, moist, steeped

maenas, adis *f* bacchante

maereō, —, — 2 to mourn, grieve, bewail

maeror, ōris *m* mourning, grief

maestitia, ae *f* sadness, grief, dejection

maestus 3 sad, dejected, gloomy

māgālia, ium *n/pl.* huts, cottages

mage = magis

magicus 3 magical, magic

magis *adv.* more, in a higher degree; rather

magister, trī *m* master, chief, director; teacher

magisterium, ī *n* direction, superintendency

magistra, ae *f* directress, instructress

magistrātus, ūs *m* civil office, magistracy; a magistrate

magn-animus 3 high-minded, high-spirited

magnificentia, ae *f* grandeur, splendour, greatness; pomposity

magni-ficus 3 splendid, fine, sumptuous; noble, distinguished

magni-loquus 3 boastful

magnitūdō, inis *f* greatness, size; number, quantity

magn-opere (*and* **magnō opere**) *adv.* very much, greatly, earnestly

magnus 3 (*comp.* **māior, ius**; *superl.* **maximus**) (*of size*) large, great, tall, long; (*of number or quantity*) abundant, much; (*of value*) high; (*of time*) aged, old; strong, intense; important; high, noble, powerful; proud, boastful; *subst.* **māiōrēs, ōrum** *m/pl.* fathers, ancestors

magus, ī *m* magician

māiestās, ātis *f* majesty, grandeur, dignity; high-treason

māior, māius, *see* **magnus**

Māius 3 of May; *subst.* ~, **ī** *m* May

māla, ae *f* cheek, jaw

male *adv.* (*comp.* **pēius,** *superl.* **pessimē**) badly, wickedly; unfortunately, unsuccessfully; excessively, greatly; scarcely, not at all

male-dīcō 3 to speak ill of, abuse

male-dictum, ī *n* abusive language, curse

male-dicus 3 abusive

maleficium, ī *n* evil deed, wickedness, injury

male-ficus 3 vicious, wicked

malevolentia, ae *f* ill will, malevolence

male-volus 3 ill-disposed, malevolent

malignitās, ātis *f* malice; niggardliness

malignus 3 wicked, malicious; niggardly, scanty

malitia, ae *f* malice, roguery

malitiōsus 3 wicked, malicious

malleolus, ī *m* fire-dart

mālō, māluī, mālle to choose rather, prefer

mālum¹, ī *n* apple

malum², ī *n* evil, misfortune, calamity; hurt, harm, injury

malus¹ 3 (*comp.* **pēior, us,** *superl.* **pessimus** 3) bad, wicked, wrong; unfortunate; injurious, destructive

mālus², ī *m* pole, mast; *f* apple-tree

malva, ae *f* mallow

mamilla, ae *f* breast

mamma, ae *f* breast

manceps, cipis *m* purchaser, contractor

mancipium, ī *n* right of possession; slave

mancipō 1 to sell

mancus 3 maimed, defective

mandātū *abl.* by order

mandātum, ī *n* charge, order, commission

mandō 1 to commit to the charge of, order, commission

mandō², ndī, ānsum 3 to chew, eat

māne *n* (*indecl.*) the early morning; *adv.* early in the morning

maneō, mānsī, mānsum 2 to stay, remain, last, persist; to await, expect

mānēs, ium *m/pl.* ghosts of the departed; the lower world

mangō, ōnis *m* slave-dealer

manicae, ārum *f/pl.* long sleeves; handcuffs

mani-festus 3 convicted of; clear, plain

manipulāris, -plus, *see* **manipul...**

manipulāris, e of a company; *subst.* **manipulāris, is** *m* common soldier

manipulātim *adv.* in maniples

manipulus, ī *m* a handful, bundle; maniple *or* company of footsoldiers

mannus, ī *m* small Gallic horse

mānō 1 to flow, run, trickle; to spread

mānsiō, ōnis f a remaining, stay [tame]

mānsuē-faciō 3 to make

mānsuēscō, suēvī, suētum 3 to become tame or gentle

mānsuētūdō, inis f mildness, gentleness, clemency

mānsuētus 3 gentle, mild, quiet

mantēle, is n towel, napkin

mantica, ae f wallet

manubiae, ārum f/pl. money from booty, spoils, plunder

manubrium, ī n handle, hilt

manū-mittō 3 to set free

manu-pretium, ī n pay, reward

manus, ūs f hand; force, power; band, body of men

mapālia, ium n/pl. huts, cottages

mappa, ae f napkin

marceō, —, — 2 to be faint, feeble, languid

marcēscō, —, — 3 to become languid or weak

mare, is n the sea, ocean

margarīta, ae f pearl

margō, inis m (and f) border, edge

marinus 3 = maritimus

marīta, ae f, see maritus

marītālis, e matrimonial, nuptial

maritimus (-umus) 3 of the sea, marine

maritus 3 nuptial, wedded; subst. ~, ī m husband, -a, ae f wife

marmor, oris n marble; statue; surface of the sea

marmoreus 3 made of marble; marble-like

Mārs, tis m the God of War; war, battle; fortune of war

Mārtius 3 of Mars; subst. ~, ī March

mās, maris m man; adj. male, manly

masculus 3 male, manly

massa, ae f lump, mass

māter, tris f mother; origin, source

mātercula, ae f little mother

māteria, ae and -iēs, ēī f stuff, materials, timber; subject, theme; occasion, cause; disposition, abilities

māternus 3 maternal, motherly

mātrimōnium, ī n wedlock, marriage

mātrōna, ae f wife, matron; woman of rank, lady

mātrōnālis, e of a matron

mātūrēscō, ruī, — 3 to become ripe

mātūritās, ātis f ripeness, perfection

mātūrō 1 to make ripe; to hasten, accelerate

mātūrus 3 ripe, mature; advanced in life; seasonable, timely, early, premature

mātūtīnus 3 of the morning, early

maximē (-umē) adv. in the highest degree, most, especially; just, precisely; certainly

maximus (-umus) 3, *superl.* of magnus

meātus, ūs *m* a going, course, path

medeor, — 2 to heal, cure; to relieve, restore

medicāmen, inis *and* medicāmentum, ī *n* remedy, medicine; drug, poison

medicīna, ae *f* the healing art, medicine; remedy

medicō 1 to add drugs *or* poison to; to dye

medicor 1 to heal, cure

medicus 3 healing; *subst.* ~, ī *m* physician, surgeon

mediocris, e middling, moderate, ordinary

mediocritās, ātis *f* moderation, mean

meditātiō, ōnis *f* preparation, exercise

medi-terrāneus 3 inland

meditor 1 to contemplate, reflect; to plan, design; to study, practise

medius 3 middle, in the midst; neutral, undecided; *subst.* medium, ī *n* the middle, centre; the public, community

medulla, ae *f* marrow, inmost part

mehercule *int.* by Hercules!

mēiō, —, — 3 to make water

mel, mellis *n* honey, sweetness

melior, *comp. of* bonus

mellītus 3 honey-sweet

melos (*pl.* melē) *n* tune, song

membrāna, ae *f* skin; parchment

membrum, ī *n* limb; part, portion

meminī —, isse to remember, think of

memor, oris mindful, remembering, recalling

memorābilis, e memorable, remarkable

memoria, ae *f* memory, recollection; record, historical account; period of recollection, time

memoriter *adv.* with a good memory

memorō 1 to call to mind, mention, relate

mendācium, ī *n* lie, falsehood

mendāx, ācis given to lying, false; feigned, counterfeit

mendīcitās, ātis *f* beggary

mendīcō 1 to beg

mendīcus 3 beggarly, needy; *subst.* ~, ī *m* beggar

mendōsus 3 faulty, incorrect

mendum, ī *n* fault, error

mēns, tis *f* mind, intellect, understanding; character, heart, soul; spirit, courage; thought, plan, purpose

mēnsa, ae *f* table; meal, course

mēnsārius, ī *m* banker

mēnsis, is *m* month

mēnsor, ōris *m* measurer, surveyor

mēnstruus 3 monthly, lasting a month

mēnsūra, ae f a measuring, measure; extent, limit

mentiō, ōnis f a calling to mind, mention

mentior, ītus sum 4 to lie, feign, deceive, cheat

mentum, ī n chin

meō 1 to go, pass

merācus 3 unmixed, pure

mercātor, ōris m trader, merchant

mercātūra, ae f trade, commerce

mercātus, ūs m trade, traffic; market, fair

mercēn(n)ārius 3 hired, paid, mercenary

mercēs, ēdis f reward, price, pay, wages; rent, revenue

mercor 1 to trade, buy

mereō 2 and **mereor, ritus sum** 2 to deserve, merit; to earn, acquire

meretrīcius 3 of a harlot

meretrīcula, ae f prostitute

meretrix, īcis f prostitute

mergō, rsī, rsum 3 to dip in, immerse, sink, overwhelm

mergus, ī m diver, gull

merīdiēs, ēī m midday; south

meritō adv. deservedly, justly

meritum, ī n merit, worth; kindness, service; fault, offence

mersō 1, intens. of **mergo**

merus 3 unmixed, pure; nothing but, mere; genuine, true; subst. **merum, ī** n unmixed wine

merx, cis f goods, merchandise

messis, is f harvest, crops

messor, ōris m reaper

met (enclitic suffix) self, own

mēta, ae f turning post, goal; end, extremity

metallum, ī n metal; mine

mētior, mēnsus sum 4 to measure; to distribute; to pass over, traverse; to estimate, value

metō (messuī) messum 3 to reap, gather, harvest; to cut down, destroy

mētor 1 to measure out, lay out

metuō, uī, — 3 to fear

metus, ūs m fear, dread, anxiety

meus 3 my, mine

mīca, ae f grain, bit

micō, cuī, — 1 to quiver, shake; to shine, flicker, flash

migrātiō, ōnis f removal, migration

migrō 1 to depart, emigrate

mīles, itis m (f) soldier; army

mīliēs = **millies**

mīlitāris, e of a soldier, military, warlike

mīlitia, ae f military service, warfare; soldiers, militia

mīlitō 1 to serve as a soldier

mīlle indecl. (pl. **mīlia, ium**) n a thousand; innumerable

mīllēsimus 3 the thousandth

mīlliē(n)s *adv.* a thousand times

mīluus (mīlvus), ī *m* bird of prey, kite

mīma, ae *f* mime-actress

mīmus, ī *m* mime-actor; mime, farce

mina, ae *f* a mina (*100 denarii*)

minae, ārum *f/pl.* threats, menaces

mināx, ācis overhanging; threatening

mingō, nxī, (n)ctum 3 to make water

minimus 3, *superl. of* parvus

minister, trī *m* attendant, servant, assistant

ministerium, ī *n* attendance, service, employment

ministra, ae, *fem. of* minister

ministrō 1 to attend, serve; to furnish, provide

minitābundus 3 threatening

minitor 1, *intens. of* minor[1]

minor[1] 1 to project; to threaten

minor[2], us, *comp. of* parvus

minuō, uī, ūtum 3 to lessen, diminish; to weaken, abate

minusculus 3 rather little

minūtātim *adv.* little by little, gradually

minūtus 3 little, small, trifling

mīrābilis, e wonderful, marvellous; extraordinary, strange

mīrāculum, ī *n* wonder, marvel

mīrandus 3 wonderful

mīrātor, ōris *m* admirer

mīri-ficus 3 = mirabilis

mirmillō, ōnis *m* gladiator with Gallic arms

mīror 1 to wonder at; to admire

mīrus 3 = mirabilis

misceō, cuī, xtum 2 to mix, mingle, join; to disturb, throw into confusion

misellus 3, *dim. of* miser

miser, era, erum wretched, unfortunate, lamentable; worthless

miserābilis, e miserable, wretched; plaintive

miserandus 3 = miserabilis

miserātiō, ōnis *f* pity, compassion

misereor, ritus sum 2 to feel pity, commiserate

miserēscō, —, — 3 = misereor

miseret me I feel pity for

miseria, ae *f* wretchedness, misery, distress

misericordia, ae *f* compassion, pity, mercy

miseri-cors, dis pitiful, merciful

miseror 1 to lament; to pity

missilis, e that may be thrown; *subst.* missile, is *n* missile, javelin

missiō, ōnis *f* a sending away; discharge from service

missus, ūs *m* a sending, dispatching

mītēscō *and* -īscō, —, — 3 to grow mild, gentle, ripe

mītigō 1 to make mild, soothe, assuage

mītis, e mellow, ripe; mild, gentle, kind

mitra, ae *f* head-band, turban

mitto, mīsī, missum 3 to send; to throw, hurl; to produce; to put forth, utter; to let go, release, dismiss; to omit, pass over

mōbilis, e movable, quick, pliant; changeable, inconstant

mōbilitās, ātis *f* mobility, quickness; fickleness

moderāmen, inis *n* rudder, helm

moderātiō, ōnis *f* guidance, government; moderation, self-control

moderātor, ōris *m* manager, ruler

moderātrīx, īcis *f* controller

moderātus 3 moderate, restrained

moderor 1 to restrain, limit; to govern, direct

modestia, ae *f* moderation, discretion, modesty

modestus 3 moderate, gentle, modest, discreet

modicus 3 moderate, temperate; mean, scanty

modius, ī *m* (*a measure, about 2 gallons*)

modo *adv.* only, but; *with subj.* if only, provided that; (*of time*) just now, lately

modulor 1 to modulate, sing, play

modulus, ī *m* measure

modus, ī *m* measure, quantity; rhythm, melody; bound, limit, moderation; way, manner

moecha, ae *f* adulteress

moechor 1 to commit adultery

moechus, ī *m* adulterer

moenia, ium *n/pl.* city-walls, ramparts, fortifications; city

mola, ae *f* millstone, grindstone; spelt

molāris, is *m* millstone; molar tooth

mōlēs, is *f* heavy mass, bulk; massive structure, foundation; weight, power; difficulty, labour

molestia, ae *f* trouble, annoyance, vexation

molestus 3 troublesome, grieving, annoying

mōlīmen, inis *and* mōlīmentum, ī *n* exertion, effort

mōlior 4 to set in motion, remove, wield; to set about, attempt; to build, make; to toil

mollēscō, —, — 3 to become soft

molliō 4 to soften; to mitigate, moderate

mollis, e soft, pliant; mild, tender, gentle; effeminate, weak

mollitia, ae *f and* mollitiēs, ēī *f* softness, tenderness; weakness, effeminacy molō, uī, itum 3 to grind

mōmentum, ī n weight, influence, cause, importance; motion, alteration; moment, instant

moneō, uī, itum 2 to remind, warn, advise; to teach, foretell

monēta, ae f mint; coin

monīle, is n necklace

monimentum, ī n = monumentum

monitor, ōris m admonisher, reminder; teacher

monitum, ī n advice; prophecy

monitus, ūs m = monitum

mōns, tis m mountain

mōnstrātor, ōris m introducer, inventor

mōnstrō 1 to show, point out; to ordain, appoint

mōnstrum, ī n omen, miracle; monster

montānus 3 of a mountain, mountainous

mont(u)ōsus 3 mountainous

monumentum, ī n memorial, monument; chronicle, record

mora, ae f delay; obstruction, hindrance

mōrātus 3 mannered, constituted [ease]

morbus, ī m sickness, dis-

mordāx, ācis biting, stinging, sharp

mordeō, momordī, mørsum 2 to bite, chew; to pain, hurt

mordicus adv. by biting, with the teeth

moribundus 3 dying; mortal

mōri-geror 1 to comply with, humour

morior, mortuus sum 3 to die; to pass away

moror 1 to delay, linger; to hinder

mōrōsus 3 peevish, morose

mors, tis f death; corpse

morsus, ūs m a biting, bite; sting, pain

mortālis, e mortal, human; subst. mortālis, is m man, human being

morti-fer 3 deadly

mortuus 3, see morior

mōs, mōris m habit, custom; will, humour; quality, nature; pl. conduct, morals, character

mōtō 1 to move about

mōtus, ūs m motion, movement; dancing; passion, emotion; inspiration; tumult, commotion

moveō, mōvī, mōtum 2 to move, stir, disturb, remove; to excite, inspire; to trouble, torment; to cause, begin

mox adv. soon, presently; then, thereupon

mūcrō, ōnis m sharp point, sword

mūgiō 4 to low, bellow, roar

mūgītus, ūs m a lowing, bellowing, roaring

mūla, ae f she-mule

mulceō, sī, sum 2 to stroke; to soothe, delight

mulcō 1 to beat, maltreat

mulgeō, lsī, — 2 to milk

muliebris, e of a woman, feminine; effeminate

mulier, eris *f* woman, wife

muliercula, ae *f* (weak) woman

mūliō, ōnis *m* muleteer

mullus, ī *m* red mullet

mulsum, ī *n* honey-wine

multa, ae *f* penalty, fine

multāticius 3 accruing from fines

multifāriam *adv.* in many places

multi-modīs *adv.* in many ways

multi-plex, icis manifold, numerous, various; versatile, changeable

multiplicō 1 to multiply, increase

multitūdō, inis *f* multitude, crowd, mob

multō 1 to punish

multum *adv.* much, very much, greatly; *comp.* **plūs, plūris** *n* more, a greater part; *adv.* **plūs** more, in a higher degree; *superl. adv.* **plūrimum** very much, for the most part

multus 3 much, many, abundant, extensive; *comp.* **plūrēs, a** more; *superl.* **plūrimum** 3 very much, most

mūlus, ī *m* mule

munditia, ae *f* cleanliness; neatness, elegance

mundus¹ 3 clean, nice, neat, elegant

mundus², ī *m* the universe, world; mankind

mūneror 1 to reward, bestow

mūnia *n/pl.* duties, functions

mūni-ceps, cipis *m (and f)* citizen of a *munciipium*; fellow-citizen

mūnicipālis, e belonging to a *municipium*, provincial

mūnicipium, ī *n* self-governing town

mūni-ficus 3 liberal, bountiful

mūnīmen, inis *and* **mūnīmentum, ī** *n* defence, fortification

mūniō 4 to wall, fortify, defend

mūnītiō, ōnis *f* a fortifying; fortification, rampart

mūnītor, ōris *m* fortifier, engineer

mūnus, eris *n* duty, office, service; present, gift; public show

mūnusculum, ī *n* small gift

mūrālis, e of a wall, mural

mūrex, icis *m* purple-fish; purple dye

murmillō, ōnis *m* = **mirmillo**

murmur, uris *n* murmur, humming, roaring

murmurō 1 to murmur, roar

murra, ae *f* myrrh-tree, myrrh

murtētum, ī *n* grove of myrtles

murteus 3 of myrtle

murtus, ī (*and* **ūs**) *f* myrtle

mūrus, ī *m* wall

mūs, mūris *m* mouse

Mūsa, ae *f* a muse; song, poem, sciences

mūscōsus 3 mossy

mūscus, ī *m* moss

mūsicus 3 musical, poetic

mussitō 1 to mutter, grumble

mussō 1 to murmur, mutter; to wonder, brood

mustum, ī *n* must

mūtābilis, e changeable

mūtātiō, ōnis *f* change, alteration; interchange

mutilō 1 to maim, mutilate

mutilus 3 maimed, mutilated

mūtiō 4 = **muttio**

mūtō 1 to move; to change, alter; to exchange

muttiō 4 to mutter, mumble

mūtuātiō, ōnis *f* a borrowing

mūtuor 1 to borrow, obtain

mūtus 3 dumb, silent

mūtuus 3 borrowed, lent; mutual, reciprocal

myrīca, ae *f* tamarisk

myrmillō, ōnis *m* = **mirmillo**

myrrha, ae *f* = **murra**

myrt..., *see* **murt...**

mystērium, ī *n* secret, mystery

mysticus 3 mystic, secret

N

naenia, ae *f* = **nenia**

naevus, ī *m* birth-mark, mole

Nāias, adis *and* **Nāis, idis** *f* water-nymph, Naiad

nam *cj.* for

nam-que *cj.* = **nam**

nancīscor, nactus *and* **nanctus sum** 3 to light upon, meet with, find, obtain

narcissus, ī *m* narcissus, daffodil

nardum, ī *n and* **nardus, ī** *f* nard

nāris, is *f* nostril; *pl.* the nose

nārrātiō, ōnis *f* a relating

nārrō 1 to tell, relate

nāscor, nātus sum 3 to be born, spring from, rise

nāsus, ī *m* nose

nātālicius 3 of a birthday

nātālis, e of birth; *subst.* **nātālis, is** *m* birthday

nātiō, ōnis *f* nation, people

natis, is *f* (*usu. pl.*) buttocks

nātīvus 3 inborn, natural

natō 1 to swim, float; to be flooded

nātūra, ae *f* nature, quality, character; laws of nature

nātūrālis, e natural, by birth

nātus[1] 3 born, destined; *subst. m* son, *f* daughter

(nātus[2]**) ūs** *m* birth, age); **grandis nātū** old, aged

nau-archus, ī *m* captain of a vessel

nau-fragium, ī *n* shipwreck; ruin, loss; remnants

nau-fragus 3 shipwrecked, ruined; causing shipwreck

nausea, ae *f* sea-sickness, nausea

nauseō 1 to be sea-sick, vomit

nauta, ae *m* sailor

nauticus 3 nautical, naval

nāvālis, e of ships, naval; *subst.* **nāvāle, is** *n* (*usu pl.*) dockyard, rigging

nāvicula, ae *f* little ship, boat

nāviculārius, ī *m* shipowner

nāvi-fragus 3 causing shipwreck

nāvigābilis, e navigable

nāvigātiō, ōnis *f* a sailing, voyage

nāvigium, ī *n* vessel, ship

nāvigō 1 to sail, voyage, navigate

nāvis, is *f* vessel, ship

nāvita, ae *m* = *nauta*

nāviter, *adv. of* navus

nāvō 1 to do zealously, accomplish

nāvus 3 active, diligent

nē¹ *int.* verily, truly

-ne² *interrog. particle*

nē³ *particle of negation and cj.* not, lest, so that not

nebula, ae *f* mist, cloud, smoke

nebulō, ōnis *m* worthless fellow, idler

nec *and* **neque** and not, nor, neither

necessāriō *adv.* necessarily

necessārius 3 necessary, inevitable; *subst.* **~, ī** *m* relation, friend

necesse esse to be necessary *or* inevitable

necessitās, ātis *f* necessity, compulsion; fate; need; want

necessitūdō, inis *f* necessity, need; relationship, friendship

nec-ne or not

necō 1 to kill, slay

nec-opīnātus 3 unexpected

nectar, aris *n* nectar, drink of the gods

nectō, nex(u)ī, nexum 3 to tie, bind, connect; to fetter, confine; *subst.* **nexum, ī** *n* assignment of the person for debt

nē-cubi *cj.* lest anywhere

nē-dum *cj.* much less, not to speak of; *adv.* not to say, much more

ne-fandus 3 = *nefarius*

ne-fārius 3 abominable, impious

ne-fās *n* (*indecl.*) unlawful, criminal, sinful thing

ne-fāstus 3 forbidden, unholy; unlucky, inauspicious; wicked

neglegentia, ae *f* carelessness, negligence

neg-legō, lēxī, lēctum 3 to neglect, disregard, despise

negō 1 to say no, deny, refuse

negōtiātor, ōris *m* merchant, banker

negōtior 1 to carry on business, trade

negōtiōsus 3 busy, occupied

neg-ōtium, ī *n* business, occupation, affair; difficulty, trouble

nēmō (nūllīus, nēminī, nē-minem, nūllō) no one, nobody

nemorālis, e of a grove *or* wood, sylvan

nemorōsus 3 full of woods *or* trees

nem-pe *adv.* certainly, of course, indeed

nemus, oris *n* wood, grove, forest

nēnia, ae *f* funeral song, dirge; lullaby

neō, nēvī, nētum 2 to spin, weave

nepōs, ōtis *m* grandson, descendant; spendthrift

neptis, is *f* granddaughter

nē-quam (*indecl.*) worthless, bad, wicked

nē-quāquam *adv.* by no means

ne-que, *see* nec

ne-queō, īvī *and* iī, itum, īre to be unable

nē-quīquam *adv.* in vain, to no purpose

nēquitia, ae (*and* nēquitiēs, ēī) *f* worthlessness, wickedness

nervus, ī *m* sinew, tendon; cord, string; bowstring; prison; vigour, strength; penis

ne-sciō 4 not to know, be ignorant

ne-scius 3 unknowing, ignorant; unable

neu, *see* neve

neuter, tra, trum neither of the two

nē-ve *and* neu *cj.* and not, nor, and lest

nex, necis *f* murder, violent death

nexilis, e bound together

nexum, ī *n, see* necto

nexus, ūs *m* a binding together, entwining

ni *cj.* unless, if not

nīdor, ōris *m* steam, smell

nīdus, ī *m* nest; dwelling, home

niger, gra, grum black, dark; gloomy, unlucky; wicked

nigrēscō, gruī, — 3 to become black

nigrō 1 to be black

nihil (*indecl.*) nothing

nihilum, ī *n* nothing; nihilō(-)minus *adv.* nevertheless

nīl = nihil; nīlum = nihilum

nimbōsus 3 cloudy, stormy

nimbus, ī *m* cloud, raincloud; rain-storm; mass, multitude

nī-mīrum *adv.* without doubt, certainly, to be sure

nimis *adv.* too much, excessively; greatly, very much

nimius 3 too great, too much

ni-si *cj.* if not, unless; except, but

nīsus, ūs *m* a pressing, striving, exertion

niteō, uī, — 2 to shine, be bright; to be in good condition, flourish

nitēscō, tuī, — 3 to begin to shine

nitidus 3 shining, bright; sleek, handsome

nitor¹, ōris *m* brightness, splendour; beauty, elegance

nitor², nīxus *or* **nisus sum** 3 to rest *or* support oneself upon; to press forward, climb; to strive, endeavour; to rely upon

nivālis, e snowy; snow-white

niveus 3 = nivalis

nivōsus 3 full of snow, snowy

nix, nivis *f* snow

nō 1 to swim

nōbilis, e well-known, famous; noble, highborn; excellent

nōbilitās, ātis *f* noble, birth; the nobility; excellence

nōbilitō 1 to make famous

nocēns, tis injurious; culpable, criminal

noceō, uī, itum 2 to harm, hurt, injure

nocti-vagus 3 night-wandering

noctū *adv.* at night, by night

nocturnus 3 by night, nocturnal

nōdō 1 to knot

nōdōsus 3 knotty

nōdus, ī *m* knot; bond, obligation; difficulty, impediment

nōlō, luī, —, nōlle not to wish, be unwilling

nōmen, inis *n* name; fame, renown; pretext, pretence; bond, debt

nōminātim *adv.* by name, expressly

nōminō 1 to name

nōn *adv.* not

Nōnae, ārum *f/pl.* the nones (*the fifth* or *seventh day of a month*)

nōnāgintā ninety

nōn-dum *adv.* not yet

nōngentī 3 nine hundred

nōn-ne *adv. interrog.* not?

nōn-nūllus 3 some, several

nōn-numquam *adv.* sometimes

nōnus 3 the ninth

norma, ae *f* standard, rule, precept

nōs we; I

nōscitō 1 to observe, recognize

nōscō, nōvī, nōtum 3 to become acquainted with; *perf.* to know; to allow, admit

noster, tra, trum our, ours

nostrās, ātis *f* of our country, native

nota, ae *f* mark, token, sign; written character; reproach, disgrace

notābilis, e remarkable, extraordinary

notātiō, ōnis *f* a marking; degradation by a censor; a noticing

nothus 3 bastard

nōtiō, ōnis *f* examination, inquiry; idea, conception

nōtitia, ae *f* acquaintance; fame; knowledge; conception, idea

notō 1 to mark; to denote, indicate; to observe; to blame, censure

notus[1], ī *m* the south wind

nōtus[2] 3 known, familiar; notorious

novācula, ae *f* razor

novālis, is *f* and novāle, is *n* fallow land; cultivated land

novellus 3 new, young

novem (*indecl.*) nine

November, bris, bre *of* November; *subst.* Novembris, is *m* November

noven-diālis, e *of* nine days

noverca, ae *f* step-mother

novīcius 3 new, fresh

novitās, ātis *f* newness, strangeness

novō 1 to renew, renovate; to change, alter

novus 3 new, fresh, recent; strange, unusual; unaccustomed

nox, noctis *f* night; darkness; death

noxa, ae *f* harm, injury; crime, fault; punishment

noxia, ae *f* guilt, crime; hurt, injury

noxius 3 hurtful; criminal, guilty

nūbēs, is *f* cloud; multitude

nūbi-fer 3 cloud-bearing

nūbi-gena, ae *m, f* cloud-born

nūbilis, e marriageable

nūbilus 3 cloudy dark, gloomy; *subst.* -a, ōrum *n/pl.* clouds

nūbō, nūpsī, ptum 3 to marry (*of a bride*)

nu-diūs it is now the ... day

nūdō 1 to bare, uncover; to leave undefended; to plunder; to disclose

nūdus 3 naked, bare; deprived of, needy, poor; simple, unadorned

nūgae, ārum *f/pl.* jests, trifles; foolish, trifling fellow

nūgātor, ōris *m* babbler, trifler

nūgātōrius 3 trifling, worthless

nūgor 1 to trifle, be frivolous

nūllus 3 none, no, not any, nobody; of no account, worthless

num *interrog. particle* really?; surely not?; whether

nūmen, inis *n* divine will, divinity, god

numerō 1 to count, reckon, number; to pay down; to consider, regard; numerātus 3 in ready money

numerōsus 3 numerous; measured, rhythmical

numerus, ī *m* measure, rhythm, harmony; num-

ber; class, category; mass,
quantity

nummārius 3 of money;
bribed

nummātus 3 provided with
money

nummulus, ī *m* paltry
money

nummus, ī *m* coin, sesterce;
pl. money

numquam *adv.* never

num-quid *interrog. particle*

nunc *adv.* now, at present;
under these circumstances

nunciam = nunc

nuncupō 1 to name; to vow

nūndinae, ārum *f/pl.* mar-
ket-day, market, trade,
traffic

nūndinātiō, ōnis *f* trade,
buying and selling

nūndinor 1 to trade, pur-
chase

nunquam = numquam

nūntia, ae *f* female messenger

nūntiō 1 to announce, re-
port, give orders

nūntius, 3 announcing;
subst. ~, ī *m* messenger;
message, news; command

nū-per *adv.* newly, lately

nuptiae, ārum *f/pl.* marriage, wedding

nuptiālis, e nuptial

nurus, ūs *f* daughter-in-law;
young married woman

nusquam *adv.* nowhere

nūtō 1 to nod, totter, waver

nūtrīcula, ae *f* nurse

nūtrīmentum, ī *n* nourishment

nūtriō 4 to suckle, nourish,
bring up; to cherish, cultivate

nūtrīx, īcis *f* nurse

nūtus, ūs *m* a nodding;
gravity; command, will

nux, nucis *f* nut; nut-tree

nympha, ae *and* nymphē, ēs
f bride, young woman;
nymph

O

ō *int.* o!, oh!

ob *prep.* with *acc.* before,
in front of; on account of,
because of   [debt]

ob-aerātus 3 involved in]

ob-ambulō 1 to walk before
or up and down

ob-dō, didī, ditum 3 to put
before, to shut

ob-dūcō 3 to bring for-
ward; to cover over

ōb-dūrēscō, ruī, — 3 to become hard *or* insensitive

ob-dūrō 1 to hold out, persist

ob-eō, iī (īvī), itum, īre to
die; to go to, visit, travel
over; to survey, review; to
surround; to engage in,
perform

ob-equitō 1 to ride up to

ob-ēsus 3 fat, plump

ōbex, icis *m and f* bolt, bar,
barrier

ob-iaceō 2 to lie against

ōb-iciō, iēcī, iectum 3 to

throw against or before, to oppose; to offer, expose; to taunt, reproach

ob-iectō 1 to set against; to abandon, expose; to reproach with

ob-iectus, ūs m a putting against, opposing

ob-itus, ūs m a setting (of sun, etc.); destruction, death

ob-iūrgātiō, ōnis f reproof, scolding

ob-iūrgātor, ōris m chider, blamer

ob-iūrgō 1 to chide, scold, reprove

(obiectāmen, inis and) **oblectāmentum, ī** n delight, pleasure

oblectātiō, ōnis f a delighting, delight

ob-lectō 1 to delight, please, amuse

ob-ligō 1 to bind, put under obligation; to pledge

ob-linō 3 to daub, smear over, cover; to stain, pollute

oblīquō 1 to turn sideways

ob-līquus 3 slanting, oblique

ob-litterō 1 to blot out of memory

oblīviō, ōnis f forgetfulness, oblivion

oblīviōsus 3 forgetful, causing forgetfulness

ob-līvīscor, oblītus sum 3 to forget

oblīvium, ī n = oblivio

ob-longus 3 oblong

ob-loquor 3 to speak against; to accompany in song

ob-luctor 1 to struggle against

ob-mūtēscō, tuī, — 3 to become dumb

ob-nītor 3 to press against, resist

ob-noxius 3 liable to, addicted to; subject, servile; obliged, indebted

ob-nūntiātiō, ōnis f announcement of evil omens

ob-nūntiō 1 to announce bad omens

ob-oedio, īvī, ītum 4 to obey

ob-orior 4 to arise, appear

ob-rēpō, rēpsī, rēptum 3 to creep up, come up suddenly

ob-rigēscō, guī, — 3 to become stiff

ob-rogō 1 to repeal a law by another

ob-ruō 3 to cover over, hide, bury; to overwhelm, weigh down, oppress

ob-saepiō 4 to hedge in, enclose

obscaenus 3 = obscenus

obs-cēnitās, ātis f impurity, lewdness

obs-cēnus 3 filthy, repulsive, impure, indecent; ill-omened

obscūritās, ātis f obscurity, indistinctness

obscūrō 1 to darken, obscure; to hide, conceal; to cause to be forgotten ob-scūrus 3 dark, obscure; reserved; unknown, ignoble, mean

ob-secrātiō, ōnis f earnest entreaty; public prayer

ob-secrō 1 to entreat, implore

ob-secundō 1 to be compliant

obsequium, ī n compliance, obedience, indulgence

ob-sequor 3 to comply with, obey, indulge in

ob-serō[1] 1 to bolt, shut up

ob-serō[2], sēvī, situm 3 to sow, cover over, fill

observantia, ae f respect, esteem

observātiō, ōnis f an observing, watching

ob-servō 1 to observe, watch; to attend to, keep; to respect, honour

ob-ses, idis m, f hostage; pledge, security

ob-sessiō, ōnis f = obsidio

obsessor, ōris m besieger

ob-sideō, sēdī, sessum 2 to sit, stay; to besiege, blockade; to occupy, fill

obsidiō, ōnis f siege, blockade

ob-sīdō, sēdī, sessum 3 to beset, occupy

ob-signātor, ōris m sealer, witness

ob-signō 1 to seal, attest under seal

ob-sistō, stitī, — 3 to stand in the way, withstand, resist

obsolēscō, lēvī, (lētum) 3 to decay, fall into disuse; obsolētus 3 worn out, decayed; common, mean

obsōnium, ī n relish, victuals

obsōnō 1 to buy provisions

ob-stetrīx, īcis f midwife

obstinātus 3 resolved, persistent, stubborn

ob-stō, stitī, (stātūrus) 1 to resist, hinder, obstruct

ob-strepō 3 to make a noise at; to drown with clamour, shout down

ob-stringō 3 to bind, tie, put under an obligation

ob-struō 3 to build against, block up, hinder

ob-stupefaciō 3 to astonish, amaze

ob-stupēscō, puī, — 3 to become senseless or astounded

ob-sum, fuī, esse to hinder, injure

ob-tegō 3 to cover, protect, conceal

ob-temperō 1 to comply, obey

ob-tendō, ndī, ntum 3 to spread before; to hide

ob-tentus, ūs m a spreading before, cover

ob-terō 3 to trample, crush, destroy

ob-testātiō, ōnis f adjuration, entreaty

ob-testor 1 to call to witness; to implore, entreat

ob-ticēscō, cuī, — 3 to become silent

ob-tineō, tinuī, tentum 2 to occupy, possess, keep; to maintain; to obtain

ob-tingō, tigī, — 3 to fall to the lot of, happen

ob-torpēscō, puī, — 3 to grow stiff or insensible

ob-torqueō 2 to twist round

ob-trectātiō, ōnis f detraction, disparagement

ob-trectātor, ōris m detractor, disparager

ob-trectō 1 to disparage

ob-trūdō 3 to thrust upon

ob-truncō 1 to kill, slaughter

ob-tundō, tudī, tū(n)sum 3 to make blunt or dull; to stun, deafen, annoy

ob-turbō 1 to disturb, trouble

ob-tūrō 1 to stop up, close

ob-tūtus, ūs m a looking at, gaze

ob-umbrō 1 to overshadow, darken; to conceal, cover

ob-uncus 3 hooked

ob-ustus 3 burnt into, hardened by fire

ob-veniō 4 to occur, fall to the lot of

ob-versor 1 to hover before, appear

ob-vertō 3 to turn towards or against

ob-viam adv. in the way, towards; obviam ire to come to meet

obvius 3 in the way, meeting; exposed to

ob-volvō 3 to wrap round, envelop

oc-caecō 1 to make blind; to darken, hide

occāsiō, ōnis f opportunity, favourable moment

oc-cāsus, ūs m setting; the west; downfall

occidēns, tis m the west

occidiō, ōnis f massacre

oc-cidō[1], cidī, (cāsūrus) 3 to fall down; to perish, die, be ruined

oc-cīdō[2], cidī, cīsum 3 to cut down, kill

occiduus 3 setting, western

oc-cipiō, cēpī, ceptum 3 to begin

oc-cīsiō, ōnis f slaughter

oc-clūdō, sī, sum 3 to shut up, close

oc-cubō, —, — 1 to lie down, lie dead

oc-culō, culuī, cultum 3 to hide, conceal

occultātiō, ōnis f concealing

occultō 1, intens. of occulo

occultus 3 hidden, secret

oc-cumbō, cubuī, cubitum 3 to fall in death, die

occupātiō, ōnis f business, employment

occupātus 3 busy, engaged

occupō 1 to take possession of, seize; to fill, occupy; to fall upon, attack; to anticipate, do first

oc-currō, currī, cursum 3 to run to meet, meet; to attack; to present itself, appear, occur; to resist, oppose; to assist; to reply

occursātiō, ōnis f a running to meet, attention

oc-cursō 1 to go to meet; to attack

oc-cursus, ūs m a meeting

ocellus, ī m little eye

ōcior, us (comp.) swifter; comp. adv. ōcius (more) swiftly

ocrea, ae f metal greave

octāvus 3 the eighth

octō (indecl.) eight

October, bris, bre of October; subst. Octobris, is m October

octōnī 3 eight each

oculus, ī m eye

ōdī, ōdisse (ōsūrus) to hate, dislike [annoying]

odiōsus 3 hateful, odious,∫

odium, ī n hatred, enmity, aversion; object of hatred

odor, ōris m smell, odour; perfume, spice; scent, suspicion

odōrātus 3 fragrant

odōri-fer 3 fragrant

odōror 1 to smell out, scent

odōrus 3 sweet-smelling; keen-scented

oeno-phorum, ī n wine-basket

offa, ae f ball of meal

of-fendō, endī, ēnsum 3 to hit, strike; to come upon, meet with; to offend, blunder, displease; to suffer disaster

offēnsa, ae f offence, disfavour, displeasure

offēnsiō, ōnis f illness; hatred, aversion, disgust; accident, misfortune

of-ferō, obtulī, oblātum, offerre to bring to, present, show, offer; to cause, occasion

officīna, ae f workshop

of-ficiō, fēcī, fectum 3 to hinder, oppose

officiōsus 3 obliging, courteous, dutiful

officium, ī n service, kindness, attention; employment, work; duty, function; sense of duty

of-firmō 1 to hold fast to

of-fundō 3 to spread over, cover

ōhē int. oh!, ah!

olea, ae f = oliva

oleaster, trī m wild olive-tree

olēns, tis fragrant; stinking

oleō, oluī, — 2 to emit a smell, smell

ol-faciō 3 to smell, scent out

olidus 3 smelling, stinking

ōlim adv. formerly, of old; one day, hereafter; at times, often

olitor, ōris m kitchen-gardener

olīva, ae f olive; olive-tree

olīvētum, ī n olive-garden

olīvi-fer 3 olive-bearing

olīvum, ī n olive-oil

ōlla, ae f pot, jar

olle and ollus (obsolete) = ille

olor, ōris m swan

olus, **eris** n vegetables, cabbage

olusculum, **ī** n = olus

omāsum, **ī** n bullock's tripe

ōmen, **inis** n omen, sign, token, foreboding

ōminor 1 to forebode, prophesy

o-mittō 3 to let go, let fall; to give up, leave off; to omit, overlook

omnīnō adv. altogether, entirely; in general; to be sure   [ful]

omni-potēns, **tis** all-power-)

omnis, **e** all, every; whole

onerārius 3 of burden

onerō 1 to load, burden; to weigh down, oppress

onerōsus 3 heavy, burdensome

onus, **eris** n load, burden; trouble, difficulty; tax, expense

onustus 3 loaded, burdened

opācō 1 to shade, overshadow

opācus 3 shady, dark

opera, **ae** f pains, effort, work; service; leisure; workman, hired assistant

operārius 3 working; subst. **,, ī** m workman

operiō, **eruī**, **ertum** 4 to cover, shut; to hide, conceal

operor 1 to work, labour; to be engaged in worship or sacrifice

operōsus 3 painstaking, busy; troublesome, difficult; elaborate

opēs, **um** f/pl., see ops

opi-fex, **icis** m, f worker, artisan

opīmus 3 fat; fertile; rich, copious

opīniō, **ōnis** f opinion, supposition, belief; reputation; report

opīnor 1 to believe, think, suppose

opitulor 1 to help, aid

oportet, **uit**, — 2 it is necessary, proper, becoming

op-perior, **pertus sum** 4 to wait (for)

op-petō 3 to encounter, suffer

oppidānus 3 of a (small) town

oppidō adv. exceedingly, exactly

oppidulum, **ī** n little town

oppidum, **ī** n town

op-pleō, **ēvī**, **ētum** 2 to fill up

op-pōnō 3 to put opposite or before, oppose; expose; to bring forward, allege

opportūnitās, **ātis** f fitness, convenience; advantage

op-portūnus 3 fit, suitable; favourable, advantageous

op-positus, **ūs** m a placing against, opposition

op-pressiō, **ōnis** f force, violent seizure

op-primō, **pressī**, **pressum** 3 to press down, crush; to conceal, hide; to overthrow, subdue; to fall upon, seize op-probrium, ī *n* reproach, abuse; disgrace, dishonour

op-pugnātiō, ōnis *f* a storming, assault

op-pugnātor, ōris *m* attacker

op-pugnō 1 to attack, assault

ops, opis *f* might, power, strength; assistance, aid; *pl.* opēs, um wealth, riches, resources

optābilis, e desirable

optimās, ātis of the best; *subst.* ~, ātis *m* aristocrat

optimus 3 *superl. of* bonus

optiō, ōnis *f* choice, option

optō 1 to choose, select; to wish, desire

opulentia, ae *f* riches, wealth

opulentus 3 rich, wealthy; powerful

opus, eris *n* work, labour; deed, achievement; artistic work; book, composition; building, fortification; opus est there is need

opusculum, ī *n* a little work

ōra, ae *f* edge, border; sea-coast; region, country

ōrāc(u)lum, ī *n* oracle, prophecy

ōrātiō, ōnis *f* language, expression; speech, oration

ōrātor, ōris *m* speaker, orator; negotiator, spokesman

orbis, is *m* circle, ring, orbit; the earth the universe

orbita, ae *f* rut, track

orbitās, ātis *f* bereavement, childlessness

orbō 1 to bereave, deprive

orbus 3 deprived, destitute, bereaved

orchēstra, ae *f* place where the senate sat in the theatre

Orcus, ī *m* (the god of) the underworld; death

ōrdinārius 3 ordinary, regular

ōrdinātim *adv.* in succession, in good order

ōrdinō 1 to set in order, arrange

ōrdior, ōrsus sum 4 to begin

ōrdō, inis *m* line, row, order, rank, class; band, troop; centurionship, command; regularity, sucession

orgia, ōrum *n/pl.* orgies, festival of Bacchus

ori-chalcum, ī *n* copper, brass

oriēns, tis *m* the east, orient

orīgō, inis *f* origin, source, descent, birth

orior, ortus sum (oritūrus) 4 to rise; to spring from, be born from, originate

ōrnāmentum, ī *n* ornament, decoration; honour, distinction

ōrnātus, ūs *m* dress, attire; ornament, decoration

ōrnō 1 to equip, fit out,

supply; to adorn, em-bellish; to honour, praise

ornus, ī *f* mountain-ash

ōrō 1 to plead, argue; to beg, pray, entreat

ortus, ūs *m* a rising, sun-rise; east; birth, origin

ōs[1], ōris *n* the mouth; an opening; face, expres-sion; boldness

os[2], ossis *n* bone; marrow, inmost part [augury]

os-cen, inis *m* bird of [augury]

ōs-citō 1 to yawn, be list-less

ōsculor 1 to kiss, caress

ōsculum, ī *n* little mouth; kiss

os-tendō, ndī, ntum (*and* nsum) **3** to show, display, disclose; to indicate, de-clare

ostentātiō, ōnis *f* a boasting, ostentation; false show, pretence

ostentātor, ōris *m* displayer, boaster

os-tentō 1 to show, exhibit; to boast of; to promise, threaten [portent]

ostentum, ī *n* prodigy,]

ōstium, ī *n* door; entrance, mouth

ostrea, ae *f and* **-um, ī** *n* mussel, oyster

ostrum, ī purple(-dye); purple dress *or* covering

ōtiōsus 3 idle, at leisure; free from public affairs; quiet, calm; indifferent, neutral

ōtium, ī *n* leisure, idleness, ease; rest, quiet, peace

ovīle, is *n* sheepfold; en-closure for voting in the Campus Martius

ovis, is *f* sheep

ovō 1 to rejoice, exult, triumph

ōvum, ī *n* egg

P

pābulātiō, ōnis *f* a foraging

pābulātor, ōris *m* forager

pābulor 1 to forage

pābulum, ī *n* fodder, food

pācālis, e of peace, peace-ful

pācātus 3 pacified, peace-ful

pāci-fer 3 peace-bringing

pāci-ficō 1 to make peace, reconcile

pacīscor, pactus sum 3 to make a contract, agree, stipulate, betroth

pācō 1 to pacify, subdue

pactiō, ōnis *f* agreement, contract, treaty

pactum, ī *n* agreement; (*abl. only*) way, means

paeān, ānis *m* hymn (to Apollo)

paed-agōgus, ī *m* slave in charge of children

paelex, icis *f* concubine, mistress

paene *adv.* nearly, almost

paenite̅ō, uī, — 2 to repent, regret; to displease

paenula, ae f travelling-cloak, mantle

pāgānus 3 of a village, rustic

pāgina, ae f page, sheet

pāgus, ī m district, canton, village

palaestra, ae f wrestling-school, wrestling

palam adv. openly, public-ly; prep. with abl. in the presence of

Palātīnus 3 of the Palatine hill

Palātium, ī n the Palatine hill; palace

palātum, ī n the palate

palea, ae f chaff

palear, āris n dew-lap

palla, ae f long robe, mantle [Pallas]

Palladium, ī n image of Pallas

palleō, uī. — 2 to be pale; to be anxious

pallēscō, luī, — 2 to turn pale, grow yellow

palliātus 3 dressed in a Greek robe

pallidus 3 pale, wan

palliolum, ī n little Greek mantle

pallium, ī n Greek cloak

pallor, ōris m paleness

palma¹, ae f palm, hand

palma², ae f palm-tree; palm-wreath, prize

palmes, itis m vine-shoot

pālor 1 to wander about, roam, straggle

palpor 1 to stroke; to flatter

palūdāmentum, ī n military cloak

palūdātus 3 clothed in a military cloak

palumbēs, is m, f wood-pigeon, ring-dove

pālus¹, ī m stake

palūs², ūdis f swamp, marsh, pool

palūster, tris, tre marshy, swampy

pampineus 3 of vine (shoots)

pampinus, ī m (f) vine-shoot, tendril

pandō, pandī, passum 3 to extend, spread out; to throw open, disclose

pandus 3 bent, curved

pangō, pepigī, pāctum 3 to make, compose; to settle, agree upon

pānis, is m bread, loaf

pannōsus 3 ragged

pannus, ī m piece of cloth, rag, patch

panthēra, ae f panther

papae int. indeed!, strange!

papāver, eris n poppy

papilla, ae f nipple, breast

papȳrus, ī f papyrus, paper

pār, paris equal, like, a match; suitable, proper; subst. m and f comrade, mate; n a pair

para-situs, ī m parasite

parātus¹ 3 prepared, ready, provided, equipped, skilled

parātus², ūs m preparation; outfit

parcō, pepercī, (parsūrus) 3 to spare; to abstain, desist, cease

parcus 3 sparing, frugal; scanty, little, niggardly

parēns, tis *m and f* parent, father, mother; ancestor; founder, inventor, author

parentālis, e of parents, parental

parentō 1 to sacrifice in honour of parents *or* relatives; to revenge

pāreō, uī, (**pāritūrus**) 2 to appear, be evident; to obey, submit to, yield

pariēs, etis *m* wall

parilis, e like, equal

pariō, peperī, partum (paritūrus) 3 to bring forth, bear, produce; to get, acquire

pariter *adv.* equally, alike; at the same time, together

parma, ae *f* small round shield

parō 1 to prepare, furnish, provide; to intend, be about; to acquire, obtain

par-ochus, ī *m* purveyor; host

parri-cīda, ae *m and f* parricide; traitor

parricidium, ī *m* murder of a parent *or* relation; treason

pars, tis *f* part, portion, share; region; direction; respect; party, faction; *pl.* character (*on the stage*), duty, function

parsimōnia, ae *f* thriftiness, parsimony

parti-ceps, cipis sharing, partaking

participō 1 to impart, share with

particula, ae *f* small part, particle

partim *adv.* partly

partior (*and* **partiō**) 4 to divide, distribute, share

partītiō, ōnis *f* a sharing, division

parturiō 4 to be in labour; to team with; to brood over, meditate

partus, ūs *m* a bringing forth, birth; offspring, child

parum *adv.* too little, not enough; *comp.* minus less; *superl.* minimē least of all, not at all

parum-per *adv.* for a little while

parvulus 3 very little *or* small; very young

parvus 3 *adj.* little, small (*comp.* minor, us, *superl.* minimus 3); young; short; trifling, unimportant; low, mean, poor

pāscō, pāvī, pāstum 3 to feed, pasture, nourish; to feast, gratify

pāscuus 3 fit for pasture; *subst.* pāscua, ōrum *n/pl.* pastures

passer, eris *m* sparrow

passim *adv.* scattered about, here and there, in every direction

passus[1] *adj.* 3 spread out

passus[2], ūs *m* step, pace

pāstor, ōris *m* herdsman, shepherd

pāstōrālis, e, pāstōricius 3, pāstōrius 3 of a shepherd, pastoral

pāstus, ūs *m* food, pasture

pate-faciō 3 to throw open, expose, reveal

patella, ae *f* pan, sacrificial dish

pateō, uī, — 2 to be open, lie open; to be accessible; to extend; to be visible *or* manifest

pater, tris *m* father; *pl.* senators

patera, ae *f* sacrificial dish

paternus 3 fatherly, paternal; native

patēscō, tuī, — 3 to lie open; to extend

patiēns, tis bearing, enduring, patient

patientia, ae *f* endurance, patience; forbearance, indulgence; subjection

patina, ae *f* dish, pan

patior, passus suni 3 to suffer, bear, undergo; to allow, permit

patria, ae *f* fatherland, native land, home

patricius 3 patrician, noble; *subst.* ~ī *m* a patrician, nobleman

patrimōnium, ī *n* inheritance, patrimony, estate

patrius 3 of a father, paternal; inherited, ancestral

patrō 1 to accomplish, perform

patrōcinium, ī *n* protection, patronage; defence in court

patrōna, ae *f* protectress, patroness

patrōnus, ī *m* protector, patron; advocate

patruēlis, e of a father's brother; of a cousin

patruus, ī *m* paternal uncle; censor; *adj.* 3 of an uncle

patulus 3 standing open; spreading

paucitās, ātis *f* small number, fewness

pauc, ulī, *usu. pl.* few

paucus 3 *usu. pl.* few

paul(l)ātim *adv.* gradually, little by little

paul(l)is-per *adv.* a little while

paul(l)ulus 3, *dim. of* paul(l)us

paul(l)ulus 3 small, little

pauper, eris poor; scanty, meagre

pauperculus 3 poor

pauperiēs, ēī *f* = paupertas

paupertās, ātis *f* poverty

paveō, —, — 2 to tremble, be afraid

pavidus 3 quaking, frightened

pavīmentum, ī *n* pavement

pavitō 1 to tremble with fear

pāvō, ōnis *m* peacock

pavor, ōris *m* a trembling, terror, dread; excitement

pāx, pācis *f* peace, tranquillity; favour (*of the gods*)

peccātum, ī *n* fault, error, sin

peccō 1 to commit a fault, to sin, offend

pecten, inis *m* comb; reed of a loom; quill for striking a lyre

pectō, pexī, pexum 3 to comb

pectus, oris *n* breast; heart, feelings; mind, understanding

pecū *pl.* pecua *n* flocks, herds

pecuārius 3 of cattle; *subst.* ~ ī *m* cattle-breeder

pecūlātus, ūs *m* embezzlement [special]

pecūliāris, e one's own, ∫

pecūlium, ī *n* personal property

pecūnia, ae *f* wealth, money

pecūniārius 3 of money, pecuniary

pecūniōsus 3 rich, wealthy

pecus[1], oris *n* cattle, sheep

pecus[2], udis *f* domestic animal (cattle, sheep &c.); wild animal

pedes, itis *m* walker; footsoldier; infantry

pedester, tris, tre on foot; on land; simple, prosaic

pede-temptim *adv.* step by step, slowly, cautiously

pedica, ae *f* fetter, snare

peditātus, ūs *m* infantry

pē-i(i)erō 1 to swear falsely, forswear oneself

pēior, *see* malus

pelagus, ī *n* sea, ocean

pēlex, icis *f* = paelex

pel-legō = perlego

pel-liciō, lexī, lectum 3 to allure, entice

pellicula, ae *f* small skin

pellis, is *f* hide, skin; leather

pellītus 3 clothed in hides

pellō, pepulī, pulsum 3 to strike, push; to move, impress; to drive out, expel; to put to flight

pelta, ae *f* light shield

penātēs, ium *m/pl.* the Penates (*guardian gods of the household*); a dwelling, home

pendeō, pependī, — 2 to hang; to hover, be poised; to depend upon; to be in suspense *or* undecided

pendō, pependī, pēnsum 3 to pay (out); to ponder, consider; to value, esteem; *subst.* pēnsum, ī *n* portion (*of wool*) weighed out, day's work, task

pendulus 3 hanging

penes *prep.* with *acc.* in the possession *or* power of; with

penetrābilis, e piercing

penetrālis, e inward, internal; *subst.* penetrāle, is *n* (*mostly pl.*) inner room, sanctuary

penetrō 1 to enter, penetrate

pēnis, is *m* the penis

penitus *adv.* inwardly, deeply; thoroughly, entirely

penna, ae *f* feather, wing

pennātus 3 winged

pēnsilis, e hanging

pēnsiō, ōnis *f* payment

pēnsitō 1 to weigh, consider; to pay

pēnsō 1 to weigh; to compensate, repay; to ponder, consider

pēnsum, see **pendo**

pēnūria, ae f want, scarcity

penus, oris n and **ūs** f, **ī** m provisions, victuals

per prep. with acc. (of space) through, along, over; (of time) during, in the course of; (of agency) through, by means of; under pretence of; for the sake of; (of manner) by, through, with

per-acūtus 3 very sharp, clear

per-aequē adv. equally

per-agō 3 to pierce through; to complete, finish, accomplish; to pass through; to go through, describe

per-agrō 1 to go over, traverse

per-ambulō 1 to travel through

per-angustus 3 very narrow

per-antīquus 3 very old

per-arō 1 to furrow; to write

per-bonus 3 very good

per-brevis, e very short

per-cārus 3 very dear

per-celebrō 1 to speak of frequently

per-cellō, culī, culsum 3 to beat, strike down, overthrow; to scare, unnerve

per-cēnseō 2 to count over; to survey; to travel through

per-cipiō, cēpī, ceptum 3 to seize, take; to receive,

harvest; to perceive, feel, know, understand

percitus 3 aroused, excited

per-commodus 3 very convenient

percontātiō, ōnis f inquiry

per-contor 1 to ask, inquire

per-crēb(r)ēscō, b(r)uī, — 3 to become frequent, spread abroad

per-cunctor 1 = **percontor**

per-currō, (cu)currī, cursum 3 to run along or over, traverse

percussiō, ōnis f a striking, beating

percussor, ōris m murderer

per-cutiō, cussī, cussum 3 to strike through, pierce; to beat, hit; to kill; to affect, astound

per-difficilis, e very difficult   [oughly]

per-discō 3 to learn thoroughly]

perditor, ōris m ruiner, destroyer

per-dō, didī, ditum 3 to destroy, ruin, squander, lose; **perditus 3** lost, ruined, profligate

per-doceō 1 to teach thoroughly

per-domō 1 to tame or subdue thoroughly

per-dūcō 3 to lead or bring to; to carry on, prolong; to persuade, win over

per-duelliō, ōnis f high-treason

per-duellis, is m enemy

per-edō 3 to consume, devour

per-egrē *adv.* (from) abroad, in a foreign country

peregrīnātiō, ōnis *f* sojourn abroad, travelling

peregrīnor 1 to be abroad, travel about; to be a stranger

peregrīnus 3 foreign, strange; *subst.* ~, ī *m* foreigner, stranger

perendiē *adv.* on the day after tomorrow

perendinus 3 after to-morrow

per-ennis, e everlasting, unceasing

per-eō, iī, itum, īre to pass away, perish, die; to be desperately in love; to be wasted

per-equitō 1 to ride through *or* about

per-errō 1 to wander through, roam over

per-exiguus 3 very small

per-facētus 3 very witty

per-facilis, e very easy

per-familiāris, e very intimate

perfectiō, ōnis *f* perfection, completion

perfectus 3 perfect, complete, finished

per-ferō, tulī, lātum, ferre to carry *or* bring to; to announce; to complete, accomplish; to bear, endure

per-ficiō, fēcī, fectum 3 to carry out, accomplish, achieve; to finish; to cause

perfidia, ae *f* faithlessness, treachery

perfidiōsus 3 = perfidus

per-fidus 3 faithless, treacherous

per-flō 1 to blow through *or* over

per-fodiō 3 to dig through, pierce

per-forō 1 to bore *or* pierce through

per-fricō 1 to rub over, scratch

per-fringō, frēgī, frāctum 3 to break to pieces, shatter; to violate

per-fruor 3 to enjoy fully

per-fuga, ae *m* deserter

per-fugiō 3 to flee for refuge; to desert

perfugium, ī *n* refuge, asylum, shelter

per-fundō 3 to soak, wet, besprinkle, bathe; to inspire, imbue

per-fungor 3 to perform, discharge; to endure; to come to the end of

per-furō 3 to rage furiously

pergō, perrēxī, perrēctum 3 to continue, go on, march

per-grandis, e very large

per-grātus 3 very pleasant

per-gravis, e very heavy *or* important

per-hibeō 2 to adduce, say, assert

per-honōrificus 3 very honourable *or* respectful

per-horrēscō 3 to shudder, tremble

per-hūmānus 3 very kind

perīclitor 1 to try, test; to be in danger, run risk

perīculōsus 3 dangerous, perilous

perīculum (and perīclum), ī n trial, experiment; danger, peril, risk

per-ierō 1 = peiero

per-imō, ēmī, ēmptum 3 to destroy, kill; to prevent

per-inde adv. in the same manner [skill]

perītia, ae f experience,∫

perītus 3 experienced, expert, skilled

per-iūcundus 3 very agreeable

per-iūrium, ī n perjury

per-iūrō = peiero

per-iūrus 3 perjured, lying

per-lābor 3 to glide over or through

per-legō 3 to examine all over; to read through, peruse

per-levis, e very (s)light

per-līberālis, e well-bred

per-liciō 3 = pellicio

per-litō 1 to sacrifice with favourable omens

per-longus 3 very long

per-lūceō 2 to shine through; to be transparent or clear

per-lūcidus 3 transparent

per-luō 3 to wash off, bathe

per-lūstrō 1 to wander through; to examine, survey

per-magnus 3 very great

per-maneō 2 to remain, stay, continue, persist

per-mānō 1 to flow through, penetrate

per-mānsiō, ōnis f a remaining

per-meō 1 to go through

per-mētior 4 to traverse

per-mīrus 3 very wonderful

per-misceō 2 to mix together; to throw into confusion

per-missū m (only abl.) by permission

per-mittō 3 to let go; to give up, yield, intrust; to permit, allow

per-modestus 3 very modest

per-molestus 3 very troublesome

per-moveō 2 to move thoroughly, excite, induce, prevail on

per-mulceō 2 to stroke; to please, charm, soothe, appease

per-multus 3 very much, very many

per-mūniō 4 to fortify completely

per-mūtātiō, ōnis f change, exchange [change]

per-mūtō 1 to change, ex-∫

per-necessārius 3 very intimate

per-negō 1 to deny obstinately

per-niciēs, ēī f destruction, ruin, death

perniciōsus 3 destructive, ruinous

pernĭcĭtās, ātis f swiftness, briskness

pernix, icis swift, nimble

per-noctō 1 to pass the night

per-nōscō 3 to learn thoroughly   [night]

per-nox, ctis through the

pērō, ōnis *m* rustic boot

per-opportūnus 3 very convenient

per-ōrātiō, ōnis *f* peroration

per-ōrō 1 to speak to the end; to end, conclude

per-ōsus 3 hating

per-parvus 3 very little

per-paucī 3 very few

per-pellō 3 to drive on, urge, compel

perpendiculum, ī *n* plumbline

per-pendō, pendī, pēnsum 3 to weigh carefully

perperam *adv.* wrongly, falsely

perpessiō, ōnis *f* a suffering

per-petior, pessus sum 3 to bear *or* suffer steadfastly

per-petrō 1 to complete, achieve, perform

perpetuitās, ātis *f* uninterrupted duration, continuity

perpetuō *adv.* uninterruptedly, for ever

perpetuus 3 uninterrupted, continuous, entire; perpetual, permanent

per-plexus 3 entangled, confused, obscure

per-poliō 4 to polish thoroughly, make perfect

per-populor 1 to ravage completely

per-pōtō 1 to continue drinking

per-pūrgō 1 to cleanse thoroughly; to explain

per-quam *adv.* exceedingly

per-quīrō, quīsīvī, quīsītum 3 to search for eagerly, inquire diligently

per-rārus 3 very rare

per-rēptō 1 to crawl (over)

per-rumpō 3 to break through, overcome

per-saepe *adv.* very often

per-scindō 3 to tear to pieces

per-scrībō 3 to write at length; to register, record; to pay by draft; to recount

per-scrīptiō, ōnis *f* a writing down, entry

per-scrūtor 1 to search through, examine

per-sentiō 4 to feel *or* perceive distinctly

per-sequor 3 to follow after, pursue, chase; to punish, prosecute judicially; to imitate, copy; to carry out, perform; to overtake; to relate, describe

per-sevērō 1 to persevere in, persist, continue

per-sīdō, sēdī, sessum 3 to settle down, penetrate

per-similis, e very like

per-solvō 3 to pay; to render, discharge; to suffer (punishment)

persōna, ae *f* mask (*of actors*); character, person

persōnātus 3 masked; in an assumed character

per-sonō 1 to resound, re-echo; to shout

perspicāx, ācis sharp-sighted, acute

per-spiciō, spexī, spectum 3 to look through, see, examine; to observe, perceive

perspicuus 3 clear, evident

per-stō, stitī (stātūrus) 1 to stand firm; to persist, persevere

per-stringō 3 to touch lightly, graze; to affect deeply, move

per-suādeō 2 to persuade, induce, convince

per-sultō 1 to leap about

per-taedet, taesum est 2 it wearies, disgusts

per-temptō 1 to prove, test; to affect deeply, try severely

per-tendō, tendī, (tēnsum or) tentum 3 to push on, proceed

per-tenuis, e very weak, very slight

per-terreō 2 to terrify

per-timēscō, muī, — 3 to be very much afraid

pertinācia, ae f stubbornness, perseverance

per-tināx, ācis persevering, firm, stubborn

per-tineō, tinuī, — 2 to reach, extend, stretch; to belong, pertain, concern; to be suitable, tend, conduce

per-tractō 1 to handle, study

per-trahō 3 to draw along, entice

per-tundō, tudī, tūsum 3 to thrust or bore through

per-turbātiō, ōnis f confusion, disorder, revolution; passion, emotion

per-turbō 1 to confuse, disturb, disquiet

per-ungō 3 to besmear, anoint

per-urbānus 3 very refined, witty

per-ūrō 3 to burn, inflame

per-ūtilis, e very useful

per-vādō 3 to go or pass through, extend; to arrive

per-vagor 1 to wander about; to spread out

per-vāstō 1 to devastate

per-vehō 3 to carry through, bring

per-vellō 3 to pinch, excite

per-veniō 4 to come, arrive, reach

perversitās, ātis f perversity

per-versus 3 awry, perverse, wrong

per-vertō 3 to overthrow, destroy, ruin

per-vestigō 1 to investigate, search into

per-vetus, eris very old

per-vicācia, ae f persistence, stubbornness

per-vicāx, ācis persevering, obstinate

per-videō 2 to survey, perceive

per-vigil, is ever watchful

per-vigilō 1 to remain awake all night

per-vincō 3 to conquer completely; to effect

per-vius 3 passable, accessible

per-volitō 1 to fly through

per-volō¹ 1 to fly through *or* about

per-volō², voluī, velle to wish greatly

per-vulgō 1 to make public, publish   [(*nautical*)]

pēs, pedis *m* foot; sheet

pessimus 3, *superl. of* malus

pessulus, ī *m* bolt (*of a door*)

pessum *adv.* to the ground; ~ dare to destroy, ruin

pesti-fer 3 fatal, injurious

pestilēns, tis unhealthy, deadly

pestilentia, ae *f* unhealthy air; plague, pestilence

pestis, is *f* plague, pestilence; destruction, ruin; curse, bane

petītiō, ōnis *f* attack, blow; application for office, candidature; claim, plaintiff

petītor, ōris *m* seeker, candidate; plaintiff

petō, tīvī (*or* tiī), tītum 3 to seek, aim at; to fall upon, attack; to fetch; to demand, claim; to ask, request

petorritum, ī *n* open carriage

petulāns, tis pert, wanton, impudent

petulantia, ae *f* impudence, forwardness

phalanx, angis *f* band of soldiers, phalanx

phalārica, ae *f* = falarica

phalerae, ārum *f*/*pl*. metal ornament worn on the breast

phalerātus 3 wearing the *phalerae*

pharetra, ae *f* quiver

pharetrātus 3 wearing a quiver

pharmaco-pōla, ae *m* seller of drugs, quack

phasēlus, ī *m* and *f* kidney-bean; swift-sailing yacht

philo-sophia, ae *f* philosophy   [losophy]

philosophor 1 to study phi-

philo-sophus, ī *m* philosopher

philyra, ae *f* bark of a linden-tree

phōca, ae *f* seal

phoenix, īcis *m* phœnix

physicus 3 of nature, physical; *subst.* ~, ī *m* natural philosopher; physica, ōrum *n*/*pl*. physics

piāculāris, e atoning, expiating

piāculum, ī *n* expiatory sacrifice, expiation; sin, guilt

picea, ae *f* pitch-pine

piceus 3 pitch-black

pictor, ōris *m* painter

pictūra, ae *f* painting, picture

pīcus, ī *m* wood-pecker

pietās, ātis *f* sense of duty, piety, devotion; filial love, patriotism; justice

piger, gra, grum slow, dull, lazy, indolent

piget, uit (and itum est) 2 it grieves, troubles, displeases

pigmentum, ī n colour, ornament

pignerō 1 to pledge, pawn

pignus, oris (or eris) n pledge, security; hostage; wager, assurance, proof; pl. pledges of love (children)

pigritia, ae (and -iēs, ēī) f laziness, indolence

pīla¹, ae f pillar

pila², ae f (game of) ball

pilentum, ī n carriage, coach

pilleātus 3 wearing a felt cap

pilleus, ī m and -um, ī n felt cap

pilōsus 3 hairy, shaggy

pīlum, ī n heavy javelin

pilus¹, ī m hair; trifle

pīlus², ī m a maniple of the triarii

pīneus 3 of pine

pingō, pinxī, pictum 3 to paint, colour; to depict, portray; to embroider; to decorate, embellish

pinguēscō, —, — 3 to grow fat or fertile

pinguis, e fat, plump; rich, fertile; dull, stupid; calm, quiet

pīni-fer 3 pine-bearing

pinna¹, ae f = penna

pinna², ae f pinnacle, battlement

pinnātus 3 = pennatus

pīnus, ūs and ī f pine, fir; ship

piō 1 to appease, propitiate; to atone for, expiate

piper, eris n pepper

pīrāta, ae m pirate

pīrāticus 3 of pirates

pirum, ī n pear

piscātor, ōris m fisherman

piscātōrius 3 of fishermen

piscīna, ae f fish-pond

piscis, is m fish

piscor 1 to fish

piscōsus 3 abounding in fish

pistor, ōris m baker

pistrīnum, ī n corn-mill

pītuīta, ae f phlegm, catarrh

pius 3 dutiful, pious, religious; affectionate, filial; holy, sacred, just

pix, picis f pitch

plācābilis, e easily appeased, placable; effective in appeasing

placenta, ae f cake

placeō, uī and placitus sum, itum 2 to please, be agreeable; placet it seems good, it is resolved

placidus 3 gentle, quiet, peaceful, mild

placitus 3 pleasing, agreeable

plācō 1 to quiet, soothe, calm, appease; to reconcile

plāga¹, ae f blow, stroke, wound; misfortune, disaster

plaga², ae f net, snare, trap

plaga³, ae f region, district

plangō, anxī, anctum 3 to

strike, beat; to lament, bewail

plangor, ōris *m* a beating; lamentation, wailing

plānitia, ae *and* **plānitiēs**, ēī *f* level ground, plain

planta[1], ae *f* shoot for propagation, cutting

planta[2], ae *f* sole of the foot

plantāria, ium *n/pl.* young plants

plānus[1], ī *m* impostor

plānus[2] 3 level, flat; plain, distinct; *adv.* **plānē** clearly, distinctly, entirely, quite

platanus, ī *f* plane-tree

platēa (*and* **platea**) ae *f* street

plaudō, sī, sum 3 to clap, beat; to applaud, approve

plaustrum, ī *n* wagon, cart

plausus, ūs *m* a clapping, applause

plēbēcula, ae *f* rabble, mob

plēbēius 3 of the common people, plebeian; common, vulgar

plēbēs, (e)ī *f* = plebs

plēbi-cola, ae *m* friend of the common people

plēbs, is *f* the common people, populace, lower class

plector, — 3 to be beaten *or* punished

plectrum, ī *n* plectrum for striking a stringed instrument; lyre, lute

plēnus 3 full, filled; abundant, copious; entire, complete

plērus-que, **plēraque**, plē-

rumque a very great part, most; *adv.* **plērumque** for the most part, commonly

plicō, —, ātum 1 to fold, coil up

plōrō 1 to wail, lament

pluit, pluit (plūvit) 3 it rains

plūma, ae *f* feather, down

plumbeus 3 of lead

plumbum, ī *n* lead

plūrēs, **plūrimus**, *see* multus

plūs, *see* multum

plūsculus 3 a little more

pluteus, ī *m* penthouse, shed; parapet, breast-work

pluvia, ae *f* rain

pluviālis, e = pluvius

pluvius 3 rainy

pōculum, ī *n* drinking vessel, cup; drink, drinking-bout

podagra, ae *f* gout

poēma, atis *n* poem

poena, ae *f* recompense, punishment, penalty

poeniō *and* **-ior** = punio(r)

poēsis, is *f* poetry, poem

poēta, ae *m* poet

poēticus 3 poetic

pol *int.* by Pollux!, indeed!, truly!

poliō 4 to adorn, polish, refine

polleō, (uī), — 2 to be strong *or* powerful

pollex, icis *m* the thumb

pol-liceor, licitus sum 2 to offer, promise

pollicitātiō, ōnis *f* promise

pollicitor 1 to promise repeatedly

pol-luŏ, uī, ūtum 3 to defile, pollute, violate

polus, ī *m* pole of the earth; the sky, heavens

pŏlypus, ī *m* polypus

pōmārium, ī *n* orchard

pōm(o)ērium, ī *n* open space on each side of the walls of a city

pōmi-fer 3 fruit-bearing

pompa, ae *f* solemn procession; retinue; display, ostentation

pōmum, ī *n* fruit

pŏnderō 1 to weigh, ponder, consider

pondō (*abl. sg.*) in weight; (*with libra understood*) pound(s)

pondus, eris *n* weight; balance; burden, load; consequence, importance

pōne *adv. and prep.* with *acc.* behind

pōnō, posuī, positum 3 to put, place, set; to lay out, bury; to invest; to spend (*time*); to set up, build; to lay down, remove; to fix, ordain; to reckon, regard; to assert, assume; to dismiss, leave off

pōns, tis *m* bridge; passage

ponti-fex, icis *m* high priest

pontificālis, e *and* **-ficius** 3 pontifical, of the high priest

pontificātus, ūs *m* office of a high priest

pontus, ī *m* the sea

popīna, ae *f* eating-house, low tavern

poples, itis *m* (hollow of) the knee

populāris, e of the people, popular, democratic; of the same people *or* country, native

populātiō, ōnis *f* devastation

populātor, ōris *m* devastator, plunderer

pōpuleus 3 of a poplar

populor *and* **-lō** 1 to lay waste, plunder, destroy

populus1, ī *m* a people, the citizens; crowd, throng

pōpulus2, ī *f* poplar

porca, ae *f* sow

porcus, ī *m* hog, pig

por(r)iciō, —, rēctum 3 to offer as a sacrifice

por-rigō, rēxī, rēctum 3 to stretch out, extend; offer, present

porrō *adv.* forward, onward; henceforward; besides, moreover

porrum, ī *n* leek

porta, ae *f* gate, entrance

por-tendō, ndī, ntum 3 to point out, indicate, foretell

portentum, ī *n* marvel, portent; monster, monstrosity

porticus, ūs *f* colonnade, portico

portiō, ōnis *f* share, portion; proportion

portitor, ōris *m* ferryman; custom-house officer

portō 1 to carry, convey

portōrium, ī *n* tax, toll, duty

portuōsus 3 having many harbours

portus, ūs *m* harbour, haven; refuge

poscō, poposcī, — 3 to beg, demand, request; to require, need

positor, ōris *m* founder, builder

positus, ūs *m* position, situation, arrangement

possessiō, ōnis *f* a taking possession; possession, property

possessor, ōris *m* possessor

pos-sideō, sēdī, sessum 2 to possess, have

pos-sīdō, sēdī, sessum 3 to occupy, take possession of

possum, potuī, posse to be able; to avail, have influence

post *adv.* behind; afterwards; *prep.* with *acc.* behind; after, since

post-eā *adv.* after that, afterwards

posteritās, ātis *f* posterity, future generations

posterus 3 coming after, following, next; *comp.* posterior, ius later, posterior, inferior, worse; *superl.* postrēmus 3 hindmost, last, lowest, worst; *adv.* postrēmum for the last time; postrēmō at last, finally; postumus 3 last born, posthumous

post-habeō 2 = postpono

post-hāc *adv.* henceforth, after this

postīcus 3 hinder, back

post-illā *adv.* afterwards

postis, is *m* door-post, door

post-līminium, ī *n* right to return home with citizenrights

pos(t)-merīdiānus 3 in the afternoon

post-modo *and* -modum *adv.* soon after, presently

post-pōnō 3 to put after, esteem less, disregard

post-quam *cj.* after, when

postrēmus 3, *see* posterus

postrī-diē *adv.* on the following day

postulātiō, ōnis *f* claim, demand

postulātum, ī *n* demand

postulō 1 to demand, claim, request; to prosecute, ask leave to prosecute

postumus 3, *see* posterus

pote, *see* potis

potēns, tis mighty, powerful, ruling over; able, capable

potentātus, ūs *m* power, dominion

potentia, ae *f* power, might, force; rule, command

potestās, ātis *f* ability, capacity; power, authority, rule; office, magistracy, magistrate; opportunity

pōtiō, ōnis *f* a drinking, drink; poisonous draught

potior, tītus sum 4 to become master of, obtain, acquire; to possess, hold

potis, pote able, capable,

possible; *comp.* **potior**, us better, preferable, more important; *adv.* **potius** rather, more; *superl.* **potissimus 3** chief, principal; *adv.* **potissimum** especially, above all

pōtō, āvi, pōtum *or* **pōtātum 1** to drink, absorb

pōtor, ōris *m* drinker, drunkard

prae *adv.* before, in front; *prep.* with *abl.* before, in front of; in comparison with; because of, on account of

prae-acūtus 3 sharp, pointed

prae-altus 3 very high *or* deep

prae-beō, uī, itum 2 to hold forth, offer, furnish; to occasion, cause; to show, exhibit

prae-caveō 2 to take care, be on one's guard

prae-cēdō 3 to go before, precede; to surpass

prae-cellō, —, — 3 to surpass, excel

prae-ceps, cipitis headlong; steep, precipitous; hasty, rash

praeceptiō, ōnis *f* precept

praeceptor, ōris *m* teacher, instructor

praeceptum, ī *n* order, injunction; rule, maxim

prae-cīdō, cīdī, cīsum 3 to cut off; to cut short, abridge

prae-cingō 3 to gird about

prae-cinō, cinuī, centum 3 to recite *or* play before

prae-cipiō, cēpī, ceptum 3 to take in advance, anticipate; to advise, instruct, prescribe, command

praecipitō 1 to cast down headlong; to hasten; *intr.* to rush headlong, sink to ruin

praecipuē *adv.* chiefly, especially

praecipuus 3 particular, especial; principal, distinguished

prae-clārus 3 splendid, noble, admirable, famous

prae-clūdō, sī, sum 3 to shut off, shut, close

praecō, ōnis *m* crier, herald; auctioneer

praecōnium, ī *n* proclamation, publication; laudation

prae-cordia, ōrum *n/pl.* midriff; internal organs; breast, heart

prae-currō, (cu)currī, cursum 3 to run before, precede, anticipate

prae-cursor, ōris *m* advanced guard, scout

praeda, ae *f* booty, plunder; prey, game; gain, profit

praedātor, ōris *m* plunderer

praedātōrius 3 plundering

praediātor, ōris *m* dealer in estates

praedicātiō, ōnis *f* proclamation; praise

praedicātor, ōris *m* commender

prae-dīcō[1] 1 to publish, proclaim, assert; to praise

prae-dīcō[2] 3 to say before, foretell, predict; to order

prae-dictum, ī n prediction; command [or estate]

praediolum, ī n small farm

prae-ditus 3 endowed or provided with

praedium, ī n farm, estate

prae-dīves, itis very rich

praedō, ōnis m plunderer, robber

praedor 1 to plunder, rob

prae-dūcō 3 to draw or construct in front

prae-dūrus 3 very hard or tough

prae-eō, iī, itum, īre to go before, lead the way; to dictate

prae-fātiō, ōnis f religious form of words, formula

praefectūra, ae f command, administration; city governed by a prefect

praefectus, ī m overseer, commander, governor

prae-ferō, tulī, lātum, ferre to carry before; to show, display; to prefer

prae-ferōx, ōcis very defiant or headstrong

prae-ficiō, fēcī, fectum 3 to set over, appoint to command

prae-fīgō 3 to fix or fasten in front; to point with

prae-fīniō 4 to determine beforehand, prescribe

prae-fluō, —, — 3 to flow by

prae-for 1 to say beforehand; to utter a preliminary prayer

prae-fringō, frēgī, frāctum 3 to break off

prae-fulgeō 2 to shine forth

prae-gestiō 4 to desire greatly

prae-gnā(n)s, (n)tis pregnant

prae-gravis, e very heavy

prae-gravō 1 to oppress with, weigh down

prae-gredior, gressus sum 3 to go before or in advance

prae-gustō 1 to taste beforehand

prae-iūdicium, ī n previous judgment, precedent

prae-iūdicō 1 to judge or decide beforehand

prae-lābor 3 to glide or flow past

prae-lūceō 2 to shine before; to outshine

prae-mātūrus 3 untimely, premature

prae-meditor 1 to consider beforehand

prae-mittō 3 to send in advance

praemium, ī n advantage, prerogative; reward, recompense; prize, booty

prae-moneō 2 to forewarn; to foretell

prae-morior 3 to die prematurely

prae-mūniō 4 to fortify, protect; to place before as a defence prae-nōmen, inis *n* first *or* personal name

prae-nōscō 3 to learn beforehand

prae-nūntius, ī *m* and -nūntia, ae *f* foreteller, foreboder

prae-occupō 1 to seize before; to anticipate, prevent

prae-optō 1 to prefer

prae-parō 1 to prepare, provide

prae-pediō 4 to shackle, hinder, obstruct

prae-pendeō, pendī, — 2 to hang down in front

prae-pes, petis quick, fleet; auspicious (*bird*)

prae-polleō 2 to be very powerful

prae-pōnō 3 to put before, set over, place at the head of; to prefer

prae-posterus 3 reversed, inverted, perverse

prae-potēns, tis very powerful

prae-properus 3 too hasty

prae-ripiō, ripuī, reptum 3 to seize first *or* prematurely; to forestall

prae-rogātīvus 3 voting before others; *subst.* prae-rogātīva, ae *f* century that voted first; previous choice [short]

prae-rumpō 3 to break off

praes, praedis *m* surety, bondsman

praesaepe, is *n* stall, stable, fold

prae-saepiō 4 to barricade

prae-sāgiō 4 to forebode

praesāgium, ī *n* presentiment, foreboding

prae-sāgus 3 foreboding, predicting

prae-scīscō, īvī, (iī), — 3 to learn beforehand

prae-scius 3 knowing beforehand

prae-scrībō 3 to prefix in writing; to order, direct, prescribe

prae-scrīptiō, ōnis *f* title; order, rule [rule]

prae-scrīptum, ī *n* order,

prae-secō 1 to cut off

praesēns, tis present, in person; immediate, prompt, efficacious; propitious; resolute

praesentia, ae *f* presence

prae-sentiō 4 to feel *or* perceive beforehand

praesēpe, is *n* = praesaepe

praesertim *adv.* especially, chiefly

prae-ses, sidis *m* and *f* protector, guardian; chief, ruler

prae-sideō, sēdī, (sessum) 2 to protect, guard; to preside over, govern

praesidium, ī *n* protection, defence, aid; guard, garrison; camp, fortification

prae-signis, e remarkable

praestābilis, e = praestans

praestāns, tis distinguished, excellent

praestantia, ae *f* excellence, superiority

praest(r)īgiae, ārum *f/pl.* deceptions, trickery

prae-stitūō, uī, ūtum 3 to determine beforehand

prae-stō[1] *adv.* at hand, ready, present, at one's service

prae-stō[2], stitī, stitum (stātūrus) 1 to stand out, excel, be superior; praestat it is preferable *or* better; *trans.* to perform, fulfil; to show, exhibit, prove; to answer, be responsible for

praestōlor 1 to wait for, stand ready for

prae-stringō 3 to blunt, dazzle, weaken

prae-struō 3 to block up

prae-sum, fuī, (futūrus), esse to be leader, preside, rule, command

prae-sūmō 3 to take beforehand, anticipate

prae-temptō 1 to feel *or* test beforehand

prae-tendō, ndī, ntum 3 to stretch forth; to spread before; to pretend, offer as a pretext

prae-tentō 1 = praetempto

praeter *adv.* unless it be, except; *prep.* with *acc.* past, in front of; except; above, besides; beyond, contrary to

praeter-eā *adv.* besides, further, moreover; henceforth

praeter-eō, iī, itum, īre to go by, pass; to neglect, omit

praeter-gredior, gressus sum 3 to walk by

praeter-lābor 3 to glide past

praeter-mittō 3 to let pass, omit, neglect

praeter-quam *cj.* except, beyond

praeter-vehor 3 to pass by

praeter-volō 1 to fly by, escape

prae-texō 3 to fringe, border, adorn; to conceal

praetextātus 3 wearing a *toga praetexta*; under age

praetor, ōris *m* leader, chief; praetor, magistrate; governor

praetōrius 3 of a praetor; of a general; *subst.* -ium, ī *n* a general's tent; council of war; residence of a governor; palace

praetūra, ae *f* praetorship

prae-ustus 3 burned at the end

prae-valeō, uī, — 2 to be very strong; to be stronger

prae-validus 3 very strong

praevāricātor, ōris *m* collusive advocate, sham accuser

prae-vehor 3 to drive *or* ride in front

prae-veniō 4 to come before, get the start of, forestall

prae-vertō *and* -vertor 3 to do in preference, attend to first; to precede, outrun; to anticipate, prevent prae-videō 2 to see first, foresee

prae-vius 3 going before

prae-vortō = prae-verto

prandeō, ndī, ānsum 2 to lunch (on)

prandium, ī n lunch

prātum, ī n meadow

prāvitās, ātis f deformity; viciousness, wickedness

prāvus 3 deformed; perverse, bad, vicious

precārius 3 obtained by entreaty; uncertain

precātiō, ōnis f an entreating, prayer

precātor, ōris m pleader, intercessor

precēs, um f/pl. (sg. rare) entreaty; prayer; curse

precor 1 to beg, pray, entreat

prehendō, ndī, ēnsum 3 to grasp, seize; to arrest, detain

premō, pressī, pressum 3 to press, press out; to burden, load, oppress; to cover, bury; to press hard upon, pursue, importune; to depress, lower; to plant; to impress, mark; to degrade, humble; to check, restrain; to prune

prēndō = prehendo

prēnsō 1 to grasp, seize; to canvass

pressō 1 to press

pressus 3 compressed; concise; restrained

pretiōsus 3 valuable, costly

pretium, ī n value, price;

wages; reward; punishment

prīdem adv. long ago, long since

prī-diē adv. on the day before

prīm-aevus 3 youthful

prīmārius 3 of the first rank, excellent

prīmi-pīlus, ī m the first centurion of a legion

prīm-itiae, ārum f/pl. first-fruits [ning, origin)

prīm-ōrdium, ī n begin-

prīmōris, e first, chief, principal

prīmus 3 first; chief, principal, most'excellent; adv. prīmum for the first time, firstly; prīmō at first

prīn-ceps, ipis adj. = primus; subst. ~, ipis m author, founder; leader, chief, ruler, emperor; prīncipēs, um m/pl. soldiers of the second line

prīncipātus, ūs m the first place, pre-eminence, chief command

prīncipium, ī n a beginning, commencement; element, principle; pl. front line of soldiers; pl. headquarters

prior, us comp. former, prior, first; better, superior; adv. prius earlier, previously

prīscus 3 of former times, old, venerable; previous

prīstinus 3 former, primitive, original

prius-quam *cj.* before

prīvātim *adv.* apart from state affairs, privately

prīvātus 3 apart from the state, private, personal; out of office; *subst.* ~, ī *m* private individual; **-um, ī** *n* private property, privacy

prīvignus, ī *m* step-son

prīvi-lēgium, ī *n* law relating to a single person only

prīvō 1 to deprive of; to free, release

prīvus 3 each; private, particular

prō¹ *int.* oh!, ah!, alas!

prō² *prep.* with *abl.* (*of place*) before, in front of; (*of relation*) for, on behalf of; in the place of, instead of, as good as; in exchange *or* return for; in proportion to, according to

pro-avus, ī *m* great grandfather; ancestor

probābilis, e pleasing, acceptable; credible likely

probātiō, ōnis *f* proving, examination; approval

probātor, ōris *m* approver

probitās, ātis *f* honesty, uprightness

probō 1 to try, test; to approve; to represent *or* commend as good; to show, prove, demonstrate

probrōsus 3 shameful, infamous

probrum, ī *n* shameful deed, disgrace, infamy; reproach, insult

probus 3 good, honest, virtuous

procāx, ācis bold, insolent

prō-cēdō 3 to proceed, advance; to appear; to pass, elapse; to continue; to turn out, succeed, prosper

procella, ae *f* storm, tempest, attack

procellōsus 3 stormy

procerēs, um *m/pl.* chiefs, nobles, princes

prōcēritās, ātis *f* height, length

prō-cērus 3 tall, long

prōcessus, ūs *m* advance, progress

prō-cidō, cidī, — 3 to fall down *or* forward

prō-clāmō 1 to call out, cry out

prō-clīnō 1 to turn, incline

prō-clīvis, e sloping down; inclined, prone to; easy

prō-cōnsul, ulis *m* proconsul

prōcōnsulāris, e proconsular

prō-crāstinō 1 to put off till tomorrow

prō-creō 1 to beget, produce, cause

prō-cūdō 3 to forge, hammer out

procul *adv.* far off, at a distance

prō-culcō 1 to tread down, trample upon

prō-cumbō, cubuī, cubitum 3 to lean *or* fall forward, sink down

prōcūrātiō, ōnis *f* admini-

stration, charge; ex-
piation

prō-cūrātor, ōris m manager, administrator, agent

prōcūrātiō, ōnis f administration, charge; expiation

prō-cūrō 1 to take care of,
attend to; to expiate

prō-currō, (cu)currī, cursum 3 to run forward; to
project

prō-cursus, ūs m a running
forward, attack

prō-curvus 3 curved for-
ward

procus, ī m wooer, suitor

prōd-eō, iī, itum, īre to go
or come forth, appear; to
advance

prō-dīcō 3 to put off, defer

prōdigiōsus 3 wonderful,
strange, unnatural

prōdigium, ī n prodigy,
portent, omen; monster

prōdigus 3 wasteful, prodigal; rich, generous

prōditiō, ōnis f betrayal,
treachery

prōditor, ōris m betrayer,
traitor

prō-dō, didī, ditum 3 to
produce, bear; to hand
down, transmit, report;
to appoint; to reveal,
betray, surrender

prō-dūcō 3 to lead forth,
bring out; to produce,
cause to appear; to pro-
mote, advance; to draw
out, lengthen; to beget,
bring up

proelior 1 to fight

proelium, ī n battle, fight

prō-fānō 1 to desecrate,
profane

prō-fānus 3 not sacred,
profane; impious; ill-
boding

profectiō, ōnis f a setting
out, departure

prō-fectō adv. truly, really,
indeed

prōfectus, ūs m advance,
increase

prō-ferō, tulī, lātum, ferre
to carry or bring forth,
move forward; to extend,
enlarge; to make known,
discover, reveal; to quote,
mention; to put off, postpone

professiō, ōnis f public
acknowledgment, declara-
tion

prō-fēstus 3 not festival,
common

prō-ficiō, fēcī, fectum 3 to
make progress, effect or
gain something; to be
useful or serviceable

prō-ficīscor, fectus sum 3
to set out, march, depart;
to spring or arise from

prō-fiteor, fessus sum 2 to
declare, acknowledge, confess; to offer, promise; to
make a return (of pro-
perty, &c.)

prōflīgātus 3 degraded,
abandoned

prō-flīgō 1 to strike to the
ground, overcome, destroy;
to bring nearly to an end

prō-flō 1 to blow or breathe
forth

prō-fluō 3 to flow forth

pro-for 1 to say *or* speak out

pro-fugiō 3 to flee away, escape

pro-fugus 3 fleeing, fugitive; banished

pro-fundō 3 to pour out; to utter; to spend, lavish, squander

pro-fundus 3 deep, profound, immoderate; *subst.* **-um, ī** *n* the deep, sea

pro-fūsus 3 lavish, excessive

prōgeniēs, ēī *f* descent, race; offspring

prō-gignō 3 to beget, bear, produce

prō-gnātus 3 born, descended

prō-gredior, gressus sum 3 to go forth *or* out, advance; to go on, proceed

prōgressiō, ōnis *f*, *fig.* = **progressus**

prō-gressus, ūs *m* advance, progress, growth, increase

pro-hibeō, uī, itum 2 to hold back, keep off, prevent, hinder; to preserve, defend

prō-iciō, iēcī, iectum 3 *to* throw forth *or* before, to thrust, extend; to banish; to throw away, abandon, give up

prō-iectus 3 stretched out, projecting; conspicuous; contemptible

proin, proinde *adv.* therefore, so; just so

prō-lābor 3 to glide forward; to go on, proceed; to fall down, decline, go to ruin; to fail, err

prō-lātiō, ōnis *f* extension; a putting off, delay

prō-lātō 1 to delay, postpone

prōlēs, is *f* offspring, race, stock

prō-lixus 3 well-disposed, favourable

prō-logus, ī *m* preface, prologue

prō-loquor 3 to speak out, declare

prō-lūdō 3 to practise beforehand

prō-luō, uī, ūtum 3 to wash (off), wet, moisten

prō-luviēs, ēī *f* overflow; refuse

prō-mereor 2 to deserve, merit, earn

prō-mineō, —, — 2 to stand out, project, overhang, extend

prō-miscuus (*and* **-cus**) 3 mixed, indiscriminate, in common

prō-missiō, ōnis *f* a promising

prōmissum, ī *n* promise

prō-mittō 3 to let grow, let hang down; to promise, give hope of

prōmō, mpsī, mptum 3 to take out, produce, bring to light

prō-moveō 2 to move forward, push onward; to extend

prōmptus¹ 3 visible, apparent; at hand, ready, inclined, disposed; courageous; easy, practicable

prōmptus² , ūs *m; only in* prōmptū public, visible; ready, at hand

prōmulgātiō, ōnis *f* public announcement

prō-mulgō 1 to publish, promulgate

prōmunturium, ī *n* headland, promontory

pro-nepōs, ōtis *m* great grandson

prō-nuba, ae *f* bride's attendant

prō-nūntiātiō, ōnis *f* publication, proclamation

prō-nūntiō 1 to publish, announce; to relate, report; to decide, pronounce judgment

prōnus 3 inclined forward, face downwards; flying headlong; setting; sloping; inclined, disposed; easy

pro-oemium, ī *n* introduction, preface

propāgātiō, ōnis *f* an extending, enlarging; propagation

pro-pāgō¹ (*and* prō-), inis *f* sucker, shoot; offspring, posterity

pro-pāgō² (*and* prō-) 1 to propagate; to enlarge, prolong

prō-palam *adv.* publicly, openly

prō-patulus 3 open in front; in prōpatulō in the open air

prope (*comp.* propius, *superl.* proximē *and* -umē) *adv.* near, at hand; nearly, almost; *prep.* with *acc.* near, close to; *adj. comp.* propior, ius nearer; later, more recent; more like, more intimate; *superl.* proximus (*and* -umus) 3 the nearest, next

prope-diem *adv.* very soon

prō-pellō, pulī, pulsum 3 to drive or push forward, drive out; to move, impel

prope-modum *adv.* nearly, almost

prō-pēnsus 3 approaching; inclined, disposed, willing

properanter *adv.* hastily, quickly

properō 1 to hasten, be quick

properus 3 hastening, quick

prō-pexus 3 combed forward, hanging down

prō-pīnō (*and* prō-) 1 to drink to one's health

propinquitās, ātis *f* nearness; relationship

propinquō 1 to come near, approach

propinquus 3 near, neighbouring; kindred, related; *subst. m* and *f* relation

propior, ius, *see* prope

propitiō 1 to appease

propitius 3 favourable, gracious

prō-pōnō 3 to put forth, expose to view; to publish, declare; to propose, offer; to threaten; to imagine, conceive; to purpose, intend

prō-positum, ī *n* purpose, intention; main point, theme

prō-praetor, ōris *m* propraetor

propriē *adv.* personally, as one's own, individually; properly, accurately

proprietās, ātis *f* a property, peculiar quality

proprius 3 lasting, permanent; one's own, peculiar, proper, personal; characteristic, essential

propter *adv.* near, hard by; *prep.* with *acc.* near, close to; on account of, because of

propter-eā *adv.* therefore, on that account

prōpugnāculum, ī *n* bulwark, rampart; defence, protection

prō-pugnātiō, ōnis *f* defence

prō-pugnātor, ōris *m* defender, protector

prō-pugnō 1 to go forth to fight; to fight in defence

prō-pulsō 1 to drive back, ward off   [ship)]

prōra, ae *f* prow, bow (of

prō-rēpō 3 to creep forward

prō-ripiō, ripuī, reptum 3 to snatch, drag, tear forth

prō-rogō 1 to prolong, protract

prōrsus (*and* prōrsum) *adv.* straight forward; utterly, entirely; in short

prō-rumpō 3 to burst forth, break out

prō-ruō 3 to throw down, pull down

pro-scaenium, ī *n* the stage

prō-scindō 3 to plough

prō-scrībō 3 to make public, advertise; to confiscate; to proscribe, outlaw

prō-scriptiō, ōnis *f* advertisement of sale; proscription

prō-secō 1 to cut off

prō-sequor 3 to follow, attend; to pursue, attack; to honour, wait upon; to go on, continue

prō-siliō, siluī, — 4 to leap forth, start out, rush

prō-spectō 1 to look forth, see afar off, look at; to await, expect

prōspectus, ūs *m* (distant) view, prospect; (faculty of) sight

prō-speculor 1 = prospecto

prosper 3 = prosperus

prosperō 1 to make successful *or* happy

prosperus 3 fortunate, according to one's wishes, favourable, prosperous

prō-spiciō, spexī, spectum 3 to look forward, look out; to exercise foresight, provide for; to see afar; to foresee; to procure

prō-sternō 3 to throw to the ground, cast down; to destroy, ruin

prō-stituō, uī, ūtum 3 to prostitute

prō-stō, stitī, — 1 to be on sale

prō-sum, prōfuī, (prōfutūrus), prōdesse to be useful, be of use

prō-tegō 3 to cover, protect, defend

prō-tendō, ndī, ntum 3 to stretch forth or out

prō-terō 3 to tread upon, trample, crush

prō-terreō 2 to frighten away

protervitās, ātis f boldness, impudence, wantonness

protervus 3 vehement; bold, impudent, wanton

prō-tinam = protinus

prō-tinus adv. forward, further on; immediately, at once; continuously, uninterruptedly

prō-trahō 3 to drag forth; to bring to light, reveal

prō-trūdō 3 to push forward

prō-turbō 1 to drive on or away

pro-ut cj. according as, just as

prō-vehō 3 to carry forward, lead on; to promote, exalt; **P.** to go on, ride, drive, advance

prō-veniō 4 to come forth, appear; to thrive, prosper

prōventus, ūs m growth, produce; issue, result, success

prō-verbium, ī n old saying, proverb

prōvidentia, ae f foresight, precaution, providence

prō-videō 2 to see from afar; to foresee; to take care, care for; to provide

prōvidus 3 foreseeing; cautious, prudent

prōvincia, ae f duty; office; province, administration of a province

prōvinciālis, e provincial

prō-vīsiō, ōnis f = prōvidentia

prō-vīsō 3 to go to see

prō-vocātiō, ōnis f appeal (in law)

prō-vocō 1 to call forth, summon, incite, challenge; to appeal (in law)

prō-volō 1 to fly forth, rush forth

prō-volvō 3 to roll forward or along

proximē, see prope

proximitās, ātis f nearness

proximus 3, superl. of prope

prūdēns, tis knowing, with intention; skilled, practised; wise, discreet, prudent

prūdentia, ae f knowledge, skill; prudence, discretion

pruīna, ae f hoar-frost, rime

pruīnōsus 3 covered with hoar-frost

prūna, ae f burning coal

prūnum, ī n plum

prūriō 4 to itch; to long for

prytanēum, ī *n* town hall, council-hall

psallō, lī, — 3 to play on *or* sing to the cithara

psaltria, ae *f* female player on the cithara

-pte (*suffix*) self, own

pūbēns, tis mature, exuberant

pūbēs[1], is *f* the genitals; young men; people

pūbēs[2], eris adult, grown up

pūbēscō, buī, — 3 to grow up, arrive at maturity

pūblicānus, ī *m* farmer of state-revenues

pūblicātiō, ōnis *f* confiscation

pūblicē *adv.* in the name *or* interest of the state

pūblicitus *adv.* = publice

pūblicō 1 to make public; to confiscate

pūblicus 3 of the people, state *or* community; in the name *or* at the cost of the state; public, common, general; rēs pūblica commonwealth, republic, state; public interest; *subst.* pūblicum, ī *n* state property; public revenue, treasury; public place

pudeō 2 to be ashamed; to make ashamed (*mostly impers.*); pudēns, tis bashful, modest, chaste

pudibundus 3 shamefaced, bashful

pudīcitia, ae *f* modesty, chastity, virtue

pudīcus 3 bashful, modest, chaste, virtuous

pudor, ōris *m* sense of shame, honour, modesty, decency; shame, disgrace

puella, ae *f* girl, maiden

puellāris, e girlish, maidenly

puellula, ae *f*, *dim. of* puella

puer, erī *m* child; boy, youth; servant, slave

puerīlis, e boyish, childish, youthful

pueritia, ae *f* boyhood, childhood

puer-pera, ae *f* woman in childbirth

pugil, ilis *m* boxer, pugilist

pūgiō, ōnis *m* dagger, poniard

pugna, ae *f* fight, battle, contest

pugnātor, ōris *m* fighter, combatant

pugnāx, ācis fond of fighting, warlike; obstinate

pugnō 1 to fight, struggle, contend

pugnus, ī *m* fist

pulcher, chra, chrum beautiful, fair, handsome; fine, glorious, noble

pulchritūdō, inis *f* beauty; excellence

pullārius, ī *m* feeder of fowls

pullulō 1 to shoot up, sprout

pullus[1], ī *m* young animal, chicken

pullus[2] 3 dark grey, gloomy

pulmentum, ī n portion of food

pulmō, ōnis m lung

pulpāmentum, ī n meat, food

pulpitum, ī n platform, stage

puls, tis f thick pap, porridge

pulsātiō, ōnis f a striking

pulsō 1 to beat, strike; to move, agitate

pulsus, ūs m a beating, striking

pultō 1 = pulso

pulvereus 3 full of dust, dusty

pulverulentus 3 dusty

pulvīnar, āris n couch of the gods, cushioned seat

pulvīnus, ī m cushion, pillow

pulvis, eris m dust, sand, ashes; arena; field; toil

pūmex, icis m pumice-stone; lava bed

punctum, ī n voting-mark; small portion of time, moment

pungō, pupugī, punctum 3 to prick, puncture; to sting, vex, afflict

pūniceus 3 bright red

pūniō and **pūnior 4** to punish; to avenge

pūpilla, ae f orphan-girl

pūpillus, ī m orphan-boy; ward

puppis, is f stern, poop; ship

pūpula, ae f (pupil of) the eye

pūrgāmen, inis and **pūrgāmentum, ī** n filth, dirt, sweepings; means of purgation

pūrgātiō, ōnis f a purging; justification

pūrgō 1 to cleanse, purge, purify, expiate; to excuse, justify; to disprove

purpura, ae f purple; purple garment

purpurātus 3 clad in purple; *subst.* ~, **ī** m high officer, courtier

purpureus 3 violet, crimson, purple; clad in purple; bright, beautiful

pūrus 3 pure, clean; clear; spotless, undefiled, chaste; unadorned, plain

pusillus 3 tiny, petty

pūsiō, ōnis m little boy

puteal, ālis n stone-enclosure

pūteō 2 to stink

puter, tris, tre rotten, decaying, stinking; crumbling, soft

pūtēscō, tuī, — 3 to rot, decay

puteus, ī m pit; well

pūtidus 3 rotten, decaying; disgusting, affected

putō 1 to prune; to estimate, reckon, consider; to think, believe, suppose

putre-faciō 3 to make rotten

putridus 3 = puter

pyra, ae f funeral pyre

pyxis, idis f small box, casket

Q

quā (*interrog. and relat.*) by what way, on which side, where; in so far as; in what manner, in any manner; quā ... quā partly ... partly, as well ... as

quā-cumque by whatever way, wherever

quadra, ae *f* a quarter (of a circular loaf, cake, &c.)

quadrāgēnī 3 forty each

quadrāgintā (*indecl.*) forty

quadrāns, tis *m* quarter (of an as)

quadrātus 3 squared, square

quadri-duum, ī *n* space of four days

quadri-ennium, ī *n* period of four years

quadri-fidus 3 split into four parts

quadrīgae, ārum *f/pl.* four-horse chariot

quadri-iugus 3 (*and* -iugis, e) of a team of four

quadrīmus 3 four years old

quadringentī 3 four hundred

quadri-partītus *or* -pertītus 3 divided into four parts

quadri-rēmis, is *f* vessel with four banks of oars

quadrō 1 to complete, arrange; *intr.* to agree, fit, accord

quadru-pedāns, tis *m* galloping

quadru-pēs, pedis four-footed; *subst. m* and *f* quadruped, horse

quadruplātor, ōris *m* informer

quadru-plex, icis fourfold

quaeritō 1 to seek eagerly

quaerō, sīvī *and* siī, situm 3 to seek, search for; to miss, want; to get, acquire; to ask, inquire, demand; to investigate, examine

quaesītor, ōris *m* president of a criminal investigation

quaesītus 3 far-fetched, affected; *subst.* quaesītum, ī *n* question; gain

quaesō 3 to beg, beseech, entreat

quaestiō, ōnis *f* question, examination; judicial inquiry; subject of investigation, case, dispute

quaestor, ōris *m* quaestor (Roman public official)

quaestōrius 3 of a quaestor

quaestuōsus 3 gainful, profitable

quaestūra, ae *f* office of quaestor

quaestus, ūs *m* gain, profit, advantage; business, trade

quālis, e of what sort or kind or nature; of such a kind as, such as

quālis-cumque 2 of whatever kind or sort; any ... whatever

quālus, ī *m* wicker-basket

quam how greatly, how much, how; as; (*after comp.*) than

quam-libet *adv.* however much

quam-ob-rem on what account?, why?; wherefore; therefore

quam-quam *cj.* though, although; however, yet

quam-vīs *adv.* and *cj.* as you will, however (much), although

quandō *adv.* and *cj.* at what time, when; at any time, ever; since, as

quandō-cumque whenever, as often as; at some time or other

quandō-que *cj.* and *adv.* whenever; since, as; at some time

quandō-quidem *cj.* since, as

quanquam = quamquam

quantopere how greatly, how much

quantulus 3 how little, how small

quantus 3 how great, how much; as great as, as much as

quantus-cumque 3 however great; however small

quantus-libet = quantusvis

quantus-vīs 3 as great as you will

quā-propter wherefore?; therefore

quā-rē whereby; wherefore, why; therefore

quārtāna, ae *f* quartan fever

quārtus 3 the fourth

quā-si *cj.* and *adv.* as if, as though, as, so to speak; nearly, almost

quassō 1 to shake, toss; to shatter

quā-tenus how far, up to what point; in so far as, since

quater *adv.* four times

quaternī 3 four each

quatiō, —, quassum 3 to shake, brandish; to beat, strike, drive; to crush, shatter; to agitate, affect, trouble, vex

quattuor (*indecl.*) four

quattuor-decim (*indecl.*) fourteen

-que *cj.* and; **que ... que** both ... and

quem-ad-modum in what manner, how; as, just as

queō, quīvī (or **iī), itum, īre** to be able, I can

quercus, ūs *f* oak

querēl(l)a, ae *f* complaint; wailing, cry

querimōnia, ae *f* = querela

quernus 3 of oak

queror, questus sum 3 to complain, lament, bewail

querulus 3 complaining, querulous, plaintive

questus, ūs *m* a complaining, complaint

quī[1], quae, quod *interrog.* what?; what kind of a?; *relat.* who, which, what, that

quī[2], qua (*and* quae), quod *indef.* any, some, any one

quī[3] *interrog.* how?; why?; *relat.* by which, with which; somehow; oh that! (in wishes) quia *cj.* because

quianam? why?

quī-cumque, quae-, quod-whoever, whatever, all that; any, every possible

quī-dam, quae-dam, quid-dam (*subst.*) *and* quoddam (*adj.*) a certain (one), somebody, something; a kind of, so to speak

quidem *adv.* certainly, indeed, at least, in truth; for example; ne ... quidem not even ...

quid-nī *adv.* why not?

quiēs, ētis *f* rest, repose, quiet; sleep; peace

quiēsco, ēvī, ētum 3 to rest, repose, keep quiet, be calm

quiētus 3 quiet, inactive, peaceful, calm

quī-libet, quae-libet, quid-libet (*subst.*) *and* quod-libet (*adj.*) any one, any thing you please

quīn *adv.* why not?; rather, nay, indeed; *cj.* that not, without; that, but that

quī-nam 3 who, which, what?

Quīnctīlis, e, = Quīntilis

quīnc-ūnx, ūncis *m* five twelfths; a quincunx (five objects arranged like the five pips on dice)

quīn-decim (*indecl.*) fifteen

quīngentī 3 five hundred

quīnī 3 five each

quīnquāgintā (*indecl.*) fifty

quīnquātrūs, uum *f/pl.*

festival in honour of Minerva

quīnque (*indecl.*) five

quīnquennālis, e occurring every five years; lasting five years

quīnqu-ennis, e five years old

quīnqu-ennium, ī *n* period of five years

quīnque-rēmis, is *f* vessel with five banks of oars

quīnque-vir, ī *m* one of a commission of five

quīnquiē(n)s *adv.* five times

Quīntilis, e of July; *subst*

Quīntilis, is *m* July

quīntus 3 the fifth

quippe *adv.* of course, to be sure, naturally, indeed; since, inasmuch as

Quirīs, ītis *m* Roman citizen

quis (*subst.* and *adj.*), quid (*subst.*) (*interrog.*) who?; which one?; what?; (*indef.*) anyone, anybody, anything; someone, something

quis-nam, quid-nam who then?; what then?

quis-piam, quae-piam (*subst.* and *adj.*), quid-piam *or* quippiam (*subst.*) *and* quodpiam (*adj.*) someone, something

quis-quam, quid-quam *or* quic-quam (*subst.* only) anyone, anything

quis-que, quae-que, quid-que (*subst.*) *and* quod-que (*adj.*) each, every, every one, every thing

quisquis, quidquid *or* **quicquid** (*subst.*) whoever, whatever

qui-vīs, quae-vīs, quid-vīs (*subst.*) *and* **quod-vīs** (*adj.*) whoever *or* whatever you please, any (one), anything

quō *adv.* to what place, where; to what purpose; by which means, whereby; to any place, anywhere; *cj.* (in order) that, that thereby

quoad as long as, until, as far as

quō-circā *adv.* therefore

quō-cumque whithersoever

quod (*relat. pron.* and *cj.*) (as to) the fact that, in so far as, because, on the ground that

quom (*archaic*) = **cum**

quō-minus *cj.* by which ... not, so that ... not

quō-modo how

quō-nam *adv.* whither?

quondam *adv.* once, former-ly; sometimes; at som, future time

quon-iam *cj.* since, seeing that

quō-quam *adv.* to any place

quoque *adv.* also, too

quō-quō whithersoever

quōquō-versus *and* **-versum** *adv.* in every direction

quōrsum *and* **-us** *adv.* whither?, to what purpose?

quot (*indecl.*) how many?; as many as

quot-annīs *adv.* every year, yearly

quotīdiānus, quotīdie, *see* cot-...

quotiē(n)s *adv.* how often?, how many times?; as often as

quotiē(n)s-cumque *adv.* however often, as often as

quot-quot (*indecl.*) however many

quotus 3 which? (in the series 1st, 2nd, 3rd, &c.)

quo-usque *adv.* how long?, until when?

R

rabidus 3 furious, raving, mad

rabiēs, (ēī) *f* rage, frenzy, anger, fury, fierceness

rabiōsus 3 = **rabidus**

racēmi-fer 3 cluster-bearing

racēmus, ī *m* cluster of grapes

rādīcitus *adv.* with the root, utterly

radiō *and* **radior** 1 to shine

radius, ī *m* spoke of a wheel; measuring-rod; weaver's shuttle; beam, ray of light

rādīx, īcis *f* root; radish; foot (*of a hill*); basis, origin, source

rādō, sī, sum 3 to scrape, shave, smooth; to touch in passing, graze

raeda, ae *f* travelling-carriage

rāmālia, ium *n/pl.* branches, twigs, brushwood

rāmōsus 3 full of boughs, branching

rāmus, ī *m* branch, bough

rāna, ae *f* frog

rancid(ul)us 3 stinking, tainted

rānunculus, ī *m* little frog

rapāx, ācis grasping, rapacious, greedy

rapidus 3 snatching, seizing; impetuous, whirling, rapid

rapīna, ae *f* robbery, plundering

rapiō, puī, ptum 3 to snatch, seize, drag, carry off, plunder, ravage; *subst.* raptum, ī *n* plunder, booty

raptim *adv.* hastily, hurriedly

raptō 1 to carry away, drag; to plunder

raptor, ōris *m* robber, abductor

raptus, ūs *m* abduction, rape; plunder

rāpulum, ī *n* turnip

rārēscō, —, —3 to grow thin; to widen out

rārus 3 thin, wide apart, scattered; scanty, few, rare; uncommon, remarkable

rāsilis, e polished, smoothed

rāstrum, ī *n* and **rāster, trī** *m* toothed hoe

ratiō, ōnis *f* a reckoning, account, calculation; trans-action, business, affair; relation, reference; respect, consideration, concern; interest, advantage; judgment, understanding, reason; manner, course, method, plan; reason, motive; theory, doctrine, science; rule, order, principle

ratiōcinātor, ōris *m* reckoner, computer

ratiōcinor 1 to reckon, calculate; to argue, reason

ratis, is *f* raft, float; boat, ship

ratiuncula, ae *f* little reckoning *or* account; slight reason

ratus 3 calculated, fixed, settled, confirmed, certain, valid

raucus 3 hoarse; roaring, ringing

rāvus 3 yellowish-grey

rea, ae *f*, *see* reus

reāpse *adv.* indeed, really

rebelliō, ōnis *f* renewal of war, revolt, rebellion

rebellis, e insurgent, rebellious

re-bellō 1 to renew a war, revolt

re-boō 1 to resound, echo

re-calfaciō 3 to make warm again

re-candēscō, duī, — 3 to glow, grow white

re-cantō 1 to recall, recant; to charm away

re-cēdō 3 to retire, withdraw, retreat, be distant;

to go away, depart, disappear

recēns, tis lately arisen, modern, fresh, vigorous, young, recent; *adv.* **recēns** recently, newly

re-cēnseō, suī, sum (*or* **situm**) 2 to count, survey, review; to go over, reckon up, recount

receptāculum, ī *n* receptacle; place of refuge; retreat, shelter

re-ceptō 1 to take back; to receive, harbour

receptum, ī *n* obligation

receptus, ūs *m* a retiring, retreat; refuge

recessus, ūs *m* a retiring, retreat; nook, recess, retired spot [newed]

recidīvus 3 restored, renew(e(c)cidō, re(c)cidī, recāsūrus** 3 to fall back, return, be thrown back, relapse, sink, fall into

re-cīdō, cīdī, cīsum 3 to cut away *or* down *or* off; to extirpate, prune away

re-cingō 3 to ungird

re-cinō, —, — 3 to (cause to) resound; to celebrate, praise

reciperō 1 = **recupero**

re-cipiō, cēpī, ceptum 3 take, get, bring, draw back; to rescue, regain, recover, seize, occupy; to admit, accept, receive, welcome; to take upon oneself, assume; to guarantee, promise

reciprocō 1 to move backwards and forwards, to turn back

recitātiō, ōnis *f* a reading aloud

recitātor, ōris *m* reader, reciter

re-citō 3 to read aloud

re-clāmō to cry out against, contradict

re-clīnis, e leaning back

re-clīnō 1 to bend back, cause to lean back

re-clūdō, sī, sum 3 to open, disclose

re-cognōscō 3 to recall to mind, recognize; to review, examine

re-colligō 3 to collect again, regain

re-colō 3 to cultivate again; to practise again, renew; to think over again

re-conciliātiō, ōnis *f* a reconciling; restoration

re-conciliō 1 to restore, reunite, reconcile

re-conditus 3 hidden, far removed; profound, abstruse

re-condō 3 to put away, store away, hide, conceal

re-coquō 3 to cook *or* boil again; to melt *or* forge again

re-cordātiō, ōnis *f* recollection, remembrance

re-cordor 1 to remember, recollect, think over

re-creō 1 to revive, restore, refresh

re-crēscō 3 to grow again

re-crūdēscō, duī, — 3 to break open afresh, break out again

rēctā (sc. viā) adv. straight, right on

rēctor, ōris m controller, director, governor, steersman

rēctus 3 straight, upright; right, correct, proper, suitable; honest, virtuous, good; subst. **rēctum, ī** n the right, the good, virtue; adv. **rēctē**

re-cubō, —, — 1 to lie back, recline

re-cumbō, cubuī, — 3 to lie down, recline (at table); to fall, sink down

recuperātor, ōris m judicial umpire, arbitrator

recuperō 1 to regain, recover

re-currō, currī, cursum 3 to run back, hasten back, return

re-cursō 1 to run back, return

re-cursus, ūs m a running back, return, retreat

re-curvō 1 to bend backward

re-curvus 3 bent back

re-cūsātiō, ōnis f a declining, refusal; objection

re-cūsō 1 to decline, refuse, reject

red-arguō, uī, — 3 to refute, contradict

red-dō, didī, ditum 3 to give or put back, restore, return; to recite, rehearse; to render, make, cause to be; to take vengeance for; to deliver, grant, render; to reply; to imitate, represent; to translate

red-ēmptiō, ōnis f a ransoming; bribing; farming

red-ēmptor, ōris m contractor, farmer

red-eō, iī, itum, īre to go or come back, return; to be brought to, have recourse to

red-igō, ēgī, āctum 3 to drive, bring, lead back; to collect, raise; to bring or reduce to a state or condition, force, make; to lessen

redimīculum, ī n band, fillet

redimiō 4 to bind or wreathe round, crown

red-imō, ēmī, ēmptum 3 to buy back, redeem, ransom, set free; to buy off, avert; to buy, purchase, hire, contract for

red-integrō 1 to restore, renew, refresh

red-itiō, ōnis f return

red-itus, ūs m return; income, revenue

red-oleō, uī, — 2 to smell of

re-dūcō 3 to bring, lead, draw back; to restore

re-ductus 3 retired, remote

red-undō 1 to stream over, overflow; to abound in, be in excess

re-dux, ucis bringing back; brought back, returned

re-fellō, fellī, — 3 to refute, rebut

re-ferciō, rsī, rtum 4 to stuff full, fill up; refertus 3 crammed, filled

re-feriō, —, — 4 to strike back

re-ferō, rettulī, relātum, referre 3 to bear, carry, bring back; to report, announce, tell, say; to call to mind, think over; to repay, to, assign to; to repay, give back; to reply, answer; to restore, renew, repeat, recall; to register, record; to bring before, refer

rē-fert, rē-tulit, rē-ferre it matters, concerns, is of advantage or importance

refertus 3, see referciō

re-ficiō, fēcī, fectum 3 to make again, restore, repair, refresh, revive

re-fīgō, xī, xum 3 to unfasten, unloose; to abolish, repeal

re-flectō 3 to bend or turn backward; to change, bring back

re-flō 1 to blow against or contrary

re-fluō 3 to flow back

refluus 3 flowing back

re-formīdō 1 to dread, shun

re-foveō 2 to refresh, revive

re-frāgor 1 to oppose, withstand

re-frēnō 1 to bridle, check

re-fricō, cuī, cātum 1 to rub or scratch open again; to tear

re-frīgerō 1 to make cool

re-frīgēscō, frīxī, — 3 to grow cool, lose vigour, abate, fail

re-fringō, frēgī, frāctum 3 to break up, off, open; to check, destroy

re-fugiō 3 to flee away, escape; to avoid, shun

re-fugus 3 receding; fugitive

re-fulgeō, fulsī, — 2 to shine or gleam back

re-fundō 3 to cause to flow back, overflow

re-fūtō 1 to repel, resist; to confute, refute

rēgālis, e kingly, princely

re-gerō 3 to carry or bring back, return

rēgia, ae f royal palace, castle, residence; court, courtiers

rēgi-ficus 3 splendid, magnificent

regimen, inis n a guiding, government; rudder

rēgīna, ae f queen, princess, lady

regiō, ōnis f direction, line; boundary; region, tract, territory, district, province

rēgius 3 of a king, royal; splendid, magnificent; despotic

rēgnātor, ōris m = rex

rēgnō 1 to be king, rule, reign; to be master, domineer

rēgnum, ī n royal power, sovereignty, despotism; kingdom, realm

regō, rēxī, rēctum 3 to guide, conduct, direct; to rule, govern, control

re-gredior, gressus sum 3 to go back, retreat, withdraw

re-gressus, ūs *m* return, retreat

rēgula, ae *f* model, pattern, example

rēgulus, ī *m* petty king, chieftain, prince

re-gustō 1 to taste repeatedly

rē-iciō, iēcī, iectum 3 to throw back, repel, drive back; to reject, refuse, disdain; to put off, defer; to refer

rēiectiō, ōnis *f* rejection

re-lābor 3 to slide, glide, sink back

re-languescō, guī, — 3 to grow languid *or* faint

re-lātiō, ōnis *f* report, proposition, motion

relātus, ūs *m* report; recital

re-laxātiō, ōnis *f* relaxation, easing

re-laxō 1 to loosen, open; to relax, abate, ease, relieve, release

relēgātiō, ōnis *f* banishment

re-lēgō 1 to send away, dispatch; to banish; to put aside, reject

re-legō 3 to gather together again; to travel over again; to read again; to consider again

re-levō 1 to lift up, raise; to relieve, alleviate, free from, lighten

relictiō, ōnis *f* a forsaking, abandoning

relicuus 3 = **reliquus**

religiō, ōnis *f* superstitious awe, religious scruples, conscientiousness; reverence of the gods, religion, piety, devoutness; worship of the gods, religious observance; religious system, faith, cult; sacredness, sanctity; sacred obligation; holy object, sacred place

religiōsus 3 anxious, scrupulous; pious, devout, religious, superstitious; holy, sacred; forbidden by religious scruples

re-ligō 1 to bind back *or* fast

re-linquō, līquī, lictum 3 to leave behind; to bequeath; to let remain, suffer to be; to abandon, forsake, desert, neglect

reliquiae, ārum *f/pl.* remainder, remains, rest

reliquus 3 left behind *or* over, remaining; other, rest; subsequent, future; *subst.* reliquum, ī *n* rest, remainder; reliquī, ōrum *pl.* 3 the others, the rest

re-lūceō, xī, — 2 to shine back

re-luctor 1 to strive *or* struggle against

re-maneō 2 to stay behind, be left, remain

re-mānsiō, ōnis f a staying behind, remaining

re-medium, ī n remedy, medicine

re-meō 1 to go back, return

re-mētior 4 to go over again, retrace

rēmex, igis m rower

rēmigium, ī n a rowing; oars; rowers

rēmigō 1 to row

re-migrō 1 to wander back, return

re-miníscor, — 3 to call to mind, remember

re-misceō 2 to mix up, mingle

re-missiō, ōnis f a sending back; a relaxing, slackening; recreation

re-missus 3 relaxed; mild, gentle, yielding; gay, merry; slack, careless

re-mittō 3 to send back, throw back; to give out, yield; to give back, reject, resign; to loosen, relax, slacken; to leave off, abate; to pardon, remit; to give up, concede; to cease, omit

re-mollēscō, —, — 3 to become soft again; to be moved or influenced

re-mordeō, mordī, morsum 2 to bite back; to torment, vex

re-moror 1 to stay, linger; to detain, delay, hinder

re-mōtus 3 distant, far off; remote, free from

re-moveō 2 to move back

or away, withdraw, remove, abolish

re-mūgiō 4 to bellow back; to resound

remulcum, ī n towing cable

remūnerātiō, ōnis f recompense, reward

re-mūneror 1 to repay, reward, recompense

rēmus, ī m oar

re-nārrō 1 to relate again

re-nāscor 3 to be born again, to rise or grow again

rēnēs, um and ium m/pl. the kidneys

re-nīdeō, —, — 2 to shine or gleam back; to beam, smile   [ing]

re-novātiō, ōnis f a renew-]

re-novō 1 to renew, restore, repeat; to refresh, revive

re-nūntiātiō, ōnis f proclamation, report

re-nūntiō 1 to bring back word, report, announce, proclaim; to revoke, renounce

re-nuō, uī, — 3 to deny (by nodding), refuse

reor, ratus sum 2 to think, believe, suppose

repāgula, ōrum n/pl. bars, bolts, barrier

re-parābilis, e reparable, retrievable

re-parō 1 to get back, restore, repair, renew; to refresh, revive

re-pellō, reppulī, repulsum 3 to drive back or away, keep off, remove; to reject, spurn

7*

re-pendō, pendī, pēnsum 3 to weigh in return, pay in equal weight; to repay, requite, recompense

repēns, tis sudden, unexpected; *adv.* repēnte

repentīnus 3 unexpected, sudden, hasty

re-percutiō 3 to strike, throw *or* drive back

re-periō, repperī, repertum 4 to find (out), discover; to perceive, learn; to acquire, obtain; to invent, devise

repertor, ōris *m* discoverer, inventor, author

re-petō 3 to attack again; to seek again, return; to fetch back; to repeat, renew, begin again; to think over again; to ask back, demand satisfaction, claim; to derive, trace from

re-pleō, plēvī, plētum 2 to fill again, fill up, replenish

re-plicō 1 to unroll, open

rēpō, rēpsī, — 3 to crawl, creep

re-pōnō 3 to put back, replace, restore; to lay, place; to lay up, store; to give back, requite, make compensation; to repeat, renew; to count, reckon, class

re-portō 1 to carry *or* bring back; to report

re-poscō, —, — 3 to demand back, claim

re-praesentātiō, ōnis *f* payment in cash

re-praesentō 1 to display, show; to pay in ready money; to perform immediately, realize, hasten

re-prehendō 3 to hold fast, check; to blame, censure

reprehēnsiō, ōnis *f* blame, censure

reprehēnsor, ōris *m* blamer, censurer

re-prēndō 3 = reprehendo

re-primō, pressī, pressum 3 to press *or* hold back, restrain, check, confine

re-prōmittō 3 to promise in return [slowly]

rēptō 1 to crawl, walk

repudiātiō, ōnis *f* refusal

re-pudiō 1 to reject, refuse, disdain

repudium, ī *n* a casting off, divorce

re-puerāscō, —, — 3 to become a boy again

re-pugnantia, ae *f* contradiction

re-pugnō 1 to resist, oppose; to be inconsistent *or* incompatible

repulsa, ae *f* rejection, repulse, refusal, denial

re-pūrgō 1 to cleanse again, clear away

re-putō 1 to think over, consider

re-quiēs, ētis *f* rest, repose, recreation

re-quiēscō, quiēvī, — 3 to rest, repose; to be relieved

re-quīrō, sīvī or siī, sītum 3 to seek again, search for; to miss, want, demand; to ask for, inquire after

rēs, rēī (*and* reī) *f* thing, matter, affair; condition, circumstances; respect, relation; fate, lot; matter of business; lawsuit, action; commonwealth, state, public interest, government, = rēs publica (*see* publicus); profit, advantage, interest; property, possessions, estate; deed, action; battle; event, facts, history; reality, truth; *pl.* the world, the universe, nature

re-sarciō 4 to patch up, repair

re-scindō 3 to tear open, break up; to annul, repeal

re-scīscō 3 to find out, ascertain

re-scrībō 3 to write back; to re-enlist; to place to someone's credit, pay back

re-secō 1 to cut off; to curtail, check

re-sequor 3 to answer, reply

re-serō 1 to unlock, open, reveal

re-servō 1 to keep back, reserve, save

re-ses, idis inactive, lazy

re-sideō, sēdī, sessum 2 to be seated, rest; to reside, be left, remain

re-sīdō, sēdī, sessum 3 to sit down, settle; to sink, fall; to abate, grow calm

residuus 3 remaining, left behind

re-signō 1 to unseal, open; to reveal; to pay back, resign   [spring back]

re-siliō, luī, — 4 to leap or]

re-sipīscō, pīvī (piī *and* puī), — 3 to recover one's senses

re-sistō, stitī, — 3 to stand back, halt, stop; to pause, stay; to resist, oppose

re-solvō 3 to untie, loosen, free, open; to relax, unnerve; to annul, cancel

re-sonō 1 to resound, echo; to cause to resound

re-sonus 3 resounding

re-sorbeō, —, — 2 to suck back, swallow again

re-spectō 1 to look back or about; to gaze at, look upon; to regard, care for; to look for, expect

respectus, ūs *m* a looking back or about; regard, consideration; refuge, retreat

re-spergō, rsī, rsum 3 to besprinkle, bestrew

re-spiciō, exī, ectum 3 to look back or about; to reflect upon, consider, care for, regard

re-spīrāmen, inis *n* windpipe

re-spīrātiō, ōnis *f* a breathing (out); a taking breath

re-spīrō 1 to breathe out; to take or recover breath, to revive, be refreshed; to abate, cease re-spondeō, ndī, ōnsum 2 to answer, reply; to give decisions, give advice; to answer to one's name, appear; to correspond, agree, be equal *or* a match for

re-spōnsiō, ōnis *f* answer, reply

respōnsō 1 to answer, echo; to withstand, defy

respōnsum, ī *n* answer

rēs-pūblica, ae *f*, *see* publicus

re-spuō 3 to spit out; to reject, refuse, spurn

re-stāgnō 1 to overflow

re-stinguō, īnxī, īnctum 3 to quench, extinguish; to mitigate, appease; to destroy

restis, is *f* rope, cord

restitō 1 to tarry, hesitate

re-stituō, uī, ūtum 3 to replace, bring back, restore, deliver up; to renew, revive, repair; to revoke, reverse

restitūtiō, ōnis *f* a reinstating, restoring

restitūtor, ōris *m* restorer

re-stō, stitī, — 1 to withstand, resist; to be left, remain

re-strictus 3 tight, close; strict; niggardly, stingy

re-stringō 3 to bind back *or* fast, tighten, restrict

re-sultō 1 to rebound, spring back; to resound

re-sūmō 3 to take again *or* back, renew

re-supīnō 1 to throw down (on the back)

re-supīnus 3 lying on the back

re-surgō 3 to rise up again, reappear

re-suscitō 1 to rouse again

re-tardō 1 to delay, detain, hinder

rēte, is *n* net

re-tegō 3 to uncover, open, reveal

re-temptō 1 to try again

re-tendō, ndī, ntum *or* ēnsum 3 to unbend

re-tentiō, ōnis *f* a keeping back

re-tentō[1] 1 to hold back *or* fast

re-tentō[2] 1 = retemptō

re-texō 3 to unweave, unravel; to annul, cancel; to weave anew, repeat

reticentia, ae *f* silence

re-ticeō, cuī, — 2 to be silent; to keep secret

rēticulum, ī *n* net-bag

retināculum, ī *n* band, halter, rope, cable

re-tineō, tinuī, tentum 2 to hold back, detain, restrain; to keep, preserve, maintain

re-torqueō 2 to twist *or* turn back

re-tractātiō, ōnis *f* drawing back, refusal

re-tractō 1 to draw back, refuse; to handle again, go over again, renew; to consider again, revise

retractus 3 retired, remote

re-trahō 3 to draw or drag back; to keep back, prevent

re-trectō 1 = retracto

re-tribuō 3 to give back, restore

retrō adv. backwards, back, behind; in the past

retrōrsum (and -us) adv. = retro

re-trūdō 3 to push back, hide

re-tundō, rettudī, retū(n)sum 3 to beat back, blunt, make dull; to check

reus, ī m and rea, ae f accused person, defendant; one who is bound or answerable for something

re-vehŏ 3 to carry back

re-vellŏ 3 to tear or pluck off or away; to abolish

re-vēlŏ 3 to unveil, uncover

re-veniō 4 to come back, return

reverentia, ae f reverence, awe, respect

re-vereor 2 to feel awe or respect, to fear

re-versiŏ, ōnis f a turning back, return

re-vertor (rarely -ŏ), perf. revertī, reversum 3 to turn back, return

re-vinciō 4 to bind back, bind fast, fasten

re-vincŏ 3 to conquer; to convict, refute

re-virēscŏ, ruī, — 3 to become green, young, vigorous again

re-vīsŏ, sī, — 3 to revisit, go back to see

re-vīvīscŏ, vixī, victum 3 to come to life again, revive

re-vocābilis, e revocable

re-vocāmen, inis n and re-vocātiŏ, ōnis f a calling back

re-vocŏ 1 to call back, recall, withdraw, check, divert; to renew, restore; to revoke, cancel; to apply, reduce, refer

re-volŏ 1 to fly back

re-volūbilis, e that may be rolled back

ro-volvŏ 3 to roll back, unroll; to read over, repeat, think over; P. to return, recur

re-vomŏ 3 to vomit up

re-vors-, -vort- = re-vers-, -vert-

rēx, rēgis m king, prince; despot, tyrant; high priest; leader, chief, master, great man, patron

rhētor, oris m teacher of rhetoric

rhētoricus 3 rhetorical, of an orator

rhombus, ī m a magician's circle; turbot

rictum, ī n and rictus, ūs m wide open mouth

rīdeŏ, sī, sum 2 to laugh, smile; to be favourable; to laugh at, mock

rīdiculus 3 funny, amusing, droll; subst. ridiculum, ī n jest, joke

rigeō, guī, — 2 to be stiff or

numb; to stand on end, bristle up

rigēscō, riguī, — 3 to become stiff

rigidus 3 stiff, hard, inflexible; stern, rough, cruel

rigō 1 to wet, moisten, water

rigor, ōris *m* stiffness; cold, chilliness; hardness, sternness

riguus 3 watering; watered

rīma, ae *f* chink, fissure, cleft

rīmor 1 to lay open, cleave; to pry into, search, examine

rīmōsus 3 full of chinks or fissures

ringor, — 3 to show the teeth, snarl

rīpa, ae *f* bank of a river

rīsus, ūs *m* laughter, laugh; object of laughter

rīte *adv.* according to (*religious*) usage or ceremonies, properly, rightly, duly; fortunately

rītus, ūs *m* religious usage, ceremony, rite; custom, usage, manner

rīvālis, is *m* rival, competitor

rīvulus, ī *m* rivulet, streamlet

rīvus, ī *m* brook, stream

rixa, ae *f* quarrel, brawl, dispute

rixor 1 to quarrel, brawl

rōbīgō, inis *f* rust, blight, mildew

rōborō 1 to strengthen, invigorate

rōbur, oris *n* hard-wood, oakwood, oak-tree; dungeon; hardness, firmness, strength; the best or strongest part, the pick

rōbustus 3 oaken; hard, firm, strong, vigorous

rōdō, sī, sum 3 to gnaw, consume; to slander, disparage

rogātiō, ōnis *f* proposed law, bill; entreaty, request

rogātor, ōris *m* collector of votes

rogātus, ūs *m* request, entreaty

rogitō 1 to ask (repeatedly)

rogō 1 to ask, question; to beg, entreat, request

rogus, ī *m* funeral pile

rōrō 1 to drop dew; to trickle, drip, moisten

rōs, rōris *m* dew; moisture, water

rosa, ae *f* rose

rosārium, ī *n* rose-garden

rōscidus 3 dewy, dripping, wet

roseus 3 rosy

rōstrātus 3 having a beak

rōstrum, ī *n* beak, snout; beak of a ship; *pl.* platform for speakers in the Forum

rota, ae *f* wheel; chariot; alternation, fickleness

rotō 1 to turn or swing round

rotundō 1 to make round, round off

rotundus 3 round, circular, spherical; rounded, elegant

rube-faciō 3 to make red

rubeō, uī, — 2 to be red; to blush

ruber, bra, brum red, ruddy

rubēscō, buī, — 3 to grow or turn red

rubēta, ae f toad

rubētum, ī n bramble-thicket

rubicundus 3 red

rubor, ōris m redness; blush; bashfulness, modesty; shame, disgrace

rubus, ī m bramble-bush, blackberry

rūctō 1 to belch

rudēns, tis m rope, cable

rudīmentum, ī n first attempt, trial, beginning

rudis[1], is f gladiator's practice-foil

rudis[2], e unwrought, rough, untilled; unskilled, inexperienced, uncultured

rudō, īvī, — 3 to roar, bellow

rūfus 3 red(-haired)

rūga, ae f wrinkle, frown

rūgōsus 3 wrinkled

ruīna, ae f a falling down, fall; disaster, overthrow, ruin, destruction; fallen building, ruins

ruīnōsus 3 fallen, ruined

rūminō 1 to chew again

rūmor, ōris m common talk, report, hearsay; common opinion, fame

rumpō, rūpī, ruptum 3 to break, burst, tear, break open or through; to violate, destroy, annul, interrupt

ruō, ruī, rutum (ruitūrus) 3 to hasten, run, rush; to fall, tumble down, go to ruin; to cause to fall, cast down; to throw up in a heap

rūpēs, is f rock, cliff

ruptor, ōris m breaker, violator

rūri-cola, ae m and f rural, rustic

rūrsus and rūrsum adv. back, backwards; again, anew; on the contrary, on the other hand, in return

rūs, rūris n the country, fields; country-seat, farm

rūscum, ī n butcher's-broom

rūsticānus 3 of the country, rustic

rūsticitās, ātis f rustic behaviour, boorishness

rūsticor 1 to live in the country

rūsticus 3 of the country, rural, rustic; simple, plain; boorish, awkward, rude, coarse; subst. ~, ī m countryman

rūta, ae f rue (a herb)

rutilō 1 to redden

rutilus 3 reddish yellow, golden red

S

sabbata, ōrum *n/pl.* Sabbath; Jewish festival

saburra, ae *f* sand; ballast

sacculus, ī *m* small bag

saccus, ī *m* sack, bag, purse

sacellum, ī *n* little sanctuary, chapel

sacer, cra, crum holy, sacred, consecrated; accursed, execrable; *subst.*

sacrum, ī *n* sacred *or* holy thing; sanctuary; sacrifice, holy rite; worship

sacerdōs, ōtis *m* and *f* priest, priestess

sacerdōtium, ī *n* priesthood

sacrāmentum, ī *n* money deposited by the parties in a suit; civil suit; military oath of allegiance; oath, obligation

sacrārium, ī *n* shrine, chapel, sanctuary

sacrificium, ī *n* sacrifice

sacrificō 1 to sacrifice

sacrificulus, ī *m* sacrificing priest

sacri-ficus 3 sacrificial

sacrilegium, ī *n* temple-robbery, sacrilege

sacri-legus 3 robbing a temple, sacrilegious; impious, wicked

sacrō 1 to consecrate, dedicate, render inviolable; to immortalize

sacrō-sānctus 3 most holy, inviolable

sacrum, ī, *see* sacer

saec(u)lum, ī *n* generation, age, lifetime; century

saepe *adv.* often, frequently

saepe-numerō *adv.* often

saepēs, is *f* hedge, fence

saepiō, psī, ptum 4 to fence in, enclose; to protect

saeptum, ī *n* (*usu. pl.*) fence, enclosure

saeta, ae *f* stiff hair, bristle

saeti-ger 3 bristle-bearing

saetōsus 3 bristly

saeviō 4 to rage, be furious *or* fierce

saevitia, ae *f* fury, fierceness, savageness

saevus 3 raging, furious, fierce, cruel, savage

sāga, ae *f* female soothsayer

sagācitās, ātis *f* keenness, sagacity, acuteness

sagātus 3 clothed in a military cloak

sagāx, ācis keen in the scent; acute, sagacious, clever

sagina, ae *f* a feeding; food

saginō 1 to feed, fatten, cram

sagitta, ae *f* arrow, bolt

sagittārius, ī *m* archer

sagitti-fer 3 arrow-bearing

sagmina, um *n/pl.* tuft of sacred grass

sagulum, ī *n* = sagum

sagum, ī *n* (military) cloak

sāl, salis *m* (*and n*) salt; saltwater, sea; acuteness, cunning, wit, sarcasm

salārius 3 of salt

salāx, ācis lustful, lecherous

salebra, ae f roughness

salictum, ī n willow planta-}

salignus 3 of willows [tion}

Saliī, (ōr)um m/pl. priests of Mars

salīnae, ārum f/pl. salt-works, salt-pits

salīnum, ī n salt-cellar

saliō, luī or **liī, —** 4 to leap, spring, jump

salīva, ae f spittle, saliva; taste, appetite

salix, icis f willow

salsāmentum, ī n salted fish; brine

salsus 3 salted, salt; sharp, witty, satirical

saltātiō, ōnis f a dancing, dance

saltātor, ōris m dancer

saltem adv. at least

saltō 1 to dance

saltuōsus 3 well-wooded

saltus[1]**, ūs** m forest- or mountain-pasture, wooded upland; mountain-pass

saltus[2]**, ūs** m a leaping, leap

salūbris, e healthful, wholesome, salutary; sound, vigorous

salūbritās, ātis f wholesomeness, healthiness

salum, ī n open sea, sea

salūs, ūtis f health; welfare, good fortune, safety, deliverance; salutation, greeting

salūtāris, e healthful, wholesome, beneficial

salūtātiō, ōnis f a greeting, saluting; visit

salūtātor, ōris m one who salutes; caller

salūti-fer 3 health-bringing

salūtō 1 to greet, salute; to wait upon, visit

salveō, —, — 2 to be well, be in good health; **salvē!** greeting! hail!; farewell!

salvus 3 safe, unhurt, sound

sanciō, sanxī, sānctum 4 to make sacred or inviolable; establish, decree, confirm, ratify; to forbid under penalty

sānctimōnia, ae f = sanctitas

sānctiō, ōnis f ordinance; penal clause, declaration of a penalty

sānctitās, ātis f sacredness, sanctity; holiness, purity, virtue

sānctus 3 sacred, inviolable; venerable, divine; holy, pious; innocent, pure; just

sandўx, ўcis f vermilion

sānē adv. indeed, truly, by all means, to be sure, certainly; then, if you will; extremely

sanguen, inis n = sanguis

sanguineus 3 bloody, of blood; blood-red; blood-thirsty

sanguinolentus 3 = sanguineus

sanguĭs (and -īs), inis m

blood; bloodshed; vigour, life; consanguinity, race, family; descendant, off-spring

saniēs, ēī *f* corrupted blood, venom, poison

sănitās, ātis *f* health; soundness of mind, good sense

sănō 1 to heal, cure; to restore, repair

sānus 3 sound, healthy, whole; sober, reasonable, discreet

săpiēns, tis wise, knowing, sensible, discreet; *subst.* ⁓, tis *m* a wise man, philosopher

săpientia, ae *f* good sense, prudence, wisdom; philosophy

săpiō, iī, — 3 to have taste; to be sensible *or* wise; to understand

săpor, ōris *m* taste, flavour; delicacy

sarcina, ae *f* bundle, pack, load, burden

sarcinula, ae *f* bundle, small baggage

sarciō, rsī, rtum 4 to patch, mend, make good, make amends for; sartus 3 in good condition, in good repair

sarculum, ī *n* hoe

sardonyx, ychis *m* and *f* sardonyx

saris(s)a, ae *f* Macedonian lance

sarmentum, ī *n* (*pl.*) twigs, brushwood, faggots

sat *adv.* = satis

sata, ōrum *n/pl.* standing corn, crops

satelles, itis *m* and *f* attendant, escort, life-guard; partner, accomplice

satiās, (ātis) *f* = satietas

satietās, ātis *f* satiety, fulness, loathing, disgust

satiō[1] 1 to fill, satisfy, satiate, appease; to overfill, disgust

satiō[2], ōnis *f* a sowing, planting

satira, ae *f* = satura

satis *adv.* enough, sufficiently, sufficient; moderately, pretty well, somewhat; *comp.* satius better, preferable

satis-dō 1 to give bail *or* security

satis-faciō 3 to satisfy; to pay; to apologize, make excuse, make amends

satis-factiō, ōnis *f* reparation; apology

sator, ōris *m* sower; father, creator

satur, ra, rum full, sated; rich, fertile, abundant

satura, ae *f* discursive composition, satire

saturō 1 = satiō[1]

satus[1], ūs *m* a sowing, planting; a begetting, origin, race

satus[2] 3, *see* sero[2]

satyrus, ī *m* Satyr

sauciō 1 to wound, hurt

saucius 3 wounded, hurt, weakened

sāv-, *see* suāv-

saxeus 3 rocky, stony

saxi-ficus 3 turning into stone

saxōsus 3 stony, rocky

saxum, ī *n* large stone, rock

scaber, bra, brum rough, scurfy, untidy

scabiēs, ēī scurf, scab, mange

scaena, ae *f* stage, theatre; publicity, public

scaenicus 3 of the stage, dramatic, theatrical; *subst.*

~, ī *m* actor

scālae, ārum *f/pl.* flight of steps, staircase, ladder

scalmus, ī *m* thole, rowlock

scalpō, psī, ptum 3 to scratch, cut, carve

scalprum, ī *n* chisel, knife

scamnum, ī *n* bench, stool

scandō, ndī, (ānsum) 3 to climb, mount, ascend

scapha, ae *f* boat, skiff

scaphium, ī *n* drinking-vessel, basin

scapulae, ārum *f/pl.* the shoulder-blades, shoulders

scarus, ī *m* (*a sea-fish*)

scateō 2 (*and* scatō 3) to bubble *or* gush up; to swarm, abound

scelerātus 3 polluted, defiled; wicked, vicious

scelerō 1 to pollute, defile

scelerōsus 3 wicked

scelestus 3 wicked, villainous, accursed

scelus, eris *n* wicked deed, crime, impiety; villain, scoundrel

scēptrum, ī *n* sceptre; dominion, kingdom, rule

schola, ae *f* learned lecture *or* dispute; school

sciēns, tis knowingly, purposely, intentionally; knowing, skilled, expert

scientia, ae *f* knowledge, science, skill

sci-licet *adv.* of course, obviously, naturally, certainly; namely

scindō, idī, issum 3 to cut, tear, split, cleave, divide

scintilla, ae *f* spark

scintillō 1 to sparkle, flash

sciō, scīvī *and* sciī, scītum 4 to know, perceive, understand, be skilled in

scīpiō, ōnis *m* staff

scirpus, ī *m* rush, bulrush

sciscitor 1 to seek to know, inquire, question, examine

sciscō, scīvī, scītum 3 to decree, ordain, assent to, vote for

scītor 1 = sciscitor

scītum, ī *n* decree, ordinance

scītus 3 knowing, clever, shrewd, skilful; pretty, elegant

scobis, is *f* sawdust, filings

scōpae, ārum *f/pl.* twigs, broom, besom

scopulōsus 3 rocky, craggy

scopulus, ī *m* rock, crag, cliff; difficulty, danger

scorpiō, ōnis *and* scorpius, ī *m* scorpion; a military engine

scortor 1 to whore

scortum, ī n whore, prostitute

scrība, ae m clerk, secretary

scrībō, psī, ptum 3 to scratch, engrave, draw; to write; to compose, draw up, to write of, describe; to enroll

scrīnium, ī n chest, box, case

scrīptiō, ōnis f written composition, text

scrīptitō 1 to write often or continually, compose

scrīptor, ōris m writer, scribe; author, composer

scrīptum, ī n writing, composition, treatise, book

scrīptūra, ae f a writing, composition; pasture tax

scrīpulum, ī n = scrupulum

scrobis, is m and f ditch, trench

scrūpulum, ī n the 24th part of an ounce

scrūpulus, ī m uneasiness, anxiety, scruple

scrūtor 1 to search carefully, examine, explore, investigate

sculpō, psī, ptum 3 to carve, cut, form, fashion

scurra, ae m buffoon, jester; dandy, man about town

scurror 1 to play the buffoon, be a parasite

scūtāle, is n thong of a sling

scūtātus 3 armed with a shield

scutica, ae f lash, whip

scūtum, ī n (oblong) shield

scyphus, ī m cup, goblet

sē acc., abl. himself, herself, itself

sē-cēdō 3 to go away or apart, withdraw, retire

sē-cernō 3 to sever, divide, separate; to discern

sē-cessiō, ōnis f a going aside, withdrawal; secession, schism

sē-cessus, ūs m retirement, solitude; retreat, hiding-place

sē-clūdō, sī, sum 3 to shut up or apart, seclude, separate

secō, cuī, ctum 1 to cut, cut off, up, down; to tear, wound; to divide, cleave, separate; to cut or pass through, traverse; to decide

sē-crētus 3 severed, separated; retired, remote, solitary; secret, hidden; subst. **sēcrētum**, ī n retirement, solitude; secret; adv. **sēcrētō**

secta, ae f way; manner, party, school, sect

sectātor, ōris m follower, attendant   [divided]

sectilis, e (that can be) cut,]

sectiō, ōnis f buying or confiscated goods

sector[1] ōris m cutter; purchaser of confiscated goods

sector[2] 1 to follow continually, attend, accompany; to pursue, chase

sē-cubitus, ūs *m* a lying *or* sleeping alone

sē-cubō, buī, — 1 to sleep alone

secundānī, ōrum *m*/*pl.* soldiers of the second legion

secundō 1 to favour, further

secundum *prep.* with *acc.* along; beside; after; next to, in accordance with; in favour of

secundus 2 following, next, second; secondary, inferior; accompanying; favourable, propitious, fortunate

secūris, is *f* axe, hatchet; blow, wound; *pl.* authority, sovereignty

sēcūritās, ātis *f* freedom from care, peace of mind; safety

sē-cūrus 3 free from care, fearless, composed; cheerful, bright, serene; safe

secus[1] *n* (*indecl.*) sex

secus[2] *adv.* otherwise, not so; not well, wrongly; *comp.* sequius *or* secius (*see also* sētius)

sed *cj.* but, yet, however

sēdātiō, ōnis *f* an allaying, assuaging

sēdātus 3 composed, quiet, calm

sē-decim (*indecl.*) sixteen

sedeō, sēdī, sessum 2 to sit; to remain, stay, be inactive; to remain encamped; to hold fast, be fixed *or* established; to sink, subside

sēdēs, is *f* seat; dwelling-place, home; place, spot; foundation

sedīle, is *n* seat, stool, chair

sēd-itiō, ōnis *f* separation, dissension, quarrel; insurrection, mutiny

sēditiōsus 3 factious, seditious, mutinous

sēdō 1 to soothe, allay, appease, stop

sē-dūcō 3 to lead aside, take apart; to separate, sever

sēdulitās, ātis *f* assiduity, zeal, application

sēdulus 3 busy, diligent, zealous; officious, obtrusive; *adv.* sēdulō

seges, etis *f* cornfield, standing corn, crop; multitude

segmentum, ī *n* strip of brocade, &c., used as trimming

sēgnis, e slow, sluggish, lazy, lingering

sēgnitia, ae (*and* -tiēs, ēī) *f* slowness, sluggishness, inactivity

se-gregō 1 to set apart, separate, remove

sē-iungō 3 to disjoin, sever, separate

sē-lēctiō, ōnis *f* selection

sē-ligō, lēgī, lēctum 3 to choose out, select

sella, ae *f* seat, chair; official chair of a magistrate

sēmanimis, -us, *see* sēmi...

semel *adv.* a single time, once; once for all; first

sēmen, inis *n* seed; stock; race; descendant, offspring; origin, ground, cause, element

sēmentis, is *f* a sowing

sēmermis, e = semiermis

sē-mēn(s)tris, e of six months, half-yearly

sēm-ēsus 3 half-consumed

sē-met = se (*strengthened*)

sēmianimis, e *and* -mus 3 half-alive, half-dead

sēmi-bōs, bovis *m* half-ox

sēmi-caper, prī *m* half-goat

sēmi-deus 3 half-divine

sēmiermis, e half-armed

sēmiēsus 3 = semesus

sēmi-fer 3 half-man and half-beast

sēmi-homō, inis half-human

sēmi-mās, maris *m* half-male, hermaphrodite; castrated

sēminārium, ī *n* nursery

sēmi-nex, nicis half-dead

sēminō 1 to sow, produce

sēmi-nūdus 3 half-naked

sēmi-plēnus 3 half-manned

sēmi-rutus 3 half-ruined

sēmis, issis *m* a half; half an as

sēmi-somnus 3 half-asleep

sēmi-supīnus 3 half on one's back

sēmita, ae *f* narrow way, footpath, lane

sēmi-ust-, *see* sem-ust-

sēmi-vir, ī *m* half-man (half-beast); castrated; effeminate

sēmi-vīvus 3 half-alive, half-dead

sē-moveō 2 to move apart *or* away, sever

semper *adv.* always, ever

sempiternus 3 everlasting, perpetual

sēm-uncia, ae *f* half an ounce

sēm-ustulātus, -ustilātus, *and* sēm-ustus 3 half-burned

senātor, ōris *m* senator

senātōrius 3 senatorial

senātus, ūs *m* senate, council of state; meeting of the senate

senecta, ae *f* = senectus

senectūs, ūtis *f* old age

senēscō, nuī, — 3 to grow old; to decay, waste away

senex, senis old, aged (*comp.* senior); *subst.* senex, is *m and f* old man *or* woman

sēnī 3 six each

senīlis, e of an old man, of old age, senile

senium, ī *n* weakness *or* decay of old age; trouble, affliction; moroseness

sēnsim *adv.* gradually, by degrees, gently

sēnsus, ūs *m* perception, sensation, sense; understanding; feeling, common sense; opinion, view, notion; meaning; inclination, disposition, mode of thinking

sententia, ae *f* opinion, thought, purpose; way of thinking, judgment; decision, sentence, vote; meaning, signification; maxim, saying

sententiōsus 3 full of meaning, sententious

sentīna, ae *f* bilge-water; ship's hold; dregs, rabble

sentiō, sēnsī, sēnsum 4 to feel, perceive, discern; to experience, suffer; to understand, observe; to think, suppose, believe, mean; to vote, declare

sentis, is *m* (*f*) thorn-bush, briar

sentus 3 rough, thorny

se-orsum *and* **-sus** *adv.* apart, separately

sēparātim, *adv. of* separatus

sēparātiō, ōnis *f* a severing, separation

sēparātus 3 separated, apart, distinct, different

sē-parō 1 to separate, divide

sepeliō, pelīvī, pultum 4 to bury (*also* to cremate); to destroy, ruin, suppress

sē-pōnō 3 to put *or* lay aside *or* apart; to keep back, reserve; to separate, pick out; to exclude

septem (*indecl.*) seven

September, bris, bre of September; *subst.* **September, bris** *m* September

semptem-geminus 3 sevenfold

septem-plex, icis sevenfold

septem-triō = septentrio

septem-vir, ī *m* one of a college of seven

septemvirālis, e of the *septemviri*

septen-decim (*indecl.*) seventeen

septēnī 3 seven each; seven at once

septentriō, ōnis *m* (*usu. pl.*) the seven stars of the Great *or* Little Bear; the north; north-wind

septiē(n)s *adv.* seven times

septimus 3 the seventh

septingentī 3 seven hundred

septuāgintā (*indecl.*) seventy

septumus 3 = septimus

sepulcrālis, e funeral

sepulcrum, ī *n* burial-place, grave, tomb

sepultūra, ae *f* burial

sequāx, ācis following, pursuing

sequester, tris, tre (*and* tra, trum) mediating; *subst.* **sequester, trī** *and* **tris** *m* mediator, go-between

sequius *adv., comp. of* secus[2]

sequor, cūtus sum 3 to follow, come after; to accompany; to pursue; to go to, aim at, seek; to accede to, imitate; to fall to the share of

sera, ae *f* bar, bolt

serēnitās, ātis *f* clearness, fair weather

serēnō 1 to make clear *or* bright

serēnus 3 clear, bright, serene; cheerful, glad

sēria, ae *f* earthen vessel, jar

sēricus 3 of silk

seriēs, ēī *f* succession, chain, series

sērius 3 serious, earnest; *adv.* sēriō

sermō, ōnis *m* talk, conversation, discourse, discussion; language; diction; common talk, rumour

sermunculus, ī *m* report, rumour, gossip

serō[1], (ruī), rtum 3 to join together, combine, entwine; to compose; *subst.* serta, ōrum *n/pl.* garlands, wreaths

serō[2], sēvī, satum 3 to sow, plant; to beget, bring forth; to spread abroad, cause

serpēns, tis *f and m* snake, serpent

serpō, psī, — 3 to crawl, creep, move slowly; to extend gradually, spread abroad

serpyllum, ī *n* wild thyme

serra, ae *f* saw

serta, ōrum *n/pl.*, see serō[1]

serum, ī *n* whey

sērus 3 late, too late; *adv.* sērō

serva, ae *f*, see servus

servātor, ōris *m* preserver, saviour

servātrīx, īcis *f of* servator

servīlis, e servile, of slaves

serviō 4 to serve, be a slave *or* servant; to comply with, gratify, assist; be governed by

servitium, ī *n* slavery; servants, slaves

servitūs, ūtis *f* slavery, servitude, subjection

servō 1 to observe, pay heed to, watch; to keep, preserve, guard; to lay up, reserve, store; to keep safe, rescue; to keep to, stay in

servulus (-volus), ī *m* young slave

servus 3 servile, slavish, subject; *subst.* servus, ī *m*, serva, ae *f* slave, servant

ses-centī 3 six hundred; countless

sēsē = se

sēsqui-pedālis, e one foot and a half long

sessiō, ōnis *f* a sitting; seat

sēs-tertius, ī *m* sesterce (*a small silver coin*); sēstertium, ī *n* (*usu. pl.*) a thousand sesterces

sēta, ae *f* = saeta

sētius *adv.* (confused with *sequius*, see secus[2]) otherwise; not well, ill

seu = sive

sevēritās, ātis *f* seriousness, severity, sternness

sevērus 3 serious, grave, strict, stern, harsh

sē-vocō 1 to call aside *or* away, withdraw

sex (*indecl.*) six

sexāgēsimus 3 the sixtieth

sexāgiē(n)s *adv.* sixty times

sexāgintā (*indecl.*) sixty

sex-ennium, ī *n* period of six years

sexiē(n)s *adv.* six times

sextāns, tis m the sixth part (*of an as, &c.*)

sextārius, ī m (*a liquid measure*) pint

Sextīlis, e of August; *subst.* **Sextīlis, is** m August

sextus 3 the sixth

sexus, ūs m sex

sī *cj.* if, if only, even if; in case, in the hope that

sībilō 1 to hiss, whistle

sībilus¹ 3 hissing, whistling

sībilus², ī m (*pl. also* **sībila** n) a hissing, whistling, rustling

Sibylla, ae f prophetess

Sibyllīnus 3 Sibylline

sīc *adv.* so, thus, in this manner; on this condition; so much; yes

sīca, ae f dagger

sīcārius, ī m assassin, murderer

siccitās, ātis f dryness, drought

siccō 1 to dry, dry up, drain

siccus 3 dry; thirsty; sober

sīcine *adv.* thus?, indeed?

sī-cubī *cj.* if anywhere

sī-cunde *cj.* if from anywhere

sīc-ut(ī) *adv.* so as, just as, as; as it were, just as if

sīdereus 3 starry, of stars

sīdō, sēdī *and* **sīdī, sessum 3** to sit down, settle, sink

sīdus, eris n constellation, star, heavenly body; sky, heavens; time of year; climate, weather; glory

sigillātus 3 adorned with little figures

sigillum, ī n small figure *or* image

signātor, ōris m one who seals, witness

signi-fer 3 bearing figures, starry; *subst.* ~, **ī** m standard-bearer

significātiō, ōnis f a pointing out, indicating, sign, token; approbation, applause

signi-ficō 1 to give a sign, indicate, point out; to foreshow; to mean

signō 1 to mark, mark out, designate; to seal; to stamp, coin, imprint; to notice

signum, ī n sign, mark, token; signal, order, password; standard, banner; company, maniple; figure, statue, picture; seal, signet; constellation

silentium, ī n silence, stillness; repose, leisure

sileō, uī, — 2 to be still *or* silent; to be inactive, rest; *trans.* to be silent about

silēscō, luī, — 3 to become silent

silex, icis m (*and* f) flint, rock, crag

siliqua, ae f husk, pod; *pl.* pulse

silua, ae f = silva

silva, ae f wood, forest, grove; crowd, mass; materials

silvestris, e of a wood *or* forest, wooded; wild

silvi-cola, ae *m* inhabitant of the woods

sīmia, ae *f* (*and* **-ius, ī** *m*) ape

similis, e like, resembling, similar; *adv.* **similiter**

similitūdō, inis *f* likeness, resemblance; comparison

sim-plex, icis simple, single, plain; open, frank, sincere; *adv.* **simpliciter**

simplicitās, ātis *f* simplicity, candour

simul *adv.* at once, at the same time, together; *cj.* **simul ac, simul atque** as soon as

simulācrum, ī *n* likeness, image, portrait, statue; shade, phantom; appearance, imitation

simulātiō, ōnis *f* false show, feigning, pretence, deceit

simulātor, ōris *m* imitator; feigner, pretender

simulō 1 to make like, imitate, copy; to pretend, feign, counterfeit

simultās, ātis *f* jealousy, rivalry, enmity, quarrel

sīn *cj.* if however, but if

sincērus 3 pure, uninjured, whole; candid, sincere, genuine

sine *prep.* with *abl.* without

singillātim *adv.* one by one, singly

singulāris, e one by one, alone, single; singular, unique, extraordinary

singulī, ae, a one each; single, several

singultō 1 to sob, gasp

singultus, ūs *m* a sobbing, gasping

sinister, tra, trum left, on the left hand; awkward, perverse; unfavourable, unlucky; favourable, auspicious; *subst.* **sinistra, ae** *f* left hand

sinistrōrsum *and* **-sus** *adv.* to the left.

sinō, sīvī, situm 3 to let, allow, permit

sinuō 1 to bend, wind, curve

sinuōsus 3 full of curves, sinuous

sinus, ūs *m* curve, fold, hollow; bay, gulf; valley; fold of a garment, bosom, lap; purse; love, affection, protection; inmost part, heart

si-quidem *cj.* if indeed; since, inasmuch as

Sīrius, ī *m* the Dog-star

sīs = sī vīs if you will, please

sistō, stitī *and* **stetī, statum 3** to cause to stand, place, put, set up; to convey, bring; to cause to appear before a court; to stop, check, arrest; *intr.* to stand, endure, remain; **status 3** set, fixed, appointed

sīstrum, ī *n* metal rattle

sitiō 4 to be thirsty; to be dry *or* parched; to be eager for

sitis, is *f* thirst; dryness,

drought; eager desire, greediness

situs¹, ūs *m* situation, position; neglect; mould, dirt, rust; inactivity, sloth

situs² 3 placed, lying, situated; buried

sī-ve *or* **seu** *cj.* or if; or; **sīve ... sīve** whether ..., or ...

smaragdus, ī *m and f* emerald (*and other jewels*)

sobrīnus, ī *m* cousin

sōbrius 3 not intoxicated; sober, moderate; sensible, cautious

soccus, ī *m* light shoe; comedy

socer, erī *m* father-in-law

sociālis, e of allies *or* partners; conjugal

societās, ātis *f* union, fellowship, association, partnership; political league, alliance

sociō 1 to join, unite, associate; to hold in common, share

socius 3 associated, allied; shared, joint; *subst.* socius, ī *m and* -ia, ae *f* companion, partner, ally

socordia, ae *f* dulness, indolence

so-cors, rdis stupid; indolent

socrus, ūs *f* mother-in-law

sodālicium, ī *n* = sodalitas

sodālis, e of companions, friendly; *subst.* sodālis, is *m* comrade, companion; member of a priesthood

sodālitās, ātis *f* companionship, friendship; association; secret society

sōdēs = si audes if you please

sōl, sōlis *m* the sun; sunshine, heat of the sun; day

sōlācium, ī *n* consolation, comfort, relief, solace

sōlāmen, inis *n* comfort, consolation

sōlārium, ī *n* sun-dial; clock

soldus 3 = solidus

solea, ae *f* sole, sandal

soleātus 3 wearing sandals

soleō, solitus sum 2 to be accustomed *or* wont; solitus 3 usual, customary

solidō 1 to make dense *or* firm, strengthen

solidus 3 dense, massive, firm, solid; whole, complete, entire; true, real, enduring, trustworthy

sōlitārius 3 solitary, alone, lonely

sōlitūdō, inis *f* loneliness, solitude; desert; destitution, deprivation

solitus 3, *see* soleo

solium, ī *n* seat, chair; throne, royal power

sōli-vagus 3 wandering alone

soll-emnis 3 periodic; established; ceremonial, religious, solemn; usual, customary; *subst.* sollemne, is *n* festival, solemnity, sacrifice; custom

soll-ers, rtis clever, skilful, adroit

soll-ertia, ae f skill, cleverness, ingenuity

sollicitātiō, ōnis f an inciting

sollicitō 1 to move, agitate, shake; to disturb, trouble, annoy; to stir up, incite

sollicitūdō, inis f uneasiness, anxiety, care

solli-citus 3 tossed, agitated; troubled, disturbed, anxious; causing trouble, painful; busy

sōlor 1 to comfort, console; to soothe, assuage, lessen

sōlstitiālis, e of the summer solstice, of midsummer

sōl-stitium, ī n (summer) solstice, summer time

solum[1], ī n bottom, ground, foundation, floor; soil, land, country

sōlum[2] adv., see solus

sōlus 3 alone, only, single, sole; lonely, solitary; adv. **sōlum** only, merely; non **sōlum ... sed etiam** not only ... but also

solūtiō, ōnis f a loosening; payment

solūtus 3, see solvo

solvō, solvī, solūtum 3 to loosen, unbind, release, set free; to pay, fulfil, perform; to acquit, absolve; to remove, break up, separate; to relax, weaken, dissolve; to solve, explain; **solūtus** 3 loosened, unbound, free; unburdened,

independent; unrestrained, wanton, lax, careless; without metre, prose, irregular

somni-fer 3 sleep-bringing

somniō 1 to dream; to talk foolishly

somnium, ī n dream; fancy, nonsense

somnus, ī m sleep; drowsiness, laziness

soni-pēs, pedis m horse, steed

sonitus, ūs m sound, noise, din

sonō, nuī, (sonātūrus) 1 intr. to make a noise, resound, roar; trans. to speak, sound; to sing, celebrate; to mean

sonor, ōris m = sonitus

sonōrus 3 sounding, resounding

sōns, sontis guilty; subst. ~, **sontis** m criminal

sonus, ī m sound, noise

sōpiō 4 to lull, put to sleep; to stun, stupefy; to calm, still, quiet

sopor, ōris m deep sleep

sopōrātus 3 put to sleep; soporific

sopōri-fer 3 causing sleep

sopōrus 3 sleep-bringing

sorbeō, buī, — 2 to suck in, swallow

sordeō, (uī), — 2 to be dirty or despised

sordēs, is f (usu. pl.) dirt, filth; mourning clothes; meanness, low condition, baseness, stinginess; rabble sordidātus 3 in mourning attire

sordidus 3 dirty, foul, filthy; mean, despicable, vile; poor; niggardly, stingy

soror, ōris f sister

sorōrius 3 of or for a sister

sors, rtis f lot, a casting lots; money, capital; fate, destiny, chance; duty; pl. oracle, prophecy

sorti-legus 3 prophetic

sortior 4 to draw lots; to assign by lot, get by lot; to gain by fate, receive; to choose

sortītiō, ōnis f a casting lots

sortītō adv. by lot, by destiny

sortītus, ūs m = sortitio

sospes, itis safe and sound, unhurt, fortunate

sospita, ae f she who saves

sospitō 1 to save, protect

spadō, ōnis m eunuch

spargō, rsī, rsum 3 to strew, scatter, sprinkle; throw; to spread abroad, disperse, divide

sparus, ī m hunting-spear

spatior 1 to walk about; to spread out

spatiōsus 3 roomy, wide, spacious; lasting long

spatium, ī n room, extent, size, length; interval, distance; race-course; walk, promenade; public place; period, time, leisure, opportunity

speciēs, ēī f sight, look, view; appearance, mien,

exterior; vision, dream; beauty, splendour, show; seeming, resemblance; idea, notion

specimen, inis n mark, token, proof; pattern, model, example

speciōsus 3 fair, beautiful, splendid; for show, specious, plausible

spectābilis, e visible; worth seeing, admirable

spectāculum, ī n seat in a theatre; show, sight, spectacle; stage-play

spectātiō, ōnis f a looking at, beholding

spectātor, ōris m observer, spectator; connoisseur

spectātus 3 well tried or tested; excellent

spectō 1 to look, view, observe, gaze at; to try, prove; to bear in mind, aim at, look for; to tend towards; to look or face towards

spēcula¹, ae f slight hope

specula², ae f height, eminence, watch-tower

speculātor, ōris m watcher, spy, scout, explorer

speculātōrius 3 of spies, of scouts

speculor 1 to look around, spy, watch, explore

speculum, ī n mirror

specus, ūs m (and n) cave, grotto; ditch, pit, canal

spēlunca, ae f cave, grotto

spernō, sprēvī, sprētum 3 to reject, disdain, despise

spērō 1 to expect; to hope; to trust in

spēs, ēī f expectation, hope; fear; anticipation

sphaera, ae f ball, sphere

spīca, ae f ear of corn, point

spīceus 3 of ears of corn

spīculum, ī n point, sting; arrow, dart, javelin

spīna, ae f thorn, prickle; backbone; perplexity, difficulty, anxiety

spīnōsus 3 thorny; crabbed, obscure

spīra, ae f coil, twist, fold

spīrābilis, e that can be breathed; life-giving

spīrāculum, ī n air-hole, vent

spīrāmentum, ī n air-hole, pore

spīritus, ūs m breath, air; life; spirit, inspiration, courage; haughtiness, pride

spīrō 1 to breathe, be alive; to blow; to exhale, emit; to be inspired with, aim at; to express

spissus 3 thick, crowded, dense; tardy, slow

splendeō, (uī), — 2 to shine, be bright; to be glorious

splendēscō, duī, — 3 to become bright

splendidus 3 bright, shining; splendid, magnificent, noble, distinguished

splendor, ōris m brightness; splendour, magnificence, honour

spoliātiō, ōnis f a plundering, robbery

spoliātor, ōris m plunderer

spoliō 1 to strip; to plunder, rob, despoil

spolium, ī n skin, hide; pl. plunder, booty, arms taken from an enemy

sponda, ae f bed, sofa

spondeō, spopondī, spōnsum 2 to promise, engage, pledge oneself; to be a security; to betroth; to forebode; subst. spōnsus, ī m bridegroom; spōnsa, ae f bride

spongia (and -ea), ae f sponge

spōnsa, ae f, see spondeo

spōnsālia, ium n/pl. betrothal

spōnsiō, ōnis f solemn promise, engagement, pledge; legal wager

spōnsor, ōris m surety

spōnsum, ī n solemn promise

spōnsus, ī m, see spondeo

sponte f (abl. sg.) of one's own accord, willingly, freely; without aid, alone; of itself

sportula, ae f little basket; gift, present

spūma, ae f foam, froth, scum

spūmeus 3 foaming

spūmi-fer 3 foaming

spūmō 1 to foam, froth

spūmōsus 3 foaming

spuō, uī, ūtum 3 to spit (out)

spurcō 1 to defile

spurcus 3 dirty, foul, impure

squāleō, —, — 2 to be rough *or* stiff; to be dirty, neglected, foul; to mourn in squalid garments

squālidus 3 rough, stiff; dirty, filthy, neglected

squālor, ōris *m* filthiness, foulness; mourning attire

squāma, ae *f* scale

squāmeus 3, squāmi-ger 3, squāmōsus 3 scaly

squilla, ae *f* a shell-fish

stabiliō 4 to make firm, support, establish

stabilis, e firm, steadfast, lasting, immutable

stabilitās, ātis *f* stability, durability, firmness

stabulor *and* -lō 1 to be stabled, dwell

stabulum, ī *n* stable, stall, fold; brothel

stadium, ī *n* race-course; stade (*about 600 feet*)

stāgnō 1 to form a pool, overflow

stāgnum, ī *n* lake, pond, pool; water

stāmen, inis *n* warp of a web; thread, string

statārius 3 standing firm

statim *adv.* at once, immediately

statiō, ōnis *f* a standing; station, position, abode; post, watch, guard; roadstead, anchorage

statīvus 3 fixed, standing still

stator, ōris *m* attendant of a magistrate; supporter (*title of Juppiter*)

statua, ae *f* statue, image

statuō, uī, ūtum 3 to set up, erect, build, found; to fix, appoint, determine, decide, ordain; to resolve, purpose; to believe, judge, consider   [stature

statūra, ae *f* height, size,}

status[1] 3, *see* sisto

status[2], ūs *m* a standing, position, attitude; condition, state, circumstances

stēlla, ae *f* star

stēllāns, tis starry

stēllātus 3 starry, shining

stemma, atis *n* pedigree

stercus, oris *n* dung, manure

sterilis, e barren; vain

sterilitās, ātis *f* unfruitfulness, barrenness

sternō, strāvī, strātum 3 to stretch out, extend, strew, scatter; to throw down; to level, smooth, pave; to cover

sternuō, uī, — 3 to sneeze

stertō, —, — 3 to snore

stigma, atis *n* brand

stillō 1 to drip; to let drop, distil

stilus, ī *m* pointed instrument for writing; writing, composition; style

stimulō 1 to torment, trouble; to incite, spur, stimulate

stimulus, ī *m* prick, goad; pointed stake; sting, pain; spur, incitement

stīpātor, ōris *m* attendant, satellite

stipendiārius 3 liable to tribute, tributary

stipendium, ī *n* pay of a soldier; military service, campaign; tax, tribute

stīpes, itis *m* log, stump, trunk of a tree

stīpō 1 to press *or* crowd together, cram, stuff; to surround, attend

stips, ipis *f* contribution in money, gift, alms

stipula, ae *f* stalk, stem, straw

stipulātiō, ōnis *f* agreement, covenant

stipulor 1 to stipulate, bargain

stirps, is *f* (and *m*) lowest part of tree-trunk, root; plant, tree; family, lineage; source, beginning; descendant, offspring

stīva, ae *f* plough-handle

stō, stetī (stātūrus) 1 to stand; to be stationed; to stand out, bristle up; to cost; to stand by, adhere to; to rest upon, depend on; to stand firm, endure, persist; to be fixed *or* determined; to keep the stage

stola, ae *f* woman's gown, long robe

stolidus 3 stupid, dull, rude

stomachor 1 to be angry *or* irritated

stomachōsus 3 angry, irritable

stomachus, ī *m* stomach; taste, liking; anger, irritation

storea *and* -ia, ae *f* straw-mat, rush-mat

strabō, ōnis *m* squinter

strāgēs, is *f* overthrow, ruin, defeat, slaughter; fallen mass, confused heap

strāgulus 3 for spreading out; strāgula vestis blanket, carpet

strāmen, inis *n* straw, litter

strāmentum, ī *n* straw, litter

strāmineus 3 of straw

strangulō 1 to choke, strangle; to torment, torture

strātum, ī *n* covering, blanket; bed, couch; horse-cloth, saddle

strēnuus 3 active, quick, ready

strepitō 1 to make a loud noise

strepitus, ūs *m* noise, din, rustling, sound

strepō, puī, (pitum) 3 to make a noise, rustle, rattle, roar; to resound

strictim *adv.* briefly, superficially

strīdeō, —, — 2 *and* strīdō, dī, — 3 to creak, hiss, hum, rustle

strīdor, ōris *m* a creaking, hissing, humming, grunting

strīdulus 3 rustling, hissing, creaking

strigilis, is *f* skin-scraper

stringō, strinxī, strictum 3 to touch lightly, graze; to wound, affect, move; to strip off, pluck, draw; to draw tight, tie together

strix, igis f screech-owl

strūctor, ōris m builder, mason; head-waiter

structūra, ae f building, construction; arrangement

struēs, is f heap

strūma, ae f tuberculous tumour

struō, -uxī, -uctum 3 to heap up, pile; to build, construct; to prepare, arrange; to contrive, cause

studeō, uī, — 2 to give attention to, apply oneself to, be busy with, strive after, desire; to be favourable to, to side with

studiōsus 3 zealous, eager, diligent; studious; friendly, favourable, devoted

studium, ī n zeal, eagerness, enthusiasm, desire, study; favour, attachment, devotion, partiality; employment, pursuit; literary occupation, research

stultitia, ae f foolishness, silliness, stupidity

stultus 3 foolish, stupid, silly

stupe-faciō 3 to stun, stupefy

stupeō, uī, — 2 to be stunned, benumbed, amazed

stupidus 3 senseless, amazed; stupid, foolish

stupor, ōris m senselessness, dulness; astonishment, stupidity, foolishness

stuppa, ae f coarse flax, tow

stuppeus 3 of tow, flaxen

stuprō 1 to defile, ravish

stuprum, ī n a debauching; unchastity

Stygius 3 of the Styx, of the nether world, infernal

Styx, ygis f a river in Hades

suādeō, sī, sum 2 to advise, exhort, suggest, persuade; to impel, induce; to promote, support

suāsiō, ōnis f a recommending; persuasive eloquence

suāsor, ōris m adviser, exhorter

suāvior 1 to kiss

suāvis, e sweet, pleasant, delightful, attractive

suāvitās, ātis f sweetness, pleasantness, agreeableness

suāvium, ī n kiss

sub prep. 1. with acc. (of place) under; up towards; close up to; (of time) about, just before; 2. with abl. (of place or condition) under, beneath, at the foot of; behind; (of time) at, at the same time as

sub-accūsō 1 to blame a little

sub-auscultō 1 to listen secretly

sub-c..., see succ...

sub-dō, didī, ditum 3 to put

or set under, apply; to substitute, forge

sub-dolus 3 cunning, crafty

sub-dubitō 1 to doubt a little

sub-dūcō 3 to draw *or* take away, remove, lead away, steal; to balance, calculate; to draw up, lift up

sub-eō, iī, itum, īre to go *or* come under, enter; to undergo, submit to, sustain, endure; to go up, climb; to approach, advance; to steal into; to come into one's mind; to come after, follow

sūber, eris *n* cork-oak; cork

sub-f...., *see* suff...

sūb-iciō (*and* sūb-), iēcī, iectum 3 to throw, put, lay under; to subject, subdue; to substitute, forge; to place near *or* by, present; to suggest, prompt, propose; to put after, append; to subordinate, comprise in; to throw up, raise; subiectus 3 lying under *or* near; subjected, subject

sub-iectō 1 to throw up; to place underneath

sub-iectus 3, *see* subicio

sub-igō, ēgī, āctum 3 to drive *or* bring up; to force, compel, constrain; to overcome, conquer; to plough, dig; to sharpen; to discipline, train

sub-inde *adv.* immediately after; from time to time, repeatedly

sub-īrāscor 3 to be a little angry   [done hastily)

subitārius 3 collected *or*)

subitus 3 sudden, unexpected; *adv.* subitō

sub-iungō 3 to join, yoke; to subdue, subject

sub-lābor 3 to glide, fall down, sink

sub-lātus 3 elated, proud, haughty

sub-legō 3 to gather, pick up, choose

sub-levō 1 to lift up, raise; to support, assist, encourage; to lessen, mitigate

sublica, ae *f* stake, pile

sub-ligō 1 to bind below

sublīmis, e high, lofty; aloft; exalted, distinguished

sub-lūceō, —, — 2 to shine forth, glimmer

sub-luō 3 to wash underneath

sub-lūstris, e glimmering

sub-m...., *see* summ...

sub-nectō 3 to tie under, bind on, fasten

sub-nīsus *and* -nīxus 3 resting *or* leaning on; relying on

sub-olēs, is *f* offspring, descendant

sub-ōrnō 1 to furnish, supply; to instruct privately, suborn

sub-p...., *see* supp...

sub-rēpō 3 to creep up (to), steal upon

sub-rīdeō 2 to smile

sub-rigō 3 to raise up

sub-ripiō 3 = surripio

sub-rogō 1 = surrogo

sub-rubeō 2 to be reddish, blush

sub-ruō 3 to dig under, undermine, overthrow, destroy

sub-scrībō 3 to write beneath; to sign a charge; to support, assent to

sub-scrīptiō, ōnis f a writing beneath; a noting down

sub-scrīptor, ōris m joint accuser

sub-secō 1 to cut off, clip

sub-sellium, ī n bench, seat; pl. court, tribunal

sub-sequor 3 to follow, come after, attend; to follow up, support

sub-sicīvus 3 left over, odd, spare

subsidiārius 3 of a reserve; subst. subsidiariī, ōrum m/pl. reserve-troops

sub-sidium, ī n reserve forces; aid, help, relief

sub-sīdō, sēdī, sessum 3 to sit down, crouch down; to sink, subside; to settle down, stay; to lie in wait for

sub-sistō, stitī, — 3 to stand still, stop, halt, remain; to resist, withstand

sub-sortior 4 to substitute by lot

sub-sortītiō, ōnis f a choosing of substitutes by lot

sub-sternō 3 to spread or place under

sub-stituō, uī, ūtum 3 to put under, present; to put instead of, substitute

sub-stringō 3 to bind or draw up

sub-strūctiō, ōnis f foundation, substructure

sub-strūō 3 to build beneath, lay (the foundation)

sub-sum, —, — to be under or behind; to be concealed in; to be near or at hand

sub-tēmen, inis n woof, weft; thread, yarn

subter adv. and prep. with acc. and abl. below, beneath, under

subter-fugiō, fūgī, — 3 to flee in secret, escape, shun

subter-lābor 3 to glide or flow under

sub-terrāneus 3 underground

sub-texō 3 to draw before, cover, veil

subtilis, e fine, thin; precise, exact; keen, delicate, refined; plain, unadorned

subtilitās, ātis f exactness, discernment, subtlety; plainness, simplicity

sub-trahō 3 to draw from under, take away, remove

sub-urbānus 3 near the city, suburban; subst. -um, ī n estate near Rome

sub-vectiō, ōnis f a carrying, conveying

sub-vectō 1 to carry, convey

sub-vehō 3 to bring up, convey, transport

sub-veniō 4 to come to help, assist, aid; to relieve, cure

sub-vertō 3 to overturn, overthrow, ruin, destroy

sub-volō 1 to fly up

sub-vortō 3 = subverto

suc-cēdō 3 to go under or into, enter; to submit to; to go to, approach, advance; to turn out well, prosper, succeed; to go up, ascend; to come after, follow, come into the place of, relieve

suc-cendō, ndī, ēnsum 3 to set on fire, kindle, inflame

succēnseō 2 = suscenseo

suc-cessiō, ōnis f a succeeding, succession

successor, ōris m successor, heir

successus, ūs m advance; good progress, success

suc-cīdō[1], cīdī, cīsum 3 to cut off below, cut down or through

suc-cīdō[2], cīdī, — 3 to sink down

succiduus 3 sinking down

suc-cingō 3 to tuck up the clothes; to gird, surround; to furnish, equip

suc-cipiō 3 = suscipio

suc-clāmātiō, ōnis f a shouting, acclamation

suc-clāmō 1 to shout to

suc-crēscō 3 to grow up

suc-cumbō, cubuī, cubitum

3 to sink down, be overcome, yield

suc-currō, currī, cursum 3 to run to help, hasten to aid, assist; to come to mind, suggest itself

sūcus, ī m juice, sap, moisture; medicinal drink; taste, flavour; vigour, force

sudis, is f stake

sūdō 1 to sweat; to drip, be wet; to toil hard

sūdor, ōris m sweat; moisture; exertion

sūdus 3 clear, serene

suēscō, ēvī, ētum 3 to become accustomed; suētus 3 accustomed, wont, customary

suf-ferō, sufferre to bear, endure, suffer

suf-ficiō, fēcī, fectum 3 to supply, furnish; to choose as a substitute; to be sufficient, suffice, avail; to stain

suf-fīgō 3 to fix beneath, fasten to

suf-fiō 4 to perfume, fumigate

suffīāmen, inis n drag, brake

suf-fōcō 1 to choke, strangle

suf-fodiō 3 to dig under, undermine; to pierce from below

suffrāgātiō, ōnis f favourable vote, support

suffrāgātor, ōris m voter, supporter

suffrāgium, ī n voting-tablet; vote, suffrage; right of voting; approbation, assent

suf-frāgor 1 to vote for, support, favour

suf-fugiō, fūgī, — 3 to flee

suf-fugium, ī *n* place of refuge

suf-fundō 3 to pour under, into, upon, overspread, suffuse

sug-gerō 3 to put under; to furnish, supply, add, subjoin

suggestum, ī *n and* **-us, ūs** *m* elevated place, platform, stage

sūgō, xī, ctum 3 to suck (in)

sulcō 1 to furrow, plough, sail over

sulcus, ī *m* furrow; trench, ditch; track, trail

sulfur, uris *n* = sulp(h)ur

sulp(h)ur, uris *n* brimstone, sulphur

sulpureus 3 sulphurous

sum, fuī, esse to be, exist, live; to happen, occur; to be present, be found, stay; to be abroad, be the case that ...; to belong or pertain to, be peculiar to, be characteristic of, be the duty of; to be valued at, cost

summa, ae *f* sum, amount, contents, substance, quantity, whole; chief point, chief thing, principal matter; pre-eminence, first rank

summātim *adv.* generally, summarily

summē *adv.* exceedingly, very much

sum-mergō 3 to dip, plunge under, overwhelm, drown

sum-ministrō 1 to furnish, supply

sum-missiō, ōnis *f* a letting down, lowering

sum-missus 3 lowered; low, soft, gentle, calm; mean, abject; humble, submissive

sum-mittō 3 to let down, lower, sink; to moderate, abate; to submit, bring down, humble; to dispatch secretly, send as aid or reinforcement; to rear, produce

sum-moveō 2 to move up or away, remove, dislodge; to banish; to keep away from, withhold, force from

summus 3, *superl. of* superus

sūmō, mpsī, mptum 3 to take, take up or in hand; to put on, wear, eat, consume; to exact (*punishment*); to take for granted, suppose, assert, cite, mention; to take, choose, select, purchase; to undertake, begin; to claim, appropriate

sūmptuārius 3 of expense

sūmptuōsus 3 expensive, costly; extravagant, prodigal

sümptus, ūs *m* charge, expense, cost [stitch]

suō, suī, sūtum 3 to sew,

su-ove-taurīlia, ium *n/pl.* sacrifice of a pig, a sheep and a bull

supellex, ectilis *f* household goods, furniture

super *adv.* over, above; besides, moreover; *prep.* with *acc.* and *abl.* over, above; during; about, concerning; beyond; more than

superābilis, e that may be surmounted *or* overcome

super-addō 3 to add over and above

superātor, ōris *m* conqueror

superbia, ae *f* pride, haughtiness, insolence

superbiō, —, — 4 to be proud *or* haughty, boast

superbus 3 haughty, proud, arrogant; fastidious; distinguished, splendid, magnificent

super-cilium, ī *n* eyebrow; severity, sternness; pride, haughtiness; ridge, summit

super-ēminō 2 to overtop, surmount

super-ficiēs, ēī *f* building with its ground

super-fluō, —, — 3 to overflow, abound

super-fundō 3 to pour upon *or* over, cover

super-iaciō, iēcī, iectum 3 to throw over *or* upon; to surmount; to exceed

super-impōnō 3 to place upon

super-incidō 3 to fall upon from above

super-iniciō 3 to throw *or* cast over

super-insternō 3 to spread over

superne *adv.* from above, above

supernus 3 on high, upper, celestial

superō 1 to be above, project; to abound; to remain, survive; to surmount, mount, ascend; to surpass, excel, prevail; to sail past, go by; to conquer, overcome, subdue

super-sedeō 2 to forbear, desist, refrain

super-stes, stitis surviving, outliving, remaining

super-stitiō, ōnis *f* superstition, excessive religious awe

superstitiōsus 3 superstitious

super-stō, —, — 1 to stand over *or* upon

super-sum, —, -fuī, -esse to remain, be left; to survive, outlive; to abound, be equal to

superus 3 what is above, upper, higher; *subst.* superī, ōrum *m/pl.* the celestial gods; *comp.* superior, us higher, upper; past, former, older; superior, nobler, more important, conqueror; *superl.* suprēmus 3 highest, uppermost, supreme; extreme, last; *superl.* summus 3 highest, topmost, highest part of, top of, surface of; extreme, last; greatest, most important, most distinguished, best, chief; whole, entire

super-vacăneus 3 over and above, superfluous, needless, useless

super-vacuus 3 = super-vacaneus

super-vādō 3 to climb or pass over

super-veniō 4 to follow up, overtake, come on by surprise, come on the scene

super-volō 1 to fly over

supīnō 1 to turn up or over

supīnus 3 lying on the back, face upwards; sloping or flowing up

sup-peditō 1 to furnish, supply; to be available, be at hand, abound, be sufficient

sup-petō 3 to be available, be at hand, be sufficient

sup-plēmentum, ī n supply, reinforcement

sup-pleō, ēvī, ētum 2 to fill up, supply, complete, recruit

sup-plex, icis kneeling, suppliant, entreating, humble, submissive

sup-plicātiō, ōnis f public thanksgiving

supplicium, ī n humble

entreaty; public thanksgiving; punishment, execution; torture, pain, distress

sup-plicō 1 to kneel down to, beseech humbly; to pray, worship

sup-pōnō 3 to put or lay under; to make subject, submit; to annex, subjoin; to substitute, forge

sup-portō 1 to carry, bring up, convey

sup-primō, pressī, pressum 3 to press down, sink; to hold back, restrain, stop; to suppress, hide

sup-pudet 2 me I am somewhat ashamed

suprā adv. above, over, on the top; before, previously; more, further, beyond; prep. with acc. above, over; beyond; before; more than

suprēmus 3, superl. of superus

sūra, ae f calf of the leg

surculus, ī m shoot, sprout, sucker

surdus 3 deaf; unheeding, regardless; silent, noiseless

surgō, surrēxī, surrēctum 3 to rise, arise, get up; to grow up, appear, spring up; to mount up, ascend

sur-rēpō 3 = subrepo

sur-rigō 3 = subrigo

sur-ripiō, ripuī, reptum 3 to snatch or take away secretly, steal, pilfer sur-rogō 1 to cause to be chosen as substitute

sūrsum (and sūrsus) adv. upwards; above, on high

sūs, suis f and m sow, swine, pig, hog

sus-cēnseō, uī, — 2 to be angry or enraged

susceptiō, ōnis f an undertaking

sus-cipiō, cēpī, ceptum 3 to catch, support; to take up a new-born child; acknowledge; to have or beget a child; to take, receive; to undertake, begin; to submit to; to assume; to answer

sus-citō 1 to raise or stir up, lift up; to awake, excite, incite

su-spectō 1 to look up at; to suspect, mistrust

su-spectus[1], ūs m height; admiration

su-spectus[2] 3 suspected, mistrusted

sus-pendium, ī n a hanging, hanging oneself

sus-pendō, ndī, ēnsum 3 to hang up, hang; to raise, prop up; to keep in suspense, make doubtful

sus-pēnsus 3 suspended, hanging; poised, light; resting or depending upon; uncertain, doubtful, wavering, anxious

su-spiciō[1], exī, ectum 3 to look up (at); to honour, admire

su-spiciō[2], ōnis f suspicion, mistrust; notion, idea

suspiciōsus 3 full of suspicion, mistrustful; causing suspicion, suspected

suspicor 1 to suspect, conjecture, suppose

su-spīritus, ūs m deep breath, sigh

suspīrium, ī n deep breath, sigh

su-spīrō 1 to breathe deeply, heave a sigh, long for

sus-tentō 1 to hold up, sustain, maintain, preserve; to hold out, suffer, endure; to check, put off, delay

sus-tineō, nuī, — 2 to hold up, support, sustain; to bear, endure, withstand; to maintain, nourish; to hold back, restrain, defer, delay   [or lift up]

sus-tollō, —, — 3 to raise

susurrō 1 to whisper, murmur

susurrus, ī m a whispering, murmuring, humming

sūtilis, e sewed together, fastened together

sūtor, ōris m shoemaker

sūtōrius 3 of a shoemaker

suus 3 poss. adj. his, her, its, their (own); proper, peculiar, suitable; appointed; favourable; independent, free; subst. suī, ōrum m/pl. one's own troops, friends, dependents; suum, ī n one's own property

sȳcophanta, ae *m* false accuser, slanderer

syllaba, ae *f* syllable

sym-bola, ae *f* contribution, share of cost of a meal

sym-phōnia, ae *f* concerted music (vocal *or* instrumental)

symphōniacus 3 musical

syn-grapha, ae *f* written agreement to pay, bond

syrma, atis *n* (tragic actor's) robe; tragedy

syrtis, is *f* sandbank in the sea (*esp.* two off the coast of North Africa)

T

tabella, ae *f* small board; little painting; writing-tablet; letter; document, record; votive tablet; voting-tablet

tabellārius 3 relating to voting; *subst.* ~, ī *m* letter-carrier

tābeō, —, — 2 to melt, waste away, be consumed

taberna, ae *f* hut, shed; tavern, shop, stall

tabernāc(u)lum, ī *n* tent; place for observing the auspices

tabernārius, ī *m* shopkeeper

tābēs, is *f* a melting away, putrefaction, decay; pestilence, plague

tābēscō, buī, — 3 to melt, waste away, decay; to pine away

tābidus 3 melting, decaying; corrupting, destructive

tabula, ae *f* board, plank; picture, painting; writing-tablet; table of the law; auction; document, record, list; will; account-book

tabulārium, ī *n* archives

tabulātum, ī *n* floor, story

tābum, ī *n* corrupt moisture, putrid gore; plague, pestilence

taceō, uī, itum 2 to be silent *or* still; to pass over in silence

taciturnitās, ātis *f* silence, taciturnity [quiet]

taciturnus 3 silent, still,|

tacitus 3 silent, quiet; kept secret, unmentioned; secret, hidden

tāctus, ūs *m* a touching, touch; influence; sense of touch, feeling

taeda, ae *f* pine-tree; pine-wood; torch; nupital torch, wedding

taedet, uit *or* taesum est 2 to cause weariness *or* disgust

taedium, ī *n* disgust, loathing, weariness

taenia, ae *f* band, fillet, ribbon

taeter, tra, trum nasty, foul, hideous, abominable

tālāris, e of *or* reaching to the ankles; *subst.* tālāria, ium *n/pl.* winged sandals *or* shoes tālārius 3 of dice

tālea, ae *f* stake, bar

talentum, ī *n* talent (*weight or money*)

tālis, e such, of such a kind; so distinguished or remarkable; so bad or blamable

talpa, ae *f* (and *m*) mole

tālus, ī *m* ankle; heel; kind of dice

tam *adv.* so, so very, to such a degree

tam-diū *adv.* so long

tamen *adv.* nevertheless, notwithstanding; yet at least, still [though]

tam-etsī *cj.* though, although

tam-quam *adv.* as, just as; *cj.* as if, as though

tandem *adv.* at last, finally; pray, then, now

tangō, tetigī, tāctum 3 to touch; to come to, reach; to border on; to taste, eat, drink; to moisten, dye; to strike, hit; to move, affect, impress; to mention

tan-quam = tamquam

tantis-per *adv.* just so long

tant-opere *adv.* so much, to such a degree

tantulus 3 so little, so small

tantus 3 so great, so much, so important; *subst.* tantum, ī *n* so much, such a quantity, so high a degree; so little; *adv.* tantum so much, so far; only so much, so little; only, merely; tantummodo only, merely

tantundem, tantīdem *n* just as much; *adv.* just as far

(tapēs), ētis *m* and tap(p)ēte, is *n* carpet, coverlet, tapestry

tarditās, ātis *f* slowness, tardiness; dulness, stupidity

tardō 1 to stop, hinder, delay

tardus 3 slow, sluggish; long, lasting; late; dull, stupid

taureus 3 of a bull *or* bull's hide

taurīnus 3 of bulls *or* oxen

taurus, ī *m* bull, ox

taxus, ī *f* yew-tree

tech(i)na, ae *f* trick, artifice

tēctōrium, ī *n* plaster, stucco, fresco-painting

tēctum, ī *n* roof; ceiling; room, dwelling; house

tēctus 3 covered, roofed, decked; concealed, secret; reserved, cautious

teges, etis *f* mat

tegimen, inis *n* cover, protection

tegimentum, tegmentum, ī *n* cover, covering

tegmen, inis *n* = tegimen

tegō, tēxī, tēctum 3 to cover; to hide, conceal, dissemble; to protect, defend

tēgula, ae *f* tile; tiled roof

tegumen, tegumentum = tegimen(tum)

tēla, ae *f* web; warp; loom

tellūs, ūris *f* the earth; soil, ground; land, country, district

tēlum, ī *n* missile weapon, spear, javelin; sword, dagger

temerārius 3 rash, thoughtless, foolhardy

temere *adv.* by chance, accidentally, casually; inconsiderately, rashly; **non temere** not easily, hardly

temeritās, ātis *f* chance, accident; rashness, haste, thoughtlessness

temerō 1 to violate, defile, disgrace

tēmētum, ī *n* wine, intoxicating drink

temnō, —, — 3 to contemn, despise

tēmō, ōnis *m* pole or beam of a wagon; wagon

temperāmentum, ī *n* right proportion, measure, moderation

temperāns, tis moderate, sober, temperate

temperantia, ae *f* moderation, temperance, continence

temperātiō, ōnis *f* just proportion, composition, proper regulation

temperātus 3 moderate, temperate, mild, calm

temperī *adv.* in due time

temperiēs, ēī *f* = temperatio

temperō 1 to mingle in due proportion, qualify, temper; to arrange, order, regulate, govern; to use with moderation; to keep back, restrain; to be moderate, forbear, abstain, spare

tempestās, ātis *f* weather; bad weather, storm; calamity, misfortune, danger, period of time, season

tempestīvus 3 seasonable, opportune, appropriate, timely, ripe; early

templum, ī *n* open space; sanctuary, temple, shrine

temptāmen, inis *and* **temptāmentum, ī** *n* = temptatio

temptātiō, ōnis *f* trial, attempt, proof

temptō 1 to touch, handle, feel; to attack, assail; to try, prove, test, attempt; to tempt, incite, disturb, tamper with

tempus¹, oris *n* time, period *or* point of time; proper time, right occasion, opportunity; circumstances, the times, state of things; crisis, misfortune, calamity, extremity

tempus², oris *n* temple on the forehead

tēmulentus 3 drunken, intoxicated

tenāx, ācis holding fast, gripping, tenacious; firm, steadfast, persisting; obstinate; stingy, niggardly

tendō, tetendī, tentum (and tēnsum) 3 to stretch, stretch out, distend, extend; to hold out, offer, present; to direct, turn; *intr.* to encamp; to travel, hold a course, direct one-

self, move, march; to be
inclined, tend; to strive,
struggle, contend, fight

tenebrae, ārum *f/pl.* darkness; night; lurking place,
haunts; obscurity

tenebricōsus 3 dark, gloomy,
obscure

tenebrōsus 3 dark, gloomy

teneō, tenuī, (tentum) 2 to
hold, keep, grasp; to un-
derstand, comprehend,
know; to hold one's course,
steer, arrive at; to gain,
acquire; to possess, be
master of, occupy; to
comprise, include; to hold
back, detain, fetter, control, restrain; to preserve,
maintain keep to; to re-
member; to last, endure;
to bind, oblige

tener, era, erum soft, delicate, tender; young,
youthful; effeminate;
yielding

tenor, ōris *m* uninterrupted
course, continuance, duration, career

tēnsa, ae *f* chariot bearing
images of the gods

tentāmen, inis *n* = tempt-
amen

tentīgō, inis *f* passion, lust

tentō 1 = tempto

tentōrium, ī *n* tent

tenuis, e thin, slender, fine,
small; subtle, exact, nice;
weak; insignificant, tri-
fling; miserable, poor,
mean

tenuitās, ātis *f* thinness,

fineness; poverty, in-
digence; simplicity

tenuō 1 to make thin or
fine; to lessen, diminish,
weaken

tenus *prep.* with *abl.* and
gen. up to, as far as, unto

tepe-faciō 3 to make warm

tepeō, uī, — 2 to be warm;
to be in love

tepēscō, puī, — 3 to grow
warm

tepidus 3 tepid, warm; cool,
faint, languid

tepor, ōris *m* lukewarmness,
moderate heat

ter *adv.* thrice, three times

ter-deciē(n)s *adv.* thirteen
times

terebrō 1 to bore, pierce,
perforate

teres, etis rounded or
polished, smooth; grace-
ful, elegant

ter-geminus 3 = trigemi-
nus

tergeō, sī, sum 2 to wipe off,
dry, clean

tergiversātiō, ōnis *f* evasion,
subterfuge

tergiversor 1 to make ex-
cuses, practise evasion

tergum, ī *n* back, rear;
surface; hide, leather

tergus, oris *n* = tergum

Terminālia, ium *n/pl.* festival of the god Terminus

termīnātiō, ōnis *f* a limiting,
determining

termīnō 1 to bound, limit,
confine; to determine, define; to end

terminus, ī m boundary; limit, end, term

ternī 3 three each; triple

terō, trīvī, trītum 3 to rub, rub off; to polish, burnish; to thrash out, grind; to consume, waste, wear out; to use often, frequent; to spend, pass

terra, ae f the earth, world; land; ground, soil; country, region

terrēnus 3 of earth, earthen; of the earth, terrestrial

terreō, uī, itum 2 to frighten, terrify, alarm; to scare away, deter

terrestris, e of the earth, terrestrial, of the land

terribilis, e terrible, frightful, dreadful

terriculum, ī n something that causes fright, bugbear

terri-ficō 1 = terreo

terri-ficus 3 = terribilis

terri-gena, ae m and f earthborn

territō 1 to frighten, terrify

terror, ōris m terror, fear, dread

tertius 3 the third; adv. tertiō and -um

ter-uncius, ī m a quarter of an as; trifle

tesqua (or tesca), ōrum n/pl. deserts, wastes

tessera, ae f cube, dice; tablet containing watchword or orders

testa, ae f tile, brick; earthen vessel, pot; potsherd; shell, shell-fish

testāmentārius 3 of a testament or will; subst. ~, ī m forger of a will

testāmentum, ī n testament, last will

testātus 3 attested, manifest, evident

testificātiō, ōnis f a bearing witness; proof, evidence

testi-ficor 1 to call to witness; to bear witness, testify; to show, prove, declare

testimōnium, ī n testimony, evidence; proof

testis, is m and f witness; spectator

testor 1 = testificor; intr. to make a will

testūdineus 3 made of tortoise-shell

testūdō, inis f tortoise; tortoise-shell; arched room, vault; shelter, covering of shields; stringed instrument, lyre

tēter 3 = taeter

tetrachmum, ī n fourdrachma piece

tetrarchēs, ae m tetrarch

tetrarchia, ae f tetrarchy

tetricus 3 gloomy, harsh, grim

texō, xuī, xtum 3 to weave, plait; to construct, make, compose

textilis, e woven

textor, ōris m weaver

textrīnum, ī n a weaver's shop

textum, ī n web, cloth; texture, construction

thalamus, ī *m* bedchamber; brida! bed, marriage

theātrālis, e theatrical

theātrum, ī *n* theatre, play-house; stage; spectators, audience

thēca, ae *f* case, covering

thēnsaurus, ī *m* = thesaurus

thēsaurus, ī *m* treasure, hoard, store; treasury, storehouse

thiasus, ī *m* Bacchic dance *or* troop of dancers

tholus, ī *m* (round building with a) dome

thōrāx, ācis *m* breastplate, cuirass

thūs, ūris *n* = tus

thȳias, adis *f* Bacchant

thymum, ī *n* thyme

thyrsus, ī *m* staff of Bacchus; goad

tiāra, ae *f and* tiārās, ae *m* turban, tiara, diadem

tībia, ae *f* flute, pipe

tībī-cen, inis *m* piper, flute-player; pillar, prop

tībicina, ae *f* female flute-player [wood]

tigillum, ī *n* little beam of

tignum, ī *n* beam, log

tigris, idis *or* is *m and f* tiger, tigress

tilia, ae *f* linden-tree, lime-tree

timeō, uī, — 2 to fear, dread, be anxious

timiditās, ātis *f* fearfulness, timidity

timidus 3 fearful, timid, cowardly

timor, ōris *m* fear, dread, alarm; object of fear

tinea, ae *f* grub, worm

ting(u)ō, tīnxī, tīnctum 3 to moisten, wet, imbue, dip in; to stain, dye

tinnītus, ūs *m* a ringing, tinkling, jingling

tinnulus 3 ringing, tinkling

tīrō, ōnis *m* young soldier, recruit; beginner, novice

tīrōcinium, ī *n* first service of a soldier; recruits

titillātiō, ōnis *f* a tickling

titillō 1 to tickle

titubō 1 to totter, stagger; to stammer, falter; to hesitate, be perplexed

titulus, ī *m* inscription, title; bill, placard; title of honour *or* dignity; pretext, pretence [stone]

tōfus, ī *m* tufa, volcanic

toga, ae *f* toga (*upper garment of a Roman*)

togātus 3 wearing the toga, in Roman dress; in the garb of peace; *subst.* ~, ī *m* Roman citizen

togula, ae *f* little toga

tolerābilis, e bearable, tolerable, passable

tolerō 1 to bear, endure, sustain; to maintain, support

tollēnō, ōnis *m* see-saw, swingbeam

tollō, sustulī, sublātum 3 to lift *or* take up, raise, exalt, elevate; to take away, remove, destroy, ruin; to annul, cancel

tondeō, totondī, tōnsum 2 to shear, clip, shave, cut; to reap, pluck, crop, graze

tonitrus, ūs *m and* **tonitruum**, ī *n* thunder

tonō, uī, — 1 to thunder; to resound, roar

tōnsa, ae *f* oar

tōnsor, ōris *m* barber

tōphus, ī *m* = tofus

torāl, ālis *n* couch-covering

toreuma, atis *n* embossed work, work in relief

tormentum, ī *n* windlass, pulley, engine for hurling, missile; torture, rack, anguish

tornō 1 to turn in a lathe, round off

tornus, ī *m* lathe; chisel

torpeō, —, — 2 to be stiff *or* inert; to be stupefied, dull, languid

torpēscō, puī, — 3 to become stiff, inert, dull

torpidus 3 stiff, benumbed

torpor, ōris *m* numbness, languor, dulness

torqueō, torsī, tortum 2 to wind, twist, turn; to hurl, fling, whirl; to wrest, distort, torture; to test, examine; to harass, distress

torquis (*and* -ēs), is *m* (*and* f) twisted neck-chain, necklace, collar

torrēns, tis burning, hot; rushing, roaring; *subst.* ~, tis *m* stream, torrent

torreō, torruī, tostum 2 to dry, parch, burn, roast

torridus 3 parched, dry; frost-bitten

torris, is *m* firebrand

tortilis, e twisted

tortor, ōris *m* torturer

tortuōsus 3 full of windings, tortuous; intricate, involved

tortus, ūs *m* a winding

torus, ī *m* muscle; cushion, couch, bed

torvus 3 stern, grim, fierce,}

tot (*indecl.*) so many [wild}

toti-dem (*indecl.*) just so many

totiē(n)s *adv.* so often, so many times

tōtus (*gen.* -īus, *dat.* -ī) 3 whole, entire, all

toxicum, ī *n* poison

trabālis, e of beams

trabea, ae *f* robe of state

trabeātus 3 in a robe of state

trabs, abis *f* beam of wood; tree; ship

tractābilis, e that can be handled, manageable; pliant, yielding

tractātiō, ōnis *f* a handling, management, treatment

tractim *adv.* gradually, continuously

tractō 1 to drag, pull; to touch, handle; to manage, exercise, practise; to treat, use; to examine, discuss

tractus, ūs *m* a drawing, dragging; track, course; district, tract

trāditiō, ōnis *f* a giving up, surrender

trā-dō, didĭ, ditum 3 to give up, hand over, deliver, intrust; to surrender, betray; to bequeath, hand down, relate, recount; to teach

trā-dūcō 3 to bring, carry, lead over or across; to transfer, win over, convert; to spend, pass; to expose to ridicule

trā-ductiō, ōnis f a transferring, removal; course of time

tragĭcus 3 of tragedy, tragic; lofty, sublime; horrible

tragoedia, ae f tragedy; tumult, disturbance

tragoedus, ī m tragic actor

trāgula, ae f javelin

trahō, traxī, tractum 3 to draw, drag, haul, pull; to consider, weigh; to allure, attract, influence; to appropriate, ascribe, refer; to carry off, plunder; to lead; to distract; to take in, quaff, inhale; to take on, acquire; to derive; to lengthen, protract, delay

trā-iciō, iēcī, iectum 3 to throw, shoot, bring or carry across or over; to transfer; to cross, pass through, go over; to transfix, pierce

trā-iectiō, ōnis f passage

trā-iectus, ūs m passage

trā-l..., see trans-l...

trā-m..., see trans-m...

trāmes, itis m by-way, path, road, course

trā-natō and trā-nō 1 to swim over or across; to pass through, penetrate

tranquillĭtās, ātis f quietness, stillness, calmness, peace

tranquillō 1 to calm, still, allay

tranquillus 3 quiet, calm, still

trāns prep. with acc. across, over; beyond, to or on the other side

trāns-abeō, iī, —, īre to pass by; to pierce

trāns-adigō 3 to thrust or pierce through

trāns-alpīnus 3 beyond the Alps

trānscendō, ndī, ēnsum 3 to climb or pass over, cross, surmount; to transcend, transgress

trānscrībō 3 to transfer in writing; to make over, assign, give over

trāns-currō, (cu)currī, cursum 3 to run over or across; to pass over, traverse

trāns dō 3, trāns-dūcō 3 = trado, traduco

trāns-eō, iī, itum, īre to go or pass over or through; to desert; to be transformed or turned; to elapse; to transgress, violate; to go through briefly; to omit, leave unnoticed

trāns-fĕrō 3 to carry, bring,

convey over or across; to transfer, transport, turn; to copy; to translate; to use figuratively; to put off, defer; to carry along or in procession

trāns-fīgō 3 to pierce; transfix

trāns-fodiō 3 = transfigo

trāns-fōrmis, e transformed

trāns-fōrmō 1 to transform

trāns-fuga, ae m deserter

trāns-fundō 3 to transfer

trāns-gredior, gressus sum 3 to step or pass over

trāns-gressiō, ōnis f a going over; transposition

trāns-iectiō, -iectus, see trā-i...

trāns-igō, ēgī, āctum 3 to drive through, pierce; to carry through, finish, accomplish; to settle a difference, agree; to pass, spend

trāns-iciō 3 = tra-icio

trānsiliō, siluī, — 4 to leap or spring over; to pass by, neglect

trāns-itiō, ōnis f a passing over; desertion

trāns-itus, ūs m a passing over or by, passage

trāns-lātīcius 3 traditional, customary, usual

trāns-lātiō, ōnis f a transferring, shifting; metaphor

trāns-marīnus 3 beyond sea

trāns-migrō 1 to migrate

trāns-missiō, ōnis f and -missus, ūs m a passing over, passage

trāns-mittō 3 to send over or across, transmit, transfer; to entrust; to travel, pass over

trāns-mūtō 1 to change, transpose [tranato]

trāns-natō, trāns-nō 1 =

trāns-portō 1 to carry or bring over, transport

trānstrum, ī n bench for rowers

trāns-vehō 3 to carry or convey over, transport; P. to travel over, go or pass by

trāns-verberō 1 to strike through, pierce

trāns-versus 3 lying across, transverse, athwart

trāns-volō 1 to fly over or across

trā-v..., see trans-v...

tre-cēnī 3 three hundred each

tre-centī 3 three hundred

tre-decim (indecl.) thirteen

tremebundus 3 trembling, shaking

treme-faciō 3 to cause to tremble or quake

tremendus 3 terrible, frightful

tremēscō and **-īscō, — —** 3 to tremble, quake (at)

tremō, uī, — 3 to tremble (at), quake, quiver

tremor, ōris m a trembling, quaking; earthquake

tremulus 3 trembling, quivering

trepidātiō, ōnis f confused hurry, agitation, alarm

trepidō 1 to hurry with alarm, be agitated, be in confusion, tremble; to waver, hesitate

trepidus 3 agitated, alarmed, restless, disturbed; boiling, bubbling; perilous, critical

trēs, tria, ium three

trēs-virī, triumvir(ōr)um *m/pl.* board of three men

triāriī, ōrum *m/pl.* soldiers of the third rank, the reserve

tribūlis, is *m* fellow tribesman [thistle]

tribulus, ī *m* a kind of

tribūnal, ālis *n* raised platform for magistrates, judgment seat, tribunal

tribūnātus, ūs *m* office of a tribune

tribūnicius 3 of a tribune, tribunicial

tribūnus, ī *m* tribune (*title of various Roman magistrates and officers*)

tribuō, uī, ūtum 3 to divide, distribute, assign, give; to concede, allow; to ascribe, attribute

tribus, ūs *f* tribe

tribūtim *adv.* by tribes

tribūtum, ī *n* tribute, tax

tribūtus 3 arranged in tribes

trīcae, ārum *f/pl.* nonsense; tricks

tri-ceps, cipitis three-headed

tricēsimus (or **-cēns-**) 3 thirtieth

tri-clīnium, ī *n* table-couch; dining-room

tri-corpor, oris having three bodies

tri-dēns, entis three-pronged; *subst.* ~, **entis** *m* trident

trī-duum, ī *n* space of three days

tri-ennium, ī *n* space of three years

triēns, tis *m* third part (*esp. of an as*)

trietēricus 3 happening every third year

trifāriam *adv.* in three places, on three sides

tri-fōrmis, e having three shapes

tri-geminus 3 threefold

trīgintā (*indecl.*) thirty

tri-linguis, e three-tongued

trīmus 3 three years old

trīnī 3 three each; triple, threefold

triōnēs, um *m/pl.* the constellation of the two Bears

tri-partītus 3 divided into three parts, threefold; *adv.* tripartītō

tri-pertītus 3 = tripartitus

tri-pēs, pedis three-footed

tri-plex, icis threefold, triple

tripudiō 1 to beat the ground with the feet, dance

tri-pudium, ī *n* a dancing, solemn dance

tripūs, odis *m* three-footed seat, tripod; (the Delphic) oracle

tri-quetrus 3 triangular

tri-rēmis, e with groups of three oars; *subst.* **-rēmis, is** *f* trireme

trīs *acc.* = **tres**

tristis, e sad, sorrowful, melancholy; bringing sorrow, saddening; dismal; gloomy, morose, stern, harsh; disagreeable

tristitia, ae *f* sadness, sorrow, grief; moroseness, sternness

tri-sulcus 3 threefold, three-pronged

trīticeus 3 of wheat

trīticum, ī *n* wheat

trītus 3 trodden, frequented; much used, usual, commonplace; expert

triumphālis, e of a triumph, triumphal

triumphō 1 to celebrate a triumph, triumph over; to exult, rejoice

triumphus, ī *m* triumph, triumphal procession

trium-vir, ī *m* triumvir, one of three associates in office

trivium, ī *n* place where three roads meet; street-corner

trochus, ī *m* boy's hoop

tropaeum, ī *n* trophy, memorial of victory; victory; monument, sign

trucīdātiō, ōnis *f* a slaughtering, massacre

trucīdō 1 to cut down, slaughter, massacre, ruin

truculentus 3 grim, harsh, savage, fierce

trūdō, sī, sum 3 to thrust, push, drive forward

trulla, ae *f* ladle; fire-pan

truncō 1 to cut off, maim

truncus[1], ī *m* trunk (of tree or body)

truncus[2] 3 maimed, mutilated, imperfect

trutina, ae *f* balance, pair of scales

trux, ucis fierce, grim, rough, savage, wild

tū thou, you

tuba, ae *f* trumpet

tūber, eris *n* swelling, bump, tumour

tubi-cen, inis *m* trumpeter

tueor, tuitus sum 2 to look at, gaze upon; to watch over, protect, defend, maintain, support

tugurium, ī *n* hut, cottage

tum *adv.* then, at that time; thereupon, afterwards, next 　　　　　[swell]

tume-faciō 3 to cause to

tumeō, —, —2 to be swollen *or* blown *or* puffed up; to swell with anger, be excited

tumēscō, muī, — 3 to begin to swell

tumidus 3 swollen; puffed up, proud, pompous; causing to swell

tumor, ōris *m* a swelling, tumour; commotion, excitement, anger

tumulō 1 to bury, inter

tumultuārius 3 hurried, confused, disorderly; levied suddenly tumultuor 1 to be in confusion, be in an uproar

tumultuōsus 3 confused, noisy, tumultuous

tumultus, ūs *m* noise, uproar, confusion; insurrection, revolt, civil war; storm

tumulus, ī *m* mound, hill; grave

tunc *adv.* then, at that time; thereupon, afterwards

tundō, tutudī, tū(n)sum 3 to beat, strike, pound; to importune

tunica, ae *f* undergarment, shirt; skin, peel

tunicātus 3 clothed in a tunic

tuor 3 = tueor

turba, ae *f* tumult, noise, confusion; crowd, throng, multitude, mob

turbātor, ōris *m* disturber

turbidus 3 confused, disturbed, stormy; muddy, turbid; impetuous, excited, troubled, astonished

turbō¹, inis *m* a whirling, spinning, revolution; whirlwind, storm; spinning-top; wheel

turbō² 1 to throw into confusion, disturb, trouble, amaze

turbulentus 3 restless, disturbed, confused; causing disturbance, seditious

turdus, ī *m* thrush

tūreus 3 of frankincense

turgeō, (rsī), — 2 to be swollen

turgēscō, —, — 3 to begin to swell

turgidus 3 swollen, inflated

tūri-cremus 3 incense-burning

turma, ae *f* division of cavalry; squadron, troop, band

turmālis, e of the same squadron

turmātim *adv.* by squadrons

turpis, e ugly; filthy, foul; disgraceful, shameful, base, indecent

turpitūdō, inis *f* baseness, disgrace, dishonour

turpō 1 to make ugly, deform, defile

turri-ger 3 tower-bearing, turreted

turris, is *f* tower; castle, palace

turrītus 3 furnished with towers; lofty

turtur, uris *m* turtle-dove

tūs, tūris *n* incense, frank-\
tussis, is *f* cough [incense\

tū-te (*emphatic*) = tu

tūtēla, ae *f* care, charge, protection; wardship, guardianship; guardian, protector; ward

tūtō, *adv., see* tutus

tūtor¹, ōris *m* protector; guardian, tutor

tūtor² 1 to guard, protect, defend, watch

tūtus 3 safe, secure, protected; watchful, cautious, prudent; *adv.* tūtō tuus 3 thy, thine, your, yours

ty(m)panum, ī n drum, tambourine; wheel

tyrannicus 3 tyrannical, despotic

tyrannis, idis f tyranny, arbitrary or despotic power

tyrannus, ī m monarch, absolute ruler, king; tyrant, despot

U

über¹, eris n teat, udder, breast; fertility, richness

über², eris fertile, fruitful; rich, abounding, plentiful

übertās, ātis f fruitfulness, fertility; fulness, plenty, richness

ubī (and ubi) interrog. adv. where?; relat. cj. where; when, as soon as, whenever

ubi-cumque (or -cunque) wherever

ubi-nam interrog. where?

ubi-que adv. everywhere, anywhere

ubi-vīs adv. where you will, everywhere

ūdus 3 moist, wet

ulcerō 1 to cause to ulcerate, make sore

ulcīscor, ultus sum 3 to avenge; to avenge oneself; to take vengeance on, punish, requite

ulcus, eris n ulcer, sore

ūlīgō, inis f moisture, dampness

ūllus 3 any, any one

ulmus, ī f elm

ulna, ae f arm; ell.

ulterior, ius comp. farther, on the further side, be-

yond, more distant; superl.

ultimus 3 farthest, most distant, extreme; earliest, oldest, first; last, latest; utmost, greatest, highest; worst, lowest

ultiō, ōnis f an avenging, revenge

ultor, ōris m avenger, punisher

ultrā adv. beyond; further, moreover, besides (comp. ulterius); prep. with acc. beyond, past, over, across; more than, above

ultrīx, īcis adj./f avenging

ultrō adv. to the farther side, beyond; even, moreover, actually; of one's own accord, voluntarily, spontaneously

ulutātus, ūs m a howling, shrieking, wailing

ululō 1 to howl, shriek, wail

ulva, ae f sedge

umbilīcus, ī m navel; middle, centre; (end of a) stick on which a manuscript was rolled

umbō, ōnis m knob, boss; shield

umbra, ae f shade, shadow,

darkness; uninvited guest; departed spirit, ghost; shelter, protection; rest, leisure; semblance, show, pretext

umbrāculum, ī *n* shady place, bower; school; parasol

umbrātilis, e retired, contemplative; scholastic

umbri-fer 3 shady

umbrō 1 to shade, overshadow, cover

umbrōsus 3 shady, giving shade

ūmectō 1 to moisten, wet

ūmeō, —, — 2 to be moist, wet, damp

umerus, ī *m* shoulder, upper arm

ūmidus 3 moist, wet

ūmor, ōris *m* moisture, liquid, fluid

umquam *adv.* ever, at any time

ūnā *adv.*, *see* unus

ūn-animus 3 of one mind, concordant

uncia, ae *f* twelfth part; ounce

unciārius 3 containing a twelfth

unctus 3 anointed, oiled, greasy; rich, luxurious, sumptuous

uncus[1], ī *m* hook, barb

uncus[2] 3 hooked, crooked, curved

unda, ae *f* wave; stream, water; agitation; surge; throng

unde (*interrog.* and *relat.*)

from which place, whence, from whom

ūn-decim (*indecl.*) eleven

ūn-decimus 3 eleventh

ūn-dēnī 3 eleven each

ūn-dē-vīgintī (*indecl.*) nineteen

undique *adv.* from all parts or sides; on all sides, everywhere; in all respects

undō 1 to rise in waves, surge, swell; to wave, undulate

undōsus 3 full of waves

ungō, unxī, unctum 3 to anoint

unguen, inis *n* = unguentum

unguentārius, iī *m* dealer in ointments

unguentum, ī *n* ointment, perfume

unguiculus, ī *m* finger-nail, toe-nail

unguis, is *m* finger-nail, toe-nail; claw, hoof

ungula, ae *f* hoof; claw, talon

unguō, unxī, unctum 3 = ungo

ūnicus 3 one only, single; singular, unique, unparalleled

ūni-gena, ae born of the same parentage

ūniversitās, ātis *f* the whole

ūni-versus 3 whole, entire, all together

unquam *adv.* = umquam

ūnus 3 one, a single, only one; one and the same, the same, common; *adv.*

ūnā at the same place, at the same time, together, at once; **ūnus quisque** each single, every one

urbānitās, ātis *f* life in Rome; city manners, refinement, elegance, politeness; wit, humour

urbānus 3 of the city (*Rome*), urban; refined, elegant, polished; witty, pleasant; bold, forward

urbs, urbis *f* city, capital; Rome

urce(ol)us, ī *m* pitcher, water-pot

urgeō, ursī, — 2 to push, press, drive, urge; to oppress, weigh down, burden, beset; to crowd, hem in; to insist upon; to stick to, apply oneself to

ūrīna, ae *f* urine

urna, ae *f* pitcher, jug, jar; voting-urn, urn for lots; urn for ashes of the dead

ūrō, ussī, ustum 3 to burn, destroy by fire; to harass, distress, vex; to dry up, parch, scorch; to pinch with cold, chafe, rub sore; to burn with passion, inflame

ursa, ae *f* she-bear; the Bear (*constellation*)

ursus, ī *m* bear

urtīca, ae *f* (stinging-) nettle; itching desire

ūrus, ī *m* wild ox

ūsitātus 3 usual, customary, common, familiar

uspiam *adv.* anywhere

usquam *adv.* anywhere; in any thing, in any way; to any place

usque *adv.* all the way, right (up), continuously, all the while; **usque quāque** everywhere, on all occasions

ustor, ōris *m* burner of dead bodies

ūsū-capiō 3 to acquire by use *or* prescription

ūsūra, ae *f* use, enjoyment; interest, usury

ūsūrpātiō, ōnis *f* a making use of, employment

ūsūrpō 1 to use, employ, practise, enjoy; to seize, usurp; to name, call

ūsus, ūs *m* a using, use, practice, exercise; skill, experience; usage, custom; intercourse, familiarity; usefulness, advantage, profit; occasion, need, necessity

ut *adv.* how; as, just as; although; as being, inasmuch as; seeing that, since; as for example; *cj.* when, as soon as; that, in order that, for the purpose of; so that (in consequence); although, granting that

ut-cumque *adv.* in whatever way, however; somehow; whenever

ūtēnsilia, ium *n/pl.* necessaries, materials, utensils

uter[1], tris *m* leather bag *or* bottle

uter[2], utra, utrum which of two, which; either

uter-cumque 3 whichever of the two

uter-libet 3 either of the two

uter-que 3 each of two, both

uterus, ī m belly, paunch; womb

uter-vīs 3 which of the two you will, either of the two

utī = ut

ūtilis, e useful, serviceable, suitable, fit, profitable

ūtilitās, ātis f usefulness, use, profit, advantage

uti-nam adv. would that!, oh that!

uti-que adv. at any rate, by all means, certainly; at least; especially

ūtor, ūsus sum 3 to use,

employ; to enjoy, have, take advantage of; to practise, exercise, perform; to be intimate with, associate with

ut-pote adv. seeing that, inasmuch as, as being, as

utrim-que adv. from or on both sides

utrobīque adv. = utrubique

utrō-que adv. to both sides; in both directions

utrubīque adv. on both sides

utrum adv. whether

ut-ut = utcumque

ūva, ae f grape

ūvēscō, —, — 3 to become wet

ūvidus 3 moist, wet; drunken

uxor, ōris f wife, mate

uxōrius 3 of a wife; devoted to one's wife, uxorious

V

vacātiō, ōnis f freedom from, immunity; exemption from military service

vacca, ae f cow

vaccīnium, ī n a purple flower

vacillō 1 to waver, totter, hesitate

vacō 1 to be empty, vacant, unoccupied; to be ownerless; to be free from, be without; to be disengaged, be at leisure for, have time for

vacuitās, ātis f freedom (from), exemption

vacuus 3 void, empty, free from, exempt; vacant, unoccupied; disengaged, at leisure, idle; quiet, calm

vadimōnium, ī n bail, security

vādō 3 to go, walk

vador 1 to bind over to appear in court

vadōsus 3 full of shallows

vadum, ī n shallow water, shoal; ford; water, sea, stream

vae int. woe!, ah!, oh!

vae-cors, vaesānus, see ve-...

vafer, fra, frum cunning, crafty, artful, subtle

vāgīna, ae *f* scabbard, sheath

vāgiō 4 to cry, scream, whimper

vāgītus, ūs *m* a crying, screaming

vagor 1 to rove, roam, wander about

vagus 3 wandering, strolling, roving; unsteady, inconstant, indefinite, vague

vāh *int.* ah!, oh!

valdē *adv.* vehemently, strongly, very much

valēns, tis strong, powerful; in good health, robust, vigorous

valeō, uī, itūrus 2 to be strong; to be well *or* in health; to be powerful, have weight *or* influence, prevail, avail, succeed; to be able *or* capable; to mean, signify; **valē** farewell, good-bye

valētūdō, inis *f* state of health; good health; ill health, sickness, weakness

validus 3 strong, vigorous, healthy, sound; powerful, mighty, efficacious

vallēs *and* **-is, is** *f* valley, vale

vallō 1 to fortify with a rampart, entrench; to protect, defend

vallum, ī *n* palisaded rampart, fortification; protection

vallus, ī *m* stake; pole; palisade; rampart, stockade

valvae, ārum *f/pl.* leaves of a folding door

vānēscō, —, — 3 to fade away, vanish

vāni-loquus 3 boasting

vānitās, ātis *f* emptiness, unreality, vanity, deception; a boasting, vainglory

vānus 3 empty, void; vain, groundless, fruitless, to no purpose; false, lying, deceitful, boastful; *subst.* **vānum, ī** *n* emptiness, mere show

vapor, ōris *m* vapour, steam, smoke; heat, warmth

vapōrō 1 to heat with steam *or* smoke, to warm

vappa, ae *f* spoiled *or* flat wine; a good-for-nothing

vāpulō 1 to be flogged *or* whipped

varietās, ātis *f* variety, difference; vicissitude, change; difference in opinion; fickleness

variō 1 to diversify, variegate, change, alter, interchange; *intr.* to be different *or* diverse, waver, change, vary

varius 3 variegated, mottled; different; diverse, varying, changeable; fickle, inconstant

vārus 3 bent, crooked; knock-kneed

vas¹, vadis *m* surety, bail

vās², vāsis *n* vessel, utensil; **vāsa**, ōrum *n/pl.* baggage, equipment

västātiō, ōnis *f* a laying waste

västātor, ōris *m* ravager, devastator

västitās, ātis *f* desolation, devastation, ruin, waste, desert

västō 1 to make empty, lay waste, desolate, ravage

västus[1] 3 waste, desolate, empty, devastated; rough, rude, uncouth

västus[2] 3 vast, huge, monstrous

vātēs, is *m* and *f* soothsayer, diviner, prophet; singer, bard, poet

vāticinātiō, ōnis *f* prediction, prophecy

vāticinor 1 to foretell, prophesy; to rave, talk idly

vāti-cinus 3 prophetic

ve *cj. enclitic* or, or perhaps

vēcordia, ae *f* madness, foolishness

vē-cors, rdis mad, foolish, frantic [income, rents]

vectīgal, ālis *n* tax, duty;]

vectīgālis, e paid in taxes; liable to taxes, tributary

vectis, is *m* lever; crowbar; bar, bolt

vectō 1 to carry, convey

vector, ōris *m* bearer, carrier; passenger, rider

vectūra, ae *f* a carrying, conveyance, transport

vegetus 3 vigorous, quick, active

vehemēns, tis violent, furious, impetuous; strong, powerful, vigorous; *adv.* **vehementer** strongly, violently, exceedingly, very much

vehiculum, ī *n* vehicle, conveyance

vehō, **vēxī**, **vectum** 3 to carry, bear, convey, draw; P. to ride, drive, travel

vel *(particle)* or, or rather; even, actually; for example; **vel ... vel** either ... or

vēlāmen, inis *n* veil, covering, clothing

vēlāmentum, ī *n* olive-branch wound round with wool

vēles, itis *m* skirmisher

vēli-fer 3 sail-bearing

vēli-ficor *(and* -ficō) 1 to sail (through); to be zealous for

vēlitāris, e of skirmishers

vēli-volus 3 flying *or* winged with sails

vellicō 1 to criticize, rail at, taunt

vellō, **vellī** *(and* **vulsī**), **vulsum** *and* **volsum** 3 to pluck (out), pull, twitch; to tear down

vellus, eris *n* wool, fleece, sheepskin; skin of an animal

vēlō 1 to veil, cover, surround, conceal

vēlōcitās, ātis *f* quickness, swiftness [rapid]

vēlōx, ōcis quick, swift,]

vēlum[1], ī *n* sail

vēlum[2], ī *n* drapery, curtain, awning, veil

vel-ut(ī) as, even as, just as; for instance

vēmēns, tis = vehemens

vēna, ae *f* vein, blood-vessel; metallic vein; inmost nature, interior; talent, natural bent, genius

vēnābulum, ī *n* hunting-spear

vēnālis, e on sale; venal, that may be bribed; *subst.* vēnālis, is *m* slave

vēnāticus 3 for hunting

vēnātiō, ōnis *f* a hunting, chase; hunting spectacle, wild beast fight; game

vēnātor, ōris *m* hunter

vēnātrīx, īcis *f* huntress

vēnātus, ūs *m* a hunting, chase

vendibilis, e on sale, salable; popular, acceptable

venditātiō, ōnis *f* a boasting, vaunting

venditiō, ōnis *f* a selling, sale

venditō 1 to offer for sale; to barter away, give for a bribe; to praise, recommend

venditor, ōris *m* seller

vendō, didī, ditum 3 to sell; to betray, give for a bribe; to cry up, praise

venē-fica, ae *f* poisoner, sorceress, witch

venēficium, ī *n* a poisoning; magic, sorcery

venē-ficus 3 poisoning,

magical; *subst.* ~, ī *m* poisoner, sorcerer

venēnātus 3 poisoned, poisonous

venēnō 1 to poison

venēnum, ī *n* dye, drug; poison; magic potion, charm

vēn-eō, iī, —, īre to be on sale, be sold [venerable]

venerābilis, e reverend,

venerābundus 3 respectful, reverent

venerātiō, ōnis *f* reverence, respect

venereus *and* venerius 3 dedicated to Venus; of sexual love

veneror 1 to revere, worship, adore; to implore, beseech

venia, ae *f* favour, grace, indulgence, permission; pardon, forgiveness

veniō, vēnī, ventum 4 to come, come to, arrive; to advance, approach, appear; to grow

vēnor 1 to hunt; to pursue, strive after

venter, tris *m* belly, paunch; womb, foetus; a swelling, protuberance

ventilō 1 to wave in the air, fan

ventitō 1 to come often

ventōsus 3 full of wind, windy; swift as the wind; vain, conceited; fickle, inconstant

ventus, ī *m* wind; fortune, circumstances

vēnum (*acc.*), **vēnō** (*dat.*), sale; **vēnum dō** = vendo; **vēnum eō** = veneo

venus, eris *f* love; beloved person; loveliness, beauty, charm; Venus goddess of love; the highest throw in dice-play

venustās, ātis *f* loveliness, charm, beauty; elegance, politeness

venustus 3 charming, lovely; attractive, fine

veprēs, is *m* thorn-bush, brier, bramble

vēr, vēris *n* spring-time

vērāx, ācis truthful

verbēna, ae *f* (*usu. pl*) sacred herbs *or* branches

verber, eris *n* blow, lash; a thrashing, flogging; whip, scourge; thong

verberō[1], **ōnis** *m* scoundrel

verberō[2] 1 to beat, strike, whip; to chastise, assail, harass

verbōsus 3 wordy, verbose

verbum, ī *n* word, expression; *pl*. talk, speech; proverb; mere word, mere talk

vērē *adv.*, *see* verus

verēcundia, ae *f* respect, awe, shyness, modesty; shame

verēcundus 3 bashful, modest; moderate

vereor, veritus sum 2 to fear, shrink from, hesitate; to reverence, respect, stand in awe of

vergō, (rsī), — 3 to incline

or turn (to); to lie *or* be situated towards; to decline

vēri-dicus 3 = verax

vērī-similis, e probable, likely

vēritās, ātis *f* truth; reality, real life; sincerity, truthfulness; honesty, integrity

verna, ae *m* (and *f*) home-born slave

vernāculus 3 native, indigenous, Roman

vernō 1 to become spring-like, be renewed, grow green

vernus 3 of spring, spring-like

vērō *adv.*, *see* versus

verrēs, is *m* boar

verrō, —, versum 3 to sweep (out), brush, clean

versātilis, e revolving; versatile

versi-color, ōris changing in colour; particoloured

versiculus, ī *m* little verse

versō 1 to turn about, turn hither and thither, roll, bend, shift; to disturb, harass, vex; to handle, deal with; to consider, meditate; P. **versor** 1 to stay, dwell, live; to be in a certain condition; to be occupied, busied, engaged in

versūra, ae *f* the borrowing of money to pay a debt; a borrowing, loan

versus[1] 3, *part. of* verto *and* verro

versus² *adv.* towards, in the direction of

versus³, ūs *m* row, line; verse, poetry

versūtus 3 cunning, crafty, dexterous

vertex, icis *m* whirlpool, eddy; whirlwind; top, summit, head

vertīgō, inis *f* a turning or whirling round; giddiness, dizziness

vertō (*archaic* vortō), rtī, rsum 3 to turn, turn round, up, back; to direct, convert; to ascribe, impute; to change to; to dig up, plough; to overthrow, destroy, ruin; to alter, change, transform; to translate; *intr. and* P. to turn *or* direct oneself; to turn out, result; to be in a certain condition *or* state; (*of time*) revolve, come round; to depend, rest upon

verū, ūs *n* spit; javelin

vērus 3 true, real, actual; truthful, upright; fitting, reasonable, just, proper; *subst.* **vērum**, ī *n* truth, reality, fact; *adv.* **vērē** truly, rightly, in fact, really; **vērō** in truth, really, indeed, certainly; but in fact, but indeed; **vērum** yes, certainly; but, but in truth, but still

verūtum, ī *m* javelin

vē-sānus 3 mad, insane, raging

vescor, —, — 3 to feed on, eat; to use, enjoy

vēscus 3 thin, slender, feeble

vēsīca, ae *f* bladder

vesper, erī (*and* -eris) *m* the evening-star; evening; the west

vespera, ae *f* the evening

vespertīnus 3 of the evening; western

Vesta, ae *f* the goddess Vesta; fire on the hearth

Vestālis, e of Vesta; *subst.* **Vestālis**, is *f* priestess of Vesta, Vestal virgin

vester, tra, trum *pron.* yours

vestibulum, ī *n* entrance court, court-yard, porch; entrance

vestīgium, ī *n* foot-print, step, track; trace, mark, sign; sole of the foot; moment, instant

vestīgō 1 to track, follow the trail of; to investigate, search out

vestīmentum, ī *n* garment, clothing

vestiō 4 to clothe, dress; to cover, deck, adorn

vestis, is *f* clothes, clothing, dress; carpet, tapestry

vestītus, ūs *m* clothing, dress, attire

veterānus 3 (*and subst. m*) veteran

veterātor, ōris *m* old hand, old fox

veterātōrius 3 cunning, crafty

veternus, ī *m* lethargy, drowsiness, laziness

vetō, uī, itum 1 to forbid, prohibit, prevent

vetulus 3 old

vetus, eris (*comp.* vetustior, *superl.* veterrimus) old, aged; of long standing, ancient; *subst.* veterēs, um *m/pl.* forefathers, men of old

vetustās, ātis *f* old age, long existence, length of time; antiquity; late posterity

vetustus 3 old, aged, ancient

vexātiō, ōnis *f* hardship, trouble; ill-treatment, vexation

vexātor, ōris *m* harasser, disturber

vexillārius, ī *m* standard-bearer; *pl.* reserve of veterans

vexillum, ī *n* standard, flag; signal-flag; company, troop

vexō 1 to move violently, shake; to harass, trouble, disturb, damage, attack, abuse

via, ae *f* way, road, street, path; march, journey; manner, method

viāticum, ī *n* money for a journey

viātor, ōris *m* traveller, wayfarer; messenger of a magistrate

vibrō 1 to shake, brandish; to hurl; *intr.* to tremble, quiver; to flash, glitter

vīcānus 3 of a village

vicārius 3 substituted, vicarious; *subst.* ~, ī *m* substitute, deputy

vīcātim *adv.* from street to street; in villages

vice *and* vicem, *see* vicis

vīcēnī 3 twenty each

vīcēnsimus 3 = vicesimus

vīcēsimus 3 twentieth; *subst.* -a, ae *f* five per cent

vicia, ae *f* vetch (tax)

vīciē(n)s *adv.* twenty times

vīcīnia, ae *f and* vīcīnitās, ātis *f* neighbourhood; neighbours

vīcīnus 3 neighbouring, near; *subst.* ~, ī *m*, -a, ae *f* neighbour

vicis (*gen.*), *acc.* em, *abl.* e, *pl.* vicēs, *abl.* vicibus *f* change, interchange, alternation; turn; reply, requital, compensation; lot, fate, fortune; position, office, post, duty; *adv.* vicem *and* vice for the sake of, on account of, like; in vicem by turns, mutually; instead of

vicissim *adv.* in turn, again; on the other hand

vicissitūdō, inis *f* change, alternation, vicissitude

victima, ae *f* beast for sacrifice, victim; sacrifice

victor, ōris *m* conqueror, victor; *adj./m* victorious

victōria, ae *f* victory, conquest

victrix, īcis *adj./f* (*and n*) victorious

victus, ūs *m* means of living, nourishment, food; manner of life

vicus, ī *m* village, hamlet; estate, farm; district of a town, street

vidē-licet *adv.* clearly, plainly, obviously; of course, to be sure; namely

videō, vīdī, vīsum 2 to see, perceive, discern, observe; to visit; to let pass, permit; to perceive mentally, understand, consider, reflect upon; to see to, take care, provide for; P. **videor**, **vīsus sum** 2 to be seen, appear, be evident, seem; **vidētur** it seems proper, right, good, it pleases

vidua, ae *f* widow

viduitās, ātis *f* widowhood

viduō 1 to deprive *or* bereave of

viduus 3 widowed; deprived, destitute; without; solitary

viētus 3 shrivelled, withered

vigeō, uī, — 2 to be lively, vigorous, strong; to flourish, bloom, be esteemed

vīgēsimus 3 = vicesimus

vigil, ilis *m* watchman, sentinel; *adj.* watchful, awake

vigilāns, tis watchful, careful

vigilantia, ae *f* wakefulness; watchfulness

vigilia, ae *f* sleeplessness;

a keeping watch, guard; watchmen, sentinels; a watch (*a fourth part of the night*); watchfulness, vigilance

vigilō 1 to keep awake; to watch, be vigilant; to perform watching, execute by night

vīgintī (*indecl.*) twenty

vigor, ōris *m* vigour, energy, liveliness

vīlicus, ī *m* overseer, steward

vīlis, e cheap, paltry, worthless, mean

vīlitās, ātis *f* cheapness, low price

vīlla, ae *f* country-house, farm

vīllōsus 3 hairy, shaggy, rough

vīllula, ae *f* small country-house *or* villa

vīllus, ī *m* shaggy hair, tuft of hair; nap of cloth

vīmen, inis *n* pliant twig, withe, osier

vīmineus 3 made of osiers, of wicker-work

vīnārius 3 of *or* for wine

vinciō, vīnxī, vīnctum 4 to bind, tie, fetter; to surround, encircle; to restrain, confine

vinclum, ī *n* = vinculum

vincō, vīcī, victum 3 to conquer, overcome, be victorious; to prevail, succeed, win; to surpass, exceed, excel; to show conclusively, carry a point vinculum, ī *n* band, tie, rope, fetter; *pl.* bonds, prison

vīn-dēmia, ae *f* vintage; grapes, wine

vindex, icis *m* protector, champion; avenger, punisher

vindiciae, ārum *f/pl.* legal claim

vindicō 1 to demand formally, claim, assume; to champion, rescue, deliver, defend; to avenge, punish, take vengeance on

vindicta, ae *f* a freeing, rescue; liberating-rod; vengeance, punishment

vīnea, ae *f* vineyard; shed for shelter, penthouse

vīnētum, ī *n* vineyard

vīnitor, ōris *m* vine-dresser

vīnolentia, ae *f* wine-drinking, intoxication

vīnolentus 3 drunken, given to wine

vīnōsus 3 full of wine, drunken, given to wine

vīnum, ī *n* wine

viola, ae *f* violet; violet-colour; gillyflower

violābilis, e easily injured

violārium, ī *n* bed of violets

violātiō, ōnis *f* a violating

violātor, ōris *m* violator, profaner

violēns, tis = violentus

violentia, ae *f* violence, impetuosity; fury

violentus 3 violent, impetuous, boisterous, harsh

violō 1 to treat with vio-

lence, injure, hurt, dishonour, violate; to defile, profane; to transgress

vīpera, ae *f* viper, adder, snake

vīpereus 3 of a viper *or* snake

vīperīnus 3 = vipereus

vir, virī *m* a man; husband; man of courage, hero; soldier; *pl.* human beings, mortals

virāgō, inis *f* a manlike woman, female warrior

vireō, uī, — 2 to be green; to be blooming, fresh, vigorous

virēscō, ruī, — 3 to grow green

virga, ae *f* twig, rod, wand, staff

virgeus 3 of rods *or* twigs

virginālis, e maidenly, of a maiden

virgineus 3 of a virgin, maidenly

virginitās, ātis *f* maidenhood, virginity

virgō, inis *f* maiden, virgin; young woman

virgula, ae *f*, *dim. of* virga

virgultum, ī *n* thicket, shrubbery, shrub; slip for planting

viridis, e green; fresh, youthful

viriditās ātis *f* greenness, verdure; freshness

viridō 1 to be green

virīlis, e of *or* like a man, manly, male; courageous, vigorous; adult

viritim *adv.* man by man, singly, separately

virtūs, ūtis *f* manhood, manliness, strength, courage, bravery; excellence, worth, virtue, goodness

vīrus, ī *n* slime; poison; saltiness

vis (*acc.* **vim**, *abl.* **vī**; *pl.* **vīrēs, ium**) *f sg.* force, power, strength; violence, attack, compulsion; influence, potency; meaning, nature, sense, import; quantity, number, abundance; *pl.* military forces, troops

viscātus 3 smeared with bird-lime

viscerātiō, ōnis *f* public distribution of meat

viscum, ī *n* mistletoe; bird-lime

viscus, eris *n* (*usually pl.*) flesh; internal organs; children; inmost part, heart, centre, life

vīsiō, ōnis *f* apparition, appearance; idea, conception

vīsō, sī, — 3 to look at carefully, view; to go to see, visit

vīsum, ī *n* sight, appearance, vision

vīsus, ūs *m* a seeing, look, sight; appearance, thing seen

vīta, ae *f* life, lifetime; soul; way of life, manners

vītābundus 3 avoiding, shunning

vītālis, e of life, vital, living

vītātiō, ōnis *f* an avoiding

vitellus, ī *m* yolk of an egg

vitiō 1 to spoil, corrupt, injure, damage, defile; to falsify

vitiōsus 3 faulty, defective, bad; vicious, wicked

vītis, is *f* vine, vine-branch; centurion's staff

vitium, ī *n* fault, defect, blemish; error, offence, crime, vice

vītō 1 to shun, avoid

vitreus 3 of glass; glassy, transparent, brilliant

vītricus, ī *m* stepfather

vitrum, ī *n* glass

vitta, ae *f* ribbon, band, fillet

vitula, ae *f* calf, heifer

vitulīnus 3 of a calf

vitulus, ī *m* calf; foal

vituperātiō, ōnis *f* a blaming, blame; blamable conduct

vituperātor, ōris *m* blamer, censurer

vituperō 1 to blame, scold, censure

vīvārium, ī *n* park, preserve, fishpond

vīvāx, ācis long-lived, lively, vigorous; lasting

vīvidus 3 lively, animated, vigorous

vīvō, vīxī, vīctūrus 3 to live, be alive; to enjoy life; to live on, last, continue; to live upon, support life

vīvus 3 living, alive; fresh, active, lasting

vix *adv.* with difficulty,

hardly, scarcely, barely, just

vix-dum *adv.* scarcely yet

vocābulum, ī *n* name, appellation

vōcālis. e uttering sounds, sounding, sonorous, singing [invoking]

vocātus, ūs *m* a calling,

vōciferātiō, ōnis *f* an exclaiming, outcry, clamour

vōciferor (*and* **-rō**) 1 to cry aloud, exclaim, shout, scream

vocitō 1 to (be wont to) call

vocō 1 to call, summon; to cite; to invite; to challenge, defy, urge, stimulate; to call by name, name; to bring into a certain condition

vōcula, ae *f* weak voice

volāticus 3 volatile, fickle

volātilis, e flying, winged; swift

volātus, ūs *m* a flying, flight

volēns, tis willing, with purpose, of one's own accord; kind, favourable, propitious; acceptable, pleasing

volgus, volgāris (*archaic*) = vulgus, vulgaris

volitō 1 to fly about, flit, hover

volnerō, volnus (*archaic*) = vulnero, vulnus

volō¹ 1 to fly; to hasten

volō², luī, velle to be willing, wish, choose, intend, desire; to command, appoint, determine; to be-

lieve, pretend, maintain, say; to mean, signify

volō³, ōnis *m* volunteer

volpēcula, volpēs (*archaic*) = vulpecula, vulpes

voltur-, voltus (*archaic*) = vultur-, vultus

volūbilis, e turning, rolling, revolving; fluent, rapid

volūbilitās, ātis *f* a rapid turning, whirling; fluency, volubility

volucer, cris, cre flying, winged; rapid, quick; transient, changeable; *subst.* volucris, is *f* bird

volūmen, inis *n* coil, whirl, fold; book, roll, volume

voluntārius 3 willing, voluntary; *subst.* ~, ī volunteer

voluntās, ātis *f* will, freewill; wish, desire, purpose; good-will, favour, affection; inclination

volup *adv.* pleasantly, agreeably

voluptārius 3 giving enjoyment, pleasurable; devoted to pleasure, voluptuous

voluptās, ātis *f* pleasure, enjoyment, delight; desire, passion

volūtō 1 to roll, turn, roll about; to turn over in the mind, consider, weigh

volva, ae *f* womb

volvō, lvī, lūtum 3 to roll, turn round, whirl round; to roll along, bring on; to utter fluently; to consider, ponder, meditate

vōmer, eris *m* ploughshare

vōmis, eris *m* = vomer

vomō, uī, itum 3 to vomit, throw up

vorāgō, inis *f* chasm, abyss; whirlpool

vorāx, ācis greedy, vora-}
vorō 1 to devour, swallow {cious}

vors..., see vers...

vortex, vortō (*archaic*) = vertex, verto

vōs you (*pl.*)

voster (*archaic*) = vester

vōtīvus 3 vowed, votive, devoted

vōtum, ī *n* votive offering, gift; vow, promise to a god; wish, longing, prayer

voveō, vōvī, vōtum 2 to vow, promise solemnly, pledge; to wish, desire

vōx, vōcis *f* voice; sound, cry, call; word, saying, speech, proverb; language

vulgāris, e common, usual, vulgar

vulgātus 3 public, known to all, notorious

vulgō¹, see vulgus

vulgō² 1 to spread abroad, make common, communicate; to prostitute; to publish, divulge

vulgus, ī *n* the people, public, mob, rabble; mass, crowd, throng; **vulgō** openly, everywhere, generally

vulnerātiō, ōnis *f* a wounding, wound, injury

vulnerō 1 to wound; to hurt, injure, grieve

vulni-ficus 3 inflicting wounds

vulnus, eris *n* wound; cut, blow, stroke; misfortune, calamity, defeat, disaster; grief, pain

vulpēcula, ae *f* little fox

vulpēs, is *f* fox

vultur, uris *m* vulture

vulturius, ī *m* vulture

vultus, ūs *m* face, countenance, features, mien, look, appearance

vulva, ae *f* = volva

X

xystus, ī *m* (*and* -um, ī *n*) walk in a garden, promenade

Z

zephyrus, ī *m* west-wind

zōna, ae *f* girdle, belt (*of women*); zone of the earth, climatic region

A

a: twice a day bis in die
abandon (*a person*) relinquo 3, desero 3; (*a task*) omitto 3; ~ed perditus
abase summitto 3
abash ruborem inicio 3 (*alci*)
abate *r/t.* imminuo 3; *v/i.* remitto 3; ~ment remissio *f*
abbey abbatia *f*
abbreviat|e imminuo 3; ~ion contractio *f*
abdicat|e abdico 1 (*me magistratu*); ~ion abdicatio *f*
abduct rapio 3
aberration error *m*
abet adiuvo 1; ~tor minister *m*
abeyance: be in ~ iaceo 2 (*leges*)
abhor abhorreo 2 (ab); ~rence odium *n*; ~rent (to) alienus (ab)
abide habito 1, maneo 2; ~ by sto 1 (*abl.*, *in re*)
ability facultas *f*, ingenium *n*
abject humilis
abjure eiuro 1
able potens, potis, pote; ingeniosus; ~-bodied validus; be ~ possum
aboard in nave; go ~ navem conscendo 3

abode domicilium *n*
abolish tollo 3, aboleo 2
abomin|able infandus, detestabilis; ~ate abominor 1; ~ation nefas *n*
aboriginal indigena *m and f*
abortion abortus, us *m*
abortive irritus
abound abundo 1, circumfluo 3 (*abl.*); ~ing in abundans (*abl.*)
about *prep.* circa, circum (*acc.*); de (*abl.*); *adv.* circa, fere
above *prep.* super, supra (*acc.*); ~ all ante omnia; *adv.* supra
abreast a latere (*alcis*)
abridge contraho 3; ~ment epitoma *f and* -e *f*
abroad foris, peregre; be ~ peregrinor 1
abrogat|e abrogo 1, rescindo 3; ~ion abrogatio *f*
abrupt repentinus, subitus; ~ly subito
abscess vomica *f*
abscond lateo 2, latito 3
absence absentia *f*; leave of ~ commeatus, us *m*
absent absens; ~-minded obliviosus; be ~ absum
absolute purus, absolutus; ~ power infinita potestas *f*; ~ly plane, prorsus

absolve absolvo 3

absorb bibo 3; ~ent bibulus; ~ed occupatus

abstain abstineo 2 (abl.)

abstemious abstemius

abstinen|ce abstinentia f; ~t abstinens

abstract separo 1; adj. cogitatione perceptus

abstruse reconditus, abstrusus

absurd absurdus, ineptus; ~ity ineptia f

abundan|ce affluentia f, abundantia f; ~t amplus, largus

abus|e abusus 3 (abl.); maledico 3 (alci); contumelia f; ~ive contumeliosus

abut adiaceo 2 (ad alqd, dat.); ~ting finitimus

abyss vorago f, barathrum n

accede assentior 4 (alci)

accelerate accelero 1

accent sonus m (vocis); ~uate syllabam acuo 3

accept accipio 3; ~able gratus, acceptus; ~ance approbatio f

access aditus, us m; ~ible pervius (dat.); facilis (homo)

accessory adiunctus; conscius m

accident casus, us m; by ~ casu; ~al fortuitus

acclamation clamor m

accommodat|e accommodo 1 (alqd alci, ad alqd); ~ing comis; ~ion deversorium n; accommodatio f

accompaniment: to the ~ of ad (acc.)

accompany comitor 1, prosequor 3

accomplice conscius m

accomplish conficio 3, efficio 3; ~ed politus; ~ments artes f/pl.

accord v/t. concedo 3; v/i. consentio 1; subst. consensus, us m; of one's own ~ sua sponte, ultro; ~ance with ex (abl.); ~ing to pro (abl.); ~ingly itaque

accost appello 1

account numero 1, duco 3; ~ for causam affero 3; ratio f; narratio f; on ~ of ob, propter (acc.); on no ~ nullo modo; ~ant ratiocinator m; ~-book tabulae f/pl.

accoutrements arma n/pl.

accrue cedo 3 (alci or in alqm)

accumulat|e cumulo 1; ~ion congestus, us m

accura|cy subtilitas f; ~te subtilis; ~tely accurate

accursed sacer, exsecratus

accus|ation accusatio f; ~e accuso 1 (alqm rei); ~ed reus m; ~er accusator m

accustom assuefacio 3 (alqm re); be ~ed soleo 2

acerbity acerbitas f

ache doleo 2; dolor m

achieve perficio 3; ~ment res f gesta

acid acidus

acknowledge fateor 2 (acc.

c. *inf.*); agnosco 3 (*acc.*);
~ment confessio *f*
acme culmen *n*
acorn glans *f*
acquaint certiorem facio 3
(*alqm*); ~ance consuetudo
f, cognitio *f*
acquiesce acquiesco 3 (*abl.*),
contentus sum
acqui|re acquiro 3; ~sition
comparatio *f*
acquit absolvo 3 (*de re*);
~tal absolutio *f*
acre iugerum *n* (= ⅔ *acre*)
acrimonious acerbus
across trans (*acc.*)
act ago 3, me gero 3; *thea.*
ago (*play or part*); factum
n; *thea.* actus, us *m*; ~ of
Parliament lex *f*; ~ion
actio *f* (*also jur.*)
activ|e impiger, industrius;
~ity industria *f*
actor histrio *m*; **actress**
mima *f*
actual verus; ~ly re vera
acumen ingenii acies *f*
acute acer
adage proverbium *n*
adapt accommodo 1
add addo 3
adder vipera *f*
addicted to deditus (*dat.*)
addition accessio *f*
address alloquor 3; allo-
quium *n*
adduce profero 3
adept peritus
adequate par, satis magnus
adhere haereo 2 (*in, ad*);
sto (*ab*); ~nt assectator *m*
adhesive tenax

Uni Engl.-Lat.

adieu vale(te)
adjacent finitimus
adjoin adiaceo 2 (*dat., ad*)
adjourn *v/t.* differo 3 (till
in + acc.) [*alqd*)\
adjudge adiudico 1 [*alci*)
adjure obsecro 1
adjust accommodo 1, compono 3
adjutant optio *m*
administer administro 1;
~ an oath (*alqm*) iure
iurando adigo 3
administ|ration procuratio
f; ~rator procurator *m*
admir|able admirabilis; ~a-
tion admiratio *f*; ~e admiror 1
admiral praefectus *m* classis
admit (of) recipio 3; ~tance
aditus, us *m*
admonish admoneo 2; ~-
ment monita *n/pl.*
ado negotium *n*
adolescent adulescens *m*
adopt adopto 1; ~ion adoptio *f*; ~ive adoptivus
adore veneror 1
adorn decoro 1
adrift: be ~ fluctuo 1
adroit callidus; ~ness sollertia *f*
adulation assentatio *f*
adult adultus
adulterate corrumpo 3
adulter|er adulter *m*; ~ess
adultera *f*; ~y adulterium
n; **commit ~y** adultero 1
advance *v/t.* promoveo 2;
v/i. progredior 3; ~ed
(*lime*) provectus; ~ment
honor *m*

9

advantage bonum *n*, commodum *n*; **~ous** utilis; be **~ous** prosum

adventure casus, us *m*

advers|ary adversarius *m*; **~e** adversus; **~ity** res *f/pl.* adversae

advert to attingo 3 (*acc.*)

advertise proscribo 3; **~ment** proscriptio *f*

advice consilium *n*

advise suadeo 2, moneo 2; **~dly** consulto; **~r** consiliarius *m*

advoca|cy suasio *f*; *jur.* patrocinium *n*; **~te** *v/t.* suadeo 2; *subst. jur.* patronus *m*

aedile aedilis *m*; **~ship** aedilitas *f*

aegis aegis *f*

aerial aerius, aetherius

afar procul

affab|ility comitas *f*; **~le** comis

affair res *f*, negotium *n*; love **~** amor *m*

affect afficio 3, moveo 2; simulo 1; **~ation** simulatio *f*; **~ed** molestus

affection affectus, us *m*, amor *m*; **~ate** amans

affiance spondeo 2

affinity cognatio *f*

affirm affirmo 1

affix affigo 3

afflict afflicto 1; **~ed with** affectus (*abl.*); **~ion** miseria *f*

affluen|ce divitiae *f/pl.*; **~t** dives

afford praebeo 2

affront offendo 3; contumelia *f*

afloat: be **~** navigo 1

afoot pedibus; set **~** moveo 2

aforesaid supra commemoratus

afraid timidus, pavidus; be **~** timeo 2; metuo 3

afresh de integro

after *prep.* post, secundum (*acc.*); *cj.* postquam; **~noon** post meridiem; *adj.* postmeridianus; **~wards** post, postea

again iterum, rursus, rursum; **~ and ~** etiam atque etiam

against contra, adversus, in (*acc.*)

agape hians

age aetas *f*, saeculum *n*; (*of things*) vetustas *f*; old **~** senectus, utis *f*; 4 years of **~** quattuor annos natus

aged senex, provectae aetatis

agen|cy opera *f* (*chiefly in abl.*); **~t** actor *m*; minister *m*

aggrandize augeo 2

aggravate aggravo 1

aggregate summa *f*

aggress|ion incursio *f*; **~ive** infestus; be the **~or** ultro arma infero 3

aggrieve laedo 3

aghast attonitus

agil|e pernix; **~ity** pernicitas *f*

agitat|e agito 1, perturbo 1; **~ed** sollicitus; **~ion** agitatio *f*, perturbatio *f*

ago abhinc (acc.); long ~ iam pridem, iam dudum; some time ~ dudum

agony cruciatus, us m, acerbissimus dolor m

agrarian agrarius

agree consentio 4 (cum alqo, de re); congruo 3, assentior 4; ~ upon compono 3; ~able gratus, commodus, suavis; be ~d constat; be ~d upon convenit; ~ment consensus, us m, conventum n; pactio f

agricultur|al rusticus, agrestis; ~e agri cultura f, res f/pl. rusticae

aground: run ~ sido 3

ague febris f

ah int. ah, a, heu

ahead: go ~ antecedo 3 (dat., acc.); anteeo (dat., acc.)

aid adiuvo 1 (acc.), succurro 3 (dat.); auxilium n

aide-de-camp optio m

ail doleo 2, aegroto 1; ~ing aegrotus, aeger; ~ment morbus m

aim intendo 3 (alqd, in alqd, alci), peto 3 (alqm); fig. affecto 1, peto 3; finis m, consilium n

air aer m, aether m, aura f; species f, modus m; in the open ~ sub divo; take the ~ deambulo 1; put on ~s me iacto 1; ~ing ambulatio f; ~y aerius

aisle ala f

akin finitimus (dat.)

alacrity alacritas f

alarm terreo 2; be ~ed perturbor 1; trepidatio f, tumultus, us m, terror m

alas heu, eheu, hei

albeit etsi

alcove angulus m; recessus, us m

alder alnus, i f

ale fermentum n

alert alacer, vigil

alien externus, alienus; peregrinus m; ~ate (ab)alieno 1; ~ation alienatio f

alight descendo 3 (ad pedes); desilio 4; set ~ incendo 3

alike par, similis; adv. pariter

aliment alimentum n

alive vivus; be ~ vivo 3

all omnis, cunctus, totus; ~ together universus; ~ the better tanto melius; nothing at ~ nihil omnino; in ~ omnino

allay levo 1, sedo 1

allegation affirmatio f; ~e praetendo 3 (acc.); refero 3 (acc. c. inf.)

allegiance fides f; take oath of ~ in verba alicuius iuro 1

allegory translationes f/pl.

alleviat|e levo 1; ~ion levatio f

alley angiportus, us m

alli|ance societas f, foedus n, coniunctio f; ~ed socius, foederatus

allot distribuo 3, assigno 1, do 1; ~ment assignatio f

allow confiteor 2; patior 3

9*

(acc. c. inf.; ut), sino 3
(inf.; acc. c. inf.), permitto
3 (ut, inf.); ~able permis-
sus; ~ance diarium n;
make ~ances for ignosco 3
(dat.); it is ~ed licet 2

alloy corrumpo 3, misceo 2
allude to tango 3, designo 1
allur|e allicio 3; ~ement
blanditia f; ~ing blandus
ally socio 1; socius m

almanac fasti m/pl.
almighty omnipotens
almond amygdala f
almost paene, fere, ferme
alms stips f
aloft sublime, in sublime,
alte
alone solus, unus; let ~
abstineo 2 (ab)
along praeter (acc.), secundum (acc.), per (acc.)
aloof procul; keep ~ re-
moveo 2 me (ab alqo)
aloud clare
alphabet litterae f/pl.
alpine alpinus
already iam
also etiam, quoque
altar ara f, altaria n/pl.
alter v/t. muto 1; v/i. mutor 1; ~ation mutatio f
altercation iurgium n
alternat|e vario 1; alternus;
~ely alternis, invicem; ~ion
vicissitudo f; have an ~ive
optio est (alci)
although quamquam, quam-
vis, (tam)etsi
altogether omnino
always semper
amalgamate misceo 2

amanuensis librarius m
amass coacervo 1
amatory amatorius
amaz|e obstupefacio 3; be
~ed stupeo 2; ~ement stu-
por m; ~ing mirus
ambassador legatus m
amber sucinum n
ambigu|ity ambiguitas f;
~ous ambiguus
ambitio|n ambitio f; ~us
cupidus gloriae
ambrosia ambrosia f
ambuscade, ambush insi-
dior 1 (dat.); insidiae f/pl.
amenable oboediens (dat.)
amend corrigo 3, emendo 1;
make ~s satisfacio 3 (alci
de re)
amiab|ility suavitas f; ~le
suavis
amicable amicus
amid(st) inter (acc.)
amiss perperam; take ~
moleste fero 3
amity amicitia f
ammunition apparatus, us
m; arma n/pl.
amnesty venia f
among inter (acc.); apud
(acc.)
amorous amatorius
amount summa f; ~ to efficio 3, summa est
amphitheatre amphithea-
trum n
ampl|e amplus; ~ify dilato
1; ~y abunde
amputate seco 1
amuse oblecto 3, delecto 1;
~ oneself ludo 3; ~ment
delectatio f

analogy similitudo, inis *f*, comparatio *f*

analyse subtiliter dissero 3

anarch|ical turbulentus; ~y licentia *f*

ancest|or avus *m*, proavus *m*; *pl.* maiores *m/pl.*; ~ral avitus

anchor ancora *f*; weigh ~ ancoram tollo 3, ~age statio *f* [priscus]

ancient antiquus, vetus, and et, ac, atque, ...que

anecdote fabula *f*

anew denuo, de integro

angel angelus *m*

anger irrito 1; ira *f*

angle piscor 1; angulus *m*; ~r piscator *m*

angr|ily iracunde; ~y iratus; be ~y irascor 3

anguish angor *m*

angular angulatus

animadver|sion animadversio *f*; ~t animadverto 3

animal animal *n*; pecus, udis *f*; fera *f*

animat|e animo 1, excito 1; ~ed alacer; ~ion animatio *f*, vis *f*

animosity odium *n*

ankle talus *m*

annals annales *m/pl.*

annex addo 3, subicio 3

annihilate deleo 2; ~ion internecio *f*

anniversary dies *m* anniversarius

annotate commentarium scribo 3 (*in alqd*)

announce (pro)nuntio 1; ~ment pronuntiatio *f*

annoy offendo 3, vexo 1; ~ance molestia *f*, vexatio *f*; be ~ed moleste fero 3; ~ing molestus

annual anniversarius, annuus; ~ly quotannis

annuity annua *n/pl.*

annul tollo 3; ~ment abrogatio *f*

anoint ungo 3; ~ing unctio *f*

anon statim, mox

anonymous sine auctoris nomine

another alius; one after ~ alius ex alio; at ~ time alias; one ~ inter se; ~'s alienus

answer respondeo 2 (*alci alqd*; *de re*), scribo 3; ~ for praesto 1 (*alqm*; *alqd alci*); responsum *n*

ant formica *f*

antagonis|m odium *n*; ~t adversarius *m*

antechamber atriolum *n*

anthem carmen *n*

anticipate antevenio 4 (*dat.*; *acc.*); anteverto 3 (*dat.*); praecipio 3

antics ineptiae *f/pl.*

antidote remedium *n*

antipathy odium *n*

antiquarian antiquarius

antiqu|e antiquus, priscus; ~ity antiquitas *f*

antithesis *rhet.* contentio *f*

antler cornu, us *n*

anvil incus, udis *f*

anxi|ety sollicitudo *f*, cura *f*; ~ous anxius, sollicitus; be ~ous to laboro 1 (*ut*, *inf.*)

any ullus; qui, qua *or* quae, quod; aliqui, aliqua, aliquod; ~how saltem, certe; ~one aliquis; quis; quisquam; ~onesoever quilibet, quivis; ~thing aliquid; quid; quidquam

apart separatim, seorsum: ~ from praeter (*acc.*), extra (*acc.*); ~ment conclave *n*

apath|etic languidus; ~y stupor *m*

ape simia *f*

aperture foramen *n*, hiatus, us *m*

aphorism sententia *f*

apiary alvus, i *f*

apolog|ist defensor *m*; ~ise excuso 1 (*me*, *alqd*); veniam peto 3 (*gen.*, *quod*); ~y excusatio *f*

appal exterreo 2

apparatus apparatus, us *m*

apparel vestio 4; vestis *f*

apparent apertus, manifestus; simulatus, fictus; be ~ appareo 2; ~ly specie

apparition simulacrum *n*

appeal appello 1, provoco 1 (*also jur.*); obsecro 1, testor 1; obsecratio *f*; *jur.* appellatio *f*, provocatio *f*

appear appareo 2, me ostendo 3; *jur.* adsum, me sisto 3; videor 2; ~ance species *f*, aspectus, us *m*

appease placo 1, sedo 1

appellant appellator *m*

append addo 3; ~age appendix *f*

appertain pertineo 2 (*ad alqd*)

appetite appetitus, us *m*; cupiditas *f*, fames *f*

applau|d (ap)plaudo 3, faveo 2; ~se plausus, us *m*; clamor *m*

apple malum *n*

applica|ble commodus(*dat.*); ~nt petitor *m*; ~tion petitio *f*; studium *n*

apply *v/t.* adhibeo 2, admoveo 2; me confero 3 (*ad alqd*); *v/i.* pertineo 2 (*ad*); aggredior 3 (*alqm*)

appoint creo 1, facio 3, praeficio 3 (*to dat.*), constituo 3; ~ment creatio *f*, constitutum *n*

apportion divido 3

apposite aptus

appraise aestimo 1

appreciate aestimo 1

apprehen|d comprehendo 3, percipio 3; metuo 3; ~sive timidus

apprentice discipulus *m*

apprize certiorem facio 3

approach accedo 3 (*ad*, *acc.*, *dat.*); appropinquo 1 (*ad alqd*, *dat.*); accessus, us *m*; aditus, us *m*

approbation approbatio *f*

appropriate mihi arrogo 1, mihi ascisco 3, sumo 3; proprius, congruens (*dat.*)

approv|al approbatio *f*; ~e laudo 3, approbo 1

approximate accedo 3 (*ad*, *dat.*); proximus

April Aprilis *m*

apt aptus, idoneus, pronus (*ad*); ~itude ingenium *n*

aquatic aquatilis

aqueduct aquae ductus, us *m*

aquiline aduncus

arable land arvum *n*

arbiter arbiter *m*

arbitr**|**ily ad libidinem (*alcs*); ~y libidinosus

arbitrat**|**e discepto 1; ~or arbiter *m*

arbour umbraculum *n*

arc arcus, us *m*

arcade porticus, us *f*

arch fornix *m*, arcus, us *m*; lascivus; ~ed fornicatus

archer sagittarius *m*

architect architectus *m*; ~ure architectura *f*

archives tabulae *f/pl.*

archon archon *m*

arctic septentriones *m/pl.*; septentrionalis

ard**|**ent ardens, vehemens; ~our ardor *m*

arduous arduus

area area *f*; regio *f*

arena arena *f*

argu**|**e disputo 1, dissero 3; ~ment argumentum *n*, ratio *f*, disputatio *f*

aria canticum *n*

arid aridus; ~ity ariditas *f*

aright recte

arise (con)surgo 3; exorior 4 (*ex*); nascor 3

aristocra**|**cy optimates *m/pl.*; ~tic nobilis

arithmetic arithmetica *n/pl.*

ark arca *f*

arm[1] bracchium *n*, lacertus *m*

arm[2] *v/t.* armo 1; *v/i.* arma

capio 3; *subst.* arma *n/pl.*; tela *n/pl.* ~s; be under ~s sum in armis; lay down ~s arma pono 3

armature copiae *f/pl.*

armistice induiae *f/pl.*

armour arma *n/pl.*; ~-bearer armiger *m*; ~er faber *m*; ~y armamentarium *n*

armpit ala *f*, axilla *f*

army exercitus, us *m*; agmen *n*; acies *f*

aroma odor *m*; ~tic odoratus

around *prep.* circum, circa (*acc.*); *adv.* circa

arouse suscito 1, excito 1

arraign accuso 1

arrange instruo 3, dispono 3, compono 3, ordino 1; ~ment collocatio *f*, institutio *f*

array instruo 3; battle-~ acies *f*

arrears reliqua *n/pl.*

arrest comprehendo 3; comprehensio *f*

arriv**|**al adventus, us *m*; ~e advenio 4, pervenio 4 (*in*, *ad*)

arroganc**|**e arrogantia *f*, superbia *f*; ~t arrogans

arrogate sumo 3 (*mihi*)

arrow sagitta *f*; ~-head cuspis, idis *f*

arsenal armamentarium *n*

arson incendium *n*

art ars *f*; artificium *n*; opus *n*

artery vena *f*

artful callidus, vafer; ~ness calliditas *f*

artic|le res *f*, merx *f*. articulus *m*; ~ulate distinctus; articulo 1; ~ulation explanatio *f*

artifice dolus *m*; ~r artifex *m and f*

artificial artificiosus, manu factus

artillery tormenta *n/pl.*

artisan opifex *m and f*

artist artifex *m and f*; pictor *m*; ~ic artificiosus

artless simplex

as (*in comparisons*) atque, et, quam, ut; ~ ... ~ tam ... quam; just ~ velut, tamquam; sicut; (*temporal*) dum; (*causal*) cum, quoniam; ~ regards de (*abl.*), quod

.ascen|d ascendo 3 (*in, ad*); ~dency potentia *f*; ~t ascensus, us *m*

ascertain comperio 4, cognosco 3

ascetic austerus; ~ism austeritas *f*

ascribe ascribo 3, assigno 1

ash(-tree) fraxinus, i *f*; mountain ash ornus, i *f*

ashamed: be ~ pudet 2 (*alqm, alcis rei*)

ashes cinis, eris *m*

ashore in terram, in terra

ask rogo 1 (*alqd ab alqo; ut*); peto 3 (*ut*); quaero 3 (*alqd; de re*)

askance limus, obliquus

aslant obliquus

asleep: be ~ dormio 1; fall ~ obdormio 4

aspect facies *f*, aspectus, us *m*, vultus, us *m*

aspen populus, i *f*

asperity acerbitas *f*

aspersions: cast ~ on calumnior 1

aspir|ation studium *n*; ~e aspiro 1 (*in, ad alqd*), peto 3; ~ing appetens (*alcis rei*)

ass asinus *m*

assail oppugno 1; invehor 3; ~ant oppugnator *m*

assassin percussor *m*, sicarius *m*; ~ate caedo 3; ~ation caedes *f*

assault adorior 4; oppugnatio *f*, vis *f*

assembl|e *v/t.* cogo 3, convoco 1; *v/i.* convenio 4; ~y coetus, us *m*

assent assentior 4; assensus, us *m*

assert affirmo 1, vindico 1; ~ion affirmatio *f*

assess aestimo 1; ~ for taxes censeo 2; ~ment aestimatio *f*, census, us *m*; ~or *jur.* assessor *m*

assets bona *n/pl.*

asseverate assevero 1

assidu|ity diligentia *f*; ~ous sedulus

assign (at)tribuo 3; *jur.* delego 1; ~ation constitutum *n*; ~ment assignatio *f*

assist (ad)iuvo 1; ~ance auxilium *n*, (ops,) opis *f*; ~ant adiutor *m*, minister *m*

assizes conventus, us *m*

associate *v/i.* ~ with utor 3 (*abl.*); socius *m*

association societas *f*

assort *v/i.* congruo 3; ~ment varietas *f*

assuage levo 1

assum|e suscipio 3, induo 3, sumo 3 (*mihi; acc. c. inf.*); ~ption arrogantia *f*; opinio *f*

assur|ance fides *f*, fiducia *f*; ~e confirmo 1, promitto 3; be ~ed confido 3; ~edly profecto

astern in puppi

asthma anhelitus, us *m*

astonish obstupefacio 3; be ~ed admiror 1, obstupesco 3; ~ment admiratio *f*, stupor *m*

astound obstupefacio 3; be ~ed obstupesco 3

astray: go ~ erro 1; lead ~ in errorem induco 3

astringent asper

astrolog|er astrologus *m*; ~y astrologia *f*

astronomer astrologus *m*

astute callidus

asunder: burst ~ dissilio 4

asylum perfugium *n*

at ad; apud; in (*abl.*); ~ the house of apud (*alqm*); ~ home domi; ~ Rome Romae; ~ daybreak prima luce; ~ the age of five quinque annos natus; ~ a high price magno pretio

atheist impius

athlet|e athleta *m*; ~ic robustus

atmosphere aer *m*, caelum *n*

atom atomus, i *f*; corpora individua *n/pl.*

atone expio 1 (*alqd*); luo 3 (*alqd*); ~ment piaculum *n*

atroci|ous immanis; ~ty atrocitas *f*

attach adiungo 3, applico 1 (*ad alqd, alci rei*); ~ importance to mea interest; ~ed to devinctus (*alci*); ~ed by alligatus (*abl.*); ~ment caritas *f*

attack adorior 4, oppugno 1, aggredior 3; *fig.* invehor 3 (*in alqm*) *med.* tempto 1; impetus, us *m*

attain consequor 3, pervenio 4 (*ad, in alqd*); adipiscor 3

attempt conor 1, molior 4; conatum *n*

attend prosequor 3 (*acc.*): intersum (*in re, dat.*); ~ to animadverto 3, curo 1; ~ance assectatio *f*; ~ant assectator *m*

attent|ion attentus animus *m*; observantia *f*; pay ~ to operam do 1, studeo 2 (*dat.*); ~ive attentus, observans

attenuate extenuo 1

attest testificor 1

attic cenaculum *n*

attire vestio 4; vestitus, us *m*

attitude status, us *m*; adopt an ~ me gero 3

attorney cognitor *m*

attract (at)traho 3; ~ion illecebrae *f/pl.*; ~ive blandus

attribute (at)tribuo 3; be an

~ of insum (in re; dat.); proprium est (gen.)

auburn fulvus

auction auctio f; sell by ~ sub hasta vendo 3; ~eer praeco m

audac|ious audax, confidens; ~ity audacia f, con-)

audible clarus [fidentia f]

audience audiens m/pl., auditores m/pl.; grant ~ to admitto 3

audit dispungo 3

auditor auditor m

augment augeo 2; ~ation incrementum n

augur auguror 1, vaticinor 1; augur m; ~y augurium n; take the ~ies auguror 1

august augustus

August (mensis) Sextilis m, Augustus m

aunt (paternal) amita f; (maternal) matertera f

auspices auspicium n; take the ~ auspicor 1

auspicious faustus

auster|e severus, austerus; ~ity severitas f

authentic verus; well ~ated quod constat

author auctor m, scriptor m; ~ity auctoritas f, potestas f; ~ities magistratus m/pl.; ~ize potestatem do 1 (alci)

autograph chirographum n

autonomy libertas f

autumn autumnus m; ~al autumnus

auxiliar|y auxiliaris; ~ies auxilia n/pl.

avail: o.s. of utor 3 (abl.); it ~s prodest; be of no ~ nihil valeo 2; ~able expeditus, in expedito

avaric|e avaritia f; ~ious avarus

aveng|e ulciscor 3 (acc.); ~er ultor m; ~ing ultrix

avenue aditus, us m; xystus m

average: on the ~ circa

averse aversus (dat.); be ~ to abhorreo 2 (a re)

aver|sion odium n; ~t averto 3; ~t from prohibeo 2 (abl.)

avidity aviditas f

avocation officium n

avoid vito 1, (de)fugio 3; ~ance fuga f

avow confiteor 2; ~al confessio f

await exspecto 1, maneo 2 (acc.)

awake v/t. excito 1, exsuscito 1; v/i. expergiscor 3; be ~ vigilo 1

award adiudico 1; addictio f

aware gnarus; be ~ of sentio 4; become ~ of cognosco 3

away: be ~ absum; ~ with you! abi

awe reverentia f; stand in ~ of vereor 2; ~-struck pavidus

awful verendus

awhile paulisper

awkward laevus, rusticus; ~ness inscitia f

awning velum n

awry perversus

axe securis *f*

axiom sententia *f*, pronuntiatum *n*

axis, axle axis *f*

aye ita, semper

azure caeruleus

B

baa balo 1

babbl|e garrio 4; ~ing garrulus

baboon simia *f*

baby infans *m*, parvulus *m*; ~hood infantia *f*; ~ish infans

bacchan|al Bacchanalia *n/pl.*; ~te Baccha *f*

bachelor caelebs

back *v/t.* adsum, adiuvo 1; *v/i.* pedem refero 3; ~ water inhibeo 2 (*navem*); tergum *n*, dorsum *n*; behind one's ~ clam (*alqm*); ~bite rodo 3; ~bone spina *f*; ~door posticum *n*; ~slide deficio 3; ~ward piger; ~wardness pigritia *f*; ~wards retro, retrorsum

bacon laridum *n*

bad malus, improbus, pravus

badge insigne *n*

badger maeles *f*

badness malitia *f*, nequitia *f*

baffle eludo 3

bag saccus *m*, culleus *m*; ~gage sarcinae *f/pl.*

bail spondeo 2 (*pro alqo*); vadimonium *n*

bailiff vilicus *m*

bait esca *f*

bake coquo 3, torreo 2; ~r pistor *m*

balance libro 1; compenso 1; ~ accounts rationes dispungo 3; libra *f*, trutina *f*

balcony maenianum *n*

bald calvus; *fig.* aridus; ~ness calvitium *n*

baldric balteus *m*

bale egero 3; fascis *m*; ~ful funestus

balk frustror 1

ball globus *m*, pila *f*

ballad nenia *f*

ballast saburra *f*

ballot suffragium *n*, tabella *f*; ~box cista *f*

balm balsamum *n*, solatium *n*; ~y suavis

balustrade cancelli *m/pl.*

ban interdico 3; interdictio *f*

band vinculum *m*; manus *f*, caterva *f*; ~ together coniuro 1

bandage alligo 1; fascia *f*

bandit latro *m*

bandy-legged valgus

bane venenum *n*, pernicies *f*; ~ful perniciosus

bang percutio 3, verbero 1; sonitus, us *m*

banish aqua et igni interdico 3, eicio 3, pello 3; ~ment eiectio *f*; exsilium *n*

banister cancelli *m/pl.*

bank ripa *f*, tumulus *m*; argentaria *f*; ~ money pecunias depono 3; ~er argentarius *m*; ~rupt decoctor *m*; be ~rupt conturbo 1, decoquo 3

banner vexillum *n*

banquet epulor 1; convivium *n*, epulae *f/pl.*

banter cavillor 1, iocor 1; iocus *m*

bar obsero 1, intercludo 3, obsto 1; claustra *n/pl.*; vectis *m*; *fig.* impedimentum *n*; *jur.* cancelli *m/pl.*; at the ~ forensis (*adj.*)

barb uncus *m*, hamus *m*; ~ed hamatus

barbar|ian barbarus *m*; ~ic barbarus; ~ous immanis, ferus

barber tonsor *m*

bard vates *m and f*

bare nudus; *v/t.* aperio 4, nudo 1; ~faced impudens; ~foot nudo pede; ~ly vix

bargain paciscor 3; pactio *f*, pactum *n*

barge linter, tris *f*

bark latro 1; latratus, us *m*; cortex *m and f*, liber *m*

barley hordeum *n*

barm fermentum *n*

barn horreum *n*, granaria *f*

baron princeps *m* [*n/pl.*]

barque ratis *f*

barracks castra *n/pl.*

barrel dolium *n*, cupa *f*

barren sterilis; ~ness sterilitas *f*

barricade obstruo 3; munimentum *n*

barrier saepta *n/pl.*; claustra *n/pl.*

barrister advocatus *m*; patronus *m*

barrow ferculum *n*; tumulus *m*

barter muto 1 (*alqd alqa re*); paciscor 3; permutatio *f*

base humilis, turpis; ~ money nummus *m* adulterinus; basis *f*; fundamentum *n*; be ~d on nitor 3; ~less vanus; ~ness turpitudo *f*

bashful verecundus, pudens; ~ness pudor *m*

basilica basilica *f*

basin crater *m*

bask apricor 1

basket canistrum *n*, fiscina *f*

bas-relief toreuma *n*

bass *mus.* gravis

bastard nothus

baste verbero 1

bastion castellum *n*

bat vespertilio *m*

bath balneum *n*, lavatio *f*; ~tub alveus *m*; ~keeper balneator *m*

bathe *v/t.* lavo 1; *v/i.* lavor 1

battalion cohors *f*

batter percutio 3; ~ing-ram aries *m*

battle pugna *f*, proelium *n*, acies *f*; join ~ proelium committere; ~cry clamor *m*; ~field acies *f*; ~ment pinna *f*

bawd lena *f*

bawl clamito 1

bay badius *m*; latro 1; sinus, us *m*; laurus, i *f*

be sum; exsisto 3, me habeo 2

beach litus *n*

beacon ignis *m*

bead lapillus *m*

beak rostrum *n*; ~ed rostratus; ~er poculum *n*

beam refulgeo 2; iubar *n*, radius *m*; tignum *n*, trabs *f*; ~ing lucidus

bean faba *f*

bear fero 3; patior 3; pario 3; ~ with morem gero 3 (alci); ursus *m*

beard barba *f*; ~ed barbatus; ~less imberbis

bear|er baiulus *m*; ~ing gestus, us *m*; have ~ing on pertineo 2 ad

beast belua *f*, bestia *f*, fera *f*; ~ly inmundus

beat v/t. caedo 3, verbero 1; supero 1; v/i. palpito 1; ~ against incutio 3; ~ing ictus, us *m*; verbera *n*/pl.

beauti|ful pulcher, formosus; ~fy orno 1

beauty pulchritudo *f*

beaver castor *m*

because quia, quod; ~ of propter (acc.)

beck nutus, us *m*; ~on innuo 3 (alci)

becom|e flo 3; impers. decet 2 (alqm); convenit 4; ~ing decorus, decens

bed cubile *n*, lectus *m*; go to ~ cubitum eo 4; ~chamber cubiculum *n*; ~clothes stragulum *n*; ~post fulcrum *n*

bedeck orno 1

bedew perfundo 3

bee apis *f*; ~hive alvearium *n*

beech fagus, i *f*

beef bubula *f*

beer fermentum *n*

beet beta *f*

beetle scarabaeus *m*

befall contingo 3 (alci); evenio 4 (alci; ut)

befit deceo 2

befool ludificor 1

before prep. ante, ob (acc.); prae (acc.), pro (abl.); apud (acc.); coram (abl.); adv. ante, antea, antehac

befoul inquino 1

befriend adiuvo 1

beg orm 1 (alqm alqd; ut); rogo 1 (alqd ab alqo; ut); peto 3 (ut); mendico 1

beget gigno 3; procreo 1

beggar mendicus *m*; egens; ~ly mendicus

begin coepi 3; incipio 3; exorior 4; ~ner tiro *m*; ~ning initium *n*; principium *n*

begone abi!

begrudge invideo 2 (alci, alci rei)

beguile fallo 3

behalf: on ~ of pro (abl.)

behave me gero 3; ~ towards utor 3 (abl.)

behaviour mores *m*/pl.

behead securi ferio 4, percutio 3

behind prep. post (acc.); adv. post, a tergo

behold conspicio 3, tueor 2; exclam. ecce, en

behove oportet 2 (*acc. c. inf.*)

being homo *m*

belabour mulco 1

belch (e)ructo 1

beleaguer obsideo 2

belie dissimulo 1

belie|f opinio *f*; fides *f*; ~ve credo 3 (*alci, acc. c. inf.*); puto 1; fidem habeo 2| (*dat.*))

bell tintinnabulum *n* [(*dat.*))

belligerent bellicosus

bellow mugio 4; ~ing mugitus, us *m*

bellows follis *m*

belly venter, tris *m*, alvus, i *f*; ~ out tumeo 2

belong|to esse (*alcis, alci*); ~ings bona *n/pl.*

beloved dilectus

below infra (*acc.*); subter (*acc.*)

belt cinctus, us *m*; cingulum *n*

bemoan gemo 3

bench subsellium *n*; transtrum *n*; *jur.* subsellia *n/pl.*

bend *v/t.* flecto 3, curvo 1; *v/i.* flector 3; flexus, us *m*, flexio *f*

beneath sub (*abl.*); infra, subter (*acc.*)

benefaction donum *n*

benefi|cence beneficentia *f*; ~cent beneficus; ~cial salutaris; ~t prosum (*dat.*); beneficium *n*; for the ~t of gratia (*gen.*)

benevolen|ce benevolentia *f*; ~t benevolus

benign benignus

bent curvus; ~ on attentus (*dat.*)

benumb stupefacio 3; be ~ed torpeo 2

bequ|eath lego 1; ~est legatum *n*

ber|eave orbo 1; ~eft orbus (*abl.*)

berry baca *f*

berth statio *f*

beseech oro 1, obsecro 1

beset obsideo 2, circumvenio 4

beside ad, prope, iuxta (*acc.*); ~s *prep.* praeter (*acc.*); *adv.* praeterea

besiege obsideo 2, circumsedeo 2; ~r obsessor *m*

besom scopae *f/pl.*

besotted demens

bespatter aspergo 3

besprinkle aspergo 3, irroro 1

best optimus

bestir oneself expergiscor 3

bestow dono 1, largior 4; confero 3 (*in alqm*); impertio 4

bet pignus do 1; pono 3; pignus *n*; sponsio *f*

betake oneself me confero 3

bethink oneself respicio 3

betimes mature

betoken denuntio 3

betray prodo 3; ~al prodi-tio *f*; ~er proditor *m*

betroth (de)spondeo 2 (*alci alqm*); ~al sponsalia *n/pl.*; ~ed sponsa *f*; pactus

better melior; it is ~ praestat; satius est; get the ~ of vinco 3 between inter (*acc.*)

beverage potio *f*

bevy grex *m*

bewail deploro 1

beware caveo 2 (*acc.*; *ab re*; *ut, ne*)

bewildered perturbatus

bewitch fascino 3

beyond *prep.* ultra (*acc.*), extra (*acc.*), supra (*acc.*), praeter (*acc.*); *adv.* ultra, supra

bias inclino 1; inclinatio *f*

bicker rixor 1; ~ing altercatio *f*

bid iubeo 2; ~ a price liceor 2; voco 1; ~ farewell valedico 3; ~ding licitatio *f*; at the ~ding of iussu

bier ferculum *n*

big ingens, magnus

bilberry vaccinium *n*

bile bilis *f*

bilge-water sentina *f*

bilk fraudo 1

bill rostrum *n*; libellus *m*; syngrapha *f*; rogatio *f*; lex *f*; titulus *m*

billet hospitium *n*

bill-hook falx *f*

billow fluctus, us *m*; ~y undosus

bin arca *f*

bind vincio 4, necto 3; *fig.* obligo 1, obstringo 3; ~ over vador 1; ~ing fascia *f*

birch betula *f*

bird avis *f*; ales *m and f*; volucris *f*; ~-cage cavea *f*; ~-catcher auceps *m*; ~-lime viscum *n*; ~'s nest nidus *m*

bireme biremis *f*

birth ortus, us *m*; genus *n*; partus, us *m*; give ~ to pario 3; ~day dies *m* natalis

bit frenum *n*; frustum *n*; offa *f*

bit|e mordeo 2; morsus, us *m*; ~ing asper

bitter amarus, acerbus; ~ness amaritudo *f*; acerbitas *f*

blab vulgo 1

black niger, ater; ~ and blue lividus; ~-berry rubus *m*; morum *n*; ~-bird merula *f*; ~en maledico 3 (*alci*); ~ing atramentum *n*; ~-smith faber *m* (ferrarius)

bladder vesica *f*

blade herba *f*; lamina *f*

blame reprehendo 3; accuso 1; culpa *f*; reprehensio *f*; ~less innocens, integer; ~worthy noxius

bland mitis

blandishment blanditia *f*; lenocinium *n*

blank purus; vacuus

blanket stragula *f*, vestis *f*

blaspheme maledico 3 (*alci*)

blast uro 3; perdo 3; flatus, us *m*

blaze ardeo 2, flagro 1; ignis *m*

bleach candidum facio 3

bleak tristis, frigidus

blear-eyed lippus

bleat balo 1

bleed *v/t.* sanguinem mitto 3; *v/i.* sanguis fluit

blemish macula *f*; vitium *n*

blend commisceo 2

bless benedico 3; fortuno 1; ~ed beatus; ~ing bonum *n*

blight lues *f*; uredo *f*

blind caecus; caeco 1; velum *n*; ~-fold oculos obligo 1; ~ly temere; ~ness caecitas *f*

blink nicto 1

bliss beatitudo *f*; ~ful beatus

blister pustula *f*

blithe hilarus

bloat tumefacio 3; ~ed tumidus

block moles *f*; massa *f*; ~ up obstruo 3; ~ade obsideo 2; obsessio *f*; ~head stipes *m*

blood sanguis *m*; cruor *m*; ~less exsanguis, incruentus; ~-red sanguineus; ~shed caedes *f*; ~-stained cruentus; ~-thirsty cruentus; ~-vessel vena *f*

bloom floreo 2; flos *m*; ~ing florens

blot litura *f*; labes *f*, macula *f*; ~ out deleo 2, extinguo 3

blow flo 1; spiro 1; inflo 1; ~ one's nose emungo 3; ~ inflo 1; ~ upon afflo 1; plaga *f*, ictus, us *m*

bludgeon fustis *m*

blue caeruleus

bluff impolitus; abruptum *n*

bluish lividus

blunder erro 1; error *m*; ~ing mendosus

blunt hebes; inurbanus; *v/t.* hebeto 1; retundo 3

blush erubesco 3; ~ at pudet (*alqm, alcs rei*); rubor *m*

bluster declamito 1; declamatio *f*

boar verres *m*; aper, apri *m*

board tabula *f*; mensa *f*, victus, us *m*; consilium *n*, collegium *n*; go on ~ navem conscendo 3; ~ over contabulo 1

boast glorior 1 (*de re, re*); me iacto 1; iactatio *f*; ~ful gloriosus

boat scapha *f*; navicula *f*; ~man nauta *m*

bode vaticinor 1

bodily corporeus

body corpus *n*; globus *m*; manus, us *f*; collegium *n*; ~-guard stipatores *m/pl.*, satellites *m/pl.*

bog palus, udis *f*; ~gy paluster

boil *v/t.* (aqua ferventi) coquo 3; *v/i.* ferveo 2; aestuo 1; vomica *f*; ~ed elixus

boisterous turbidus

bold audax, ferox; ~ness audacia *f*

bolster pulvinus *m*; ~ up fulcio 4

bolt obsero 1; fulmen *n*; telum *n*; repagula *n/pl.*; claustra *n/pl.*; clavus *m*

bombastic tumidus

bond vinculum *n*; nodus *m*; syngrapha *f*; ~age servitus, utis *f*

bone os *n*

bonnet mitra *f*

bony osseus

book liber, bri m; libellus m; volumen n; codex m; ~binder glutinator m; ~case foruli m/pl.; ~seller librarius m

boom mugio 4

boon beneficium n; ~companion sodalis m

boorish agrestis

boot calceus m; caliga f

booth taberna f

booty praeda f

booze poto 1

border ora f; margo m and f; finis m; ~ on attingo 3, contingo 3; ~ed with praetextus; ~ing finitimus

bor|e perforo 1; obtundo 3; foramen n; ~ing importunus, odiosus

born natus; be ~ nascor 3, orior 4

borough municipium n

borrow ' mutuor 1; ~ed mutuus; alienus; ~ing mutuatio f

bosom sinus, us m; gremium n; pectus n

boss bulla f; umbo m

both ambo; uterque; in ~ directions utroque

both ... and et ... et; cum ... tum

bother vexo 1

bottle ampulla f, amphora f

bottom fundus m; imus, infimus

bough ramus m; frons f

boulder saxum n

bounce salio 4

bound v/i. exsilio 4; v/t. finio 4, termino 1; finis m;

modus m; terminus m; be ~ to debeo 2; be ~ for tendo 3 (in, ad); ~ary finis m; ~less infinitus

bount|iful benignus, liberalis; ~y liberalitas f; praemium n

bout certamen n

bow flecto 3, inclino 1; demitto 3; saluto 1; arcus, us m; ~ed curvus; ~legged valgus; ~man sagittarius m

bowels alvus, i f; viscera n/pl.

bower umbraculum n

bowl crater m; patera f; ~ along volvo 3

bows prora f

box arca f; cista f; colaphus m; pugnis certo 1; ~er pugil m; ~ing glove caestus, us m; ~tree buxus, i f

boy puer, eri m; ~hood pueritia f

brace firmo 1; fibula f; fascia f

bracelet armilla f

brag glorior 1; ~gart gloriosus

braid necto 3; intexo 3; limbus m

brain cerebrum n; ~less socors

brake dumetum n

bramble dumus m; sentis m

bran furfur m

branch ramus m; frons f; ~ into dividor 3; ~ing ramosus

brand inuro 3; noto 1; torris m; stigma n

brandish vibro 1; iacto 1

brass aes *n*; orichalcum *n*

brav|e fortis, acer; experior 4; **~ery** fortitudo *f*, virtus, utis *f*

brawl rixor 1; rixa *f*

brawn lacertus *m*; **~y** lacertosus

bray rudo 3

brazen aeneus, aeratus; impudens

breach discutio 3; frango 3; violo 1; violatio *f*

bread panis *m*; victus, us *m*

breadth latitudo *f*

break frango 3; rumpo 3; violo 1; **~ down** *v/i.* haereo 2; *v/t.* frango 3; **~ in** domo 1; **~ into** irrumpo 3; **~ off** dirumpo 3; **~ up** dissolvo 3; **~fast** prandium *n*; **~water** moles *f*

breast mamma *f*; pectus *n*; **~plate** lorica *f*

breath spiritus, us *m*, anima *f*; out of **~** exanimatus; **~e** spiro 1; anhelo 1; **~ing** respiratio *f*; **~ing-space** respirandi spatium *n*

breeches bracae *f/pl.*

breed pario 3; genero 1; alo 3; genus *n*

breeze aura *f*

brevity brevitas *f*

brew coquo 3

brib|e (pecunia) corrumpo 3; largior 4; **~ery** largitio *f*; praemium *n*, donum *n*

brick later *m*; **~layer** structor *m*; **~work** latericium *n*

bridal nuptialis; nuptiae *f/pl.*

bride nupta *f*; sponsa *f*; **~groom** sponsus *m*

bridge pons *m*; pontem facio 3 (*in flumine*)

bridle infreno 1; frenum *n*

brief brevis; *jur.* causa *f*; in **~** ne multa

brier vepres *m*

brigade legio *f*

brigand latro *m*; **~age** latrocinium *n*

bright clarus, lucidus, nitidus; **~en** splendesco 3; **~ness** fulgor *m*, candor *m*

brillian|cy splendor *m*, nitor *m*; **~t** splendidus, luculentus

brim ora *f*; labrum *n*

brimstone sulpur *n*

brine muria *f*

bring affero 3; adveho 3; **~ about** efficio 3; **~ forth** prodo 3; **~ forward** (a law) fero 3; **~ out** effero 3; **~ up** the rear agmen claudo 3

brink margo *m*

brisk alacer

bristl|e horreo 2; seta *f*; **~y** setiger, hirsutus

brittle fragilis

broad latus, amplus

broil torreo 2

broken confectus

broker interpres *m*

bronze aes *n*; aeneus, aeratus

brooch fibula *f*

brood|(over) incubo 1 (*alci rei*); agito 1 (*rem*); fetus, us *m*

brook rivus *m*; patior 3
broom scopae *f/pl.*
broth ius *n*
brothel lustrum *n*
brother frater *m*; ~hood sodalitas *f*; ~ly fraternus
brow supercilium *n*; frons *f*
brown fuscus
browse upon pascor 3; tondeo 2
bruise contundo 3; contusum *n*
bruit abroad vulgo 1
brush detergeo 2; verro 3; scopae *f/pl.*; peniculus *m*; ~wood virgula *n/pl.*
brut|al saevus, inhumanus; ~ality inhumanitas *f*; ~e fera *f*
bubble bulla *f*; ~ up scateo 2
buck cervus *m*
bucket hama *f*
buckle fibula *f*
bucolic rusticus
bud gemma *f*; gemmo 1
budge me moveo 2
buffet colaphus *m*; tundo 3
buffoon scurra *m*
bug cimex *m*; ~bear terricula *n/pl.*
bugle tuba *f*; bucina *f*
build aedifico 1; construo 3; condo 3; ~ upon confido 3 (*alci*); ~er aedificator *m*; ~ing aedificium *n*
bulb bulbus *m*
bulge tumeo 2; tumor *m*
bulk magnitudo *f*, moles *f*; maior pars *f*; ~y magnus
bull taurus *m*; ~ock iuvencus *m*
bulrush iuncus *m*

bulwark munimentum *n*, propugnaculum *n*
bump offendo 3; tuber *m*
bumpkin rusticus *m*
bunch racemus *m*
bundle fascis *m*; sarcina *f*
bung obturamentum *n*
buoy fulcio 4; ~ancy levitas *f*; ~ant levis
bur lappa *f*
burden onero 1, opprimo 3; onus *n*; beast of ~ iumentum *n*; ~some gravis, molestus
burgher municeps *m*
burglar fur *m*
burial funus *n*; sepultura *f*; ~-place sepulcrum *n*
burn *v/t.* uro 3, incendo 3; *v/i.* flagro 1, ardeo 2; ~ing ardens
burnish polio 4
burnt-offering hostia *f*
burrow cuniculus *m*; ~ under suffodio 4
burst *v/t.* (di)rumpo 3; *v/i.* dissilio 4; ~ into *fig.* effundo 3 in
bury sepelio 4, humo 1; condo 3
bush dumus *m*; frutex *m*
bushel medimnum *n*
bushy fruticosus
business negotium *n*; res *f*; occupatio *f*; quaestus, us *m*; ars *f*
buskin cothurnus *m*
bust imago *f* [us *m*]
bustle trepido 1; tumultus,]
busy occupatus, negotiosus
but sed, at, verum, autem; all ~ tantum non

butcher lanius m; obtrunco 1; ~y caedes f
butler promus m
butt fig. ludibrium n
butter butyrum n
butterfly papilio m
buy emo 3, paro 1; ~ back, off redimo 3; ~er emptor m
buzz bombus m

by ad (acc.), secundum (acc.), praeter (acc.); ab (abl.); per (acc.); day ~ day in dies; ~ night de nocte; ~ the gods per deos; ~ your leave bona tua venia; ~gone praeteritus, priscus; ~road deverticulum n; ~standers circumstantes m/pl.

C

cab cisium n
cabal coniurati m/pl.
cabbage brassica f; caulis m
cabin casa f; cella f
cabinet conclave n; armarium n; consilium n
cable ancorale n; funis m; rudens m and f
cackle strideo 2; strepitus, us m
cadaverous cadaverosus
cage cavea f; claustra n/pl.; includo 3 (in)
cajole blandior 4; ~ry blanditia f
cake libum n; placenta f; v/i. concresco 3
calamit|ous funestus, exitiosus; ~y calamitas f, clades f; malum n
calculat|e computo 1; subduco (rationem) 3; ~ion ratio f; calculus m
calendar fasti m/pl.
calends Calendae f/pl.
calf vitulus m; sura f
call appello 1, nomino 1; (ad)voco 1; be ~ed audio 4; ~ in advoco 1; vox f;

salutatio f; pay a ~ saluto 1; ~ing quaestus, us m; artificium n
callo|sity callum n; be ~us obduresco 3, occalesco 3
callow rudis
calm placidus, tranquillus; sedo 1; tranquillitas f; malacia f
calumn|iate criminor 1, calumnior 1; ~y criminatio f
camel camelus m
camp castra n/pl.; break up ~ castra moveo 2; pitch ~ castra pono 3
campaign expeditio f; stipendium n
can possum; queo 4; scio 4; hama f
canal fossa f
cancel induco 3; tollo 3
cancer cancer, cri m
candid apertus, sincerus
candidat|e candidatus m; be a ~e for peto 3; ~ure petitio f
candle candela f; cereus m; ~stick candelabrum n

candour candor *m*

cane harundo *f*; virga *f*; verbero 1

canine caninus

canister pyxis *f*

canker robigo *f*

cannon tormentum *n*

cannot non possum, nequeo 4; nescio 4

canoe scapha *f*

canon norma *f*

canopy aulaea *n/pl.*

canton pagus *m*

canvas linteum *n*

canvass ambio 4; ambitio *f*

cap pilleus *m*

capab|ility facultas *f*; ~le capax

capaci|ous amplus, capax; ~ty captus, us *m*

cape promontorium *n*; sagum *n*

caper exsulto 1; capparis *f*

capital centurio *m*; prae- fectus *m*; nauarchus *m*; magister, tri *m*

captious captiosus

captivate delenio 4

captiv|e captivus; ~ity cap- tivitas *f*

capture capio 3

car currus, us *m*

caravan commeatus, us *m*

carcass cadaver, eris *n*, cor- pus *n*

card pecto 3; pecten *f*

care cura *f*, sollicitudo *f*; curatio *f*; take ~ (of) caveo 2 (*alqd*); take ~ (lest) caveo 2 (*ne*); ~ for curo 1; I don't ~ for (about) nihili facio 1 (*alqd*)

career cursus, us *m*

care|ful diligens, attentus, curiosus; ~less securus; neglegens; ~lessness in- curia *f*, neglegentia *f*

caress blandior 4; mulceo 2; blanditia *f*

cargo onus *n*

carnage strages *f*

carol carmen *n*

carouse poto 1; comissor 1; ~r comissator *m*

carp at carpo 3, vellico 1

carpenter faber *m* tigna- rius

carpet stragulum *n*

carriage raeda *f*, vehiculum *n*

carry fero 3, gero 3, veho 3; porto 1; ~ away aufero 3; ~ on gero 3; ~ out exse- quor 3; ~ through perfero 3

cart plaustrum *n*

carve caelo 1, sculpo 3; seco 1; ~r carptor *m*

carving caelatura *f*; ~-knife culter *m*

cascade deiectus, us *m* aquae

case res *f*, causa *f*; tempus *n*; involucrum *n*; it is the ~ that accidit ut

casement fenestra *f*

cash nummi *m/pl.*; pecunia *f*; numeratum *n*

cashier exauctoro 1

cask cupa *f*; ~et arcula *f*

cast iacio 3, conicio 3; fundo 3; ~ off exuo 3; ~ upon confero 3; iactus, us *m*

castanet crotalum *n*

castaway naufragus

caste ordo *m*

castigate castigo 1

castle castellum *n*; arx *f*

casual fortuitus; ~ty casus, us *m*

cat felis *f*

cataract cataracta *f*

catarrh gravedo *f*

catastrophe ruina *f*

catch capio 3; deprehendo 3; excipio 3; ~ fire ignem concipio 3; ~ a disease morbum contraho 3; praeda *f*

cater obsono 1; ~er obsonator *m*

cattle boves *m and f*; pecus *n*; pecudes *f/pl.*

cauldron lebes *m*; cortina *f*

cause facio 3, efficio 3 (*alqd, ut, ne*); curo 1; creo 1; pario 3; causa *f*, materia *f*, effectio *f*; with good ~ iure; be the ~ of per (*alqm*) fit ut, stat quominus; ~less vanus; ~way agger, |

caustic acerbus [eris *n*]

cauterize aduro 3

caution cautio *f*; cura *f*; moneo 1; ~ous cautus, consideratus

cavalry equitatus, us *m*;

equites *m/pl.*; equestris; ~-squadron turma *f*; ~ man eques *m*

cave specus, us *m*; spelunca *f*; antrum *n*

cavil at vellico 1

cavity caverna *f*

caw crocio 4

cease desino 3 (*alcis rei, inf.*); desisto 3 (*re, inf.*); omitto 3 (*alqd, inf.*); consisto 3; ~less perpetuus

cedar cedrus, i *f*

ceiling lacunar *n*, tectum *n*

celebrate celebro 1; ~ed celeber; ~ion celebratio *f*

celery apium *n*

celestial caelestis

celibacy caelibatus, us *m*; ~te caelebs

cell cella *f*

cellar cella *f*

cement ferrumen *n*; ~ together conglutino 1

cemetery sepulcra *n/pl.*

censor censor *m*; noto 1; ~ship censura *f*

censure vitupero 1; vituperatio *f*

census census, us *m*; hold the ~ censum habeo 2

centaur centaurus *m*

central medius; ~e medium *n*; ~e upon situm esse (*in re*)

centurion centurio *m*; ~ship centuriatus, us *m*; ordo *m*

century centuria *f*; ordo *m*; saeculum *n*

ceremonial sollemnis; ~y caerimonia *f*; ritus, us *m*

certain certus, exploratus;

a ~ quidam; consider as ~
pro certo habeo 2; be ~
certo scio 4; ~ly sane,
profecto

certify recognosco 3; certiorem facio 3

cessation intermissio f

chafe v/t. attero 3; v/i.
stomachor 1

chaff palea f; acus n; fig.
quisquiliae f/pl.

chagrin dolor m

chain catena f; vinculum n;
fig. series f; throw into ~s
catenas inicio 3 (alci)

chair sella f; cathedra f;
~man magister, tri m

chalk creta f

challenge provoco 1

chamber conclave n; cubi-
culum n; cella f; ~servant
cubicularius m; ancilla f

champion propugnator m

chance fors f; casus, us m;
spes f; by ~ forte, casu;
it ~d accidit (ut)

chandelier candelabrum n

change v/t. (com)muto 1;
verto 3; v/i. mutor 1; me
verto 3; (com)mutatio f;
vicis (gen.) f; vicissitudo f;
~able mutabilis; ~ling
subditus

channel canalis m; fretum n

chant canto 1; cantus, us m

chapel aedicula f; sacellum
n

chaplet sertum n

chapter caput n

char amburo 3

character littera f; mores
m/pl.; habitus, us m; thea.

persona f; partes f/pl.; of
good ~ honestus; ~istic
proprius (gen.)

charcoal carbo m

charge incurro 3; signa infero 3 (in); mando 1, committo 3 (alci ut); arguo 3
(alqm alcis rei; acc. c. inf.);
impetus, us m; mandatum
n; cura f (gen.); crimen n;
sumptus, us m; be in ~ of
praesum

chariot currus, us m; ~eer
auriga m; quadrigarius
m

cnarit|able benignus, mitis;
~y benignitas f; stips f

charm fascino 1; delenio 4;
cantio f; dulcedo f; ~ing
suavis, lepidus

chart tabula f

chase caelo 1; sector 1;
agito 1; venatio f; vena-
tus, us m

chasm hiatus, us m

chaste castus, pudicus,
purus

chastise castigo 1

chastity castitas f

chat garrio 4; ~ter effutio 4;
clamor m; crepitus, us m

cheap vilis; ~ly bene; ~ness
vilitas f

cheat fraudo 1; circum-
venio 4; fraudator m

check cohibeo 2, contineo
2, retineo 2; comprimo 3;
incommodum n

cheek gena f, mala f, bucca
f

cheer v/t. erigo 3, hilaro 1;
v/i. plaudo 3; clamorem

tollo 3; clamor *m*; be of
good ~ bono animo sum;
~ful alacer, hilaris
cheese caseus *m*
chequer vario 1; ~ed varius
cherish foveo 2; colo 3
cherry cerasus, i *f*
chess-board latruncularia
tabula *f*
chess-man latrunculus *m*
chest arca *f*; armarium *n*;
pectus *n*
chestnut castanea *f*
chew mando 3
chicanery calumnia *f*
chicken pullus *m*
chick-pea cicer *n*
chide obiurgo 1
chief princeps, praecipuus,
summus; princeps *m*;
procer *m*; dux *m*
child puer, eri *m*; infans *m*;
~birth partus, us *m*; ~hood
pueritia *f*; ~ish puerilis;
~ren liberi *m/pl.*
chill refrigero 1; frigidus;
frigus *n*
chime sono 1
chimera commentum *n*
chimney caminus *m*
chin mentum *n*
china fictilia *n/pl.* tenuia
chine tergum *n*
chink rima *f*
chip assula *f*
chirp pipilo 1
chisel scalprum *n*
choice delectus, us *m*; conquisitus
choir chorus *m*
choke strangulo 1; suffoco 1
choleric iracundus

choose deligo 3, eligo 3;
~ rather malo
chop dolo 1; caedo 3; ~ off
detrunco 1; ~per securis *f*
chord chorda *f*; nervus *m*
chorus chorus *m*
Christian christianus; ~
name praenomen *n*
chronic diuturnus
chronicles annales *m/pl.*
chuckle rideo 2
church ecclesia *f*; aedes *f*
churlish inhumanus, agre-
stis
cinder cinis, eris *m*
cipher numerus *m*; nota *f*
circle orbis *m*; circulus *m*;
corona *f*
circuit ambitus, us *m*; make
a ~ circumeo 4
circula|r rotundus; ~te dif-
fundo 3; percrebresco 3
circumcise circumcido 3
circum|ference ambitus, us
m; ~locution ambages
f/pl.; ~navigate circum-
vehor 3; ~scribe circum-
scribo 3; ~spect cautus;
~stance res *f*; tempus *n*;
~vent circumscribo 3
circus circus *m*
cistern cisterna *f*
citadel arx *f*
cite profero 3
cithern cithara *f*
citizen civis *m and f*; ~ship
civitas *f*
city urbs *f*; urbanus
civil civilis; comis; ~ian
civis, is *m and f*; civilis;
~ization cultus, us *m*;
~ized humanus

clad vestitus (*abl.*)

claim postulo 1; exigo 1; vindico 1; postulatio *f*; ~ant petitor *m*

clamber scando 3

clammy umidus

clamour clamor *m*; ~ for flagito 1

clamp confibula *f*

clan gens *f*

clandestine clandestinus

clang strepo 3; clangor *m*

clansman gentilis *m*

clap plaudo 3; ~ping plausus, us *m*

clarify explano 1

clash concrepo 1; configo 3; crepitus, us *m*

clasp complector 3; necto 3; fibula *f*; amplexus, us *m*

class genus *n*; ordo *m*; ~ification discriptio *f*; ~ify discribo 3

clause articulus *m*; incisum *n*; caput *n*

claw unguis *m*

clay lutum *n*; argilla *f*

clean mundus, purus; (per-)purgo 1; detergeo 2; ~liness munditia *f*

clear liquidus, serenus; clarus; purus; apertus; expedio 4, purgo 1; ~ oneself me purgo 1; it is ~ apparet; ~ up explano 1; ~ness claritas *f*

cleave findo 3, scindo 3; ~ to adhaereo 2

cleft hiatus, us *m*; rima *f*

clemency clementia *f*

clench comprimo 3

clerk scriba *m*

clever sollers, callidus, ingeniosus; vafer; ~ness calliditas *f*

click crepo 1

client cliens *m and f*; consultor *m*

cliff cautes *f*; scopulus *m*

climate caelum *n*

climax gradatio *f*

climb scando 3, ascendo 3

cling adhaereo 2 (*dat.*)

clip tondeo 2

clique factio *f*; globus *m*

cloak pallium *n*; lacerna *f*; dissimulo 1

clock horologium *n*; clepsydra *f*

clod glaeba *f*

clog impedio 4; sculponeae *f/pl.*

cloister porticus, us *f*

close claudo 3; comprimo 3; coeo 4; confertus, densus, creber; *adv.* prope, iuxta; finis *m*; exitus, us *m*; ~ to iuxta (*acc.*), prope (*acc.*)

closet cella *f*

clot concresco 3

cloth textile *n*; ~e vestio 4; induo 3; ~ed in amictus; ~es vestis *f*; vestitus, us *m*; vestimenta *n/pl.*

cloud nubes *f*; nubila *n/pl.*; storm-~ nimbus *m*; ~ over nubem induco 3; ~y nubi-

cloven bisulcus [lus]

clown scurra *m*

club fustis *m*; clava *f*; sodalitas *f*; collegium *n*

clue *fig.* indicium *n*

clums|iness inscitia *f*; ~y inscitus; rusticus

cluster racemus *m*

clutch arripio 3; ~es manus, us *f*

coach currus, us *m*; raeda *f*; ~man raedarius *m*

coagulate concresco 3

coal carbo *m*

coalition societas *f*; coitio *f*

coarse crassus, rudis; incultus

coast ora *f*; litus *n*; ~ along lego 3; praetervehor 3

coat lacerna *f*; tegmentum *n*; illino 3

coax palpo 1; blandior 4; ~ing blandimentum *n*

cobble sarcio 4; ~r sutor *m*

cobweb aranea *f*

cock gallus *m*; game ~ gallus *m* rixosus; mas; erigo 3; ~roach blatta *f*; ~scomb crista *f*

code leges *f/pl.*

coerce cogo 3

coeval aequalis (*dat.*)

coffer arca *f*

coffin sarcophagus *m*

cog dens *m*

cogent gravis

cognizance cognitio *f*

cognomen cognomen *n*

cohere cohaereo 2; ~nce contextus, us *f*

cohort cohors *f*

coil spira *f*; ~ up glomero 1

coin nummus *m*; signo 1; novo 1; ~age moneta *f*

coincide concurro 3; congruo 3; by ~nce forte

colander colum *n*

cold frigidus; frigus *n*; gravedo *f*; be ~ frigeo 2

collapse concido 3

collar collare *n*; monile *n*; comprehendo 3

colleague collega *m*

collect colligo 3, congero 3; ~ion congeries *f*; collectio *f*; ~ive universus; ~or exactor *m*

college collegium *n*

colli|de confligo 3, concurro 3; ~sion concursus, us *m*

colloquial familiaris, vulgaris

collu|de colludo 3; ~sion collusio *f*; praevaricatio *f*

colonel praefectus *m*; tribunus *m*

colon|ial colonicus; ~ist colonus *m*; ~izing deductio *f*

colonnade porticus, us *f*

colony colonia *f*; found a ~ coloniam deduco 3

colossal vastus

colour color *m*; pigmentum *n*; *fig.* species *f*; ~s signum *n*; coloro 1; inficio 3; rubesco 3; ~ed coloratus

colt eculeus *m*

column columna *f*; *mil.* agmen *n*

comb pecto 3; pecten *m*

combat repugno 1; pugna *f*; proelium *n*; certamen *n*

combin|ation coniunctio *f*; conspiratio *f*; ~e (con)iungo 3; confero 3 (in unum); conspiro 1

come (per)venio 4; advehor 3; ~! age, agite; ~ about fieri; ~ down descendo 3; ~ forth prodeo 4; ~ in in-

cedo 3; ~ up with conse-
quor 3   [comoedia *f*]
comedian comoedus *m*; ~y
comely pulcher
comet cometes, ae *m*
comfort consolor 1; sola-
tium *n*; consolatio *f*; ~able
commodus; ~er consolator
m
comic comicus; ridiculus
command impero 1 (*dat.*);
iubeo 2 (*acc.*); praesum
(*dat.*); imperium *n*, mandatum *n*, iussum *n*; put in
~ praeficio 3; ~er imperator *m*, dux *m*
commemorate celebro 1
commence incipio 3; exor-
dior 4; ~ment initium *n*
commend commendo 1
(*alci alqd*); laudo 1 (*acc.*);
~able laudabilis
commensurate dignus (*abl.*)
comment sententia *f*; dictum *n*; ~ary commentarii
m/pl.
commerce mercatura *f*,
mercatus, us *m*; commer-
cium *n*
commission mandatum *n*;
mando 1 (*alci*)
commit mando 1, committo
3 (*alci alqd*); ~ (a crime)
committo 3; be ~ted to
obligor 1 (*dat.*)
commodity merx *f*
common communis; publi-
cus; vulgaris; in ~ in commune; communiter; ~s
plebs *f*; populus *m*; ~-
wealth res *f* publica; civitas *f*

commotion motus, us *m*;
tumultus, us *m*; turba *f*
commune colloquor 3
communicate impertio 4;
communico 1; ~tion com-
municatio *f*; commercium
n
commun|ion communio *f*;
societas *f*; ~ity commune
n; civitas *f*
compact solidus, compac-
tus; pactum *n*, foedus *n*
companion socius *m*; comes
m and *f*; ~ship sodalitas *f*
company coetus, us *m*; con-
vivae *m/pl.*; mil. mani-
pulus *m*; societas *f*
compar|e comparo 1, con-
fero 3 (*alqd cum re*; *dat.*);
~ison comparatio *f*; in
~ison with ad, adversus
(*acc.*)
compartment pars *f*
compass spatium *n*; ~es
circinus *m*
compassion misericordia *f*;
~ate misericors
compatible conveniens
compatriot civis *m* and *f*,
popularis *m* and *f*
compel cogo 1, subigo 3
compendium summarium *n*
compensat|e compenso 1
(*alqd re*); ~ion compensatio
f
compete certo 1; contendo
3; ~ for peto 3; ~nt capax;
locuples
competit|ion certamen *n*;
~or competitor *m*
compile compono 3
complain (con)queror 3

(*alqd, de re*); ~t querela *f*,
querimonia *f*

complaisan|ce obsequium
n; ~t commodus

complement supplementum
n

complete plenus, integer;
perfectus; compleo 2, ex-
pleo 2; ~ly omnino, pror-
sus

complex multiplex; ~ion
color *m*

complian|ce obtemperatio
f; ~t facilis

complicat|ed involutus;
~ion implicatio *f*

complicity conscientia *f*

compliment laudo 1; offi-
cium *n*; pay one's ~s to
saluto 1

comply with pareo 2, ob-
tempero 1 (*dat.*)

component pars *f*; elementum *n*

compos|e compono 3; sedo
1; be ~ed of consto 1 (*ex,
in; abl.*); ~ed placidus;
~er auctor *m*; ~ition compositio *f*; scriptio *f*; scrip-
tum *n*; ~ure aequus ani-
mus *m*

compound misceo 2; ~ in-
terest anatocismus *m*

comprehen|d percipio 3, in-
tellego 3, comprehendo 3;
~sion intellectus, us *m*

compress concludo 3, coarto 1

comprise comprehendo 3;
contineo 2

compromise implico 1;
transigo 3 (*rem*)

compulsion vis *f*, necessitas
f

compunction paenitentia *f*

compute computo 1

comrade sodalis *m*, contu-
bernalis *m*

concave (con)cavus

conceal celo 1 (*alqd, alqm*);
abdo 3; occulto 1; ~ment
occultatio *f*; latebra *f*

concede permitto 3, con-
cedo 3

conceit superbia *f*; ~ed
superbus

conceive concipio 3; com-
prehendo 3

concentrate cogo 3, con-
traho 3; operam do 1;
intendo 3 animum

concept, conception imago
f, notio *f*

concern attinet, pertinet
(*ad*); interest, refert; ~
oneself about curo 1
(*alqd*); be ~ed in versor 1;
be ~ed about sollicitus
sum; negotium *n*; cura *f*;
sollicitudo *f*; ~ing de
(*abl.*)

concert concentus, us *m*

concession concessio *f*

conciliate concilio 1

concise brevis, concisus;
~ness brevitas *f*

conclu|de concludo 3; per-
ficio 3; ~sion conclusio *f*;
finis *m*; ~sive certus

concord concordia *f*

concourse concursus, us *m*;
frequentia *f*

concubine concubina *f*,
paelex *f*

concur concurro 3; assentior 4

condemn damno 1, condemno (*alcis rei, de re*); improbo 1; ~ation damnatio *f*

condense spisso 1; premo 3; ~d densus

condescend descendo 3; me demitto 3

condition status, us *m*; sors *f*, fortuna *f*; condicio *f*; lex *f*; on ~ that ea condicione ut

condole consolor 1; ~nces consolatio *f*

condone condono 1

conduce to conducit (*dat.*); proficit (*ad*); ~ive utilis (*ad*)

conduct adduco 3, perduco 3; ~ oneself me gero 3; mores *m/pl.*; vita *f*; administratio *f*, ~or dux *m*

conduit aquaeductus, us *m*; canalis *m*

cone conus *m*

confectioner pistor *m*; libarius *m*; ~y crustum *n*

confedera|cy foedus *n*; foederatae civitates *f/pl.*; ~te foederatus; socius *m*

confer *v/t.* confero 3, tribuo 3 (*alci alqd*); *v/i.* colloquor 3; ~ence colloquium *n*; congressus, us *m*

confess confiteor 2, fateor 2; ~ion confessio *f*

confid|ant conscius *m*; familiaris; ~e *v/i.* confido 3 (*dat., abl.*); *v/t.* committo 3; ~ence fides *f*; fiducia *f*; confidentia *f*; ~ent confidens; ~ential secretus

confine includo 3, coerceo 2, contineo 2; ~d artus; ~ment vincula *n/pl.*; partus, us *m*

confirm confirmo 1; comprobo 3

confiscat|e proscribo 3; publico 1; ~ion proscriptio *f*

conflagration incendium *n*

conflict certamen *n*; pugna *f*; ~ with repugno 1

confluence confluens *m*

conform| (to) accommodo 1 (*me ad, dat.*); ~ity convenientia *f*; in ~ity with ex (*abl.*), secundum (*acc.*)

confound confundo 3, misceo 2; obstupefacio 3

confront compono 3; me oppono 3

confus|e confundo 3; ~ion perturbatio *f*; stupor *m*

confute confuto 1

congeal concresco 3

congenial commodus

congratulat|e gratulor 1; ~ion gratulatio *f*

congregat|e (me) congrego 1; ~ion coetus, us *m*

congress conventus, us *m*

conjectur|al opinabilis; ~e conicio 3; coniectura *f*

conjugal coniugalis; maritus

conjuncture discrimen *n*

conjur|ation carmen *n*; obsecratio *f*; ~e obtestor 1; ~er praestigiator *m*

connect conecto 3, coniungo 3 (*cum re, dat.*); be ~ed with

contingo 3 (*alqm*); ~ion colligatio *f*; necessitudo *f*

connive coniveo 2 (*in alqa re*)

connoisseur intellegens *m and f*

conquer vinco 3, supero 1; ~or victor *m*, victrix *f*

conquest victoria *f*

conscien|ce conscientia *f*; religio *f*; ~tious religiosus; diligens

conscious conscius (*alcis rei, alci rei*); ~ness conscientia *f*

conscript tiro *m*; ~ion dilectus, us *m*

consecrate consecro 1, dedico 1

consecutive continuus

consent annuo 3; ~ to accipio 3; ~ that permitto 3 (*ut*); consensus, us *m*

consequence eventus, us *m*; it is of no ~ nihil refert; be the ~ of consequor 3

consequently ergo, igitur

consider cogito 1 (*de*); considero 1 (*alqd, de*); delibero 1 (*alqd, de*); rationem habeo 2 (*alcis rei*); ~able aliquantus; ~ate humanus; ~ation respectus, us *m*; deliberatio *f*

consign committo 3

consist consto 1 (*ex, in re*; *abl.*); consisto 3 (*in, abl.*); ~ency constantia *f*; ~ent consentaneus (*dat.*); be ~ent with consentio 4

consol|ation solatium *n*; ~e consolor 1

consolidate stabilio 4

consort coniunx *m and f*; ~ with utor 3 (*abl.*)

conspicuous insignis, conspectus

conspir|acy coniuratio *f*; ~ator coniuratus *m*; ~e coniuro 1

constable vigil *m*

constan|cy constantia *f*; fides *f*; ~t constans; fidelis; perpetuus

constellation sidus *n*

consternation pavor *m*; perturbatio *f*

constitut|e constituo 3; statuo 3; compono 3; ~ion habitus, us *m*; natura *f*; res *f* publica; civitas *f*; ~ional legitimus, innatus

constrain cogo 3; ~t necessitas *f*

construct (con)struo 3; facio 3; ~ion constructio *f*; structura *f*

construe interpretor 1

consul consul *m*; ~ar consularis; ~ate consulatus, us *m*

consult *v/t.* consulo 3 (*alqm de re*); *v/i.* consulto 1; ~ation deliberatio *f*

consum|e consumo 3; abutor 3; conficio 3; edo 3; ~er emptor *m*

consummate perficio 3; perfectus

consumption tabes *f*

contact, contagion contagio *f*

contain capio 3; contineo 2

contaminate contamino 1
contemplat|e intueor 2;
considero 1; ~ion contemplatio f
contemporary aequalis
contempt contemptio f;
~ible abiectus, contemptus; ~uous fastidiosus
contend contendo 3; certo
1; ~ against adversor 1
content contentus (abl.);
be ~ satis habeo 2 (inf., si);
~ion discordia f; controversia f; ~ious pugnax;
~ment aequus animus m
contest contendo 3 (cum
algo de re); certamen n;
contentio f; be ~ed in controversiam venio 4
contiguous confinis (dat.)
continen|ce continentia f;
~t continens; continens f
contingen|cy casus, us m;
~t fortuitus
continu|al perpetuus; assiduus; ~ance perpetuitas f;
~ation continuatio f; ~e
v/i. persevero 1 (inf., in
re); permaneo 2 (in); pergo 3; v/t. continuo 1; prorogo 1; ~ous continens,
perpetuus; ~ously continenter
contort contorqueo 2
contour forma f
contraband illicitus
contract contraho 3; astringo 3; ~ a debt aes alienum
contraho 3; ~ for loco 1;
conduco 3; locatio f;
pactio f; ~or conductor m;
redemptor m

contradict adversor 1 (dat.);
repugno 1; ~ion repugnantia f; ~ory repugnans
contrary contrarius, diversus, adversus; ~ to contra
(acc.); contrarium n (gen.);
on the ~ contra; immo
contrast confero 3; discrepo
1 (cum, a re); discrepantia f
contravene violo 1
contribut|e confero 3; affero 3 (ad); ~ion collatio f;
collecta f; stips f
contriv|ance excogitatio f;
ars f; machina f; ~e struo
3; machinor 1; invenio 4;
~er machinator m
control moderor 1 (dat.);
coerceo 2; moderatio f;
potestas f
controversy concertatio f,
controversia f
contumacious contumax
contumel|ious contumeliosus; ~y contumelia f
convalesce convalesco 3;
~nt convalescens
convene (con)voco 1
convenien|ce commoditas f;
opportunitas f; utilitas f;
at your, his ~ce commodo
tuo, suo; ~t commodus;
opportunus
convention conventus, us
m; pactio f; mos m; ~al
usitatus
converge in unum tendo 3
convers|ant peritus (gen.);
~ation colloquium n; sermo m, ~e colloquior 3 (cum);
congressus, us m; contrarium n

convert (com)muto 1

convex convexus

convey (ad)veho 3; conveho 3; deporto 1; significo 1; ~ance vehiculum *n*

convict convinco 3 (*alqm alcs rei*); condemno 1; ~ion damnatio *f*

convince persuadeo 2 (*alci*); be ~d persuasum habeo 2

conviviality convivia *n/pl.*

convoy commeatus, us *m*

convulse concutio 3; ~ion perturbatio *f*

coo queror 3

cook coquo 3; coquus *m*; coqua *f*

cool frigidus; impavidus; *v/t.* refrigero 1; *v/i.* refrigesco 3; ~ness frigus *n*; impudentia *f*

coop cavea *f*; ~ up includo 3

cooperat|e adiuvo 1; operam confero 3; ~ion auxilium *n*; opera *f*

coot fulica *f*

cope (with) contendo 3 (*cum*)

copious largus, uber, abundans

copper aes *n*; aenum *n*; aeneus

copse fruticetum *n*, dumetum *n*

copulate coeo 4

copy describo 3, exscribo 3; imitor 1; exemplar *n*; similitudo *f*; ~ist librarius *m*

coral corallium *n*

cord funis *m*; constringo 3; ~age rudentes *m/pl.*

cordial benignus

cordon corona *f*

core medulla *f* [*m*]

cork suber, eris *n*; cortex *f*

corn frumentum *n*; frumentarius; standing ~ seges *f*; ~-merchant frumentarius *m*; ~ supply, price of ~ annona *f*

corner angulus *m*; recessus, us *m*

cornet bucina *f*

coronet diadema *n*

corpor|ation collegium *n*; municipium *n*; ~eal corporeus

corpse cadaver, eris *n*, corpus *n*

corpulen|ce opimus habitus, us *m*; ~t pinguis

correct rectus, accuratus; corrigo 3; emendo 1; ~ion correctio *f*; castigatio *f*

correspond congruo 3 (*cum, inter se, dat.*); respondeo 2 (*dat.*); litteras scribo 3; ~ence convenientia *f*; litterae *f/pl.*; ~ing par (*dat.*)

corroborate confirmo 1

corrode erodo 3

corrugate corrugo 1

corrupt corrumpo 3; depravo 1; putridus; corruptus; ~er corruptor *m*; ~ible venalis; ~ion corruptio *f*; corruptela *f*; largitio *f*

corselet lorica *f*; thorax *m*

cosmetics medicamina *n/pl.*; fucus *m*

cosmopolitan mundanus *m*

cost (con)sto 1; pretium *n*; impensa *f*; damnum *n*;

at what ~? quanti?; ~ly
pretiosus; carus

costume vestitus, us m

cot lectulus m

cottage casa f

couch lectus m; cubile n;
subsido 3; (in language)
dico 3

cough tussis f; tussio 4

council concilium n, consilium n; ~ of war praetorium n; **town-~lor** decurio
m

counsel moneo 2; consilium n; patronus m; **~lor**
consiliarius m

count numero 1; duco 3;
~ **upon** fidem habeo 2
(alci)

countenance vultus, us m;
facies f; indulgeo 2

counter calculus m; mensa
f; **run ~ to** repugno 1;
~act occurro 3; **~balance**
compenso 1 (alqd cum);
~feit simulo 1; adulterinus; fictus; **~pane** stragulum n

countless innumerabilis

countrified agrestis

country rus n; agri m/pl.;
terra f; fines m/pl.; native
~ patria f; **in the ~** ruri;
~-house, ~ **seat** villa f;
~man rusticus m; homo m
agrestis

coup d'état res f/pl. novae

couple copulo 1; par n;
iugum n; bini, ae, a (adj.)

courage virtus, utis f; animus m; **~ous** fortis, animosus

courier nuntius m

course venor 1; curro 3;
cursus, us m; iter, ineris n;
curriculum n; ratio f, consilium n; **race-~** circus m;
in the ~ of in (abl.), inter
(acc.); **of ~** sane; scilicet;
videlicet

court peto 3; ambio 4;
capto 1; aula f; atrium n;
regia f; **law-~** basilica f;
subsellia n/pl.; iudicium
n; **~eous** comis, **~esy** comitas f; **~esan** meretrix f;
~ier comes m; **~ing** am-
bitio f   [consobrina f]

cousin consobrinus m;}

cove sinus, us m

covenant stipulor 1; pactum n

cover (in)tego 3; operio 4;
obduco 3; velo 1; opercu-
lum n; praesidium n; **~ing**
tegmen n, tegimentum n;
~let stragulum n; **~t** occultus; obliquus; dumetum n

covet concupisco 3; **~ous**
avarus; **~ousness** avaritia f

cow vacca f, bos f; terreo 2;
~herd pastor m, armentarius m

coward|ice ignavia f; **~ly**
ignavus, timidus

cower tremo 3

coxcomb crista f (galli);
nugator m

coy verecundus

crab cancer, cri m; **~bed**
morosus

crack findo 3; dissilio 4;
concrepo 1; rima f; crepitus, us m

cradle cunae *f/pl.*; incunabula *n/pl.*; foveo 2

craft ars *f*; artificium *n*; dolus *m*; scapha *f*; ~sman artifex *m*, opifex *m*; ~y callidus

crag scopulus *m*; ~gy asper

cram refercio 4; stipo 1; sagino 1

cramp comprimo 3

crane grus, gruis *f*; tolleno *n*

crash fragor *m*; ~ down ruo 3

crate corbis *f*

crater crater, eris *m*

crav|e oro 1, obsecro 1 (*alqm alqd*); ~en ignavus; ~ing desiderium *n*

crawl repo 3; serpo 3

craz|iness furor *m*; ~y imbecillus

creak strideo 2; concrepo 1

cream flos *m* lactis

crease corrugo 1; ruga *f*

creat|e creo 1; pario 3; fingo 3; ~ion mundus *m*; opus *n*; ~or genitor *m*; procreator *m*; auctor *m*; ~ure animal *n*; animans *m and f*

creden|ce fides *f*; ~tials auctoritates *f/pl.*

credible credibilis

credit fides *f*; existimatio *f*; gratia *f*; be to one's ~ honori esse alci; fidem habeo 2 (*alci*); ~able honestus; ~or creditor *m*

credul|ity credulitas *f*; ~ous credulus

creek aestuarium *n*

creep serpo 3, repo 3; ~ up

on obrepo 3 (*dat., ad, in*)

cremate cremo 1

crescent luna *f*; lunatus

crest crista *f*; iuba *f*; vertex *m*; ~ed cristatus; ~fallen demissus

crevice rima *f*

crew nautae *m/pl.*; remiges *m/pl.*; remigium *n*

crib praesaepe *n*; lectulus *m*

cricket cicada *f*

crier praeco *m*

crim|e facinus *n*; scelus *n*; ~inal nefarius; sons *m*

crimson coccineus; coccum *n*

cring|e adulor 1 (*alqm, alci*); ~ing proiectus

cripple *fig.* accido 3; ~d claudus; mancus

crisis discrimen *n*; tempus *n*

criterion obrussa *f*

criti|c iudex *m*, criticus *m*; ~cal intellegens; dubius; ~cism iudicium *n*; ~cise iudico 1 (*de*); reprehendo 3

croak cano 3; crocio 4; occino 3; ~ing clamor *m*

crock olla *f*; ~ery fictilia *n/pl.*

crocodile crocodilus *m*

crone anus, us *f*

crook pedum *n*; ~ed pravus

crop seges *f*; fruges *f*; carpo 3; tondeo 2

cross transeo 3; me traicio 3; obsto 1 (*alci*); ~ the mind occurro 3 (*animo*); crux *f*; quincunx *m*; transversus; difficilis; ~examination interrogatio

f; ~ing transitus, us m;
trivium n
crouch subsido 3
crow cornix f; cano 3
crowd turba f; vulgus, i n;
frequentia f; stipo 1; compleo 2; ~ around circumfundor 3 (alci); ~ together
conglobo 1 (me); ~ed celeber; frequens
crown corona f; diadema n;
fig. cumulus m; diadema
impono 3 (capiti); cingo 3
crucify cruce afficio 3
crude rudis
cruel crudelis, atrox; ~ty
crudelitas f
cruise (per)vagor 1
crumb frustum n; ~le frio
1; contero 3; corruo 3
crumpled rugosus
crush opprimo 3; frango 3
crust crusta f; ~ of bread
frustum n
crutch baculum n
cry clamo 1; fleo 2; vagio 4;
~ out ac acclamo 1; clamor m; vox f
crystal crystallum n
cub catulus m
cuckoo cuculus m
cucmber cucumis m
cudgel fustis m; baculum n;
fuste verbero 1
cue signum n; give a ~
innuo 3
cuff colaphus m
cuirass lorica f
cull lego 3
culmination fastigium n;
summum n

culp|able nocens; ~rit noxius m
cultivat|e colo 3; ~ed cultus; ~ion cultura f; cultus, us m; ~or cultor m
culture cultura f (animi)
cumbersome inhabilis
cumin cuminum n
cunning callidus, dolosus;
astutia f
cup poculum n, calix m;
~board armarium n
cupidity cupiditas f
cur canis m
curable sanabilis
curator curator m
curb (re)freno 1; coerceo 2;
frenum n; crepido f
curdle v/t. coagulo 1; v/i.
concreso 3
cure medeor 2 (dat.); sano
1; sanatio f; remedium n
curio|sity curiositas f; cura
f, ~us curiosus; elaboratus; rarus
curl torqueo 2; cincinnus
m; cirrus m; ~y crispus,
cincinnatus; ~ing iron
calamister m
currant acinus m
curren|cy moneta f; ~t
vulgaris, usitatus; be ~t
vigeo 2; percrebresco 3;
flumen n; aestus, us m;
~t of air aura f
curse execror 1; exsecratio
f; preces f/pl.
curtail coarto 1
curtain aulaeum n
curve sinus, us m; flexus,
us m; flecto 3; curvo 1;
~d curvatus; sinuosus

cushion pulvinus *m*

custod|ian curator *m*; ~y custodia *f*

custom mos *m*; consuetudo *f*; institutum *n*; commercium *n*; ~ary translaticius; usitatus; ~er emptor *m*

cut caedo 3; seco 1; ~ down excido 3; ~ off praecido, intercludo 3; vulnus *n*;

a short ~ via *f* compendiaria

cutter celox *f*

cutting acerbus

cuttle-fish sepia *f*

cycle orbis *m*

cylinder cylindrus *m*

cymbal cymbalum *n*

cynical mordax

cypress cupressus, i *f*

D

dabble tingo 3

dagger pugio *m*, sica *f*

daily cotidianus, diurnus; *adv.* cotidie; in dies

daint|iness fastidium *n*; ~ies cuppedia *n/pl.*; ~y fastidiosus; delicatus

dall|iance lusus, us *m*; ~y ludo 3; moror 1

dam moles *f*; mater *f*; ~ up obstruo 3

damage laedo 3; affligo 3; damnum *n*; incommodum *n*; ~s *jur.* damnum *n*

dame matrona *f*

damp umidus; umor *m*; restinguo 3

damsel virgo *f*

dance salto 1; saltatus, us *m*; ~r saltator *m*; saltatrix *f*

dandruff porrigo *f*

dandy (homo) delicatus *m*

danger periculum *n*; discrimen *n*; ~ous periculosus; gravis

dangle pendeo 2 (*ab, de re*)

dank umidus

dappled varius; maculosus

dare *v/i.* audeo 2; *v/t.* provoco 1 (*alqm in pugnam*)

daring audax; audacia *f*

dark obscurus; ater; it grows ~ advesperascit 3; after ~ de nocte; keep in the ~ celo 1 (*alqm alqd*); ~en obscuro 1, occaeco 1; ~ness tenebrae *f/pl.*; caligo *f*

darling deliciae *f/pl.*

darn sarcio 4

dart iaculor 1; provolo 1; emico 1; telum *n*, iaculum *n*

dash ruo 3; ~ against affligo 3 (*ad*); ~ to pieces elido 3; have one's hopes ~ed spe depellor 3; impetus, us *m*; ~ing animosus

dastardly ignavus

date dies *m and f*; tempus *n*; (*fruit*) palmula *f*; diem ascribo 3; ~ from incipio 3 (*abl.*)

daub illino 3 (*alqd re*)

daughter filia *f*; ~-in-law nurus, us *f*

daunt percello 3; ~**less**
ferox, impavidus

dawdle cesso 1

dawn (prima) lux f; aurora
f; dilucesco 3

day dies m and f; lux f;
~ **after** ~ diem ex die;
every ~ in dies; **every
other** ~ alternis diebus;
the ~ **before pridie; the** ~
after postridie; ~**light** dies
m and f, lux f

dazz∥le perstringo 3; ~**ling**
splendidus

dead mortuus; **the** ~ **manes**
m/pl.; inferi m/pl.; ~ **of
night** nox f intempesta;
~**en** obtundo 3; ~**ly** funestus; capitalis

deaf surdus; ~**en** obtundo 3;
~**ness** surditas f

deal infligo 3 (alci); ~ **out**
dispertio 4; ~ **with** tracto 1
(alqm); ~**er** negotiator m,
mercator m; ~**ings** commercium n

dear carus; pretiosus; ~**ness**
caritas f

dearth inopia f

death mors f; letum n;
obitus, us m

debar prohibeo 2

debase adultero 3

debate disputo 1 (alqd, de
re); controversia f

debauch stupro 1; perdo 3;
~**ery** stuprum n

debilitate debilito 1 [(alci)]

debit expensum fero 3]

debt aes n alienum; debitum n; **be in** ~ in aere
alieno sum; ~**or** debitor m

decant diffundo 3

decapitate securi ferio 4;
detrunco 1

decay tabesco 3; putesco 3;
minuor 3; tabes f; senium
n

decease obitus, us m; ~**d**
demortuus

deceit fraus f; dolus m;
~**ful** fallax, dolosus

deceive decipio 3; fallo 3

December december, bris m

decemvir decemvir m; ~**ate**
decemviratus, us m

decen∥cy pudor m; honestas f; ~**t** honestus;
decens

deception fraus f; dolus m

decide v/t. decerno 3; di-
iudico 1; v/i. constituo 3

decimate decimo 3

decisi∥on decretum n, arbitrium n, iudicium n;
~**ve** supremus (proelium);
certus

deck orno 1; pons m

declaim declamo 1; ~
against invehor 3 (in);
~**er** declamator m

declar∥ation professio f;
~**e** v/t. declaro 1; renuntio
1; v/i. affirmo 1; ~**e war**
bellum indico 3

decline v/i. senesco 3, deficio 3; v/t. recuso 1 (alqd;
inf.); deminutio f

decompose putesco 3

decorat∥e (ex)orno 1; ~**ion**
decus n; ornamentum n;
insigne n

decorous decorus

decoy illicio 3

decrease (de)minuor 3;
imminutio *f*

decree decerno 3; censeo 2;
decretum *n*; **~of the senate**
senatus consultum *n*

decrepit decrepitus

decry obtrecto 1

dedicat|e dedico 1 (*dat.*);
~ion dedicatio *f*

deduce concludo 3

deduct deduco 3; **~ion** deductio *f*; conclusio *f*

deed factum *n*; res *f*;
facinus *n*; tabula *f*

deem existimo 1

deep altus, profundus; altum *n*; **an** altiorem
facio 3; **~ly** penitus

deer cervus *m*

deface deformo 1

defam|ation obtrectatio *f*;
~e maledico 3 (*dat.*)

defeat vinco 3; supero 1;
frustror 1; clades *f*; repulsa *f*

defect vitium *n*; **~ion** defectio *f*; **~ive** vitiosus

defence defensio *f*; tutela *f*;
jur. patrocinium *n*; praesidium *n*; **~less** inermis

defend defendo 3; tueor 2;
~ant reus *m*; rea *f*; **~er**
propugnator *m*

defer differo 3 (*alqd in*);
~ to obtempero 1; **~ence**
observantia *f*

defian|ce: in ~ce of contra
(*acc.*); **~t** ferox

deficien|cy inopia *f*; **be ~t**
desum 1

defile contamino 1; angustiae *f/pl.*

defin|e circumscribo 3; de-
finio 4; **~ite** definitus,
certus; **~ition** definitio *f*

deflect deflecto 3

deform deformo 1; **~ed**
pravus; **~ity** pravitas *f*

defraud fraudo 1 (*alqm
alqa re*)

defray suppedito 1

deft scitus

defy provoco 1; contemno 3

degenerate degenero 1 (*ab*);
perditus

degrad|ation ignominia *f*;
~e moveo 2 (*abl.*); abicio
3; **~ing** indignus

degree gradus, us *m*; **in
some ~** aliquantum; **by ~s**
gradatim

deign dignor 1 (*inf.*)

deity deus *m*; dea *f*; numen
n

dejected demissus

delay moror 1; cunctor 1;
mora *f*

delegat|e defero 3 (*ad*); le-
gatus *m*; **~ion** legatio *f*

delete deleo 2

deliberat|e consulo 3, deli-
bero 1 (*de*); cogitatus;
~ely consulto; **~ion** deliberatio *f*

delica|cy humanitas *f*; cup-
pedia *n/pl.*; **~te** subtilis,
tener, suavis

delicious suavis

delight v/t. delecto 1; v/i.
gaudeo 2 (*abl., inf., quod*);
delectatio *f*; voluptas *f*;
~ful iucundus

delineate describo 3

delinquent noxius *m*

deliver libero 1; eripio 3; reddo 3, trado 3; ~ a speech orationem habeo 3; ~ance salus, utis *f*; ~y *rhet.* actio *f*; *med.* partus, us *m*

dell vallis *f*

delude decipio 3

deluge inundatio *f*; inundo 1

delusion error *m*; ~ve fallax

demagogue contionator *m*

demand postulo 1, flagito 1; postulatio *f*

demean me demitto 3; ~our habitus, us *m*

demented demens

demesne ager, gri *m*

demigod semideus *m*

demise obitus, us *m*

democracy civitas *f* popularis; ~tic popularis

demolish demolior 4

demonstrate demonstro 1; ~ion indicium *n*

demur dubito 1; haesito 1; dubitatio *f*

demure verecundus

den latibulum *n*

denial negatio *f*

denizen incola *m*

denote indico 1, significo 1

denounce defero 3 (*nomen alcis*)

dense densus, confertus

dent vulnus *n*

denude (de)nudo 1

denunciation delatio *f*; accusatio *f*

deny nego 1; infitior 1; abnuo 3

depart abeo 4, discedo 3 (*ab, ex, de*); *fig.* descisco 3

(*ab*); ~ment provincia *f*; munus *n*; ~ure discessus, us *m*

depend pendeo 2 (*abl., ex*); nitor 3 (*abl.*); consisto 3 (*in re*); ~ant cliens *m*; ~ent (on) obnoxius (*dat.*)

depict (de)pingo 3; describo 3

deplorable miserabilis; ~e deploro 1; miseror 1

deploy explico 1

depopulate vasto 1; depopulor 1; ~ion vastatio *f*

deport relego 1; ~ation relegatio *f*; exsilium *n*; ~ment habitus, us *m*

depose abrogo 1 (*magistratum alci*); moveo 2; testificor 1

deposit depono 3 (*apud alqm*); depositum *n*; pignus *n*

depot horreum *n*

deprave corruptus; ~ity pravitas *f*

deprecate deprecor 1 (*alqd ab alqo*)

depreciate detraho 3 (*de*)

depredation direptio *f*

depress deprimo 3; ~ed fractus; ~ion tristitia *f*

deprive privo 1 (*abl.*); adimo 3 (*alqd alci*); ~d of orbus (*abl.*)

depth altitudo *f*; ~s altum *n*; in ~ in agrum

deputation legatio *f*; ~e mando 1 (*dat.*); ~y procurator *m*; legatus *m*

derange perturbo 1; ~d insanus

deri|de derideo 2; ~sion irrisus, us *m*

deriv|ation declinatio *f*; ~e duco 3, traho 3 (*originem ab, ex*)

derogatory indignus

descend descendo 3 (*de, ex, in, ad*); degredior 3; pervenio 4; ~ant progenies *f*; ~ants posteri *m/pl.*; ~ed ortus (*abl.*)

descent descensus, us *m*; genus *n*

describe describo 3; exprimo 3; expono 3

descry conspicio 3

desecrate violo 1

desert desero 3, relinquo 3; desertus, vastus; deserta *n/pl.*; ~s meritum *n*; ~er desertor *m*, perfuga *m*

deserve mereor 2; dignus sum; ~dly merito, iure

design describo 3; formo 1, cogito 1; descriptio *f*; consilium *n*; ~ate designo 1; ~edly consulto; ~er architectus *m*; auctor *m*

desir|able optabilis; ~e cupio 3, (ex)opto 1; gestio 4; cupiditas *f*; studium *n*; libido *f*; ~ous cupidus (*gen.*)

desist desisto 3 (*re, inf.*)

desk scrinium *n*

desolat|e vastus, desertus; orbus; vasto 1; ~ion vastatio *f*; solitudo *f*

despair despero 1 (*de; alqd; acc. c. inf.*); desperatio *f*

despatch mitto 3; perficio 3, conficio 3; litterae *f/pl.*

desperate desperatus, periculosus

despise contemno 3, sperno 3

despite *prep.* etiamsi; *cj.* quamvis

despoil spolio 1

despond despero 1, animum demitto 3

despot tyrannus *m*; ~ic tyrannicus

dessert bellaria *n/pl.*

destin|e destino 1; ~ed fatalis (*ad*); ~y fatum *n*

destitut|e inops, egens, expers; ~ion egestas *f*, inopia *f*

destroy deleo 2, everto 3, perdo 3; ~er perditor *m*

destruct|ion pernicies *f*; exitium *n*; ~ive exitialis

desultory inconstans

detach eximo 3, abripio 3; disiungo 3; removeo 2; ~ment manus, us *f*

detail enarro 1; ~s singula *n/pl.*; in ~ singillatim

detain teneo 2; retineo 2

detect deprehendo 3; comperio 4

deter deterreo 2 (*a re, ne*)

deteriorate corrumpo(r) 3

determin|ate certus; ~ation sententia *f*; constantia *f*; ~e statuo 3, constituo 3 (*inf., ut*); decerno 3 (*alqd; acc. c. inf.; ut*); ~ed firmus, constans

detest odi; abominor 1; ~able foedus, detestabilis

dethrone regno expello 3

detonation fragor *m*

detour circuitus, us *m*

detract detraho 3, derogo 1 (*de*); ~or obtrectator *m*

detriment damnum *n*, detrimentum *n*

devastat|e vasto 1, populor 1; ~ion vastatio *f*

develop *v/t.* dilato 1, explico 1; amplifico 1; alo 3; *v/i.* cresco 3; ~ment incrementum *n*

deviat|e declino 1 (*de*); ~ion declinatio *f*

device insigne *n*; artificium *n*

devil diabolus *m*

devise excogito 1; fingo 3

devoid expers (*gen.*); vacuus (*abl.*)

devolve *v/t.* defero 3 (*alci*); *v/i.* pervenio 4 (*ad*); obvenio 4 (*dat.*)

devot|e devoveo 2 (*dat.*); confero 3 (*dat.*); ~e oneself to incumbo 3 (*in, ad*); ~ed sacer; studiosus (*gen.*); ~ion studium *n*; ~ions preces *f/pl.*

devour devoro 1

devout pius

dew ros *m*; dew-lap palearia *n/pl.*; ~y roscidus

dexter|ity calliditas *f*; ~ous callidus

diadem diadema *n*

diagram descriptio *f*

dial solarium *n*

dialect lingua *f*; ~ical dialecticus; ~ics dialectica *f*

dialogue sermo *m*; dialogus *m*

diamond adamas *m*

diaphragm praecordia *n/pl.*

diary ephemeris *f*

dice tali *m/pl.*; tesserae *f/pl.*; game of ~ alea *f*; ~-board alveus *m*; ~-box fritillus *m*

dictat|e impero 1; praescribo 3; dicto 1; praeceptum *n*; ~ion arbitrium *n*; ~or dictator *m*; ~orial arrogans; ~orship dictatura *f*

diction dictio *f*

die talus *m*; tessera *f*; morior 3; obeo4; pereo 4; ~ out obsoleto 3

diet cibus *m*; victus, us *m*; diaeta *f*

differ differo 3, discrepo 1, disto 1 (*ab, inter se*); ~ence differentia *f*, distantia *f*; it makes a ~ence interest (*utrum ... an*); ~ent diversus, varius, alius, dispar

difficult difficilis, arduus; ~y difficultas *f*; angustiae *f/pl.*; with ~y aegre, vix

diffident verecundus

diffuse diffundo 3; diffusus, verbosus

dig fodio 3

digest concoquo 3

dignif|ied gravis; ~y honesto 1 [*f*]

dignity dignitas *f*, maiestas]

digress digredior 3, declino 1; ~ion digressio *f*

dike fossa *f*; agger, eris *n*

dilapidated ruinosus

dilate (upon) dilato 1

dilatory tardus

dilemma complexio *f*; angustiae *f/pl.*

diligen|ce diligentia *f*; **~t** diligens, industria *f*; **~t** diligens, industrius

dilute diluo 3

dim obscurus, hebes; obscuro 1; **~ grow ~** hebesco 3

dimension modus *m*; amplitudo *f*

dimin|ish minuo 3; levo 1; **~utive** parvus, exiguus

dimness obscuritas *f*

dimple gelasinus *m*

din sonitus, us *m*; strepitus, us *m*

dine ceno 1

dingy squalidus

dining|-couch, ~-room triclinium *n*

dinner cena *f*

dint ictus, us *m*; **by ~ of** per (acc.)

dip tingo 3; mergo 3 (abl.); **me incline** 1; **~ into** perstringo 3

diplomatist legatus *m*

dire dirus

direct rectus; dirigo 3; intendo 3 (in, ad); doceo 2; rego 3; iubeo 2; **~ion** cursus, us *m*; iter, ineris *n*; administratio *f*; praeceptum *n*; inscriptio *f*, **in all ~ions** passim; **in the ~ion of** in, ad, ... versus; **~ly recta**; statim; **~or** magister, tri *m*; curator *m*

dirge nenia *f*

dirt sordes *f*; caenum *n*, lutum *n*; **~y** sordidus, squalidus; foedo 1

disable debilito 1; **~d** mancus, debilis

disabuse errorem tollo 3

disadvantage incommodum *n*; **~ous** incommodus, iniquus

disaffect alieno 1; **~ion** alienatio *f*; seditio *f*

disagree dissentio 4, dissideo 2 (ab, cum, inter se); **~able** molestus, difficilis; **~ment** dissensio *f*; discordia *f*

disappear evanesco 3; dilabor 3

disappoint fallo 3; **~ing** fallax

disapprov|al reprehensio *f*; **~e** improbo 1

disarm exuo 3 armis

disarrange turbo 1

disast|er clades *f*; calamitas *f*; **~rous** calamitosus

disavow infitior 1 (alqd)

disband dimitto 3

disbelieve fidem non habeo 2

disburse expendo 3; **~ment** erogatio *f*

discard excutio 3

discern discerno 3 (alqd a re); dispicio 3; **~ing** acutus; **~ment** iudicium *n*

discharge evomo 3; (im-)mitto 3; mil. dimitto 3; exauctoro 1; (per-)fungor 3 (abl.); coniectus, us *m*, missio *f*; jur. absolutio *f*

disciple discipulus *m*

discipline disciplina *f*; **good ~** modestia *f*; coerceo 2

disclaim infitior 1

disclos|e patefacio 3; ostendo 3; **~ure** indicium *n*

dis|colour infusco 1; ~comfit perturbo 1; ~comfort vexatio f; ~composed commotus; ~concert perturbo 1; ~consolate maerens

discontent molestia f; ~ed iniquus (*animus*)

discontinue desisto 3 (*abl., inf.*)

discord discordia f; ~ant discors

discount deduco 3; decessio f; ~enance perturbo 1

discourage animum frango 3; (*alqm a re, ne*); be ~d animum demitto 3

discourse sermo m; oratio f; ~ upon dissero 3 (*de*)

discourteous inhumanus

discover invenio 4; reperio 4; deprehendo 3; ~er inventor m; ~y inventum n

discredit invidia f; fidem non habeo 2 (*alci*); ~able inhonestus

discreet prudens

discrepancy discrepantia f

discretion prudentia f; arbitratus, us m; arbitrium n; at his ~ arbitratu, arbitrio suo

discriminat|e diiudico 3 (*acc., inter*); ~ing acutus; ~ion discrimen n

discuss disputo 1, dissero 3 (*de*); ~ion disceptatio f

disdain despicio 3; contemno 3; fastidium n; ~ful fastidiosus

disease morbus m; ~d aeger, morbo affectus

disembark v/t. expono 3; v/i. egredior 3 (ex navi)

disengage expedio 4

disentangle explico 1

disfavour offensio f

disfigure deformo 1

disfranchise civitatem adimo 3 (*alci*)

disgorge evomo 3

disgrace dedecoro 1; ignominia f, turpitudo f; dedecus n; be ~d infamiam habeo 2, capio 3; ~ful turpis, foedus

disguise dissimulo 1; persona f; simulatio f

disgust fastidium n, taedium n; fastidium pario 3, affero 3; taedet (*me alcis rei*); ~ing foedus

dish patina f, lanx f

dishearten exanimo 1

dishevelled passus

dishonest fraudulentus, mendax; ~y fraus f, improbitas f

dishonour dedecoro 1; stupro 1; ignominia f; stuprum n; ~able inhonestus

disinclined: be ~ abhorreo 2 (*a re*)

disinherit exheredo 1

disinterested integer

disjointed disiunctus

dislike odi; abhorreo 2 (*ab*)

dislocate extorqueo 2

dislodge (sum)moveo 2; deicio 3

disloyal perfidus

dismal tristis, maestus

dismay percello 3; perturbo 1; perturbatio f; pavor m

dismember discerpo 3

dismiss (di)mitto 3; moveo 2; **~al** missio *f*

dismount descendo 3 (*ex equo*); desilio 4

disobey non pareo 2

disobliging inhumanus

disorder perturbo 1; perturbatio *f*, turba *f*; **~ly** inordinatus, turbulentus

disown infitior 1

disparage detraho 3 (*de*)

dispel dispello 3

dispens|ation immunitas *f*; **~e** tribuo 3; **~e with** remitto 3   [dilabor 3]

disperse *v/t.* dissipo 1; *v/i.*)

displace summoveo 2

display praebeo 2; ostendo 3; ostentatio *f*

displeas|e displiceo 2; **be ~ed** aegre fero 3; **~ure** offensio *f*

dispos|al dispositio *f*; dicio *f*; **~e** ordino 1; **~ed** propensus (*in, ad*); inclinatus(*ad*); **~ition** natura *f*; indoles *f*

dispossess expello 3

disproportionate inaequalis

dispute discepto 1 (*de*); altercor 1 (*cum alqo*); controversia *f*

disqualif|ication impedimentum *n*; **~y** impedio 4; impedimento est (*alci*)

disquiet sollicito 1; sollicitudo *f*

dis|regard neglego 3; **~reputable** infamis; **~repute** infamia *f*; **~respectful** contumeliosus; **~robe** vestem detraho 3

dissatisf|action molestia *f*; **be ~ied** me paenitet (*alcis rei*)

dissemble dissimulo 1; obtego 3

disseminate dissemino 1

dissen|sion dissensio *f*; **~t** dissentio 4 (*ab alqo*)

dissertation schola *f*

dissimilar dissimilis (*gen., dat.*)

dissipat|e dissipo 1; **~ed** dissolutus; **~ion** libidines *f/pl.*

dissociate separo 1

dissol|ute dissolutus; **~ve** (dis)solve 3

dissuade dissuadeo 2 (*ne*)

distan|ce spatium *n*; at a **~ce** longe, procul; a **~t** disiunctus; longinquus; be **~t** absum; disto 1 (*ab*)

distaste fastidium *n*; **~ful** odiosus

distend distendo 3

distil stillo 1

distinct clarus; distinctus; alius (*ac, atque*); **~ion** discrimen *n*; distinctio *f*; honor *m*; **~ive** proprius; **~ly** clare; diserte

distinguish discerno 3; distinguo 3 (*alqd ab alqo*); **~ oneself** emineo 2; **~ed** insignis, egregius

distort detorqueo 2

distract distraho 3; **~ed** amens; **~ion** perturbatio *f*

distress affligo 3; ango 3; dolor *m*, angor *m*; **~ing** miser

distribut|e distribuo 3; dispertio 4; **~ion** partitio *f*

district regio *f*; tractus, us *m*; ager, gri *m*

distrust diffido 3 (*dat.*); diffidentia *f*

disturb perturbo 1; sollicito 1; **~ance** turba *f*; tumultus, us *m*; perturbatio *f*

disunite dissocio 1

disuse desuetudo *f*; **fall into ~** obsolesco 3

ditch fossa *f*

ditty nenia *f*

dive mergo(r) 3 (*in rem, in re*); **~r** urinator *m*

diverge decedo 3 (*de via*); deflecto 3 (*a, de*); **~ing** diversus

divers|e varius, diversus; **~ion** derivatio *f*; oblectamentum *n*

divert derivo 1; averto 3; oblecto 3; *mil.* distinguo 3; **~ing** festivus, facetus

divest exuo 3, depono 3; **~ oneself of** exuo 3 (*alqd*)

divide seco 1; divido 3; dispertio 4

divin|ation divinatio *f*; **~e** divino 1 (*alqd, acc. c. inf.*); conicio 3; divinus; sacer; **~ely** infinitus; **~ity** numen *n*. deus *m*

division partitio *f*, discidium *n*; pars *f*; (*for voting*) discissio *f*

divorce divortium *n*; divortium facio 3

divulge divulgo 1

dizziness vertigo *f*

do facio 3; ago 3; **have to**

~ with rationem habeo 2 (*cum*); **how ~ you ~?** quid agis?; **~ without** careo 2

docile tractabilis

dock navalia *n*/*pl.*; cancelli *m*/*pl.*; **subduco** 3 navem, praecido 3

doctor medicus *m*

doctrine ratio *f*; disciplina *f*

document tabula *f*

dodge elabor 3 (*ex*); declino 1 (*alqd*)

doe cerva *f*

dog canis *m and f*; investigo 1; **~ged** pertinax; **~matic** arrogans; **~star** Sirius *m*

doing factum *n*

dole diurnum *n*; diurnus cibus *m*; stips *f*; **~ out** divido 3; **~ful** maestus

doll pupa *f*

dolphin delphinus *m*

dolt baro *m*

domain regnum *n*; dicio *f*

dome tholus *m*

domestic domesticus, familiaris; famulus *m*; famula *f*

domicile domus, us *f*; domicilium *n*

dominat|e regno 1, dominor 1 (*in*); **~ion** dominatio *f*

domineering imperiosus

dominion imperium *n*; potestas *f*

donation stips *f*

done: well ~ euge!

donkey asinus *m*

doom fatum *n*; exitium *n*; condemno 1; **~ed** fatalis

door ianua *f*; fores *f*/*pl.*; ostium *n*. **in ~s** domi; **out**

of ~s foris; back~ posti-
cum n; ~keeper ianitor m;
~way limen n

dose medicamentum do 1

dot punctum n

dot|age deliratio f; ~ard se-
nex m delirus; ~e upon depereo 4

double duplex, geminus,
duplum n; duplico 1;
flecto 3; ~-dealing fraus f;
versutus

doubt dubito 1 (de re; quin);
dubitatio f; without ~ sine
dubio; ~ful dubius, incertus; anceps; ~less nimi-
rum; scilicet

dove columba f

down¹ lanugo f; plumae f/pl.

down² prep. de (abl.); ~
stream secundum flumen
adv. deorsum; ~cast de-
missus; ~fall ruina f; ~
hill declivis; ~right merus;
plane, prorsus

dowry dos f; having a ~
dotata

doze dormito 1

drag traho 3; ~on draco m

drain sicco 1; (ex)haurio 4;
cloaca f

drama fabula f; ~tic scaenicus; ~tist poeta m

drapery amictus, us m

draught potio f; game of ~s
latrunculi m/pl.

draw traho 3; educo 3
(gladium); haurio 4
(aquam); duco 3 (spiritum);
~ back pedem refero 3;
~ near appropinquo 1;
~ up (in words) concipio 3;

mil. instruo 3; ~ing tabula
f; descriptio f

dread formido 1; formido f;
~ful terribilis, atrox

dream somnio 1; somnium
f; dreary vastus; tristis

dregs faex f; sentina f

drench perfundo 3

dress induo 3 (sibi, alci,
alqd); vestio 4 (alqm
veste); como 3 (capillos);
obligo 1 (vulnera); vestis
f; vestitus, us m; habitus,
us m; ~ing fomentum n

drift deferor 3 vento

drill perforo 1; exerceo 2;
terebra 3; exercitium n

drink bibo 3; potio f; potus,
us m; ~ to propino 3 (alci);
~er potator m; ~ing-bout
potatio f

drip stillo 1; mano 1 (alqa
re); ~ping (with) madidus
(abl.)

drive v/t. ago 3; v/i. vehor 3;
~ away abigo 3; ~ back
repello 3; ~ from, out
exigo 3; pello 3; ~r agita-
tor m, auriga m

droll ridiculus

drone fucus m; bombus m

droop v/i. pendeo 2; langueo
2; v/t. demitto 3; ~ing
languidus, fractus

drop v/t. demitto 3; v/i.
stillo 1; delabor 3; decido
3; ~ in on venio 4 (ad);
gutta f

dropsy hydrops m

drought siccitas f

drove grex m; ~r pastor m;
armentarius m

drown summergo 3; *fig.* mergo 3

drows|iness somnus *m*; ~y somniculosus

drudge mediastinus *m*; ~ry labor *m*

drug medicamentum *n*, venenum *n*; medico 1 (*alqd*)

druids Druides *m/pl.*

drum tympanum *n*

drunk ebrius; ~ard ebriosus *m*; ~enness ebrietas *f*

dry siccus, aridus; ~ land aridum *n*, *v/t.* sicco 1; abstergeo 2; *v/i.* aresco 3; ~ness siccitas *f*

dubious dubius

duck anas *f*; summergor 3

due debitus, meritus; debitum *n*; vectigal *n*, portorium *n*; in ~ time tempore, tempori

duel certamen *n*

dug uber, eris *n*

dull hebes; tardus; obtusus; subnubilus; frigidus; obtundo 3; hebeto 1; ~ness tarditas *f*

dumb mutus; ~founded obstupefactus

dun fuscus

dung stercus *n*

dungeon carcer, eris *n*

dunghill sterquilinum *n*

dupe ludifico 1; credulus (*homo*)

duplicate exemplar *n*

duplicity fraus *f*

dura|ble firmus, stabilis; ~tion spatium *n*; tempus *n*; of long, short ~tion diuturnus, brevis

during per (*acc.*), inter (*acc.*); in (*abl.*); *cj.* dum

dusk crepusculum *n*; ~y fuscus, obscurus

dust pulvis *m*; tergeo 2; verro 3; ~y pulverulentus

dutiful pius; officiosus; ~ness pietas *f*

duty officium *n*; munus *n*; *mil.* on ~ in statione (*esse*); pay ~ vectigal pendo 3; it is my ~ debeo 2

dwarf pumilio *m* and *f*

dwell habito 1 (*in*); incolo 3; ~ upon commoror 1; ~ing domicilium *n*; habitatio *f*

dwindle decresco 3, minuor 3

dye tingo 3; inficio 3; color *m*; ~r infector *m*

dynasty domus, us *f*

E

each quisque; ~ and every unus quisque; ~ of two uterque; ~ other inter se; one ~ singuli

eager avidus, cupidus (for *gen.*); acer; ~ness aviditas *f*; studium *n*

eagle aquila *f*; ~-bearer aquilifer *m*

ear auris *f*; give ~ to aures do 1, praebeo 2 (*alci*); ~ of corn spica *f*

earliness maturitas *f*

early matutinus, maturus;

antiquus; *adv.* mane, mature [quor 3]

earn mereo(r) 2; conse-]

earnest acer; serius; arrhabo *m*; ~ly magnopere, vehementer

earnings merces *f*

earth terra *f*, tellus *f*; ~en fictilis; ~enware fictilia *n/pl.*; ~ly terrestris; humanus; ~quake terrae motus, us *m*; ~work agger, eris *m*

ease remitto 3; relaxo 1; levo 1; otium *n*; quies *f*; facilitas *f*; at ~ otiose

east oriens *m*; solis ortus, us *m*; ~er pascha *f*; ~ern Eous; ~ wind eurus *m*

easy facilis; expeditus; commodus

eat edo 3; vescor 3 (*abl.*); ~ up comedo 3; consumo 3; ~ables epulae *n/pl.*; ~ing-house popina *f*

eaves-drop subausculto 1

ebb recedo 3; *fig.* decresco 1; (aestus) recessus, us *m*; be at a low ~ iaceo 2

ebony ebenum *n*

echo imago *f*; refero 3; resono 1; itero 1

eclipse defectio *f*; obscuro 1; be ~d deficio 3

eclogue ecloga *f*

econom|ical parcus; ~y parsimonia *f*

ecsta|sy insania *f*; laetitia *f*; ~tic insanus

eddy vertex *m*

edge ora *f*; margo *m*; cutting ~ acies *f*; praetexo 3

edible esculentus

edict edictum *n*

edifice aedificium *n*

edify excolo 3

edit edo 3

educat|e educo 1; instituo 3; ~ion educatio *f*; disciplina *f*

eel anguilla *f*

efface deleo 2; oblittero 1

effect efficio 3; effectus, us *m*; eventus, us *m*; vis *f*; in ~ reapse, re vera; have ~ on valeo 2 (*apud*); ~ive efficax; ~s bona *n/pl.*

effeminate effeminatus, mollis, muliebris

effervesce effervesco 3; ~nce fervor *m*

efficac|ious efficax; ~y vis *f*

efficient idoneus

effigy imago *f*

effort conatus, us *m*; labor *m*

effrontery impudentia *f*; os *n*

egg ovum *n*; ~ on incito 1; ~-shell ovi putamen *n*

egregious insignis

eight octo; ~een duodeviginti; ~eenth duodevicesimus; ~-fold octuplus; ~h octavus; ~y octoginta

either alteruter; utervis, uterlibet; on ~ side utrimque; ~ ... or aut ... aut; vel ... vel

ejaculate exclamo 1

eject deicio 3

eke out parco 3

elaborate expolio 4; elaboratus, accuratus

elapse praetereo 4

elated elatus (gaudio, superbia)

elbow cubitum n

elder maior natu; ~ly aetate provectus; the ~ly seniores m/pl.

elect creo 1; deligo 3; designatus; ~ion suffragium n; comitia n/pl.; ~ioneering petitio f, ambitio f; ~or suffragator m

elegan|ce munditia f; urbanitas f; ~t elegans, urbanus

eleg|iacs elegi m/pl.; ~y elegia f

element elementum n; ~s principia n/pl.; elementa n/pl.; ~ary simplex

elephant elephantus m

elevat|e effero 3; excolo 3; ~ed celsus, elatus; ~ion elatio f

eleven undecim; ~th undecimus

elicit elicio 3 [cimus]

eligible optabilis

eliminate tollo 3

ell ulna f

elm ulmus, i f

elocution pronuntiatio f

elope (ef)fugio 3

eloquen|ce eloquentia f, facundia f; ~t eloquens, disertus, copiosus

else alioqui(n); aliter; some one ~ alius; ~where alibi

elucidate illustro 3

elu|de effugio 3; elabor 3 (abl.); eludo 3; ~sive fallax

emaciat|e macero 1; ~ion macies f

emanate emano 1

emancipat|e manumitto 3; libero 1; ~ion manumissio f

emasculate enervo 1

embalm condio 4

embankment agger, eris m; moles f

embargo prohibitio f

embark v/t. impono 3 (in navem); v/i. navem conscendo 3; ~ upon ineo 4 (alqd)

embarrass impedio 4; implico 1; be ~ed haereo 2; perturbor 1; ~ment scrupulus m; angustiae f/pl.

embassy legatio f

embellish orno 1; ~ment ornamentum n

embers cinis, eris m

embezzle averto 3; ~ment peculatus, us m; ~r peculator m

embitter exacerbo 1

emblem indicium n

embolden confirmo 1

embrace amplector 3, complector 3; complexus, us m

embroider pingo 3

embroil implico 1

emerald smaragdus, i m and f

emerge emergo 3, exsisto 3 (ex); ~ncy tempus n, discrimen n

emigrat|e (e)migro 1; ~ion migratio f

eminen|ce tumulus m; praestantia f; ~t praeclarus; nobilis

emissary legatus m

emit emitto 3; iacio 3

emotion motus, us *m*; commotio *f*

emperor imperator *m*, princeps *m*

emphasis vis *f*; ~size vehementer dico 3

empire imperium *n*; regnum *n*

employ utor 3; adhibeo 2; ~ment quaestus, us *m*

empower potestatem do 1 (*alci*)

empt|iness inanitas *f*; ~y vacuus; inanis; vanus; exinanio 4; exhaurio 4

emulat|e aemulor 1 (*acc.*); ~ion aemulatio *f*

enable facultatem do 1 (*alci*)

enact sancio 4 (*legem, lege alqd, ut*); scisco 3 (*alqd, ut*); constituo 3; get ~ed perfero 3; ~ment lex *f*; scitum *n*

enamoured: be ~ depereo 2 (*alqm*)

encamp castra pono 3; consido 3

enchant fascino 1; capio 3; ~ing venustus; ~ment carmen *n*; ~ress venefica *f*

encircle cingo 3; circumdo 1 (*alqd re*)

enclos|e includo 3; ~ure saepta *n/pl.*

encore revoco 1

encounter offendo 3; congredior 3; oppeto 3 (*mortem*); experior 4 (*periculum*); congressus, us *m*

encourage confirmo 1; hortor 1; ~ment cohortatio *f*

encroach upon occupo 1; imminuo 3 (*ius etc.*)

encumb|er impedio 4; ~rance impedimentum *n*

end finis *m*; make an ~ finem facio 3 (*gen.*); put an ~ to finem affero 3 (*dat.*); dirimo 3; in the ~ postremo; to no ~ frustra; to this ~ ideo; extremus; *v/t.* finio 4; *v/i.* desino 3

endanger periclitor 1

endeavour conor 1; conatum *n*

end|ing exitus, us *m*; ~less infinitus

endow dono 1 (*alqm re*); instruo 3; ~ed praeditus

endur|ance patientia *f*; fortitudo *f*; ~e patior 3; (per)fero 3; duro 1; ~ing patiens (*gen.*); perennis

enemy hostis *m and f*, inimicus *m*

energ|etic acer; strenuus; ~y vis *f*; impetus, us *m*

enervate enervo 1

enfeeble debilito 1

enforce exerceo 2

enfranchise civitatem do 1 (*alci*)

engage *v/t.* conduco 3; *v/i.* congredior 3 (*cum hostibus*); (*in me*) recipio 3; promitto 3 (*acc. c. inf.*); ~ in suscipio 3; ~d occupatus (*in re*); sponsus; ~ment sponsio *f*; negotium *n*; proelium *n*

engender gigno 3

engin|e machina *f*; tormentum *n*; ~eer machinator *m*

engrave incido 3; caelo 1; ~r sculptor *m*, sculptor *m*

engross occupo 3

engulf devoro 3

enhance amplifico 1; augeo 2; ~ment amplificatio *f*

enigma aenigma *n*

enjoin praecipio 3 (*alci alqd*)

enjoy fruor 3, utor 3 (*abl.*); delector 1 (*abl.*); ~ment gaudium *n*; voluptas *f*

enlarge augeo 2; dilato 1; ~ upon uberius loquor 3, dico 3

enlighten erudio 4; certiorem facio 3

enlist *v/t.* conscribo 3; *v/i.* nomen do 1, edo 3, sacramentum dico 3

enliven exhilaro 1

enmity inimicitia *f*; simultas *f*

enormity immanitas *f*; scelus *n*; ~ous ingens; immanis

enough satis; ~ and to spare satis superque; not ~ parum

enrage exaspero 1

en|rapture delecto 1; ~rich locupleto 1, ~rol ascribo 3 (*in, dat.*); ~sconce oneself consido 3

ensign signum *n*; vexillum *n*

enslave in servitutem abduco 3, abstraho 3; ~ment servitus, utis *f*

ensnare irretio 4

ensue sequor 3

ensure curo 1; provideo 2 (*ut, ne*)

entail affero 3

entangle implico 3

enter ingredior 3 (*intra, in*); venio 4 (*in*); intro 1 (*alqd, in, ad*); refero 3 (*alqd in libellum*); ~ upon ineo 4 (*alqd*); ~prise inceptum *n*, consilium *n*; audacia *f*; ~prising promptus, audax

entertain excipio 3; invito 1; oblecto 1; ~ment hospitium *n*; epulae *f/pl.*

enthusias|m studium *n*; ardor *m*; ~tic studiosus (*gen.*); be ~tic ardeo 2 (*studio*)

entic|e allicio 3, illicio 3; ~ement illecebra *f*; ~ing blandus

entire totus; integer; universi; ~ly omnino; plane

entitle inscribo 3; be ~d to ius habeo 2 (*gen.*); dignus sum (*abl., qui*)

entrails viscera *n/pl.*

entrance introitus, us *m*; aditus, us *m*; capio 3

entreat oro 1, obsecro 1; flagito 1; ~y preces *f/pl.*; obsecratio *f*

entrust credo 3 (*alqd alci*)

entry introitus, us *m*; aditus, us *m*; make an ~ refero 3 (*alqa re*)   [*alqd*]

entwine implico 3 (*alqd*)

enumerate enumero 1

envelop involvo 3; ~e involucrum *n*

envi|able fortunatus; ~ous invidus; ~oy legatus *m*; ~y invidia *f*; invideo 2 (*dat.*)

ephemeral caducus, brevis
epic epos n; epicus
epigram epigramma n
epistle epistula f
epitaph elogium n
epoch tempus n; saeculum n
equable aequus
equal aequus; aequalis;
par; (ad)aequo 1; aequi-
pero 1; ~ity aequabilitas f;
~ize aequo 1
equanimity aequus animus
m
equestrian equester; eques
m
equinox aequinoctium n
equip orno 1; instruo 3;
~ment arma n/pl.; appa-
ratus, us m; instrumentum
n
equit|able aequus; ~y aequi-
tas f
equivocal ambiguus
equivocate tergiversor 1
era tempus n
eradicate exstirpo 1
eras|e deleo 2; induco 3;
~ure litura f
ere prius, ante quam
erect exstruo 3; statuo 3;
erectus; ~ion aedificatio f;
aedificium n
erotic amatorius
err erro 1; pecco 1
errand mandatum n; ~-boy
nuntius m
err|atic vagus; ~oneous fal-
sus; ~or error m; erratum
n; peccatum n
erudit|e doctus, eruditus;
~ion eruditio f
eruption eruptio f

escape effugio 3; elabor 3
(ex); it ~s one's notice
fallit; praeterit; affugium
n
escort prosequor 3; deduco
3; praesidium n; comita-
tus, us m
especial praecipuus; ~ly
praecipue; praesertim
espy conspicor 1
essay tento 1; periculum n
essen|ce substantia f; ~tial
necessarius
establish instituo 3; statuo
3; stabilio 4; ~ that vinco 3
(acc. c. inf.); ~ment con-
stitutio f; familia f
estate status, us m; ager m;
fundus m
esteem diligo 3; magni
facio 3; existimatio f
estimat|e aestimo 1; iudi-
cium n; aestimatio f; ~ion
existimatio f; opinio f
estrange alieno 1; ~ment
alienatio f
estuary aestuarium n
etern|al aeternus; sempi-
ternus; ~ity aeternitas f
ether aether, eris m; ~eal
aetherius
ethic|al moralis; ~s philoso-
phia f moralis
etiquette mos n
eulog|ize laudo 1; ~y lau-
datio f; laus f
eunuch eunuchus m
evacuate vacuefacio 3; mil.
deduco 3 praesidium; ex-
cedo 3 (abl.)
evade subterfugio 3; frau-
dem facio 3 (legi)

evaporate exhalo 1

evasion ambages *f/pl.*; practise ~ tergiversor 1

eve: on the ~ of pridie (*gen.*)

even aequus, planus; *adv.* etiam; vel; not ... ~ ne ... quidem; ~ if etiamsi

evening vesper *m*; in the ~ vesperi; vespertinus; ~ star Hesperus *m*

evenness aequitas *f* (animi)

event res *f*; eventus, us *m*; at all ~s certe; ~ful memorabilis; ~ually postremo; ad postremum

ever semper; if ~ si quando; nor ... ~ nec ... umquam; ~ since ex eo tempore quo; ~lasting sempiternus

every quisque; omnis; any and ~ quivis; ~ day cotidie; ~ year quotannis; ~body quisque; omnes; nemo ... non; ~thing quidque; omnia *n/pl.*; ~where ubique; passim

evidence testimonium *n*; indicium *n*; argumentum *n*; give ~ testificor 1

evident manifestus; apertus; evidens; it is ~ appaeret 2; ~ly aperte; scilicet

evil malus; improbus; pravus; malum *n*; incommodum *n*

evince praesto 1

evoke evoco 1

ewe ovis *f*

ewer urceus *m*

exact exigo 3; impero 1; sumo 3 (*poenas*); subtilis;

accuratus; diligens; ~itude diligentia *f*

exaggerate augeo 2; exaggero 1; in maius (vero) fero 3, extollo 3

exalt effero 3; augeo 2; ~ed celsus

examin|ation investigatio *f*; interrogatio *f*; probatio *f*; ~e investigo 1; interrogo 1; quaero 3; probo 1

example exemplum *n*; exemplar *n*; documentum *n*; for ~ verbi causa

exasperate irrito 1

excavat|e (ex)cavo 1; ~ion cavum *n*

exceed egredior 3 (*extra*, *acc.*); ~ingly valde

excel praesto 1 (*dat.*); excello 3 (*dat.*); ~lence virtus, utis *f*; excellentia *f*; ~lent optimus; praestans

except excipio 3; nisi quod; nisi ut; praeter (*acc.*); ~ing you two exceptis vobis duobus; ~ion exceptio *f*; without ~ion omnes; ~ional rarus; eximius

excess nimium *n*; luxuria *f*; ~ive nimius; immoderatus

exchange muto 1 (*alqd alqa re*); inter se dare; permutatio *f*; ~ of money collybus *m*

exchequer aerarium *n*; fiscus *m*

excise vectigalia *n/pl.*

excit|able fervidus; ~e commoveo 2; excito 1, concito 1 (ad); ~ement commotio f; perturbatio f

exclaim exclamo 1; conclamo 1; ~ against acclamo 1 (dat.). [matio f]

exclamation vox f; exclaー

exclu|de prohibeo 2; excludo 3; ~sion interdictio f; ~sive proprius

excrement stercus n

excruciating acerbissimus

exculpate purgo 1

excus|able venia dignus; ~e me purgo 1, excuso 1 (alci); veniam do 1; ignosco 3; excusatio f; venia f

execrate exsecror 1

execut|e exsequor 3; perficio 3; supplicium sumo 3 (de); supplicio afficio 3; ~ion supplicium n; mors f; ~ioner carnifex m

exempl|ary egregius; ~ify exemplum do 1, prodo 1

exempt libero 1; solvo 3 (alqm alqa re); immunitatem tribuo 3; immunis (abl.); ~ion immunitas f; vacatio f

exercise exerceo 2; exercitatio f; take ~ ambulo 1

exert exerceo 2; utor 3; ~ oneself nitor 3; laboro 1; ~ion contentio f

exhal|ation exhalatio f; ~e exhalo 1

exhaust exhaurio 4; defatigo 1; debilito 1; be ~ed deficio 3; ~ed confectus; defessus; effetus; ~ion lassitudo f

exhibit propono 3; expono 3; exhibeo 2; praesto 1; ostento 1; ~ion spectaculum n; munus n

exhilarate exhilaro 1

exhort (ad-, co-)hortor 1; ~ation hortatio f

exigency necessitas f

exile eicio 3; aqua et igni interdico 3; pello 3; exsilium n; exsul m and f; extorris; be an ~ live in ~ exsulo 1; go into ~ solum verto 3

exist sum; exsisto 3; exsto 1; ~ence vita f

exit exitus, us m

exonerate libero 1 (culpa)

exorbitant immodicus

exordium exordium n

expan|d pando 3; extendo 3; ~se spatium n

expect exspecto 1 (alqd); spero 1 (alqd, acc. c. inf.); credo 3 (acc. c. inf.); ~ation exspectatio f; spes f; contrary to ~ation praeter spem

expedien|cy utilitas f; ~t utilis; be ~t expedit

expedite maturo 1; ~ion expeditio f

expel (ex)pello 3; eicio 3

expen|d impendo 3; ~se impensa f; sumptus, us m; ~sive sumptuosus; carus

experience experior 4; patior 3; usus, us m, peritia f; ~d peritus (gen.)

experiment periculum n; experimentum n (facio 3)

expert peritus (*gen.*), sciens (*gen.*); **~ness** peritia *f*

expiate expio 1 (*alqd alqa re*); **~ion** expiatio *f*

expire exspiro 1; animam, vitam edo 3; exeo 2

expl|ain explico 1; explano 1; expono 3; **~anation** explanatio *f*; ratio *f*; **~icit** apertus

explode dirumpor 3; explodo 3 (*sententiam*)

exploit res *f* gesta; facinus *n*

explore exploro 1; speculor 1

explosion fragor *m*

export exporto 1

expos|e expono 3; profero 3 (*rem*); nudo 1; **~e** to obicio 3; **~ed** apertus; obnoxius (*dat.*); **~ition** explicatio *f*; **~tulate** expostulo 1 (*cum alqo de, acc. c. inf.*); **~ure** frigus *n*

expound expono 3

express effero 3; dico 3; significo 1; **~ion** verba *n/pl.*; oratio *f*; vultus, us *m*; significatio *f*; **~ive** significans; **~ly** diserte

exquisite conquisitus, exquisitus

extant: be **~** exsto 1

extempor|ary subitus; **~e** subito

extend extendo 3, distendo 3; porrigo 3; propago 1

extens|ion propagatio *f*; **~ive** amplus, latus

extent spatium *n*; to this **~** that hactenus ... ut; to what **~** quatenus

extenuate levo 1

exterior exterior; species *f*

exterminate ad internecionem deleo 2, redigo 3; deleo 2

external externus; **~ things** quae extra sunt

extinct mortuus; **~ion** interitus, us *m*

extinguish exstinguo 3

extirpate exstirpo 1

extol laudo 1; laudibus effero 3

extort extorqueo 2; exprimo 3; **crime of ~ion** (pecuniae) repetundae *f/pl.*; **~ionate** rapax

extra praecipuus; *adv.* praeterea

extract extraho 3; exprimo 3; **make an ~** excerpo 3; **~ion** evulsio *f*; genus *n*

extraneous alienus

extraordinar|ily extra ordinem *or* modum; **~y** extraordinarius; insolitus

extravagan|ce luxuria *f*; sumptus *m/pl.*; **~t** immodicus; prodigus, profusus

extreme extremus; summus; ultimus; **~s** extrema *n/pl.*

extricate (me) expedio 4, extraho 3

exuberan|ce hilaritas *f*; **~t** laetus; luxuriosus

exude sudo 1

exult gestio 4; exsulto 1; gaudeo 2 (*abl.*); **~ant** laetus; **~ation** laetitia *f*

eye oculus *m*; lumen *n*;

before one's ~s ante ocu-
los, in oculis, in conspectu;
aspicio 3; ~ball pupula f;

~brow supercilium n; ~lid
palpebra f; ~sight acies f,
~witness arbiter, tri m

F

fable fabula f; ~d fabulosus
fabric textile n; textum n;
fabrica f; ~ate fig. com-
miniscor 3; ~ation com-
mentum n
fabulous commenticius, fabulosus
face os n; facies f; vultus,
us m; frons f; ~ to ~ coram
(abl.); in the ~ of in (abl.);
obviam eo 4 (dat.); me oppono 3, offero 3 (dat.); ~
(towards) aspecto 1 (acc.);
vergo 3 (in, ad); ~ about
signa converto 3
facetious facetus
facil|itate facilius reddo 3;
~ity facilitas f; facultas f
facing adversus (acc.)
fact res f; factum n; in ~ in
re vera
facti|on factio f; pars f;
~ous factiosus
factor procurator m; ~y
officina f
faculty facultas f; ingenium
n
fade palleo 2; pallesco 3;
cado 3   [n/pl.]
faggot fascis m; sarmenta
fail v/i. deficio 3; desum
(dat.); cado 3; male eve-
nit; v/t. destituo 3; without ~ certe; ~ure defectio f
fain: I would ~ velim, vel-
lem

faint hebes; languidus; confectus; intermorior 3; animus relinquit (alqm); ~
hearted ignavus; ~ness
languor m
fair candidus; pulcher; su-
dus, serenus (tempestas);
mediocris; secundus (ven-
tus); aequus; nundinae
f/pl.; ~ly satis; ~ness
aequum n; candor m;
~ weather sudum n
faith fides f; put ~ in fidem
habeo 2 (dat.); keep good ~
fidem servo 1; break ~
fidem violo 1; in good ~
ex bona fide; ~ful fidelis;
fidus; ~less perfidus
fall cado 3; labor 3; praecipito 1; ruo 3; ~ away de-
scisco 3 (ab); ~ in with incido 3 (in c. acc.); ~ out
dissideo 2 (inter se); ~
short of desum (dat.); ~ to
obtingit (sors, etc., alci);
accidit (alci); ~ upon invado 3 (in c. acc.); casus,
us m; lapsus, us m; ruina
f; deminutio f; water~
defectus, us m (aquae)
fallac|ious fallax; ~y cap-
tio f
fallow novalis, inaratus;
~ land novalis f; novale n;
lie ~ cesso 1
fals|e falsus; fictus; men-

dax; perfidus; **~ehood**
mendacium *n*; commen-
tum *n*; **~ify** corrumpo 3;
vitio 1

falter titubo 1; haereo 2

fame gloria *f*; fama *f*; nomen *n*

familiar familiaris (with
dat.); notus; **be on ~
terms** with familiariter
utor 3 (*alqo*); **~ity** familiaritas *f*; usus, us *m*; **~ize**
assuefacio 3 (*alqm alqa re*)

family domus, us *f*; mei,
tui, sui; familia *f* (*of common descent*); domesticus;
gentilis

famine fames *f*

famished fame confectus

famous clarus, praeclarus,
celeber, nobilis

fan flabellum *n*; ventilo 1

fancy fingo 3 (cogitatione,
animo); puto 1; cogitatio
f; somnium *n*; species *f*;
libido *f*; **as I ~** ut libet
(*mihi*)

fang dens *m*

fantastic commenticius;
vanus

far procul; longe; **by ~**
longe, multo; **be ~** (removed) **from** longe absum (ab);
as ~ as tenus (*abl.*); *adv.*
quatenus, quoad; **thus ~**
hactenus, **~-fetched** arcessitus; **~-off** longinquus

farce mimus *m*

fare me habeo 2 (*bene,
male*); mihi evenit; cibus
m; vectura *f*; **~well** vale

farm fundus *m*; praedium

---

n; ager, gri *m*; colo 3;
conduco 3 (*vectigalia*); **~
out** loco 1; **~er** agricola *m*;
colonus *m*; **~house** villa *f*;
~ing agri cultura *f*

farthing: **not a ~** nullus
teruncius *m*; **I don't care
a ~** non flocci facio 3

fasces fasces *m/pl.*

fascinate capio 3; delenio
4; **~ion** blanditiae *f/pl.*

fashion fabricor 1; effingo
3; forma *f*; mos *m*; **after
the ~ of** more (*gen.*); **~able**
elegans; **be ~able** moris est

fast firmus; stabilis; celer;
velox; ieiunus sum; ieiu-
nium *n*; **make ~** deligo 1;
be ~ asleep arte dormio 4

fasten figo 3 (*alqd in re*);
annecto 3 (*ad alqd*: *dat.*);
deligo 1 (*ad*); **~ing** claustra
n/pl.; vinculum *n*

fastidious fastidiosus

fat pinguis; opimus, obesus; pingue *n*; adeps *m
and f*

fatal fatalis; funestus; perniciosus; **~ity** fatum *n*

fate fatum *n*; **~d** fatalis (*ad*)

father pater *m*; parens;
~-in-law socer *m*; **~less**
orbus; *gt.*; paternus

fathom *fig.* mente comprehendo 3; **~less** profundus

fatigue fatigo 1; (de)fati-
gatio *f*

fatness pinguitudo *f*; obe-
sitas *f*

fatt|en sagino 1; farcio 4;
~y pinguis

fatuous fatuus

fault culpa *f*; delictum *n*; peccatum *n*; vitium *n*; find ~ with accuso 1; commit a ~ pecco 1; it is my ~ per me stat (*quominus, ne*); ~less emendatus; perfectus; ~y mendosus, vitiosus

favour faveo 2, foveo 2, studeo 2 (*dat.*); gratia *f*; studium *n*; beneficium *n*; confer a ~ beneficium confero 3; win the ~ of gratiam ineo 4 (*ab, apud*); in ~ of pro (*abl.*); ~able prosperus; secundus; ~ite gratus; carus; dilectus; deliciae *f/pl.*; ~itism studium *n*

fawn hinnuleus *m*; ~ upon adulor 1 (*alqm*)

fear timeo 2, metuo 3; vereor 2; ~ for diffido 3 (*dat.*); metus us, *m*, timor *m*; ~ful timidus; atrox; ~less fidens

feast convivium *n*; epulae *f/pl.*; dies *m* festus; epulor 1; convivor 1

feat factum *n*; res *f*

feather penna *f*, pluma *f*

feature proprium *n*; ~s vultus, us *m*; lineamenta *n/pl.*

February Februarius *n*

fecundity fecunditas *f*

federation civitates *f/pl.* foederatae

fee merces *f*

feeble infirmus; imbecillus; ~ness imbecillitas *f*

feed *v/t.* alo 3; nutrio 4;

pasco 1; *v/i.* vescor 3 (*abl.*); pascor 1

feel tento 1; tango 3; contrecto 1; sentio 4; percipio 3; ~ing tactus *m*; sensus, us *m*; ~ings animus *m*

feign fingo 3; simulo 1

felicitate gratulor 1 (*alci de re, quod*)

fell dirus; caedo 3

fellow socius *m*; homo *m*; ~-citizen civis *m* and *f*; ~-countryman popularis *m*; ~-slave conservus *m*; ~ship societas *f*; sodalitas *f*; ~-soldier commilito *m*

felt coactum *n*

female femineus; femina *f*

feminine muliebris; femineus

fen palus, udis *f*

fence saepes *f*; saepta *n/pl.*; rudibus certare; ~ in saepio 4

ferment fermentum *n*; *fig.* aestus, us *m*; fermentor 1; be in a ~ ferveo 2

fern filix *f*

ferocious trux; ~ty atrocitas *f*

ferret out eruo 3

ferry transveho 3; ~man portitor *m*

fertile fertilis; fecundus; ~ity fecunditas *f*; ~ize laetifico 1

fervent ardens; ~our ardor *m*

fester suppuro 1

festival dies *m* festus; sollemne *n*; feriae *f/pl.*; ~e

festus; festivus; ~ity sol-
lemnia *n/pl.*

festoon serta *n/pl.*

fetch fero 3; accesso 3

fetid fetidus

fetter compes *m;* vinculum
n; catena *f;* catenas inicio
3 (*alci*)

feud simultas *f*

fever febris *f;* ~ish *fig.*
furiosus

few pauci; aliquot; rarus

fibre fibra *f*

fickle levis; mobilis; ~ness
levitas *f*

ficti|on commentum *n;* fa-
bula *f;* ~tious fictus

fidelity fidelitas *f*

field ager, gri *m;* arvum *n;*
fig. campus *m;* locus *m;*
~ of battle acies *f;* in the ~
militiae

fiendish inhumanus

fierce atrox; saevus; acer;
~ness atrocitas *f*

fiery igneus, ardens; ferox

fif|teen quindecim; ~teenth
quintus decimus; ~th quintus; ~tieth quinquagesi-
mus; ~ty quinquaginta

fig ficus, i *and* us *f*

fight pugno 1; dimico 1;
(con)certo 1; ~ a battle
proelium committo 3;
pugna *f;* certamen *n;* ~er
pugnator *m*

figur|ative translatus; ~e
figura *f;* forma *f;* signum
n; ~e of speech translatio *f*

filament filum *n*

filch surripio 3

file lima *f; mil.* ordo *m;*

rank and ~ gregarii mili-
tes *m/pl.;* limo 1

filial pius

fill impleo 2, compleo 2
(*alqd alqa re*); celebro 1
(*locum, aures* etc.); inicio 3
(*spem,* etc. *alci*)

fillet vitta *f;* fascia *f*

film membrana *f*

filter liquo 1; colum *n*

filth sordes *f/pl.;* caenum *n;*
illuvies *f;* ~iness squalor
m; ~y sordidus; spurcus;
foedus

final ultimus, extremus; ~ly
ad extremum; postremo;
denique

finance pecuniam solvo 3
(*pro re*); (public) ~s aerarium *n*

find invenio 4; reperio 4;
nanciscor 3; ~ guilty damno 1; ~ out comperio 4;
~ing inventum *n*

fine praeclarus; pulcher;
bellus; tenuis; subtilis;
multo 1 (*alqm pecunia*);
multa *f;* ~ness tenuitas *f;*
~sse argutiae *f/pl.*

finger digitus *m;* attrecto 1;
~tips extremi digiti
m/pl.

finish conficio 3, perficio 3;
perago 3; finio 4; ~ off
absolvo 3; absolutio *f;* ~ed
perfectus

fir abies *m;* pinus, us *f;* of
~wood abiegnus

fire ignis *m;* incendium *n;*
ardor *m;* set on ~ incendo
3; be on ~ ardeo 2; catch ~
exardesco 3; ~-brand fax

f; ~-place focus m; ~wood ligna n/pl.

firm firmus, stabilis; constans; societas f; **make** ~ firmo 1; **stand** ~ sto 1; ~ament caelum n; ~ness firmitas f; constantia f

first primus; princeps; at ~ primo; ~ly, in the ~ place primo, primum; for the ~ time prinum; ~-fruits primitiae f/pl.

fish piscis m; piscor 1; ~ for capto 1; ~erman piscator m; ~ing boat piscatoria navis f; ~ing rod harundo f; ~monger cetarius m; ~pond piscina f

fist pugnus m

fit aptus (alci; ad alqd); idoneus; accommodatus; v/t. accommodo 1 (alci ad alqd); v/i. convenio 4 (ad); ~ out instruo 3; impetus, us m; ~ful incertus; ~ting decens; it is ~ting oportet

five quinque; ~ times quinquies

fix figo 3; constituo 3; destino 1; defigo 3 (oculos in alqd); ~ed certus; constans

flabby, flaccid mollis; enervatus

flag languesco 3; refrigesco 3; vexillum n, signum n

flagon lagoena f

flame flamma f; flagro 1; ~-coloured flammeus

flamen flamen m

flank latus n; ilia n/pl.; mil. on the ~s a lateribus

flap v/t. plaudo 3 (pennis etc.); v/i. fluito 1; lacinia f

flare flagro 1

flash fulgeo 2; corusco 1; mico 1; fulgor m; lightning ~ fulgur n

flask ampulla f

flat aequus; planus; campester; pronus; fig. frigidus; campus m; ~ness planities f; ~ten complano 1

flatter adulor 1 (acc.); blandior 4, assentor 1 (dat.); ~er assentator m; ~ing blandus; ~y adulatio f

flatulent inflatus

flaunt ostento 1

flavour sapor m; have a ~ sapio 3 (acc.)

flaw vitium n, mendum n; ~less emendatus

flax linum n; carbasus, i f; ~en flavus

flay pellem deripio 3

flea pulex m

flee fugio 3; in fugam me do 1, confero 3

fleece vellus n; expilo 1; ~y laniger

fleet celer; classis f; ~ing fugax; ~ness velocitas f

flesh caro f; corpus n

flexib|**ility** mollitia f; ~le flexibilis, lentus

flicker mico 1; corusco 1

flight volatus, us m; lapsus, us m; fuga f; **put to** ~ in fugam do 1, conicio 3 (alqm); ~ of stairs scalae f/pl.; ~y levis

flimsy subtilis; pertenuis

finch abhorreo 2 (*ab*)

fling iacio 3; ~ away pro-, ab-icio 3

flint silex *m*; ~y *fig.* ferreus

flippant nugax

flit volito 1

float fluito 1; inno 1; fluo 3; ratis *f*

flock grex *m*; pecus *n*; floccus *m*; ~ to, towards, together conftuo 3; congregor 1

flog verbero 1; ~ging verberatio *f*; verbera *n/pl.*

flood diluvies *f*, diluvium *n*; unda *f*; *fig.* flumen *n*; inundo 1

floor solum *n*; pavimentum *n*; contignatio *f*

florid rubicundus; floridus

flounce instita *f*

flounder mergor 3; haereo 2

flour farina *f*

flourish floreo 2; vigeo 2; iacto 1; flos *m*; clangor *m* (*tubarum*)

flout contemno 3

flow fluo 3; mano 1; ~ down, into, past de-, in-, praeterfluo 3; flumen *n*; lapsus, us *m*; accessus, us *m* (*aestus*)

flower flos *m*; flosculus *m*; floreo 2; ~y floreus; floridus

fluctuate me iacto 1; nato 1

fluen(*cy*) copia *f*, facultas *f* dicendi; ~t volubilitas, copiosus

fluid liquidus; liquor *m*

flurry trepidatio *f*; trepido

1

flush rubeo 2; rubor *m*; flos *m*; planus

flute tibia *f*; ~-player tibicen *m*

flutter volito 1; trepidatio *f*

fly volo 1; fugio 3; ~ at involo 1; ~ open dissilio 4; musca *f*; ~ing volucer

foal eculeus *m*

foam spumo 1; spuma *f*; ~ing spumeus, spumosus

fodder pabulum *n*

foe hostis *m*; inimicus *m*

fog caligo *f*, nebula *f*; ~gy caliginosus

foil eludo 3; rudis *f*; lamina *f*

fold complico 1; ruga *f*, sinus, us *m* (*vestis*); saepta *n/pl.*; ovile *n*; ~ing-doors valvae *f/pl.*

foliage frondes *f/pl.*

folk vulgus, i *n*

follow (con-, in-)sequor 3; insisto 3 (*rationem, etc.*); utor 3 (*consiliis*); as ~s in hunc modum; it ~s that sequitur ut; ~er assectator *m*; the ~ing proximus; ~ing comitatus, us *m*

folly stultitia *f*

foment *fig.* concito 1

fond amans, studiosus (*gen.*); indulgens (*in alqm; dat.*); be ~ of amo 1 (*acc., inf.*); ~le mulceo 2; blandior 4

food cibus *m*; alimentum *n*; pabulum *n*; victus, us *m*

fool stultus *m*; ludificor 1 (*alqm*), ludo 3 (*alqm*); ~ery ineptiae *f/pl.*; ~hardy temerarius; ~ish stultus, ineptus

foot pes m; mil. pedes m/pl.; pedites m/pl.; imum n (adj.) imus; at the ~ of sub (abl.); on ~ pedibus; pedestris; pedes; ~ing status, us m; ~man pedisequus m; ~path semita f; ~print vestigium n; ~stool scamnum n

foppish delicatus

for prep. pro (abl.); ob, propter (causam); in, ad (acc.); ~ my part pro mea parte; leave ~ dead pro occiso relinquo 3; cj. nam; enim; quippe

forage pabulor 1; frumentor 1; pabulum n

forbear mitto 1, desino 3 (inf.); ~ance patientia f

forbid veto 1 (acc. c. inf.); impero 1 (ne)

force vis f; be in ~ valeo 2; v/t. cogo 3 (ut, inf.); ~ a way through. out of perrumpo 3 per, erumpo 3 ex; ~ out of extorqueo 2; ~d accessitus; ~s copiae f/pl.

forcible vehemens; gravis

ford vadum n; vado transeo 4

fore|bode portendo 3; praesentio 4; ~cast praevideo 2; ~fathers maiores m/pl.; ~finger digitus m index; ~go dimitto 3; ~head frons f

foreign externus; peregrinus; ~ to abhorrens ab;

~er advena m; peregrinus m

fore|knowledge providentia f; ~man procurator m; ~most princeps, primus; ~see provideo 2; ~sight providentia f

forest silva f

fore|stall anteverto 3 (dat.); ~tell praedico 3

forfeit multor 1 (abl.); multa f; commissus

forge fabricor 1 (gladium); subicio 3; fornax f

forget obliviscor 3 (gen., acc.); ~ful immemor (gen.); obliviosus

forgive ignosco 3 (alci alqd); ~ness venia f

fork furca f; ~ed bifurcus

forlorn destitutus; miser

form forma f, figura f, species f; genus n; ritus, us m; scamnum n; for ~'s sake dicis causa; (con-) formo 1; fingo 3; instruo 3 (aciem); ineo 4 (consilium)

formal|ities ritus m/pl.; iusta n/pl.; ~ly rite

former prior; superior; pristinus; the ~ ille; ~ly olim, quondam

formidable gravis

formula formula f; carmen n; praefatio f

forsake desero 3

forsooth scilicet, nempe

forswear eiuro 1 (alqd); ~ oneself periuro 1

fort castellum n

forth foras; from that time ~ inde; ~with protinus

fortieth quadragesimus

fortif|ication munitio *f*; munimentum *n*; moenia *n/pl.*; **~y** munio 4

fortress castellum *n*; arx *f*

fortuitous fortuitus; **~ly** fortuito, forte

fortun|ate felix; fortunatus; **~e** fortuna *f* (*secunda, adversa*); fors *f*; **good ~** felicitas *f*; res *f/pl.* secundae; divitiae *f/pl.*, fortunae *f/pl.*; res *f* (*familiaris*); **~e-teller** hariolus *m*

forty quadraginta

forum forum *n*

forward porro, ante; **thence~** iam inde; protervus; promptus; adiuvo 1; perfero 3 (*litteras*); **~ness** protervitas *f*

foster foveo 2; nutrio 4; **~-child** alumnus *m*; **~-mother** nutrix *f*

foul foedus; taeter; inquino 1; **~ness** foeditas *f*

found condo 3, constituo 3; deduco 3 (*coloniam*), **~ation** fundamentum *n*; sedes *f*; **~er** conditor *m*; auctor *m*; summergor 3

foundry fornax *f*

fountain fons *f*

four quattuor; **~ each** quaterni; **~ times** quater; **~ hundred** quadringenti; **~fold** quadruplus; quadruplum *n*; **~footed** quadrupes; **~teen** quattuordecim; **~teenth** quartus decimus; **~th** quartus; **~thly** quarto

fowl volucris *f*; gallina *f*; **~er** auceps *m*; **~ing** aucupium *n*

fox vulpes *f*; **old ~** veterator *m*; vulpinus

fract|ion pars *f*; **~ure** fran-)
fragile fragilis   [go 3*J*

fragment fragmentum *n*

fragran|ce suavis odor *m*; **~t** odorus, suavis

frail infirmus, fragilis

frame compages *m*; forma *f*; **~ of mind** affectio *f*; animus *m*; compono 3; fabricor 1; formo 1; concipio 3 (*ius iurandum*); forma includo 3 (*tabulam*)

franchise civitas *f*; suffragium *n*

frank liber; simplex; sincerus; **~ness** libertas *f*

frantic fanaticus; insanus

fratern|al fraternus; **~ity** sodalitas *f*

fraud fraus *f*; dolus *m*; **~ulent** fraudulentus

fray rixa *f*; detero 3

freak monstrum *n*; **~ish** inconstans

freckle macula *f*

free liber (*re, a re*); vacuus (*a re*); expers (*gen.*); **be ~ from** careo 2 (*abl.*); **~ from blame** extra culpam; **~ from care** securus; **of one's own ~ will** sua sponte; libero 1 (*alqm re, a re*); manumitto 3 (*servum*); vindico 1 (*ab*); **~booter** latro *m*; **~born** ingenuus; **~dman** libertus *m*; **~dom** libertas *f*; vacuitas *f*

freeze congelo 1; concresco 3; conglacio 1

freight onus *n*; navem onero 1

frenz|ied furiosus, insanus; ~y furor *m*

frequen|cy crebritas *f*; frequentia *f*; ~t creber; frequens; celebro 1; ~ted celeber; ~tly crebro

fresh recens; integer; a~ de integro; ~en increbresco 3 (*ventus*); ~ness viriditas *f*

fret sollicito 1; doleo 2; ~ful morosus

friction tritus, us *m*

friend amicus *m*; familiaris *m*; ~ly comes; benevolus, amicus (*erga, dat.*); ~ship amicitia *f*; familiaritas *f*

fright terror *m*; ~en (per-)terreo 2; ~ful terribilis; atrox

frigid frigidus

frill segmenta *n/pl.*

fringe fimbriae *f/pl.*; limbus *m*

fritter away dissipo 1

frivol|ity levitas *f*; ~ous levis; nugax

fro: to and ~ ultro citroque

frock stola *f*

frog rana *f*

frolic ludo 3; lascivio 4; lascivia *f*

from a, ab (*abl.*); de (*abl.*); e, ex (*abl.*); ~ all sides undique; ~ day to day in dies; ~ that place hinc, illinc

front frons *f*; ~ of a column primum agmen *n*; in ~

a fronte; in ~ of pro (*abl.*); ante (*acc.*); in ~ (*adj.*) adversus; obviam eo 4 (*alci*); aspecto 3 (*alqd*); ~ier finis *m*; ~ing adversus (*acc.*)

frost gelu *n*; pruina *f*; ~bitten praeustus; ~y gelidus

froth spuma *f*; spumo 1

frown frontem contraho 3; contractio *f* frontis

frozen glacie, frigore concretus

frugal frugi; parcus; ~ity parsimonia *f*

fruit fructus, us *m*; pomum *n*; fruges *f/pl.*; baca *f*; ~erer pomarius *m*; ~ful fructuosus; fruger; fecundus; ~less irritus; ~tree pomum *n*

frustrate dirimo 3; disturbo 1

fry frigo 3; ~ing-pan sartago *f*

fuel ligna *n/pl.*; gather ~ lignor 1; *fig.* add ~ to faces subicio 3 (*dat.*)

fugitive caducus; fugax; profugus *m*; fugitivus *m*

fulfil expleo 2; perfungor 3; exsequor 3

full plenus (*abl.*); refertus (*abl., gen.*); frequens; satur (*cibo*); ~y copiose

fulminate intono 1

fume fumus *m*; stomachor 1

fumigate fumigo 1; vaporo 1

fun iocus *m*; ludus *m*

function officium *n*, munus *n*; ~ary magistratus, us *m* fund copia *f* (pecuniae); ~amental ultimus

funeral funus *n*; exsequiae *f/pl.*; funebris

funnel infundibulum *n*

funny ridiculus

fur pellis *f*; villi *m/pl.*, pili *m/pl.*\]

furbish interpolo 1 \[*m/pl.*\]

furious iratus; furibundus

furlong stadium *n*

furlough commeatus, us *m*

furnace fornax *f*

furnish praebeo 2; suppedito 1; orno 1 (*alqd re*)

furniture supellex *f*

furrow sulcus *m*; sulco 1

furry villosus

further ulterior; consulo 3 (*dat.*); *adv.* longius; praeterea; amplius; ~more porro

furtive furtivus

fury furor *m*; rabies *f*; furia *f*

fuse fundo 3; *fig.* confundo 1

fuss perturbatio *f*

fustian *fig.* tumor *m*; tumidus

futile futilis; vanus

future futurus; in, for the ~ in futurum, in posterum; futura *n/pl.*

G

gable fastigium *n*

gad-fly asilus *m*

gag praelego 1; obturamentum *n*

gage pignus *n*

gaiety hilaritas *f*

gain lucror 1; consequor 3, pario 3; paro 1; lucrum *n*; quaestus, us *m*; ~ful lucrosus

gainsay nego 1; contra dico 3

gait incessus, us *m*

gale ventus *m*

gall fel *n*; bilis *m*; mordeo 2

gallant fortis; amator *m*; ~ry virtus, utis *f*

gallery porticus, us *f*; pinacotheca *f*

galley navis *f* longa

galling mordax

gallop: at a ~ citato equo

gallows crux *f*; patibulum *n*

gambl|e alea ludo 3; ~er aleator *m*; ~ing alea *f*

gambol lascivio 4

game ludus *m*; lusus, us *m*; venatio *f*

gaming alea *f*

gammon perna *f*

gander anser, eris *m*

gang caterva *f*; operae *f/pl.*

gaol carcer, eris *m*; ~er custos *m*

gap lacuna *f*; ~e dehisco 3; hio 1; stupeo 2 (at *alqd*)

garb vestitus, us *m*

garbage quisquiliae *f/pl.*

garden hortus *m*; ~er hortulanus *m*

garland corona *f*; sertum *n*

garlic allium *n*

garment vestimentum *n*

garnish decoro 1

garret cenaculum *n*

garrison praesidium *n*; praesidio confirmo 1

garrulous loquax

garter periscelis, idis *f*

gash plaga *f*; vulnus *n*; seco 1

gasp anhelo 1; anhelitus, us *m*

gate porta *f*; ~post postis *m*; ~way limen *n*

gather colligo 3; confero 3; cogo 3; lego 3; *fig.* conicio 3 (*ex re*); in meto 3; ~ing coetus, us *m*

gaudy versicolor

gauge metior 4; modulus *m*

gauntlet caestus, us *m*

gay hilaris, hilarus; festus

gaze intueor 2; contemplo 1; obtutus, us *m*

gazette acta *n/pl.* diurna

gear instrumentum *n*

gelding canterius *m*

gem gemma *f*

gender genus *n*

general generalis; communis; universus: dux *m*, imperator *m*; become ~ increbresco 3; in ~ ad summam; ~ities loci *m/pl.* communes; ~ize universe loquor 3; ~ly plerumque; vulgo

generat|e pario 3; genero 1; ~ion saeculum *n*; aetas *f*

gener|osity liberalitas *f*; ~ous liberalis, generosus

genial benignus, comis

genius ingenium *n*

genteel politus

gentile gentilis

gentle lenis, mitis; nobilis;

~man generosus *m* (homo); ~manly honestus; ~ness lenitas *f*; mansuetudo *f*

genuine sincerus, verus, merus

geography geographia *f*

geomet|er geometres, ae *m*; ~ry geometria *f*

germ germen *n*; semen *n*; ~ane affinis; ~inate germino 1

gest|iculate gestum ago 3; ~iculation gestus, us *m*; iactatio *f*; ~ure gestus, us *m*; motus, us *m*

get adipiscor 3; nanciscor 3; pario 3; percipio 3 (*fructus*); impetro 1 (*quod postulo*); ~ something done curo 1 alqd faciendum; *v/impers.* fit; ~ abroad percrebresco 3; ~ along, on procedo 3; ~ back recupero 1; ~ out descendo 3 (*e curru*); ~ to pervenio 4 (*ad*); ~ up surgo 3

ghastly pallidus; foedus

ghost umbra *f*; Manes *m/pl.*; larva *f*

giant vir *m* eximia corporis magnitudine; praegrandis

gibbet furca *f*; patibulum *n*

gidd|iness vertigo *f*; ~y levis

gift donum *n*; munus *n*; facultas *f*; ~ed praeditus (*alqa re*); ingeniosus

gig cisium *n*

gigantic immanis

giggle cacchinno 1

gild inauro 1

gill quartarius *m*

gilt aureus, inauratus

gimlet terebra *f*

gin pedica *f*, plaga *f*

gingerly pedetemptim

gird cingor 3 (*alqa re*); ~le cingulum *n*

girl puella *f*; virgo *f*; ~ish virginalis

girth cingula *f*

gist summa *f*

give do 1; dono 1; tribuo 3; ~ one's word fidem interpono 3; ~ place, way to (de)cedo 3 (*alci*); ~ away largior 4; ~ back reddo 3; ~ in me dedo 4 (*alci*); ~ out me fero 3; ~ up trado 3; dimitto 3; ~ way to indulgeo 2 (*dat.*)

glad laetus; be ~ gaudeo 2, ~den hilaro 1

glade saltus, us *m*; nemus *n*

gladiator gladiator *m*; of a ~ gladiatorius

gladly libenter

glance oculos adicio 3 (*dat.*); aspectus, us *m*

gland glandula *f*

glar|e torvis oculis aspicio 3; fulgor *m*; ~ing fulgens; *fig.* manifestus

glass vitrum *n*; drinking ~ poculum *n* (vitreum); looking ~ speculum *n*; ~ware vitrea *n/pl.*; of ~ vitreus

gleam fulgeo 2; fulgor *m*, nitor *m*; ~ing nitidus

glean spicas lego 3; colligo 3

glee hilaritas *f*

glen convallis *f*

glib blandus; volubilis

glide labor 3

glimmer subluceo 2

glimpse conspicio 3; aspectus, us *m*

glitter fulgeo 2; corusco 1; fulgor *m*

gloat pascor (*alqa re*)

globe globus *m*; orbis *m* (terrarum)

gloom tenebrae *f/pl.*; caligo *f*; ~y tenebricosus, tenebrosus; tristis; ater

glori|fy celebro 1; augeo 2; ~ous praeclarus, amplus

glory gloria *f*; decus *n*; ~ in glorior 1 (*in re*)

gloss nitor *m*; interpretatio *f*; ~y nitidus

gloves manicae *f/pl.*

glow candeo 2, caleo 2; *fig.* ardeo 2; calor *m*; ardor *m*; ~worm cicindela *f*

glue gluten *n*; ~ together coagmento 1

glut satio 1; satietas *f*; ~ton helluo *m*; lurco *m*; ~tony edacitas *f*; gula *f*

gnarled nodosus

gnash frendeo 2

gnat culex *m*

gnaw rodo 3

go eo 4; vado 3; ~ well bene procedit 3 (*alci*); let ~ dimitto 3, omitto 3; ~ astray erro 1; ~ away discedo 3; ~ before anteeo 4 (*dat., acc.*); ~ by praetereo 4; sequor 3; ~ on flo 3; ~ over transeo 4; ~ up to subeo 4

goad stimulus *m*; ~ on stimulo 1 (*ad, in, ut*)

goal meta *f*; calx *f*
goat caper, pri *m*; capra *f*
go-between internuntius *m*
gobble devoro 1
goblet poculum *n*; scyphus *m*
god deus *m*; numen *n*; ~dess dea *f*; ~less impius; ~like divinus
gold aurum *n*; aureus; ~leaf brattea *f*; ~smith aurifex *m*
good bonus; probus; utilis (*ad*); bonum *n*, commodum *n*; ~s bona *n*/*pl*.; merx *f*; a ~ deal aliquantum (*gen*.); a ~ many complures; do ~ to prosum (*dat*.); make ~ sarcio 4; ~bye vale; ~day salve; ~for-nothing nequam; ~natured comis; ~will benevolentia *f*
goose anser, eris *m*
gore cruor *m*
gorge fauces *f*/*pl*.; ingurgito 1 (*me re*)
gorgeous magnificus
gormandise helluor 1
gory cruentus
gossip rumor *m*; sermo *m*; sermonem confero 3 (*cum alqo*); garrio 4; ~ing garrulus
gourd cucurbita *f*
gout podagra *f*; ~y arthriticus
govern impero 1 (*dat*.); rego 3, guberno 1, moderor 1 (*acc*.); ~ment administratio *f*; imperium *n*; res *f* publica; qui rei publicae

praesunt; ~or gubernator *m*; proconsul *m* or pro consule; praetor *m*; legatus *m*; praefectus *m*; be ~or praesum (*dat*.)
gown stola *f*; palla *f*
grace gratia *f*; venia *f*; elegantia *f*; decoro 1 (*alqd alqa re*); get into the good ~s of gratiam concilio 1 (*alcs*); ~ful decorus, venustus
gracious propitius, benignus
grade gradus, us *m*; locus *m*
gradually gradatim; paulatim; sensim
graft insero 3; surculus *m*
grain frumentum *n*; granum *n*, mica *f*
grammar grammatica *f*; ~ian grammaticus *m*
granary horreum *n*
grand grandis; magnificus; sublimis; ~daughter neptis *f*; ~eur maiestas *f*; ~father avus *m*; ~iloquent grandiloquus; ~mother avia *f*; ~son nepos *m*
grange villa *f*
grant concedo 3; permitto 3; tribuo 3
grape uva *f*; acinus *m* and ~um *n*; ~vine vitis *f*
graphic vividus
grapple luctor 1 (*cum*); ~ing-iron manus *f* ferrea
grasp comprehendo 3, complector 3 (*also fig*.); complexus, us *m*; manus, us *f*; ~ at appeto 3; ~ing avarus

grass gramen *n*; herba *f*;
~y herbidus, herbosus
grate (con)tero 3; strideo 2;
focus *m*
grateful gratus; be ~ gratiam habeo 2 (*alci*)
grati|fication expletio *f*;
voluptas *f*; ~fy gratificor 1
(*alci*); morem gero 3
(*alci*); expleo 2; ~fying
gratus; ~tude gratia *f*
gratuit|ous gratuitus; ~y
corollarium *n*
grave gravis, serius; austerus; sepulcrum *n*; from
the ~ ab inferis
gravel glarea *f*
grave|stone monumentum
n; ~yard sepulcra *n/pl.*
gravity gravitas *f*, severitas
f; momentum *n*
gravy ius *n*
graze *v/t.* pasco 3; perstringo 3 (*alqd alqa re*);
v/i. pascor 3
grease adeps *m and f*;
pingue *n*; ungo 3
great magnus; ingens; grandis; as, how ~ quantus; so
~ tantus; ~grandfather
proavus *m*; ~ly magno-
pere; valde; ~ness magni-
tudo *f*, amplitudo *f*
greed avaritia *f*; edacitas *f*;
~y avarus, avidus; cupidus
(*gen.*)
green viridis; prasinus;
crudus; ~s olus *n*; be ~
vireo 2; ~horn tiro *m*;
~ness viriditas *f*; cruditas
f; ~sward herba *f*; caespes
m

greet saluto 1; ~ing salutatio *f*
grey canus, albus; glaucus;
~ hair cani capilli *m/pl.*;
canities *f*
grief dolor *m*; luctus, us *m*;
maeror *m*
griev|ance querel(l)a *f*;
iniuria *f*; ~e *v/t.* dolore
afficio 3 (*alqm*); ango 3;
v/i. doleo 2 (*acc., abl.,
quod*); piget 2 (*me alcs
rei*); ~ous acerbus, gravis
grill torreo 2
grim torvus, atrox
grimace os torqueo 2
grimy squalidus
grin rideo 2
grind (con)tero 3; molo 3;
frendeo 2 (*dentibus*); ~
down opprimo 3; ~stone
cos *f*
grip comprehendo 3; ma-
nus, us *f*
grisly horridus
grizzled canus
groan (in)gemo 3 (*alqd*);
gemitus, us *m*
groin inguen *n*
groom agaso *m*
groove canalis *m*
grope praetento 1 (*iter*)
gross crassus; indecorus;
~ness magnitudo *f*; turpitudo *f*
grotto antrum *n*
ground terra *f*; solum *n*;
humus, i *f*; locus *m* (*aequus
etc.*); ~s causa *f*, ratio *f*;
on, to the ~ humi; gain ~
percrebresco 3 (*rumor*);
proficio 3; ~less vanus,

inanis; ~work fundamentum *n*

group circulus *m*; globus *m*; dispono 3

grove lucus *m*; nemus *n*

grovel me abicio 3 (*ad pedes*); ~ling humilis

grow *v/i.* cresco 3; adolesco 3; nascor 3; *fig.* fio 3; *v/t.* colo 3, sero 3; ~ long promitto 3 (*capillos etc.*) [*m*]

growl fremo 3; fremitus, us*]

grow|n up adultus; ~th incrementum *n*; auctus, us *m* [eruo 3]

grub vermiculus *m*; ~ up]

grudge invideo 2 (*dat.*); simultas *f*; bear a ~ against successeo 2 (*alci*)

gruel puls *f*

gruff asper

grumble murmuro 1

guarantee fides *f*; pignus *n*; fidem do 1 (*alci*); satisdo 1

guard custodio 4; tueor 2; praesideo 2 (*dat.*); custodia *f*; praesidium *n*; custos *m*; vigiliae *f/pl.* (*by night*); mount ~ custodiam ago 3; be on one's ~ caveo 2 (*alqd*); off one's ~ incautus; ~ed cautus; ~ian praeses *m and f*; tutor *m*

guess conicio 3; divino 1; coniectura *f*

guest hospes *m*; hospita *f*; conviva *m*

guidance consilium *n*

guide duco 3; rego 3; dux *m*

guild sodalitas *f*, societas *f*; collegium *n*

guile dolus *m*; ~ful dolosus

guilt noxa *f*; scelus *n*; culpa *f*; ~less innocens; ~y noxius, sons, nocens

guise species *f*

gulf sinus, us *m*, gurges *m*

gull mergus *m*; ludificor 1

gullet gula *f*

gullible credulus

gully fauces *f/pl.*

gulp singultus, us *m*; ~ down absorbeo 2

gum gingiva *f*; gummi *n*; lacrima *f*

gurgle murmuro 1 [1]

gush me profundo 3; emico]

gust aura *f*; flatus, us *m*; ~y ventosus

gut intestina *n/pl.*, viscera *n/pl.*; exintero 1

gutter fossa *f*; cloaca *f*; imbrex *f*

gymnas|ium palaestra *f*, gymnasium *n*; ~tic gymnicus; ~tics palaestra *f*

H

habit mos *m*; consuetudo *f*; habitus, us *m*; be in the ~ of soleo 2; ~ation domicilium *n*; ~ual usitatus

hack concido 3; caballus *m*; ~neyed tritus

haft manubrium *n*

hag anus, us *f*; ~gard macie confectus

hail saluto 1; salvere iubeo 2 (*alqm*); *int.* salve; grando *f*; *it* ~s grandinat hair capillus *m*; crinis *m*; pilus *m*; **~dresser** tonsor *m*; cinerarius *m*; **~less** glaber, calvus; **~y** pilosus, villosus

hale validus

half dimidius; dimidia pars *f*; dimidium; **~-breed** hibrida *m and f*; **~ hour** semihora *f*; **~-moon** luna *f* dimidia; **~-pound** selibra *f*; **~-witted** stultus; **~yearly** semestris

hall atrium *n*

hallow sacro 1; **~ed** sanctus

hallucination error *m* (mentis); somnium *n*

halo corona *f*

halt *v/t.* constituo 3; *v/i.* consisto 3; haesito 1; claudico 1; claudus; **~er** capistrum *n*

ham perna *f*; poples *m*

hamlet viculus *m*

hammer malleus *m*; tundo 3 (malleo)

hamper qualus *m*; impedio 4

hamstring poplites succido 3 (*alci*)

hand manus, us *f*; palma *f*; right, left **~** dext(e)ra, laeva; at **~** praesto, ad manum; be at **~** adsum (*dat.*); by **~** manu; in **~** in manibus; on the one **~** ... on the other **~** quidem ... sed, at ... contra; **~ to** comminus (*pugnare*); come to **~** venire ad manum; have a **~ in** intersum (*dat.*); **~ down, over** trado

3; **~ in** profiteor 2 (*nomen etc.*); **~ round** circumfero 3; **~book** libellus *m*; **~cuff** manicae *f/pl.*; **~ful** manipulus *m*

handi|craft artificium *n*; **~work** opus *n*

handkerchief sudarium *n*

handle tracto 1; ansa *f*; manubrium *n*

hand|maid ancilla *f*; **~some** pulcher, decorus, speciosus; liberalis; **~writing** chirographum *n*; manus, us *f*; **~y** habilis, dexter

hang *v/t.* suspendo 3 (*alqm, alqd, re, rex, de, in re*); affigo 3 (*ad, dat.*); *v/i.* pendeo 2; **~ back** dubito 1; **~ over** immineo 2 (*dat.*); let **~** demitto 3; **~er-on** assecla *m*; **~ing** suspendium *n*; **~ings** aulaea *n/pl.*; **~man** carnifex *m*

hanker after cupio 3

hap|hazardly temere; **~less** nfelix, **~ly** fortasse

happ|en accido 3 (that *ut*); contingo 3 (*dat.*); evenio 4; fio

happ|iness felicitas *f*; **~y** felix, beatus, fortunatus

harangue contionor 1 (*apud*); contio *f*

harass sollicito 1; vexo 1; fatigo 1

harbinger (prae)nuntius *m*

harbour portus, us *m*; *fig.* refugium *m*; excipio 3

hard durus; asper; difficilis, arduus; *adv.* valde, sedulo; **~ by** prope, iuxta; be **~**

pressed premor 3; ~en duro 1; become ~ened obduresco 3; ~hearted ferreus; ~ly vix, aegre; ~ness duritia f; ~ship iniuria f; labor m; ~ware ferramenta n/pl.; ~y robustus

hare lepus, oris m

harlot meretrix f

harm laedo 3; noceo 2 (dat.); iniuria f; incommodum n; ~ful nocens; ~less innocens

harmon|ious concors; ~ise concino 3; consentio 4; ~y concentus, us m; concordia f

harness freni m/pl.; frenos impono 3

harp cithara f; ~ upon canto 1

harrow rastrum n; occo 1

harsh asper, austerus, durus

hart cervus m

harvest messis f; demeto 3, percipio 3; ~er messor m

hast|e propero 1, festino 1; festinatio f; celeritas f; ~en accelero 1, maturo 1; ~ily propere, raptim; ~y properus, praeceps; iracundus

hat petasus m

hatch excludo 3; coquo 3 (consilium)

hatchet securis f

hate odi; ~ful invisus, odiosus; be ~ful to odio sum (alci)

hatred odium n

haught|iness superbia f,

arrogantia f; ~y superbus, arrogans

haul traho 3, rapio 3; ~ down, up de-, sub-duco 3 (naves); praeda f

haunch clunis f or m

haunt celebro 1, frequento 1; inquieto 1; latebra f

have habeo 2; teneo 2; est mihi; utor 3; I ~ to do this hoc mihi faciendum est

haven refugium n

havoc caedes f, clades f

hawk accipiter m; v/i. exscreo 1; v/t. vendito 1; ~er institor m

hay faenum n; ~-loft faenilia n/pl.

hazard in discrimen committo 3, voco 1; in aleam do 1; periculum n; alea f; ~ous periculosus

haze nebula f

hazel corylus, i f

he ille; ~ who is qui; ~ himself ipse

head caput n; vertex m; princeps m; be ~ of praesum (dat.); mil. ~ of a column primum agmen n; ~ foremost pronus; be brought to a ~ in discrimen adducor 3; hang over one's ~ supra caput est; lay ~s together capita conferre; make ~way proficio 3; ~ache capitis dolor m; ~band vitta f; ~land promontorium n; ~long praeceps; ~quarters principia n/pl.; ~strong pervicax

heal sano 1; medeor 2 (dat.);

coeo 4 (*vulnera*); ~er medicus *m*; ~ing sanatio *f*; salutaris

health sanitas *f*, valetudo *f*; **good, bad** ~ bona, infirma valetudo *f*; **drink one's** ~ propino 1 (*salutem alci*); ~ful salubris, salutaris; ~y sanus, validus

heap acervus *m*; cumulus *m*; ~ **up** coacervo 1; ~ **upon** congero 3 (*in alqm*)

hear audio 4 (*acc., acc. c. inf.*); percipio 3; *fig.* cognosco 3; give a ~ing aures praebeo 2 (*alci*)

hearken ausculto 1 (*alci*)

hearsay auditio *f*; rumor *m*

heart cor *n*; *fig.* pectus *n*; animus *m*; viscera *n/pl.*; **know by** ~ memoria teneo 2; ~**breaking** miserabilis; ~**felt** sincerus; ~**en** confirmo 1

hearth focus *m*

heart|ily summo studio; vehementer; ~**iness** studium *n*; ~**less** ferreus; ~**y** sincerus, comis

heat calor *m*, ardor *m*; aestus, us *m*; calefacio 3

heath planum *n*; loca *n/pl.* virgultis obsita

heathen paganus, barbarus

heave *v/i.* tumeo 2; tumesco 3; *v/t.* tollo 3; ~ **a** groan, sigh gemitum, suspirium do 1, duco 3

heaven caelum *n*; *fig.* superi *m/pl.*, di *m/pl.* immor-

tales; ~**ly** caelestis, divinus

heav|iness gravitas *f*; ~**y** gravis; crassus; aeger (*animi*); magnus (*imber etc.*)

hecatomb hecatombe *f*

hectic febriculosus; *fig.* incitatus

hedge saepes *f*; saepio 4; ~**hog** erinaceus *m*

heed oboedio 4 (*dat.*); take ~ curo 1; caveo 2; ~**ful** memor, cautus; ~**less** immemor (*gen.*); incautus

heel calx *f*; take to one's ~s me in pedes conicio 3

heifer iuvenca *f*

height altitudo *f*; proceritas *f*; locus *m* editus, superior; *fig.* fastigium *n*; summus; ~**en** amplifico 1; augeo 2

heinous atrox, nefarius

heir heres *m and f*

hell inferi *m/pl.*; ~**ish** infernus; nefandus

helm gubernaculum *n*; clavus *m*

helmet galea *f*, cassis *f*; ~**ed** galeatus

helmsman gubernator *m*

help adiuvo 1; subvenio 4 (*dat.*); opem fero 3; porrigo 3 (*cibus*); **I can't** ~ facere non possum quin; auxilium *n*, ops *f*; ~**er** adiutor *m*; ~**ful** utilis; ~**less** inops

hem ora *f*, instita *f*, ~ in circumsedeo 2; claudo 3

hemlock cicuta *f*

hemp cannabis *f*

hen gallina *f*

hence hinc; ita, ex quo; ~forth dehinc, posthac

her suus; eius

herald praeco *m*; praenuntio 1

herb herba *f*

herd grex *m*; pecus *n*; ~sman pastor *m*

here hic; ~ and there passim; be ~ adsum; ~abouts hic alicubi; ~after posthac, aliquando

hereditary hereditarius; paternus

here|sy prava opinio *f*; ~tical pravus

hereupon hic

heritage hereditas *f*

hermit homo *m* solitarius

hero heros *m*; vir *m* fortissimus; ~ic heroicus; ~ine heroina *f*, herois *f*; ~ism virtus, vis *f*, fortitudo *f*

heron ardea *f*

herself ipsa

hesita|ncy haesitatio *f*; ~te dubito 1; haesito 1, cunctor 1; ~tion haesitatio *f*

hew caedo 3; dolo 1

hiccup singulto 1, singultus, us *m*

hide *v/t.* celo 1; abdo 3, condo 3; dissimulo 1; *v/i.* lateo 2; corium *n*; pellis *f*

hideous foedus, taeter, informis

hiding verbera *n/pl.*; ~place latebrae *f/pl.*

high altus; (ex)celsus; sublimis; *fig.* summus, amplus; magnus (*price, etc.*);

~born generosus; ~lands loca *n/pl.* montuosa; ~ly magni (*aestimo*); ~priest pontifex *m*; ~-spirited ferox; ~way via *f*; ~wayman latro *m*

hilarity hilaritas *f*

hill collis *m*; clivus *m*; tumulus *m*; ~y clivosus

hilt manubrium *n*

himself ipse; se(met); by ~ solitarius, solus

hind cerva *f*; posterior

hind|er impedio 4 (*alqm a re*; *ne, quin, quominus*); obsto 1 (*alci*; *ne, quominus*); ~rance impedimentum *n*, mora *f*

hinge cardo *m*; ~ on vertor 3 (*in re*)

hint significo 1; significatio *f*; signum *n*

hip coxendix *f*

hire conduco 3; merces *f*; ~ling mercenarius *m*

his suus; eius

hiss sibilo 1; ~ off explodo 3; ~ing sibilus, us *m*

histor|ian rerum scriptor *m*; ~ical historicus; ~y historia *f*; res *f/pl.* (gestae)

hit ferio 4; percutio 3; ~ upon invenio 4; plaga *f*

hitch impedimentum *n*; ~ up succingo 3

hither huc; ~to adhuc; antehac

hive alvearium *n*

hoard recondo 3; thesaurus *m*

hoar|frost pruina *f*; ~iness canities *f*

hoarse raucus

hoary canus; priscus

hoax fallo 3; fallaciae *f/pl.*

hobble claudico 1

hobby studium *n*

hoe sarculum *n*

hog porcus *m*

hoist tollo 3; ~ sail vela do 1

hold teneo 2; gesto 1; capio 3; habeo 2, possideo 2; gero 3 (*magistratum*); ~ the belief that existimo 1, censeo 2; ~ good convenit 4 (*ad*); ~ one's tongue conticesco 3; ~ out sustineo 2; ~ with consentio 4; ~ na *f*; catch ~ of comprehendo 3; arripio 3

hole cavum *n*; foramen *n*

holiday feriae *f/pl.*; dies *m* festus; keep ~ ferior 1; ferias ago 3

holiness sanctitas *f*; numen *n*

hollow cavus; *fig.* vanus; fucatus; caverna *f*, cavum *n*; ~ out (ex)cavo 1

holy sanctus, divinus

homage observantia *f*, veneratio *f*

home domus, us *f*; domicilium *n*; at ~ domi; ~ (wards) domum; from ~ domo; drive, strike ~ adigo 3; domesticus; ~ly rusticus; ~sickness suorum desiderium *n*

honest probus, sincerus; ~y probitas *f*

honey mel *n*; ~comb favus *m*; ~ed mellitus

honorary honorarius

honour honor *m*; dignitas *f*; honestas *f*; word of ~ fides *f*; ~s iusta *n/pl.*; honoro 1; honesto 1; in honore habeo 2; orno 1, colo 3; ~able honestus

hood cucullus *m*; ~wink ludificor 1

hoof ungula *f*

hook hamus *m*; uncus *m*; hamo capio 3; ~ed aduncus

hoop circulus *m*

hoot cano 3; *fig.* obstrepo 3 (*alci*)

hop salio 4

hope spero 1 (*alqd, acc. c. inf.*); expecto 1 (*alqd*); spes *f*; lose, give up ~ despero 1

horizon prospectus, us *m*; ~tal aequus

horn cornu *n*; bucina *f*; corneus; ~ed cornutus

horri|ble horribilis, atrox, foedus; ~fy terreo 2; per-cello 3

horror horror *m*, pavor *m*

horse equus *m*; on ~back (in) equo; ~man eques *m*; ~-race certamen *n* equorum; ~shoe solea *f*; ~-whip flagellum *n*

hose tibiale *n*

hospit|able hospitalis; ~al valetudinarium *n*; ~ality hospitium *n*; liberalitas *f*

host hospes *m*; multitudo *f*; ~age obses *m*; ~elry caupona *f*; ~ess hospita *f*

hostil|e hostilis; inimicus, infestus, infensus; ~ity

inimicitiae *f/pl.*; ~ities
bellum *n*

hot calidus; aestuosus; be ~
caleo 2; aestuo 1; ~-headed
fervidus, calidus

hound canis *m or f* (venati-
cus); ~ on stimulo 1,
agito 1

hour hora *f*; half an ~ semihora *f*; from ~ to ~ in
horas; ~-glass horologium
n

house domus, us *f*; domicilium *n*; aedes *f*; tectum *n*;
at my ~ apud me; domo
excipio 3; condo 3; ~-
breaker fur *m*; ~hold familia *f*; ~hold gods Lares
m/pl., Penates *m/pl.*; ~-
keeper dispensator *m*; ~-
maid ancilla *f*; ~wife ma-
terfamilias *f*

hovel gurgustium *n*

hover (circum)volito 1; *fig.*
obversor 1 (*alci*; *ante alqm*)

how quomodo, quemadmo-
dum; *int.* quam, ut; ~
much quantus; ~ many
quot; ~ever utcumque;
tamen

howl ululo 1; ululatus, us *m*

hubbub clamor *m*

huckster institor *m*

huddled together confertus

hue color *m*

huff: be in a ~ stomachor 1

hug amplector 3; com-
plexus, us *m*   [manis]

huge ingens, vastus, im-}

hull alveus *m* (navis)

hum murmuro 1; musso 1;
bombus *m*; fremitus, us *m*

human humanus; ~ beings
homines *m/pl.*; ~e huma-
nus; ~ity humanitas *f*;
genus *n* humanum

humble humilis; demissus;
deprimo 3

humbug tricae *f/pl.*

humid umidus

humiliate deprimo 3; ~a-
tion dedecus *n*; ~ating
indignus; ~ty modestia *f*

humorous facetus, festivus

humour ingenium *n*; facetiae *f/pl.*; be in the ~ to
libet 2 (*alci c inf.*); morem
gero 3 (*alci*); gratificor 1

hump gibba *f*

hunchbacked gibber

hundred centum; a ~ times
centies, ~th centesimus

hunger fames *f*; inedia *f*;
esurio 4

hungry ieiunus

hunt venor 1; venatus, us
m, venatio *f*; ~er venator
m; ~ing spear venabulum
n; ~ress venatrix *f*

hurdle crates *f*

hurl conicio 3 (*in*); iaculor 1

hurricane procella *f*

hurr|ied praeceps; prae-
properus; ~iedly raptim; ~y
v/i. festino 1, propero 1,
curro 3; *v/t.* rapio 3; festi-
natio *f*

hurt noceo 2; laedo 3; doleo
2; be ~ acerbe fero 3 (*alqd*);
~ful noxius

husband maritus *m*; vir *m*;
~man agricola *m*; ~ry agri
cultura *f*; parsimonia *f*

hush st!, tace, tacete; sedo 1; ~ up celo 1

husk folliculus *m*; vagina *f*

husky raucus

hustle trudo 3

hut tugurium *n*; casa *f*

hutch cavea *f*

hyena hyaena*f*

hymeneal nuptialis

hymn carmen *n*; cano 3

hyperbole superlatio *f*

hypocri|sy (dis)simulatio *f*; ~te (dis)simulator *m*; ~tical simulatus, fictus

hypothesis sumptio *f*; on this ~ hoc posito

I

I ego

ic|e glacies *f*; ~icle stiria *f*; ~y glacialis, gelidus

idea notio *f*; notitia *f*; imago *f*; ~l perfectus; exemplum *n*

identi|cal idem; ~fy agnosco 3

ides idus, uum *f/pl.*

idiocy fatuitas *f*

idiom proprietas *f* (linguae); ~atic proprius

idiot imbecillus, fatuus (homo *m*)

idle otiosus, vacuus; deses, ignavus; (*of things*) vanus, irritus; be ~ cesso 1, vaco 1; ~ness pigritia *f*, desidia *f*

idol simulacrum *n*; *fig.* deliciae *f/pl.*; ~ise veneror 1

if si; ~ not sin, si minus; ~ ... not nisi; ~ only dummodo; but, even ~ quod si, etiamsi; I ask ~ rogo 1 num

ignite *v/t.* accendo 3; *v/i.* exardesco 3

ignoble ignobilis; turpis

ignominious turpis

ignor|ance ignoratio *f*, ignorantia *f*; inscitia *f*; ~ant ignarus, imprudens (*gen.*);

rudis; be ~ant ignoro 1; nescio 4; ~e praetereo 4; neglego 3

ill aeger, aegrotus; malus; malum *n*; be ~ aegroto 1; laboro 1; morbo afficior 3; speak ~ of maledico 3 (*alci*); ~-advised temerarius; ~-bred inhumanus, agrestis

illegal contra leges

illegitimate spurius, haud legitimus

ill-|fated infelix; ~ health valetudo *f* [tus]

illiterate illiteratus, indoc-*f*

ill|natured malevolus; ~omened dirus, infaustus; ~ temper stomachus *m*; ~-tempered iracundus, difficilis

illuminate illustro 1

illus|ion error *m*; species *f*; ~ory vanus

illustrat|e illustro 1; ~ion exemplum *n*

illustrious praeclarus, illustris

image imago *f*; simulacrum *n*, effigies *f*; species *f*

imagin|ary commenticius; ~ation cogitatio *f*; ~e animo fingo 3; puto 1

imbue imbuo 3, inficio 3 (*alqd alqa re*)

imitat|e imitor 1; effingo 3; ~ion imitatio *f*; imago *f*; ~or imitator *m*

immaculate integer

immature crudus

immeasurable immensus

immediate praesens; proximus; ~ly statim, protinus, continuo

immense ingens, immanis

immerse mergo 3

immigrant advena *m*

imminent praesens; be ~ immineo 2

immoderate immoderatus, nimius

immodest impudicus

immoral pravus, turpis; ~ity pravitas *f*; luxus, us *m*

immortal immortalis; aeternus; ~ity immortalitas *f*

immovable immobilis

immun|e immunis; ~ity immunitas *f*

immure includo 3

impair infringo 3; imminuo 3; elevo 1

impart impertio 4 (*alci alqd*); communico 1 (*cum alqo*)

impartial aequus, integer; ~ity aequitas *f*

impassable invius

impatien|ce ardor *m*; ~t impatiens (*gen.*); avidus (for *gen.*); be ~t for gestio 4 (*inf.*)

impeach accuso 1; postulo 1

impediment impedimentum *n*; ~ of speech haesitantia *f* (linguae)

impel impello 3 (*ad alqd, ut*)

impend impendeo 2; ~ing praesens, futurus

impenetrable invius, inaccessus

imperative necessarius

imperceptibly sensim

imperfect imperfectus; mancus, mendosus; ~ion vitium *n* [gustus]

imperial imperatorius; au-*f*

imperious imperiosus

imperishable immortalis

impersonate partes sustineo 2 (*alcs*)

impertinen|ce contumelia *f*; os *n*; ~t contumeliosus

imperturbable tranquillus

impervious (to) surdus (ad)

impetuous acer, fervidus

impetus vis *f*

impious nefarius, impius

implacable implacabilis; atrox

implant insero 3

implement instrumentum *n*

implicate implico 1; be ~d affinis, conscius sum

implicit tacitus

implore oro 1, obsecro 1

imply|y: be ~ied in inest (in)

impolite inhumanus

import importo 1 (*in*); significatio *f*; ~s merces *f/pl.* (importaticiae)

importan|ce momentum *n*, pondus *n*; be of ~ce interest (to me mea); ~t gravis, magnus; amplus

importun|ate improbus; ~e flagito 1

impos|e impono 3 (alqd alci); ~e upon impono 3 (alci); ~ition fraus f

impossible: it is ~ fieri non potest (quin)

impostor planus m

imprecation preces f/pl.

impregna|ble inexpugnabilis; ~te inicio 3

impress (per)moveo 2; inculco 1; imprimo 3; ~ion impressio f; opinio f; ~ive gravis

imprison in vincula, carcerem conicio; includo 3; ~ment vincula n/pl.

improbable haud veri similis

improper indecorus

improve v/t. corrigo 3; meliorem facio 3, reddo 3; v/i. melior fio; proficio 3

improvident improvidus

imprudence temeritas f, imprudentia f

impuden|ce impudentia f; os n; ~t impudens

impugn impugno 1

impulse impulsus, us m; impetus, us m

impunity: with ~ impune

impure impurus

impute do 1, attribuo 3, imputo 1 (alqd alqd)

in in (abl.); ~ Rome Romae; ~ summer aestate; ~ the writings of apud (alqm); ~ that quod

in|accessible invius; difficilis; ~accurate parum di-

ligens; ~action otium n; ~active iners; ~activity inertia f

in|adequate impar (dat.); ~advertently per imprudentiam; ~animate inanimus; ~appropriate parum aptus

inasmuch as quoniam; ~ he quippe qui

in|attentive parum attentus; ~augural aditialis; ~augurate inauguro 1; ~auspicious dirus; ~cantation carmen n

incapa|ble: be ~ble of non possum; alienus sum (ab); ~city inscitia f

in|cautious incautus; ~cense tus n; incendo 3 (ira); ~centive incitamentum n; ~cessant continuus, assiduus; ~cest incestum n

inch uncia f

incident casus, us m; res f; ~ally casu

incite incito 1; ~ment stimulus m

in|civility inhumanitas f; ~clement asper

inclin|ation voluntas f; animus m; studium n; ~e inclino 1; induco 3; clivus m; be favourably ~ed to inclinor 1 ad; I am ~ed to think haud scio 4 an, nescio 4 an

include includo 3; ascribo 3

incom|e vectigal n; ~parable singularis; ~patible repugnans; ~petence inscitia f; ~plete imperfectus incon|clusive infirmus; be ~gruous discrepo 1; ~siderate inconsideratus; ~sistent inconstans; absonus, alienus (ab); ~stant inconstans, levis; ~venience incommodum n; incommodo 1 (alci); ~venient incommodus

in|corporate contribuo 3; ascribo 3; ~correct falsus, mendosus; ~correctly perperam, prave; ~corrigible perditus; ~corruptible integer

increase v/t. augeo 2; amplifico 1; v/i. cresco 3; incrementum n

incred|ible incredibilis; ~ulous incredulus

in|criminate culpam (in alqm) transfero 3; ~culcate inculco 1

incur suscipio 3; incurro 3 (alqd)

in|curable insanabilis; ~cursion incursio f

indebted obnoxius; be ~ pecuniam debeo 2 (alci); fig. acceptum refero 3 (alqd alci) [turpis]

indecen|cy turpitudo f; ~t]

indeci|sion dubitatio f; ~sive dubius, anceps

indeed quidem; vero; ain' (vero)?

inde|fatigable impiger; ~finable nescio quis; ~finite infinitus

indelicate putidus

indemnify damnum sarcio 4; remuneror 1

independen|ce libertas f; ~t liber, solutus; sui iuris (homo)

inde|structible perennis; ~terminate anceps, dubius

index index m

indicat|e indico 1, significo 1; ~ion indicium n; signum n

indict accuso 1: reum facio 3; ~ment accusatio f; crimen n

indifferen|ce aequus animus m; neglegentia f; ~t neglegens; (of things) indifferens; be ~t to parvi facio 3 (alqd)

indi|genous indigena; ~gent inops; ~gestible gravis; ~gestion cruditas f

indign|ant: be ~ indignor 1 (alqd); stomachor 1 (alqa re); grave indignatio f; ira f; ~ity contumelia f, indignitas f

indirect obliquus

indis|creet imprudens; ~criminate promiscuus; adv. passim

indispos|ed aegrotus; ~ition valetudo f

indis|putable certus; ~tinct obscurus, obtusus

individual proprius; singuli

indolen|ce inertia f; ~t iners

indomitable invictus

indoor domesticus; ~s domi

induce adduco 3, induco 3 (alqm ut); persuadeo 2 (alci ut); ~ment praemium n; illecebra f

indulge indulgeo 2 (*dat.*);
morem gero 3 (*alci*); expleo 2 (*alqd*); ~nce in-
dulgentia; venia *f*, ~nt
indulgens, remissus

industr|ious industrius, se-
dulus, navus; ~y indu-\
striae [stria *f*]

inebriated ebrius

in|effectual irritus; ~effi-
cient invalidus; ~ept ineptus; ~ert segnis, immobilis;
~ertness segnitia *f*; ~evit-
able necessarius; ~ex-
haustible inexhaustus; ~exor-
able inexorabilis, durus;
~expensive vilis

inexper|ience imperitia *f*;
~ienced imperitus, rudis
(*gen.*); ~t inscitus

in|explicable inexplicabilis;
~expressible infandus; ~-
fallible certus

infam|ous infamis; flagitio-
sus; ~y flagitium *n*

infan|cy (prima) pueritia *f*,
infantia *f*; ~t infans *m*
and *f*; ~tile infans; ~try
pedes *m/sg.* and *pl.*, pedites *m/sg.* and *pl.*; pedita-
tus, us *m*; pedester

infatuat|ed demens; ~ion
dementia *f*

infect inficio 3; ~ion contagio *f*

infer colligo 3; ~ence coniectura *f*

inferior inferior, deterior;
impar (*dat.*)

infernal infernus; ~ regions
inferi *m/pl.*

infinit|e infinitus, immen-
sus; ~y infinitas *f*

infirm infirmus, imbecillus;
~ity infirmitas *f*

inflam|e in~, ac~cendo 3;
be ~ed flagro 1; ~matory
turbulentus

inflat|e inflo 1; be ~ed tur-
geo 2; ~ion tumor *m*

inflexib|ility pertinacia *f*;
~le obstinatus, rigidus

inflict infero 3; impono 3
(*alqd alci*); ~ punishment
poenam sumo 3 (*de
alqo*)

influen|ce momentum *n*;
auctoritas *f*; have ~ce
with possum apud; moveo
2; ~tial gravis, amplus

inform certiorem facio 3
(*alqm*); doceo 2; be ~ed
cognosco 3; ~ against no-
men defero 3 (*alcis*); ~ant
nuntius *m*; ~er delator *m*,
index *m*

infringe violo 1, imminuo
3; ~ment imminutio *f*

infuse infundo 3

ingen|ious sollers; ~uity
sollertia *f*; ~uous ingenuus

inglorious inglorius, turpis

ingrained insitus

ingrati|ate gratiam ineo 4
(*apud alqm*); ~tude in-
gratus animus *m*

inhabit teneo 2, incolo 3;
habito 1; able habitabi-
lis; ~ant incola *m* and *f*

inhere inhaereo 2 (*re, in re*);
insum

inherit hereditatem adeo 4,
capio 3; ~ance hereditas *f*;
~ed hereditarius

inhospitable inhospitalis; inhumanus

inhuman immanis, crudelis

iniquit|ous improbus; ~y scelus n

initia|l primus; ~te initio 1 (alqm alci rei)

injudicious inconsultus

injunction mandatum n

injur|e noceo 2, obsum (dat.); laedo 3; ~ious noxius, gravis; ~y damnum n, incommodum n; vulnus n; iniuria f

injustice iniustitia f; iniuria f

ink atramentum n

inland mediterraneus, interior

inlet aestuarium n

inmate inquilinus m

inmost intimus

inn caupona f; deversorium n

innate insitus, innatus

inner interior

innkeeper caupo m

innocen|ce innocentia f; ~t innocens; insons; castus

innovat|e novo 1; ~ion res f/pl. novae

innumerable innumerabilis

inoffensive innocens

inopportune inopportunus

inordinate immoderatus

inquir|e quaero 3 (alqd ab, de, alqo); percontor 1 (alqd ab alqo; alqm de re); interrogo 1 (alqm); ~e into inquiro 3 (in alqd); ~y percontatio f, interrogatio f; quaestio f

inquisitive percontator m

inroad incursio f; make an ~ incurro 3 (in)

insan|e insanus, vecors; ~ity insania f

insatiable insatiabilis

inscri|be inscribo 3 (alqd in re); ~ption inscriptio f; titulus m

insect insectum n

insecure instabilis

insensib|ility lentitudo f; ~le lentus

insert insero 3 (alqd in alqd, dat.); includo 3 (in re, in rem)

inside intra (acc.); adv. intus; interiora n/pl.

insight cognitio f

insignia insignia n/pl.

in|significant exiguus; nullius momenti; ~sincere fictus, simulatus

insinuate me insinuo 1 (alci); significo 1

insipid insulsus, frigidus

insist flagito 1; urgeo 2; insto 1

insolen|ce insolentia f, contumacia f; ~t superbus

insolvent: be ~ decoquo 3

insomuch adeo (ut)

inspect inspicio 3; recenseo 2 (exercitum); ~ion recensio f, recognitio f; ~or curator m

inspir|ation afflatus, us m; instinctus, us m; ~e fig. inicio 3, incutio 3 (alci alqd); ~ed instinctus (re)

instal|l inauguro 1; ~ment pensio f

instance *n* exemplum; for ~ verbi gratia

instant praesens; momentum *n* (temporis); ~ly continuo, statim

instead of pro (*abl.*); loco (*gen.*)

instigat|e instigo 1; at your ~ion instigante, auctore te

instil instillo 1

instinct impetus, us *m*; natura *f*; ~ive naturalis

institut|e in-, con-stituo 3; ~ion institutum *n*

instruct instituo 3; doceo 2; praecipio 3; mando 1 (*alci ut*); ~ion institutio *f*; mandatum *n*; ~ive utilis; ~or magister *m*

instrument instrumentum *n*; organum *n*; machina *f*; ~ality: by your ~ tua opera

insubordinate seditiosus

insufferable intolerabilis

insufficien|cy inopia *f*; ~t non satis (magnus)

insulate segrego 1

insult probrum *n*; contumelia *f*; contumeliam impono 3 (*alci*), iacio 3 (*in alqm*); ~ing contumeliosus

insupportable intolerabilis

insure caveo 2 (*ut*)

insur|gent turbulentus, seditiosus; ~rection tumultus, us *m*; defectio *f*

intact integer, incolumis

integr|al necessarius; ~ity integritas *f*, innocentia *f*

intell|ect mens *f*; ingenium *n*; ~igence mens *f*; intelligentia *f*; ingenium *n*; sollertia *f*; ~igent intellegens; ingeniosus

intempera|nce intemperantia *f*; ~te intemperans, immoderatus

intend in animo habeo 2, in animo est (mihi) (*inf.*); destino 1 (*alqd*)

intense magnus, acer

intens|ify incendo 3; ~ity vis *f*; ardor *m*

intent intentus (*re, in re*); totus (*in re*); be ~ on animum intendo 3 in (*re*); ~ion consilium *n*; ~ionally consulto; de industria; ~ness intentio *f*

inter sepelio 4

intercalary intercalarius

intercede deprecor 1 (for alqm; *ut, ne*)

intercept intercipio 3; excipio 3

intercession deprecatio *f*

interchange commuto 1 (*inter se*); vices *f/pl.*; vicissitudo *f*

intercourse usus, us *m*; consuetudo *f*; commercium *n*

interdict interdico 3 (*alci alqa re, alci alqd*)

interest delecto 1; capio 3; ~ oneself incumbo 3 (*dat.*); utilitas *f*; commodum *n*; it is of ~ interest (alicis, ad alqd); studium *n*; faenus *n* (on money); gain the ~ of gratiam concilio 1 (*alcis*); ~ing iucundus

interfere me interpono 3

(*dat.*, *in alqd*); intercedo 3, intervenio 4 (*dat.*); **~nce** intercessio *f*

interim: in the **~** interim

interior interior; **pars** *f* interior; interiora *n/pl.*

interlude *thea.* embolium *n*

intermedia|ry internuntius *m*; **~te** medius

interment sepultura *f*

intermingle misceo 2

intermission intermissio *f*; without **~** assidue

internal intestinus, domesticus; interior

interpose interpono 3, intercedo 3

interpret interpretor 1; explano 1; **~ation** interpretatio *f*; **~er** interpres *m*

interrogat|e interrogo 1; **~ion** interrogatio *f*; quaestio *f*

interrupt interrumpo 3 (*orationem*, *etc.*); interpello 1 (*alqm*); **~ion** interpellatio *f*

intersperse misceo 2

interval spatium *n* (*inter*); intervallum *n*; after an **~** of a year anno interiecto; in the **~** interim

interven|e intercedo 3, intersum; interpello 1; intervenio 4; **~ing** medius; **~tion** intercessio *f*

interview admitto 3; colloquor 3 (*cum alqo*, *inter se*); colloquium *n*

intestate intestatus

intestines intestina *n/pl.*

intima|cy familiaritas *f*, necessitudo *f*; **~te** familiaris; intimus *m*; significo 1; intimus *n*; **~tion** denuntiatio *f*

intimidat|e terreo 2; **~ion** minae *f/pl.*

into in (*acc.*)

intolera|ble intolerabilis; **~nt** intolerans

intoxicat|ed ebrius; **~ion** ebrietas *f*

intrench vallo et fossa munio 4; **~ment** vallum *n*, munimentum *n*

intrepid intrepidus, fortis; **~ity** fortitudo *f*

intricate implicatus

intrigue dolus *m*; fallaciae *f/pl.*

introduc|e intro-, in-duco 3; inveho 3; **~tion** inductio *f*; *liter.* prooemium *n*, exordium *n*; praefatio *f*; give an **~ion** commendo 1 (*alqm alci*); letter of **~ion** litterae *f/pl.* commendaticiae

intrude inculco 1 (*me alci*)

inundat|e inundo 1; **~ion** diluvies *f*, diluvium *n*

inure duro 1

invade invado 3 (*in*); bellum infero 3 (*dat.*)

invalid aegrotus (*homo*); irritus; **~ate** infirmo 1; labefacto 1

invaluable inaestimabilis

invariable constans

invasion irruptio *f*

invective convicium *n*

inveigh against invehor 3 (*in*); insector 1, incesso 3

inveigle pellicio 3

invent reperio 4; excogito 1; ⁓ion inventum *n*; commentum *n*; ⁓or inventor *m*, auctor *m*

invert inverto 3

invest inauguro 1 (*alqm magistratum*); addo 3 (*alqd alci rei*); circumsedeo 2 (*urbem, etc.*); colloco 1 (*pecuniam in re*)

investigat|e investigo 1; quaero 3; ⁓ion investigatio *f*; quaestio *f*

inveterate inveteratus

invidious invidiosus, invisus

invigorate corroboro 1; confirmo 1

in|vincible invictus; ⁓violate** inviolatus, sacrosanctus; ⁓visible** obscurus, caecus

invit|ation invitatio *f*; ⁓e** invito 1, voco 1 (*alqm in, ad*); accerso 3; ⁓ing** gratus, blandus

invoke invoco 1, imploro 1

involuntar|y coactus, ⁓ily** imprudenter; haud sponte

involve contineo 2; affero 3; admisceo 2; be ⁓d** in versor 1, implicor 1 (*abl.*)

inward interior, ⁓ly** penitus

irascible iracundus

ire ira *f*

irk piget 2 (*me alcs rei*); ⁓some** molestus

iron ferrum *n*; ferreus; ⁓s** vincula *n/pl.*; ⁓mongery** ferramenta *n/pl.*

irony ironia *f*; dissimulatio *f*

irrational fatuus; brutus

irreconcilable repugnans

ir|recoverable irreparabilis; ⁓refutable** certissimus

irregular inaequabilis, incompositus, tumultuarius (*milites*)

irrelevant: be ⁓ nihil attinet

ir|religious impius; ⁓reparable** irreparabilis; ⁓reproachable** integer; ⁓resistible** invictus; ⁓resolute** dubius; ⁓revocable** irrevocabilis

irrigat|e irrigo 1; ⁓ion** irrigatio *f*

irrita|ble stomachosus; ⁓te** stomachum moveo 2 (*alci*); irrito 1; ⁓tion** stomachus *m*

island insula *f*; ⁓er** insulanus *m*

isolate intercludo 3; secerno 3

issue *v/i.* evenio 4; *v/t.* edo 3; metior 4 (*frumentum*); ⁓ forth** egredior 3; eventus, us *m*; exitus, us *m*; egressus, us *m*; res *f*; liberi *m/pl.*; the main ⁓ summa *f*

it id

itch prurio 4; *fig.* gestio 4; prurigo *f*

iterat|e itero 1; ⁓ion** iteratio *f*

itinerant vagus

ivory ebur *n*; eburneus

ivy hedera *f*

J

jackdaw monedula *f*
Jack-of-all-trades omnis Minervae homo *m*
jaded defessus
jagged scopulosus
jail carcer, eris *n*; ~er custos *m*
jam conditae baccae *f/pl.*
jamb postis *m*
January Ianuarius *m*
jar discrepo 1; olla *f*; cadus *m* (wine); a~ semiapertus; ~ring discors, dissonus
jaunty hilaris
javelin pilum *n*, iaculum *n*
jaw malae *f/pl.*; maxilla *f*; *fig.* fauces *f/pl.*
jealous invidus, aemulus; be ~ of invideo 2 (*alci*); ~y invidia *f*, aemulatio *f*
jeer cavillor 1, derideo 2; irrisio *f*
jeopard|ise periclitor 1; ~y periculum *n*
jest iocor 1; cavillor 1; iocus *m*; in ~ per iocum; ~er cavillator *m*, sannio *m*, scurra *m*
jet: ~ of water aqua *f* saliens; ~black niger; ~ty moles *f*, crepido *f*
Jew Iudaeus *m*
jewel gemma *f*; ~led gemmeus; ~ler aurifex *m*
Jewish Iudaicus
jibe convicium *n*
jilt repudio 1
jingle tinnio 4
job opus *n*; negotium *n*

jockey eques *m*
joc|ose iocosus; ~und hilaris
join (con)iungo 3; connecto 3; me adiungo 3 (*alci, ad*); ~ in intersum (*dat.*); ~ together coeo 4; ~er faber, bri *m*
joint commissura *f*; articulus *m*; nodus *m*; com]
joist tignum *n* [munis]
joke iocus *m*; iocatio *f*; iocor 1 (*de*); cavillor 1
jolly hilaris, festivus
jolt quasso 1, iacto 1; iactatio *f*
jostle trudo 3
jot: not a ~ ne pilus quidem; I don't care a ~ non pili facio 3 (*alqd*)
journal ephemeris *f*; commentarii *m/pl.*
journey iter, ineris *n*; iter facio 3; proficiscor 3
jovial hilaris
joy gaudium *n*; laetitia *f*; gaudeo 2; ~ful laetus
jubilant exsultans
judge iudico 1; reor 2, existimo 1, aestimo 1; iudex *m*, quaesitor *m*; existimator *m*; ~ment iudicium *n*; arbitrium *f*; pronounce ~ment ius dico 3; good ~ment consilium *n*
judic|ial iudicialis, iudiciarius, forensis; ~ious prudens

juic|e sucus *m*; ~y suco-
sus

jug urceus *m*

juggl|er praestigiator *m*;
~ing praestigia *f/pl.*

July Quintilis *m*; Iulius *m*

jumble confundo 3

jump salio 4; saltus, us *m*

juncture tempus *n*

June Iunius *m*

jungle loca *n/pl.* obsita
(*virgultis etc.*)

junior minor natu

juniper iuniperus, i *f*

juris|consult iuris consultus

m; ~diction iurisdictio *f*;
~t iuris consultus *m*

jur|or iudex *m*; ~y iudices
m/pl.

just iustus, aequus; meritus; *adv.* vix; modo; ~ as
perinde ac; ~ when cum
maxime; commodum ...
cum

just|ice iustitia *f*; ~ifiably
iure; ~ification purgatio *f*;
~ify purgo 1, excuso 1

jut| out exsto 1; promineo
2; ~ting proiectus

juvenile iuvenilis

K

keel carina *f*

keen acer, sagax; studio-
sus; ~ness sagacitas *f*,
acies *f*

keep teneo 2, retineo 2;
servo 1 (*fidem etc.*); habeo
2; custodio 4; condo 3
(*frumentum etc.*); ~ ac-
counts tabulas conficio 3;
~ away abstineo 2 (*me,
alqm*); ~ company con-
gregor 1 (*cum*); ~ holiday
festum diem celebro 1; ~
in the dark cælo 1 (*alqd
alqm*); ~ off arceo 2; ~ up
tueor 2; ~up with subse-
quor 3; arx *f*; ~er custos
m; ~ing custodia *f*; in ~ing
with convenies (*dat.*);
~sake pignus *n*

keg cadus *m*

kennel cubile *n*

kerchief sudarium *n*

kernel nucleus *m*

kettle olla *f*

key clavis *f*; ~hole foramen
n

kick calce ferio 4, peto 3;
calx *f*

kid haedus *m*

kidnap surripio 3

kidneys renes *m/pl.*

kill interficio 3, occido 3,
caedo 3; neco 1; ~ing
caedes *f*

kiln fornax *f*

kin propinqui *m/pl.*, necessarii *m/pl.*

kind benignus, comis; ge-
nus *n*; of this ~ huiusmodi; of such a ~ talis ...
(qualis)

kindle *v/t.* ac~, in~cendo 3;
inflammo 1; *v/i.* exar-
desco 3

kindness benignitas *f*, comitas *f*; beneficium *n*; officium *n*

kindred propinqui *m/pl.*; necessarii *m/pl.*; cognatus, consanguineus; *fig.* finitimus

king rex *m*; be ~ regno 1; ~dom regnum *n*; ~ly regius

kinsman necessarius *m*

kiss suavior 1, osculor 1; suavium *n*, osculum *n*

kitchen culina *f*

kite milvus *m*

knack sollertia *f*

knapsack sarcina *f*

knav|e nebulo *m*, furcifer *m*, scelestus *m*; ~ery nequitia *f*; ~ish nequam, improbus

knead subigo 3

knee genu *n*; ~l nitor 3 genibus

knife culter *m*

knight eques *m*; ~ly equester

knit: ~ the brows supercilium contraho 3

knob bulla *f*; umbilicus *m*; nodus *m*

knock pulso 1; ferio 4; ~ at the door fores pulso 1; ~ down sterno 3; (*at an auction*) addico 3 (*alci alci*); pulsatio *f*; ~-kneed varus

knot nodus *m*; *fig.* vinculum *n*; (*of people*) corona *m*; nodo 1; ~ty nodosus

know scio 4; (*cog*)nosco 3; not to ~ nescio 4, ignoro 1; be ~n constat 1; make ~n declaro 1; ~ledge scientia *f*; cognitio *f*; doctrina *f*; without the ~ledge of clam (*abl.*); to my ~ledge quod sciam; well-~n notus, celeber

L

label titulus *m*

laborious operosus

labor laboro 1; contendo 3 (*inf.*); labor *m*; opera *f*; partus, us *m*; ~er operarius *m*, mercenarius *m*

lace necto 3; alligo 1

lacerate lacero 1

lack egeo 2, careo 2; mihi deest; inopia *f*; defectio *f*

lackey pedisequus *m*

lacking: be ~ deficio 3, desum [sum]

lad puer *m*

ladder scalae *f/pl.*

lade onero 1; ~n onustus, gravis

ladle trulla *f*

lady matrona *f*, mulier *f*; ~ship domina *f*, era *f*

lag cesso 1; ~gard cessator *m*

lake lacus, us *m*; stagnum *n*

lamb agnus *m*; (*meat*) agnina *f*

lame claudus *m*; be ~ claudico 1; ~ness claudicatio *f*

lament lugeo 2; miseror 1; lamentor 1; ~able miserandus; ~ation lamentatio *f*; plangor *m*

lamp lucerna *f*; ~stand lychnuchus *m*

lampoon versus *m/pl.* probrosi, famosi

lamprey murena *f*

lance hasta *f*, lancea *f*; telum *n*; incido 3

land terra *f*, tellus, uris *f*; solum *n*; ager, gri *m*; terrestris; *v/t.* expono 3; *v/i.* egredior 3 (e nave)

land|ing egressus, us *m*; ~lady caupona *f*; ~lord caupo *m*; ~mark lapis *m*; ~owner (agri) possessor *m*; ~slide lapsus, us *m* terrae; ~tax vectigal *n*

lane angiportus, us *m*

language lingua *f*; oratio *f*, verba *n/pl.*, sermo *m*

langu|id languidus; be ~id langueo 2; ~ish tabesco 3; ~or lassitudo *f*

lank strigosus

lantern lanterna *f*

lap gremium *n*; sinus, us *m*; lambo 3

lapse labor 3; error *m*; ~ of time spatium *n*

larceny furtum *n*

lard adeps *m*; laridum *n*; ~er carnarium *n*

large magnus, grandis, amplus, ingens; ~ss donativum *n*; largitio *f*

lark alauda *f*

lascivious libidinosus

lash flagello 1; flagellum *n*; verbera *n/pl.*

lass puella *f*

lassitude lassitudo *f*

last ultimus, postremus; extremus, ~ night proxima nocte; in the ~ three days his tribus diebus; ~ but one proximus a postremo; forma *f*; at ~ postremo, ad extremum, demum, denique; duro 1; maneo 2; ~ing diuturnus; ~ly denique

late serus; ~ at night sera, multa nocte; ~ in life provecta iam aetate; the ~ (de)mortuus (*alqs*), recens (*alqd*); *adv.* sero; ~ly nuper, modo, recens

Latin Latinus; speak ~ Latine loquor 3

latitude libertas *f*

latter posterior; the ~ hic; ~ly nuper

lattice cancelli *m/pl.*

laudable laudabilis

laugh rideo 2; cachinno 1; ~ at irrideo 2 (*acc.*); risus, us *m*; ~able ridiculus; ~ing-stock ludibrium *n*

launch deduco 3 (*naves*); ~ at iaculor 1 (*in*); inmitto 3 (*in*)

laurel laurus, i *f* (*tree and wreath*); laureus

lavish pro-, ef-fusus; profundo 3; largior 4 (*alqd alci*)

law lex *f*; the ~ ius *n*; go to ~ litem intendo 3 (*alci*); propose, enact a ~ fero 3, scisco 3 legem; ~ful legitimus; ~less seditiosus; ~lessness licentia *f*

lawn pratum *n*

lawsuit lis *f*

lawyer iuris consultus *m*

lax dissolutus, remissior, neglegens; ~ness neglegentia *f*

lay pono 3; loco 1; edo 3 (*ova*); ~ aside repono 3; ~ before defero 3, propono 3; ~ down arms ab armis discedo 3; ~ hold of prehendo 3; ~ plans consilium capio 3, ineo 4; ~ siege to obsideo 2; ~ waste vasto 1; cantus,\

layer tabulatum *n* [us *m*]

laziness pigritia *f*; ~y ignavus, piger

lead¹ plumbum *n*; plumbeus

lead² duco 3; ~ back, out, round re-, e-, circum-duco 3; ~ a life vitam ago 3; ~er dux *m*; be ~er praesum (*dat.*)

leading primus, princeps; ~ men principes *m/pl.*

leaf folium *n*; (*of book*) scheda *f*, pagina *f*; (*of door*) foris *f*; be in ~ frondesco 3; ~y frondosus

league societas *f*; be in ~ conspiro 3, coniuro 1

leak perfluo 3; rima *f*; ~y rimosus

lean macer; (in)nitor 3 (*abl.*); incumbo 3 (*in alqd*); ~ness macies *f*

leap salio 4; saltus, us *m*

learn disco 3; cognosco 3, certior fio; be ~ed doctus, eruditus; ~ing doctrina *f*, eruditio *f*

lease conduco 3; loco 1; locatio *f*

least minimus; at ~ saltem, certe

leather corium *n*; scorteus

leave relinquo 3, destituo 3 (*acc.*); discedo 3 (*ab, ex*); excedo 3 (*ex loco*); (*at death*) lego 1; ~ off desino 3; ~ out omitto 3; potestas *f*; ~ of absence commeatus, us *m*; by your ~ bona tua venia

lecherous salax

lecture schola *f*, acroasis *f*; scholas habeo 2; ~room schola *f*

ledge tabula *f*; pluteus *m*; ~r codex *m*

leech hirudo *f*

leek porrum *n*

lees faex *f*

left laevus, sinister; ~ over reliquus; be ~ over resto 1

leg crus, uris *n*

legacy legatum *n*; ~-hunter captator *m*

legal legitimus; ex lege

legate legatus *m*; legatio *f*

legend fabula *f*; ~ary commenticius

legion legio *f*; ~ary legionarius *m*

legislate leges scribo 3

legitimate legitimus; germanus

leisure otium *n*; at ~ otiosus, vacuus; be at ~ vaco 1; ~ly lentus

lend mutuum (*alqd*) do 1 (*alci*); commodo 1 (*alqd alci*)

length longitudo *f*; diurnitas *f* (temporis); at ~ tandem; demum; late, fuse (*loqui*); ~en produco 3; ~wise in longitudinem

lenient mitis, lenis

lentil lens *f*

less minor; *adv.* minus; much, still ~ nedum (*subj.*); ~ee conductor *m*; ~en minuo 3

lesson *fig.* documentum *n*; take ~s disco 3; audio 4)

lessor locator *m* [(*alqm*)

lest ne

let permitto 3; sino 3; loco 1 (*agrum etc.*); ~ alone abstineo 2 (*me re*); ~ down demitto 3; ~ loose, go emitto 3

lethargy veternus *m*

letter littera *f*; epistola *f*, litterae *f/pl.*; ~-carrier tabellarius *m*

lettuce lactuca *f*

level planus, aequus; ~ place planities *f*; *fig.* gradus, us *m*; make ~ with exaequo 1 (*alqd alci rei*); sterno 3 (*muros*)

lever vectis *f*

levity iocatio *f*

levy delectus, us *m*; delectum habeo 2, scribo 3; impero 1 (*alqd alci*)

lewd incestus

liable obnoxius (*dat.*)

liar (homo *m*) mendax

libation libamentum *n*; make ~ libo 1

libel diffamo 1; libellus *m* (*famosus*)

liberal liberalis, benignus; ~ity liberalitas *f*

liberat|e solvo 3; libero 1; ~ion liberatio *f*

liberty libertas *f*; be at ~ to licet 2 (*dat. c. inf.*)

library bibliotheca *f*

licen|ce potestas *f*; venia *f*; licentia *f*; ~se potestatem do 1 (*alci*); ~tious libidinosus

lick lambo 3, lingo 3

lictor lictor *m*

lid operculum *n*; eye~ palpebra *f*

lie mentior 4 (*in alqa re*); iaceo 2; cubo 1, recumbo 3; (*of places*) situm esse; as far as in me ~s quantum in me est; ~ in wait insidior 1 (*dat.*); mendacium *n*

lieu: in ~ of loco (*gen.*)

lieutenant legatus *m*

life vita *f*; anima *f*; vigor *m*, viriditas *f*; ~(time) aetas *f*; in his ~time vivus (*adj.*); ~less exanimis; frigidus

lift tollo 3; levo 1; sublevo 1; effero 3

ligature ligamentum *n*

light lux *f*; lumen *n*; see in a good, unfavourable ~ in mitiorem, deteriorem partem accipio 3 (*alqd*); set ~ to accendo 3; illustris; levis; grow ~ lucesco 3; make ~ illustro 1; make ~ of contemno 3; ~ upon offendo 3 (*acc.*); ~-armed troops levis armatura *f*; velites *m/pl.*

lighten *v/t.* levo 1; *v/i.* fulguro 1, fulgeo 2

light|house pharus, i *f*; **~ness** levitas *f*; **~ning** fulmen *n*

like similis (*gen.*); par (*dat.*); *adv.* similiter (*ac*); modo, ritu (*gen.*); velut(i); me iuvat 1; amo 1 (*inf.*); mihi libet 2, placet 2; **~ly** veri similis; it is **~ly** fieri potest (*ut*); **~n** comparo 1; **~ness** similitudo *f*; effigies *f*; **~wise** item

liking animus *m*

lily lilium *n*

limb membrum *n*; articulus *m*

lime calx *f*; **bird-~** viscum *n*; **~ tree** tilia *f*

limit finis *m*; modus *m*; terminus *m*; finio 4; circumscribo 3; **~ed** circumscriptus, certus; **~less** infinitus

limp claudico 1; languidus; **~et** lepas *f*

limpid liquidus

line linea *f*; (*battle*) acies *f*; (*of march*) agmen *n*; (*poetry*) versus, us *m*; **~s** ordines *m/pl.*; **~ up** in ordinem instruo 3, dispono 3

line|age genus *n*; **~ament** lineamentum *n*

linen linteum *n*; linteus, lineus

linger moror 1, cunctor 1; **~ing** tardus

link connecto 3; iungo 3; vinculum *n*

lion leo *m*; **~ess** leaena *f*

lip labrum *n*; *fig.* os *n*

liqu|efy liquefacio 3; **~id** liquidus; liquidum *n*; liquor *m*

lisping blaesus

list tabula *f*; index *m*

listen ausculto 1; audio 4; **~er** auditor *m*

listless languidus

literal|ly ad litteram; **~ture** litterae *f/pl.*

litigate litigo 1

litter lectica *f*; fetus, us *m*

little parvus, exiguus; (*time*) brevis; **for a ~** time paulisper; **a ~** paulum; too **~** parum

live vivo 3, spiro 1; vitam ago 3; **~ in** habito 1 (*acc.*); **~ on, off** vescor 3 (*abl.*); vivus

livel|ihood victus, us *m*; **~iness** alacritas *f*; **~y** alacer, laetus

liver iecur *n*

livid lividus

living vivus; victus, us *m*

lizard lacerta *f*

lo ecce, en

load onero 1 (*abl.*); *fig.* congero 3 (*alqd in alqm*); onus *n*; **~ed** onustus

loaf panis *m*

loam lutum *n*

loan: make a ~ mutuum do 1 (*alqd*); **obtain a ~** mutuor 1 (*alqd*)

loath invitus

loath|e odi; fastidio 4; **~ing** fastidium *n*; **~some** foedus, taeter

lobby vestibulum *n*

lobster locusta *f*

locality locus *m*

lock obsero 1; sera *f*; floccus *m*; ~ out excludo 3; ~ up concludo 3; ~s crines *m/pl.*

locust locusta *f*

lodge deversor 1, deverto 3 (*in*, *apud*); maneo 2; ~r inquilinus *m*; deversor *m*

lodging deversorium *n*, hospitium *n*

loft cenaculum *n*; ~iness excelsitas *f*; ~y excelsus, altus, sublimis

log tignum *n*; stipes *m*

loggerheads: be at ~ discordo 1 (*ab*, *inter se*)

logic dialectica *f*; ~al dialecticus; ~ian dialecticus *m*

loin lumbus *m*

loiter cunctor 1, cesso 1

lonel|iness solitudo *f*; ~y solus, solitarius

long longus; procerus; (*time*) diuturnus; promissus (*capillus*); *adv.* diu; ~ ago iam pridem; ~ after, before multo ante, post; how ~ quamdiu; ~ to aveo 2, gestio 4 (*inf.*); ~ for desidero 1; ~ed-for exspectatus; ~ing desiderium *n*

look speciem habeo 2, praebeo 2 (*honesti, ridentis, etc.*); ~ (at) aspicio 3; intueor 2 (*alqd*); ~ after colo 3; ~ down (on) despicio 3 (*acc.*); ~ for quaero 3; ~ forward exspecto 1; ~ out! cave; ~ round circumspicio 3; ~ towards specto 1; ~ up (to) suspicio 3; aspectus, us *m*; obtutus, us *m*; vultus, us *m*; ~er-on spectator *m*; ~ing-glass speculum *n*

loom tela *f*

loop retinaculum *n*; ~hole fenestra *f*; locus *m*

loose laxus, solutus; mobilis; *fig.* dissolutus; let ~ emitto 3; ~n laxo 1; remitto 3; solvo 3; ~ness pravitas *f*

lop amputo 1; ~-sided inaequalis

loquacious loquax

lord dominus *m*; ~ it over dominor 1 (*in*), ~ly regius, superbus

lore doctrina *f*

lose amitto 3; perdo 3; ~ heart animo deficio 3; ~ an opportunity tempori desum; ~ the day vincor 3

loss damnum *n*, detrimentum *n*; be at a ~ haereo 2

lot sors *f*; *fig.* fortuna *f*; by ~ sorte, sortito; cast ~s (for) sortibus utor 3; sortior 4 (*acc.*); it falls to my ~ mihi contingit 3

loud magnus, clarus

lounge otior 1; desideo 2

louse pediculus *m*; pedis *m*

love amo 1, diligo 3; me iuvat 1, cordi est mihi (*alqd, inf.*); amor *m*; studium *n*; caritas *f*; fall in ~ with adamo 1; ~-affair amor *m*; ~liness venustas f; ~ly venustus, amabilis; ~r amator m; amans m

loving amans

low humilis, demissus; ‡gravis; summissus; obscurus; sordidus, abiectus; mugio 4; ~born ignobilis; ~er inferior; demitto 3; abicio 3; ~ering minax; ~est infimus, imus; ~ing mugitus, us m; ~lands loca n/pl. campestria; ~spirited demissus

loyal fidelis, fidus; ~ty fides f

lozenge pastillus m

lubricate ungo 3

lucid lucidus, clarus

luck fors f, fortuna f; good ~ felicitas f; ~less infelix; ~y felix, fortunatus; faustus

lucrative fructuosus

ludicrous ridiculus

luggage impedimenta n/pl.; sarcinae f/pl.

lukewarm tepidus; frigidus

lull sedo 4; sopio 4; ~aby nenia f

lumber scruta n/pl.

lumin|ary lumen n; ~ous lucidus

lump massa f; glaeba f; ~ish crassus

lun|acy insania f; ~ar lunaris; ~atic insanus

lunch prandium n; ~ (on) prandeo 2

lung pulmo m

lurch: leave in the ~ derelinquo 3

lure pellicio 3; esca f; illecebrae f/pl.

lurk lateo 2; latito 1

luscious praedulcis

lust libido f; ~ful libidinosus

lustra|l lustralis; ~tion lustratio f

lustre nitor m, splendor m

lusty validus

luxuri|ant luxuriosus; ~ous lautus, delicatus

luxury luxuria f, lautitia f; luxus, us m

lying mendax; ~in puerperium n

lynx lynx m and f; ~eyed lynceus

lyre lyra f, cithara f; fides f/pl.; ~player citharoedus m

lyric lyricus; carmen n lyricum

M

machin|ations fallaciae f/pl., artes f/pl.; ~e machina f; ~ery machinatio f

mackerel scomber, bri m

mad insanus; be ~ furo 3

madam domina f

mad|den mentem alieno 1

(alci); irrito 1; ~man homo m furiosus; ~ness insania f; furor m

magazine armamentarium n

maggot vermiculus m [n]

magic magicus; magica ars f; ~ian magus m

magist|erial imperiosus;
~racy magistratus, us *m*;
~rate magistratus, us *m*

magnanim|ity magnanimitas *f*; ~ous magnanimus

magnet lapis *m* magnes

magnificen|ce magnificentia *f*; ~t splendidus, lautus

magni|fy amplifico 1; ~tude magnitudo *f*

magpie pica *f*

maid virgo *f*, puella *f*;
~enly virginalis, puellaris;
~servant ancilla *f*

mail squamae *f/pl.*; spongia *f*; litterae *f/pl.*; tabellarius

maim mutilo 1; ~ed mancus, truncus

main praecipuus, primus;
~ point summa *f*; ~ road via *f*; pontus *m*; ~land continens *f*; ~ly plerumque, praecipue

maintain conservo 1; sustineo 2; contendo 3, affirmo 1 (*alqd, acc. c. inf.*)

majest|ic augustus, regius;
~y maiestas *f*

major|-domo dispensator *m*; ~ity plerique *m/pl*.;
maior pars *f*

make facio 3; fingo 3; reddo 3 (*mare tutum, alqm iratum*); cogo 3 (*alqm alqd facere*); ~ as if simulo 1 (*acc. c. inf.*); ~ away with tollo 3; ~ for peto 3; ~ good sarcio 4; ~ light of contemno 3; ~ much of magni facio 3; ~ up expleo 2 (*numerum*); ~ up one's mind certum est (*inf.*); ~

war bellum infero 3; ~ way decedo 3 (*alci*); ~r fabricator *m*, creator *m*

malady morbus *m*

male mas, virilis

malediction dirae *f/pl.*

malevolen|ce malevolentia *f*; ~t malevolus

malice malitia *f*

malign obtrecto 1

malleable ductilis, lentus

mallet malleus *m*

maltreat vexo 1

man homo *m*; genus *n* humanum, mortales *m/pl.*;
vir *m*; our men nostri *m/pl.*; compleo 2 (*naves*);
~servant servus *m*

manacle manica *f*

manage curo 1; administro 1; gero 3; tracto 1; ~able tractabilis; ~ment cura *f*, administratio *f*; ~r (pro-)curator *m*; magister, tri *m*

mane iuba *f*

manful fortis

manger praesaepe *n*

mangle lanio 1

manhood: reach ~ togam virilem sumo 3; in ~ iuvenis, vir

mania insania *f*

manifest manifestus, apertus; declaro 1, ostendo 3

manifold multiplex, varius

maniple manipulus *m*

manipulate tracto 1

man|kind genus *n* humanum; ~liness fortitudo *f*;
~ly fortis

manner modus *m*; ratio *f*;

mos m; ~s mores m/pl.;
~ed affectatus
manœuvre decursio f
manor praedium n
mansion domus, us f
manslaughter caedes f
mantle palla f
manual libellus m
manufacture fabrica f;
fabricor 1
manumi|ssion manumissio
f; ~t manumitto 3
manure stercus n
many multi, plerique; a
good ~ complures; how ~
quot
map tabula f; ~ out describo 3
maple acer, eris n
mar deformo 1, corrumpo 3
marauding praedatorius
marble marmor n; mar-
moreus
March Martius m
march iter facio 3; progredior 3; incedo 3; iter, ineris
n; agmen n; on the ~ in
itinere
mare equa f
margin margo f
marigold caltha f
mari|ne marinus; (miles m)
classicus; ~ner nauta m;
~time maritimus
mark nota f, operam do 1
(dat.); nota f; signum n,
indicium n; ~ out denoto
1; ~ed gravis
market forum n, macellum
n; mercatus, us m; ~ (day)
nundinae f/pl.; nundinor
1; obsono 1

marriage coniugium n;
matrimonium n; nuptiae
f/pl.; ~able nubilis; ~-con-
tract pactio f nuptialis
marrow medulla f
marry (in matrimonium)
duco 3 (alqm uxorem);
nubo 3 (alci viro); colloco
1 (in matrimonium) (fi-
liam); matrimonio iungor
3
marsh palus, udis f; ~y
paluster
marshal instruo 3
martial bellicosus, bellicus
marvel miror 1 (at alqd);
~lous mirus
masculine virilis, masculi-
nus
mash farrago f; contundo 3
mask persona f; fig. integu-
mentum n; dissimulo 1
mason structor m
mass moles f; multitudo f;
vulgus, i n; congrego(r) 1
massacre trucido 1; caedes f
massive solidus
mast malus m; glans f
master dominus m, erus m;
magister, tri m (societatis,
ludi, navis); potens (gen.);
peritus (in re); be ~ of
potior 4 (abl.); domo 1;
~ful imperiosus; ~ly artificiosus; ~y potestas f,
victoria f
masticate mando 3
mat teges f; storea f
match (ex)aequo 1, comparo 1; par sum; certa-
men n; ~less singularis
mate socius m; coeo 4

material corporeus; materia *f*; textile *n*

maternal maternus

mathematic|al mathematicus; ~ian mathematicus *m*

matrimony matrimonium *n*

matron matrona *f*; ~ly matronalis

matter corpus *n*; res *f*; materia *f*; what is the ~? quid est?; it ~s refert 3 (*parvi, magni, etc.*)

mattress culcita *f*

matur|e adultus; maturus; maturo 1; ~ity maturitas *f*

maxim sententia *f*; praeceptum *n*

May Maius *m*

may licet 2 (*alci*); possum (*inf.*); ~be forsitan, fortasse

mayor praefectus *m* urbi(s)

maze labyrinthus *m*

me me; to ~ mihi

meadow pratum *n*

meagre exilis, exiguus

meal prandium *n*; farina *f*; chief ~ cena *f*

mean humilis; illiberalis; medius; in animo est (*mihi inf.*); significo 1, volo (mihi) (*verba etc.*); dico 3; medium *n*; mediocritas *f*; ~s modus *m*; by all ~s omnino; by no ~s haudquaquam, nullo modo; by ~s of per (*acc.*); ~ing significatio *f*; sententia *f*; ~ness sordes *f*; humilitas *f*; ~while interea, interim

measure metior 4; mensura *f*; modus *m*; consi-

lium *n*; in some ~ aliqua ex parte; take ~s provideo 2 (*ut, ne*); ~d moderatus; ~ment mensura *f*

meat caro, carnis *f*

mechani|c faber, bri *m*; ~sm machina *f*

meddle me immisceo 2 (*alci rei*)

mediat|e me interpono 3; ~or deprecator *m*; intercessor *m*

medic|al medicinus; ~ate medico 1; ~ine medicina *f*; medicamentum *n*, medicamen *n*

mediocr|e mediocris; ~ity mediocritas *f*

meditat|e volvo 3; cogito 1 (*de*); in animo est mihi (*inf.*); ~ion cogitatio *f*

medium medius, mediocris; modus *m*

medley farrago *f*

meed praemium *n*

meek mitis, demissus; ~ness animus *m* demissus

meet aptus, accommodatus (*ad*); obviam fio (*alci*); convenio 4 (*alqm*); incido 3 (*alci*); oppeto 3 (*mortem etc.*); go to ~ obviam eo 4 (*alci*); ~ together convenio 4; ~ing coetus, us *m*; conventus, us *m*; contio *f*

melancholy tristis; tristitia *f*

mellow mitis, maturus, lenis; maturesco 3

melod|ious canorus; ~y modus *m*; cantus, us *m*

melon melopepo *m*

melt *v/t.* liquefacio 3; *v/i.*

liquefio, liquesco 3; ~ away dilabor 3

member membrum n; socius m

memor|able memorabilis; insignis; ~ial monumentum n; ~y memoria f; recordatio f

menac|e minor 1 (alci alqd); minae f/pl.; ~ing minax

mend v/t. sarcio 4; emendo 1; corrigo 3; v/i. melior fio

mendacious mendax

mendicant mendicus

menial sordidus; mediastinus m

mention (com)memoro 1; mentionem facio 3 (gen., de); not to ~ ne dicam; mentio f

mercenary mercenarius, conductus (miles m)

merchan|dise merx f; res f/pl. venales; ~t mercator m; ~t-ship navis f oneraria

merc|iful clemens, misericors; ~iless durus; ~y misericordia f, venia f; show ~y ignosco 3

mere merus, unus; lacus, us m

merge confundo 3

merit mereo(r) 2; meritum n; virtus, utis f; ~ed meritus

merry hilarus, festivus

mesh macula f; plaga f

mess squalor m

mess|age nuntius m; ~enger nuntius m; tabellarius m

metal metallum n

metamorphose transformo 1; verto 3

metaphor translatio f; ~ical translatus

meteor fax f

methinks ut mihi videtur

method ratio f; modus m; ~ically disposite

metonymy immutatio f

metr|e numerus m; ~ical metricus

metropolis caput n; urbs f

mettle ferocitas f; ~some ferox, animosus

mews stabula n/pl.

mid medius; ~day meridies m; meridianus

middle medius; medium n; ~-aged senior

middling mediocris

midge culex m

mid|land mediterraneus; ~night media nox f; ~riff praecordia n/pl.

midst medius

mid|summer media aestas f; ~wife obstetrix f; ~winter bruma f

might vis f, potestas f; ~y validus, (prae)potens

migrate migro 1

mild mitis, clemens, facilis; tepidus

mildew robigo f; situs, us m

mildness lenitas f, mansuetudo f

mile mille passuum; ~stone milliarium n

military militaris, bellicus; militares copiae f; ~ service militia f

militate against contra facio 3 *(alqm)*

milk mulgeo 2; lac *n*; ~y lacteus

mill tero 3; mola *f*; pistrinum *n*; ~er pistor *m*; ~stone mola *f*

millet milium *n*

million decies centena milia

mime imitor 1; mimus *m*

mince conseco 1; not to ~ matters ut plane aperteque dicam; ~d **meat** minutal *n*

mind curo 1; ~ one's own business meum negotium ago 3; mens *f*; animus *m*; ingenium *n*; sensus, us *m*; sententia *f*; be out of one's ~ insanio 4; bear in ~ memini; call to ~ recordor 1; change one's ~ sententiam muto 1; have a ~ to mihi libet; mihi in animo est; to my ~ ex mea sententia; ~ful memor *(gen.)*

mine meus; (ef)fodio 4; *mil.* cuniculos ago 3; metallum *n*; cuniculus *m*; ~r metallicus *m*; ~ral metallum *n*

mingle (im)misceo 2 *(alqd alci rei)*; confundo 3 *(alqd in alqd)*

miniature minutus

minimum minimus

minion minister, tri *m*; satelles *m*

minister praefectus *m*; ~ to servio 4 *(dat.)*; prosum *(dat.)*

ministry ministerium *n*

minor minor; filius *m* familias; ~ity minor pars *f*

minstrel vates *m*

mint cudo 3; moneta *f*; mentha *f*

minus sine *(abl.)*

minute minutus, pusillus; subtilis; momentum *n* (temporis); commentarius *m*

mirac|le miraculum *n*, prodigium *n*; ~ulous mirus

mire lutum *n*

mirror speculum *n*; imaginem reddo 3

mirth hilaritas *f*, laetitia *f*; ~ful hilarus

misadventure casus, us *m*

misanthropic inhumanus

misapply abutor 3

mis|apprehension error *m*; ~behave indecore me gero 3

miscalculat|e erro 1; ~ion error *m*

miscarriage abortus, us *m*

miscellan|eous promiscuus, varius; ~y farrago *f*

mischance incommodum *n*

mischie|f incommodum *n*; maleficium *n*; pestis *f*; ~vous improbus, noxius

miscon|duct peccatum *n*; ~strue male interpretor 1

misdeed delictum *n*

miser homo *m* avarus; ~able miser; ~y miseria *f*, angor *m*

misfortune adversa *n/pl.*; incommodum *n*; calamitas *f*

misgivings: have ~ diffido 3

mis|govern male administro

1; ~guided demens; ~hap
incommodum n; ~inter-
pret male interpretor 1;
male iudico 1; ~lay amitto
3; ~lead decipio 3; ~repre-
sent in deteriorem partem
interpretor 1; ~rule male
administro 1

miss aberro 1 (abl.); frustra
mittor 3 (telum etc.); amitto 3 (occasionem etc.);
desidero 1 (alqm); requiro
3 (alqd); puella f; domina f

misshapen deformis, pravus

missile telum n, missile n

missing: be ~ desideror 1;
desum

mission legatio f; officium n

mist nebula f; caligo f

mistake error m; erratum n;
mendum n; by ~ for pro
(abl.); be ~n erro 1, fallor 3
(in re)

mistletoe viscum n

mistress era f, domina f,
mater f familias; puella f,
amica f

mistrust diffido 3; diffidentia f

misty nebulosus

misunderstand haud recte
intellego 3; ~ing error m

misuse iniuriose tracto 1

mite teruncius m

mitigat|e mitigo 1; levo 1;
~ion levamentum n

mix (ad)misceo 2 (alqd re);
commisceo 3 (alqd cum re);
~ed promiscuus, varius;
~ture mixtura f

moan gemo 3; gemitus, us
m

moat fossa f

mob turba f; multitudo f;
vulgus, i n; circumfundor 3
(dat.)

mobile mobilis

mock irrideo 2, derideo 2
(acc.); illudo 3 (dat.); fictus; ~er derisor m; ~ery
irrisio f; irrisus, us m;
ludificatio f

mode modus m; ratio f

model exemplum n, exem-
plar n; fingo 3

moderat|e modicus, mode-
ratus, modestus; tempero
1, mitigo 1; moderor 1
(dat.); ~ion modus m; mo-
deratio f, mediocritas f

modern recens, novus

modest modicus; verecun-
dus, demissus; ~y vere-
cundia f; pudor m

modify tempero 1; immuto
1; accommodo 1 (alqd: to
suit ad alqd)

modulat|e flecto 3; ~ion
flexio f

moist umidus, ~en made-
facio 3; rigo 1; ~ure umor|

molar molaris m   [m|

mole talpa f; moles f; naevus m

molest vexo 1, sollicito 1;
~ation vexatio f

mollify mitigo 1

moment punctum n, mo-
mentum n (temporis); in
a ~ statim; at the ~ when
cum maxime; of great ~
magni momenti; ~ary bre-
vis; ~ous maximi momenti;
~um impetus, us m

monarch rex *m*, princeps *m*; ~ical regius; ~y regnum *n*

monastery monasterium *n*

money pecunia *f*; nummi *m/pl.*; nummarius; ~bag fiscus *m*; ~changer nummularius *m*; ~lender faenerator *m*; ~ed pecuniosus

mongrel hibrida *m and f*

monkey simia *f*

monograph libellus *m*

monoton|ous similis, ~y similitudo *f*

monster, monstrosity belua *f*; monstrum *n*

monstrous monstruosus, portentosus; nefarius

month mensis *m*; ~ly menstruus

monument monumentum *n*

mood animus *m*; mens *f*; affectus, us *m (mentis etc.)*; ~y morosus [lumen *n*]

moon luna *f*; ~light lunae]

moor religo 1, deligo 1; loca *n/pl.* patentia; ~ings retinacula *n/pl.*; statio *f*

mop detergeo 2

moral moralis; probus; ~s mores *m/pl.*; officia *n/pl.*; the ~ is significat; ~ity honestas *f*

morbid morbosus, insanus

more plus, magis; ultra *(acc., quam)*; amplius; no ~ non iam, non diutius; ~over praeterea

morning matutinum tempus *n*; in the ~ mane; matutinus; good morning! salve

morose tristis, difficilis

morrow posterus dies *m*; crastinus dies *m*

morsel offa *f*; frustum *n*

mortal mortalis; mortifer, funestus; ~ity mortalitas *f*; mortes *f/pl.*

mortar mortarium *n*; calx *f*

mortgage pignus *n*; pignero 1

mortif|ication offensio *f*; indignitas *f*; ~y *v/t.* offendo 3 *(alqm)*; *v/i.* putresco 3

mosaic tessellatus *(opus, pavimentum, etc.)*

mosquito culex *m*

moss muscus *m*; ~y muscosus

most plurimus; plerique; *adv.* maxime, plurimum; at the ~ summum; for the ~ part plerumque, fere, maximam partem

moth blatta *f*

mother mater *f*; of a ~ maternus; ~in-law socrus, us *f*; ~ tongue patrius sermo *m*

motion motus, us *m*; agitatio *f*; rogatio *f*; sententia *f*; adopt a ~ in sententiam *(alcs)* discedo 3; innuo 3 *(dat.)*; ~less immotus

motive causa *f*, ratio *f*

motley, mottled versicolor; varius, maculosus

motto sententia *f*

mould fingo 3; formo 1; forma *f*; robigo *f*; situs, us *m*; ~er putresco 3; ~ering, ~y puter, mucidus

moult pennas exuo 3

mound tumulus *m*; agger, eris *m*

mount scando 3, conscendo 3 (*alqd*); ascendo 3 (*alqd, in alqd*); equum conscendo 3; ~ guard in statione sum

mountain mons *m*; ~eer montanus (homo *m*); ~ous montuosus; ~ range iugum *n*

mourn lugeo 2, maereo 2, doleo 2 (*acc.*); ~ful tristis, luctuosus; lugubris; ~ing luctus, us *m*; squalor *m*; sordes *f/pl.*; be in ~ing squaleo 2; go into ~ing vestitum muto 1

mouse mus *m*; ~-trap muscipula *f*

moustache labri superioris capilli *m/pl.*

mouth os *n*; rostrum *n*; ostium *n*; ~ful bucca *f*

move *v/t.* moveo 2; commoveo 2 (*alqm ad*); (re-)fero 3 (*legem, rogationem, etc.*); *v/i.* moveor 2, me moveo 2; migro 1; ~ables bona *n/pl.* (mobilia); ~ment motus, us *m*

moving miserabilis, flebilis

mow seco 1, meto 3

much multus; multum *n*; *adv.* multum; multo (*with comparatives*); as ~ as tantus ... quantus; how ~ quantus; too ~ nimius; nimium *n*; ~ less nedum

mud lutum *n*, caenum *n*; limus *m*; ~dle confundo 3;

perturbo 1; ~dy lutulentus, limosus; turbidus

muffle involvo 3, obvolvo 3

mug poculum *n*; ~gy umidus

mulberry morum *n*; ~-tree morus, i *f*

mule mulus *m*; ~teer mulio) mulish pervicax　　　　[*m*)

mullet mullus *m*

multi|ply *v/t.* multiplico 1, augeo 2; *v/i.* cresco 3; ~tude multitudo *f*; vis *f*; vulgus, i *n*

mumble murmuro 1; musso 1

munch mando 3

municipal municipalis; ~ity municipium *n*

munificen|ce liberalitas *f*; ~t liberalis

murder neco 1; interficio 3; obtrunco 1; caedes *f*, nex *f*; ~er homicida *m*; sicarius *m*; percussor *m*; ~ous cruentus

murky caliginosus, obscurus

murmur murmuro 1; fremo 3 (*acc. c. inf.*); murmur *n*; fremitus, us *m*

musc|le lacertus *m*; nervus *m*; ~ular lacertosus

muse meditor 1, cogito 1; Musa *f*

mushroom fungus *m*; boletus *m*

music musica *f and n/pl.*; cantus, us *m*; modi *m/pl.*; ~al musicus, canorus; ~ sicorum studiosus; ~ian musicus *m* muslin sindon *f*

must debeo 2 (*inf*.); oportet me (*inf*.); necesse est mihi (*inf*., *ut*); I ~ go eundum est mihi; mustum *n*

mustard sinapi *indecl. n*, sinapis *f*

muster nomen *n*, vocabulum *n*; *v*/*t*. cogo 3; lustro 1; *v*/*i*. congregor 1; recensio *f*

musty mucidus

mutability inconstantia *f*

mute mutus, tacitus

mutilate mutilo 1, (de-) trunco 1

mutin|ous seditiosus, turbulentus; ~y seditio *f*; seditionem facio 3

mutter murmuro 1, musso 1; murmur *n*

mutton ovilla (caro) *f*

mutual mutuus

muzzle os *n*; fiscella *f*

my meus

myriad sescenti

myrrh murra *f*

myrtle myrtus, i *f*; myrteus

myself (me) ipse

myster|ious occultus, arcanus; ~y arcanum *n*; res *f* occulta

mystic mysticus

mystification ambages *f*/*pl*.

myth fabula *f*; ~ical fabulosus

N

nag caballus *m*

nail unguis *m*; clavus *m*; clavis (con)figo 3 (*dat*.)

naive simplex

naked nudus; apertus

name nomen *n*, vocabulum *n*; family ~ sur~ cognomen *n*; first ~ praenomen *n*; good ~ fama *f*, existimatio *f*; in ~ nomine; in my ~ meis verbis; in the ~ of per (*deos*); nomino 1, appello 1, nuncupo 1; dico 3; ~ly dico, inquam

nap villus *m*; brevis som-)

nape cervix *f*　　　[nus *m*)

napkin mappa *f*

narcotic somnifer

nard nardum *n*

narrat|e (e)narro 1; ~ion, ~ive narratio *f*; historia *f*; ~or narrator *m*

narrow angustus, artus; angustior fio; ~ly diligenter; haud multum abest quin ...; ~ness, ~s angustiae *f*/*pl*.

nasty foedus, taeter

natal natalis

nation gens *f*, natio *f*; populus *m*; cives *m*/*pl*.; res *f* publica; ~al communis; ~al assembly concilium *n* populi

native indigena *m and f*; be a ~ of natus sum; ~ land patria *f*; ~ language patrius sermo *m*

natural naturalis; nativus; proprius (*gen*.); ~ parts ingenium *n*; ~ize civitatem do 1 (*alci*); ~ly natura, naturaliter

nature natura *f* (rerum);

ingenium *n*; indoles *f*; vis *f*

naught nihil; set at ~ parvi facio 3, contemno 3; ~y improbus

nause|a nausea *f*; fastidium *n*; ~ate fastidium facio 3; ~ating taeter, foedus

nautical nauticus

naval navalis, maritimus

navel umbilicus *m*

naviga|ble navigabilis; ~te navigo 1; ~tor nauta *m*, gubernator *m*

navy classis *f*

nay immo; minime (vero)

near prope, ad, iuxta (*acc.*); propinquus, vicinus; *adv.* prope, iuxta; appropinquo 1 (*ad*; *dat.*); be ~ at hand adsum; advento 1 (*tempus*)

nearer propior; *adv.* propius

nearest proximus; *adv.* proxime

near|ly prope, paene, fere, ferme; haud multum afuit quin ...; ~ness propinquitas *f*

neat mundus, nitidus; ~ness munditia *f*

necessary necessarius; it is ~ necesse est (*inf.*); opus est (*nom.*; *abl.*)

necess|aries necessaria *n/pl.*; ~itate cogo 3 (*inf.*); ~ity necessitas *f*; egestas *f*; res *f* necessaria; tempus *n*

neck cervix *f*; collum *n*; angustiae *f/pl.*; ~lace monile *n*

nectar nectar *n*

need egeo 2 (*abl.*); requiro 3

(*alqd*); egestas *f*, inopia *f*; there is ~ of (mihi) opus est (*nom.*; *abl.*); there is no ~ nihil attinet 2 (*inf.*); ~ful opus; necessarius

needle acus, us *f*

need|less sine causa; ~y egens

nefarious nefarius

negat|ion negatio *f*; ~ive negans; give a ~ive answer nego 1; intercedo 3 (*dat.*)

neglect neglego 3, praetermitto 3; desum (*dat.*); incuria *f*, neglegentia *f*; ~ful of neglegens (*gen.*)

negligen|ce neglegentia *f*; ~t remissus

negotiat|e ago 3 (*de re*); ~ion pactio *f*

negro Aethiops *m*

neigh hinnio 4; hinnitus, us *m*

neighbour vicinus *m*; *fig.* alter *m*; ~hood vicinitas *f*; ~ing vicinus, finitimus, propinquus

neither neuter, neutri; ~ ... nor neque ... neque, nec ... nec; neve ... neve

nephew fratris or sororis filius *m*

nerv|e nervus *m*; ~ous anxius, trepidus; ~ousness metus, us *m*; anxietas *f*

nest nidus *m*; nidum facio 3

net rete *n*; plaga *f*; plagis capio 3

nether infernus; ~most infimus, imus

nettle urtica *f*

neuter neuter

neutral medius; neutrius partis; **remain** ~ quiesco 3

never numquam; **and** ~ nec umquam; **nevermore** numquam posthac; **~the-less** nihilominus, (at)tamen, veruntamen

new novus, recens; **~comer** adven *m*; **~ly** nuper, modo, recens; **~ness** novitas *f*

news nuntius *m*; **what** ~? quid novi?; **~ was brought** nuntiatum est (*acc. c. inf.*); **~paper** acta *n/pl.* diurna

newt lacertus *m*

next proximus (*dat.*); insequens; posterus; **on the ~ day** postridie; *adv.* deinceps, proxime; **~ before** proximus ante; **~ after, to** secundum (*acc.*); iuxta (*acc.*); deinde, postea

nib acumen *n*

nibble rodo 3; **~ at** arrodo 3

nice subtilis, exquisitus; elegans; suavis, dulcis; **to a ~ty** ad unguem

niche angulus *m*

nick incido 3; **in the ~ of time** in ipso articulo temporis

nickname cognomen *n*

niece fratris *or* sororis filia *f*

niggardly sordidus, parcus

night nox *f*; **all ~** pernox; **at ~ fall** sub noctem; **by ~** noctu, de nocte; nocturnus; **~ingale** luscinia *f*; **~watch** vigiliae *f/pl.*, excubiae *f/pl.*

nimble pernix

nine novem; ~ **hundred** nongenti; ~ **times** novies; **~teen** undeviginti; **~teenth** undevicesimus; **~th** nonus; **~tieth** nonagesimus; **~ty** nonaginta

nip mordeo 2; vellico 1; uro 3; **~pers** forceps *f*

nipple papilla *f*

nitre nitrum *n*

no nullus; immo; minime (vero); ~ **one** nemo; **and ~ one** nec quisquam; ~ **more than** nihilo magis quam; ~ **news** nihil novi; ~ **sooner ... than** ubi primum

nob|ility nobilitas *f*; nobiles *m/pl.*; generosus animus *m*; **~le** nobilis, generosus, excelsus; praeclarus; **~leman** vir *m* nobilis

nobody nemo

nocturnal nocturnus

nod nuto 1; nutus, us *m*; ~ (**assent**) **to** annuo 3 (*alci; alqd alci*); **~ding** nutans

nois|e sonitus, us *m*; strepitus, us *m*; crepitus, us *m*; **~e abroad** effero 3; **~eless** tacitus, silens; **~ome** taeter, foedus; **~y** clamosus, tumultuosus, argutus

nomadic vagus

nominally nomine; verbo; specie (*gen.*)

nominat|e nomino 1, dico 3; **~ion** nominatio *f*

none nemo; nullus; ~ **the less** nihilominus

nones nonae *f/pl.*

nonsens|e nugae *f/pl.*, ineptiae *f/pl.*; ~ical absurdus, ineptus

nook angulus *m*

noon meridies *m*; ~day meridianus

noose laqueus *m*

nor neque, nec; neu

normal solitus

north septentrio *m*; septentriones *m/pl.*; septentrionalis; ~-east inter septentriones et orientem; ~-east wind aquilo *m*; ~-west inter septentriones et occasum solis; ~-west wind caurus *m*; ~-wind aquilo *m*

nose nasus *m*; nares *f/pl.*; ~gay fasciculus *m* (florum)

nostril naris *f*

not non; haud; minus; and ~ neque, nec; ~ even ne ... quidem; ~ that ... but non quod ... sed; ~ yet nondum

nota|ble memorabilis; ~ry scriba *m*; ~tion notatio *f*

notch incisura *f*

note nota *f*; codicilli *m/pl.*; vox *f*; ~s commentarius *m*; noto 1; animadverto 3, intellego 3; ~book pugillares *m/pl.*; ~d insignis; ~worthy memorabilis

nothing nihil; nihilum *n*

notice animadverto 3; proscriptio *f*; titulus *m*; attract ~ conspicior 3; escape ~ fallo 3 (*alqm*; *acc. c. inf.*); lateo 2; give ~ denuntio 1, praenuntio 1; ~able notabilis

notif|ication denuntiatio *f*; ~y denuntio 1

notion notio *f*, suspicio *f*

notor|iety infamia *f*; ~ious notus, infamis, famosus

notwithstanding nihilominus, attamen

noun nomen *n*

nourish nutrio 4; alo 3; ~ment alimentum *n*; cibus *m*

novel novus; ~ty novitas *f*, insolentia *f*

November November, bris *m*

novice tiro *m*

now nunc, iam, hodie; ~ ... ~ modo ... modo; ~ (for a long time) iam diu, iam pridem; *particle* quidem, nunc; ~adays nunc; hodie; ~ and then aliquando

no|where nusquam; ~wise haudquaquam

noxious nocens

nude nudus

nudge fodico 1

nuisance: be a ~ molestum est

null irritus; ~ify infirmo 1; irritum facio 3

numb torpens; be ~ torpeo 2

number numerus *m*; a ~ pars *f*; a considerable ~ aliquot; large ~s, a large ~ multi *m/pl.*, complures *m/pl.*; multitudo *f*, copia *f*: what, such a ~ quot?, tot; (e)numero 1; ~less innumerabilis

numbness torpor m
numerous multi, plurimi, plures
nuptial nuptialis; ~s nuptiae f/pl.
nurse nutrix f; fig. altrix f; nutrio 4, alo 3; assideo 2

(aegrotanti); ~ry (for plants) seminarium n
nurture educatio f
nut nux f
nutri|ment, ~tion alimentum n; cibus m; ~tious alibilis

O

O, oh! o
oak quercus, us f; ilex f; aesculus, i f; quern(e)us; aesculeus; ~wood robur n
oar remus m; ~blade palma f; ~sman remex m
oat avena f; avenaceus
oath ius n iurandum; military ~ sacramentum n; swear an ~ to iuro 1 in verba (alcs); tender, take an ~ ius iurandum defero 3 (alci), accipio 3
obdurate obstinatus, durus
obedien|ce oboedientia f; ~t oboediens (dat.); dicto audiens (alci)
obese obesus
obey pareo 2, oboedio 4, obtempero 1 (dat.)
object| (to) improbo 1, gravor 1 (acc.); repugno 1 (dat.); recuso 1 (alqd, ne; after neg.: quin, quominus); res f; consilium n; finis m; I have no ~ion per me licet (inf., subj.); ~ionable ingratus; ~ive externus
obligat|ion officium n; be under an ~ion obnoxius, obligatus sum (alci); lay under an ~ion obligo 1,

obstringo 3; ~ory necessarius
oblig|e cogo 3; gratificor 1 (alci); beneficium confero 3 (in alqm); gratum facio 3 (alci); ~ing comis, facilis
oblique obliquus
obliterate deleo 2; oblittero 1
oblivi|on oblivio f; ~ous immemor, ignarus (gen.)
obloquy vituperatio f
obnoxious ingratus, invisus; nocens
obscen|e obscenus, turpis; ~ity obscenitas f
obscur|e obscurus, reconditus; ignobilis; obscuro 1; ~ity obscuritas f; tenebrae f/pl.
obsequies exsequiae f/pl.
obsequious obsequens, ambitiosus
observ|ance conservatio f; mos m; ~ation observatio f, contemplatio f; sententia f; ~e observo 1, contemplor 1; dico 3; conservo 1
obsolete obsoletus; become ~ obsolesco 3

obstacle impedimentum *n*

obstina|cy pertinacia *f*, pervicacia *f*; ~te pertinax, pervicax, obstinatus

obstruct *v/t.* obstruo 3 (*dat.*); *v/i.* obsto 1 (*dat.*); ~ion impedimentum *n*

obtain adipiscor 3, consequor 3; nanciscor 3; obtineo 2; impetro 1

obtru|de inculco 1 (*alqd, se, alci*); ingero 3 (*alqd alci*); ~sive molestus

obtuse hebes, obtusus

obviate occurro 3 (*dat.*)

obvious apertus, manifestus

occasion occasio *f*; tempus *n*; causa *f*; efficio 3; ~ally per occasionem, aliquando

occult arcanus

occup|ation occupatio *f*, possessio *f*; negotium *n*; quaestus, us *m*; ~y occupo 1; obsideo 3; possideo 3; teneo 2; be ~ied with versor 1 (*in re*); totum sum in (*re*)

occur accido 3, contingo 3; evenio 4; in mentem venio 4, occurro 3 (*dat.*); ~rence res *f*

ocean oceanus *m*

October October, bris *m*

odd impar; insolitus, mirus; ridiculus; subsicivus (*tempus etc.*); be at ~s with dissideo 2 (*ab; inter se*)

ode carmen *n*

odi|ous invisus, odiosus; ~um invidia *f*

odour odor *m*; be in bad ~

with invidiam suscipio 3 (*apud alqm*)

of (*abl.*), ex (*abl.*): each ~ you uterque vestrum; one ~ you unus ex vobis

off: (the coast of) prope, propter (*acc.*); be well ~ for abundo 1 (*abl.*); far ~ longe (*ab*); make ~ me concicio 3 (*in*); some way ~ procul (*ab*)

offal quisquiliae *f/pl.*

offen|ce delictum *n*, peccatum *n*; offensio *f*; ~d offendo 3 (*acc.*); laedo 3; pecco 1; ~d against violo 1 (*ius etc.*); ~sive odiosus, molestus; putidus; take the ~sive bellum, signa infero 3 (*in*)

offer offero 3, defero 3; porrigo 3; adhibeo 2 (*preces etc.*); macto 1 (*hostia*); condicio *f*; ~ing donum *n*

office officium *n*, munus *n*; magistratus, us *m*; ministerium *n*; hold ~ magistratum obtineo 2; ~r praefectus *m*

official publicus, civilis; minister, tri *m*; lictor *m*

officious molestus

offset compenso 1 (*alqd alqua re, cum alqua re*)

offspring progenies *f*; liberi *m/pl.*

often saepe, saepenumero; as ~ as quotiescumque; how ~ quoties; so ~ toties

ogre larva *f*

oil oleum *n*; of ~ olearius

ointment unguentum *n*;
eye ~ collyrium *n*

old vetus, antiquus, vetustus; senex, senior; **four years** ~ quattuor annos natus; ~ **age** senectus, utis *f*; ~**er** maior natu; ~**-fashioned** priscus, pristinus; obsoletus; ~ **man** senex *m*; ~ **woman** anus, us *f*

olive (tree) olea *f*, oliva *f*; ~**-oil** oleum *n*

omen omen *n*; auspicium *n*; **obtain good** ~**s** lito 1

ominous infaustus, infelix

omission praetermissio *f*

omit praetermitto 3, omitto 3; praetereo 4; relinquo 3

on in (*abl.*); super (*acc.*); ~ **all sides** undique; ~ **foot** pedibus; ~ **the right** a dextra parte; ~, **the subject of** de (*abl.*); *adv.* porro

once semel; **at** ~ simul, uno tempore; ilico, statim; ~ (**upon a time**) olim, quondam

one unus; ~ **and all** cuncti; ~ **and the same** idem; ~ **another** inter se; ~ **by** ~ singuli; singillatim; ~ **day** olim, aliquando; ~ **of** unus ex, quidam ex (*abl.*); ~ **or two** unus vel alter; ~ ... ~ alius ... alius; ~ **who is** qui; ~**-eyed** luscus; ~**-sided** inaequalis, iniquus

onerous gravis

onion caepa *f*, caepe *n*

only unus, solus, unicus; *adv.* solum, modo, tantum

onset, onslaught impetus, us *m*; incursus, us *m*

onward porro

ooze mano 1

opaque caecus

open apertus, patens; manifestus; simplex; patefacio 3; aperio 4; pando 3; *fig.* exordior 4 (*orationem*); **be, lie** ~ pateo 2; **in the** ~ **air** sub divo; ~**ing** exordium *n* (*orationis*); foramen *n*; os *n*; *fig.* ansa *f*, opportunitas *f*; ~**ly** palam, aperte

operat|e ago 3, facio 3; *med.* seco 1; ~**e upon** moveo 2; ~**ion** res *f*; actio *f*; ~**ive** efficax

opin|e opinor 1; ~**ion** opinio *f*, sententia *f*; **good** ~**ion** existimatio *f*; **give an** ~**ion on** censeo 2 (*de*)

opponent adversarius *m*

opportun|e opportunus, idoneus, tempestivus; ~**ity** occasio *f*, opportunitas *f*; tempus *n*

oppose *v/t.* oppono 3 (*alq̄d alci, alci rei*); *v/i.* adversor 1, repugno 1, obsto 1 (*dat.*)

opposit|e adversus, contrarius, diversus; ~**e to** contra (*acc.*); **e regione** (*gen.*); adversus (*acc.*); ~**ion** repugnantia *f*; adversarii *m/pl.*

oppress premo 3; affligo 3; vexo 1; **injur|ies** iniuriae *f/pl.*; ~**ive** iniquus, gravis, acerbus

opprobrious turpis

option optio *f* (eligendi)

opulen|ce divitiae *f/pl.*; ~t locuples, dives

or aut; either ... ~ aut ... aut; vel ... vel; whether ... ~ sive ... sive, seu ... seu; *interrog.* utrum ... an; ~ not annon (*direct*); necne (*indirect*)

oracle oraculum *n*; responsum *n*

orally voce, verbis

orange (-coloured) luteus

orat|ion oratio *f*; contio *f*; ~or orator *m*; ~orical oratorius; ~ory rhetorica *f*; eloquentia *f*, facundia *f*

orb orbis *m*; ~it orbis *m*; ambitus, us *m*

orchard pomarium *n*

orchestra symphoniaci pueri *m/pl.*, servi *m/pl.*

ordain sancio 4; statuo 3; decerno 3

ordeal discrimen *n*

order dispono 3; iubeo 2 (*acc. c. inf.*); impero 1 (*alci ut*); edico 3 (*ut*); ordo *m*, descriptio *f*; iussum *n*, mandatum *n*; imperium *n*, imperatum *n*; ~ of battle acies *f*; the equestrian ~ equester ordo *m*; the lower ~s vulgus, i *n*; by, without ~ of iussu, iniussu (*gen.*); money ~ perscriptio *f*; in good ~ ordine, in ordinem, ex ordine; ~ly compositus; modestus

ordinance edictum *n*

ordinary usitatus, cottidianus, vulgaris; mediocris

ore metallum *n*

organ pars *f*; membrum *n*; organum *n*; ~isation descriptio *f*, temperatio *f*; ~ise dispono 3, compono 3; tempero 1; ~ism animal *n*; animans *n*

orgies orgia *n/pl* ; *fig.* comissatio *f*

orient oriens *m*

orifice os *m*

origin origo *f*; principium *n*; primordia *n/pl.*; genus *n*; ~al pristinus; principalis; exemplar *n*, exemplum *n*; ~ate *v/t.* instituo 3; *v/i.* orior 4 (*ex, ab*); principium, initium duco 3 (*ab*); nascor 3 (*ex*); ~ator auctor *m*

ornament ornamentum *n*; ornatus, us *m*; *fig.* decus *n*; lumen *n*

ornate pictus

orphan orbus

oscilla|te agitor 1, iactor 1, ~ion agitatio *f*

osier vimen *n*; vimeneus

ostensibly per speciem

ostentat|ion ostentatio *f*; ~ious gloriosus

ostler agaso *m*

ostrich struthiocamelus *m*

other alius, (than *atque*); the ~ (of two) alter; the ~s ceteri *m/pl.*, reliqui *m/pl.*; of ~s alienus; ~wise aliter, secus; alioquin, sin aliter

otter lutra *f*

ought debeo 2 (*inf.*); oportet (*acc. c. inf.*)

ounce uncia *f*

our noster; ~selves (nos) ipsi

oust eicio 3

out foris (esse, cenare, etc.); foras (ire); ~ of e, ex (abl.); (one) ~ of, (made) ~ of de (abl.); ~ of fear per, propter metum; ~break impetus, us m; ~cast extorris; ~cry clamor m; acclamatio f; ~do supero 1; vinco 3; ~doors foris, foras

outer exterior; ~most extremus

out|fit apparatus, us m; ~house tugurium n; ~landish barbarus; ~law proscribo 3; proscriptus m; latro m; ~lay impensa f; ~let exitus, us m; emissarium n; ~line lineamenta n/pl.; ~live supersum; ~look prospectus, us m; ~number superiores esse (numero); ~post statio f

outrage vexo 1; violo 1; iniuria afficio f; vexatio f; iniuria f; facinus n; ~ous indignus, turpis

out|right plane, prorsus; ~set principium n; ~side extra (acc.); adv. extrinsecus, foris; externus; species f; ~skirts suburbanus; be ~spoken aperte loquor 3; ~standing reliquus; praestans; ~strip supero 1; ~ward externus; ~wardly specie; ~weigh praepondero 1; antiquius sum (alqd alci); ~wit decipio 3; ~work munitio f

oven furnus m; fornax f

over super (acc. and abl.); supra (acc.); trans (flumen, etc.); plus (numbers); per (Alpes, etc.); ~ and above praeter (acc.); ~ and ~ (again) saepenumero, identidem; be ~ praesum (dat.); it is all ~ with actum est de (alqo); place, appoint ~ praeficio 3 (alqm alci rei)

over|awe deterreo 2; ~bearing insolens; ~burden praegravo 1; ~cast obscuratus, obductus; ~coat (cloak) lacerna f; ~come vinco 3; supero 1; ~flow me effundo 3; redundo 1; ~grown obsitus (abl.); ~hang immineo 2 (dat.); ~head insuper; ~hear excipio 3; ~lay induco 3 (alqd re); ~look prospicio 3; coniveo 2; ignosco 3 (alci alqd); ~much nimis; nimium; ~power opprimo 3; ~reach circumvenio 4; ~run percurro 3 (alqd); potior 4 (abl.); ~seer curator m; ~shadow obscuro 1, obumbro 1; ~take consequor 3 (alqm); fig. deprehendo 3, opprimo 3; ~throw everto 3, prosterno 3; ruina f

overtly aperte

overtures: make ~ of peace condicionem fero 3; make ~ to sollicito 1 (alqm)

over|turn everto 3; ~whelm obruo 3, opprimo 3

owe debeo 2 (alqd alci)

owing to propter (acc.); be ~ stat 1 (per alqm quominus)

owl bubo m, noctua f

own meus, tuus, suus, etc.; meus ipsius; (meus) proprius; possideo 2, teneo 2, habeo 2; ~ that confiteor 2 (acc. c. inf.); ~er dominus m

ox bos m

oyster ostrea f

P

pace passua, us m; gradus, us m; spatior 1; incedo 3

pacify paco 1, sedo 1

pack colligo 3 (sarcinas etc.); stipo 1; sarcina f; grex m, turba f; ~et fasciculus m; ~horse iumentum n

pact pactio f; pactum n

pad farcio 4; ~ding tomentum n

paddle remus m; remigo 1

paddock saeptum n

page pagina f; puer, eri m

pageant spectaculum n

pail hama f

pain dolor m; mental ~ aegritudo f; be in ~ doleo 2; v/t. dolore afficio 3 (alqm); ~ful acerbus; ~s opera f; take ~s operam do 1 (ut, ne); elaboro 1 (in alqa re; ut); ~staking operosus, industrius

paint pingo 3; fuco 1; pigmentum n; ~brush penicillus m; ~er pictor m; ~ing tabula f; art of ~ing pictura f

pair par n; bini, ae, a; iungo 3; compono 3 (combatants etc.)

palace regia f

palat|able iucundus; ~e palatum n

pale pallidus, albus; palus m; obscuror 1; grow, be ~ palleo 2

palisade vallum n

pall pallium n; satietatem pario 3

pallet grabatus m

palliate lenio 4; extenuo 1

pallor pallor m

palm palma f; ~ off upon suppono 3 (alqd alci)

palpable manifestus

palpitate salio 4; palpito 1

palsy paralysis f

paltry vilis, exiguus

pamper indulgeo 2 (dat.); foveo 2 (acc.)

pamphlet libellus m

pan patina f, patella f; frying~ sartago 2

pander leno m

panegyric laudatio f

panel tabula f; ~led laqueatus; ~led ceiling lacunar n

pang dolor m

panic pavor m; ~stricken pavidus, exterritus

pannier clitellae f/pl.

pansy viola f

pant anhelo 1; ~ing anhelitus, us m

panther panthera *f*

pantry cella *f* (penaria)

pap puls *f*

paper charta *f*; papyrus, i *f*; libellus *m*

papyrus papyrus, i *f*

parade pompa *f*; mil. decursus, us *m*; ostento 1; mil. decurro 3

paragon specimen *n*

paralys|e debilito 1; *fig.* percello 3; ~is paralysis *f*

paramount summus; antiquissimus

paramour adulter *m*; meretrix *f*

parapet pluteus *m*

paraphernalia apparatus, us *m*

paraphrase interpretor 1

parasite parasitus *m*

parasol umbraculum *n*

parcel fasciculus *m*; ~ out partior 4

parch torreo 2; uro 3; ~ed torridus, aridus

parchment membrana *f*

pardon ignosco 3 (alci alqd); veniam do 1 (alci); venia *f*, excusatio *f*

pare reseco 1; circumcido 3

parent parens *m and f*; genitor *m*, genetrix *f*; ~age genus *n*; stirps *f*; ~al patrius

park horti *m/pl.*; vivarium *n*

parlance sermo *m*

parley colloquor 3; colloquium *n*

parliament concilium *n*; senatus, us *m*

parlour conclave *n*

parody per iocum imitor 1

parole fides *f*

parricide parricida *m*; parricidium *n*

parrot psittacus *m*

parry eludo 3; propulso 1

parsimon|ious parcus; ~y parsimonia *f*; sordes *f/pl.*

part pars *f*; *thea.* partes *f/pl.*; persona *f*; ~s loca *n/pl.*; in, to, foreign ~s peregre; for my ~ equidem; for the most ~ plerumque; in great ~ magna ex parte; do one's ~ officium servo 1; play a ~ partes ago 3; take in good, bad, ~ in bonam, malam, partem accipio 3 (alqd); take ~ in intersum (dat.); me immisceo 2 (dat.); attingo 3 (alqd); have no ~ in expertem sum (gen.); it is my ~ meum est; it is the ~ of a king regis est; v/t. seiungo 3; separo 1; divido 3; v/i. ~ from discedo 3, digredior 3 (ab)

partake particeps sum (gen.); intersum (dat.)

partial cupidus; iniquus; ~ity studium *n*; ~ly ex aliqua parte

particip|ant particeps; ~ate particeps sum

particle particula *f*

particular proprius; praecipuus; subtilis; ~ly praecipue, praesertim

parting digressus, us *m*

partisan fautor *m*; be a ~ of
studiosus sum (*gen.*)

partition partitio *f*; paries *m*

partly partim; (aliqua) ex
parte

partner socius *m*; consors;
~ship societas *f*

partridge perdix *f*

party pars *f*, factio *f*;
convivium *n*; ~ to affinis
(*dat.*)

pass *v/t.* ago 3, dego 3
(*tempus*); trado 3 (*alci
alqd*); perfero 3 (*legem*);
v/i. intercedo 3; transeo 4
(*dies, etc.*); pervenio 4
(*hereditas, etc.*); ~ away intereo 4; ~ by praetereo 4,
praetervehor 3 (*acc.*); ~ for
habeor 2 (*pro algo*); ~ on
v/t. trado 3; *v/i.* pergo 3;
~ over transeo 4 (*alqd; ad*);
praetermitto 3. come to ~
fio, evenio 4; angustiae
f/pl., fauces *f/pl.*; discri-

passable tolerabilis [men *n f*]

passage transitus, us *m*;
via *f*; iter, ineris *n*; trans-
itio *f*; (*of book*) locus *m*

passenger vector *m*

passer-by qui praeterit

passion (*animi*) motus *m/pl.*;
cupiditas *f*; libido *f*; ira *f*;
iracundia *f*; studium *n*;
~ate ardens, vehemens;
iracundus

passive iners, lentus

password tessera *f*

past praeteritus; praeterita
n/pl.; praeteritum tempus
n; *prep.* praeter, ultra
(*acc.*)

paste gluten *n*

pastille pastillus *m*

pastime ludus *m*

pastoral pastoralis

pastry crustum *n*; ~cook
pistor *m*; crustularius *m*

pastur|age pabulum *n*;
pastus, us *m*; ~e pascuum
n; pasco 3

pat permulceo 2; palpo 1

patch sarcio 4; pannus *m*;
~work cento *m*

patent apertus, manifestus;
diploma *n*, privilegium *n*

paternal paternus, patrius

path semita *f*; trames *m*;
via *f*; iter, ineris *n*

pathetic miser, miserabilis

pathless invius

patien|ce patientia *f*; with
~ce aequo animo; ~t pa-
tiens; aeger *m*, aegro-
tus *m*

patrician patricius

patriot bonus, optimus civis
m; ~ic amans patriae

patrol custodiae *f/pl.*, vigiliae *f/pl.*

patron patronus *m*; praeses
m; ~age patrocinium *n*;
clientela *f*; ~ize faveo 2
(*dat.*)

pattern exemplar *n*, exemplum *n*, specimen *n*;
signum *n*

paucity paucitas *f*

paunch venter, tris *m*

pauper inops

pause subsisto 3; inter-
mitto 3; intermissio *f*

pave munio 4; ~ment pavi-
mentum *n*

pavilion tabernaculum *n*

paw pes *m*; pulso 1

pawn (op)pignero 1; pignus *n*

pay solvo 3; pendo 3 (*pecuniam pro*); ~ down, out numero 1; ~ off exsolvo 3 (*aes alienum, etc.*); ~ penalty poenas do 1; ~ respects saluto 1 (*alqm*); merces *f*; soldier's ~ stipendium *n*; ~master tribunus *m* aerarius; ~ment solutio *f*

pea pisum *n*

peace pax *f*; otium *n*; ~ of mind securitas *f*; tranquillus; ~ful pacatus, placidus

peach Persicum *n*

peacock pavo *m*

peak cacumen *n*; vertex *m*

peal sono 1; fragor *m*

pear pirum *n*; ~tree pirus, i *f*

pearl margarita *f*

peasant rusticus, agrestis

pebble calculus *m*

peck vellico 1; modius *m*

peculation peculatus, us *m*

peculiar proprius; singularis; ~ity proprium *n*; proprietas *f*

pedant scholasticus *m*; ~ry proprium *n*

peddle vendito 1

pedestal basis *f*

pedestrian pedester

pedigree stemma *n*

pediment fastigium *n*

peel cutis *f*; membrana *f*; reseco 1

peep strictim aspicio 3 (at *alqd*)

peer rimor 1 (at *alqd*); par; ~less unicus

peevish stomachosus, morosus

peg clavus *m*

pell-mell passim

pelt iacio 3 (*alqd in alqm*); peto 3 (*alqm telis, etc.*)

pen calamus *m*; (*for animals*) saepta *n/pl.*; scribo 3; includo 3

penalty poena *f*; supplicium *n*, damnum *n*; pay, exact the ~ poenas do 1, sumo 3

pencil penicillus *m*

pending dum

penetrate|pervado 3 (*ad, per*); penetro 1, pervenio 4 (*in, ad*); ~ion sagacitas *f*

peninsula paeninsula *f*

penitent: be ~ paenitet (*me alcs rei, quod, inf.*)

pennant vexillum *n*

penniless inops

penny as *m* (*a copper coin*)

pension annua *n/pl.*

penthouse vinea *f*

penur|ious inops; ~y egestas *f*

people homines *m/pl.*; populus *m*; common ~ plebs *f*; vulgus, i *n*; incolo 3; frequento 1; of the ~ publicus

pepper piper *n*

perceive percipio 3; sentio 4; intellego 3

perch insido 3 (*dat.*); sedile *n* (avium)

perchance forte

percussion ictus, us *m*

perdition exitium *n*

peremptorily praecise

perfect perfectus; integer; merus, perficio 3; **~ion** perfectio *f*, absolutio *f*; **~ly** plane, prorsus

perfid|ious perfidus; **~y** perfidia *f*

perforate perforo 1

perforce per vim; invitus

perform persequor 3; exsequor 3; fungor 3 (*abl.*); praesto 1 (*munus, fidem, etc.*); *thea.* ago 3; **~ance** functio *f*

perfume odor *m*; unguentum *n*; **~d** odoratus

perhaps fortasse; forsan, forsitan; forte, nescio an; haud scio an

peril periculum *n*, discrimen *n*; **~ous** periculosus

period tempus *n*; aetas *f*; spatium *n* temporis

perish pereo 4, intereo 4; **~able** caducus

peristyle peristylum *n*

perjur|ed periurus; **~y** periurium *n*; commit **~y** peiero 1

permanen|ce stabilitas *f*; **~t** diuturnus, mansurus; **~tly** perpetuo

permeate permano 1 (*in*)

permission potestas *f*; with your **~** bona tua venia; without the **~** of iniussu (*alcs*); invito (*alqo*); give **~** potestatem facio 3 (*alci faciendi*); have **~** licet (*per alqm*)

permit permitto 3 (*alci ut*); sino 3 (*inf.*; *acc. c. inf.*); it is **~ted** licet (*alci inf.*; *acc.c.inf.*)

pernicious perniciosus

peroration peroratio *f*

perpendicular (di)rectus

perpetrate committo 3; admitto 3 (*facinus*; *facinus in me*)

perpetua|l perennis, sempiternus, perpetuus; **~te** perpetuo 1

perplex distraho 3; sollicito 1; be **~ed** haereo 2; **~ity** dubitatio *f*

persecut|e insector 1; **~ion** insectatio *f*; **~or** insectator *m*

persever|ance perseverantia *f*; **~e** persevero 1, persto 1 (*in re*); **~ing** pertinax

persist persto 1, persevero 1 (*in re*); permaneo 2; **~ent** pertinax

person homo *m*; caput *n*; persona *f*; in **~** ipse; **~age** persona *f*; **~al** privatus; proprius; **~al appearance** habitus, us *m*; **~ality** mores *m/pl.*

perspicaci|ous perspicax; **~ty** acumen *n*

perspir|ation sudor *m*; **~e** sudo 1

persuade persuadeo 2 (*alci ut, ne*); adduco 3 (*alqm in, ad, ut*)

pert procax

pertain attineo 2, pertineo 2 (*ad*)

pertinacious pertinax

pertinent aptus, appositus
pertness procacitas *f*
perturb (per)turbo 1; sollicito 1; ~ation perturbatio *f*
perus|al pellectio *f*; ~e per-
lego 3
pervade permano 1 (*in, ad*);
pervado 3 (*acc., in, per*)
perverse perversus, pravus;
pertinax
perver|sion depravatio *f*;
~t depravo 1; corrumpo 3
pest pestis *f*; ~er vexo 1;
~ilence pestilentia *f*
pestle pilum *n*
pet deliciae *f/pl.*; amores
m/pl.
petition preces *f/pl.*; libellus *m*; libellum do 1 (*alci*);
~er supplex *m*
petrify in lapidem me verto 3; *fig.* be ~ied obstupesco 3
petticoat tunica *f*
pettish stomachosus
petty minutus, angustus
petulant stomachosus
pew subsellium *n*
phantom simulacrum *n*
pheasant phasianus *m*
phenomenon res *f* (mirabilis, nova)
phial laguncula *f*
philanthrop|ic beneficus,
humanus; ~y humanitas *f*
philolog|ical grammaticus;
~ist grammaticus *m*; ~y
grammatica *f*
philosoph|er philosophus *m*;
sapiens *m*; ~ize philosophor 1; ~y philosophia *f*
philtre amatorium *n*

phlegm pituita *f*; ~atic
lentus
phoenix phoenix *m*
phrase verba *n/pl.*; dico 3,
loquor 3
physic medicamentum *n*;
~al physicus; ~al strength
corporis vires *f/pl.*; ~ian
medicus *m*; ~s physica
n/pl.
physiognomy vultus, us *m*;
oris lineamenta *n/pl.*
pick carpo 3, lego 3; ~ out
vello 3; eligo 3; ~ up tollo
3, colligo 3; the ~ of the
troops robur *n* militum;
~axe dolabra *f*; ~ed lectus,
electus; ~et statio *f*; sta-
tionem dispono 3
pickle condo 3; condio 4;\
pickpocket fur *m* [muria *f*]
picture tabula *f*; depingo 3;
fingo 3 (animo)
pie crustum *n*
piece frustum *n*; *thea.* fabula *f*; *mus.* carmen *n*;
~ of money nummus *m*;
sarcio 4; break in ~s comminuo 3; fall to ~s dis-
solvor 3; tear in ~s discerpo 3; lanio 1
pied versicolor
pier moles *f*; pila *f*
pierce|confodio 4, traicio 3;
perforo 1, terebro 1; *fig.*
ango 3; ~ing acutus, acer
piety pietas *f*
pig porcus *m*; sus *f and m*;
porcinus
pigeon columba *f*; palum-
bes *m and f*
pigmy pumilio *m and f*

pigsty hara *f*

pike hasta *f*; (*fish*) lupus *m*

pile acervus *m*; cumulus *m*; strues *f*; palus *m*; sublica *f*; *funeral* ~ rogus *m*; (*of cloth*) villus *m*; ~ up congero 3, exstruo 3; coacervo 1

pilfer surripio 3 (*alqd alci*); ~er fur *m*

pill pilula *f*

pillage *v/t.* diripio 3; populor 1; *v/i.* praedor 1; rapina *f*, direptio *f*

pillar columna *f*; *fig.* columen *n*

pillow pulvinus *m*; cervical *n*

pilot gubernator *m*; guberno 1

pimp leno *m*

pimple pusula *f*, pustula *f*

pin acus, us *f*; fibula *f*; affigo 3 (*alqd ad alqd, dat.*)

pincers forceps *f*

pinch vellico 1; uro 3 (*frigus, calcei, etc.*); urgeo 2 (*inopia*)

pine tabesco 3; consenesco 3; pinus, us *f*

pinion vincio 4; pinna *f*

pink roseus

pinnacle fastigium *n*

pint sextarius *m*

pious pius, religiosus

pip semen *n*; granum *n*

pipe fistula *f*; tibia *f*; tubus *m*; tubulus *m*; *reed* ~ calamus *m*; tibia cano 3; ~r fistulator *m*; tibicen *m*

piquant acer; salsus

pique offensio *f*

pira|cy latrocinium *n*; ~te praedo *n*; pirata *m*; piraticus

pit fovea *f*, fossa *f*; barathrum *n*; *arm.* ala *f*; excavo 1; ~ against oppono 3 (*dat.*)

pitch pono 3 (*castra*); conicio 3; pix *f*; *to such a* ~ eo (*gen.*); *highest* ~ fastigium *n*; *musical* ~ vox *f*; ~ed battle universae rei dimicatio *f*; ~er urceus *m*; ~fork furca *f*; ~pipe fistula *f*; ~y piceus

piteous miserabilis

pitfall *fig.* laqueus *m*; plaga *f*

pith medulla *f*; *fig.* summa *f*; ~y sententiosus

pit|iable, ~iful miserabilis, afflictus; ~iless durus, ferreus

pittance mercedula *f*

pity misereor 2 (*gen.*); me miseret (*gen.*); misericordia *f*; miseratio *f*; ~ing misericors

pivot cardo *m*

placard libellus *m*

placate placo 1

place locus *m*; sedes *f*; gradus, us *m*; officium *n*; *in this, that* ~ hic, illic; *in the same* ~ ibidem; *in the* ~ *of* loco (*gen.*); *take* ~ fio; accido 3; *out of* ~ ineptus; pono 3; (*coll*)loco 1; statuo 3

placid placidus, tranquillus

plagiari|sm furtum *n*; ~ze compilo 1 (*alqd*)

plague pestilentia *f*; pestis *f*; molestus sum; vexo 1

plain planus, manifestus, apertus, clarus; inornatus, subtilis, purus, simplex; campus *m*; planities *f*; aequum *n*; ~ly simpliciter (*loqui, etc.*); ~ness simplicitas *f*

plaint querela *f*

plaintiff petitor *m*, actor *m*, accusator *m* [bilis]

plaintive querulus, misera-*f*

plait intexo 3, nodo 1

plan consilium *n*; ratio *f*; descriptio *f*; consilium capio 3; excogito 1; describo 3

plane tero 1; rado 3; lima *f*, runcina *f*; ~tree platanus, i *f*

planet stella *f* errans

plank tabula *f*

plant sero 3, consero 3; pono 3; herba *f*; ~ation arbustum *n*; ~er sator *m*

plaster induco 3 (*alqd alci rei*); tectorium *n*

plate lamina *f*; lanx *f*, patella *f*; silver ~ argentum *n*

platform tribunal *n*; suggestus, us *m*; (*in Forum*) rostra *n/pl.*

plaudits plausus, us *m*

plausible probabilis, speciosus

play ludo 3; cano 3 (*abl.*); ago 3 (*fabulam*); ludus *m*; *thea.* fabula *f*; ~er histrio *m*; ~ful lascivus; iocosus; ~mate collusor *m*

plea excusatio *f*; *jur.* exceptio *f*; ~d excuso 1, causor 1 (*alqd*); obsecro 1 (*ut*); defendo 3 (*acc. c. inf.*); ~d a case causam dico 1, ago 3; ~der orator *m*

pleasant iucundus, amoenus; suavis; ~ry facetiae *f/pl.*

please placeo 2 (*dat.*); delecto 1 (*acc.*); gratificor 1 (*alci*); ~! quaeso 3; as you ~ quod libet; if you ~ si libet

pleas|ing gratus; be ~ing cordi est (*alci*); ~ure voluptas *f*; libido *f*; arbitratus, us *m*; it is the ~ure of placet 2, videtur 3 (*dat.*)

plebeian plebeius; ~ order plebs *f*

pledge spondeo 2 (*alqd alci*; *acc. c. inf.*); promitto 3; oppignero 1, obligo 1 (*alqd*); pignus *n*; fides *f*

plentiful largus, uber; ~y copia *f*; ~y of satis (*gen.*)

pliable lentus; flexibilis

plight obligo 1; miseria *f*

plot coniuro 1; molior 4; coniuratio *f*; consilium *n*; *thea.* argumentum *n*; ~ of land agellus *m*

plough aro 1; aratrum *n*; ~share vomer, eris *m*

pluck carpo, lego 3; vello 3; ~ up courage bono animo sum, utor 3 (*abl.*); ~y fortis

plug obturo 1; obturamentum *n*

plum prunum *n*; ~-tree prunus, i *f*

plumage pinnae *f/pl.*, plumae *f/pl.*

plumb(-line) perpendiculum *n*

plume penna *f*, pinna *f*; ~ oneself on me iacto 1 (*de*)

plump pinguis, nitidus

plunder praedor 1; diripio 3; praeda *f*; ~ing rapina *f*; praedatorius

plunge *v/t.* (im)mergo 3, summergo 3 (*in*); *v/i.* me mergo, *etc.* (*in*)

plural pluralis; ~ity multitudo *f*

ply exerceo 2, urgeo 2

poach furor 1; ~er fur *m*

pocket sacculus *m*; intercipio 3; ~book (tablets) pugillares *m/pl.*; ~money peculium *n*

pod siliqua *f*

poem poema, atis *n*, carmen *n*

poet poeta *m*; ~ess poetria *f*; ~ical poeticus; ~ry carmen *n*; poesis *f*; versus *m/pl.*

poignant acerbus

point acumen *n*; mucro *m*; punctum *n*; locus *m*; res *f*; the main ~ summa *f*; caput *n*; to this ~ huc; to such a ~ eo; on the ~ of speaking locuturus; be to the ~ attineo 2; ~ out (de)monstro 1; designo 1; significo 1; ostendo 3; ~ed (prae-)acutus; salsus; ~er index *m*; ~less frigidus, insulsus, ineptus

poise libro 1

poison venenum *n*; venenum do 1 (*alci*); veneno 1 (*alqd*); ~er veneficus *m*; ~ing veneficium *n*; ~ous venenatus

poke fodio 3; fodico 1; ~r rutabulum *n*

polar septentrionalis

pole contus *m*; axis *m*; ~cat feles *f*

polemics controversiae *f/pl.*

police vigiles *m/pl.*

policy consilia *n/pl.*; ratio *f*

polish polio 4; *fig.* limo 1; nitor *m*; lima *f*; ~ed (per-)politus

polite comis, humanus; urbanus; ~ness comitas *f*; humanitas *f*

politic prudens

politic|al civilis, politicus; ~s res *f* publica; take part in ~s in re publica versor 1

poll suffragium *n*

pollut|e inquino 1, contamino 1; polluo 3; ~ion colluvio *f*

pomp pompa *f*; apparatus, us *m*; ~osity magnificentia *f*; ~ous inflatus

pond stagnum *n*

ponder considero 1; animo voluto 1; ~ous gravis

poniard pugio *m*

pony mannus *m*

pool stagnum *n*; lacus, us *m*

poop puppis *f*

poor pauper, inops, egens; miser; exilis

pop crepito 1; ~ out exsilio 4; crepitus, us *m*

pope pontifex *m*

poplar populus, i *f*; populeus

poppy papaver, eris *n*

populace plebes *m/pl.*; vulgus, i *n*

popular popularis; gratus, acceptus; vulgaris; ~ party populares *m/pl.*; ~ity favor *m* (populi); studium *n*; ~ly populariter

population populus *m*

populous frequens, celeber

porcelain fictilis

porch vestibulum *n*; porticus, us *f*

porcupine hystrix *f*

pore foramen *n*; ~ over animum, considerationem intendo 3 (*in alqd*)

pork porcina *f*

porridge puls *f*

port portus, us *m*

portal porta *f*

portcullis cataracta *f*

portend portendo 3; significo 1

portent prodigium *n*, portentum *n*, monstrum *n*; ~ous prodigiosus

porter ianitor *m*; ostiarius *m*; baiulus *m*

portfolio scrinium *n*

portico porticus, us *f*

portion pars *f*; divido 3; partior 4; marriage ~ dos *f*

portly plenus

portmanteau mantica *f*

portrait imago *f*

portray pingo 3; depingo 3, describo 3

pose *v/t.* (pro)pono 3

(*quaestionem*); *v/i.* simulo 1 (*acc. c. inf.*); status, us *m*

position locus *m*; situs, us *m*; *fig.* status, us *m*; gradus, us *m*

positive certus, firmus; be ~ that pro certo habeo 2

possess possideo 2, habeo 2, teneo 2; est mihi; ~ed insanus; ~ion possessio *f*; take ~ion of occupo 1, capio 3 (*locum, animum, etc.*); ~ions bona *n/pl.*

possible: it is ~ fieri potest (*ut*); as quickly as ~ quam celerrime

possibly fortasse; fieri potest (*ut*)

post (col)loco 1; constituo 3 (*milites*); do 1 (*litteras*); ~ up propono 3, figo 3 (*in publicum*); palus *m*; cippus *m*, statio *f*, locus *m*, praesidium *n*; officium *n*; door~ postis *m*; tabellarius

posterior posterior; ~ty posteri *m/pl.*; posteritas *f*

postman tabellarius *m*

postpone differo 3, profero 3

postulate pono 3

posture status, us *m*

pot olla *f*

potency vis *f*; ~t efficax, potens; ~tate princeps *m*, rex *m*

potion potio *f*

potsherd testa *f*

potter figulus *m*; ~y fictilia *n/pl.*

pouch pera *f*; sacculus *m*

poultry altiles *m/pl.*

pounce upon insilio 4; involo 1 (in alqm)

pound tero 3, tundo 3; libra f

pour fundo 3; ~ down v/i. me deicio 3; v/t. praecipito 1; ~ forth, out v/t. profundo 3; v/i. me eicio 3, effundor 3

poverty paupertas f, egestas f

powder pulvis m; tero 3 (in pulverem)

power vis f; ops f; potestas f, potentia f; imperium n, dicio f; be in one's ~ in manu sum (alcs); ~ful validus; potens, valens; efficax; be very, most ~ful multum, plurimum possum; be ~less nihil possum

practical experience, practice usus, us m; tractatio f; exercitatio f

practise exerceo 2; celebro 1; meditor 1; ~d exercitatus, peritus

praetor praetor m; ~ian guard praetoriani m/pl.; praetorium n; ~ship praetura f

praise laudo 1; celebro 1 (laudibus); laus f; ~worthy laudabilis, laudandus

prance exsulto 1

prank iocus m

prate, prattle garrio 4, blatero 1

pray precor 1, obsecro 1; oro 1 (alqm, alqd, ut);

quaeso 3 (alqd ab alqo, ut); ~ to the gods adoro 1 (acc.); supplico 1 (dat.); ~er preces f/pl.; precatio f

preach doceo 2

preamble praefatio f; exordium n

precarious incertus

precaution: take ~s praecaveo 2 (ne)

precede praeeo 4; antecedo 3 (acc., dat.); ante fio, sum (quam)

precedence: give ~ to cedo 3 (alci); praevertor 3 (alqd, alci rei)

preced|ent exemplum n; ~ing proximus, superior

precept praeceptum n

precinct templum n

precious pretiosus

precipi|ce locus m praeceps, abruptus; ~tate v/i. me praecipito 1, deicio 3; v/t. maturo 1 (alqd); praeceps, temerarius; ~tous praeceps, praeruptus

precis|e subtilis, exactus; ~ion subtilitas f; cura f

preclude prohibeo 2 (inf., ne)

precocious praecox

precon|ceived praeiudicatus; ~ception praeiudicata opinio f; ~certed compositus

pre|decessor proximus; ~determine praefinio 4; ~dicament angustiae f/pl.

predict praedico 3; ~ion praedictum n; praedictio f

pre|dilection studium n;

dominate plus, plurimum possum; superiores sunt; eminent praecipuus

preface praefatio *f*; praefor 1 (*pauca*)

prefect praefectus *m*; ure praefectura *f*

prefer malo (*alqd. inf.*); antepono 3, praepono 3 (*acc., dat.*); ~ a charge against nomen defero 3 (*alcs de re*); able potior, antiquior; ably potius

prefix praescribo 3, praepono 3

pregnan|cy graviditas *f*; t gravida, praegnans

prejud|ge praeiudico 1; ice praeiudicata opinio *f*; laedo 1

preliminary: ~ exercise prolusio *f*; make some ~ remarks pauca praefor 1

prelude proemium *n*; *fig.* prolusio *f*

premature praematurus, immaturus

premeditate praemeditor 1; dly consulto, de industria

premier princeps *m* [stria] premise propositio *f*, assumptio; s aedificia *n/pl.*

premium praemium *n*

premonition augurium *n*

preoccupied occupatus

prepar|ation praeparatio *f*; e (prae)paro 1; meditor 1; me comparo 1 (*ad alqd*)

preponderate plus, plurimum polleo 2

preposterous praeposterus, absurdus

presage portendo 3; significo 1

prescribe praescribo 3

presence praesentia *f*; conspectus, us *m*; ce of mind praesens animus *m*; praesentia *f* animi; in the ce of coram (*abl.*); in my ce me praesente

present praesens; at the ~ in praesenti; for the ~ in praesens; at the ~ day hodie; be ~ adsum, intersum (*dat.*); introduco 3; offero 3, obicio 3; praebeo 2, dono 1 (*alqm dono*); ~ itself occurro 3; obvenio 4; donum *n*, munus *n*; iment augurium *n*; ly mox, brevi

preserv|ation conservatio *f*; e (con)servo 1; tueor 2; (*fruit*) condio 4; ed conditivus; er servator *m*

preside praesideo 2 (*dat.*); ut praefectus *m*

press premo 3 (*alqd, alqm*); ~ hard urgeo 2; insto 1 (*dat.*); ~ together comprimo 3; prelum *n* (*for wine, olives, clothes, etc.*); turba *f*; ing praesens; ingly vehementer, impense; ure pressus, us *m*

prestige gloria *f*

presum|e sumo 3 (*mihi ut*); audeo 2; ption arrogantia *f*; coniectura *f*; ptuous arrogans

preten|ce simulatio *f*, species *f*; d simulo 1; dictito 1. fingo 3; der qui regnum affectat; ~sion ostentatio *f*; have ~sions to affecto 1 (*alqd*)

preternatural monstruosus; ~ly praeter modum

pretext species *f*; put forward as a ~ praetendo 3 (*alqd alci rei*)

pretty bellus, pulcher, lepidus

prevail vinco 3; valeo 2; ~ upon impetro 1 (*alqd ab alqo; ut*)

prevalent creber, vulgatus; become ~ increb(r)esco 3

prevaricate tergiversor 1

prevent prohibeo 2 (*alqm; quominus; acc. c. inf.*); obsto 1 (*dat.; quominus*)

previous proximus, superior, prior; ~ to prius quam; ~ly antea, antehac

prey praeda *f*; ~ upon praedor 1; *fig.* sollicito 1

price pretium *n*; ~ of corn, food annona *f*; sell at a high, low ~ magno, parvo vendo 3; *v/t.* pretium constituo 3; ~less pretiosissimus

prick pungo 3; *fig.* stimulo 1; ~ up one's ears aures erigo 3; stimulus *m*; aculeus *m*; ~le spina *f*; ~ly spinosus

pride superbia *f*; fastidium *n*; ~ oneself on glorior 1 (*de, in re*)

priest sacerdos *m and f*; ~hood sacerdotium *n*

prima|cy principatus, us *m*; ~ry primus

prime optimus; erudio 4 (*alqm de*); be in the ~ floreo 2, vigeo 2; ~val priscus

primitive priscus, pristinus, antiquus, principalis

prince rex *m*, princeps *m*; regulus *m*; ~ly regalis; ~ss regina *f*; regis filia *f*

principal praecipuus, primus; magister, tri *m*; (*money*) caput *n*; ~ity regnum *n*

principle principium *n*, elementum *n*; institutum *n*, decretum *n*; man of ~ vir *m* probus, integer

print imprimo 3 (*alqd in re*); nota *f* (*impressa*); tabula *f*

prior potior; ~ to ante (*acc.*)

prison carcer, eris *n*; vincula *n/pl.*; ~er captivus *m*; *jur.* reus *m*; take ~er capio 3

priva|cy solitudo *f*; secretum *n*; secessus, us *m*; ~te privatus; proprius; secretus; domesticus; in ~te privatim; secreto; ~te soldier miles *m* gregarius; ~tion inopia *f*

privet ligustrum *n*

privilege ius *n*; commodum *n*

privy secretus; ~ to conscius (*dat.*)

prize praemium *n*; praeda *f*; magni facio 3

probabl|e veri similitudo *f*; ~le veri similis; probabilis; ~ly nescio an probation rudimenta *n/pl.*; ~er tiro *m*

probe scrutinor 1; tento 1

probity probitas *f*

problem quaestio *f*

procedure ratio *f*

proceed pergo 3; procedo 3, progredior 3; ~ against persequor 3 (*alqm iudicio*); *fig.* ~ from proficiscor 3; ~ing ratio *f*; ~ings acta *n/pl.*; ~s fructus, us *m*

process *iur.* actio *f*; ~ion pompa *f*

procla|im pronuntio 1; renuntio 1, declaro 1 (*alqm consulem, etc.*); edico 3; ~mation praedicatio *f*; edictum *n*

proconsul proconsul *m*; pro consule

procrastinat|e cunctor 1; ~ion mora *f*; cunctatio *f*

procur|ator procurator *m*; ~e comparo 1, adipiscor 3; ~er leno *m*

prodigal prodigus

prodig|ious immanis; ~y portentum *n*, prodigium *n*; miraculum *n*

produce profero 3, produco 3; pario 3; (ef)fero 3; efficio 3, moveo 2; fructus, us *m*; fetus, us *m*

product fructus, us *m*; opus *n*; ~ive ferax; fecundus

profan|ation violatio *f*; ~e profanus; impius; violo 1; polluo 3

profess profiteor 2 (*alqd*; *acc. c. inf.*); ~ion professio *f*; artificium *n*

proffer polliceor 2

proficient prudens, peritus (*gen.*)

profile obliqua imago *f*

profit prosum (*dat.*); proficio 3 (*ad*); commodum *n*, bonum *n*; emolumentum *n*, lucrum *n*; quaestus, us *m*; get ~ from proficio 3 (*abl.*); ~able fructuosus, quaestuosus; ~less inutilis

profliga|cy flagitia *n/pl.*; ~te perditus

profound altus, profundus; ~ly penitus, valde

profus|e prodigus, profusus; ~ion copia *f*

progeny progenies *f*

programme consilium *n*

progress progredior 3; iter, ineris *n*; progressus, us *m*; progressio *f*; make ~ proficio 3 (*in alqa re*); progressus facio 3; ~ion progressio *f*

prohibit veto 1, prohibeo 2 (*acc. c. inf.*); interdico 3 (*alci alqd; ne*); ~ion interdictum *n*

project emineo 2 (*ex, in, super*); consilium *n*; ~ile missile *n*; ~ing eminens, projectus

proletariat vulgus, i *n*

prolific fecundus

prolix verbosus

prologue prologus *m*

prolong produco 3; prorogo 1 (*imperium*); ~ation prolatio *f*; ~ed diuturnus

prominent eminens; praestans

promise promitto 3; polliceor 2, profiteor 2; promissum *n*; keep, break a ~ fidem servo 1, fallo 3

promontory promunturium *n*

promot|e proveho 3, produco 3 (*alqm ad honorem*); servio 4, consulo 3 (*alci rei*); ~ion amplior honoris gradus, us *m*

prompt promptus, paratus (*ad*); impello 3 (*alqm in, ut*); subicio 3 (*verba etc.*); ~itude celeritas *f*

promulgate promulgo 1

prone pronus; ~ to pronus, propensus (*ad*)

prong dens *m*

pronounce pronuntio 1 (*sententiam etc.*); enuntio 1, loquor 3 (*litteras*)

pronunciation appellatio *f*

proof documentum *n*, argumentum *n*, indicium *n*; be a ~ documento sum; make ~ of experior 4; ~ against invictus (*ab, adversus*)

prop adminiculum *n*, columen *n*; ~ up fulcio 4, sustineo 2

propagat|e propago 1, dissemino 1; ~ion propagatio *f*

propel impello 3

propensity proclivitas *f*; have a ~ to propensus, pronus sum (*ad*)

proper proprius; decorus; it is ~ decet (*acc. c. inf.*); ~ly proprie; recte, commode; ~ty proprium *n*; proprietas *f*; bona *n/pl.*; res *f*; fortunae *f/pl.*

prophe|cy praedictio *f*; praedictum *n*; oraculum *n*; ~sy vaticinor 1, ominor 1, divino 1; praedico 3; ~t vates *m and f*; ~tic divinus

propinquity propinquitas *f*

propitiat|e placo 1; ~ion placatio *f*; piaculum *n*

propitious propitius, faustus, prosperus

proportion ratio *f*; in ~, ~ally pro portione; in ~ to pro (*abl.*); sense of ~ modus *m*

propos|al condicio *f*; consilium *n*; carry a ~al (*for a law*) rogationem perfero 3; ~e in animo est (*mihi*), cogito 1 (*inf.*); pono 3; fero 3, rogo 1 (*legem*); ~er lator *m* (*legis*); auctor *m*; ~ition condicio *f*; propositio *f*, propositum *n*

propound expono 3, pono 3

propriet|or dominus *m*; ~y decorum *n*

prorogue differo 3; prorogo 1

proscri|be proscribo 3; ~p-tion proscriptio *f*

prose soluta oratio *f*; solutus

prosecut|e nomen (*alcs*) defero 3, accuso 1 (*alqm rei, de re*); exsequor 3, persequor 3; ~ion accusatio *f*, delatio *f*; ~or accusator *m*, actor *m*

prospect prospectus, us *m*; spes *f*

prosper *v/t.* adiuvo 1; *v/i.* secunda, prospera fortuna utor 3; floreo 2; bene procedit (*mihi*); be ~ *ity* res *f/pl.* secundae, prosperae; ~ous secundus, prosperus, florens

prostitute vulgo 1; meretrix *f*

prostrate sterno 3; ~ oneself procumbo 3, me proicio 3, prosterno 3 (*humi, ad pedes alcs*); be ~d iaceo 2, fractus sum

protect defendo 3, tueor 2; protego 3; ~ion tutela *f*; praesidium *n*; ~or defensor *m*, praeses *m*

protest obtestor 1 (*acc. c. inf.*); ~ against recuso 1 (*ne, quominus*)

protract (pro)duco 3; ~ed diuturnus

protrude *v/t.* protrudo 3; *v/i.* emineo 2

protuberan|ce tuber, eris *n*; ~t eminens

proud superbus, arrogans; be ~ of glorior 1 (*de, in re*)

prove *v/t.* probo 1, confirmo 1, efficio 3; experior 4; *v/i.* me praesto 1, praebeo 2; evado 3

proverb proverbium *n*

provide (com)paro 1; praebeo 2; ~ against caveo 2, provideo 2 (*ne*); ~ for provideo 2 (*dat.*); ~d with instructus (*abl.*); ~d that dum(modo), modo

providen|ce providentia *f*; ~t providus; ~tially divinitus

provinc|e regio *f*; provincia *f* (*also fig.*); ~ial provincialis

provision: make ~ for provideo 2; make ~ that caveo 2 (*ut, ne*); ~s frumentum *n*; res *f* frumentaria; commeatus, us *m*; cibaria *n/pl.*; ~ally ad tempus

provocation contumelia *f*

provok|e irrito 1, lacesso 3; moveo 2 (*alqd*); ~ing molestus

prow prora *f*

prowess virtus, utis *f*

prowl vagor 1

proxim|ate proximus; ~ity propinquitas *f*

proxy procurator *m*; vicarius *m*

prude|nce prudentia *f*; ~nt cautus, prudens; ~ry pudor *m*

prun|e (am)puto 1 (*also fig.*); ~ing knife falx *f*

pry into rimor 1, exploro 1

puberty pubes aetas *f*

public publicus; ~ affairs, ~ life res *f* publica; appear in ~ prodeo 4 in publicum; in ~ in publico; at ~ expense publice; make ~ vulgo 1; the ~ populus *m*; vulgus, i *n*; ~ house caupona *f*; ~an caupo *m*; ~ity lux *f*

publish effero 3; pervulgo 1; edo 3 (*librum etc.*)

pudding placenta *f*

puddle lacuna *f*

puerile puerilis, ineptus

puff *v/t.* flo 1; *v/i.* anhelo 1; ~ out inflo 1; be ~ed up *fig.* me effero 3, tumeo 2

pugilist pugil *m*

pugnacious pugnax

pull traho 3, vello 3, rapio 3; ~ down demolior 4, destruo 3; ~ out revello 3, evello 3, eripio 3; nisus, us *m*; ~ing tractus, us *m*; ~ey troclea *f*

pulp caro *f*

puls|ate agito 1; ~e pulsus, us *m* venarum

pulverise tero 3

pumice pumex *m*

pump antlia *f*; ~ out exhaurio 4 (*sentinam, aquam, etc.*); ~kin pepo *m*

pun iocus *m*; iocor 1

punch pertundo 3, terebro 3 (*alqd alqa re*); pulso 1, ferio 4 (*alqm*); ictus, us *m*

punctilious religiosus

punctual diligens; ~ly ad tempus, praesto

punctuat|e interpungo 3; ~ion mark interpunctum *n*

puncture pungo 3; punctum *n*

pungent acer

punish punio 4; animadverto 3; poenas sumo 3, capio 3 (*de alqo*); ~ment poena *f*; supplicium *n*; animadversio *f*

puny pusillus

pupil discipulus *m*; ~ of the eye pupilla *f*, pupula *f*

puppet pupa *f*

puppy catellus *m*; catulus

purchase emo 3; comparo 1; emptio *f*; merx *f*; ~r emptor *m*

pure purus, merus; castus, integer

purge purgo 1 (*alvum, urbem, etc.*)

puri|fy purgo 1; lustro 1; ~ty castitas *f*, integritas *f*

purloin surripio 3

purple purpureus, conchyliatus; purpura *f*; conchylium *n*

purport volo (*esse etc.*); significatio *f*, sententia *f*; summa *f*; what is the ~ quo spectat?

purpose propositum *n*, consilium *n*; animus *m*; finis *m*; voluntas *f*; with this ~ eo, ideo (... *ut*); on ~ consulto; de industria; to no ~ frustra, nequicquam; it is to the ~ multum refert (*si, utrum, etc.*); in animo habeo 2, est; consilium est (*inf.*); ~less vanus, inutilis, irritus; ~ly consulto

purse crumena *f*; marsupium *n*; sacculus *m*; astringo 3

pursu|ance: in ~ance of ex (*abl.*); secundum (*acc.*); ~e (per)sequor 3, insequor 3; insisto 3 (*acc., dat.*); ~it studium *n*

purvey comparo 1; praebeo 2; ~ food obsono 1

push trudo 3, impello 3, expello 3; ~ on contendo 3, pergo 3; iter facio 3; impulsus, us *m*; impetus, us *m*

pusillanimous timidus, ignavus

puss feles *f*

put pono 3; colloco 1; ~ aside *fig.* (de)pono 3; ~ away condo 3; ~ back repono 3; ~ down depono 3; comprimo 3 (*seditionem*); ~ forth summitto 3, effero 3; ~ in impono 3, insero 3 (*alqd in rem*); ~ into shore applico 1 (*navem ad terram*); ~ off *v/t.* differo 3 (*alqd in posterum diem*); *v/i.* navem solvo 3; ~ on impono 3 (*alqd alci, in alqd*); induo 3 (*vestem alci, mihi*); ~ out eicio 3, ex-

stinguo 3 (*ignem*); effodio 3 (*oculum*); *fig.* perturbo 1 (*alqm*); ~ out of the way tollo 3; ~ to sea navem solvo 1; ~ up at deverto 3 (*ad, apud*); ~ up for peto 3 (*consulatum*); ~ up for sale propono 1 (*alqd venale*); ~ up with tolero 1, devoro 1

putr|ify putesco 3; ~id puter, putridus

puzzl|e aenigma *n*; quaestio *f*; dubium facio 3; per-turbo 1; be ~ed haereo 2, dubito 1; ~ing obscurus, ambiguus, dubius

pygmy pumilio *m*

pyramid pyramis *f*

pyre rogus *m*

Q

quack pharmacopola *m*, circulator *m*

quadrangle quadratum *n*

quadruped quadrupes *m and f*

quadruple: in ~ in quadru-plum

quaff haurio 4

quail trepido 1; ~ before pertimesco 3 (*alqd*); cotur-nix *f*

quaint facetus, insolitus

quak|e tremo 3; tremor *m*; ~ing trepidus

quali|fication potestas *f*; exceptio *f*; ~fied idoneus, aptus (*ad*); dignus (*abl.*); ~fy idoneum facio 3 (*alqm*); induo 3 (*alqd de volup-*

tate, etc.); ~ty ingenium *n*; natura *f*; virtus, utis *f*

quandary angustiae *f/pl.*

quantity magnitudo *f*; nu-merus *m*; vis *f*; small ~ aliquantulum *n*

quarrel rixor 1, altercor 1; iurgium *n*, altercatio *f*, rixa *f*; ~some litigiosus, pugnax

quarry lapicidinae *f/pl.*; praeda *f*; excido 3

quart duo sextarii *m/pl.*

quarter in quattuor partes divido 3; in hospitia de-duco 3 (*milites*); quarta pars *f*; quadrans *m*; locus *m*, regio *f*; (*of a town*) vicus *m*; ask for ~ in deditionem

venio 4; **fight without** ~
sine missione pugno 1;
give ~ parco 3, veniam do
1; ~**s hospitium** n; *mil.*
castra n/*pl.*; **general's** ~**s**
praetorium n; **come to**
close ~**s** manum consero 3
(*cum alqo*); **at close** ~**s**
comminus [facio 3]
quash rescindo 3; irritum|
quavering vibrans, tremulus, tremens
quay crepido f
queen regina f
queer insolitus; absurdus;
mirificus
quell comprimo 3; sedo 1
quench exstinguo 3; expleo 2 (*sitim*)
querulous queribundus,
querulus
query quaestio f
quest inquisitio f; **be in** ~ **of**
quaero 3 (*acc.*)
question interrogo 1, per-
contor 1 (*alqm*); dubito 1
(*de re*); (inter)rogatum n;
dubitatio f; quaestio f; res
f; **the** ~**is** quaestio est (*an*);
put someone to the ~
quaestionem habeo 2 (*de
alqo*); ~**able** anceps, incertus; ~**ing** interrogatio f
quibble captio f; captiose
dico 3; ~**ing** captiosus

quick celer, velox; alacer,
impiger; promptus (*ad*);
acutus, callidus; **be** ~ propero 1; vivum n; **cut to**
the ~ mordeo 2; ~**en** v/t.
accelero 1; excito 1; v/i.
vigeo 2; ~**ness** celeritas f,
alacritas f; acumen n;
~**silver** argentum n vivum;
~**-tempered** iracundus; ~
witted acutus, sagax
quiet quietus, tranquillus;
tacitus, taciturnus; placo
1, sedo 1; quies f, tran-
quillitas f; otium n; **be** ~
sileo 2, taceo 3; ~**ness**|
quill penna f [otium n]
quince cydonium n
quintessence medulla f
quip dictum n
quit excedo 3 (*abl., ex*);
relinquo 3 (*acc.*); ~ **of**
exemptus, solutus (*abl.*)
quite prorsus, plane, ad-
modum; omnino; **not** ~
parum
quiver tremo 3, trepido 1;
tremor m; (*for arrows*)
pharetra f; ~**ing** tremebundus, tremulus
quoit discus m
quot|ation dictum n; ~**e**
profero 3, laudo 1 (*aucto-
res, testes*)
quoth ait, inquit

R

rabbit cuniculus m
rabble turba f; colluvio f
rabid rabidus
race certo 1; gens f; genus

n; stirps f; certamen n
(*equorum etc.*); **chariot-**
curriculum n; ~**-course**
stadium n, curriculum n

rack torqueo 2; equuleus *m*; tormentum *n*; carnificina *f*; cratis *f*; be ~ed (ex)crucior 1; ~et strepitus, us *m*

racy salsus

radia|nce fulgor *m*, splendor *m*; ~nt nitidus, fulgens, splendidus; ~te fulgeo 2

radical tosus; *pol.* popularis; ~ly penitus, omnino

radish radix *f*

radius radius *m*

raft ratis *f*

rafter trabs *f*

rag pannus *m*; ~s panni *m/pl.*

rage ira *f*; furor *m*; rabies *f*; furo 3, saevio *m*

ragged pannuceus (*vestis*); pannosus (*homo*)

raid incursio *f*; incursionem facio 3 (*in*)

rail palus *m*; longurius *m*; ~at maledico 3 (*dat.*); convicium facio 3 (*alci*); ~ing pali *m/pl.*, saepes *f*; convicium *n*; ~lery iocatio *f*

raiment vestis *f*

rain pluvia *f*; imber *m*; it ~s pluit; ~bow arcus, us *m* (pluvius); ~water aquae *f/pl.* pluviae; ~y pluvius, pluvialis

raise tollo 3 (*alqd*; *clamorem*; *cachinnum*); (sub)levo 1; erigo 3 (*caput, oculos, animum*); effero 3 (*alqm ad dignitatem*); sero 3 (*fruges*); cogo 3 (*pecuniam*); conscribo 3 (*exercitum*)

raisin uva *f* passa

rake rado 3; ~ up excito 1; rastrum *n*; *fig.* ganeo *m*

rally *v/t.* restituo 3 (*ordines, aciem*); irrideo 2 (*alqm*); *v/i.* me colligo 3; concurro 3 (*milites*)

ram aries *m*; arietinus; ~ down fistuco 1

ramble vagor 1, erro 1; ~ing vagus

rampart vallum *n*; agger, eris *m*; moenia *n/pl.*

ranco|rous infensus; ~ur simultates *f/pl.*; invidia *f*

random fortuitus; at ~ temere

range *v/t.* dispono 3; *v/i.* (per)vagor 1; ordo *m*; genus *n*; *fig.* campus *m*, area *f* (*orationis etc.*); mountain ~ iugum *n*; ~ of a weapon teli iactus, us *m*

rank numero 1; habeo 2 (*alqm in numero*); ordo *m*; series *f*; gradus, us *m*; dignitas *f*; status, us *m*; luxuriosus; fetidus, rancidus; *fig.* merus

ransack diripio 3; perscrutor 1

ransom redimo 3; pretium *n*; redemptio *f*

rant bacchor 1

rap ferio 4; pulso 1; ictus, us *m*

rapaci|ous rapax; ~ty rapacitas *f*

rape rapio 3; raptus, us *m*

rapid celer, rapidus; ~ity celeritas *f*, velocitas *f*

rapier gladius *m*

rapine rapina *f*

rapt stupens; ~ure laetitia f

rar|e rarus; ~ tenuis (aer); singularis; ~efy extenuo 1; ~ely raro; ~eness raritas f, paucitas f

rascal verbero m, furcifer m; ~ly nequam, flagitiosus

rasp v/t. rado 3; v/i. strideo 2; scobina f

rat mus m

rate aestimo 1 (alqm, alqd, magni); censeo 2; increpo 1; pretium n; vectigal n; ~ of interest faenus n; at a high ~ magno; at any ~ utique, certe

rather potius, prius, libentius; quin, immo; I would ~ malo, mallem

ratif|ication sanctio f (foederis); ~y sancio 4; confirmo 1

rating aestimatio f

ration (diurnus) cibus m; soldier's ~ cibaria n/pl.

rational rationis particeps (homo); consentaneus; ~ity ratio f

rattle crepitus, us m; crotalum n; crepo 1, crepito 1

ravage vasto 1, populor 1; diripio 3

rave furo 3, bacchor 1; saevio 4

raven corvus m; ~ous rapax, edax

ravine fauces f/pl.; vallis f praerupta

raving furens, insanus, rabidus

ravish rapio 3; stupro 1; ~ing suavissimus

raw crudus; fig. rudis, imperitus; ~ soldier tiro m

ray radius m; iubar n

raze to the ground solo aequo 1 (alqd); funditus everto 3, deleo 2

razor novacula f

reach v/i. pervenio 4 (ad); attingo 3, tango 3 (alqd); v/i. pertineo 2 (ad); ~ out porrigo 3; spatium n; iactus, us m (teli); beyond ~ of extra (acc.)

react upon afficio 3 (alqm, alqd, invicem)

read lego 3 (alqd, librum); volvo 3 (librum); ~ aloud recito 1; ~ through perlego 3; ~er lector m; ~ing lectio f, recitatio f

readily ultro, libenter

ready paratus, promptus (ad); celer, facilis; be ~ praesto sum; get ~ (com-)paro 1; ~ money praesens pecunia f

real verus, germanus, solidus; ~ property fundus m; ~isation effectus, us m; ~ise v/t. perficio 3; redigo 3 (pecuniam); v/i. intellego 3: mente concipio 3; ~ity veritas f; verum n; in ~ity re vera

really re vera; vero, profecto

realm regnum n; fig. regio f

reanimate recreo 1

reap meto 1; fig. percipio 3 (fructum ex re, rei); ~er messor m

reappear redeo 4

rear *v/t.* educo 1 *and* 3; alo
3; *v/i.* me erigo 3; tergum
n; in the ~ a tergo; ~ of a
column novissimum ag-
men *n*; bring up the ~
agmen claudo 3

reason ratio *f*, mens *f*; causa
f; with ~ ratione; without
~ temere; the ~ for ... is
idcirco (*alqd facio*) ...
quod; ask the ~ for quaero
3 cur, quamobrem; by ~ of
propter (*acc.*); ratiocinor
1; disputo 1 (*de re*); dissero 3 (*de re, cum alqo*);
~able prudens; probabilis
(*coniectura*); aequus; mediocris, modicus; ~er dis-
putator *m*; ~ing ratio *f*,
ratiocinatio *f*

reass|emble redeo 4; ~ure
confirmo 1 (*animos etc.*)

rebel descisco 3 (*ab*); seditionem, rebellionem facio
3, commoveo 2; hostis *m*;
~lion seditio *f*, rebellio *f*;
defectio *f*; tumultus, us *m*;
~lious seditiosus, turbu-

rebound resilio 4 [lentus]

rebuff sperno 3, repello 3;
repulsa *f*

rebuild restituo 3, reficio 3

rebuke increpo 1; reprehendo 3; reprehensio *f*

rebut refello 3

recall revoco 1 (*ad; in animum*); reduco 3; revocatio
f; receptus, us *m*

recant revoco 1 (*alqd*)

recede recedo 3

receive accipio 3, excipio 3,
recipio 3, capio 3

recent recens; ~ly recens,
nuper

recep|tacle receptaculum *n*;
~tion aditus, us *m*; admis-
sio *f*; congressus, us *m*;
~tive studiosus, capax

recess recessus, us *m*; se-
cessus, us *m*

reciproc|al mutuus; ~ate
refero 3

reci|tal narratio *f*, enume-
ratio *f*; ~e recito 1, pronuntio 1

reckless temerarius, incautus; incuriosus (*gen.*);
~ness temeritas *f*

reckon duco 3; refero 3
(*alqm, alqd, in numero*);
ascribo 3 (*in numerum*); ~
up (e)numero 1, computo
1, aestimo 1; ~ing ratio *f*;
enumeratio *f*; numerus *m*;
~ing on fretus (*abl.*)

reclaim repeto 3, reposco 3;
recupero 1

recline recumbo 3, accum-
bo 3

recogni|se cognosco 3,
agnosco 3 (*alqm*); ~ that
intellego 3 (*acc. c. inf.*);
~tion agnitio *f*

recoil recido 3 (*in alqm*)

recollect memini; reminiscor 3; colligo 3 (*me, animum*); ~ion memoria *f*

recommence instauro 1,
redintegro 1

recommend commendo 1
(*alqm, alqd, alci*); suadeo 2
(*alci ut*); ~ation commen-
datio *f*, laudatio *f*

recompense remuneror 1

(*alqm re*); praemium *n*;
munus *n*; remuneratio *f*;
merces *f*

reconcil|e reconcilio 1; in
gratiam restituo 3; ac-
commodo 1 (*alqd ad alqd*);
be ~ed in gratiam redeo 4
(*cum*); ~iation reconcilia-
tio *f*

recondite abditus, abstrusus

reconnoitre exploro 1

reconsider reputo 1, retracto 1 (*alqd*)

reconstruct restituo 3; *fig.*
repeto 3 (*alqd memoria*)

record litteris mando 3;
refero 3; historia *f*, narra-
ratio *f*; monumentum *n*;
memoria *f*; tabula *f*; ~s
acta *n/pl.*; fasti *m/pl.*

recount enarro 1, comme-
moro 1

recourse: have ~ to decurro
3 (*ad*); descendo 3 (*ad*)

recover *v/t.* recupero 1; recipio 3; ~ oneself colligo 3
(*me, animum*); *v/i.* convalesco 3; emergo 3 (*ex*);
~y recuperatio *f* (*rei*);
refectio *f*; salus, utis *f*

recreat|e recreo 1; ~ion
remissio *f*; relaxatio *f*;
requies *f*; vacatio *f*

recruit reficio 3; *mil.* (con-)
scribo 3; comparo 1; sa-
cramento adigo 3; tiro *m*

recti|fy corrigo 3; emendo
1; ~tude probitas *f*

recur redeo 4; ~rence reditus, us *m*; assiduitas *f*

red ruber, rubens, rubicun-

dus, rufus, rutilus; be ~
rubeo 2; ~den (e)rubesco 3

redeem redimo 3; ~er liberator *m*

red-handed: catch ~ mani-
festo deprehendo 3 (*alqm*)

red|-hot candens; ~ lead
minium *n*; ~ness rubor *m*

redolent redolens (*alqd*)

redouble ingemino 1

redress corrigo 3; restituo 3

reduc|e minuo 3; redigo 3
(*alqm in alqd*); subigo 3,
vinco 3 (*alqm*); be ~ed to
recido 3 (*in alqd*); redeo 4
(*ad*); ~tion deminutio *f*

redundant supervacaneus;
be ~ redundo 1

re-echo refero 3

reed harundo *f*; calamus *m*

reef saxa *n/pl.*; scopuli
m/pl.; contraho 3 (*vela*)

reek fumo 1

reel vacillo 1, titubo 1;
fusus *m*

re|ject reficio 3; ~establish
restituo 3

refer refero 3 (*rem ad alqm,
ad alqd*); reicio 3 (*rem ad
alqm; alqm ad rem*); ~ to
memoro 1; attingo 3
(*alqd*); ~ee arbiter, tri *m*;
~ence mentio *f*; locus *m*;
have ~ence to attineo 2
(*ad*)

refill repleo 2

refine defaeco 1 (*vinum etc.*);
fig. expolio 4; excolo 3
(*alqd*); ~d humanus, politus; ~ment humanitas *f*,
urbanitas *f*

reflect reddo 3 (imaginem);

~ upon reputo 1, considero 1, recordor 1 (*alqd*); ~ion imago *f*; cogitatio *f*, deliberatio *f*; cast a ~ion upon reprehendo 3

reform emendo 1; corrigo 3; restituo 3, reficio 3; correctio *f*; ~er corrector *m*

refractory contumax

refrain (me) abstineo 1, tempero 1 (*re, a re, quin, quominus*); me contineo 2, contineor 2 (*re, a re*)

refresh recreo 1, renovo 1; reficio 3; ~ment cibus *m*

refuge perfugium *n*, refugium *n*, asylum *n*; take ~ with confugio 3 (*ad*); ~e exsul *m*; profugus *m*

refund reddo 3

refus|al recusatio *f*, repudiatio *f*, repulsa *f*; ~e recuso 1 (*acc., ne, quin, quominus*); abnuo 3 (*acc.*); nolo (*inf.*); nego 1 (*alqd alci, acc. c. inf.*); purgamentum *n*; *fig.* faex *f*; quisquiliae *f*/*pl.*

refut|ation reprehensio *f*, dissolutio *f*; ~e refello 3, refuto 3, revinco 3 (*acc.*)

regain recipio 3

regal regius; ~ia insignia *n*/*pl.* regia

regard specto 1, aspicio 3; intueor 2, respicio 3; habeo 2 (*alqm pro amico*); duco 3 (*alqm amicum etc.*); cura *f*, respectus, us *m*; honor *m*; have ~ to rationem habeo 2 (*gen.*); ~less neglegens, incuriosus (*gen.*); as ~s quod

regen|cy procuratio *f* regni; ~t procurator *m* regni

regimen victus, us *m*

regiment legio *f*, cohors *f*

region regio *f*; tractus, us *m*

regist|er in tabulas refero 3; perscribo 3; tabulae *f*/*pl.*; album *n*; ~rar actuarius *m*; ~ry tabularium *n*

regret piget 2, paenitet 2 (*me alcs rei, inf.*); doleo 2 (*acc., abl., acc. c. inf., quod*)

regular constans, certus; ordinarius; aequabilis; iustus (*bellum etc.*); status (*sacrificia, dies etc.*); ~ troops legionarii milites *m*/*pl.*; ~ity ordo *m*; constantia *f*

regulat|e ordino 1, compono 3; moderor 1 (*dat.*); administro 1; ~ion administratio *f*; praeceptum *n*, institutum *n*

rehearse meditor 1; narro 1

reign regno 1; dominor 1 (*dat.*); regnum *n*, imperium *n*

reimburse remuneror 1

rein habena *f*; frenum *n*; take, hold the ~s habenas accipio 3, teneo 2; ~ in coerceo 1, freno 1

reinforce firmo 1; ~ments subsidia *n*/*pl.*, auxilia *n*/*pl.*

reiterate itero 1

reject reicio 3; repudio 1; sperno 3; ~ion repudiatio *f*

rejoic|e *v/i.* gaudeo 2 (*acc. c. inf.; quod*); laetor 1 *(abl., acc. c. inf.); v/t.* delecto 1; ~ing laetitia *f*

rejoin redeo 4 *(ad, in alqm, alqd);* respondeo 2 *(acc. c. inf.);* ~**der** responsum *n*

rekindle suscito 1

relapse recido 3 *(in graviorem morbum)*

relate (e)narro 1, expono 3, refero 3 *(alqd);* trado 3 *(acc. c. inf.);* ~ **to** attinet 2 *(ad);* spectat 1 *(ad);* ~**d** propinquus, cognatus *(dat.);* finitimus

relation propinquus *m;* cognatus *m;* narratio *f;* ~**ship** cognatio *f,* coniunctio *f;* necessitudo *f*

relative propinquus *m;* cognatus *m;* ~**ly** mediocriter

relax *v/t.* relaxo 1; remitto 3; *v/i.* relanguesco 3; ~**ation** remissio *f,* relaxatio *f;* otium *n*

release libero 1; (ex)solvo 3; liberatio *f;* missio *f (from service)*

relent iram mitigo 1, mollio 4; ~**less** atrox, saevus

relevant quod attinet 2 *(ad)*

relia|**ble** fidus, certus; locuples; ~**nce** fiducia *f;* place ~**nce** on fidem habeo 2 *(alci)*

relic *fig.* monumentum *n;* ~**s** reliquiae *f/pl. (alcs)*

relief levamen *n,* levamentum *n (gen.); mil.* subsidium *n,* auxilium *n;* carve in ~ caelo 1

relieve (sub)levo 1; mitigo

1, exonero 1; succurro 3, subvenio 4 *(alci); (on duty etc.)* succedo 3 *(dat.);* excipio 3 *(alqm)*

religi|**on** religio *f;* sacra *n/pl.;* ~**ous** religiosus, sacer, sollemnis

relinquish remitto 3, concedo 3, relinquo 3

relish delector 1 *(re);* sapor *m;* condimentum *n*

reluctant invitus; be ~ nolo

rely confido 3 *(dat., abl.);* fidem habeo 2 *(alci);* ~**ing** on fretus *(abl.)*

remain (per)maneo 2; moror 1; resto 1; supersum 1; it ~s that restat 1 *ut;* ~**der** reliquum *n;* the ~**der** of ceteri *m/pl.;* ~**ing** reliquus, residuus, superstes; ~**s** reliquiae *f/pl.*

remark animadverto 3; dico 3; dictum *n;* ~**able** singularis, insignis

remedy remedium *n,* medicamentum *n;* medicamentum do 1; sano 1; medeor 2 *(dat.);* corrigo 3

remember memini; reminiscor 3 *(gen., acc. c. inf.);* recordor 1 *(acc.; acc. c. inf.);* memor sum *(gen.);* ~**er me to** saluta *(alqm)* ~**rance** recordatio *f,* memoria *f*

remind (ad)moneo 2, commoneo 2, commonefacio *(alqm de re, gen.)*

reminiscence recordatio *f*

remiss neglegens; ~**ion** remissio *f*

remit mitto 3 (*pecuniam*); remitto 3 (*poenam*); ~tance pecunia *f*

remnant reliquum *n*; reliquiae *f/pl.*; the ~ of reliquus, ceterus

remonstrate reclamo 1; ~ with obiurgo 1 (*alqm, quod*)

remorse conscientia *f* (for *gen.*); feel ~ for paenitet 2 (*me alcs rei, quod*); ~less immisericors

remote remotus, semotus (*abl.*); fig. alienus, disiunctus (*ab*); ~ness longinquitas *f*

remov|al amotio *f*; migratio *f*; ~e *v/t.* removeo 2, amoveo 2; tollo 3; segrego 1; *v/i.* (e)migro 1, commigro 1

remunerat|e remuneror 1 (*alqm*); ~ion remuneratio *f*; praemium *n*

rend scindo 3; lacero 1, lamio 1

render reddo 3, trado 3, tribuo 3; ago 3 (*gratias*); (*with double acc.*) facio 3, efficio 3, reddo 3; ~ up dedo 3, trado 3; ~ an account rationes reddo 3

rendezvous constitutum *n*

renew renovo 1, instauro 1, redintegro 1; ~al renovatio *f*

renounce renuntio 1, eiuro 1; abdico 1 (*me re*)

renovate renovo 1

renown gloria *f*, fama *f*; ~ed clarus

rent conduco 3; ~ out loco 1; merces *f*; vectigal *n*; ~er conductor *m*

renunciation abdicatio *f*

reopen (iterum) recludo 3

repair reficio 3, restituo 3; sarcio 4; ~ to me recipio 3 (*ad*); restitutio *f*, refectio *f*; in good ~ sartus; in bad ~ ruinosus

reparation: make ~ satisfacio 3 (*dat.*)

repast cena *f*; epulae *f/pl.*

repay refero 3 (*alqd alci*); remuneror 1 (*alqm, alqd*); ~ment remuneratio *f*; solutio *f*

repeal abrogo 1; rescindo 3

repeat itero 1, renovo 1; ~ often decanto 1: ~edly identidem: saepius, persaepe

repel repello 3; propulso 1

repent paenitet 2 (*me alcs rei, inf., quod*); ~ance paenitentia *f* [tio *f*]

repetition iteratio *f*, repeti-

repine queror 3

replace repono 3; ~ ... with substituo 3 (*alqm pro alqo, alci*); suppono 3 (*alqm pro alqo*); subrogo 1 (*alqm in locum alcs*)

reple|nish repleo 2; ~te repletus, plenus (*abl.*)

reply respondeo 2; responsum *n*

report (re)nuntio 1, refero 3 (*alqd; acc. c. inf.*); rumor *m*, fama *f*; relatio *f*, renuntiatio *f*; ~er nuntius *m*, notarius *m*

repose pono 3; quies *f*; otium *n*; **enjoy ~** otiosus sum

reprehen|d reprehendo 3; **~sible** vituperabilis

represent repraesento 1, exprimo 3, imitor 1; **propono** 3 (*acc. c. inf.*); sto 1 (*pro alqo, alqa re*); **~ation** imago *f*; **~ative** vicarius *m*; procurator *m*

repress reprimo 3; coerceo 2

reprieve supplicium differo 3; veniam do 1; parco 3 (*dat.*); dilatio *f* (supplicii); venia *f*

reprimand reprehendo 3

reprisals ultio *f*

reproach exprobro 1 (*alci alqd; quod*); obicio 3 (*alci alqd; acc. c. inf.; quod*); increpo 1 (*alqm*); opprobrium *n*, probrum *n*; vituperatio *f*; **~ful** obiurgatorius

reprobate perditus

reproduce propago 1; *fig.* refero 3; imitor 1

repro|of obiurgatio *f*, reprehensio *f*; **~ve** reprehendo 3, obiurgo 1

reptile serpens *f*

republic res *f* publica; civitas *f* (libera, popularis); **~an** popularis

repudiate repudio 3

repugnan|ce odium *n*; fastidium *n*; **~t** aversus (*ab*); **be ~t to** odio sum; repugno 1 (*dat.*)

repuls|e repello 3; offensio

---

f, repulsa *f*; **~ive** odiosus, foedus

reput|able honestus; **~ation,** **~e** fama *f*; **good ~e** existimatio *f*, laus *f*; honor *m*; **bad ~e** infamia *f*

request peto 3, posco 3 (*alqd ab alqo, ut*); rogo 1 (*alqm alqd; ut*); rogatum *n*, postulatum *n*; preces *f/pl.*

require requiro 3 (*alqd; alqd ex alqo*); quaero 3; posco 3; desidero 1

requisite necessarius

requit|al remuneratio *f*, vicis *f* (*beneficii*); ultio *f* (*sceleris*); **~e** vindico 1 (*scelus*); ulciscor 3 (*alqm pro scelere*); (com)penso 1 (*alqd alqa re*); remuneror 1 (*alqm alqa re*)

rescind rescindo 3; abrogo 1

rescue libero 1, vindico 1, eripio 3 (*alqm ab*); **come to the ~** subvenio 4 (*alci*)

research investigatio *f*

resembl|ance similitudo *f*; **~e** similis sum (*gen., dat.*); accedo 3 (*ad*)

resent aegre, moleste fero 3 (*alqd, quod*); **~ful** iracundus; **~ment** ira *f*, invidia *f*; dolor *m*

reserv|ation exceptio *f*, **~e** (re)servo 1 (*alqd, alqm, ad, dat.*); sepono 3; taciturnitas *f*; **~ed** superbus *n/pl.*; subsidiarii *m/pl.*; **~ed** tectus, taciturnus

reservoir cisterna *f*; lacus, us *m*

reside habito 1; *fig.* consto 1 (*in, ex re*); ~nce mansio *f*, habitatio *f*; domicilium *n*; domus, us *f*; ~nt habitator *m*

resign (con)cedo 3 (*alqd alci*); permitto 3, remitto 3, depono 3 (*alqd*); summitto 3 (*me, animum, ad, dat.*); ~ation abdicatio *f*; aequus animus *m*; patientia *f*; ~ed patiens

resin resina *f*

resist resisto 3, obsisto 3, repugno 1 (*dat.*)

resolute firmus, fortis, obstinatus; ~ion constantia *f*, firmitas *f*; solutio *f*; sententia *f*; pass a ~ion (de-) cerno 3

resolve (dis)solvo 3; dissipo 1; statuo 3 (*inf.; ut*); constituo 3, decerno 3 (*inf.: acc. c. inf.*); certum est, concilium est (*mihi, inf.*); consilium *n*, propositum *n*; sententia *f*

resort locus *m* celeber; ~ to decurro 3, descendo 3, confugio 3 (*ad*)

resound resono 1, persono 1 (*alqa re*)

resource auxilium *n*, subsidium *n*; ~s opes *f/pl.*, copiae *f/pl.*

respect observo 1; suspicio 3, colo 3; vereor 2; observantia *f*, honor *m*; pay one's ~s to saluto 1 (*alqm*); as ~s quod attinet 2 (*ad*); in both ~s in utramque partem; in every ~ omni-

no; in other ~s ceterum; ~ability honestas *f*; ~able honestus; ~ful observans (*gen.*), verecundus; ~ing de (*abl.*)

respiration spiritus, us *m*; respiratio *f*

respite mora *f*, intermissio *f*

resplendent splendidus

respond respondeo 2 (*dat.*)

responsibility officium *n*; cura *f*; be ~le for praesto 1 (*alqd*); hold, make ~le for rationem reposco 3 (*ab alqo alcs rei*)

rest (re)quies *f*; otium *n*; adminiculum *n*; the ~ (*adj.*) reliquus, ceterus; reliquum *n*; *v/t.* repono 3 (*alqd in re*); *v/i.* (re)quiesco 3; quietem capio 3; ~ upon nitor 3 (*abl.*); ~ with situm est (*in alqo; in re*)

restitution: make ~ satisfacio 3 (*alci*); restituo 3 (*alqd*)

restive ferox; ~less turbidus, inquietus

restoration refectio *f*; restitutio *f* (*bonorum*); ~e renovo 1, redintegro 1; restituo 3, refero 3; reddo 3; be ~ed redeo 4; ~er restitutor *m*

restrain coerceo 2, retineo 2; comprimo 3; ~t moderatio *f*; repugula *n/pl.*

restrict (de)finio 4 (*alqd*); circumscribo 3, includo 3 (*alqd*); angustus; ~ion modus *m*; finis *n*

result evenio 4 (*ex re, ut*):

evado 3 (*ex re*); fio 3 (*ut*);
nascor 3 (*ab, ex*); eventus,
us *m*; exitus, us *m*; fructus, us *m*
resume repeto 1, recolo 3
retailer venditor *m*
retain retineo 2, teneo 2;
servo 1; **~er** satelles *m* and
f
retaliat|e ulciscor 3 (*alqm,
alqd*); **~ion** vicis *f* (*gen.*);
ultio *f*
retard retardo 1
reticent taciturnus
retinue comitatus, us *m*;
satellites *m/pl.*
retire recedo 3, decedo 3;
abeo 4; me recipio 3; **~d**
remotus, quietus; **~ment**
solitudo *f*; otium *n*
retouch retracto 1
retrace repeto 3; pedem
refero 3
retract renuntio 1
retreat me recipio 3; pedem
refero 3; recedo 3; receptus, us *m*; recessus, us *m*;
latebrae *f/pl.*
retribution poena *f*; merces
f
retrieve recupero 1; sarcio 4
return *v/i.* redeo 4; revertor
3; *v/t.* reddo 3; refero 3
(*gratiam*); remitto 3; renuntio 1 (*alqm consulem*);
reditus, us *m*; regressus,
us *m*; remuneratio *f*;
quaestus, us *m*; fructus
m/ol.
reunite reconcilio 1
reveal patefacio 3; aperio
4; enuntio 1

revel comissor 1; *fig.* bacchor 1, exsulto 1; comis-
satio *f*, bacchatio *f*
revelation patefactio *f*
reveller comissator *m*
revenge ultio *f*; poena *f*;
vicis *f* (*gen.*); take **~** on
ulciscor 3 (*alqm*); take **~**
for vindico 1 (*scelus in
alqm*); **~r** vindex *m*
revenue vectigal *n*; fructus,
us *m*
revere (re)vereor 2; veneror
1; **~nce** reverentia *f*; honor
m; **~nd** venerabilis; **~nt**
pius, reverens
rever|se inverto 3; *fig.*
rescindo 3 (*legem, iudicium
etc.*); infirmo 1; conversio
f, commutatio *f*; *mil.*
clades *f*; aversus, contrarius; **~t** to redeo 4 (*ad*)
review recenseo 2, recognosco 3, lustro 1; recensio *f*, recognitio *f* (*civium
etc.*); take censor *m*
revile maledico 3 (*alci*)
revis|e corrigo 3, emendo 1;
retracto 1 (*leges*); **~ion**
emendatio *f*; lima *f*
revisit reviso 3
reviv|al renovatio *f*; **~e** *v/t.*
reficio 3, recreo 1 (*alqm ex
vulnere, morbo*); *fig.* excito
1, redintegro 1; *v/i.* me,
animum recipio 3; renas-
cor 3
revoke renuntio 1, rescindo
3
revolt deficio 3, descisco 3
(*ab alqo*); defectio *f*; tumultus, us *m*; **~ing** foedus

revolution conversio *f*; circuitus, us *m*; commutatio *f*; *pol.* res *f/pl.* novae; ~ary novus (*res*); seditiosus (*homo*); ~ise novo 1

revolve volvor 3, convertor 3; voluto 1 (*alqd animo*)

revulsion fastidium *n*

reward praemium *n*; merces *f*; fructus, us *m*; praemio afficio 3 (*alqm*); remuneror 1

rhetoric rhetorica *f*; ~al rhetoricus, oratorius; ~ian rhetor *m*

rheum pituita *f*; ~atism dolor *m* artuum

rhinoceros rhinoceros *m*

rhyme versus *m/pl.*; ~ carmen *n*

rhythm numerus *m*; modus *m*; ~ical numerosus

rib costa *f*

ribald obscenus

ribbon vitta *f*, taenia *f*

rice oryza *f*

rich dives, locuples, opulentus (*in abl.*); pretiosus; uber, fertilis (*terra etc.*); ~es divitiae *f/pl.*, opes *f/pl.*; ~ness ubertas *f*, copia *f*

rid libero 1; get ~ of exuo 3, depono 3, tollo 3

riddle aenigma *n*; ambages *f/pl.*; be ~d with confodior 3

ride vehor 3 (*equo, curru*); ~r eques *m*

ridge dorsum *n*, iugum *n*

ridicul|e risus, us *m*; irrideo 2 (*acc.*); ~ous ridiculus

rife: be ~ increbresco 3

rifle compilo 1

rift rima *f*; hiatus, us *m*

rig armo 1; ~ging armamenta *n/pl.*

right dexter (*manus etc.*); rectus, iustus, aequus; restituo 3, corrigo 3; fas *n*, iustum *n*; ius *n*; on, to the ~ dextra, dextrorsum; all ~ bene habet; be ~ recte sentio 4, facio 3; ~ hand dextra (manus) *f*; ~ on recta; ~eous integer, probus; ~ful iustus, legitimus; ~ly recte, iuste, iure

rigid rigidus; severus

rigo|rous durus, severus; ~ur duritia *f*, asperitas *f*

rill rivulus *m*

rim labrum *n*; crepido *f*

rime pruina *f*

rind crusta *f*, cutis *f*; corium *n*

ring tinnio 4, resono 1; circulus *m*; orbis *m*; (*of people*) corona *f*; (*for finger*) anulus *m*; (*for horses*) gyrus *m*; ~ing clarus (*vox etc.*); ~let cincinnus *m*

rinse eluo 3

riot turbae *f/pl.*; tumultus, us *m*; turbas efficio 3; run ~ luxurior 1; ~ous turbulentus; dissolutus

rip scindo 3; ~ up rescindo 3

ripe maturus, tempestivus, coctus; ~ for paratus (*ad*); ~n maturesco 3; ~ness maturitas *f*

ripple trepido 1

ris|e (ex)surgo 3; (ex)orior 4; me erigo 3; cresco 3; increbresco 3 (*ventus*); rebello 1; incrementum n; ortus, us m; collis m; tumulus m; **give ~e to** pario 3; **~ing** ortus, us m (*solis*); tumultus, us m; seditio f, rebellio f

risk periculum n, discrimen n; periclito 1 (**one's life** *caput* or *capite*); **run a ~** periculum facio 3, adeo 3 (*capitis*); **~y** periculosus

rite ritus, us m

rival aemulor 1 (*alqm*); aemulus m, competitor m; **~ in love** rivalis m; **~ry** aemulatio f, rivalitas f

river flumen n; amnis m; fluvius m; **~-bed** alveus m

rivet clavus m

rivulet rivus m

road via f; iter, ineris n; **~stead** statio f

roam vagor 1

roar rudo 3; fremo 3; fremitus, us m; clamor m

roast torreo 3; frigo 3; assus

rob v/t. compilo 1 (*templum*); spolio 1 (*alqm re*); adimo 3 (*alqd alci*); v/i. latrocinor 1; **~ber** latro m, fur m; **~bery** latrocinium n

robe vestis f, palla f; vestio 4

robust validus, robustus

rock v/t. agito 1; moveo 2; v/i. vacillo 1, nuto 1; rupes f, cautes f; scopu-

lum n, saxum n; **~y** saxosus, scopulosus

rod virga f; **fishing ~** harundo f

roe cerva f; (*of fish*) ova n/pl.; **~buck** cervus m

rogue veterator m, furcifer m

roll v/t. volvo 3; v/i. volvor 3; volutor 3; globus m; (*of writing*) volumen n; (*of names*) album n; **~er** (*for ships*) scutula f, phalangae f/pl.; cylindrus m

roman|ce fabula f; **~tic** commenticius

romp lascivio 4; lascivia f

roof tectum n, culmen n; tego 3

room locus m; spatium n; conclave n; cella f; **~y** amplus

roost stabulor 1

root radix f; *fig.* fons f; **take ~** coalesco 3; **become ~ed** inveterasco 3; **~ up** radicitus evello 3; **~ed** inveteratus

rope funis m; restis f; rudens m; **~-walker** funambulus m

rose rosa f

rostrum rostra n/pl.

rosy roseus

rot v/i. putesco 3; v/t. putrefacio 3; tabes f

rotat|e volvor 3; me converto 3; convertor 3; **~ion** conversio f

rotten put(r)idus

rotund rotundus

rouge fucus *m*; fuco 1

rough asper, horridus; incultus, incomptus; ~ness asperitas *f*

round globosus, rotundus; flecto 3 (*promontorium*); ambitus, us *m*; orbis *m*; anfractus, us *m*; circuitio *f* (*vigiliarum*); *adv. and prep.* circum, circa (*acc.*); ~ **about** circiter (*eandem horam*; *septuaginta*); ad (*centum*); **all the year** ~ toto anno; ~ **off** torno 1; concludo 3

round|about devius, ~**about way** circuitio *f*; ~**ly** libere, aperte

rouse suscito 1, excito 1; ~ **oneself** expergiscor 3

rout turba *f*, fuga *f*; fundo 3, fugo 1

route iter, ineris *n*

routine usus, us *m*; consuetudo *f*

rove vagor 1, erro 1

row ordo *m*; versus, us *m*; turba *f*; tumultus, us *m*; ~ **of seats** gradus, us *m*; remigo 1; ~**er** remex *m*; ~**ing** remigatio *f*

royal regius, regalis; ~**ty** regnum *n*

rub (per)frico 1; tero 3; ~ **off** detergeo 2; ~ **out** deleo 2; induco 3

rubbish quisquiliae *f/pl.*, nugae *f/pl.*

rubble rudus *n*

ruby carbunculus *m*

rude rudis, inconditus, rusticus; inhumanus, asper, insolens; ~ness rusticitas *f*; inhumanitas *f*

rudiment|s elementa *n/pl.*; ~**ary** incohatus, rudis

rue ruta *f*; paenitet 2 (*me alcs rei*); ~**ful** maestus

ruffian latro *m*; sicarius *m*

ruffle agito 1

rug stragulum *n*

rugged asper, praeruptus

ruin perdo 3; profligo 1; affligo 3; corrumpo 3; interitus, us *m*; exitium *n*; pernicies *f*; calamitas *f*, clades *f*; ~**ed** ruinosus (*aedes*); afflictus; ~**ous** exitiosus, funestus

rule *v/t.* rego 3; impero 1 (*dat.*); moderor 1; *v/i.* praesum (*dat.*); regno 1; decerno 3, edico 3 (*ut*); (*for measuring*) regula *f*; *fig.* regula *f*, norma *f*; praescriptum *n*, praeceptum *n*, institutum *n*; lex *f*; dicio *f*, imperium *n*; ~**r** moderator *m*, gubernator *m*, rector *m*; regula *f*

rumble mugio 4; murmur *m*

rumour rumor *m*; fama *f*

rumple ruga *f*

run curro 3; fluo 3 (*aqua*), labor 3, mano 1; ~ **aground** eicior 3; ~ **away** aufugio 3; ~ **out** exeo 4; ~ **over** *fig.* percurro 3; ~**away** fugitivus *m*; ~**ner** cursor *m*

rupture rumpo 3; *fig.* dissidium *n*

rural rusticus

rush iuncus *m*; impetus, us *m*; incursio *f*; concursus,

us m; ruo 3, curro 3; me
praecipito 1; ~ at me
inicio 3 (in); occurso 1
(dat.); ~ out evolo 1; me
effundo 3; ~ing praeceps;
~-basket scirpiculus m;
~y lunceus, scirpeus
russet fulvus
rust robigo f; v/i. robigine

laedor 3; v/t. robigine
laedo 3
rustic agrestis; rusticus
rustle crepo 1, crepito 1;
crepitus, us m
rusty robigine laesus
rut orbita f
ruthless immitis, saevus,
crudelis

S

Sabbath sabbata n/pl.
sable niger, ater
sabre gladius m
sack saccus m; direptio f
(urbis); diripio 3, populor
1; ~cloth vestis f canna-
bina; ~er direptor m
sacred sacer, sanctus
sacri|fice v/t. immolo 1,
fig. profundo 3 (alqd pro);
condono 1 (alqd dat.); v/i.
sacrifico 1; (sacrifium)
facio 3 (alci hostiis); sacrificium n; res f divina; fig.
iactura f; ~lege sacrilegium
n; ~sty sacrarium n
sad maestus, tristis; be ~
maereo 2; ~den contris-
to 1
saddle ephippium n; sterno
3; fig. ~ with impono 3
(alqd alci); pack-~ clitellae
f/pl.
sadness tristitia f, maestitia f
safe tutus, salvus, incolumis; cella f; (for money)
arca f; ~conduct fides f;
~guard cautio f; ~ty salus,
utis f

saffron crocum n and cro-
cus m; croceus
sagaci|ous prudens, sagax;
~ty sagacitas f
sage sapiens m
sail navigo 1; ~ round cir-
cumvehor 3; velum n;
set ~ vela do 1; navem
solvo 3; ~ing navigatio f;
~or nauta m
saintly sanctus, pius
sake: for the ~ of (alcs, rei)
causa, gratia; pro (abl.)
salamander salamandra f
salary merces f
sale venditio f; for ~ venalis; offer for ~ venum do 1;
public ~ hasta f; ~sman
venditor m
salient praecipuus
saline salsus
saliva saliva f
sallow pallidus, luridus
sally eruptio f; make a ~
eruptionem facio 3
salmon salmo m
salt sal m; ~cellar salinum
n; ~works salinae f/pl.;
~y salsus
salubrious salubris

salutary salutaris, utilis

salut|ation salutatio f; salus, utis f; ~e saluto 1

salvation salus, utis f

salve unguentum n

salver scutella f

same idem (as qui, atque)

sample exemplum n

sanct|ify sacro 1, consecro 1; ~ion ratum facio 4; sancio 4 (legem etc.); permitto 3 (alci ut); auctoritas f; confirmatio f; ~ity sanctitas f; ~uary asylum n [~pit arenaria f.]

sand arena f, saburra f;|

sandal solea f, crepida f

sandy arenosus

sane sanus

sanguine: be ~ spero 1 (acc. c. inf.); magnam spem habeo 2 [~y sanitas f]

sanit|ary purus, saluber;|

sap sucus m; subruo 3, labefacto 1; ~ling arbor f novella

sapper munitor m

sapphire sapphirus, i f

sarcas|m cavillatio f; ~tic dicax, acerbus

sardine sarda f

sash cingulum n

satchel loculus m

sate, satiate satio 1, saturo 1; expleo 2

satiety saturitas f

satir|e satura f; ~ical satiricus; dicax; ~ist saturarum scriptor m

satis|faction: give ~faction satisfacio 3 (dat.); placet 2 (dat.); ~factorily ex sen-

tentia (mea); ~factory idoneus, probabilis; ~fy expleo 2 (alci); satisfacio 3 (alci); be ~fied satis habeo 2; mihi persuasum est (acc. c. inf.)

satrap satrapes m

saturate saturo 1

satyr satyrus m

sauce ius n; condimentum n; ~pan cacabus m; ~r patella f

saucy petulans, protervus

saunter spatior 1

sausage botulus m; tomaculum n

savage ferus; immanis, saevus; homo m incultus, barbarus; ~ry feritas f, immanitas f; atrocitas f; barbaria f

sav|e servo 1; eripio 3; salutem affero 3 (alci); ~e up reservo 1; adv. and prep. praeter (acc.); nisi (quod); ~ing compendium n (alcs rei); ~iour servator m

savour sapor m; ~ of (red-) oleo 2 (alqd); ~y conditus n; ~y sapio 3; be ~y sapio 3

saw serra f; proverbium n; v/t. serra seco 1 (alqd); v/i. serram duco 3; ~dust scobis f

say dico 3; loquor 3 (alqd); ~ yes aio; ~ that ... not nego 1; said I inquam, aio; said he inquit, ait; as Homer ~s ut ait Homerus; they (men) ~ that ferunt 3, traditum est (*acc. c. inf.*); he is said to be traditur 3, dicitur 3 (esse); ~ing dictum *n*, proverbium *n*; as the ~ing is ut aiunt

scab scabies *f*

scabbard vagina *f*

scaffold machina *f*; *fig.* securis *f*, supplicium *n*

scal|e conscendo 3; lanx *f*; squama *f* (*piscis etc.*); *fig.* gradus, us *m*; modus *m*; pair of ~es trutina *f*; ~ing-ladder scalae *f*/*pl.*

scalp cutis *f* capitis

scalpel scalpellum *n*

scaly squamosus

scamp verbero *m*, furcifer *m*

scan intueor 2; contemplor 1, considero 1

scandal opprobrium *n*, dedecus *n*; ~ise offendo 3 (*dat.*); ~ous probrosus, infamis, turpis

scant|iness exiguitas *f*; inopia *f*; ~y exiguus, tenuis

scapegoat piaculum *n*

scar cicatrix *f*

scarc|e rarus; ~ely vix; ~ely yet vixdum; ~ity inopia *f*, paucitas *f*

scare terreo 2; ~crow formido *f*

scarf velamen *n*; rica *f*

scarlet coccum *n*; coccinus

scarred cicatricosus

scatter *v/t.* spargo 3; dissipo 1; disicio 3; *v/i.* dissipor 1, disicior 3; ~ing dissipatio *f*

scene locus *m*; spectaculum

n; *thea.* scaena *f*; come on the ~ intervenio 4; ~ry scaena *f*; species *f* loci

scent odoror 1 (*cibum etc.*); odor *m*; get ~ of olfacio 3, odoror 1 (*alqd*); ~ed odoratus

sceptical: be ~ dubito 1

sceptre sceptrum *n*; scipio [*m*]

schedule tabula *f*

scheme consilium *n*; ars *f*; insidiae *f*/*pl.*; ratio *f*; molior 4

scholar vir *m* doctus, eruditus; discipulus *m*; ~ly doctus; ~ship litterae *f*/*pl.*; doctrina *f*

school schola *f* (philosophorum); (*for boys*) ludus *m*; *fig.* disciplina *f*, secta *f* (*Platonis etc.*); erudio 4; ~ed expertus (*gen.*); ~fellow condiscipulus *m*; ~master magister *m*

schooner actuaria *f*

scien|ce scientia *f*, disciplina *f*, doctrina *f*; ars *f*; ratio *f*; ~ce of war res *f* militaris; ~tific physicus

scion proles *f*, progenies *f*

scissors forfex *f*

scoff at irrideo 2, derideo 2 (*acc.*); ~ing irrisio *f*; irrisus, us *m*

scold increpo 1, obiurgo 1; ~ing obiurgatio *f*

scoop ligula *f*; ~ out excavo 1 (*alqd*)

scope campus *m*; area *f*; locus *m*

scorch amburo 3; torreo 2; ~ed, ~ing torridus

score noto 1; nota *f*; (*total*) summa *f*; viginti; **reckon the ~** rationem computo 1

scorn contemno 3, sperno 3; **~er** contemptor *m*; **~ful** fastidiosus (*gen.*); arrogans, superbus

scorpion scorpio *m*

scot-free incolumis

scoundrel nebulo *m*, furcifer *m*

scour (de)tergeo 2; verro 3; *fig.* pervagor 1

scourge virgis caedo 3; verbero 1; flagellum *n*

scout explorator *m*, speculator *m*; exploro 1; repudio 1, sperno 3

scowl frontem contraho 3, frontis contractio *f*; **~ing**

scraggy strigosus (trux)

scramble (up) conscendo 3, scando 3 (*arcem etc.*)

scrap frustum *n*

scrape rado 3; angustiae *f/pl.*; **~r** strigilis *f*

scratch rado 3; seco 1; nota *f*

scream vociferor 1; clamo 1, clamito 1; ululo 1; clamor *m*; vociferatio *f*

screech ululo 1; ululatus, us *m*

screen tego 3; vela *n/pl.*; *fig.* nauseabundus

screw clavus *m*

scribe scriba *m*; librarius *m*

script scriptio *f*, scriptura *f*

scrofula struma *f*

scroll volumen *n*

scrub tergeo 2

scruple scrupulus *m*; reli-

gio *f*; cunctor 1, dubito 1 (*inf.*); **~ulous** religiosus, diligens; **~ulousness** religio *f*, diligentia *f*

scrutinise (per)scrutor 1

scuffle rixa *f*

scull palma *f*

sculp|tor sculptor *m*; **~ture** sculptura *f*; sculpo 3

scum spuma *f*; *fig.* sentina *f*; quisquiliae *f/pl.*

scurf porrigo *f*

scurrilous scurrilis, probrosus

scuttle summergo 3

scythe falx *f*

sea mare *n*; pelagus, i *n*; **by ~ and land** terra marique; **be at ~** fluctuo 1; **~** marinus, maritimus; **~ board, coast** ora *f* (maritima); **~gull** mergus *m*

seal ob)signo 1 (*epistolam, testamenta*); signum *n*; phoca *f*; **~ed** obsignatus; **~ing-wax** cera *f*

seam sutura *f*

seaman nauta *m*

sear uro 3

search (per)scrutor 1; **~ fo 1** quaero 3; indago 1; **~ into** investigo 1; **~ out** exploro 1; investigatio *f*; **~ing** diligens

seasick nauseabundus; **be ~** nauseo 1; **~ness** nausea *f*

seaside maritimus

season tempus *n*; condio 4 (*cibum*); **~able** tempestivus; **~ably** ad tempus; **~ing** condimentum *n*; sal *m*

seat sedes *f*, sella *f*; (**rows of**) **~s** subsellia *n/pl.*: **~** oneself consido 3; **be ~ed**)

seaweed alga *f* [sedeo 2]

secede descisco 3 (*ab*)

seclu|ded secretus; **~sion** solitudo *f*

second secundus (*ad, ab*); alter; **a ~ time** iterum; momentum *n* (*temporis*); adiuvo 1; **~ary** secundarius, posterior; **~er** suasor *m*; **~ly** deinde; **~rate** inferior

secre|cy secretum *n*; **~t** occultus, tectus, arcanus; clandestinus; occultum *n*; commissa *n/pl.*: **keep a ~t** occultum teneo 2 (*alqd*); **keep ~t from** celo 1 (*alqd alqm*); **~tary** scriba *m*

secrete abdo 3

secretly clam, occulte

sect secta *f*, schola *f*

section pars *f*

secure tutus; confirmo 1; tueor 2; munio 4 (*me contra alqd*)

security salus, utis *f*; cautio *f*; pignus *n*, vas *m*; **give ~** caveo 2 (*alci de re*), cautionem praesto 1; **get ~ from** caveo 2 (*ab alqd*); **be ~ for** vas fio (*alci*)

sedan-chair lectica *f*

sedate sedatus, gravis

sedentary iners

sedge ulva *f*

sediment faex *f*

sediti|on seditio *f*; tumultus, us *m*; **~ous** seditiosus, factiosus

seduc|e tempto 1; corrumpo 3; **~er** corruptor *m*; **~tion** corruptela *f*; stuprum *n*; **~tive** blandus

sedulous assiduus

see video 2; cerno 3; conspicor 1; specto 1 (*fabulam, ludos*); (*mentally*) intellego 3; percipio 3; sentio 4; **~ to** consulo 3 (*dat.*); video 2 (*alqd*); **go to ~** viso 3

seed semen *n*

seeing that quoniam, siquidem

seek quaero 3; (ex)peto 3

seem videor 2 (*inf.*); **~ing** fictus; **~ingly** ut videtur; **~ly** decens, decorus; **it is ~ly** decet 2 (*acc. c. inf.*)

seer vates *m*

seethe ferveo 2

segregate secerno 3

seiz|e rapio 3; comprehendo 3, deprehendo 3; *mil.* occupo 1; invado 3; **~ure** comprehensio *f*

seldom raro

select deligo 3, eligo 3; lectus, exquisitus; **~ion** delectus, us *m*

self ipse; **~-confidence** sui fiducia *f*; **~-control** moderatio *f*; (*mentally*) modestia *f*, moderatio *f*; **be ~ish** mea causa ago 3; **mihi** (*soli*) consulo 3

sell *v/t.* vendo 3 (*alqd auro*); *v/i.* veneo, venum eo 4; **~er** venditor *m*; **~ing** venditio *f*

semblance imago *f*, umbra *f*; simulacrum *n*

semicircle hemicyclium *n*

senat|e senatus, us *m*; patres *m/pl.*; ~e-house curia *f*; ~or senator *m*; ~ors patres *m/pl.* conscripti; ~orial senatorius

send mitto 3; ~ away dimitto 3; ~ back remitto 3; ~ for accerso 3; ~ word nuntio 1; certiorem facio 3 (*alqm*); (re)scribo 3; ~ing missio *f*

senil|e senilis; ~ity senium *n*

senior maior natu (*quam alqs, alqo*); superior (*aetate, gradu*); ~ity superior aetas *f*, gradus, us *m*

sensation sensus, us *m*

sense sensus, us *m*; mens *f*, prudentia *f*; sententia *f* (*legis*); out of one's ~s mente captus; ~less stultus, fatuus

sensible prudens; be ~ sentio 4 (*alqd*); intellego 3

sensitive tener, mollis

sensual voluptarius; ~ity voluptates *f/pl.*

sentence sententia *f*; *jur.* iudicium *n*; damno 1, condemno 1, multo 1 (*alqm morte, exsilio*); pass ~ sententiam fero 3

sentiment sensus, us *m*; opinio *f*, sententia *f*; hold the same ~s eadem sentio 4

sentinel, sentry vigil *m*, excubitor *m*; ~'s vigilia *f*, statio *f*; be on sentry duty in statione sum

separa|ble separabilis; ~te separo 1, disiungo 3 (*a re*);

divido 3 (*alqd in partes*); (*mentally*) discerno 3, secerno 3; separatus, disiunctus; ~tion disiunctio *f*

September September, bris *m*

sepulchre sepulcrum *n*

sequence ordo *m*; series *f*

sequestrate sequestro pono 3, do 1 (*alqd*)

serene tranquillus, serenu *s*

serf servus *m*; ~dom servitium *n*; servitus, utis *f*

series series *f*; a ~ of continuus

serious gravis (*homo, res*); severus (*homo*); serius (*res*); ~ matters seria *n/pl.*; ~ness gravitas *f*

sermon oratio *f*

serpent serpens *f*, anguis *m* and *f*; coluber, bri *m*, draco *m*; ~ine sinuosus, multiplex

serrated serratus

serried confertus, densus

servant famulus *m*, servu *s*; minister, tri *m*

serve servio 4 (*dat.*); prosum (*dat.*); proficio 3 (*ad, in alqd*); *mil.* stipendia mereo(r) 2, milito 1; ~ for sum (*pro re*); ~ up appono 3 (*cibum alci*)

service ministerium *n*; opera *f*; officium *n*; *military* militia *f*; stipendia *n/pl.*; good ~s merita *n/pl.*; be of ~ to prosum (*dat.*); ~able utilis; aptus (*ad*)

servi|le servilis; abiectus, humilis; ~lity humilitas *f*.

adulatio *f*; ~tude servitus,
utis *f*; servitium *n*

session sessio *f*; ~s conventus *m/pl.*

sesterce sestertius *m*; a
thousand ~s sestertium *n*

set status, ratus; series *f*;
circulus *m*, globus *m*; *v/t.*
pono 3; (col)loco 1; statuo
3; *v/i.* occido 3 (*sol*); ~
about incipio 3; ~ against
oppono 3 (*alqd alci rei*);
~ apart sepono 3; ~ at
naught contemno 3, nihili
facio 3; ~ on fire incendo 3;
~ out proficiscor 3; ~ up
statuo 3, constituo 3; ~tee
lectus *m*; ~ting occasus,
us *m*

settle *v/t.* constituo 3 (*gen-
tem, pretium*); compono 3
(*controversias*); solvo 3
(*nomen, aes alienum*); deduco 3 (*coloniam, colonos*);
v/i. consido 3 (*in*); ~d certus, ratus; ~ment deductio
f (*coloniae*); colonia *f*;
compositio *f*; ~r colonus
m; advena *m*

seven septem; ~fold sep-
templex; ~teen septende-
cim; ~th septimus; ~tieth
septuagesimus; ~ty sep-
tuaginta

sever disiungo 3

several aliquot; (com)plu-
res; singuli

sever|e durus, austerus, se-
verus; gravis, acerbus
(*poena, morbus etc.*); ~ity
severitas *f*, gravitas *f*

sew suo 3

sewer cloaca *f*

sex sexus, us *m*

shabby obsoletus; pan-
nosus (*homo*); sordidus

shackle vinculum *n*; compes *f*

shade umbra *f*; simulacrum
n; manes *m/pl.*, inferi
m/pl.; opaco 1; put in the
~ officio 3 (*alci*; *nomini*);
sun~ umbraculum *n*

shadow umbra *f*; ~y inanis,
vanus

shady opacus, umbrosus,
umbrifer

shaft telum *n*; sagitta *f*;
hastile *n*; temo *m*

shaggy villosus, hirtus

shak|e *v/t.* quatio 3, con-
cutio 3; agito 1; labefacto
1, commoveo 2; *v/i.* qua-
tior 3; *fig.* horreo 2, hor-
resco 3; ~e one's head
abnuo 3; ~y tremebundus,
instabilis

shallow brevis; *fig.* vanus,
levis; vadum *n*

sham simulatus, falsus;
simulo 1

shame pudor *m*, verecundia
f; rubor *m*; dedecus *n*,
probrum *n*; ruborem, pu-
dorem incutio 3 (*alci*); dedecoro 1 (*acc.*); feel ~
pudet 2 (*me alcs rei*); ~-
faced verecundus; ~ful
turpis, probrosus, flagi-
tiosus; ~less impudens,
improbus; ~lessness im-
pudentia *f*

shank crus, uris *n*

shape forma *f*, figura *f*,

facies *f*; fingo 3; (con-) formo 1; ~less informis, deformis; ~ly formosus

shard testa *f*

share pars *f*; partior 4, communico 1, consocio 1 (*alqd cum alqo*); ~ out divido 3; have a ~ of in partem habeo 2; intersum (*dat.*); ~d communis; ~r particeps *m*, socius *m*

shark pistrix *f*

sharp acutus; acer (*sensus*); sagax, argutus; mordax; ~en acuo 3; ~er fraudator *m*; ~ness asperitas *f*, acerbitas *f*; acumen *n*; subtilitas *f*   [quasso 1]

shatter frango 3, elido 3;

shav|e rado 3, tondeo 2; ~ings ramenta *n/pl.*

shawl palla *f*

she ea, haec, illa

sheaf manipulus *m*; fascis *m*

shear tondeo 2; ~ing tonsura *f*; ~s forfices *f/pl.*

sheath vagina *f*; ~e recondo 3 (*gladium in vaginam*)

shed profundo 3, effundo 3 (*lacrimas, sanguinem, etc.*); be ~ decido 3 (*ex alqa re*); tectum *n*, tugurium *n*

sheen fulgor *m*

sheep ovis *f*; ~fold saepta *n/pl.*

sheer abruptus, praeruptus; merus, germanus

sheet (*linen*) linteum *n*; (*paper*) scida *f*; (*metal*) lamina *f*; *naut.* bos *m*

shelf pluteus *m*; pegma *n*

shell concha *f*, testa *f*

(*ostreae etc.*); putamen *n*; crusta *f*; ~fish concha *f*

shelter tego 3, defendo 3; in tutelam recipio 3; perfugium *n*; hospitium *n*

shepherd pastor *m*

shield scutum *n*; clipeus *m*; *fig.* praesidium *n*; tego 3 (*alqd ab alqa re*)

shift *v/t.* moveo 2; (per-) muto 1; *v/i.* moveor 2, mutor 1; consilium *n*; stropha *f*; tunica *f*; mutatio *f*; make ~ provideo 2; ~y versutus, subdolus

shin crus, uris *n*; ~bone tibia *f*

shine luceo 2, fulgeo 2, niteo 2; nitor *m*

shingle calculi *m/pl.*

shining lucidus, nitidus, fulgens

ship navis *f*; merchant ~ navis *f* oneraria; war ~ navis *f* longa; in navem impono 3; ~owner navicularius *m*; ~ping naves *f/pl.*; ~wreck naufragium *n*; ~wrecked naufragus

shirt tunica *f*, subucula *f*

shiver *v/t.* comminuo 3; *v/i.* horreo 2; tremo 3; fragmentum *n*; horror *m*, tremor *m*

shoal examen *n* (*piscium*); vadum *n*; syrtis *f*

shock conflictus, us *m*; concursus, us *m*; impetus, us *m*; *fig.* offensio *f*; offendo 3; be ~ed obstupesco 3; ~ing foedus, atrox, nefarius shoe calceus m; indoor ~ horse~ solea f; calceo 1; ~maker sutor m; ~string lingula f

shoot planta f, virga f; v/t. (e)mitto 3, conicio 3 (telum); vulnero 1 (alqm); v/i. volo 1; ~ing star fax f

shop taberna f; obsono 1; ~keeper tabernarius m; ~ping obsonatus, us m

shore litus n; ora f; ~ up fulcio 4

short brevis; be ~ of egeo 2 (abl.); fall ~ of non contingo 3 (alqd); in ~ denique; ~age inopia f; ~coming delictum n; ~cut compendiaria via f; ~en contraho 3; ~hand notae f/pl.; ~hand writer notarius m; ~ly brevi, mox; breviter; ~ness brevitas f; ~sighted hebes (oculus); fig. improvidus

shot ictus, us m; within, out of, ~ intra, extra ictum (teli)

shoulder umerus m; in umeros tollo 3 (onus)

shout clamo 1, vociferor 1; clamor m

shove trudo 3

shovel rutrum n; pala f

show monstro 1 (viam etc.); praebeo 3, exhibeo 2, praesto 1 (virtutem; me fortem); ~ that demonstro 1, doceo 2 (acc. c. inf.); ~ off ostento 1 (alqd, me); ostentatio f, species f; spectaculum n

shower imber, bris m; ingero 3, fundo 3 (tela in alqm); ~y pluvius

showy magnificus, speciosus

shred conseco 1; fragmentum n

shrewd sagax, acutus; ~ness calliditas f

shrewish importunus

shriek ululo 1; ululatus, us m

shrill (per)acutus

shrine delubrum n, sacrarium n

shrink me contraho 3; ~ from refugio 3, abhorreo 2 (ab); detrecto 1, reformido 1 (alqd)

shrivel torreo 2; ~led rugosus, torridus

shroud involvo 3 (alqd alqa re)

shrub frutex m; ~bery arbustum n

shudder horreo 2; ~ at perhorresco 3 (alqd); horror m, tremor m

shuffle v/t. (per)misceo 2; v/i. tergiversor 1

shun fugio 3; vito 1

shut claudo 3, occludo 3; obsero 1 (fores); operio 4; ~ in includo 3; ~ out excludo 3; ~ter foricula f

shuttle radius m

shy timidus, verecundus; consterno 1; ~ness verecundia f

Sibyl Sibylla f; ~line Sibyllinus

sick aeger, aegrotus; be

aegroto 1; morbo afficior 3; vomo 3; nauseo 1; be ~ of taedet 2 (me alcs rei); ~en v/t. fastidium moveo 2; v/i. in morbum cado 3, incido 3

sickle falx f

sick|ly aeger, invalidus; ~ness morbus m; aegrotatio f

side latus n (corporis, collis); pars f; factio f; on this, that ~ hinc, illinc; on this, that ~ of citra (acc.), trans (acc.); on both, all ~s utrimque, undique; on, at the ~ a latere (ulcs, exercitus etc.); be on the ~ of sto 1 (ab alqo); be on neither ~ nullius partis sum; ~long obliquus, limus; ~ways in obliquum

siege obsidio f, obsessio f; lay ~ to obsideo 2 (urbem); oppugno 1; ~works opera n/pl.

sieve cribrum n

sift perscruter 1

sigh suspiro 1; gemo 3; suspirium duco 3, traho 3; suspirium n; ~ing suspiratus, us m

sight visus m; acies f (oculorum); conspectus, us m; aspectus, us m; species f; spectaculum n; at first ~ primo aspectu; in ~ of in conspectu (alcs); catch ~ of conspicio 3, conspicor 1 (alqd)

sign signum n, indicium n;

nota f; vestigium n; heavenly ~ omen n, portentum n; subscribo 3 (dat.); ~ with a seal signo 1

signal signum n; insignis, egregius; **give a** ~ signum do 1; annuo 3; mil. cano 3 (receptui etc.)

sign|ature nomen n; ~et signum n; ~et-ring anulus m

significan|ce significatio f; ~t significans (verbum)

signify significo 1; sibi vult

silen|ce silentium n; refuto 1 (alqm); **keep** ~ce taceo 2, sileo 2; ~t tacitus, silens; ~tly tacite

silk serica n/pl.; bombyx m; ~en sericus

sill limen n

sill|iness stultitia f; ~y stultus, ineptus, fatuus

silver argenteus; argentum n; argento induco 3 (alqd)

similar similis, par (gen., dat.); ~ity similitudo f

simile similitudo f

simple simplex, merus; ~-minded ineptus, credulus; ~ton stultus (homo) m

simpl|icity simplicitas f; candor m; ~ify dilucide, apertius narro 1; explano 1; ~y solum, simpliciter

simulat|e simulo 1; ~ion simulatio f

simultaneously eodem tempore; simul

sin peccatum n, delictum n; pecco 1

since ex (abl.), ab (abl.);

post (*acc.*): *conj.* postquam (*perf. indic.*); **it is many years** ~ abhinc multos annos; **long** ~ iamdudum; (*causal*) cum (*subj.*), quoniam (*indic.*)

sincer|e simplex, candidus, sincerus; ~ty probitas *f*, sinceritas *f*

sinew nervus *m*; lacertus *m*; ~y nervosus

sinful impius, pravus

sing cano 3, canto 1 (*alqd*)

singe aduro 3, amburo 3

sing|er cantator *m*, cantatrix *f*; ~ing cantus, us *m*

single unus, solus; ~ **out** eligo 3; **in** ~ **combat** comminus

singular singularis, unicus, egregius; novus, mirabilis

sinister dirus

sink *v/t.* deprimo 3 (*navem*); *v/i.* consido 3, desido 3; mergor 3 (*in aquam*); ruo 3; collabor 3

sinner peccator *m*

sinuous sinuosus

sip sorbillo 1, degusto 1

sire pater, tris *m*, genitor *m*

Siren Siren *f*

sister soror *f*

sit sedeo 2 (*in sede*); ~ **down** consido 3; ~ **up** vigilo 1 (*de nocte*)

site situs, us *m*; locus *m*

sitting (*con*)sessio *f*

situat|ed situs (*in*); **be** ~**ed** iaceo 2; ~**ion** situs, us *m*; locus *m*

six sex; ~ **hundred** sescenti; ~**teen** sedecim; ~**teenth**

sextus decimus; ~**tieth** sexagesimus; ~**ty** sexaginta

size magnitudo *f*, amplitudo *f*; **of what** ~? quantus?

skein spira *f*

skeleton ossa *n/pl.*: *fig.*

sketch adumbro 1; describo 3; adumbratio *f*; lineamenta *n/pl.*

skewer veru *n*

skiff scapha *f*, navicula *f*

skil|ful sollers, habilis; ~l sollertia *f*, peritia *f*; artificium *n*; ~led peritus (*gen., abl.*); doctus, sciens (*gen.*)

skim despumo 1; ~ **over** percurro 3, perstringo 3, rado 3 (*alqd*)

skin cutis *f*; pellis *f*, tergum *n* (*bovis etc.*); pellem detraho 3 (*alci*); **dressed in** ~s pellitus; ~ny macer

skip exsulto 1; salio 4; lascivio 4 (*agnus etc.*); *fig.* praetereo 4, transilio 4; ~**per** navicularius *m*; nauarchus *m*

skirmish proelium *n* (leve); concursatio *f*; velitor 1, concurso 1; ~**er** veles *m*, concursator *m*

skirt limbus *m*; praetereo 4; *fig.* perstringo 3

skittish lascivus

skulk lateo 2; delitesco 3 (*in re*)

skull caput *n*

sky caelum *n*; ~-**blue** caeruleus; **raise to the skies** in caelum fero 3 slab lapis *m*; tabula *f*

slack laxus, remissus; piger; ~en remitto 3; relaxo 1; ~ness pigritia *f*, remissio *f*

slake exstinguo 3, restinguo 3

slander maledico 3 (*dat.*); criminor 1, obtrecto 1 (*alqm*); maledictio *f*, criminatio *f*, obtrectatio *f*; crimen *n*; ~er obtrectator *m*; ~ous maledicus

slanting obliquus

slap alapa *f*; pulso 3

slash incido 3; plaga *f*

slate (*roof*) tegula *f*; writing-~ tabula *f*

slaughter caedo 3, concido 3; trucido 3; caedes *f*, internecio *f*

slave servus *m*; famulus *m*; home-born ~ verna *m* and *f*; female ~ ancilla *f*, serva *f*; (de)sudo 1; laboro 1; ~-dealer venalicius *m*; ~ry servitium *n*; servitus, utis *f*

slay interficio 3, caedo 3, occido 3; neco 1; interimo 3; ~er interfector *m*, percussor *m*

sledge trahea *f*; ~hammer malleus *m*

sleek nitidus, nitens

sleep dormio 4; quiesco 3; dormito 1, somnum capio 3; ~ off edormio 4; somnus *m*; quies *f*; sopor *m*; go to ~ obdormisco 3; during ~ in somnis; ~iness somni cupido *f*; ~ing-draught so-

por *m*; ~less insomnis; be ~less vigilo 1; ~lessness insomnia *f*; ~y semisomnus, somniculosus

sleet grando *f*

sleeve manicae *f/pl.*

sleight-of-hand praestigiae *f/pl.*

sleigh trahea *f*

slender gracilis, tenuis; exilis; ~ness gracilitas *f*

slice concido 3; segmentum *n*

slide labor 3; lapsus, us *m*

slight levis, exiguus, parvus; despicio 3, contemno 3, parvi facio 3; neglego 3; indignitas *f*, neglegentia *f*; ~ingly contemptim

slim gracilis, tenuis

slime limus *m*; lutum *n*; ~y limosus

sling funda *f*; mitto 3, conicio 3; suspendo 3 (*alqd re*); ~er funditor *m*

slink away nec subduco 3

slip labor 3; let ~ amitto 3 (*opportunitatem*); ~ away me subduco 3; ~ out of elabor 3; lapsus, us *m*; *fig.* error *m*; make a ~ erro 1; ~per solea *f*, crepida *f*; ~pery lubricus; ~shod dissolutus

slit incido 3, scindo 3

sloop lembus *m*

slop|e clivus *m*; fastigium *n*; vergo 3; ~ing declivis, acclivis, proclivis

sloth segnitia *f*, desidia *f*; ~ful segnis, ignavus, piger

slovenly neglegens

slow tardus, lentus, segnis; ~ness tarditas *f*, pigritia *f*

slugg|ard homo *m* ignavus; ~ish piger, ignavus

sluice cataracta *f*

slumber sopor *m*; dormio 4

slur macula *f*; cast a ~ upon maculo 1 (*alqd*)

slush tabes *f*

sly callidus, astutus, vafer

smack alapa *f*; sonus *m*; fishing-~ lenunculus *m*; ferio 4; verbero 1; ~ of sapio 3 (*alqd*); (red)oleo 2 (*alqd*)

small parvus, tenuis, brevis, exiguus; how ~ quantulus ?; ~ness exiguitas *f*, brevitas *f*

smart lautus; acer, acerbus; sagax; mordeor 2, doleo 2; poenam do 1; morsus, us *m*, dolor *m*

smash comminuo 3, confringo 3

smear lino 3 (*alqd alqa re*); illino 3 (*alqd alci rei*)

smell olfacio 3, odoror 1; ~ of (red)oleo 2 (*alqd*); odor *m*; sense of ~ odoratus, us *m*; sweet-~ing odoratus

smelt (ex)coquo 3

smile (sub)rideo 2, renideo 2; risus, us *m*

smite ferio 4

smith faber, bri *m*; ferrarius *m*; ~y officina *f* (ferraria); fabrica *f*

smok|e *v/i.* fumo 1; *v/t.* fumigo 1; fumus *m*; vapor *m*; ~y fumosus, fumidus

smooth levis, teres; glaber; placidus, tranquillus (*mare*); levo 1; polio 4; rado 3; ~ness levitas *f*, lenitas *f*; ~-tongued blandus

smother opprimo 3; suffoco 1; *fig.* reprimo 3, comprimo 3

smoulder fumo 1

smudge litura *f*

smug mihi placens

smuggle furtim, contra leges importo 1 (*alqd*)

smut fuligo *f*; ~ty *fig.* ob-snack cenula *f* [scenus]

snaffle frenum *n*

snail cochlea *f*

snak|e anguis *m and f*; coluber, bri *m*; serpens *f*; ~y anguineus, vipereus

snap *v/t.* praefringo 3; *v/i.* frangor 3, rumpor 3; crepo 1; concrepo 1 (*digitis*); ~ up corripio 3; crepitus, us *m*

snare plaga *f*, pedica *f*; laqueus *m*; *fig.* insidiae *f/pl.*; irretio 4; laqueo capto 1

snarl gannio 4; ringor 3

snatch rapio 3, carpo 3; ~ at capto 1; ~ away, from avello 3; ~ up arripio 3; in ~es carptim

sneak correpo 3 (*in, intra*); arrepo 3 (*ad*)

sneer irrideo 2, derideo 2, naso suspendo 3 (*alqm, alqd*); irrisio *f*; irrisus, us *m*

sneez|e sternuo 3; ~ing sternumentum *n*

sniff odoror 1

snip praecido 3; segmentum n

snore sterto 3

snort fremo 3; fremitus, us m

snout rostrum n

snow nix f; it ~s ningit 3; ~-white niveus, nivalis; ~y nivosus

snub contemno 3, sperno 3; ~-nosed simus, silus

snuff (out) exstinguo 3

snug commodus

so ita, tam, adeo (... ut); just ~ sic; ita; and ~ itaque, ergo, igitur; and ~ on et cetera

soak v/t. madefacio 3; macero 1; v/i. mano 1; ~ed madidus

soap sapo m

soar sublime feror 3; subvolo 1; me tollo 3

sob singulto 1; singultus, us m

sob|er sobrius, siccus; sanus; modestus, temperans; ~riety sobrietas f; continentia f, temperantia f

sociab|ility facilitas f; ~le sociabilis; comis

social communis, civilis

society societas f, communitas f, commune n; civitas f; sodalitas f, collegium n

socket cavum n; sedes f

socle basis f

sod caespes m

soda nitrum n

sodden madidus

sofa lectulus m

soft mollis, lenis, tener; mitis, mansuetus; ~en v/t. (e)mollio 4; mitigo 1 (cibum, severitatem); lenio 4, placo 1; v/i. mitesco 3, mansuesco 3; ~ness mollitia f, lenitas f

soil terra f; solum n; humus, i f; inquino 1, foedo 1

sojourn (com)moror 1; commoratio f, mansio f

solace consolor 1; consolatio f; solatium n

solder ferrumen n; ferrumino 1

soldier miles m; common ~ gregarius (miles) m; ~ly militaris; ~y miles m

sole planta f; solum n; solus, unus, unicus; ~ly solum, tantum

solemn sollemnis, festus; augustus, religiosus; severus, gravis, serius; ~ity sollemne n; gravitas f, severitas f; ~ize celebro 1

solicit peto 3 (alqd ab alqo); flagito 1, obsecro 1 (alqm; ut); ~ation flagitatio f; ~or cognitor m; iuris consultus m; ~ous officiosus; ~ude anxietas f

solid solidus; firmus, robustus; solidum n; ~ify concresco 3

soliloquize mecum loquor 3

solit|ary solitarius (homo); desertus, solus, secretus; ~ude solitudo f

solo solus

solstice: summer ~ solstitium *n*; winter ~ bruma *f*

solution dilutum *n*; explicatio *f*

solve (dis)solvo 3; enodo 1; be ~nt solvendo sum

sombre tristis, tenebrosus

some aliqui, nonnullus; aliquot (*pl.*); aliquid, aliquantum *n*; ~ ... others alii... alii; ~body, ~one aliquis, quidam, nescio quis; ~how aliqua; ~thing aliquid, nescio quid; ~time aliquando; ~times aliquando, interdum, nonnunquam; modo ... modo; ~where alicubi

son filius *m*; ~-in-law gener, eri *m*

song cantus, us *m*; carmen *n*

sonorous sonorus, clarus

soon mox, brevi, iam; ~ after paulo; as ~ as simul atque, ac; statim ut; cum primum, ubi primum; as ~ as possible quamprimum; ~er ante ... quam;

soot fuligo *f* [libentius]

soothe mitigo 1, sedo 1, placo 1

soothsayer augur *m*, haruspex *m*, vates *m*

sooty fuliginosus, fumosus

sop *fig.* delenimentum *n*

sophist sophistes *m*; cavillator *m*; ~ical captiosus; ~ry captiones *f/pl.*; ~icated urbanus

soporific soporifer, somnificus

sorcer|er veneficus *m*; magus *m*; ~ess maga *f*, saga *f*; ~y veneficia *n/pl.*

sordid sordidus

sore ulcus, eris *n*; acerbus, gravis (*dolor etc.*); be ~ doleo 2 (*caput etc.*); *fig.* aegre fero 3 (*alqd*; *quod*); ~ly graviter; ~ness dolor *m*

sorrel lapathus *m*

sorrow dolor *m*, maeror *m*; luctus, us *m*; doleo 2, lugeo 2; ~ful maestus, maerens, tristis

sorry miser, miserabilis; be ~ paenitet 2, piget 2 (*me alcs rei*; *inf.*; *quod*)

sort genus; a ~ of quidam; of this, that ~ huiusmodi, eiusmodi; of such a ~ is. talis; of all ~s omnis; digero 3, dispono 3; ~ with consentio 4 (*cum*)

sortie eruptio *f*, excursio *f*; make a ~ erumpo 3

sot potator *m*

soul animus *m*; anima *f*; with all my ~ ex animo, toto pectore; not a ~ nemo (omnium); ~less hebes

sound sanus; salvus, incolumis; artus (*somnus*); sonus *m*; sonitus, us *m*; vox *f*; *v/t.* cano 3 (*classicum*; *signum*; *fidibus*); tento 1 (*vadum*); scrutor 1 (*animos*); ~ the praises of celebro 1 (*laudem*; *alqm*); *v/i.* sono 1, cano 3; sonitum reddo 3; ~ness sanitas *f*, gravitas *f*

soup ius *n*

sour acerbus; acidus; amarus; **turn** ~ (co)acesco 3

source fons m; caput n; origo f; **have its** ~ **in** orior 4 (ab)

south meridies m; australis, meridianus; ~ **wind** auster, tri m; ~**east inter** meridiem et solis ortum; ~**east wind** eurus m; ~**pole** polus m australis; ~**west inter** meridiem et occasum solis; ~**west wind** Africus m

sovereign rex m, princeps m; potentissimus; validus; ~**ty** principatus, us m; regnum n; imperium n

sow scrofa f, porca f; (con)sero 3; ~**er** sator m; ~**ing** sementis f, satio f

spac|e locus m; spatium n, intervallum n; ~**ious** amplus, latus, capax; ~**iousness** amplitudo f

spade pala f

span palmus m; spatium n (temporis); iungo 3 (flumen ponte)

spangled distinctus (stellis etc.)

spar|e exilis; subsicuus (tempus, opera); parco 3 (dat.); ~**ing** parcus (in re; gen.)

spark scintilla f; igniculus m; ~**le** mico 1, corusco 1, scintillo 1; ~**ling** micans, coruscus

sparrow passer, eris m

sparse rarus

spasm convulsio f; ~**odic** fig. rarus

spatter aspergo 3

speak dico 3, loquor 3 (de re); ~ **out** eloquor 3; ~ **to** alloquor 3, appello 1 (alqm); ~**er** orator m

spear hasta f; telum n; hasta transfigo 3 (alqm); ~**man** hastatus m; iaculator m

special proprius, peculiaris, praecipuus, extraordinarius; **ity** proprium n; quod proprium est (gen., dat.); ~**ly** praecipue

species genus n

specif|ic peculiaris; certus; ~**ically** subtilier; diserte

specimen exemplum n, exemplar m; specimen n

specious probabilis, speciosus

speck macula f; ~**led** maculosus, varius

specta|cle spectaculum n; ~**tor** spectator m

spectre larva f; simulacrum n, imago f

specula|te cogito 1 (de re); inquiro 3 (rem); conicio 3; coniecturam facio 3; ~**ion** coniectura f

speech oratio f, lingua f; contio f; sermo m; verba n/pl.; **make a** ~ orationem, contionem habeo 2; ~**less** mutus

speed celeritas f; accelero 1, maturo 1; fortuno 1; ~**y** celer, citus

spell carmen n; cantus, us m; litteras ordino 1

spend impendo 3, insumo 3

(*alqd in alqd*); ago 3, dego 3, consumo 3 (*tempus*); **~thrift** nepos *m*; profusus (homo) *m*

spent: be ~ defervesco 3 (*ira, cupido etc.*)

spew vomo 3

sphere sphaera *f*; globus *m*; *fig.* campus *m*; provincia *f*, area *f*

sphinx Sphinx *f*

spice odor *m*; condimentum *n*; condio 4; **~d** odoratus

spider's web aranea *f*

spike clavus *m*; cuspis *f*; spica *f*

spill effundo 3; assula *f*

spin *v/t.* neo 2; deduco 3; verso 1; *v/i.* versor 1; **~ out** duco 3; **~dle** fusus *m*

spine spina *f*

spinster innupta *f*

spiral spira *f*, coc(h)lea *f*; **in a ~ shape** in cocleam

spirit animus *m*; anima *f*; mens *f*, ingenium *n*; vigor *m*; voluntas *f*, sententia *f* (*legis*); **high ~s** animi *m/pl.*, spiritus *m/pl.*; **~s of the dead** Manes *m/pl.*; **~ed** animosus, ferox, acer; **~less** ignavus, abiectus (animo)

spit spuo 3; veru (con)figo 3 (*carnem*); veru *n*

spite malevolentia *f*, malignitas *f*, invidia *f*; laedo 3; malevolentia utor 3 (*in alqm*); **~ful** malevolus, infestus

spittle sputum *n*

splash aspergo 3 (*alqm alqa re*); sonitus, us *m*

spleen lien *m*; bilis *f*; stomachus *m*

splend|id splendidus, lautus, magnificus, praeclarus; **~our** splendor *m*; lautitia *f*

splenetic stomachosus

splinter assula *f*; fragmentum *n*

split *v/t.* (dif)findo 3, scindo 3; *v/i.* dissilio 4; fissum *n*; fissura *f*

splutter crepo 1, crepito 1; balbutio 4

spoil spolio 1; corrumpo 3, vitio 1; (*nimium*) indulgeo 2 (*dat.*); praeda *f*; spolia *n/pl.*

spoke radius *m*

spokesman interpres *m*, orator *m*

spondee spondeus *m*

sponge spongia *f*; spongia detergo 3

spontaneous voluntarius; **~ly** sua sponte, ultro

spoon cochlear *n*

sporadic rarus

sport ludo *m*; ludus *m*; lusus, us *m*; ludibrium *n*; **make ~ of** ludifico 1 (*alqm*); **be the ~ of** ludibrio sum (*alcs*); **~ive** ludicer, iocosus; **~sman** venator *m*

spot macula *f*, nota *f*; locus *m*; **on the ~** ibidem; conspicio 3; **~less** integer, purus; **~ted** maculosus, varius

spouse coniunx *f and m*

spout os *n*; prosilio 4; emico 1

sprain intorqueo 2

sprawl fundor 3 (*humo*)

spray aspergo 3; aspergo *f*; ramulus *m*

spread extendo 3, pando 3; ~ **abroad** *v*/*t.* sero 3, differo 3, divulgo 1; *v*/*i.* diffundor 3; serpo 3; evagor 1; increbresco 3, percrebresco 3, peragro 1 (*rumores etc.*); ~**ing** patulus

sprig ramulus *m*

sprightly alacer, hilaris

spring ver *n*; fons *m*; saltus, us *m*; vernus; salio 4, exsilio 4; ~ **down** desilio 4; ~ **from** nascor 3 (*ab, ex re*; *alqo*); ~ **up** coorior 4 (*tempestas etc.*); exorior 4 (*seditio etc.*); exsilio 4 (*de sella*); ~**-time** vernum tempus *n*

sprinkle aspergo 3, inspergo 3 (*alqd alqa re*; *alqd alci rei*) [(*ex*); surculus *m*]

sprout cresco 3, emergo 3]

spruce nitidus, lautus

spume spuma *f*

spur calcar *n*; (*of mountains*) iugum *n*; calcaribus concito 1; calcaria subdo 1 (*equo*); *fig.* concito 1

spurious falsus

spurn aspernor 1; reicio 3

spurt emico 1; nisus, us *m*; impetus, us *m*

spy explorator *m*, speculator *m*; ~ **out** exploro 1

squabble altercor 1, rixor 1; iurgium *m*

squadron (**of cavalry**) turma *f*, ala *f*

squal|id sordidus, squalidus; ~**or** squalor *m*

squall procella *f*; vagio 4

squander effundo 3; dissipo 1; ~**er** nepos *m*

square quadratum *n*; quadratus; quadro 1; ~ **with** consentio 4 (*cum*); ~ **accounts** rationem subduco 3

squash obtero 3

squat subsido 3; consido 3; brevis, humilis

squeak strideo 2; stridor *m*

squeamish fastidiosus

squeeze comprimo 3, premo 3

squint strabonem sum; limis (oculis) intueor 2; ~**ing** strabo, paetus

squire armiger, eri *m*

squirrel sciurus *m*

stab (con)fodio 3, percutio 3; vulnus *n*

stability stabilitas *f*

stable stabilis, firmus, solidus; stabulum *n*

stablish *s. establish*

stack coacervo 1; acervus *m*; strues *f*

staff baculum *n*; scipio *m*; *fig.* columen *n*; **military** ~ legati *m*/*pl.*

stag cervus *m*

stage pulpitum *n*, proscaenium *n*; scaena *f*; gradus, us *m*

stagger titubo 1, vacillo 1

stagnant iners; *fig.* frigidus; **be** ~ stagno 1, ~ **water** stagnum *n* stagnat|e refrigesco 3, torpesco 3; ~ion cessatio *f*; torpor *m*

staid severus

stain tingo 3, inficio 3; maculo 1, foedo 1; macula *f*; *fig.* labes *f*, nota *f*; ~less purus

stair scala *f*; gradus, us *m*; ~case scalae *f/pl.*

stake palus *m*; stipes *m*; sudes *f*; pignus *n*; be at ~ in discrimen venio 4; pono 3

stale obsoletus, vulgaris; mucidus

stalk stirps *f*, caulis *m*; *v/i.* incedo 3; *v/t.* (vestigiis) persequor 3

stall stabulum *n*, tectum *n*; taberna *f*

stallion (equus) admissarius *m*

stamina robur *n*; vires *f/pl.*

stammer (lingua) haesito 1; balbutio 4; haesitatio *f*; ~ing balbus

stamp signo 1; imprimo 3; pedem supplodo 3; moneta *f*, forma *f*; nota *f*; (pedis) supplosio *f*

stand *v/i.* sto 1; *v/t.* tolero 1; patior 3, perfero 3; statio *f*; raised ~ suggestus, us *m*; be at, come to, a ~ consisto 3; bring to a ~ constituo 3; make a ~ resisto 3; ~ by adsum (*dat.*); ~ firm consisto 3; ~ for peto 3 (*magistratum*); ~ round circumsto 1 (*acc.*); ~ still subsisto 3, consisto

3; ~ thus se habet 2 (*res*): it ~s to reason dubitari non potest (*quin*); ~ up (con)surgo 3; ~ up for adsum (*dat.*)

standard signum *n*, vexillum *n*; norma *f*, regula *f*; ~-bearer aquilifer, eri *m*; signifer, eri *m*

standing status, us *m*; locus *m*

standstill: be at a ~ cesso 1; haereo 2

star stella *f*; sidus *n*, astrum *n*; *fig.* lumen *n*

starboard dextra *f*; to ~ ad dexteram; dextera

starch amylum *n*

stare stupeo 2; ~ at intueor 2 (*alqd*; *in alqd*) (oculorum) obtutus, us *m*

stark naked plane nudus

starling sturnus *m*

starry sidereus, stellans

start *v/i.* tremo 3; proficiscor 3; incipio 3 (*alqd*; *inf.*); coepi (*inf.*); *v/t.* instituo 3; aggredior 3 (*alqd, ad alqd*); ~ing-place carcer, eris *n*

startle terreo 2; timorem, metum inicio 3 (*alci*)

starv|ation fames *f*, inedia *f*; ~e fame conficior 3, consumor 3; *fig.* privo 1 (*alqm alqa re*)

state condicio *f*; status, us *m*; locus *m*; res *f* publica, civitas *f*; pompa *f*; publicus, civilis; profiteor 2; declaro 1, affirmo 1, explico 1; ~liness lautitia *f*, gravitas *f*; **~ly** magnificus, gravis; **~ment** affirmatio *f*, professio *f*; testimonium *n*; **~sman** qui in re publica versatur; vir *m* rei publicae gubernandae peritus

station locus *m*; condicio *f*; ordo *m*; statio *f*; (dis)pono 3; **~ary** fixus, immotus; **~ery chartae** *f/pl.*

statue statua *f*; signum *n*

stature statura *f*

statute lex *f*

stave scipio *m*; **~ off** arceo 2, prohibeo 2

stay *v/i.* maneo 2, commoror 1 (*apud, in*); *v/t.* moror 1; mora *f*; commoratio *f*; *fig.* columen *n*, praesidium *n*

stead: in his **~** pro eo; **~fast** constans; firmus; **~fastness** constantia *f*; **~iness** stabilitas *f*; **~y** firmus, stabilis; frugi, honestus

steak frustum *n* (*carnis*); offa *f*

steal furor 1; surripio 3; *v/t.* **~ away** me subduco 3; dilabor 3; **~ over, upon** irrepo 3 (*in alqd*); **~ up to** arrepo 3 (*ad*); **~ing** furtum *n*

stealth: **by ~** clam; furtim; **~y** furtivus, clandestinus

steam vapor *m*; *v/i.* fumo 1; *v/t.* vaporo 1

steed equus *m* (*bellator*)

steel chalybs *m*; ferrum *m*; duro 1

steep praeceps, arduus, praeruptus; madefacio 1; **~le turris** *f*

steer guberno 1; rego 3; iuvencus *m*; **~ing** gubernatio *f*; **~sman** gubernator *m*

stem stirps *f*; stipes *m*; obsisto 3, resisto 3 (*dat.*)

stench fetor *m*; foedus odor *m*

stenograph|er notarius *m*; **~y notae** *f/pl.*

step gradus, us *m*; vestigium *n*; *fig.* **~s** consilium *n*; incedo 3, ingredior 3; **~ by ~** pedetemptim; **~-daughter privigna** *f*; **~-father vitricus** *m*; **~-mother noverca** *f*; **~-son privignus** *m*

steril|e sterilis, inutilis; **~ity sterilitas** *f*

stern severus, durus, rigidus; **puppis** *f*; **~ness severitas** *f*

stew coquo 3; **caro** *f* **elixa**

steward vilicus *m*; procurator *m*

stick *v/t.* (de)figo 3 (*alqd in re*); *v/i.* haereo 2 (*re; in re*); adhaereo 2 (*in re*); adhaeresco 3 (*ad; in re*); baculum *n*; clava *f*; **~y** tenax, lentus

stiff rigidus; durus, severus; **~en rigeo** 2; rigesco 3; **~ness rigor** *m*; duritia *f*

stifle strangulo 1, suffoco 1; *fig.* reprimo 3

stigma nota *f*; stigma *n*; **~tize noto** 1

still immotus, tranquillus, quietus; placo 1, sedo 1; *adv.* adhuc, etiam; etiam

14*

nunc, etiamtum; semper, usque; nihilominus, (at-) tamen, verumtamen; ~- ness quies f; silentium n
stilted inflatus
stimul|ate excito 1, incendo 3, stimulo 1; **~us** stimulus m; incitamentum n
sting pungo 3; fig. mordeo 2, uro 3; aculeus m; mor- sus, us m
sting|iness sordes f/pl.; **~y** sordidus, parcus
stink male oleo 2; fetor m
stint parco 3 (dat.); pensum n
stipend merces f; annuum n
stipulat|e (de)paciscor 3 (ut); statuo 3 (ut); **~ion** condicio f
stir (com)moveo 2; motus, us m; tumultus, us m; turba f; **~ up** excito 1; misceo 2
stitch suo 3
stock stirps f; genus n; copia f; instrumentum n, merces f/pl.; pecus n; instruo 3, repleo 2 (alqd alqa re); tritus, usitatus; well-~ed abundans, fre- quens (abl.).
stockade vallum n
stocking tibiale n
stocks compedes f/pl.
stoic Stoicus; durus; Stoi- cus m
stole palla f
stolid hebes, stolidus
stomach stomachus m; con- coquo 3
stone lapis m; saxum n;

nucleus m (olivarum etc.); lapideus; lapidibus coope- rio 4 (alqm); **~quarry** lapicidinae f/pl.
stony lapidosus, saxosus, saxeus; **~-hearted** ferreus
stook manipulus m
stool scamnum n
stoop demitto 3, summitto 3; fig. descendo 3 (ad alqd)
stop v/t. teneo 2, retineo 2; sisto 3; fig. cohibeo 2; comprimo 3, reprimo 3; v/i. consisto 3, insisto 3, subsisto 3; maneo 2; com- moror 1 (apud alqm); de- sino 3, omitto 3 (inf.); **~ up** obturo 1, obsaepio 4; interpunctum n; **put a ~** to dirimo 3, comprimo 3; moram facio 3 (alci rei); **~per** obturamentum n
store condo 3, repono 3; copia f; **~s** commeatus, us m; **~ house** apotheca f, cella f; horreum n; **~- keeper** cellarius m
storey tabulatum n
stork ciconia f
storm tempestas f; procella f; v/t. expugno 1; v/i. saevio 4; **~ing** expugnatio f; **~y** turbulentus, turbidus
story fabula f; res f; **there is a ~** ferunt 3 (acc. c. inf.); **~-teller** narrator m
stout pinguis, opimus; vali- dus; **~-hearted** impavidus, fortis; **~ness** habitus, us m opimus (corporis)
stove caminus m; focus m

stow repono 3, condo 3; ~ away me condo 3, abdo 3

straggle vagor 1, palor 1

straight rectus, directus; *adv.* recta; ~en corrigo 3; ~forward directus, sincerus, simplex; ~way statim, continuo

strain *v/t.* contendo 3; intendo 3 (*aciem*); intorqueo 2 (*talum*); liquo 1, colo 1 (*vinum*); *v/i.* nitor 3, me intendo 3 (*ut, ne*); contentio *f*; nixus, us *m*; labor *m*; cantus, us *m*; modus *m*; ~ed arcessitus (*dictum etc.*); ~er colum *n*

strait fretum *n*; angustiae *f/pl.*; ~-laced rigidus

strand litus *n*; be ~ed eicior 3 (in litore)

strange insolitus, inusitatus, mirus, novus; peregrinus, externus; alienus (*ab; dat.*); ~ly mirabiliter; nescio quo pacto; ~ness insolentia *f*; ~r peregrinus *m*; hospes *m*; homo *m* ignotus; *fig.* a ~r to ignarus, rudis, imperitus (*gen.*)

strangle strangulo 1

strap lorum *n*; loris vincio 4, ~ping validus

stratagem insidiae *f/pl.*; machina *f*; dolus *m*

strategy consilium *n*; belli ratio *f*

straw stramentum *n*; culmus *m*; *fig.* pilus *m*; stramenticius; ~berry fragum *n*   [palor 1; errans]

stray (ab)erro 1, vagor 1,

streak linea *f*; ~ed virgatus

stream rivus *m*; flumen *n*; down ~ secundo flumine; up ~ adverso flumine; labor 3; me effundo 3; ~er vexillum *n*

street via *f*; vicus *m*; platea *f*

strength vis *f*; vires *f/pl.*; robur *n*; firmitas *f*, firmitudo *f*; ~ of mind constantia *f*; on the ~ of fretus (*abl.*); ~en (con)firmo 1; stabilio 4

strenuous acer, impiger

stress vis *f*; impetus, us *m*; pondus *n*; lay ~ on (magni) momenti facio 3 (*alqd*)

stretch *v/t.* (in)tendo 3, contendo 3; *v/i.* pateo 2; patesco 3, pando 3; ~ forth, out porrigo 3, extendo 3; contentio *f*, intentio *f*; tractus, us *m*; spatium *n*; ~er lectica *f*

strew sterno 3, spargo 3

stricken: ~ in years aetate confectus

strict severus, durus; intentus, diligens

stricture reprehensio *f*

stride magnis gradibus incedo 3; magnus gradus, us *m*

strife discordia *f*; iurgia *n/pl.*; lites *f/pl.*

strigil strigilis *f*

strike *v/t.* ferio 4; percutio 3, caedo 3, ico 3; signo 1 (*nummos*); pello 3 (*lyram, nervos*); percello 3, percutio 3 (*animum, mentem*);

incurro 3, incurso 1 (*in oculos, aures*); *v/i.* sono 1; ~ against infligo 3, offendo 3 (*alqd alci*); ~ at, down subverto 3, everto 3; ~ camp castra moveo 2; it ~s me mihi occurrit 3, venit 4 in mentem; ~ out induco 3

striking insignis, gravis, mirus

string linum *n*; nervus *m* (*lyrae, arcus*); chorda *f* (*lyrae*); shoe ~ corrigia *f*; ~ together conecto 3; ~ed instrument fides *f/pl.*

stringent severus

strip *v/t.* spolio 1, nudo 1, exuo 3 (*alqm alqa re*); vestem depono 3; ~ off stringo 3, exuo 3, detraho 3 (*alqd*); ~ of paper (papyri) scida *f*; ~ of cloth fascia *f*

stripe virga *f*; purple ~ clavus *m* (*latus, angustus*); ~s verbera *n/pl.*, vulnera *n/pl.*; ~d virgatus

striv|**e** (e)nitor 3 (*ut; ad. pro*); contendo 3 (*inf.; ut; ad. alqd; contra alqm*); conor 1 (*inf.*); ~ing contentio *f*, appetitio *f* (*gen.*)

stroke (per)mulceo 2; ictus, us *m*; plaga *f*; pulsus, us *m* (*remorum*); linea *f*

stroll inambulo 1, spatior 1; ambulatio *f*

strong validus, robustus, firmus, fortis; gravis, acer; potens; vehemens; be ~

valeo 2; ~box arca *f*; ~hold arx *f*; praesidium *n*

structure compages *f*; aedificium *n*; *fig.* ratio *f*

struggle luctor 1, pugno 1 (*cum*); nitor 3 (*ut*); contendo 3 (*inf.*); dimico 1 (*cum; de*); certamen *n*; dimicatio *f*

strut magnifice incedo 3; magnifice me iacto 1

stubble stipula *f*

stubborn pertinax, pervicax, obstinatus; ~ness pertinacia *f*

stud equaria *f*; equi *m/pl.*

studded distinctus (*alqa re*)

stud|**ent** qui studet (*litteras, doctrinas etc.*); homo *m* litterarum studiosus; ~ent of rhetoric scholasticus *m*; ~ied meditatus, exquisitus; ~ious studiosus (*litterarum, doctrinae*)

study studeo 2 (*dat.*); operam do 1, incumbo 3 (*dat.*); cognosco 3; meditor 1; meditatio *f*; studium *n*; opera *f*; litterarum studia *n/pl.*; ars *f*; bibliotheca *f* (*cubiculum n*)

stuff materia *f*; textile *n*; farcio 4, refercio 4; sagino 1; ~ing fartum *n*; (*of cushions*) tomentum *n*

stumble offendo 3 (*pedem ad alqd*); labor 3; ~ upon incido 3 (*dat.*)

stump stipes *m*

stun (ob)stupefacio 3; consterno 1; be ~ned sopior 4

stunted minutus

stupe|**faction** stupor *m*; ~fy

(ob)stupefacio 3; consterno 1; ~ndous permirus

stupid stultus, stupidus, stolidus; ~ity stultitia f

sturdy robustus, validus, firmus

sturgeon acipenser, eris m

stutter balbutio 4; haesito 1; ~ing balbus

sty hara f

styl|e ratio f; modus m; literary ~e genus n; oratio f; stilus m; sermo m; appello 1, voco 1; dico 3; ~ish lautus, magnificus

subaltern optio m

subdue subicio 3, subigo 3, redigo 3; domo 1

subject subicio 3 (alqm sub alqd; dat.); oppono 3 (alqm alci rei); subiectus, dicto audiens; ~ to obnoxius (dat.); civis m; privatus m; res f; argumentum n; materia f; quaestio f; ~ion servitus, utis f

subjoin subicio 3; ~jugate subigo 3, redigo 3; domo 1

sublim|e elatus, excelsus; ~ity elatio f

submarine marinus, summersus

submerge summergo 3, demergo 3; inundo 1

submi|ssive humilis, summissus, supplex; ~t me summitto 3, subicio 3 (dat.); (con)cedo 3 (dat.); subeo 4; perfero 3 (labores etc.); refero 3 (alqd ad alqm)

subordinate subicio 3 (alqd alci rei); secundus, inferior; minister, tri m

suborn suborno 1

subpoena testimonium denuntio 3 (alci)

subscri|be subscribo 3; assentior 4 (alci, sententiae); confero 3 (pecuniam); ~ption subscriptio f

subsequent posterior, proximus; ~ly postea, deinde

subsid|e resido 3, remitto 3; cado 3; defervesco 3 (ira etc.); ~iary secundus; subsidiarius (cohortes etc.); ~ise pecunias praebeo 2; ~y collatio f

subsist sustineor 2; consto 1; sum; ~ence victus, us m

substan|ce res f; natura f; corpus n; summa f; ~tial solidus, gravis, magnus; amplus; ~tiate probo 1 (crimen); argumentis confirmo 1

substitute vicarius m; as a ~ for pro (alqo); in vicem (alcis); substituo 3, suppono 3 (alqm, alqd, in locum alcs, pro alqo)

subterfuge tergiversatio f; dolus m

subterranean subterraneus

subtle subtilis, acutus, acer; callidus; ~ty subtilitas f; acumen n; astutia f

subtract deduco 3

suburb suburbium n; ~an suburbanus

subver|sion eversio f; ~t everto 3

succeed v/t. succedo 3 (alci); excipio 3 (annus annum; regnum); v/i. succedit 3 (mihi); prospere evenit 4 (mihi); efficio 3 (ut); ~ in perficio 3 (alqd)

success res f/pl. secundae, prosperae; felicitas f; **~ful** felix, fortunatus; secundus, bonus; ~ion continuatio f, series f; in ~ion ex ordine; **~ive** continuus; **~or** successor m

succinct brevis

succour subvenio 4, succurro 3 (dat.); auxilium n

succulent sucosus

succumb (con)cedo 3, succumbo 3 (dat.)

such talis, huiusmodi, eiusmodi; ~ a man as to is qui; ~ a good man tam bonus vir; to ~ an extent adeo; in ~ a way ita

suck sugo 3; sorbeo 2; bibo 3; **~ing** lactens; **~le** mammam do 1, praebeo 2 (dat.)

sudden subitus, repentinus, repens; **~ly** repente, subito

sue litem, actionem intendo 3 (alci); ~ **for** peto 3, rogo 1, precor 1 (alqd ab alqo)

suet sebum n

suffer subeo 4, accipio 3, patior 3, perpetior 3, (per-)fero 3 (labores etc.); permitto 3 (alci inf.; ut); sino 3 (acc. c. inf.; inf.; subj.); ~ **from** afficior 3 (abl.); laboro 1 (abl.); **~er** aeger, gri m; **~ing** miseria f; labor m; **~ing from** afflictus (abl.)

suffice sufficio 3 (dat.; ad; ut); suppeto 3 (dat.); satis sum

sufficien|cy, **~t** satis (alcs rei)

suffocate suffoco 1, strangulo 1

suffrage suffragium n

suffuse suffundo 3 (alqd alqa re)

sugar saccharon n; mel n (lit. honey)

suggest subicio 3, inicio 3 (alqd alci); admoneo 2 (ut); ~ **itself** animo occurrit 3; ~ion admonitus, us m; consilium n; **at my** ~ion me auctore

suicid|al funestus, fatalis; **~e** mors f voluntaria; **commit** ~**e** mihi mortem conscisco 3

suit v/t. accommodo 1 (alqd ad); v/i. convenio 4 (in, ad alqd; dat.; acc. c. inf.); congruo 3 (cum; dat.); decet 2 (alqm); placet 2 (alci); **~able** idoneus, aptus (ad); commodus, opportunus; dignus

suite comitatus, us m; satellites m/pl., comites

suitor procus m [m/pl.]

sulky morosus, difficilis

sullen tristis, severus, tetricus

sully contamino 1

sulphur sulfur n

sultr|iness aestus, us m; **~y** aestuosus

sum summa *f*; pecunia *f*; caput *n*; ~ **up** subduco 3; ~**marily** sine mora; ~**mary** brevis, subitus; breviarium *n*; **give a ~mary** breviter describo 3

summer aestas *f*; aestivus

summit cacumen *n*, culmen *n*; vertex *m*; summus mons *m*

summon voco 1 (*also jur.* in ius), accerso 3; appello 1; ~**s** arcessitus, us *m*

sumptuous sumptuosus, lautissimus

sun sol *m*; ~ **oneself** apricor 1; ~**beam** solis radius *m*; ~**burnt** adustus; ~**dial** solarium *n*

sunken depressus, humilis, cavus

sun|ny apricus; ~**rise** solis ortus, us *m*; ~**set** solis occasus, us *m*; ~**shine** sol *m*

sup ceno 1 [*m*; lux *f*]

superabundan|ce abundantia *f*; ~**t** abundans

superannuated qui annuum accipit 3; obsoletus

superb magnificus, lautus

super|cilious arrogans, superbus, fastidiosus; ~**ficial** levis; ~**fluous** supervacaneus; ~**human** (paene) divinus

superintend praesum (*dat.*); curo 1 (*alqd*); ~**ence** cura *f*; administratio *f*; ~**ent** (pro)curator *m*; praefectus *m*

superior superior, melior; amplior; praestans; **be ~ to** supero 1

super|lative praestans, singularis; ~**natural** divinus; ~**scription** titulus *m*; ~**stition** superstitio *f*, religio *f*; ~**stitious** superstitiosus, religiosus; ~**vision** cura *f*, curatio *f*

supine supinus, iners

supper cena *f*

supple flexibilis, lentus

supplement accessio *f*, appendix *f*

suppli|ant supplex *m and f*; ~**cate** supplico 1 (*dat.*); oro 1, obsecro 1 (*alqm*); ~**cation** preces *f/pl.*; ~**catory** supplex

supply praebeo 2, suppedito 1, ministro 1 (*alqd alci*); suppleo 2, (re)sarcio 4 (*damna*); copia *f*, facultas *f*; ~**ies** commeatus, us *m*; copiae *f/pl.*

support sustineo 2, sublevo 1; perfero 3, tolero 1 (*labores*); alo 3, sustento 1 (*familiam*); adiuvo 1 (*alqm*); adsum (*alci*); firmamentum *n*, adminiculum *n*; *fig.* columen *n*; praesidium *n*; alimentum *n*; ~**er** fautor *m*, adiutor *m*

suppose pono 3; fingo 3 (*animo*); puto 1, opinor 1; ~**ition** opinio *f*; ~**itious** subditus, subdititius

suppress reprimo 3, opprimo 3; supprimo 3, celo 1 (*famam etc.*)

suprem|acy principatus, us *m*; imperium *n*; ~**e** summus, supremus

sure certus; compertus (res); fidus (homo); be ~ pro certo habeo 2; certe scio 3; compertum habeo 2; be ~ to cura 1 (ut)!; ~ly certe, certo, nimirum; ~ty vas m, sponsor m; be ~ty for spondeo 2 (pro alqo)

surf fluctus m/pl.

surface aequor n; summum n; adj. summus

surfeit satietas f; satio 1

surge fluctus, us m; aestus, us m; aestuo 1, surgo 3

surge|on chirurgus m; ~ry chirurgia f

surl|iness morositas f; ~y morosus, difficilis

surmise suspicor 1; coniectura f

surmount transcendo 3 (alqd), fig. (ex)supero 1; vinco 3

surname cognomen n

surpass (ex)supero 1; vinco 3; praesto 1

surplus residuum m, reliquum n

surpris|e admiratio f; res f improvisa; opprimo 3, adorior 4 (alqm); occupo 1 (urbem etc.); be ~ed miror 1 (acc.; acc. c. inf.; quod; si); ~ing mirus, mirabilis

surrender v/t. cedo 3, trado 3; v/i. me dedo 3, arma trado 3; deditio f, traditio f

surreptitious furtivus, clandestinus; ~ly furtim, clam

surround circumsto 1 (acc.); circumdo 1, cingo 3 (alqd,

alqm, alqa re); circumsedeo 2 (urbem); ~ed by circumfusus, cinctus (abl.)

survey contemplor 1, considero 1; contemplatio f; mensura f (agri etc.); ~or finitor m, metator m

surviv|e supersum, superstes sum (dat.); supero 1; ~ing superstes

susceptib|ility mollitia f (animi); ~le obnoxius (dat.)

suspect suspicor 1 (alqd; acc. c. inf.); suspectum habeo 2 (alqm); be ~ed in suspicione sum (alci alcs rei); suspectus sum

suspend suspendo 3 (alqd re; e, de re); intermitto 3 (proelium etc.); moveo 2 (alqm magistratu)

suspense dubitatio f; in ~ suspensus, incertus, dubius

suspension intermissio f

suspici|on suspicio f; ~ous suspiciosus (in alqm; res)

sust|ain sustineo 2; alo 3, sustento 1; patior 3; ~enance victus, us m; alimentum n [bula n/pl.]

swaddling|clothes incuna-}

swagger magnifice incedo 3; magnifice me iacto 1

swallow hirundo f; devoro 1; haurio 3

swamp palus, udis f; inundo 1; deprimo 3 (navem); ~y paludosus

swan cygnus m

sward caespes m

swarm examen *n*; *fig.* turba *f*, multitudo *f*; congregor 1, glomeror 1; ~ out of effundor 3 (*abl.*); ~ up scando 3

swarthy fuscus, adustus

swathe fascia *f*

sway *v/t.* agito 1; *v/i.* vacillo 1, fluito 1; *fig.* dirigo 3, rego 3; imperium *n*; dicio *f*

swear iuro 1 (*per alqm*; *in alqd*; *acc. c. inf.*); iusiurandum accipio 3; ~ at exsecror 1 (*alqm*); ~ in iureiurando obstringo 3 (*alqm*); iusiurandum adigo 3 (*alqm*); ~ allegiance to iuro 1 in nomen (*alcs*); ~ing execrationes *f/pl.*

sweat sudor *m*; sudo 1

sweep verro 3 (*vias, purgamenta, etc.*); (de)tergeo 2 (*vias*); percurro 3 (*alqd oculo*); ~ings purgamenta *n/pl.*

sweet dulcis, suavis, iucundus; ~en iucundum facio 3; ~heart deliciae *f/pl.*; ~ness dulcedo *f*, suavitas *f*

swell *v/i.* tumeo 2; tumesco 3, turgesco 3; cresco 3; *v/t.* distendo 3; inflo 1; fluctus, us *m*; ~ing tumor *m*

swerve declino 1 (*ab, de*)

swift celer; velox, rapidus; ~ness velocitas *f*

swim nato 1; ~mer natator *m*; ~ming natatio *f*

swindle fraudo 1 (*alqm pecunia*); decipio 3 (*alqm*); fraus *f*; ~r fraudator *m*

swine sus *f and m*; ~herd subulcus *m*

swing *v/t.* agito 1 (*huc illuc*); *v/i.* vacillo 1, fluito 1; *fig.* ~ round me verto 3 (*in*)

swirl torqueor 3; vertex *m*

swish strepitus, us *m*

switch virga *f*; *v/t.* muto 1; *v/i.* mutor 1

swollen tumidus, turgidus

swoon collabor 3

swoop lapsus, us *m*; impetus, us *m*; ~ down (on) (de)labor 3 (*in*); ~ upon involo 1, incurro 3 (*in*)

sword gladius *m*; ferrum *n*

sycophant assentator *m*

syllable syllaba *f*

symbol signum *n*; imago *f*

symmetr|ical aequalis, congruens; ~y convenientia *f*

sympath|etic misericors; ~ise misereor 2 (*gen.*); ~y misericordia *f*; concordia *f*

symphony concentus, us *m*; symphonia *f*

symptom indicium *n*, signum *n*

syndicate societas *f*

synonymous quod idem declarat 1 (*verbum*)

synopsis epitoma *f*

syntax constructio *f* verborum

synthesis coniunctio *f*

syringe sipho *m*

system ratio *f*, institutio *f*, descriptio *f*; disciplina *f* (*philosophiae*); ~atic ordinatus; ~atise ordino 1

table   428   taper

T

table mensa *f*; *fig.* cena *f*; index *m*

tablet tabula *f*, tabella *f*, tessera *f*

tacit tacitus; ~urn taciturnus

tack *v/t.* figo 3 (*alqd in re*); ~ together, up (con)suo 3 (*alqd*); *v/i.* reciprocor 1; clavulus *m*

tackle armamenta *n/pl.*, instrumenta *n/pl.*; obviam eo 4 (*dat.*)

tact prudentia *f*, humanitas *f*; ~ful prudens

tactics belli ratio *f*; consilium *n*

tag pittacium *n*; ~ after subsequor 3 (*alqm*)

tail cauda *f*

tailor vestiarius (homo) *m*

taint contamino 1, inquino 1; imbuo 3; contagio *f*; vitium *n*

take capio 1, sumo 3; accipio 3; duco 3; ~ after similis sum (*alcs*); ~ away adimo 3, aufero 3, tollo 3 (*alqd*); ~ down detraho 3; ~ fire ignem accipio 3, concipio 3; ~ for habeo 2 (*pro amico etc.*); ~ hold of comprehendo 3; ~ in recipio 3, accipio 3 (*hospitem*); comprehendo 3, percipio 3 (*mente*); decipio 3 (*alqm dolo*); ~ off depono 3 (*vestem*); ~ out eximo 3, eripio 3; ~ (oneself) to me

confero 3; ~ place fio 3; ~ up sumo 3 (*arma*); consumo 3 (*tempus*); suscipio 3 (*bellum*, *partem alcs*)

tale fabula *f*, narratio *f*, historia *f*

talent ingenium *n*; indoles *f*; ~ed ingeniosus

talk (col)loquor 3 (*cum alqo*); sermo *m*; colloquium *n*; ~ative loquax, garrulus; ~ativeness loquacitas *f*

tall procerus; grandis; longus; ~ness proceritas *f*

tallow sebum *n*

tally convenio 4 (*cum re*); tessera *f*; ratio *f*

talon unguis *m*

tambourine tympanum *n*

tame mansuetus, cicur, domitus; ignavus; mansuefacio 3; domo 1; ~ness lentitudo *f*; ~r domitor *m*

tamper with *fig.* sollicito 1 (*alqm*)

tan pelles conficio 3; coloro 1 (*corpus*)

tangle implico 1; implicatio *f*; nodus *m*

tank lacus, us *m*; cisterna *f*; ~ard cantharus *m*

tanner coriarius *m*

tantamount idem (*ac*); par (*dat.*)

tap leviter pulso 1; ictus, us *m*

tape taenia *f*

taper cereus *m*; fastigor 1;

~ing fastigatus (*in cacumen etc.*)

tapestry tapetia *n/pl.*

tar pix *f*

tard|iness tarditas *f*; ~y tardus, lentus

tare lolium *n*

target *fig.* meta *f*

tarnish maculo 1, vitio 1

tarry (com)moror 1

tart scriblita *f*; acidus; mordax

task opus *n*, negotium *n*, pensum *n*; onus impono 3 (*alci*); ~master exactor *m* (operis)

tassels fimbriae *f/pl.*; cirri *m/pl.*

taste *v/t.* (de)gusto 1, (de)libo 1 (*alqd*); *v/i.* sapio 3 (*alqd*; *bene*); sapor *m*; gustatus, us *m*; *fig.* intellegentia *f*; iudicium *n*; elegantia *f*; ~ful elegans, intellegens; ~less insulsus

tast|er praegustator *m*; ~y sapidus, conditus

tatter pannus *m*; ~ed pannosus

tattle garrio 4

tattoo compungo 3

taunt obicio 3 (*alqd alci*); opprobrium *n*, convicium *n*

tavern caupona *f*

tawdry fucosus

tawny fulvus

tax vectigal *n*; incuso 1 (*alqm alcs rei*); vectigal impono 3 (*alci*); censeo 2 (*alqm*); ~collector exactor *m*

teach doceo 2 (*alqm alqd*; *inf.*); erudio 4, instruo 3 (*alqm alqa re*); ~er magister, tri *m*; doctor *m*, praeceptor *m*; ~ing doctrina *f*, institutio *f*; praecepta *n/pl.*

team iugum *n*

tear¹ lacrima *f*; shed ~s lacrimas fundo 3; ~ful lacrimans

tear² scindo 3; ~ to pieces lanio 1; discindo 3; convello 3; scissura *f*

tease obtundo 3 (*alqm*); vexo 1

teat mamma *f*

tedious lentus, longus, molestus

teem abundo 1, scateo 2 (*alqa re*)

tell (e)narro 1 (*rem alci*); dico 3 (*acc. c. inf.*); memoro 1 (*alqd*); iubeo 2 (*alqm alqd facere*); ~ing gravis, validus

temerity temeritas *f*

temper tempero 1; lenio 4; animus *m*; bad ~ iracundia *f*; bad-~ed morosus, difficilis; ~ament habitus, us *m*; ~ance temperantia *f*, modestia *f*; ~ate temperatus, temperans

temperature temperatura *f*; high ~ calor *m*; low ~ frigor *m*

tempest tempestas *f*; ~uous procellosus

temple templum *n*; aedes *f*; tempus *n* (*capitis*); ~keeper aedituus *m* tempor|arily ad tempus; in tempus; ~ary temporarius; ~ise cunctor 1; tempori servio 4

tempt tempto 1, sollicito 1; ~ation sollicitatio f; illecebra f; ~er temptator m; ~ing illecebrosus

ten decem; ~ times decies

tenac|ious pertinax, tenax; ~ity tenacitas f, pertinacia f

tenant conductor m; incola m

tend v/t. colo 3; curo 1; v/i. tendo 3; pertineo 2; specto 1; ~ency inclinatio f

tender tener, delicatus, mollis; defero 3, offero 3; ~ness teneritas f; indulgentia f

tendon nervus m

tendril pampinus m

tenet institutum n, dogma n

tenor cursus, us m; ratio f

tens|e tentus; intentus; tempus n; ~ion intentio f

tent tabernaculum n; general's ~ praetorium n

tentacle bracchium n

tenth decimus

tenuous exiguus, rarus

tepid tepidus

term finis m; spatium n; tempus n; verbum n; nuncupo 1, appello 1. ~s condicio f; be on good (bad) ~s (with) est mihi amicitia (inimicitia) (cum alqo)

termin|ate finio 4; concludo 3; ~ation finis m;

exitus, us m; ~ology vocabula n/pl., verba n/pl.

terrestrial terrestris, terrenus

terrible, terrific terribilis. horribilis

territory fines m/pl.; ager, gri m; terra f

terror terror m, pavor m; ~ize terreo 2

terse pressus, astrictus; ~ness brevitas f

test experior 4; tento 1, specto 1, periclitor 1; periculum n, experimentum n; obrussa f

testa|ment testamentum n; ~tor testator m

testicle testis m

testify (to) testificor 1, testor 1, declaro 1 (alqd; acc. c. inf.)

testimony testimonium n

testy stomachosus

tether religo 1

text verba n/pl.; oratio f

textile textilis; textile n

texture textus, us m; textum n

than quam, atque

thank gratias ago 3 (alci); ~ you benigne; ~ful gratus; ~less ingratus; ~s gratia f, gratiae f/pl.; ~sgiving supplicatio f, gratulatio f

that ille; is; iste; relat. qui, quae, quod; cj. ut; ~ not ut non, ne; oh ~! utinam

thatch stramentum n

thaw v/t. (dis)solvo 3; v/i. tabesco 3, resolvor 3

the ille; ~ more ... ~ more
quo magis ... eo magis

theatr|e theatrum n; scaena
f, cavea f; spectaculum n;
_ical theatralis, scaenicus

theft furtum n

their suus, sua, suum

theme propositum n, argu-
mentum n; res f

then tum, tunc; deinde,
inde, post, postea; igitur,
ergo; ~ and there ilico

thence inde, illinc; hinc;
_forth ex eo tempore,
inde

theolog|ian theologus m;
_y theologia f

theor|etically scientia; _y
ratio f; scientia f

there ibi, illic; eo; _abouts
circa, _after exinde; _fore
igitur, ergo, itaque; _upon
tum, subinde, inde

thesis propositum n, argumentum n

thick densus, crassus, artus; creber, confertus; in
the ~ of in medio (proelio
etc.); _en denso 1; _et
dumetum n; _ness crassi-
tudo f

thie|f fur m and f; _ve furor
1; _vish furax

thigh femur n

thin tenuis; rarus; gracilis;
subtilis; exilis, macer;
attenuo 1, extenuo 1

thing res f; negotium n

think cogito 1; arbitror 1,
opinor 1, puto 1, existimo
1; credo 3; censeo 2; ~
about, over cogito 1 (alqd;

de re); reputo 1 (alqd); _er
philosophus m; _ing cogi-
tatio f

third tertius; tertia pars f;
_ly tertio

thirst sitis f; sitio 4 (alqd);
_y sitiens, siccus

thirt|een tredecim; _eenth
tertius decimus; _ieth tri-
gesimus; _y triginta

this hic, haec, hoc

thistle carduus m

thither illuc, eo

thong lorum n

thorn spina f; _bush sentis
m; _y spinosus

thorough germanus, per-
fectus; _bred generosus;
_fare pervium n; _ly peni-
tus, omnino, plane

though quamquam, quam-
vis; etsi, etiamsi

thought cogitatio f; cogita-
tum n; notio f; _ful providus; _fulness cura f;
_less inconsultus, negle-
gens; _lessness temeritas f

thousand mille, pl. milia; a
~ times miliens; _th mil-
lesimus

thrall servus m

thrash tero 3, tundo 3 (frumentum); verbero 1; _ing
verbera n/pl.

thread filum n, linum n;
cursus, us m (verborum);
filum in acum conicio 3;
~ one's way me insinuo 1;
_bare obsoletus

threat minae f/pl.; _en v/t.
minor 1 (alqd alci; acc. c.
inf.); intendo 3 (alqd alci,

in alqm); denuntio 1 (alqd
alci); v/i. impendeo 2;
insto 1; ~ening minax

three tres, tria; ~ times
ter; ~ each terni; ~ days
triduum n; ~ years trien-
nium n; ~fold triplex;
~legged tripes

thresh tero 3, tundo 3;
~ing tritura f; ~ing floor
area f

threshold limen n

thrice ter

thrift frugalitas f; ~y frugi;
parcus

thrill agito 1 (alqm, mentem); commoveo 2; strin-
gor m, horror m; ~ed
attonitus

thriv|e vigeo 2, floreo 2,
vireo 2; ~ing vegetus,
vigens, laetus

throat guttur n, iugulum n;
fauces f/pl.; gula f; cut
the ~ iugulo 1

throb palpito 1; salio 4;
pulsus, us m

throes dolor m

throne solium n; fig. regnum
n

throng frequentia f, multitudo f, turba f; v/t. frequento 1, celebro 1 (locum);
v/i. confluo 3

throttle strangulo 1, suffoco 1

through per (acc.); propter
(acc.); ~out per (totam
urbem, noctem etc.); adv.
penitus, semper

throw iacio 3, conicio 3,
mitto 3; iacto 1; excutio 3,

deicio 3 (equitem); ~ across
traicio 3; ~ away proicio 3,
abicio 3; ~ oneself down
me proicio 3; iactus, us
m; coniectus, us m

thrush turdus m

thrust trudo 3, pello 3;
plaga f

thud fragor m

thumb pollex m

thump tundo 3

thunder tonitrus, us m;
tono 1; ~bolt fulmen n;
~ing tonans; ~struck attonitus, obstupefactus

thus ita, sic

thwart obsto 1 (dat.); disturbo 1 (alqd); transtrum n

thyme thymum n

thyrsus thyrsus m

tiara tiara f

tick crepito 1; pedis m

ticket tessera f

ticking crepitus, us m

tick|le titillo 1; ~ling titil-
latio f; ~lish fig. lubricus

tide aestus, us m

tid|iness munditia f; ~y
mundus

tidings nuntius m

tie (al)ligo 1; vincio 4;
vinculum n; necessitudo f,
coniunctio f (amicitiae etc.)

tier ordo m

tiger tigris m

tight strictus, contentus,
astrictus, artus; ~en
(a)stringo 3, contendo 3

tile tegula f, imbrex f;
later, eris m

till colo 3; dum, donec,
quoad; prep. (usque) ad

(*acc.*); ~er cultor *m*, arator *m*; gubernaculum *n*; clavus *m*

tilt proclino 1, inclino 1

timber materia *f*, materies *f*; ligna *n/pl.*

time tempus *n*; tempestas *f*, aetas *f*; spatium *n*; at that ~ tum; ea tempestate; at the same ~ simul; at a good ~, in ~ tempore, in tempore, ad tempus; at another ~ alias; for the first ~ primum; what is the ~ hora quota est?; keep ~ servo 1 numerum, modum; in ~ in numerum; (tempus) metior 4; ~ly tempestivus, opportunus, maturus; ~-piece horologium *n*

timid timidus, trepidus, ~ity timiditas *f*

timorous pavidus

tin stannum *n*

tincture color *m*; tingo 3

tinder fomes *m*

tinge tingo 3, imbuo 3

tingle ferveo 2

tinkle tinnio 4; crepito 1; crepitus, us *m*; tinnitus, us *m*

tinsel brattea *f*; bratteatus

tint color *m*; tingo 3

tiny parvulus, pusillus, exiguus

tip cacumen *n*; apex *m*; finger~ extremus digitus *m*; praefigo 3 (*caput hastae*); ~ up inclino 1

tipple poto 1; ~r potator *m*

tipsy ebrius, temulentus

tiptoe: stand on ~ in digitos me erigo 3

tirade declamatio *f*

tire (de)fatigo 1; I am ~d of taedet 1 me (*alcs rei*); ~d (de)fessus, lassus; ~some odiosus, molestus; laboriosus

tiro tiro *m*

tissue textus, us *m*

titbit cuppedium *n*; mattea *f*

tithe decima (pars) *f*

title titulus *m*; inscriptio *f*; nomen *n*; ~d nobilis

to ad (*acc.*), in (*acc.*); *final cj.* ut: ~ and fro huc illuc; all ~ a man omnes ad unum

toad bufo *m*, ~stool fungus *m*

toady assentor 1 (*alci*); adulor 1 (*alqm, alci*); assentator *m*

toast torreo 2; frigo 3; propino 1 (*poculum alci; salutem*); propinatio *f*

today hodie; hodiernus dies *m*

toe digitus *m*

toga toga *f*

together simul, una; ~ with (una) cum (*abl.*)

toil labor *m*; laboro 1; ~s plagae *f/pl.*

toilet ornatus, us *m*; cultus, us *m*

toilsome laboriosus

token signum *n*

tolera|ble tolerabilis; mediocris; ~bly satis; ~nce indulgentia *f*; ~nt patiens *(gen.)*; indulgens; ~te tolero 1; patior 3, fero 3; indulgeo 2 *(dat.)*

toll vectigal *n*

tomb sepulcrum *n*, monumentum *n*; ~stone lapis *m*

tomorrow cras; crastinus dies *m*; after ~ perendinus

tone sonus *m*, vox *f*; color *m*

tongs forceps *f*

tongue lingua *f*

tonight hac nocte

tonsils tonsillae *f/pl.*

too et, etiam; quoque; nimis; ~ long nimis longus; longior; ~ much nimis, nimium; ~ little parum

tool instrumentum *n*, ferramentum *n*; *fig.* minister, tri *m*

tooth dens *m*; ~less edentulus; ~pick dentiscalprum *n*

top summus; summum cacumen *n*, fastigium *n*, caput *n*, culmen *n*; vertex *m*; turbo *m*; on the ~ of the hill in summo monte

toper potator *m*

topic res *f*; locus *m*; argumentum *n*

topmost summus

topography locorum descriptio *f*

topsy-turvy sursum deorsum *(versare omnia)*

torch fax *f*; taeda *f*

torment (ex)crucio 1; ango 3; vexo 1; cruciatus, us *m*

tornado turbo *m*

torp|id piger, iners; ~or

inertia *f*, pigritia *f*; torpor *m*

torrent torrens *m*

torrid torridus

tortoise(-shell) testudo *f*

torture (ex)crucio 1; (ex-)torqueo 2; tormenta *n/pl.*; quaestio *f*, cruciatus, us *m*; ~r carnifex *m*

toss iacto 1; iactus, us *m*

total totus, cunctus; summa *f*; ~ly omnino

totter titubo 1, vacillo 1, labo 1

touch tango 3, attingo 3; *fig.* moveo 2; flecto 3, afficio 3; ~ in at navem appello 3 *(ad)*; ~ upon tango 3, attingo 3, perstringo 3; tactus, us *m*; contagio *f*; ~ing quod ad; de *(abl.)*; ~stone index *m*; *fig.* obrussa *f*; ~y difficilis stomachosus   [cilis]

tough lentus, durus; difficilis

tour iter, ineris *n*; *(abroad)* peregrinatio *f*; circuitio *f*; iter facio 3, circumeo 4; ~ist peregrinator *m*

tow stuppa *f*; (remulco) traho 3; ~line remulcum *n*

towards ad, adversus, in *(acc.)*; sub *(noctem)*; erga *(algm)*

towel mantele *n*

tower turris *f*; ~ up emineo 2

town urbs *f*; oppidum *n*; municipium *n*; urbanus; ~ councillors decuriones *m/pl.*; ~ crier praeco *m*; ~hall curia *f*; ~sman oppidanus *m*, municeps *m*

toy crepundia *n/pl*; *fig.*
ludicrum *n*, ludibrium *n*;
ludo 3

trace vestigium *n*, indicium
n; significatio *f*; habena *f*,
lorum *n* (*equi*); sequor 3;
indago 1

track vestigium *n*; callis *f*;
~ out, down odoror 1,
indago 1, vestigo 1; ~less
avius, invius

tract tractus, us *m*; regio *f*;
libellus *m*

tractable tractabilis, docilis

trade commercium *n*; mercatura *f*; negotium *n*;
artificium *n*; negotior 1;
~r mercator *m*; ~sman
caupo *m*

trading vessel navis *f* oneraria

tradition mos *m* (maiorum);
fama *f*, memoria *f*; there
is a ~ traditur; tradunt;
memoria proditum est
(*acc. c. inf.*); ~al a maiori-
bus traditus

traduce maledico 3 (*dat.*);
obtrecto 1 (*alqm*)

traffic commercium *n*; commercium habeo 2 (*cum
alqo*); (merces) muto 1

trag|edian tragoedus *m*;
~edy tragoedia *f*; ~ic tra-
gicus; *fig.* tristis, miserabilis

trail traho 3; vestigo 1,
odoror 1; vestigia *n/pl.*

train instituo 3; doceo 2,
exerceo 2; exercito 1;
assuefacio 3 (*alqm alqa re*;

inf.); pompa *f*; commeatus, us *m*; tractus, us *m*;
ordo *m*; series *f*; ~er
exercitor *m*; ~ing disciplina *f*, exercitatio *f*

trait nota *f*

traitor proditor *m*; ~ous
perfidus

trample on calco 1, con-
culco 1; obtero 3

tranquil tranquillus, placidus; ~lity otium *n*

transact transigo 3, con-
ficio 3, ago 3; ~ion res *f*,
negotium *n*

transcend supero 1

transcri|be perscribo 3;
~pt exemplar *n*

transfer traduco 3, trans-
fero 3; translatio *f*

transfix traicio 3, transfigo
3; *fig.* ~ed (ob)stupefactus

transform muto 1; verto 3

transgress violo 1; transcendo 3; ~ion violatio *f*,
delictum *n*

transient fluxus, caducus,
brevis

transit transitus, us *m*

translate converto 3, reddo
3; interpretor 1; ~or in-
terpres *m*

trans|lucent pellucidus; ~
marine transmarinus; ~
mit transmitto 3; ~parent
pellucidus; ~plant trans-
fero 3

transport transporto 1;
traicio 3, transveho 3; *fig.*
be ~ed exardesco 3, ef-
feror 3 (*gaudio etc.*);
vectura *f*; navis *f* oneraria

transverse transversus
trap pedica *f*, plaga *f*; insidiae *f/pl.*; **mouse~** muscipulum *n*; irretio 4
trappings ornatus, us *m*; insignia *n/pl.*
trash scruta *n/pl.*; quisquiliae *f/pl.*; **~y** vilis
travail dolor *m*, labor *m*
travel iter facio 3; peregrinor 1; **~ over** perlustro 1 (*acc.*); peregrinatio *f*; **~ler** viator *m*, peregrinator *m*
traverse obeo 4; perlustro 1
tray ferculum *n*, repositorium *n*
treacher|ous perfidus, perfidiosus; lubricus; **~y** perfidia *f*
tread insisto 3 (*in re*; *dat.*); **~ upon** calco 1 (*alqd*); gradus, us *m*; vestigium *n*
treason maiestas *f*; proditio *f*; **commit ~** maiestatem minuo 3, laedo 3
treasur|e thesaurus *m*; gaza *f*; coacervo 1; plurimi facio 3, aestimo 1; **~er** aerarii praefectus *m*; **~y** aerarium *n*; fiscus *m*; thesaurus *m*
treat tracto 1; accipio 3 (*alqm bene*); habeo 2 (*alqm pro amico*, *in honore*); utor 3 (*abl.*); curo 1 (*aegrotum*); dissero 3, disputo 1 (*de re*); **~ lightly** parvi facio 3 (*rem*); **~ with** ago 3, paciscor 3 (*cum alqo*); **~ise** liber, bri *m*; **~ment** tractatio *f*; curatio *f*; **~y** foedus, *n*, pactio *f*; pactum *n*

treble acutus (*sonus*); triplex
tree arbor *f*
trellis cancelli *m/pl.*
trembl|e tremo 3, contremisco 3 (*alqd*); **~ing** tremor *m*; tremens, tremulus
tremendous immanis, ingens
trem|or tremor *m*; **~ulous** tremulus
trench fossa *f*; sulcus *m*
trepidation trepidatio *f*
trespass pecco 1; **~ upon** *fig.* praesumo 3 (*alqd*); imminuo 3
tress crinis *m*; coma *f*
trial experientia *f*; periculum *n*; probatio *f*; conatus, us *m*; *jur.* iudicium *n*; quaestio *f*; **make ~ of** periclitor 1; **put on ~** postulo 1 (*alqm de re*)
triang|le triangulum *n*; **~ular** triangulus, triquetrus
tribe gens *f*, natio *f*; tribus, us *f*
tribunal iudicium *n*; quaestio *f*
tribun|ate tribunatus, us *m*; **~e** tribunus *m* (*plebis*, *militum*); **~icial** tribunicius
tribut|ary stipendiarius, vectigalis; **~e** tributum *n*, vectigal *n*; *fig.* munus *n*
trice momentum *n*
trick dolus *m*; fallacia *f*; fallo 3; ludificor 1; **~ery** dolus *m*; artificium *n*
trickle mano 1; stillo 1

tricky difficilis

trident tridens *m*

tried spectatus, probatus

trifl|e nugae *f/pl.*; nugor 1; ludo 3; ~e with illudo 3 (*acc.*); ~ing levissimus; in- constans; ineptiae *f/pl.*

trill vibro 1; ~ing tremulus

trim mundus, nitidus; ton- deo 2; puto 1; como 3 (*capillos*); ~mer qui tem- poribus servit

trip offendo 2 (pedem); *fig.* erro 1; ~ up supplanto 1 (*alqm*); iter, ineris *n*

tripartite tripartitus

tripe omasum *n*

tri|ple triplex; ~pod tripus, odis *m*; ~reme triremis *f*

trite tritus, pervulgatus

triumph victoria *f*; Roman general's ~ triumphus *m*; ovatio *f*; exsulto 1; trium- pho 1; ~ over supero 1; ~al triumphalis; ~ant victor

triumvir triumvir *m*; ~ate triumviratus, us *m*

trivial levis

troop caterva *f*, manus, us *f*; grex *m*; turma *f* (*equi- tum*); confluo 3; ~er eques *m*; ~s copiae *f/pl.*; milites

trophy tropaeum *n* [*m/pl.*]

troth fides *f*

trouble opera *f*; labor *m*; negotium *n*; molestia *f*; incommodum *n*; dolor *m*; res *f/pl.* adversae; solli- cito 1, perturbo 1; mole- stiam exhibeo 2 (*alci*); ~ oneself curo 1 (*alqd*; *ut*;

inf.); be ~d with, by laboro 1 (*morbo etc.*); ~some mole- stus, gravis

trough alveus *m*

trousers bracae *f/pl.*

truant vagus

truce indutiae *f/pl.*

truck carrus *m*

trudge pedibus eo 4

true verus; germanus, sin- cerus; fidus; rectus; be ~ of cadit 3 (*in*); convenit 4 (*dat.*)

truffle tuber, eris *n*

truly profecto

trump up comminiscor 3

trumpet bucina *f*; *mil.* tuba *f*; ~ abroad celebro 1, vulgo 1; ~er bucinator *m*, tubicen *m*

truncheon scipio *m*

trunk truncus *m*; stirps *f*; truncus *m* corporis; pro- boscis *f* (*elephanti*); arca *f*, cista *f*

truss fascia *f*; fascis *m*

trust confido 3 (*alci*; *alqa re*); fidem habeo 2 (*alci*); fides *f*; mandatum *n*, de- positum *n*; ~ful credulus; ~worthy certus, fidus, gra- vis (*auctor*, *testis*); ~y fidus, fidelis

truth veritas *f*; vera *n/pl.*; fides *f*; in ~ vero; ~ful verax

try conor 1, tento 1 (*inf.*); experior 4, periclitor 1 (*alqd*); *jur.* iudico 1; co- gnosco 3 (*causam*; *de re*); ~ing incommodus, diffi- cilis

tub labrum *n*; cupa *f*
tube fistula *f*; tubus *m*
tuck up succingo 3
tuft crista *f*; floccus *m*;
~ed cristatus
tug traho 3
tuition institutio *f*
tumble cado 3, concido 3;
casus, us *m*; ~r petaurista
m; poculum *n*
tumbrel plaustrum *n*
tumour tumor *m*
tumult tumultus, us *m*;
turba *f*; perturbatio *f*;
~uous tumultuosus, turbu-
lentus
tun dolium *n*
tune cantus, us *m*; carmen
n; numeri *m/pl.*; **keep in**
concentum servo 1; **be
out of** ~ discrepo 1; **out of**
~ absonus; tendo 3; ~ful
canorus
tunic tunica *f*
tunnel cuniculus *m*
turban mitra *f*
turbid turbidus
turbot rhombus *m*
turbulent turbulentus, tumultuosus
turf caespes *m*; herba *f*
turgid tumidus, turgidus
turmoil tumultus, us *m*;
turba *f*
turn *v/t.* (con)verto 3; verso
1; torqueo 2; flecto 3
(*oculos, equum, cursum,
promontorium*); intendo 3
(*oculos, iter, animum*); *v/i.*
(con)vertor 3; me (con)-
verto 3; fio; ~ **against**
descisco 3 (*ab*); ~ **aside**

declino 1 (*de via etc.*); ~
away aversor 1 (*ab*); ~
bad vitior 1; ~ **in** devertor
3 (*apud*); ~ **into** *v/t.* verto
3, muto 1 (*alqd in, ad*);
v/i. muto 1, mutor 1; me
converto 3; ~ **off** averto
3; ~ **out** *v/t.* eicio 3, exigo
3; moveo 2; *v/i.* cado 3,
evenio 4, accido 3 (*bene,
male, etc.*); evado 3 (*sapiens, orator*); ~ **round** verso 1, contorqueo 2 (*rotam
etc.*); ~ **sour** (co)acesco 3
(*vinum*); ~ **to use, one's
advantage** utor 3 (*abl.*);
ad utilitatem meam refero
3 (*alqd*); ~ **upon** vertor 3;
situm est (*in alqo, alqa re*);
~ **upside down** everto 3;
conversio *f*; flexus, us *m*
(*viae*); commutatio *f*, vicissitudo *f*; ambulatio *f*;
a good, bad ~ beneficium *n*,
iniuria *f*; **in** ~ invicem;
by ~s alternis; ~**ing point**
discrimen *n*
turnip rapum *n*
turnkey ianitor *m* (*carceris*)
turpentine terebinthus, i *f*
turret turris *f*
turtle-dove turtur *m*
tusk dens *m*
tutelary praeses
tutor magister, tri *m*; praeceptor *m*; doceo 2; instituo 3
twang sonitus, us *m*; sono 1
twelfth duodecimus
twelve duodecim; ~ **each**
duodeni; ~ **times** duode-
cies; ~**month** annus *m*

twentieth vicesimus

twenty viginti; ~ each viceni; ~ times vicies

twice bis; ~ as much bis tantum; ~ over semel atque iterum

twig surculus *m*; virga *f*

twilight crepusculum *n*

twin geminus

twine linum *n*; *v/t.* circumplico 1, circumplector 3 (*alqd alqa re*); *v/i.* ~ around complector 3 (*alqd*)

twinge morsus, us *m* (doloris)

twinkle mico 1, corusco 1

twirl verso 1

twist (con)torqueo 2; intorqueo 2; spira *f*

twit vellico 1; irrideo 2 (*acc.*) [motus, us *m*]

twitch vellico 1; vello 3;]

twitter pipilo 1; garrio 4

two duo, duae, duo; bini; ~ days biduum *n*; ~ years biennium *n*; ~ hundred ducenti; ~fold duplex

typ|e exemplar *n*, exemplum *n*; forma *f*; litterae *f/pl.*; ~ical proprius; ~ify exemplum sum

tyrann|ical tyrannicus, superbus; ~ize dominor 1 (*alqd*; *in alqm*); opprimo 3; ~y tyrannis *f*; dominatus, us *m*, dominatio *f*

tyrant tyrannus *m*; dominus *m*

U

udder uber, eris *n*

ugl|iness deformitas *f*; foeditas *f*; ~y deformis, informis; pravus

ulcer ulcus *n*; suppuro 1

ulterior occultus

ultimate ultimus, postremus; ~ly ad postremum

umbrage: take ~ offendor 3

umbrella umbraculum *n*

umpire arbiter, tri *m*

unabashed intrepidus, impudens

unable: be ~ nequeo 4; non possum (*inf.*)

un|acceptable ingratus, invisus; ~accountable inexplicabilis

unaccustomed]insolitus(*ad*); insolens, insuetus (*gen.*)

un|acquainted ignarus, expers (*gen.*); ~affected simplex, sincerus; ~alterable immutabilis; ~ambitious modestus

unanim|ity consensio *f*; consensus, us *m*; ~ously una voce; consensu omnium

un|armed inermis; ~asked sponte, ultro; ~assuming modestus, humilis; ~authenticated sine auctore; incertus; ~availing irritus, vanus; ~avenged inultus; ~avoidable quod vitari non potest; necessarius

unaware inscius, ignarus (*gen.*); ~s (de) improviso; take ~s imprudentem, inopinantem capio 3 (alqm)

un|bar resero 1; aperio 4; ~bearable intolerabilis; ~becoming indecorus; alienus (abl.); ~bend remitto 3; ~bending rigidus; ~biassed incorruptus; ~bidden iniussus; invocatus; ~bind (re)solvo 3; ~blemished purus, integer; ~bolt resero 1; ~born nondum natus; ~bosom oneself me patefacio 3; ~bounded infinitus; ~bridled effrenatus; ~broken continuus, perpetuus; ~burden oneself me patefacio 3; onus allevo 1; ~buried inhumatus, insepultus; ~button (re)solvo 3; ~ceasing continuus, perpetuus

uncertain dubius, incertus, anceps; be ~ dubito 1; haereo 2; it is ~ incertum est; ~ty dubium n; dubitatio f

unchange|able immutabilis; be ~d permaneo 2

un|charitable malevolus, iniquus; ~chaste impudicus; ~checked liber; ~civil inhumanus, rusticus; ~civilised barbarus,incultus

uncle patruus m (paternal); avunculus m (maternal)

un|clean impurus; ~clouded serenus; ~coil evolvo 3; ~comfortable incommodus, gravis; ~common rarus, insolens, insolitus; ~concerned otiosus; ~connected

disiunctus; ~conquered invictus

unconscious inscius, ignarus (gen.); ~ness oblivio f; defectio f (animi)

unconstitutional non legitimus; illicitus; ~ly contra rem publicam

un|controlled impotens, effrenatus; ~couple disiungo 3; ~couth incultus, rudis, inhumanus; ~cover recludo 3; aperio 4; ~cultivated incultus; ~damaged integer; ~daunted intrepidus, impavidus; ~deceive errorem tollo 3 (dat.); ~decided anceps; dubius; ~defended nudus; ~deniably certe

under sub (acc.; abl.); subter, infra (acc.); per (acc.); ~ a pretence of specie; ~ arms armatus; ~ ten days intra decem dies; ~garment subucula f; ~go subeo 4; perfero 3, patior 3; ~ground sub terra; subterraneus; ~growth virgulta n/pl.; ~hand clandestinus, perfidus; ~line noto 1; ~ling assecla m; ~mine labefacto 1; detraho 3 (alqd de re); ~neath infra, subter (acc.)

understand intellego 3, comprehendo 3; teneo 2; accipio 3, percipio 3; certior fio; audio 4; ~ing mens f; ingenium n

undertak|e suscipio 3 (alqd); spondeo 2; recipio 3, pro-

mitto 3 (*alqd; acc. c. inf.*);
~er libitinarius *m*; ~ing
inceptum *n*, facinus *n*
un|deserved immeritus; ~-
developed immaturus; cru-
dus; ~digested crudus; ~-
diminished integer; ~dis-
puted certus; ~do (dis)sol-
vo 3, resolvo 3; pessum do
1; irritum facio 3; be
~done pereo 4; leave ~done
omitto 3; ~doing dissolutio
f; ~doubted certus, haud
dubius; ~dress vestem ex-
uo 3, detraho 3; ~dressed
nudus; ~dulate fluctuo
1; ~duly nimis; ~earth de-
tego 3; ~earthly mirus,
monstruosus; ~easiness
perturbatio *f*, aegritudo *f*;
~educated indoctus, illit-
teratus, ineruditus; ~em-
ployed vacuus, otiosus
unequal impar, dispar;
~led singularis, unicus
un|equivocally plane; ~er-
ring certus; ~even inae-
quabilis, asper; ~exampled
inauditus, unicus; ~ex-
pected inopinatus, inex-
pectatus; necopinatus; im-
provisus; ~failing peren-
nis; ~fair iniquus, iniustus
unfaithful perfidus, infidus;
be ~ fidem fallo 3
un|familiar novus, insoli-
tus; ~fasten refigo 3; ~-
favourable iniquus, alie-
nus, adversus, inopportu-
nus; ~feeling durus; ~fin-
ished imperfectus, rudis;

~fit inutilis, inhabilis; indignus; ~told explico 1;
evolvo 3; ~foreseen impro-
visus; ~forgiving implacabilis, atrox; ~formed crudus, informis; ~fortunate
miser, infelix; ~founded
vanus; ~friendly inimicus;
~fulfilled inanis, vanus;
~furl solvo 3, pando 3; ~-
gainly imperitus, rusticus;
~gentlemanly illiberalis;
~godly impius; ~gracious
inhumanus; ~grateful in-
gratus; immemor (bene-
ficii); ~guarded parum
custoditus; incautus; ~-
happy miser, infelix; ~-
harmed incolumis; ~-
healthy pestilens (*locus*);
valetudine affectus; ~-
heard (of) inauditus; ~-
hesitatingly audacter; ~-
holy impius, nefarius; ~-
hurt incolumis
uniform aequabilis; orna-
tus, us *m* militaris; ~ity
aequabilitas *f*
un|impaired integer; ~im-
portant nullius momenti;
~inhabitable inhabitabilis;
~inhabited desertus; ~-
injured incolumis; ~intel-
ligible obscurus; ~inten-
tional haud meditatus,
cogitatus
union consociatio *f*; concilium *n*; societas *f*; coniunctio *f*
unique unicus, singularis
unison: in ~ una voce
unit|e *v/t.* (con)iungo 3;

consocio 1; v/i. coniuro 1;
consocior 1; ~ed consocia-
tus; ~y consensus, us m;
concordia f

univers|al communis; ~ally
in universum, universe;
~e mundus m; ~ity acade-
mia f

un|just iniquus, iniustus;
~kempt horridus, incomp-
tus; ~kind haud benignus;
crudelis, inhumanus; ~-
known ignotus, incogni-
tus; ~lace solvo 3

unlawful illicitus, vetitus;
it is ~ nefas est; ~ly contra
legem; contra ius

unless nisi, ni

un|like dissimilis, dispar
(gen., dat.); ~limited infinitus; ~load expono 3; ~lock
resero 1; ~looked-for necopinatus, inexspectatus;
~loose solvo 3; ~lucky infelix; ~manageable intrac-
tabilis; ~manly mollis;
~mannerly agrestis, inhu-
manus; ~married caelebs;
~mentionable infandus; ~-
merciful immitis; ~mind-
ful immemor (gen.); ~-
mistakeable certissimus;
~mixed merus; ~moved
immotus

unnatural immanis, nefa-
rius; arcessitus (oratio);
~ly praeter naturam

un|necessary haud neces-
sarius; supervacaneus; ~-
nerve frango 3

unnoticed: pass ~ lateo 2

un|occupied vacuus; ~-

palatable fig. molestus;
~patriotic improbus, ma-
lus; ~pleasant iniucundus,
molestus; ~polished impo-
litus, rudis

unpopular invidiosus, in-
visus, ingratus; ~ity in-
vidia f; offensio f

un|practised inexpertus; ~-
precedented inauditus, novus; ~prepossessing iniu-
cundus; ~principled im-
probus; nequam; ~propi-
tious iniquus, infaustus;
~provoked ultro (adv.);
~punished impunitus; ~-
questionably facile, certe;
~ravel retexo 3; fig. enodo
1; ~reasonable absurdus;
contra rationem

un|refined crudus; rudis;
~relenting atrox; ~remit-
ting assiduus; ~restrained
effrenatus, liber; ~ripe
crudus; ~rivalled unicus;
praestantissimus; ~roll
evolvo 3; ~ruffled aequus;
~ruly impotens; ~saddle
stratum detraho 3; ~safe
infestus, lubricus, periculosus; ~seal resigno 1;
aperio 4; ~seasonable im-
maturus, ineptus; ~seemly
indecorus; ~seen invisus;
~serviceable inutilis

unsettled dubius, perturbatus; vagus; leave ~ in
medio relinquo 3

un|sheath educo 3, eripio 3
(e vagina); ~sightly turpis,
foedus; ~skilled imperitus
(gen.); ~sociable difficilis;

~sophisticated simplex; ~sound infirmus, morbosus; ~sparing profusus, prodigus (gen.); ~speakable infandus; ~stable, ~steady instabilis, fluxus; ~successful infelix; adversus, irritus; ~suitable incommodus, ineptus; alienus (ab); ~suspecting incautus; ~thinking inconsideratus; ~tie (dis)solvo 3; laxo 1

until ad, in (acc.); cj. dum, quoad, donec; not ~ non prius (ante) ... quam

un|timely immaturus; ~tiring assiduus; ~touched intactus, integer; ~toward adversus; ~tried inexpertus; ~troubled securus, tranquillus; ~true falsus; ~truth mendacium n; ~used insuetus (gen.); insolitus (ad; gen.); integer; ~usual insolitus, insolens, novus; ~varnished haud fucatus; ~veil detego 3; fig. patefacio 3, aperio 4; ~versed in imperitus (gen.); ~warlike imbellis; ~wary imprudens, incautus; ~wearied impiger; ~welcome iniucundus, ingratus; ~well aeger; ~wholesome gravis (cibus); noxius; ~wieldy inhabilis

unwilling invitus; be ~ nolo (inf.); ~ly invitus

un|wind revolvo 3; ~wise insipiens; ~witting imprudens; ~wonted insuetus, insolitus; ~worthy indi-

gnus (abl.; qui); alienus (ab); ~wrap evolvo 3; explico 1; ~written non scriptus; ~yielding firmus, obstinatus

up sursum; ~ and down sursum deorsum; ~ in the air sublime; ~ to ad (acc.); in (acc.); ~ to this year usque ad hunc annum

up|braid obiurgo 1; ~country in interiora; ~hill acclivis, arduus; ~hold sustineo 2, sustento 1; ~land editus

upon in, super (acc., abl.); ~ the right a dextra

upper superior, superus; ~most supremus, summus

upright rectus; integer, honestus, bonus; ~ness probitas f

uproar tumultus, us m; turba f

uproot evello 3

upset everto 3, subverto 3; sollicito 1 (alqm)

upshot exitus, us m

upside: turn ~ down sursum deorsum verso 1

up|start novus homo m; terrae filius m; ~stream adverso flumine; in adversum flumen

upwards sursum; sublime; ~ of amplius, plus

urge suadeo 2 (alci ut; alqd alci); hortor 1 (alqm ut; alci alqd); impello 3 (alqm ad alqd); ~ on incito 1, impello 3; ~nt gravis, praesens; ~ntly vehementer

urn urna *f*

usage mos *m*

use utor 3 (*abl.*); adhibeo 2 (*alqd ad alqd*; *in re*); tracto 1 (*alqm*); usus, us *m*; utilitas *f*; commodum *n*; be of ~ prosum; usui sum; make ~ of utor 3 (*alqa re*); in common ~ usitatus; ~ up consumo 3; ~d to assuetus, assuefactus; ~ful utilis, commodus; ~less inutilis, vanus, irritus; it is ~less nihil prodest; ~lessly frustra

usher in introduco 3; *fig.* infero 3

usual solitus, usitatus, consuetus; be ~ soleo 2; ~ly plerumque; fere

usufruct usus, us *m*

usurer faenerator *m*; be a ~ faeneror 1

usurp invado 3 (*in alqd*; *alqd*); usurpo 1

usury faeneratio *f*; faenus *n*

utensils suppellex *f*; instrumenta *n/pl.*

utility utilitas *f*

utmost extremus, ultimus, summus; to my ~ quantum in me est; omnibus viribus

utter totus, merus, germanus; dico 3, emitto 3, loquor 3; ~ance dictum *n*; ~ly omnino, funditus; ~most ultimus, extremus

V

vacan|cy (vacuus) locus *m*; inane *n*; ~t vacuus, inanis

vacat|e vacuefacio 3; ~ion feriae *f/pl.*

vacillate vacillo 1; ~ion dubitatio *f*

vacuum inane *n*

vagabond vagus; erro *m*

vagary libido *f*

vagrant vagus; erro *m*

vague incertus, dubius; vagus; ~ness obscuritas *f*

vain vanus, inanis, irritus; levis; gloriosus (*homo*); in ~ frustra, nequiquam; ~glorious gloriosus

vale vallis *f*

valet cubicularius *m*

valiant fortis

valid firmus, certus, ratus; ~ity auctoritas *f*, gravitas *f*

valley vallis *f*

valour virtus, utis *f*

valu|able pretiosus; magni (pretii); ~ation aestimatio *f*

value aestimo 1, habeo 2, facio 3, duco 3, pendo 3 (*alqd magni, pluris, parvi, etc.*); diligo 3; pretium *n*; aestimatio *f*; virtus, utis *f*; honor *m*; be of ~ prosum (*alci*); ~less minimi pretii

vampire lamia *f*

van *mil.* primum agmen *n*

vanish evanesco 3, dilabor 3

vanity vanitas *f*; iactatio *f*, gloria *f*

vanquish vinco 3; supero 1

vapour vapor *m*; halitus, us *m*; exhalatio *f*

variable varius, mutabilis, mobilis

variance discordia *f*; discrepantia *f*; be at ~ with pugno 1 cum; at ~ with discors

variation varietas *f*, commutatio *f*

varicose varicosus; ~ vein varix *f*

var|ied varius, diversus; ~iegate vario 1; ~iety varietas *f*, diversitas *f*; ~ious varius, diversus, multiplex; ~ious opinions were expressed alius aliud dixit

varnish *fig.* fucus *m*

vary vario 1, muto 1; distinguo 3

vase amphora *f*

vast ingens, maximus, immensus

vat dolium *n*

vault salio 4; fornix *f*; camera *f*; saltus, us *m*; ~ed fornicatus

vaunt iacto 1, ostento 1 (*alqd*); glorior 1 (*acc. c. inf.*); iactatio *f*, ostentatio *f*

veal vitulina *f*

veer (me) verto 3 (*in, ad*)

vegetable planta *f*; ~s olus *n*

vehemen|ce vis *f*; ~t vehemens, ardens

vehicle vehiculum *n*

veil velum *n*, velamentum *n*; rica *f*; velo 1; tego 3

vein vena *f*

velocity velocitas *f*, celeritas *f*

venal venalis

vend vendo 3; ~or venditor *m*

venera|ble venerabilis, gravis, augustus; ~te veneror 1; ~tion veneratio *f*

vengeance ultio *f*

venison ferina *f*

venom virus, i *n*, venenum *n*; ~ous venenatus; mordax

vent foramen *n*; give ~ to erumpo 3 (*abl.*; *alqd*); erumpo 3, effundo 3 (*alqd in alqm*)

ventilat|e *fig.* in medium profero 3; ~ion perflatus, us *m*

venture audeo 2 (*alqd*; *inf.*); conor 1 (*alqd*; *inf.*); periclitor 1 (*alqd*); in periculum infero 3 (*alqm, alqd*); in aleam do 1; periculum *n*, discrimen *n*; alea *f*; at a ~ temere; ~some audax, audens

verac|ious verax, verus; ~ity fides *f*, veritas *f*

verb verbum *n*; ~ally verbum pro verbo (*reddere etc.*); sermone (*iubere*); ~atim totidem verbis; ~ose verbosus

verdict sententia *f*; iudicium *n*; pronounce ~ pronuntio 1

verdure viriditas *f*

verg|e margo *m*; ora *f*; ~ing on proximus (*dat.*)

verify probo 1, confirmo 1

vermilion miniatus

vernacular patrius sermo *m*

vernal vernus

versatile varius, multiplex

vers|e versus, us *m*; carmen *n*; **~ed** in peritus (*gen.*), exercitatus (*in re*)

vertebra vertebra *f*

vertical rectus, directus; **~ly** ad lineam

very *adv.* valde, maxime, admodum (*bonus etc.*); **not ~** non ita; **~ much** magnopere, vehementer; *adj.* germanus; **this ~** hic ipse; **at that ~ moment** ea ipsa hora

vessel vas *n*; navis *f*

vest subucula *f*

vestal vestalis (virgo) *f*

vestibule vestibulum *n*

vestige indicium *n*, signum *n*; nota *f*

vetch vicia *f*

veteran veteranus (miles) *m*; vetus

veto intercessio *f*; intercedo 3 (*dat.*)

vex sollicito 1, vexo 1; **~ation** stomachus *m*; **~atious** molestus, odiosus

vibrate tremo 3; vibro 1

vice flagitium *n*, vitium *n*; pravitas *f*, turpitudo *f*; **~roy** praefectus *m*

vicious flagitiosus, pravus, nequam

vicinity vicinitas *f*; vicinum *n*

vicissitudes vices *f/pl.*, vicissitudines *f/pl.*

victim victima *f*, hostia *f*

victor victor *m*, victrix *f*;

~ious victor; **be ~ious** vinco 3; **~y** victoria *f*; **triumphus** *m*; **gain ~y** victoriam consequor 3

victuals victus, us *m*; cibaria *n/pl.*

vie with certo 1, contendo 3 (*cum*)

view conspectus, us *m*; acies *f*; *fig.* sententia *f*, opinio *f*; iudicium *n*; **~ down**, over despectus, us *m*; **be in ~** sum in prospectu; **come into ~** venio 4 in conspectum (*alcs*); **in ~** in conspectu; ante oculos; *fig.* in my **~** meo iudicio; mihi videtur; **take the same ~** idem sentio 4 (*quod*, *atque*); **with a ~ to** ut; gratia, causa (*alcs rei*); **intueor** 2, contueor 2; specto 1, contemplor 1

vigilan|ce vigilantia *f*; **~t** vigilans, providus

vigo|rous acer, strenuus, ferox; **~ur** ferocitas *f*; vis *f*

vile turpis, perditus, nequam

vilify maledico 3 (*dat.*)

villa villa *f*

village pagus *m*; vicus *m*; **~r** rusticus *m*, agrestis *m*

villain verbero *m*, furcifer *m*; **~y** nequitia *f*; flagitium *n*

vindicate purgo 1

vine vitis *f*; **~ leaf** pampineus *m*

vinegar acetum *n*

vin|eyard vinea *f*; vinetum *n*; **~tage** vindemia *f* viol|ate violo 1; ~ater violator *m*; ~ence vis *f*, violentia *f*; ~impetus, us *m*; ~ent violentus, vehemens

violet viola *f*

viper vipera *f*

virgin virgo *f*; innupta *f*; virginalis; ~ity virgintas *f*

viril|e virilis; mas; ~ity virilitas *f*

virtue virtus, utis *f*; probitas *f*; in ~ of pro (*abl.*); per (*acc.*)

virtuous honestus, probus

virulen|ce acerbitas *f*; vis *f*; ~t acerbus, gravis

visage os *n*

viscous lentus

visible conspicuus, manifestus; be ~ appareo 2

vision visus, us *m*; aspectus, us *m*; visum *n*; imago *f*

visit (in)viso 1; saluto 1; salutatio *f*; ~or hospes *m and f*

vista prospectus, us *m*; despectus, us *m*

vital vitalis; necessarius; ~ity alacritas *f*

vitiate vitio 1

vivaci|ous alacer, acer; ~ty alacritas *f*

vivid vivus, acer

vocal sonorus

vociferously magno clamore

vogue mos *m*

voice vox *f*; *fig.* sententia *f*, opinio *f*

void inanis, vacuus; vote *n*; lacuna *f*; erumpo 3, evomo 3

volition voluntas *f*

volley *fig.* nubes *f*

voluble loquax

volum|e volumen *n*; liber, bri *m*; ~inous copiosus

volunt|arily mea (sua) sponte, voluntate; ultro; ~ary voluntarius

volunteer sponte, ultro offero 3 (*alqd*); *mil.* nomen do 1; (miles) voluntarius *m*

voluptuous voluptarius, libidinosus

vomit (e)vomo 1

voracious avidus, vorax

votary cultor *m*

vot|e suffragium *n* (*populi*); sententia *f* (*iudicis*); *v/t.* censeo 2; decerno 3; *v/i.* suffragium fero 3; ~e for suffragor 1 (*alci*); ~ing-tablet tabella *f*; ~ing urna, box cista *f*

votive votivus

vouch for praesto 1, confirmo 1 (*alqd*)

vouch|er auctoritas *f*; ~safe concedo 3 (*alqd*); permitto 3 (*ut*)

vow (de)voveo 2; promitto 3; votum *n*

vowel vocalis *f*

voyage navigatio *f*; make a ~ navigo 1

vulgar vulgaris, communis; agrestis, insulsus, ineptus; ~ity ineptiae *f/pl.*; ~ly vulgo

vulture vultur *m*

W

waddle vacillo 1

waft fero 3

wag quasso 1; moveo 2; ioculator *m*

wage gero 3 (*bellum etc. cum algo*)

wager spondeo 2; pono 3; sponsio *f*; pignus *n*

wages merces *f/pl.*; praemium *n*

waggon plaustrum *n*; carrus *m*; ~er bubulcus *m*; auriga, ae *m*

wail ploro 1; fleo 2; ploratus, us *m*; fletus, us *m*

wain plaustrum *n*

waist medium corpus *n*

wait exspecto 1, maneo 2, opperior 4 (*algd; dum*); ~ on ministro 1 (*alci*); ~er puer, eri *m*; minister, tri *m*

waive remitto 3 (*algd*)

wake *v/t.* excito 1, suscito 1; *v/i.* expergiscor 3; vigilia *f*; ~ful vigilans

walk pedibus eo 4; ambulo 1, spatior 1; ~ in inambulo 1 (*abl.*); ambulatio *f*; ~er pedes *m*; ~ing stick baculum *n*

wall murus *m*; city~ moenia *n/pl.*; house~ paries *m*; munio 4; ~ed munitus; ~et pera *f*

wallow volutor 1

walnut (tree) iuglans *f*

wan pallidus

wand virga *f*; caduceus *m*

wander erro 1, vagor 1, palor 1; ~ing vagus; erratio *f*

wane decresco 3; minuor 3

wanness pallor *m*

want volo 1; aveo 2; careo 2 (*abl.*); desidero 1; inopia *f*, egestas *f*; **there** ~**s** deest; opus est (*nom.; abl.*); **be** ~**ing** deficio 3, desum, absum

wanton libidinosus, protervus, procax; ~ness protervitas *f*

war bellum *n*; militia *f*; bello 1; **make** ~ on arma, bellum infero 3 (*alci*); **wage** ~ bellum gero 3; **declare** ~ bellum indico 3 (*alci*); **in** ~ **and peace** pace belloque; ~-cry clamor *m*

warble cano 3

ward custodia *f*; pupillus *m*, pupilla *f*; regio *f* (*urbis*); ~ **off** arceo 2; defendo 3, averto 3; ~en, ~er custos *m*, excubitor *m*; ~ship tutela *f*

wares merces *f/pl.*

war|fare militia *f*; res *f* bellica; ~like bellicosus

warm calidus, tepidus; *fig.* acer; tepefacio 3; foveo 2; ~th calor *m*, tepor *m*

warn (ad)moneo 2 (*algm algd; ut*); ~ing monitus, us *m*; admonitum *n*

warp stamen *n*; torqueo 2

warrant auctoritas *f*; man-

datum *n*; spondeo 2;
praesto 1; promitto 3

warrior bellator *m*

wary cautus, providus

wash *v/t.* lavo 1; *v/i.* lavor
1; ~ against alluo 3 (*acc.*);
~ing lavatio *f*

wasp vespa *f*

waste consumo 3; perdo 3,
tero 3 (*tempus etc.*); dissipo 1, profundo 3 (*rem*),
vastus, desertus; lay ~
vasto 3; populor 1; effusio
f; vastitas *f*, solitudo *f*;
~ful prodigus, effusus;
~fulness luxuria *f*

watch *v/t.* observo 1; custodio 4; exspecto 1; *v/i.* vigilo 1, excubo 1; vigilia *f*;
excubiae *f/pl.*; custodia *f*;
keep ~ over custodio 4;
set a ~ vigilias dispono 3;
~ful vigilans; ~man vigil
m; ~-tower specula *f*; ~
word tessera *f*

water (ir)rigo 1; aqua *f*;
sea~ aqua *f* marina; by
land and ~ terra marique;
~-carrier aquarius *m*; ~-
clock clepsydra *f*; well
~ed irriguus; ~fall desi-
liens aqua *f*; ~ing-place
aquatio *f*

wattle crates *f*

wave unda *f*; fluctus, us *m*;
v/t. iacto 1, agito 1; *v/i.*
fluctuo 1, fluito 1; ~r fluctuo 1, vacillo 1, dubito 1;
~ring dubius, incertus

wax cera *f*; *v/t.* cero 1; *v/i.*
cresco 3 (*luna*); ~en cereus

way via *f*; cursus, us *m*;

fig. modus *m*; ratio *f*; on
the ~ ex itinere; out of the
~ devius, remotus, ab-
strusus; get under ~ ancoram solvo 3; ~farer viator
m; ~lay insidior 1 (*dat.*);
~side ad viam; ~ward
pertinax, levis

we nos

weak infirmus, debilis,
imbecillus, fractus, tenuis;
~en infirmo 1; frango 3,
comminuo 3; ~ness infir-
mitas *f*

weal vibix *f*; common ~
bonum *n* publicum

wealth divitiae *f/pl.*, opes
f/pl.; copia *f*; ~y dives,
opulentus, locuples

wean lacte depello 3

weapon telum *n*; iaculum *n*;
~s arma *n/pl.*

wear *v/t.* gero 3 (*vestem*);
v/i. duro 1; ~ away (con-)
tero 3; ~ out conficio 3;
tritus, us *m*; habitus *m*;
~ied defessus; ~iness
lassitudo *f*; ~ing amictus
(*alqa veste*); ~isome operosus, laboriosus

weary defessus, defatiga-
tus; (de)fatigo 1; be ~ of
taedet 2 me (*alcs rei*)

weasel mustela *f*

weather tempestas *f*; caelum *n*; fine ~ serenitas *f*;
bad ~ foeda tempestas *f*;
fig. perfero 3; ~beaten
adustus

weave (con)texo 3; ~r textor *m*

web tela *f*; textum *n*

wed duco 3 (*uxorem*); nubo 3 (*maritum*); ~ded maritus, nupta; *fig.* ~ded to deditus (*dat.*); ~ding nuptiae *f/pl.*

wedge cuneus *m*

wedlock matrimonium *n*

weed lolium *n*; runco 1

week septem dies *m/pl.*

weep fleo 2; lacrimor 1; ~ over defleo 2 (*alqd*), illacrimo 1 (*dat.*); ~ing fletus, us *m*

weevil curculio *m*

weigh (ex)pendo 3; penso 1; *fig.* pondero 1; ~ down premo 3, opprimo 3; gravo 1; ~t pondus *n*; momentum *n*; gravitas *f*; auctoritas *f*; have great, no ~t multum, nihil valeo 2 (*apud alqm*); ~ty gravis

welcome gratus, acceptus; salvere iubeo 2 (*benigne*) excipio 3, accipio 3; saluto 1; *int.* salve!; salutatio *f*

weld ferrumino 1

welfare salus, utis *f*; bonum *n*, commodum *n*

well puteus *m*; fons *m*; *adj.* valens, salvus; *adv.* bene, probe; be ~ valeo 2; ~-being felicitas 1; ~-born nobilis; ~-bred urbanus, comis; ~-disposed to benevolus (*erga, in alqm*); ~-earned (bene) meritus; ~-known celebratus; ~-versed peritus, versatus; ~-wisher amicus *m*

west occidens *m*; occasus, us *m* (solis); ~ern ad occi-

dentem; occidentalis; ~-wards in occasum; ~ wind zephyrus *m*

wet madefacio 3; umidus, udus, madidus; be ~ madeo 2; ~ness umor *m*

whale balaena *f*, cetus *n*

wharf crepido *f*

what quid?, quod?; ~ kind of a quod?, *exclam.* qui, qualis; *relat.* quod; ~ever quisquis; quisquilis

wheat triticum *n*

wheedle blandior 4 (*dat.*)

wheel rota *f*; ~ round *v/t.* circumago 3; *v/i.* circumagor 3

whelp catulus *m*

when quando?; *cj.* cum, ubi, postquam, ut; ~ce unde?; ~ever quandocumque, quotiescumque, cum

where ubi?, quo?; *relat.* qua, ubi; ~ ... from unde?; ~ on earth ubi gentium?; ~as quoniam; ~by qua ratione; ~upon quo facto; ~ver ubicumque

whet acuo 3

whether *interrog.* num; utrum ... (an); ~ne ... (an); *cj.* ~ ... or sive ... sive; seu ... seu

whetstone cos *f*

which quis?; *relat.* qui; ~ (of two) uter?; *relat.* quis; ~ever quicumque

while *cj.* dum; donec, cum; tempus *n*; for a little parumper; ~ away dego 3

whim arbitrium *n*; libido *f*

whimper vagio 4

whimsical ridiculus

whine vagio 4

whip flagellum *n*; lora *n*/*pl.*; verbero 1

whirl turbo *m*; ~ round torqueor 2; ~pool vorago *f*, vertex *m*; ~wind turbo *m*

whiskers capilli *m*/*pl.*

whisper (in)susurro 1; susurrus *m*

whistle sibilo 1; sibilus *m*; fistula *f*

white albus, candidus; canus (*capilli*); album *n*; ~n albesco 3, canesco 3; ~ness candor *m*; ~wash dealbo 1

whither quo?

who quis?; *relat.* qui; ~ever quicumque

whole totus; cunctus, omnis; integer, solidus; totum *n*; as a ~ in universum; on the ~ ad summam; ~sale dealer mercator *m*; ~some salutaris

wholly omnino; ex omni ratione; prorsus

whoop ululo 1; ululatus, us *m*

whose cuius

why cur?, quare?, quam ob rem?; ~ not quidni?

wick filum *n*

wicked scelestus, improbus, nefarius; ~ness scelus *n*, flagitium *n*; nequitia *f*

wicker vimineus; ~work vimen *n*

wide latus, amplus; *adv.* late; ~spread (per)vulga-

tus; ~spreading patulus (*rami*); ~n laxo 1, dilato 1

widow vidua *f*; ~ed viduus; ~er viduus homo *m*

width latitudo *f*, amplitudo *f*

wield gero 3; utor 3

wife uxor *f*, coniunx *f*

wig capillamentum *n*

wild ferus, incultus; vastus; insanus; ~erness desertum *n*; vastitas *f*; ~ness feritas *f* [*f*/*pl.*]

wiles dolus *m*; fallaciae

wilful pertinax, pervicax

will voluntas *f*; consilium *n*, arbitrium *n*; testamentum *n*; against my ~ me invito; invitus (*adj.*); as you ~ ut libet

willing libens; promptus (*ad*); ~ly libenter; ~ness studium *n*

willow salix *f*

wily vafer, astutus, callidus

win vinco 3 (*in pugna etc.*); consequor 3, pario 3 (*alqd*); concilio 1 (*gratiam etc.*)

wind ventus *m*; volvo 3; glomero 1; ~ one's way into me insinuo 1 (*in*); ~ed anhelans; ~ing flexuosus; ambages *f*/*pl.*; sinus, us *m*

window fenestra *f*

wind|pipe aspera arteria *f*; ~y ventosus

wine vinum *n*; ~-cellar cella *f*; ~-press prelum *n*

wing ala *f*, penna *f*; cornu *n* (*exercitus*); volo 1; ~ed volucer, pinniger

wink nictus, us *m*; nicto 1;
~ at coniveo 2 (*dat.*)

win|ner victor *m*; ~ning
victor; blandus, suavis

winnowing fan vannus, i *f*

winter hiems *f*; hiemo 1,
hiberno 1; ~ solstice bruma
f; ~quarters hiberna *n*/*pl.*

wintry hiemalis, hibernus

wipe (de)tergeo 2; ~ out
deleo 2   [lium *n*)

wisdom sapientia *f*; consi-

wise sapiens, prudens, peritus

wish volo (*inf.*); cupio 3,
opto 1 (*inf.*); ~ for volo,
opto 1 (*alqd*); votum *n*,
optatum *n*, desiderium *n*;
optatio *f*; against my ~es
me invito

wit sal *m*; facetiae *f*/*pl.*;
ingenium *n*, acumen *n*;
to ~ scilicet

witch saga *f*; venefica *f*;
~craft veneficium *n*; ma-
gicae artes *f*/*pl.*

with cum (*abl.*); ~ me
mecum; apud me, it rests,
lies ~ me penes me est;
~draw *v*/*t.* removeo 2; abduco 3, deduco 3; *v/i.*
(re)cedo 3, me recipio 3

wither *v/t.* torreo 2; *v/i.*
languesco 3, aresco 3; ~ed
marcidus, rugosus

withhold retineo 2; sup-
primo 3, recuso 1

within in (*abl.*); intra, inter
(*acc.*); cis, citra (*acc.*); *adv.*
intus

without sine (*abl.*); *cj.* quin;
adv. extra, extrinsecus

withstand obsto 1, resisto 3,
obsisto 3 (*dat.*)

witness testis *m*; arbiter *m*;
spectator *m*; video 2;
conspicio 3; bear ~, call to
~ testor 1, testificor 1
(*alqd*; *alqm*: *acc. c. inf.*);
bear ~ against testimo-
nium dico 3 (*in alqm*)

witt|icism dictum *n*; ~y
facetus, salsus

wizard magus *m*

woad vitrum *n*

woe dolor *m*; ~ful miser,
tristis

wolf lupus *m*

woman mulier *f*, femina *f*;
old ~ anus, us *f*; young ~
puella *f*; ~ish muliebris,
effeminatus; ~ly, ~'s mu-
liebris, femineus

womb uterus *m*

wonder admiratio *f*; mira-
culum *n*; (ad)miror 1
(*alqd*; *acc. c. inf.*; *quod*);
~ful mirus, mirabilis, mirificus

wont mos *m*; be ~ soleo 2

woo peto 3; *fig.* ambio 4

wood lignum *n*; silva *f*;
nemus *n*; ~cutter lignator
m; ~ed silvestris; ~en
ligneus; ~pigeon palum-
bes *m*; ~y lignosus, sil-
vosus

wooer procus *m*

wool lana *f*; ~len laneus

word verbum *n*, vocabu-
lum *n*, nomen *n*; vox *f*; ~s
dicta *n*/*pl.*; in a ~, few ~s
paucis, breviter; have ~s
with altercor 1 (*cum alqo*)

send (back) ~ (re)nuntio 1; keep, break one's ~ fidem servo 1, fallo 3; ~y verbosus

work opus n; labor m; opera f; pensum n; ~ of art opus n; ars f; artificium n; ~s machinatio f; v/i. (e)laboro 1; v/t. subigo 3, colo 3 (terram); ~ at exerceo 2 (rem); versor 1 (in re); ~ upon flecto 3 (animum etc.); ~er opifex m, artifex m; ~house ergastulum n; ~ing cultus, us m (terrae); ~man opifex m; ~shop officina f

world mundus m; orbis m terrarum; all the ~ omnes (ad unum); nemo est quin (subj.); where in the ~ ubi gentium?; in the whole ~ usquam

worm vermis m; tinea f; ~ one's way into me insinuo 1 (in) [2; agito 1]

worry sollicito 1; exerceo

worse peior, deterior; for the ~ in deterius; grow ~ ~n ingravesco 3

worship colo 3; veneror 1; cultus, us m; veneratio f; ~per cultor m

worst pessimus, deterrimus, ultimus; get the ~ of it vincor 3

worth dignus (abl.); pretium n; dignitas f; it is ~ (while) operae pretium est (inf.); ~less nequam (homo); inutilis, vilis; ~y dignus (abl.; qui); bonus

would that utinam

wound vulnus n; plaga f; vulnero 1; saucio 4

wrangle altercor 1

wrap involvo 3, obvolvo 3 (alqd re); ~per involucrum n, tegumentum n

wrath ira f

wreath sertum n; corona f; volumen n; vertex m; ~e necto 3 (caput sertis)

wreck frango 3, illido 3; naufragium n; ~ed naufragus [(alqd alci)

wrench, wrest extorqueo 2 |

wrestl|e luctor 1; ~er luctator m; ~ing luctatio f

wretch homo m nequam, perditus; miser; ~ed infelix, miserabilis; ~edness miseria f

wriggle torqueo 2 me

wring torqueo 2, crucio 1; ~ from extorqueo 2 (alqd alci)

wrinkle ruga f; ~d rugosus

writ litterae f/pl.; mandatum n

write scribo 3; ~ back rescribo 3; ~ out perscribo 3; ~r scriptor m, auctor m

writing scriptio f, scriptura f; ~s scripta n/pl.; ~case scrinium n; ~paper charta f

wrong falsus; pravus, iniustus, iniquus; iniuriam infero 3 (alci); be ~ erro 1; ~doer maleficus m; ~ful iniustus; ~ly male, perperam, falso

wry distortus

Y

yacht phaselus *m*; celox *f*

yard area *f*, cohors *f*; antenna *f* (*navis*)

yarn linum *n*; fabula *f*

yawn oscito 1; *fig.* hio 1, dehisco 3; oscitatio *f*

yea ita, certe

year annus *m*; ~ly anniversarius; *adv.* quotannis

yearn| for desidero 1; ~ing desiderium *n*

yeast fermentum *n*

yell ululo 1; ululatus, us *m*

yellow flavus, luteus, croceus

yelp gannio 4

yes ita (vero); sane, certe, etiam; say ~ aio

yesterday heri; hesternus dies *m*; of ~ hesternus

yet tamen, vero, nihilominus, at; (*of time*) etiam

(~nunc), adhuc; not ~ nondum

yew taxus, i *f*

yield *v/t.* effero 3; *fig.* pario 3, affero 3; do 1, concedo 3, dedo 3; *v/i.* cedo 3, obsequor 3 (*dat.*); fructus, us *m*; ~ing mollis

yoke iugum *n*; iungo 3

yolk vitellus *m*

yonder *adj.* ille; *adv.* ecce, illic

yore olim, quondam

you tu, vos

young iuvenis, parvus, adolescens; partus, us *m*, fetus, us *m*; ~er iunior, minor natu

your tuus, vester

youth iuventus, utis *f*, adolescentia *f*; iuvenis *m*, adolescens *m*; ~ful iuvenilis, puerilis

Z

zeal studium *n*; ardor *m*; ~ous studiosus, acer

zephyr zephyrus *m*

zero nihil

zest gustatus, us *m*; sapor *m*; studium *n*

zigzag anfractus, us *m* (*viae etc.*); tortuosus

zone zona *f*; regio *f*

© *1966 Langenscheidt KG, Berlin and Munich*

Printed in Germany

LANGENSCHEIDT
has the great advantage of being a purely foreign languages publishing house and as such can concentrate exclusively on dictionaries and language teaching publications.

LANGENSCHEIDT considers that its duty is to maintain the highest standard in this field. Everywhere, its name stands for editorial experience, accuracy, clearness, and up-to-date completeness.